CHILTON BOOK COMPANY

REPAIR MANUAL

CHEVY/GMC PICK-UPS and SUBURBANS 1970-87

All U.S. and Canadian models of ½, ¾, and 1 ton Pick-Ups and SUBURBANS • 2- and 4-wheel drive, including diesel engines

President GARY R. INGERSOLL
Senior Vice President, Book Publishing and Research RONALD A. HOXTER
Vice President and General Manager JOHN P. KUSHNERICK
Editor-in-Chief KERRY A. FREEMAN, S.A.E.
Managing Editor DEAN F. MORGANTINI, S.A.E.
Senior Editor RICHARD J. RIVELE, S.A.E.
Senior Editor W. CALVIN SETTLE, JR., S.A.E.
Editor MARTIN J. GUNTHER

CHILTON BOOK COMPANY
Radnor, Pennsylvania
19089

CONTENTS

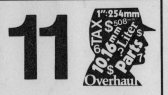

SAFETY NOTICE

Proper service and repair procedures are vital to the safe, reliable operation of all motor vehicles, as well as the personal safety of those performing repairs. This book outlines procedures for servicing and repairing vehicles using safe, effective methods. The procedures contain many NOTES, CAUTIONS and WARNINGS which should be followed along with standard safety procedures to eliminate the possibility of personal injury or improper service which could damage the vehicle or compromise its safety.

It is important to note that repair procedures and techniques, tools and parts for servicing motor vehicles, as well as the skill and experience of the individual performing the work vary widely. It is not possible to anticipate all of the conceivable ways or conditions under which vehicles may be serviced, or to provide cautions as to all of the possible hazards that may result. Standard and accepted safety precautions and equipment should be used during cutting, grinding, chiseling, prying, or any other process that can cause material removal or projectiles.

Some procedures require the use of tools specially designed for a specific purpose. Before substituting another tool or procedure, you must be completely satisfied that neither your personal safety, nor the performance of the vehicle will be endangered.

Although the information in this guide is based on industry sources and is as complete as possible at the time of publication, the possibility exists that the manufacturer made later changes which could not be included here. While striving for total accuracy, Chilton Book Company cannot assume responsibility for any errors, changes, or omissions that may occur in the compilation of this data.

PART NUMBERS

Part numbers listed in this reference are not recommendations by Chilton for any product by brand name. They are references that can be used with interchange manuals and aftermarket supplier catalogs to locate each brand supplier's discrete part number.

SPECIAL TOOLS

Special tools are recommended by the vehicle manufacturer to perform their specific job. Use has been kept to a minimum, but where absolutely necessary, they are referred to in the text by the part number of the tool manufacturer. These tools can be purchased, under the appropriate part number, from the Service Tool Division, Kent-Moore Corporation, 1501 South Jackson Street, Jackson, MI 49203. In Canada, contact Kent-Moore of Canada, Ltd., 2395 Cawthra Mississauga, Ontario, Canada L5A 3P2., or an equivalent tool can be purchased locally from a tool supplier or parts outlet. Before substituting any tool for the one recommended, read the SAFETY NOTICE at the top of this page.

ACKNOWLEDGMENTS

Chilton Book Company expresses appreciation to the Chevrolet Motor Division, General Motors Corporation, Detroit, Michigan 48202; and GMC Truck and Coach Division, General Motors Corporation, Pontiac, Michigan 48053 for their generous assistance.

Information has been selected from Chevrolet and GMC shop manuals, owner's manuals, data books, brochures, service bulletins, and technical manuals.

Chilton's Repair Manual: Chevrolet/GMC Pick-Ups and Suburban 1970–87
ISBN 0-8019-7828-9 pbk.
Library of Congress Catalog Card No. 87-47947

General Information and Maintenance

HOW TO USE THIS BOOK

Chilton's Repair Manual for ½, ¾ and 1 ton Chevrolet and GMC pick-ups and Suburbans from 1970 to 1987, is intended to help you learn more about the inner workings of your vehicle and save you money on its upkeep and operation. All of the operations apply to both Chevrolet and GMC trucks unless specified otherwise.

The first two chapters will be the most used, since they contain maintenance and tune-up information and procedures. Studies have shown that a properly tuned and maintained truck can get at least 10% better gas mileage than an out-of-tune truck. The other chapters deal with the more complex systems of your truck. Operating systems from engine through brakes are covered to the extent that the average do-it-yourselfer becomes mechanically involved. This book will not explain such things as rebuilding the differential for the simple reason that the expertise required and the investment in special tools make this task uneconomical. It will give you detailed instructions to help you change your own brake pads and shoes, replace spark plugs, and do many more jobs that will save you money, give you personal satisfaction, and help you avoid expensive problems.

A secondary purpose of this book is a reference for owners who want to understand their truck and/or their mechanics better. In this case, no tools at all are required.

Before removing any bolts, read through the entire procedure. This will give you the overall view of what tools and supplies will be required. There is nothing more frustrating than having to walk to the bus stop on Monday morning because you were short one bolt on Sunday afternoon. So read ahead and plan ahead. Each operation should be approached logically and all procedures thoroughly understood before attempting any work.

All chapters contain adjustments, maintenance, removal and installation procedures, and repair or overhaul procedures. When repair is not considered practical, we tell you how to remove the part and then how to install the new or rebuilt replacement. In this way, you at least save the labor costs. Backyard repair of such components as the alternator is just not practical.

Two basic mechanic's rules should be mentioned here. One, whenever the left side of the truck or engine is referred to, it is meant to specify the driver's side of the truck. Conversely, the right side of the truck means the passenger's side. Secondly, most screws and bolt are removed by turning counterclockwise, and tightened by turning clockwise.

Safety is always the most important rule. Constantly be aware of the dangers involved in working on an automobile and take the proper precautions. (See the section in this chapter Servicing Your Vehicle Safely and the SAFETY NOTICE on the acknowledgement page.)

Pay attention to the instructions provided. There are 3 common mistakes in mechanical work:

1. Incorrect order of assembly, disassembly or adjustment. When taking something apart or putting it together, doing things in the wrong order usually justs cost you extra time; however, it CAN break something. Read the entire procedure before beginning disassembly. Do everything in the order in which the instructions say you should do it, even if you can't immediately see a reason for it. When you're taking apart something that is very intricate (for example, a carburetor), you might want to draw a picture of how it looks when assembled at one point in order to make sure you get everything back in its proper position. (We will supply exploded view whenever possible). When making adjustments, especially tune-up adjustments,

do them in order; often, one adjustment affects another, and you cannot expect even satisfactory results unless each adjustment is made only when it cannot be changed by any order.

2. Overtorquing (or undertorquing). While it is more common for over-torquing to cause damage, undertorquing can cause a fastener to vibrate loose causing serious damage. Especially when dealing with aluminum parts, pay attention to torque specifications and utilize a torque wrench in assembly. If a torque figure is not available, remember that if you are using the right tool to do the job, you will probably not have to strain yourself to get a fastener tight enough. The pitch of most threads is so slight that the tension you put on the wrench will be multiplied many, many times in actual force on what you are tightening. A good example of how critical torque is can be seen in the case of spark plug installation, especially where you are putting the plug into an aluminum cylinder head. Too little torque can fail to crush the gasket, causing leakage of combustion gases and consequent overheating of the plug and engine parts. Too much torque can damage the threads, or distort the plug which changes the spark gap.

There are many commercial products available for ensuring that fasteners won't come loose, even if they are not torqued just right (a very common brand is Loctite®). If you're worried about getting something together tight enough to hold, but loose enough to avoid mechanical damage during assembly, one of these products might offer substantial insurance. Read the label on the package and make sure the products is compatible with the materials, fluids, etc. involved before choosing one.

3. Crossthreading. This occurs when a part such as a bolt is screwed into a nut or casting at the wrong angle and forced. Cross threading is more likely to occur if access is difficult. It helps to clean and lubricate fasteners, and to start threading with the part to be installed going straight in. Then, start the bolt, spark plug, etc. with your fingers. If you encounter resistance, unscrew the part and start over again at a different angle until it can be inserted and turned several turns without much effort. Keep in mind that many parts, especially spark plugs, used tapered threads so that gentle turning will automatically bring the part you're treading to the proper angle if you don't force it or resist a change in angle. Don't put a wrench on the part until its's been turned a couple of turns by hand. If you suddenly encounter resistance, and the part has not seated fully, don't force it. Pull it back out and make sure it's clean and threading properly.

Always take your time and be patient; once

you have some experience, working on your truck will become an enjoyable hobby.

To use this book properly, each operation should be approached logically and the recommended procedures read thoroughly before beginning the work. Before attempting any operation, be sure that you understand exactly what is involved. Naturally, it is considerably eaasier if you have the necessary tools on hand and a clean place to work.

Information in this book is based on factory sources. Special factory tools have been eliminated from repair procedures wherever possible, in order to substitute more readily available tools.

TOOLS AND EQUIPMENT

It would be impossible to catalog each tool that you would need to perform each or any operation in this book. It would also not be wise for the amateur to rush out and buy an expensive set of tools on the theory that he may need one of them at some time. The best approach is to proceed slowly, gathering together a good quality set of those tools that are used most frequently. Don't be misled by the low cost of bargain tools. Forged wrenches, 12 point sockets and fine tooth ratchets are by far preferable to their less expensive counterparts. As any good mechanic can tell you, there are few worse experiences that trying to work on your truck with bad tools. Your monetary savings will be far outweighed by frustration and mangled knuckles.

Begin accumulating those tools that are used most frequently, In addition to a basic assortment of screwdrivers and a pair of pliers, you will need the following tools for routine maintenance and tune-up jobs:

1. One set each of both metric and S.A.E. sockets, including a ⅝" spark plug socket. Various length socket drive extensions and universals are also very helpful, but you'll probably acquire these as you need them. Ratchet handles are available in ¼", ⅜" and ½" drives, and will fit both metric and S.A.E. sockets (just make sure that your sockets are the proper drive size for the ratchet handle you buy).

2. One set each of metric and S.A.E. combination (one end open and one end box) wrenches.

3. Wire-type spark plug feeler gauge.

4. Blade-type feeler gauge for ignition and valve settings.

5. Slot and Phillips head screwdrivers in various sizes.

6. Oil filter strap wrench, necessary for re-

moving oil filters (never used, though, for installing the filters).

7. Oil can filler spout, for pouring fresh oil from quart oil cans.

8. Pair of slip-lock pliers.

9. Pair of vise-type pliers.

10. Adjustable wrench.

11. A hydraulic floor jack of at least 1½ ton capacity. If you are serious about maintaining your own truck, then a floor jack is as necessary as a spark plug socket. The greatly increased utility, strength, and safety of a hydraulic floor jack makes it pay for itself many times over through the years.

12. At least two sturdy jackstands for working underneath the truck—any other type of support (bricks, wood and especially cinderblocks) is just plain dangerous.

13. Timing light, preferably a DC battery hookup type, and preferably an inductive type for use on trucks with electronic ignition.

This is an adequate set of tools, and the more work you do yourself on your truck, the larger you'll find the set growing—a pair of pliers here, a wrench or two there. It makes more sense to have a comprehensive set of basic tools as listed above, and then to acquire more along the line as you need them, than to go out and plunk down big money for a professional size set you may never use. In addition to these basic tools, there are several other tools and gauges you may find useful.

1. A compression gauge. The screw-in type is slower to use but it eliminates the possibility of a faulty reading due to escaping pressure.

2. A manifold vacuum gauge, very useful in troubleshooting ignition and emissions problems.

3. A drop light, to light up the work area (make sure yours is Underwriter's approved, and has a shielded bulb).

4. A volt/ohm meter, used for determining whether or not there is current in a wire. These are handy for use if a wire is broken somewhere and are especially necessary for working on today's electronics-laden vehicles.

As a final note, a torque wrench is necessary for all but the most basic work. It should even be used when installing spark plugs. The more common beam-type models are perfectly adequate and are usually much less expensive than the more precise click type (on which you preset the torque and the wrench clocks when that setting arrives on the fastener you are torquing).

Special Tools

Special tools are occasionally necessary to perform a specific job or are recommended to make a job easier. Their use has been kept to a minimum. When a special tool is indicated, it will be referred to by the manufacturer's part number, and, where possible, an illustration of the tool will be provided so that an equivalent tool may be used. A list of tool manufacturers and their addresses follows:

Service Tool Division
Kent-Moore Corporation
1501 South Jackson Street
Jackson, Michigan 49203

In Canada, contact Kent-Moore of Canada, Ltd., 2395 Cawthra Mississauga, Ontario, Canada L5A 3P2.

SERVICING YOUR TRUCK SAFELY

It is virtually impossible to anticipate all of the hazards involved with automotive maintenance and service, but care and common sense will prevent most accidents.

The rules of safety for mechanics range from "don't smoke around gasoline," to "use the proper tool for the job." The trick to avoiding injuries is to develop safe work habits and take every possible precaution.

Dos

● Do keep a fire extinguisher and first aid kit within easy reach.

● Do wear safety glasses or goggles when cutting, drilling, grinding or prying, even if you have 20/20 vision. If you wear glasses for the sake of vision, they should be made of hardened glass that can serve also as safety glasses, or wear safety goggles over your regular glasses.

● Do shield your eyes whenever you work around the battery. Batteries contain sulphuric acid. In case of contact with the eyes or skin, flush the area with water or a mixture of water and baking soda and get medical attention immediately.

● Do use safety stands for any undercar service. Jacks are for raising vehicles; safety stands are for making sure the vehicle stays raised until you want it to come down. Whenever the car is raised, block the wheels remaining on the ground and set the parking brake.

● Do use adequate ventilation when working with any chemicals or hazardous materials. Like carbon monoxide, the asbestos dust resulting from brake lining wear can be poisonous in sufficient quantities.

● Do disconnect the negative battery cable when working on the electrical system. The secondary ignition system can contain up to 40,000 volts.

● Do follow manufacturer's directions whenever working with potentially hazardous materials. Both brake fluid and antifreeze are poisonous if taken internally.

• Do properly maintain your tools. Loose hammerheads, mushroomed punches and chisels, frayed or poorly grounded electrical cords, excessively worn screwdrivers, spread wrenches (open end), cracked sockets, slipping ratchets, or faulty droplight sockets can cause accidents.

• Likewise, keep your tools clean; a greasy wrench can slip off a bolt head, ruining the bolt and often ruining your knuckles in the process.

• Do use the proper size and type of tool for the job being done.

• Do when possible, pull on a wrench handle rather than push on it, and adjust you stance to prevent a fall.

• Do be sure that adjustable wrenches are tightly closed on the nut or bolt and pulled so that the face is on the side of the fixed jaw.

• Do select a wrench or socket that fits the nut or bolt. The wrench or socket should sit straight, not cocked.

• Do strike squarely with a hammer; avoid glancing blows.

• Do set the parking brake and block the drive wheels if the work requires the engine running.

Don'ts

• Don't run the engine in a garage or anywhere else without proper ventilation – EVER! Carbon monoxide is poisonous; it takes a long time to leave the human body and you can build up a deadly supply of it in your system by simply breathing in a little every day. You may not realize you are slowly poisoning yourself. Always use power vents, windows, fans or open the garage doors.

• Don't work around moving parts while wearing a necktie or other loose clothing. Short sleeves are much safer than long, loose sleeves; hard toed shoes with neoprene soles protect your toes and give a better grip on slippery surfaces. Jewelry such as watches, fancy belt buckles, beads or body adornment of any kind is not safe working around a car. Long hair should be tied back under a hat or cap.

• Don't use pockets for toolboxes. A fall or bump can drive a screwdriver deep into your body. Even a wiping cloth hanging from the back pocket can wrap around a spinning shaft or fan.

• Don't smoke when working around gasoline, cleaning solvent or other flammable material.

• Don't smoke when working around the battery. When the battery is being charged, it gives off explosive hydrogen gas.

• Don't use gasoline to wash your hands; there are excellent soaps available. Gasoline may contain lead, and lead can enter the body through a cut, accumulating in the body until you are very ill. Gasoline also remove all the natural oils from the skin so that bone dry hands will such up oil and grease.

• Don't service the air conditioning system unless you are equipped with the necessary tools and training. The refrigerant, R-12, is extremely cold when compressed, and when released into the air will instantly freeze any surface it contacts, including your eyes. Although the refrigerant is normally non-toxic, R-12 becomes a deadly poisonous gas in the presence of an open flame. One good whiff of the vapors from burning refrigerant can be fatal.

• Don't use screwdrivers for anything other than driving screws! A screwdriver used as an prying tool can snap when you least expect it, causing injuries. At the very least, you'll ruin a good screwdriver.

• Don't use a bumper jack (that little ratchet, scissors, or pantograph jack supplied with the car) for anything other tan chaining a flat! These jacks are only intended for emergency use out on the road; they are NOT designed as a maintenance tool. If you are serious about maintaining your car yourself, invest in a hydraulic floor jack of a least 1½ ton capacity, and at least two sturdy jackstands.

SERIAL NUMBER IDENTIFICATION

Vehicle

The Vehicle Identification Number (V.I.N.) is on a plate attached to the left hand door pillar, or on the left top of the dashboard (visible through the windshield) on later models. The gross vehicle weight (GVW), or maximum safe total weight of the truck, cargo, and passengers, is also given on the plate.

```
MFD. BY GENERAL MOTORS CORPORATION
                                GVWR [        ]
GAWR FRONT [        ]      GAWR REAR [        ]

VIN [        ]
   CAMPER LOADING DATA
   CWR [    ]   DIM A [    ]   DIM B [    ]
   INFLATION DATA FOR TIRES FURNISHED WITH VEHICLE
   FRONT [        ]              PRESSURE [    ]
   REAR  [        ]              PRESSURE [    ]
      WARRANTY VOIDED IF LOADED IN EXCESS OF RATINGS [ ]
   SEE OWNERS MANUAL FOR OTHER LOADING AND INFLATION DATA
```

Typical vehicle identification (VIN) plate

1970

The first letter indicates the vehicle type, **C** for two wheel drive, **K** for four wheel drive. The second letter indicates the engine type, **S** for six cylinder, or **E** for V8. The first number is for the GVW range, either a **1**, indication ½ ton, or a **2**, indication ¾ ton. The second and third numbers are for the body type: **04** for fenderside, or Stepside; **34** for wideside, or Fleetside. The third letter indicates the assembly plant. The fourth letter is for the model year (Z is for 1970). The last five digits are the serial numbers.

1971

The plate is essentially the same as 1970, except that either a hyphen or a letter indicating the type of state certification appears between the body type numbers and the assembly plant letter. The model year number is 1.

1972-78

The plates for these years are the same, with the exception of the engine codes, and the model years, of course. The first letter indicates a Chevrolet (C) or GMC (T) vehicle. The second letter is the vehicle type, C or K. The third letter is the engine type. For 1972 this would be an **S** or an **E**. Later years are covered below. The first number is the GVW range, 1 (½ ton) or 2 (¾ ton). The second number is the model type, **4** for cab and pickup box. The third number is for the year, **2** for 1972, for example. The fourth letter indicates the assembly plant. The last six numbers are the serial numbers.

The following are 1973-78 engine codes:

1973 ENGINE CODES
Q: 250 six
T: 292 six
X: 307 V8
Y: 350 V8
Z; 454 V8

1974 ENGINE CODES
Q: 250 six
T: 292 six
X: 307 V8
V: 350 V8 2 barrel
Y: 350 V8 4 barrel
Z: 454 V8

1975 ENGINE CODES
Q: 250 six
T: 292 six
X: 307 V8
V: 350 V8 2 barrel
Y: 350 V8 4 barrel
M: 400 V8 4 barrel
Z: 454 V8

1976 ENGINE CODES
D: 250 six
T: 292 six
V: 350 V8 2 barrel
L: 350 V8 4 barrel
V: 400 V8 4 barrel
S: 454 V8

1977 ENGINE CODES
D: 250 six
T: 292 six
V: 350 V8 2 barrel
L: 350 V8 4 barrel
R: 400 V8 4 barrel
S: 454 V8

1978 ENGINE CODES
D: 250 six
T: 292 six
U: 305 V8
L: 350 V8
R: 400 V8
S: 454 V8
Z: 350 V8 Diesel

1979-80

The VIN is on a plate attached to the upper left hand side of the instrument panel. The interpretation for the VIN code is the same as outlined for 1972-78, except for the engine codes, which are:

1979-80 ENGINE CODES
D: 250 six
T: 292 six
U: 305 V8
M: 350 V8 2 barrel
L: 350 V8 4 barrel
R: 400 V8
S: 454 V8
Z: 350 V8 Diesel

1981 and Later

Beginning in 1981 a new 17 digit code is used. The interpretation is the same previous years except that the engine code is the eighth digit. Additional engines/codes include the 305 V8 (F and H codes); a 350 V8 (P code); a **W** — code 454 V8 and a Chevrolet built 379 cu. in. V8 diesel, in both C and J codes.

Engine

The engine number is located as follows:

• Inline six cylinder: On a pad on the right hand side of the cylinder block, at the rear of the distributor.

• V6 and V8: On a pad at the front right hand side of the cylinder block, except for 1979 and 1980 454 V8s, which have the code on a pad at the front top center of the engine block immediately forward of the intake manifold; and diesel engines, which have the code on a label attached to the rear face of the left valve cover.

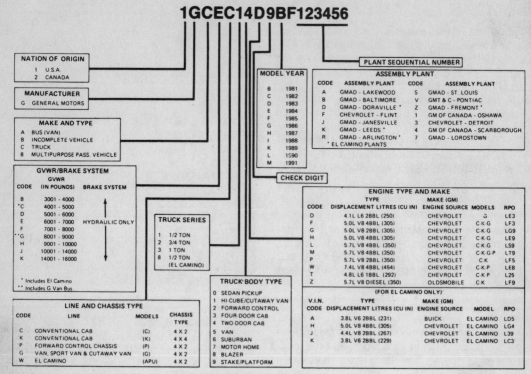

17-digit VIN, 1981 and later

Engine Cu. In. (liter)	Cylinders	1981	1982	1983	1984	1985	1986	1987
252 (4.1)	6	D	D	D	D	—	—	—
260 (4.3)	6	—	—	—	—	N	N	—
260 (4.3)	6	—	—	—	—	—	Z	Z
292 (4.8)	6	T	T	T	T	T	T	T
305 (5.0)	8	F	F	F	F	F	F	—
305 (5.0)	8	H	H	H	H	H	H	H
350 (5.7)	8	L	L	L	L	L	L	L
350 (5.7)	8	M	M	M	M	M	M	M
350 (5.7)	8	—	P	P	P	—	—	—
350 (5.7)	8	N	—	—	—	—	—	K
380 (6.2)	8	—	C	C	C	C	C	C
380 (6.2)	8	—	J	J	J	J	J	J
454 (7.4)	8	W	W	W	W	W	W	W
454 (7.4)	8	—	—	—	—	—	—	N

Engine Identification Codes by VIN Number 1981–1987

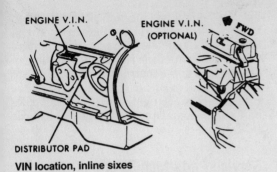

VIN location, inline sixes

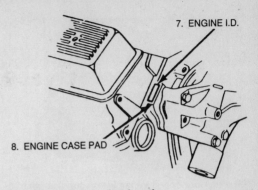

V6 engine serial number location

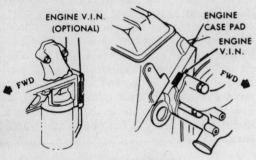

Gasoline V8 engine VIN location

Example-F1210TFA:
- F-Manufacturing Plant. F-Flint and T-Tonawanda
- 12-Month of Manufacture (December)
- 10-Day of Manufacture (Tenth)
- T-Truck
- FA-Transmission and Engine Combination

TRANSMISSION

The Muncie or Saginaw three speed manual transmission serial number is located on the lower left side of the case adjacent to the rear of the cover. The three speed Tremec transmission has the number on the upper forward mounting flange. The four speed transmission is numbered on the rear of the case, above the output shaft. The Turbo Hydra-Matic 350 serial number is on the right rear vertical surface of the fluid pan. The Turbo Hydra-Matic 400 is identified by a light blue plate attached to the right side, which is stamped with the serial number. The Powerglide transmission

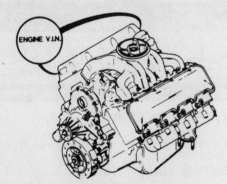

350 and 379 diesel engine VIN locations

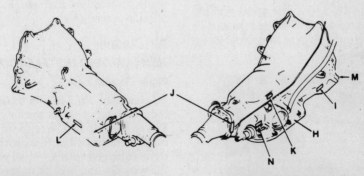

H. THM 350C stamped I.D. location
I. THM 350C VIN location
J. THM 350C optional VIN locations

K. THM 400 I.D. tag location
L. THM 400 VIN location
M. THM 700-R4 stamped I.D. location
N. THM 700-R4 VIN location

Turbo Hydra-Matic 350, 400, and 700 series I.D. locations

Three and four-speed transmission serial number location—lower left side of the case adjacent to the rear cover

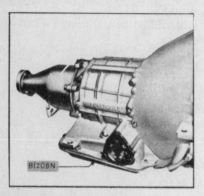

Powerglide serial number location

(through 1972 only) is stamped in the same location as the Turbo Hydra-Matic 350.

Transfer Case

The New Process 203, 205 and 208 transfer cases have a build date tag attached to the front of the case. Muncie Model 203 transfer cases have a build date on the front of the case above the output shaft.

Axles

From 1970 to 1973, the axle serial number for ½ ton Chevrolet and GMC trucks can be found on the bottom flange of the carrier hous-

Rear axle serial number location

ing. For ¾ and 1 ton, the number is stamped on the forward upper surface of the carrier. For all trucks, 1974 and later, the rear axle numbers are on the front of the right rear axle tube inboard of the upper control arm bracket, except for Dana-built axles, which are stamped on the rear surface of the right axle tube. Front axles on 4 x 4s are marked on the front of the left axle tube.

Service Parts Identification Plate

The service parts identification plate, commonly known as the option list, is usually located on the inside of the glove compartment door. On some trucks, you may have to look for it on an inner fender panel. The plate lists the vehicle serial number, wheelbase, all regular production options (RPOs) and all special equipment. Probably the most valuable piece of information on this plate is the paint code, a useful item when you have occasion to need paint.

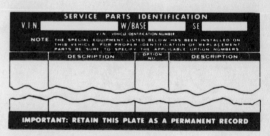

Service parts identification plate

ROUTINE MAINTENANCE

The accompanying chart gives the recommended maintenance intervals for the components covered her. Refer to the text for the applicable procedures.

Air Cleaner

REMOVAL AND INSTALLATION

Paper Element Type

Loosen the wing nut on top of the cover and remove the cover from the air cleaner housing. The element should be replaced when it has become oil saturated or filled with dirt. If the filter is equipped with a wetted wrapper, remove the wrapper and wash it in kerosene or similar solvent. Shake or blot dry. Saturate the wrapper in engine oil and squeeze it tightly in an absorbent towel to remove the excess oil. Leave the wrapper moist. Clean the dirt from the filter by lightly tapping it against a workbench to

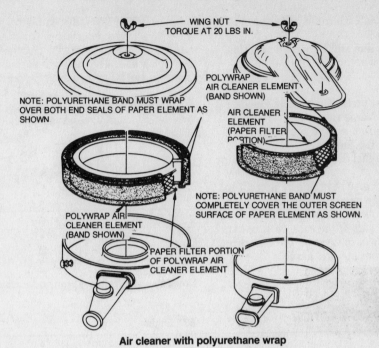

WING NUT
TORQUE AT 20 LBS IN.

POLYWRAP
AIR CLEANER ELEMENT
(BAND SHOWN)

AIR CLEANER
ELEMENT
(PAPER FILTER
PORTION)

NOTE: POLYURETHANE BAND MUST WRAP
OVER BOTH END SEALS OF PAPER ELEMENT AS
SHOWN

NOTE: POLYURETHANE BAND MUST
COMPLETELY COVER THE OUTER SCREEN
SURFACE OF PAPER ELEMENT AS SHOWN.

POLYWRAP AIR
CLEANER ELEMENT
(BAND SHOWN)

PAPER FILTER PORTION
OF POLYWRAP AIR
CLEANER ELEMENT

Air cleaner with polyurethane wrap

dislodge the dirt particles. Wash the top of the air cleaner housing and wipe it dry. If equipped, replace the crankcase ventilation filter, located in the air filter housing, if it appears excessively dirty. Replace the oiled wrapper on the air cleaner element and reinstall the element in the housing.

Fuel Pressure Release

Carbureted

To release the fuel pressure on the carbureted system, remove and replace the fuel tank cap.

Throttle Body Injection (TBI); Electronic Fuel Injection (EFI)

The 220 TBI unit used on the V6 and V8 engines contains a constant bleed feature in the pressure regulator that relieves pressure any time the engine is turned off. Therefore, no special relieve procedure is required, however, a small amount of fuel may be released when the fuel line is disconnected.

CAUTION: *To reduce the chance of personal injury, cover the fuel line with cloth to collect the fuel and then place the cloth in an approved container.*

Gasoline Fuel Filter

There are three types of fuel filters; internal (in the carburetor fitting), inline (in the fuel line) and in-tank (the sock on the fuel pickup tube).

CAUTION: *Before removing any component of the fuel system, refer to the Fuel Pressure Release procedures in this section and release the fuel pressure.*

REMOVAL AND INSTALLATION

Internal Filter

Internal filters are located in the inlet filling on all carburetors. Elements are placed in the inlet hole with the gasket surface outward. A spring holds the element outward, sealing it by compressing a gasket surface against the inlet fitting. A check valve is also built into the filter element.

1. Disconnect fuel line connection at fuel inlet filter nut.
2. Remove fuel inlet filter nut from carburetor.
3. Remove filter and spring.
4. If removed, install check valve in fuel inlet filter. The fuel inlet check valve must be installed in the filter to meet Motor Vehicle Safety Standards (M.V.S.S.) for roll-over. New service replacement filter must include the check valve.
5. Install fuel inlet filter spring, filter, and check valve assembly in carburetor. Check valve end of filter faces toward fuel line. Ribs on closed end of filter element prevent filter from being installed incorrectly unless forced.

6. Install nut in carburetor. Tighten nut to 24 N.m (18 ft.lb.).

7. Install fuel line and tighten connection.

8. Start engine and check for leaks.

Inline Filter

The inline filter on the fuel injected models is found along the frame rail.

1. Release the fuel system pressure.

2. Disconnect the fuel lines.

3. Remove the fuel filter from the retainer or mounting bolt.

4. To install, reverse the removal procedures. Start the engine and check for leaks.

NOTE: *The filter has an arrow (fuel flow direction) on the side of the case, be sure to install it correctly in the system, the with arrow facing away from the fuel tank.*

Diesel Fuel Filter

REMOVAL AND INSTALLATION

350 Engine

The diesel fuel filter is mounted on the rear of the intake manifold, and is larger than that on a gasoline engine because diesel fuel generally is dirtier (has more suspended particles than gasoline.

The diesel fuel filter should be changed every 30,000 miles or two years.

1. With the engine cool, place absorbent rags underneath the fuel line fittings at the filter.

2. Disconnect the fuel lines from the filter.

3. Unbolt the filter from its bracket.

4. Install a new filter. Start the engine and check for leaks. Run the engine for about two minutes, then shut the engine off for the same amount of time to allow any trapped air in the injection system to bleed off.

Some GM diesel trucks equipped with the 350 engine also have a fuel filter inside the fuel tank which is maintenance-free.

NOTE: *If the filter element ever becomes clogged, the engine will stop. This stoppage is usually preceded by a hesitation or sluggish running. General Motors recommends that after changing the diesel fuel filter, the Housing Pressure Cold Advance be activated manually, if the engine temperature is about 125 degrees F. Activating the H.P.C.A. will reduce engine cranking time.*

To activate the H.P.C.A. solenoid, disconnect the two-lead connector at the engine temperature switch and bridge the connector with a jumper. After the engine is running, remove the jumper and reconnect the connector to the engine temperature switch. When the new filter element is installed, start the engine and check for leaks.

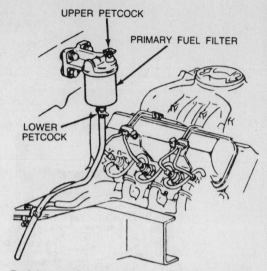

Draining water from the primary fuel filter, 379 diesel

379 Engine

On 1982-83 models, there are is a primary fuel filter attached to the firewall and a secondary fuel filter mounted to the back of the manifold. If it should be necessary to drain water from the fuel tank, also check the primary fuel filter for water and drain as outlined below.

The 1984-87 engines use an inline type filter which acts as a filter, water separator, water detector, water drain and a fuel heater.

1982-83 PRIMARY FILTER

If it should be necessary to check for water proceed as follows:

1. Open the petcock on the top of the primary filter housing.

2. Place a drain pan below the filter and open the petcock on the bottom of the drain assembly. (Attach a length of hose to the petcock and direct the fluid below the frame).

3. After all water is drained from the filter close the petcock tightly.

4. Replace the filter and fill with clean diesel fuel to prevent engine stalling.

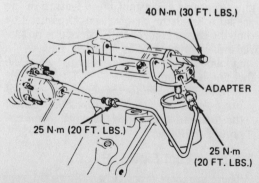

Secondary fuel filter installation, 379 diesel

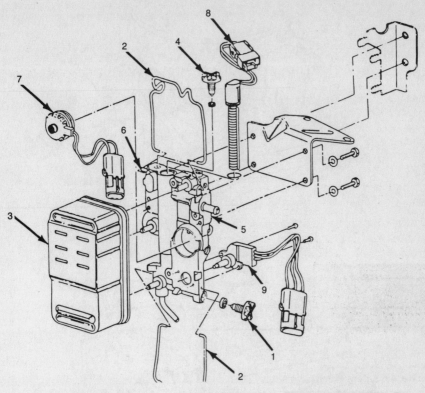

1. Water drain valve
2. Bail wires
3. Fuel filter element
4. Air bleed
5. Filter adapter
6. Air bleed port
7. Restriction switch
8. Fuel heater
9. Water sensor

Fuel filter, 1984–87 379 diesel engine

5. Close the upper petcock tightly.

6. Start the engine and let it run briefly. The engine may run roughly for a short time until the air is purged from the system.

NOTE: *If the engine continues to run roughly, check to make sure both petcocks are closed tightly.*

1982-83 SECONDARY FILTER

1. Remove the fuel filter lines from the adapter.

2. Remove the fuel filter adapter from the intake.

3. Remove the filter.

4. Replace the filter and refill with clean diesel fuel to prevent engine stalling after start up.

5. Install the fuel filter to the adapter.

6. Install the fuel filter adapter to the intake.

7. Install the fuel filter lines to the adapter.

1984-87

1. Remove the fuel filter cap to release any pressure or vacuum in the fuel tank.

2. Remove both bail wires.

3. Use a suitable container and drain the fuel from the filter by opening the air bleed and water drain valve.

4. Remove the fuel filter element.

5. Install a new filter element.

6. Install the bail wires.

7. Close the drain valve.

8. Install a ⅛" inside diameter hose to the air bleed port and the other end of the hose into a suitable container.

9. Disconnect the fuel injection pump shut-off solenoid wire.

10. Crank the engine for 10-15 seconds and then wait one minute for the starter motor to cool. Repeat until clear fuel is observed coming from the air bleed.

11. Close the air bleed.

12. Connect the injection pump solenoid wire.

13. Install the filler cap.

14. Start the engine and allow it to idle for five minutes.

15. Check the fuel filter for leaks.

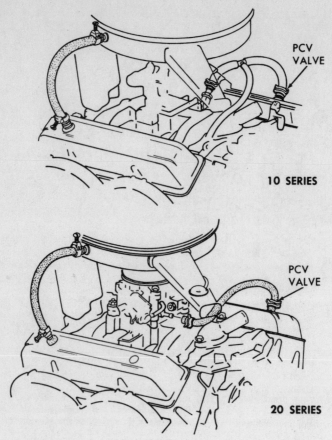

Typical PCV valve locations. Inline six valve also in valve cover

PCV Valve
REMOVAL AND INSTALLATION

The PCV valve is located on top of the valve cover. Its function is to purge the crankcase of harmful vapors through a system using engine vacuum to draw fresh air through the crankcase. The system reburns crankcase vapors, rather than exhausting them. Proper operation of the PCV valve depends on a sealed engine. If the oil begins to form sludge, which will be obvious as it is drained, and the PCV system is functioning properly, check the engine for possible causes.

Engine operating conditions that would indicate a malfunctioning PCV system are rough idle, oil present in the air cleaner, oil leaks or excessive oil sludging.

The simplest check for the PCV valve is to remove it from its rubber grommet on top of the valve cover and shake it. If it rattles, it is functioning; if not, replace it. In any event, it should be replaced at the recommended interval whether it rattles or not. Check the PCV hoses for breaks or restrictions. If necessary, the hos-es should also be replaced. The plastic T-fittings used in this system break easily, so be careful.

To replace the PCV valve:

1. Pull the valve, with the hose still attached to the valve, from the rubber grommet in the rocker cover.

2. Use a pair of pliers to release the hose clamp, remove the PCV valve from the hose.

3. Install the new valve into the hose, slide the clamp into position, and install the valve into the rubber grommet.

Evaporative Canister
SERVICING

The only regular maintenance that need be performed on the evaporative emission canister is to regularly change the filter and check the condition of the hoses. If any hoses need replacement, use only hoses which are marked **EVAP**. No other types should be used. Whenever the vapor vent hose is replaced, the restrictor adjacent to the canister should also be replaced.

The evaporative emission canister is located

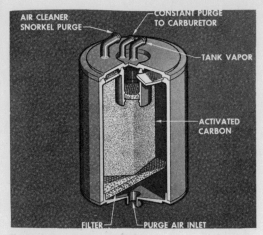

Typical evaporative canister

on the left side of the engine compartment, with a filter located in its bottom. The filter should be replaced according to the scheduled maintenance.

To service the canister filter:

1. Note the installed positions of the hoses, tagging them as necessary, in case any have to be removed.
2. Loosen the clamps and remove the bottom of the canister.
3. Pull the filter out and throw it away.
4. Install a new canister filter.
5. Install the bottom of the canister and tighten the clamps.
6. Check the hoses for cracks, restrictions or hose connection openings.

Crankcase Depression Regulator

Diesel Engines

The Crankcase Depression Regulator (CDR), found on 1981 and later diesels, and the flow control valve, used in 1980, are designed to scavenge crankcase vapors in basically the same manner as the PCV valve on gasoline engines. The valves are located either on the left rear corner of the intake manifold (CDR), or on the rear of the intake crossover pipe (flow control valve). On each system there are two ventilation filters, one per valve cover.

The filter assemblies should be cleaned every 15,000 miles by simply prying them carefully from the valve covers (be aware of the grommets underneath), and washing them out in solvent. The ventilation pipes and tubes should also be cleaned. Both the CDR and flow control valves should also be cleaned every 30,000 miles (the cover can be removed from the CDR; the flow control valve can simply be flushed with solvent). Dry each valve, filter, and hose with compressed air before installation.

NOTE: *Do not attempt to test the crankcase controls on these diesels. Instead, clean the valve cover filter assembly and vent pipes and check the vent pipes.*

Replace the breather cap assembly every 30,000 miles. Replace all rubber fittings as required every 15,000 miles.

Battery

Check the battery fluid level (except in Maintenance Free batteries) at least once a month, more often in hot weather or during extended periods of travel. The electrolyte level should be up to the bottom of the split ring in each cell. All batteries on Chevrolet and GMC trucks are equipped with an eye in the cap of one cell. If the eye glows or has an amber color to it, this means that the level is low and only distilled water should be added. Do not add anything else to the battery. If the eye has a dark appearance the battery electrolyte level is high enough. It is wise to also check each cell individually.

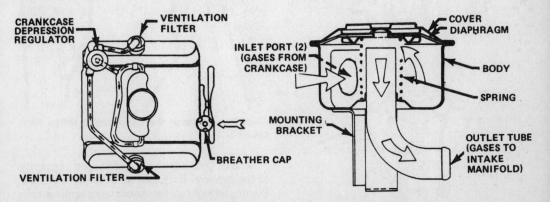

DIESEL CRANKCASE VENTILATION SYSTEM   **CRANKCASE DEPRESSION REGULATOR**

Diesel crankcase ventilation flow and depression regulator

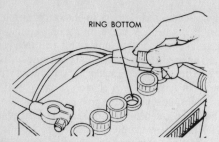

Fill each battery cell to the bottom of the split ring with distilled water

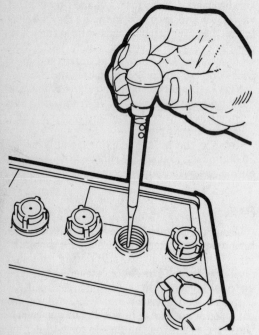

The specific gravity of the battery can be checked with a simple float-type hydrometer

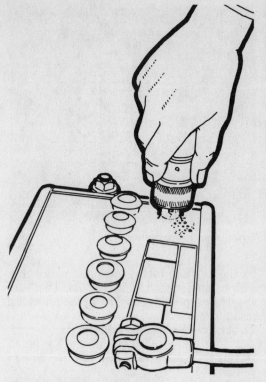

Clean the battery posts with a wire brush, or the special tool shown

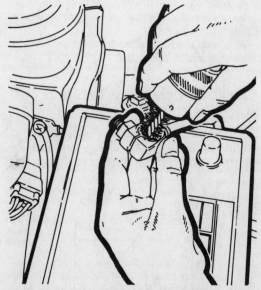

Clean the inside of the cable clamp with a wire brush

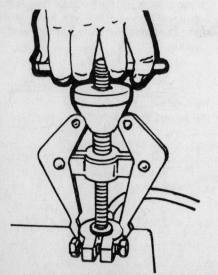

Special pullers are available to remove cable clamps

At least once a year, check the specific gravity of the battery. It should be between 1.20-1.26. Clean and tighten the clamps and apply a thin coat of petroleum jelly to the terminals. This will help to retard corrosion. The terminals can be cleaned with a stiff wire brush or with an in-

Battery State of Charge at Room Temperature

Specific Gravity Reading	Charged Condition
1.260–1.280	Fully Charged
1.230–1.250	¾ Charged
1.200–1.220	½ Charged
1.170–1.190	¼ Charged
1.140–1.160	Almost no Charge
1.110–1.130	No Charge

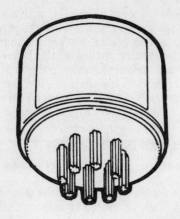

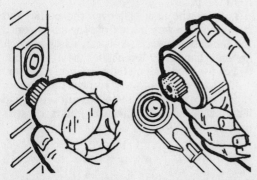

Special tools are available for cleaning the terminals and cable clamps on side terminal batteries

expensive terminal cleaner designed for this purpose.

If water is added during freezing weather, the truck should be driven several miles to allow the electrolyte and water to mix. Otherwise the battery could freeze.

If the battery becomes corroded, a solution of baking soda and water will neutralize the corrosion. This should be washed off after making sure that the caps are securely in place. Rinse the solution off with cold water.

Some batteries were equipped with a felt terminal washer. This should be saturated with engine oil approximately every 6,000 miles. This will also help to retard corrosion.

If a fast charger is used while the battery is in the truck, disconnect the battery before connecting the charger.

CAUTION: *Keep flame or sparks away from the battery; it gives off explosive hydrogen gas.*

TESTING THE MAINTENANCE FREE BATTERY

All later model trucks are equipped with maintenance free batteries, which do not require normal attention as far as fluid level checks are concerned. However, the terminals require periodic cleaning, which should be performed at least once a year.

The sealed top battery cannot be checked for charge in the normal manner, since there is no provision for access to the electrolyte. To check the condition of the battery:

1. If the indicator eye on top of the battery is dark, the battery has enough fluid. If the eye is light, the electrolyte fluid is too low and the battery must be replaced.

2. If a green dot appears in the middle of the eye, the battery is sufficiently charged. Proceed to Step 4. If no green dot is visible, charge the battery as in Step 3.

3. Charge the battery at this rate:

Charging Rate Amps	Time
75	40 min
50	1 hr
25	2 hr
10	5 hr

CAUTION: *Do not charge the battery for more than 50 amp/hours. If the green dot appears, or if electrolyte squirts out of the vent hole, stop the charge and proceed to Step 4.*

It may be necessary to tip the battery from side to side to get the green dot to appear after charging.

4. Connect a battery load tester and a voltmeter across the battery terminals (the battery cables should be disconnected from the battery). Apply a 300 amp load to the battery for 15 seconds to remove the surface charge. Remove the load.

5. Wait 15 seconds to allow the battery to recover. Apply the appropriate test load, as specified in the following chart:

Battery	Test Load
Y85-4	130 amps
R85-5	170 amps
R87-5	210 amps
R89-5	230 amps

Apply the load for 15 seconds while reading the voltage. Disconnect the load.

6. Check the results against the following chart. If the battery voltage is at or above the specified voltage for the temperature listed, the battery is good. If the voltage falls below what's listed, the battery should be replaced.

Temperature (°F)	Minimum Voltage
70 or above	9.6
60	9.5
50	9.4
40	9.3
30	9.1
20	8.9
10	8.7
0	8.5

Heat Riser
SERVICING

The heat riser is a thermostatically or vacuum operated valve in the exhaust manifold. Not all engines have one. Heat riser equipped V8s have only one valve, located in the right manifold. The valve opens when the engine is warming up, to direct hot exhaust gases to the intake manifold, in order to preheat the incoming fuel/air mixture. If it sticks shut, the result will be frequent stalling during warmup, especially in cold and damp weather. If it sticks open, the result will be a rough idle after the engine is warm. The heat riser should move freely. If it sticks, apply GM Manifold Heat Control Solvent or something similar (engine cool) to the ends of the shaft. Sometimes rapping the end of the shaft sharply with a hammer (engine hot) will break it loose. If this fails, components must be removed for further repairs.

Drive Belts
INSPECTION

At the interval specified in the Maintenance Intervals chart, check the water pump, alternator, power steering pump (if equipped), air conditioning compressor (if equipped) and air pump (if equipped) drive belts for proper tension. Also look for signs of wear, fraying, separation, glazing, and so on, and replace the belts as required.

ADJUSTMENT

Belt tension should be checked with a gauge made for the purpose. If a tension gauge is not available, tension can be checked with moderate thumb pressure applied to the belt at its longest span midway between pulleys. If the belt has a free span less than 12″, it should deflect approximately 1/8-1/4″. If the span is longer than 12″, deflection can range between 1/8″ and 3/8″.

REMOVAL AND INSTALLATION

1. Loosen the driven accessory's pivot and mounting bolts.
2. Move the accessory toward the engine until enough slack is created to remove the belt from the pulley.
3. Place the new belt over the pulley and move the accessory away from the engine until the tension is correct. You can use a wooden hammer handle, or broomstick, as a lever, but do not use anything metallic, such as a prybar.
4. Tighten the bolts and recheck the tension. If new belts have been installed, run the engine for a few minutes, then recheck and readjust as necessary.

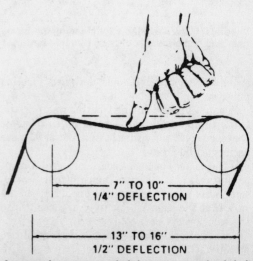

A gauge is recommended, but you can check belt tension with thumb pressure

Typical heater riser valve, six cylinder shown

HOW TO SPOT WORN V-BELTS

V-Belts are vital to efficient engine operation—they drive the fan, water pump and other accessories. They require little maintenance (occasional tightening) but they will not last forever. Slipping or failure of the V-belt will lead to overheating. If your V-belt looks like any of these, it should be replaced.

Cracking or weathering

This belt has deep cracks, which cause it to flex. Too much flexing leads to heat build-up and premature failure. These cracks can be caused by using the belt on a pulley that is too small. Notched belts are available for small diameter pulleys.

Softening (grease and oil)

Oil and grease on a belt can cause the belt's rubber compounds to soften and separate from the reinforcing cords that hold the belt together. The belt will first slip, then finally fail altogether.

Glazing

Glazing is caused by a belt that is slipping. A slipping belt can cause a run-down battery, erratic power steering, overheating or poor accessory performance. The more the belt slips, the more glazing will be built up on the surface of the belt. The more the belt is glazed, the more it will slip. If the glazing is light, tighten the belt.

Worn cover

The cover of this belt is worn off and is peeling away. The reinforcing cords will begin to wear and the belt will shortly break. When the belt cover wears in spots or has a rough jagged appearance, check the pulley grooves for roughness.

Separation

This belt is on the verge of breaking and leaving you stranded. The layers of the belt are separating and the reinforcing cords are exposed. It's just a matter of time before it breaks completely.

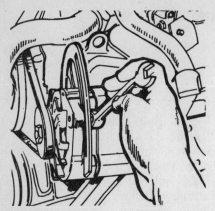

To adjust belt tension or to replace belts, first loosen the component's mounting and adjusting bolts slightly

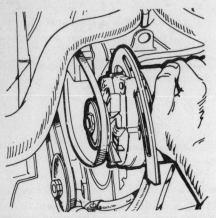

Push the component toward the engine and slip off the belt

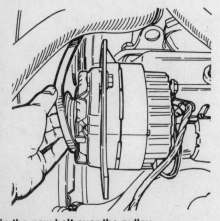

Slip the new belt over the pulley

It is better to have belts too loose than too tight, because overtight belts will lead to bearing failure, particularly in the water pump and alternator. However, loose belts place an extremely high impact load on the driven component due to the whipping action of the belt.

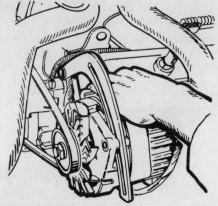

Pull outward on the component and tighten the mounting bolts

Hoses

Upper and lower radiator hoses and all heater hoses should be checked for deterioration, leaks and loose hose clamps every 15,000 miles.

REMOVAL AND INSTALLATION

1. Drain the radiator as detailed later in this chapter.

CAUTION: *When draining the coolant, keep in mind that cats and dogs are attracted by the ethylene glycol antifreeze, and are quite likely to drink any that is left in an uncovered container or in puddles on the ground. This will prove fatal in sufficient quantity. Always drain the coolant into a sealable container. Coolant should be reused unless it is contaminated or several years old.*

2. Loosen the hose clamps at each end of the hose to be removed.

3. Working the hose back and forth, slide it off its connection and then install a new hose if necessary.

4. Position the hose clamps at least ¼" from the end of the hose and tighten them.

NOTE: *Always make sure that the hose clamps are beyond the bead and place in the center of the clamping surface before tightening them.*

Air Conditioning

GENERAL SERVICING PROCEDURES

The most important aspect of air conditioning service is the maintenance of a pure and adequate charge of refrigerant in the system. A refrigeration system cannot function properly if a significant percentage of the charge is lost. Leaks are common because the severe vibration encountered in an automobile can easily cause a sufficient cracking or loosening of the air condi-

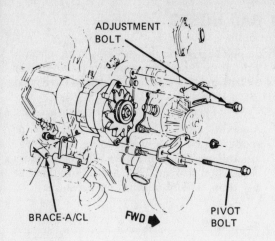

GENERATOR

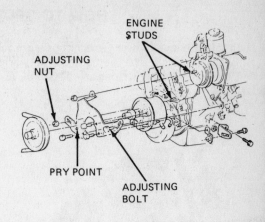

POWER STEERING

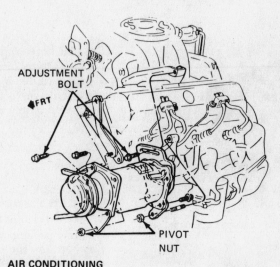

AIR CONDITIONING

379 diesel belt adjustments

tioning fittings; as a result, the extreme operating pressures of the system force refrigerant out.

The problem can be understood by considering what happens to the system as it is operated with a continuous leak. Because the expansion valve regulates the flow of refrigerant to the evaporator, the level of refrigerant there is fairly constant. The receiver/drier stores any excess of refrigerant, and so a loss will first appear there as a reduction in the level of liquid. As this level nears the bottom of the vessel, some refrigerant vapor bubbles will begin to appear in the stream of liquid supplied to the expansion valve. This vapor decreases the capacity of the expansion valve very little as the valve opens to compensate for its presence. As the quantity of liquid in the condenser decreases, the operating pressure will drop there and

throughout the high side of the system. As the R-12 continues to be expelled, the pressure available to force the liquid through the expansion valve will continue to decrease, and, eventually, the valve's orifice will prove to be too much of a restriction for adequate flow even with the needle fully withdrawn.

At this point, low side pressure will start to drop, and severe reduction in cooling capacity, marked by freeze-up of the evaporator coil, will result. Eventually, the operating pressure of the evaporator will be lower than the pressure of the atmosphere surrounding it, and air will be drawn into the system wherever there are leaks in the low side.

Because all atmospheric air contains at least some moisture, water will enter the system and mix with the R-12 and the oil. Trace amounts of moisture will cause sludging of the oil, and cor-

HOW TO SPOT BAD HOSES

Both the upper and lower radiator hoses are called upon to perform difficult jobs in an inhospitable environment. They are subject to nearly 18 psi at under hood temperatures often over 280°F., and must circulate nearly 7500 gallons of coolant an hour—3 good reasons to have good hoses.

A good test for any hose is to feel it for soft or spongy spots. Frequently these will appear as swollen areas of the hose. The most likely cause is oil soaking. This hose could burst at any time, when hot or under pressure.

Swollen hose

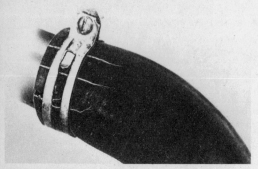

Cracked hoses can usually be seen but feel the hoses to be sure they have not hardened; a prime cause of cracking. This hose has cracked down to the reinforcing cords and could split at any of the cracks.

Cracked hose

Weakened clamps frequently are the cause of hose and cooling system failure. The connection between the pipe and hose has deteriorated enough to allow coolant to escape when the engine is hot.

Frayed hose end (due to weak clamp)

Debris, rust and scale in the cooling system can cause the inside of a hose to weaken. This can usually be felt on the outside of the hose as soft or thinner areas.

Debris in cooling system

rosion of the system. Saturation and clogging of the filter/drier, and freezing of the expansion valve orifice will eventually result. As air fills the system to a greater and greater extent, it will interfere more and more with the normal flows of refrigerant and heat.

From this description, it should be obvious that much of the repairman's time will be spent detecting leaks, repairing them, and then restoring the purity and quantity of the refrigerant charge. A list of general precautions that should be observed while doing this follows:

1. Keep all tools as clean and dry as possible.

2. Thoroughly purge the service gauges and hoses of air and moisture before connecting them to the system. Keep them capped when not in use.

3. Thoroughly clean any refrigerant fitting before disconnecting it, in order to minimize the entrance of dirt into the system.

4. Plan any operation that requires opening the system beforehand, in order to minimize the length of time it will be exposed to open air. Cap or seal the open ends to minimize the entrance of foreign material.

5. When adding oil, pour it through an extremely clean and dry tube or funnel. Keep the oil capped whenever possible. Do not use oil that has not been kept tightly sealed.

6. Use only refrigerant 12. Purchase refrigerant intended for use in only automatic air conditioning systems. Avoid the use of refrigerant 12 that may be packaged for another use, such as cleaning, or powering a horn, as it is impure.

7. Completely evacuate any system that has been opened to replace a component, or that has leaked sufficiently to draw in moisture and air. This requires evacuating air and moisture with a good vacuum pump for at least one hour. If a system has been open for a considerable length of time it may be advisable to evacuate the system for up to 12 hours (overnight).

8. Use a wrench on both halves of a fitting that is to be disconnected, so as to avoid placing torque on any of the refrigerant lines.

9. When overhauling a compressor, pour some of the oil into a clean glass and inspect it. If there is evidence of dirt or metal particles, or both, flush all refrigerant components with clean refrigerant before evacuating and recharging the system. In addition, if metal particles are present, the compressor should be replaced.

10. Schrader valves may leak only when under full operating pressure. Therefore, if leakage is suspected but cannot be located, operate the system with a full charge of refrigerant and look for leaks from all Schrader valves. Replace any faulty valves.

Additional Preventive Maintenance Checks

ANTIFREEZE

In order to prevent heater core freeze-up during A/C operation, it is necessary to maintain permanent type antifreeze protection of +15°F, or lower. A reading of −15°F is ideal since this protection also supplies sufficient corrosion inhibitors for the protection of the engine cooling system.

NOTE: *The same antifreeze should not be used longer than the manufacturer specifies.*

RADIATOR CAP

For efficient operation of an air conditioned car's cooling system, the radiator cap should have a holding pressure which meets manufacturer's specifications. A cap which fails to hold these pressures should be replaced.

CONDENSER

Any obstruction of or damage to the condenser configuration will restrict the air flow which is essential to its efficient operation. It is therefore a good rule to keep this unit clean and in proper physical shape.

NOTE: *Bug screens are regarded as obstructions.*

CONDENSATION DRAIN TUBE

This single molded drain tube expels the condensation, which accumulates on the bottom of the evaporator housing, into the engine compartment. If this tube is obstructed, the air conditioning performance can be restricted and condensation buildup can spill over onto the vehicle's floor.

SAFETY PRECAUTIONS

Because of the importance of the necessary safety precautions that must be exercised when working with air conditioning systems and R-12 refrigerant, a recap of the safety precautions are outlined.

1. Avoid contact with a charged refrigeration system, even when working on another part of the air conditioning system or vehicle. If a heavy tool comes into contact with a section of copper tubing or a heat exchanger, it can easily cause the relatively soft material to rupture.

2. When it is necessary to apply force to a fitting which contains refrigerant, as when checking that all system couplings are securely tightened, use a wrench on both parts of the fitting involved, if possible. This will avoid putting torque on refrigerant tubing. (It is advisable, when possible, to use tube or line wrenches when tightening these flare nut fittings.)

3. Do not attempt to discharge the system by merely loosening a fitting, or removing the ser-

vice valve caps and cracking these valves. Precise control is possible only when using the service gauges. Place a rag under the open end of the center charging hose while discharging the system to catch any drops of liquid that might escape. Wear protective gloves when connecting or disconnecting service gauge hoses.

4. Discharge the system only in a well ventilated area, as high concentrations of the gas can exclude oxygen and act as an anaesthetic. When leak testing or soldering, this is particularly important, as toxic gas is formed when R-12 contacts any flame.

5. Never start a system without first verifying that both service valves are back-seated, if equipped, and that all fittings throughout the system are snugly connected.

6. Avoid applying heat to any refrigerant line or storage vessel. Charging may be aided by using water heated to less than 125° to warm the refrigerant container. Never allow a refrigerant storage container to sit out in the sun, or near any other source of heat, such as a radiator.

7. Always wear goggles when working on a system to protect the eyes. If refrigerant contacts the eyes, it is advisable in all cases to see a physician as soon as possible.

8. Frostbite from liquid refrigerant should be treated by first gradually warming the area with cool water, and then gently applying petroleum jelly. A physician should be consulted.

9. Always keep refrigerant drum fittings capped when not in use. Avoid sudden shock to the drum, which might occur from dropping it, or from banging a heavy tool against it. Never carry a drum in the passenger compartment of a car.

10. Always completely discharge the system before painting the vehicle (if the paint is to be baked on), or before welding anywhere near refrigerant lines.

Air Conditioning Tools and Gauges

Test Gauges

Most of the service work performed in air conditioning requires the use of a set of two gauges, one for the high (head) pressure side of the system, the other for the low (suction) side.

The low side gauge records both pressure and vacuum. Vacuum readings are calibrated from 0 to 30 inches and the pressure graduations read from 0 to no less than 60 psi.

The high side gauge measures pressure from 0 to at least 600 psi.

Both gauges are threaded into a manifold that contains two hand shut-off valves. Proper manipulation of these valves and the use of the attached test hoses allow the user to perform the following services:

1. Test high and low side pressures.
2. Remove air, moisture, and contaminated refrigerant.
3. Purge the system (of refrigerant).
4. Charge the system (with refrigerant).

The manifold valves are designed so they have no direct effect on gauge readings, but serve only to provide for, or cut off, flow of refrigerant through the manifold. During all testing and hook-up operations, the valves are kept in a closed position to avoid disturbing the refrigeration system. The valves are opened only to purge the system of refrigerant or to charge it.

When purging the system, the center hose is uncapped at the lower end, and both valves are cracked open slightly. This allows refrigerant pressure to force the entire contents of the system out through the center hose. During charging, the valve on the high side of the manifold is closed, and the valve on the low side is cracked open. Under these conditions, the low pressure in the evaporator will draw refrigerant from the relatively warm refrigerant storage container into the system.

Service Valves

For the user to diagnose an air conditioning system he or she must gain "entrance" to the system in order to observe the pressures. There are two types of terminals for this purpose, the hand shut off type and the familiar Schrader valve.

The Schrader valve is similar to a tire valve stem and the process of connecting the test hoses is the same as threading a hand pump outlet hose to a bicycle tire. As the test hose is threaded to the service port the valve core is depressed, allowing the refrigerant to enter the test hose outlet. Removal of the test hose automatically closes the system.

Extreme caution must be observed when removing test hoses from the Schrader valves as some refrigerant will normally escape, usually under high pressure. (Observe safety precautions.)

Some systems have hand shut-off valves (the stem can be rotated with a special ratcheting box wrench) that can be positioned in the following three ways:

1. FRONT SEATED—Rotated to full clockwise position.

a. Refrigerant will not flow to compressor, but will reach test gauge port. COMPRESSOR WILL BE DAMAGED IF SYSTEM IS TURNED ON IN THIS POSITION.

b. The compressor is now isolated and ready for service. However, care must be exercised when removing service valves from the compressor as a residue of refrigerant may still be present within the compressor. Therefore, remove service valves slowly observing all safety precautions.

2. BACK SEATED – Rotated to full counter clockwise position. Normal position for system while in operation. Refrigerant flows to compressor but not to test gauge.

3. MID-POSITION (CRACKED) – Refrigerant flows to entire system. Gauge port (with hose connected) open for testing.

USING THE MANIFOLD GAUGES

The following are step-by-step procedures to guide the user to correct gauge usage.

1. WEAR GOGGLES OR FACE SHIELD DURING ALL TESTING OPERATIONS. BACKSEAT HAND SHUT-OFF TYPE SERVICE VALVES.

2. Remove caps from high and low side service ports. Make sure both gauge valves are closed.

3. Connect low side test hose to service valve that leads to the evaporator (located between the evaporator outlet and the compressor).

4. Attach high side test hose to service valve that leads to the condenser.

5. Mid-position hand shutoff type service valves.

6. Start engine and allow for warm-up. All testing and charging of the system should be done after engine and system have reached normal operation temperatures (except when using certain charging stations).

7. Adjust air conditioner controls to maximum cold.

8. Observe gauge readings.

When the gauges are not being used it is a good idea to:

a. Keep both hand valves in the closed position.

b. Attach both ends of the high and low service hoses to the manifold, if extra outlets are present on the manifold, or plug them if not. Also, keep the center charging hose attached to an empty refrigerant can. This extra precaution will reduce the possibility of moisture entering the gauges. If air and moisture have gotten into the gauges, purge the hoses by supplying refrigerant under pressure to the center hose with both gauge valves open and all openings unplugged.

SYSTEM CHECKS

CAUTION: *Do not attempt to charge or discharge the refrigerant system unless you are thoroughly familiar with its operation and the hazards involved. The compressed refrigerant used in the air conditioning system expands and evaporates (boils) into the atmosphere at a temperature of –21.7°F (–29.8°C)*

or less. This will freeze any surface that it comes in contact with, including your eyes. In addition, the refrigerant decomposes into a poisonous gas in the presence of flame.

1970-72

All Chevrolet and GMC pick-ups in these years have an air conditioning sight glass for checking the refrigerant charge.

1. Start the engine and set it on fast idle.

2. Set the controls for maximum cold with the blower on high.

3. If bubbles are present in the sight glass, the system is low on charge. If no bubbles are present in the sight glass, the system is either fully charged or empty.

4. Feel the high and low pressure lines at the compressor. The high pressure line should be warm and the low pressure line should be cool. If no appreciable temperature difference is felt, the system is empty or nearly empty.

Even though there is a noticeable temperature difference, there is a possibility of over-charge. If the refrigerant in the sight glass remains clear for more than 45 seconds before foaming and then settling away from the sight glass, an overcharge is indicated.

If the refrigerant foams and then settles away from the sight glass in less than 45 seconds, it can be assumed that the system is properly charged.

1973 and Later

These air conditioning systems have no sight glass for checking.

1. Warm the engine to normal operating temperature.

2. Open the hood and doors.

3. Set the selector lever at A/C.

4. Set the temperature lever at the first detent to the right of COLD (outside air).

5. Set the blower on HI.

6. Idle the engine at 1,000 rpm.

7. Feel the temperature of the evaporator inlet and the accumulator outlet with the compressor engaged.

Both lines should be cold. If the inlet pipe is colder than the outlet pipe the system is low on charge.

DISCHARGING THE SYSTEM

CAUTION: *Perform operation in a well ventilated area.*

When it is necessary to remove (purge) the refrigerant pressurized in the system, follow this procedure:

1. Operate air conditioner for at least 10 minutes.

2. Attach gauges, shut off engine and air conditioner.

3. Place a container or rag at the outlet of the center charging hose on the gauge. The refrigerant will be discharged there and this precaution will avoid its uncontrolled exposure.

4. Open low side hand valve on gauge slightly.

5. Open high side hand valve slightly.

NOTE: *Too rapid a purging process will be identified by the appearance of an oily foam. If this occurs, close the hand valves a little more until this condition stops.*

6. Close both hand valves on the gauge set when the pressures read 0 and all the refrigerant has left the system.

EVACUATING THE SYSTEM

Before charging any system it is necessary to purge the refrigerant and draw out the trapped moisture with a suitable vacuum pump. Failure to do so will result in ineffective charging and possible damage to the system.

Use this hook-up for the proper evacuation procedure:

1. Connect both service gauge hoses to the high and low service outlets.

2. Open high and low side hand valves on gauge manifold.

3. Open both service valves a slight amount (from back seated position), allow refrigerant to discharge from system.

4. Install center charging hose of gauge set to vacuum pump.

5. Operate vacuum pump for at least one hour. (If the system has been subjected to open conditions for a prolonged period of time it may be necessary to "pump the system down" overnight. Refer to "System Sweep" procedure.)

NOTE: *If low pressure gauge does not show at least 28 in.Hg within 5 minutes, check the system for a leak or loose gauge connectors.*

6. Close hand valves on gauge manifold.

7. Shut off pump.

8. Observe low pressure gauge to determine if vacuum is holding. A vacuum drop may indicate a leak.

SYSTEM SWEEP

An efficient vacuum pump can remove all the air contained in a contaminated air conditioning system very quickly, because of its vapor state. Moisture, however, is far more difficult to remove because the vacuum must force the liquid to evaporate before it will be able to remove it from the system. If a system has become severely contaminated, as, for example, it might become after all the charge was lost in conjunction with vehicle accident damage, moisture removal is extremely time consuming. A vacuum pump could remove all of the moisture only if it were operated for 12 hours or more.

Under these conditions, sweeping the system with refrigerant will speed the process of moisture removal considerably. To sweep, follow the following procedure:

1. Connect vacuum pump to gauges, operate it until vacuum ceases to increase, then continue operation for ten more minutes.

2. Charge system with 50% of its rated refrigerant capacity.

3. Operate system at fast idle for ten minutes.

4. Discharge the system.

5. Repeat twice the process of charging to 50% capacity, running the system for ten minutes, and discharging it, for a total of three sweeps.

6. Replace drier.

7. Pump system down as in Step 1.

8. Charge system.

CHARGING THE SYSTEM

CAUTION: *Never attempt to charge the system by opening the high pressure gauge control while the compressor is operating. The compressor accumulating pressure can burst the refrigerant container, causing sever personal injuries.*

Basic System

In this procedure the refrigerant enters the suction side of the system as a vapor while the compressor is running. Before proceeding, the system should be in a partial vacuum after adequate evacuation. Both hand valves on the gauge manifold should be closed.

1. Attach both test hoses to their respective service valve ports. Mid-position manually operated service valves, if present.

2. Install dispensing valve (closed position) on the refrigerant container. (Single and multiple refrigerant manifolds are available to accommodate one to four 15 oz. cans.)

3. Attach center charging hose to the refrigerant container valve.

4. Open dispensing valve on the refrigerant can.

5. Loosen the center charging hose coupler where it connects to the gauge manifold to allow the escaping refrigerant to purge the hose of contaminants.

6. Tighten center charging hose connection.

7. Purge the low pressure test hose at the gauge manifold.

8. Start car engine, roll down the car windows and adjust the air conditioner to maximum cooling. The car engine should be at normal operating temperature before proceeding. The heated environment helps the liquid vaporize more efficiently.

9. Crack open the low side hand valve on the

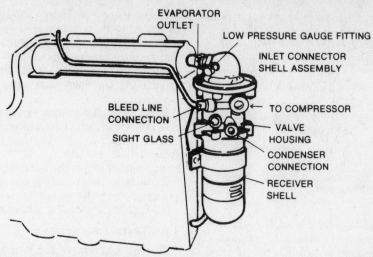

EVAPORATOR OUTLET
LOW PRESSURE GAUGE FITTING
INLET CONNECTOR SHELL ASSEMBLY
BLEED LINE CONNECTION
TO COMPRESSOR
VALVE HOUSING
SIGHT GLASS
CONDENSER CONNECTION
RECEIVER SHELL

The air conditioning sight glass on most models is located near the top of the VIR unit, mounted on the left side of the radiator

manifold. Manipulate the valve so that the refrigerant that enters the system does not cause the low side pressure to exceed 40 psi. Too sudden a surge may permit the entrance of unwanted liquid to the compressor. Since liquids cannot be compressed, the compressor will suffer damage if compelled to attempt it. If the suction side of the system remains in a vacuum the system is blocked. Locate and correct the condition before proceeding any further.

NOTE: *Placing the refrigerant can in a container of warm water (no hotter than 125°F) will speed the charging process. Slight agitation of the can is helpful too, but be careful not to turn the can upside down.*

Some manufacturers allow for a partial charging of the A/C system in the form of a liquid (can inverted and compressor off) by opening the high side gauge valve only, and putting the high side compressor service valve in the middle position (if so equipped). The remainder of the refrigerant is then added in the form of a gas in the normal manner, through the suction side only.

Systems With A Sight Glass (1970-72)

The air conditioning systems that use a sight glass as a means to check the refrigerant level, should be carefully checked to avoid under or over charging. The gauge set should be attached to the system for verification of pressures.

To check the system with the sight glass, clean the glass and start the vehicle engine. Operate the air conditioning controls on maximum for approximately five minutes to stabilize the system. The room temperature should be above 70 degrees. Check the sight glass for one of the following conditions:

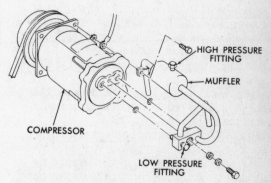

HIGH PRESSURE FITTING
MUFFLER
COMPRESSOR
LOW PRESSURE FITTING

High and low pressure lines on the 1970–72 factory-installed air conditioning compressor

1. If the sight glass is clear, the compressor clutch is engaged, the compressor discharge line is warm and the compressor inlet line is cool, the system has a full charge of refrigerant.

2. If the sight glass is clear, the compressor clutch is engaged and there is no significant temperature difference between the compressor inlet and discharge lines, the system is empty or nearly empty. By having the gauge set attached to the system a measurement can be taken. If the gauge reads less than 25 psi, the low pressure cutoff protection switch has failed.

3. If the sight glass is clear and the compressor clutch is disengaged, the clutch is defective, or the clutch circuit is open, or the system is out of refrigerant. By-pass the low pressure cut-off switch momentarily to determine the cause.

4. If the sight glass shows foam or bubbles, the system can be low on refrigerant. Occasional foam or bubbles is normal when the room temperature is above 110 degrees or below 70 degrees. To verify, increase the engine speed to

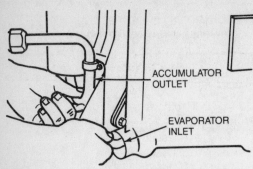

ACCUMULATOR OUTLET

EVAPORATOR INLET

Checking evaporator inlet and accumulator outlet line temperatures, 1973 and later

approximately 1,500 rpm and block the airflow through the condenser to increase the compressor discharge pressure to 225-250 psi. If the sight glass still shows bubbles or foam, the refrigerant level is low.

CAUTION: *Do not operate the vehicle engine any longer than necessary with the condenser airflow blocked. This blocking action also blocks the cooling system radiator and will cause the system to overheat rapidly.*

When the system is low on refrigerant, a leak is present or the system was not properly charged. Use a leak detector and locate the problem area and repair. If no leakage is found, charge the system to its capacity.

CAUTION: *It is not advisable to add refrigerant to a system utilizing the suction throttling valve and a sight glass, because the amount of refrigerant required to remove the foam or bubbles will result in an overcharge and potentially damaged system components.*

Systems Without A Sight Glass (CCOT System 1973 and later)

When charging the CCOT system, attach only the low pressure line to the low pressure gauge port, located on the accumulator. Do not attach the high pressure line to any service port or allow it to remain attached to the vacuum pump after evacuation. Be sure both the high and the low pressure control valves are closed on the gauge set. To complete the charging of the system, follow the outline supplied.

1. Start the engine and allow to run at idle, with the cooling system at normal operating temperature.

2. Attach the center gauge hose to a single or multi-can dispenser.

3. With the multi-can dispenser inverted, allow one pound or the contents of one or two 14 oz. cans to enter the system through the low pressure side by opening the gauge low pressure control valve.

4. Close the low pressure gauge control valve and turn the A/C system on to engage the com-

pressor. Place the blower motor in its high mode.

5. Open the low pressure gauge control valve and draw the remaining charge into the system. Refer to the capacity chart at the end of this section for the individual vehicle or system capacity.

6. Close the low pressure gauge control valve and the refrigerant source valve, on the multi-can dispenser. Remove the low pressure hose from the accumulator quickly to avoid loss of refrigerant through the Schrader valve.

7. Install the protective cap on the gauge port and check the system for leakage.

8. Test the system for proper operation.

Leak Testing the System

There are several methods of detecting leaks in an air conditioning system; among them, the two most popular are (1) halide leak-detection or the "open flame method," and (2) electronic leak-detection.

The halide leak detection is a torch like device which produces a yellow-green color when refrigerant is introduced into the flame at the burner. A purple or violet color indicates the presence of large amounts of refrigerant at the burner.

An electronic leak detector is a small portable electronic device with an extended probe. With the unit activated the probe is passed along those components of the system which contain refrigerant. If a leak is detected, the unit will sound an alarm signal or activate a display signal depending on the manufacturer's design. It is advisable to follow the manufacturer's instructions as the design and function of the detection may vary significantly.

CAUTION: *Care should be taken to operate either type of detector in well ventilated areas, so as to reduce the chance of personal injury, which may result from coming in contact with poisonous gases produced when R-12 is exposed to flame or electric spark.*

Tires and Wheels

The tires should be rotated as specified in the Maintenance Intervals chart. Refer to the accompanying illustrations for the recommended rotation patterns.

The tires on your truck should have built-in tread wear indicators, which appear as $\frac{1}{2}$" bands when the tread depth gets as low as $\frac{1}{16}$". When the indicators appear in 2 or more adjacent grooves, it's time for new tires.

For optimum tire life, you should keep the tires properly inflated, rotate them often and have the wheel alignment checked periodically. Some late models have the maximum load

Troubleshooting Basic Air Conditioning Problems

Problem	Cause	Solution
There's little or no air coming from the vents (and you're sure it's on)	• The A/C fuse is blown • Broken or loose wires or connections • The on/off switch is defective	• Check and/or replace fuse • Check and/or repair connections • Replace switch
The air coming from the vents is not cool enough	• Windows and air vent wings open • The compressor belt is slipping • Heater is on • Condenser is clogged with debris • Refrigerant has escaped through a leak in the system • Receiver/drier is plugged	• Close windows and vent wings • Tighten or replace compressor belt • Shut heater off • Clean the condenser • Check system • Service system
The air has an odor	• Vacuum system is disrupted • Odor producing substances on the evaporator case • Condensation has collected in the bottom of the evaporator housing	• Have the system checked/repaired • Clean the evaporator case • Clean the evaporator housing drains
System is noisy or vibrating	• Compressor belt or mountings loose • Air in the system	• Tighten or replace belt; tighten mounting bolts • Have the system serviced

Sight glass condition
    Constant bubbles, foam or oil streaks
    Clear sight glass, but no cold air
    Clear sight glass, but air is cold
    Clouded with milky fluid
	
	• Undercharged system
	
	• No refrigerant at all
	• System is OK
	• Receiver drier is leaking dessicant
		
		• Charge the system
		
		• Check and charge the system
		
		• Have system checked

Large difference in temperature of lines	• System undercharged	• Charge and leak test the system
Compressor noise	• Broken valves • Overcharged • Incorrect oil level • Piston slap • Broken rings • Drive belt pulley bolts are loose	• Replace the valve plate • Discharge, evacuate and install the correct charge • Isolate the compressor and check the oil level. Correct as necessary. • Replace the compressor • Replace the compressor • Tighten with the correct torque specification
Excessive vibration	• Incorrect belt tension • Clutch loose • Overcharged • Pulley is misaligned	• Adjust the belt tension • Tighten the clutch • Discharge, evacuate and install the correct charge • Align the pulley
Condensation dripping in the passenger compartment	• Drain hose plugged or improperly positioned • Insulation removed or improperly installed	• Clean the drain hose and check for proper installation • Replace the insulation on the expansion valve and hoses
Frozen evaporator coil	• Faulty thermostat • Thermostat capillary tube improperly installed • Thermostat not adjusted properly	• Replace the thermostat • Install the capillary tube correctly • Adjust the thermostat
Low side low—high side low	• System refrigerant is low • Expansion valve is restricted	• Evacuate, leak test and charge the system • Replace the expansion valve
Low side high—high side low	• Internal leak in the compressor—worn	• Remove the compressor cylinder head and inspect the compressor. Replace the valve plate assembly if necessary. If the compressor pistons, rings or

Troubleshooting Basic Air Conditioning Problems (cont.)

Problem	Cause	Solution
Low side high—high side low (cont.)		cylinders are excessively worn or scored replace the compressor
	• Cylinder head gasket is leaking	• Install a replacement cylinder head gasket
	• Expansion valve is defective	• Replace the expansion valve
	• Drive belt slipping	• Adjust the belt tension
Low side high—high side high	• Condenser fins obstructed	• Clean the condenser fins
	• Air in the system	• Evacuate, leak test and charge the system
	• Expansion valve is defective	• Replace the expansion valve
	• Loose or worn fan belts	• Adjust or replace the belts as necessary
Low side low—high side high	• Expansion valve is defective	• Replace the expansion valve
	• Restriction in the refrigerant hose	• Check the hose for kinks—replace if necessary
	• Restriction in the receiver/drier	• Replace the receiver/drier
	• Restriction in the condenser	• Replace the condenser
Low side and high side normal (inadequate cooling)	• Air in the system	• Evacuate, leak test and charge the system
	• Moisture in the system	• Evacuate, leak test and charge the system

pressures listed on the V.I.N. plate on the left door frame. In general, pressure of 28-32 psi would be suitable for highway use with moderate loads and passenger car type tires (load range B, non-flotation) of original equipment size. Pressures should be checked before dirving, since pressure can increase as much as 6 psi due to heat. It is a good idea to have an accurate gauge and to check pressures weekly. Not all gauges on service station air pumps are to be trusted. In general, truck type tires require higher pressures and flotation type tires, lower pressures.

TIRE ROTATION

It is recommended that you have the tires rotated every 6,000 miles. There is no way to give

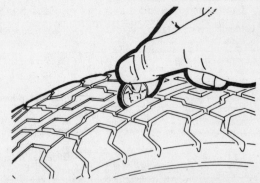

Tread depth can be checked with a penny; when the top of Lincoln's head is visible, it's time for new tires

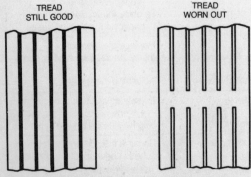

Tire tread wear indicators appear as solid bands when the tire is worn out

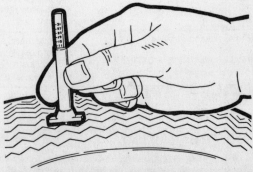

Tread depth can also be checked with an inexpensive gauge made for the purpose

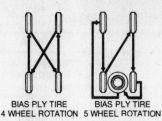

BIAS PLY TIRE   BIAS PLY TIRE
4 WHEEL ROTATION   5 WHEEL ROTATION

This rotation pattern is for bias or bias-belted tires only

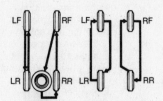

5 WHEEL ROTATION   4 WHEEL ROTATION

This rotation pattern is for radical tires; it can also be used for bias or bias-belted tires if you wish. The radial spare can be used on the left side, too, but don't change its direction of rotation once used

a tire rotation diagram for every combination of tires and vehicles, but the accompanying diagrams are a general rule to follow. Radial tires should not be cross-switched; they last longer if their direction of rotation is not changed. Truck tires sometimes have directional tread, indicated by arrows on the sidewalls; the arrow shows the direction of rotation. They will wear very rapidly if reversed. Studded snow tires will lose their studs if their direction of rotation is reversed.

NOTE: *Mark the wheel position or direction of rotation on radial tires or studded snow tires before removing them.*

If your truck is equipped with tires having different load ratings on the front and the rear, the tires should not be rotated front to rear. Rotating these tires could affect tire life (the tires with the lower rating will wear faster, and could become overloaded), and upset the handling of the truck.

TIRE USAGE

The tires on your truck were selected to provide the best all-around performance for normal operation when inflated as specified. Oversize tires (Load Range D) will not increase the maximum carrying capacity of the vehicle, although they will provide an extra margin of tread life. Be sure to check overall height before using larger size tires which may cause interference with suspension components or wheel wells. When replacing conventional tire sizes with other tire size designations, be sure to check the manufacturer's recommendations.

Interchangeability is not always possible because of differences in load ratings, tire dimensions, wheel well clearances, and rim size. Also due to differences in handling characteristics, 70 Series and 60 Series tires should be used only in pairs on the same axle; radial tires should be used only in sets of four.

The wheels must be the correct width for the tire. Tire dealers have charts of tire and rim compatibility. A mismatch can cause sloppy handling and rapid tread wear. The old rule of thumb is that the tread width should match the rim width (inside bead to inside bead) within an inch. For radial tires, the rim width should be 80% or less of the tire (not tread) width.

The height (mounted diameter) of the new tires can greatly change speedometer accuracy, engine speed at a given road speed, fuel mileage, acceleration, and ground clearance. Tire manufacturers furnish full measurement specifications. Speedometer drive gears are available for correction.

NOTE: *Dimensions of tires marked the same size may vary significantly, even among tires from the same manufacturer.*

The spare tire should be usable, at least for low speed operation, with the new tires.

TIRE TYPES

For maximum satisfaction, tires should be used in sets of five. Mixing or different types (radial, bias-belted, fiberglass belted) should be avoided. Conventional bias tires are constructed so that the cords run bead-to-bead at an angle. Alternate plies run at an opposite angle. This type of construction gives rigidity to both tread and sidewall. Bias-belted tires are similar in construction to conventional bias ply tires. Belts run at an angle and also at a 90 degree angle to the bead, as in the radial tire. Tread life is improved considerably over the conventional bias tire. The radial tire differs in construction, but instead of the carcass plies running at an angle of 90 degree to each other, they run at an angle of 90 degree to the bead. This gives the tread a great deal of rigidity and the sidewall a

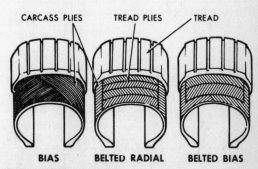

CARCASS PLIES   TREAD PLIES   TREAD

BIAS   BELTED RADIAL   BELTED BIAS

Types of tire construction

Troubleshooting Basic Wheel Problems

Problem	Cause	Solution
The car's front end vibrates at high speed	• The wheels are out of balance • Wheels are out of alignment	• Have wheels balanced • Have wheel alignment checked/adjusted
Car pulls to either side	• Wheels are out of alignment • Unequal tire pressure • Different size tires or wheels	• Have wheel alignment checked/adjusted • Check/adjust tire pressure • Change tires or wheels to same size
The car's wheel(s) wobbles	• Loose wheel lug nuts • Wheels out of balance • Damaged wheel • Wheels are out of alignment • Worn or damaged ball joint • Excessive play in the steering linkage (usually due to worn parts) • Defective shock absorber	• Tighten wheel lug nuts • Have tires balanced • Raise car and spin the wheel. If the wheel is bent, it should be replaced • Have wheel alignment checked/adjusted • Check ball joints • Check steering linkage • Check shock absorbers
Tires wear unevenly or prematurely	• Incorrect wheel size • Wheels are out of balance • Wheels are out of alignment	• Check if wheel and tire size are compatible • Have wheels balanced • Have wheel alignment checked/adjusted

great deal of flexibility and accounts for the characteristic bulge associated with radial tires.

Chevrolet and GMC trucks are capable of using radial tires and they are recommended in some years. If they are used, tire sized and wheel diameters should be selected to maintain ground clearance and tire load capacity equivalent to the minimum specified tire. Radial tires should always be used in sets of five, but in an emergency radial tires can be used with caution on the rear axle only. If this is done, both tires on the rear should be of radial design.

WARNING: *Radial tires should never be used on only the front axle.*

Radial tires must not be mounted on 16.5″ rims unless the rims are stamped with the word Radial. Ordinary rims are not strong enough to withstand the additional side loads.

Snow tires should not be operated at sustained speeds over 70 mph.

On four wheel drive trucks, all tires must be of the same size, type, and tread pattern, to provide even traction on loose surfaces, to prevent driveline bind when conventional four wheel

Troubleshooting Basic Tire Problems

Problem	Cause	Solution
The car's front end vibrates at high speeds and the steering wheel shakes	• Wheels out of balance • Front end needs aligning	• Have wheels balanced • Have front end alignment checked
The car pulls to one side while cruising	• Unequal tire pressure (car will usually pull to the low side) • Mismatched tires • Front end needs aligning	• Check/adjust tire pressure • Be sure tires are of the same type and size • Have front end alignment checked
Abnormal, excessive or uneven tire wear See "How to Read Tire Wear"	• Infrequent tire rotation • Improper tire pressure • Sudden stops/starts or high speed on curves	• Rotate tires more frequently to equalize wear • Check/adjust pressure • Correct driving habits
Tire squeals	• Improper tire pressure • Front end needs aligning	• Check/adjust tire pressure • Have front end alignment checked

Tire Size Comparison Chart

"Letter" sizes			Inch Sizes	Metric-inch Sizes		
"60 Series"	"70 Series"	"78 Series"	1965–77	"60 Series"	"70 Series"	"80 Series"
			5.50-12, 5.60-12	165/60-12	165/70-12	155-12
		Y78-12	6.00-12			
		W78-13	5.20-13	165/60-13	145/70-13	135-13
		Y78-13	5.60-13	175/60-13	155/70-13	145-13
			6.15-13	185/60-13	165/70-13	155-13, P155/80-13
A60-13	A70-13	A78-13	6.40-13	195/60-13	175/70-13	165-13
B60-13	B70-13	B78-13	6.70-13	205/60-13	185/70-13	175-13
			6.90-13			
C60-13	C70-13	C78-13	7.00-13	215/60-13	195/70-13	185-13
D60-13	D70-13	D78-13	7.25-13			
E60-13	E70-13	E78-13	7.75-13			195-13
			5.20-14	165/60-14	145/70-14	135-14
			5.60-14	175/60-14	155/70-14	145-14
			5.90-14			
A60-14	A70-14	A78-14	6.15-14	185/60-14	165/70-14	155-14
	B70-14	B78-14	6.45-14	195/60-14	175/70-14	165-14
	C70-14	C78-14	6.95-14	205/60-14	185/70-14	175-14
D60-14	D70-14	D78-14				
E60-14	E70-14	E78-14	7.35-14	215/60-14	195/70-14	185-14
F60-14	F70-14	F78-14, F83-14	7.75-14	225/60-14	200/70-14	195-14
G60-14	G70-14	G77-14, G78-14	8.25-14	235/60-14	205/70-14	205-14
H60-14	H70-14	H78-14	8.55-14	245/60-14	215/70-14	215-14
J60-14	J70-14	J78-14	8.85-14	255/60-14	225/70-14	225-14
L60-14	L70-14		9.15-14	265/60-14	235/70-14	
	A70-15	A78-15	5.60-15	185/60-15	165/70-15	155-15
B60-15	B70-15	B78-15	6.35-15	195/60-15	175/70-15	165-15
C60-15	C70-15	C78-15	6.85-15	205/60-15	185/70-15	175-15
	D70-15	D78-15				
E60-15	E70-15	E78-15	7.35-15	215/60-15	195/70-15	185-15
F60-15	F70-15	F78-15	7.75-15	225/60-15	205/70-15	195-15
G60-15	G70-15	G78-15	8.15-15/8.25-15	235/60-15	215/70-15	205-15
H60-15	H70-15	H78-15	8.45-15/8.55-15	245/60-15	225/70-15	215-15
J60-15	J70-15	J78-15	8.85-15/8.90-15	255/60-15	235/70-15	225-15
	K70-15		9.00-15	265/60-15	245/70-15	230-15
L60-15	L70-15	L78-15, L84-15	9.15-15			235-15
	M70-15	M78-15				255-15
		N78-15				

Note: Every size tire is not listed and many size comparisons are approximate, based on load ratings. Wider tires than those supplied new with the vehicle, should always be checked for clearance.

drive is used, and to prevent excessive wear on the center differential with full time four wheel drive.

Windshield Wipers

For maximum effectiveness and longest element life, the windshield and wiper blades should be kept clean. Dirt, tree sap, road tar and so on will cause streaking, smearing and blade deterioration if left on the glass. It is advisable to wash the windshield carefully with a commercial glass cleaner at least once a month. Wipe off the rubber blades with the wet rag afterwards. Do not attempt to move the wipers back and forth by hand; damage to the motor and drive mechanism will result.

If the blades are found to be cracked, broken or torn, they should be replaced immediately. Replacement intervals will vary with usage, although ozone deterioration usually limits blade life to about one year. If the wiper pattern is smeared or streaked, or if the blade chatters across the glass, the blades should be replaced. It is easiest and most sensible to replace them in pairs.

There are basically three different types of wiper blade refills, which differ in their method of replacement. One type has two release buttons, approximately $\frac{1}{3}$ of the way up from the ends of the blade frame. Pushing the buttons down releases a lock and allows the rubber blade to be removed from the frame. The new blade slides back into the frame and locks in place.

The second type of refill has two metal tabs

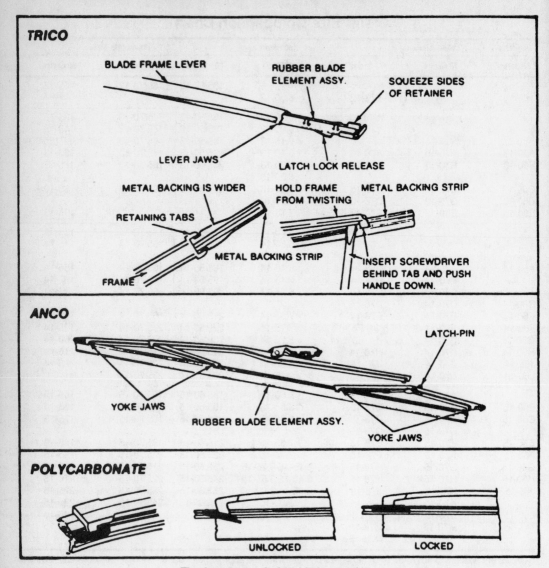

TRICO

BLADE FRAME LEVER

RUBBER BLADE ELEMENT ASSY.

SQUEEZE SIDES OF RETAINER

LEVER JAWS

LATCH LOCK RELEASE

METAL BACKING IS WIDER

HOLD FRAME FROM TWISTING

METAL BACKING STRIP

RETAINING TABS

METAL BACKING STRIP

FRAME

INSERT SCREWDRIVER BEHIND TAB AND PUSH HANDLE DOWN.

ANCO

LATCH-PIN

YOKE JAWS

RUBBER BLADE ELEMENT ASSY.

YOKE JAWS

POLYCARBONATE

UNLOCKED

LOCKED

The three types of wiper blade retention

which are unlocked by squeezing them together. The rubber blade can then be withdrawn from the frame jaws. A new one is installed by inserting it into the front frame jaws and sliding it rearward to engage the remaining frame jaws. There are usually four jaws; be certain when installing that the refill is engaged in all of them. At the end of its travel, the tabs will lock into place on the front jaws of the wiper blade frame.

The third type is a refill made from polycarbonate. The refill has a simple locking device at one end which flexes downward out of the groove into which the jaws of the holder fit, allowing easy release. By sliding the new refill through all the jaws and pushing through the slight resistance when it reaches the end of its travel, the refill will lock into position.

Regardless of the type of refill used, make sure that all of the frame jaws are engaged as the refill is pushed into place and locked. The metal blade holder and frame will scratch the glass if allowed to touch it.

FLUIDS AND LUBRICANTS

Fuel and Engine Oil Recommendations
MOTOR OIL

The SAE grade number indicates the viscosity of the engine oil, or its ability to lubricate under a given temperature. The lower the SAE grade number, the lighter the oil; the lower the

Gasoline Engine Oil Viscosity Chart

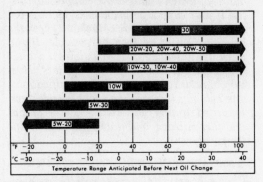

(© **Chevrolet Motor Div.**)

NOTES: 1. SAE 5W and 5W-20 are not recommended for sustained high speed driving.
2. SAE 5W-30 is recommended for all seasons in Canada

viscosity, the easier it is to crank the engine in cold weather.

The API (American Petroleum Institute) designation indicates the classification of engine oil for use under given operating conditions. Only oils designated for Service SF should be used. These oils provide maximum engine protection. Both the SAE grade number and the API designation can be found on the top of a can of oil.

NOTE: *Non-detergent should not be used.*

Oil viscosities should be chosen from those oils recommended for the lowest anticipated temperatures during the oil change interval.

The multi-viscosity oils offer the important advantage of being adaptable to temperature extremes. They allow easy starting at high speeds and engine temperatures. This is a decided advantage in changeable climates or in long distance driving.

Diesel engines also require SF engine oil. In addition, the oil must qualify for a CC rating. The API has a number of different diesel engine ratings, including CB, CC, and CD.

NOTE: *1981 and later diesel engines can use either SF/CC, SF/CD.*

The diesel engine in the Chevrolet and GMC pick-ups requires SF/CC rated oil. DO NOT use an oil if the designation CD appears anywhere on the oil can. Use SF/CC engine oil only. Do not use an oil labeled only SF or only CC. Both designations must appear.

For recommended oil viscosities, refer to the chart. 10W-30 grade oils are not recommended for sustained high speed driving.

Single viscosity oil (SAE 30) is recommended for sustained high speed driving.

Synthetic Oil

There are excellent synthetic and fuel-efficient oils available that, under the right circumstances, can help provide better fuel mileage and better engine protection. However, these advantages come at a price, which can be three or four times the price per quart of conventional motor oils.

Before pouring any synthetic oils into your car's engine, you should consider the condition of the engine and the type of driving you do. Also, check the truck's warranty conditions regarding the use of synthetics.

Generally, it is best to avoid the use of synthetic oil in both brand new and older, high mileage engines. New engines require a proper break-in, and the synthetics are so slippery that they can prevent this; most manufacturers recommend that you wait at least 5,000 miles before switching to a synthetic oil. Conversely, older engines are looser and tend to use more oil; synthetics will slip past worn parts more readily than regular oil, and will be used up faster. If your car already leaks and/or uses oil (due to worn parts and bad seals or gaskets), it

Diesel Engine Oil Viscosity Chart

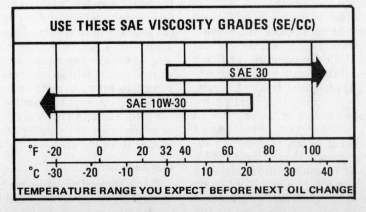

will leak and use more with a slippery synthetic inside.

Consider your type of driving. If most of your accumulated mileage is on the highway at higher, steadier speeds, a synthetic oil will reduce friction and probably help deliver better fuel mileage. Under such ideal highway conditions, the oil change interval can be extended, as long as the oil filter will operate effectively for the extended life of the oil. If the filter can't do its job for this extended period, dirt and sludge will build up in your engine's crankcase, sump, oil pump and lines, no matter what type of oil is used. If using synthetic oil in this manner, you should continue to change the oil filter at the recommended intervals.

Trucks used under harder, stop-and-go, short hop circumstances should always be serviced more frequently, and for these trucks synthetic oil may not be a wise investment. Because of the necessary shorter change interval needed for this type of driving, you cannot take advantage of the long recommended change interval of most synthetic oils.

Finally, most synthetic oils are not compatible with conventional oils and cannot be added to them. This means you should always carry a couple of quarts of synthetic oil with you while on a long trip, as not all service stations carry this oil.

FUELS

Gasoline Engines

1970-74 AND 1975 AND LATER MODELS WITHOUT CATALYTIC CONVERTER

Chevrolet and GMC trucks are designed to operate on regular grades of fuel (1970-71) commonly sold in the U.S. and Canada. In 1972-74 (and 1975 and later models without a catalytic converter), unleaded or low-lead fuels of approximately 91 octane (Research Octane) or higher are recommended. General Motors recommends the use of low-leaded or unleaded fuels (0-0.5 grams per gallon) to reduce particulate and hydrocarbon pollutants.

Use of a fuel which is too low in anti-knock quality will result in spark knock. Since many factors affect operating efficiency, such as altitude, terrain and air temperature, knocking may result even though you are using the recommended fuel. If persistent knocking occurs, it may be necessary to switch to a slightly higher grade of gasoline to correct the problem. In the case of late model engines, switching to a premium fuel would be an unnecessary expense. In these engines, a slightly higher grade of gasoline (regular) should be used only when persistent knocking occurs. Continuous or excessive knocking may result in engine damage.

NOTE: *Your engine's fuel requirement can change with time, mainly due to carbon buildup, which changes the compression ratio. If your engine pings, knocks, or runs on, switch to a higher grade of fuel and check the ignition timing as soon as possible. If you must use unleaded fuel, sometimes a change of brands will cure the problem. If it is necessary to retard the timing from specifications, don't change it more than about four degrees. Retarded timing will reduce power output and fuel mileage, and it will increase engine temperature.*

1975 AND LATER MODELS WITH CATALYTIC CONVERTER

Chevrolet and GMC trucks with Gross Vehicle Weight Ratings (GVWR) which place them in the heavy duty emissions class do not require a catalytic converter. However, almost all 1975 and later light duty emissions trucks have a catalytic converter. The light duty classification applies to all trucks with a GVWR under 6,000 lbs. through 1978, except for 1978 trucks sold in California. 1978 California models and all 1979 models with GVWR's under 8,500 lbs. fall into the light duty category. In 1980 and later, the light duty classification applies to all trucks with GVWR's under 8,600 lbs.

The catalytic converter is a muffler-shaped device installed in the exhaust system. It contains platinum and palladium coated pellets which, through catalytic action, oxidize hydrocarbon and carbon monoxide gases into hydrogen, oxygen, and carbon dioxide.

The design of the converter requires the exclusive use of unleaded fuel. Leaded fuel renders the converter inoperative, raising exhaust emissions to illegal levels. In addition, the lead in the gasoline coats the pellets in the converter, blocking the flow of exhaust gases. This raises exhaust back pressure and severely reduces engine performance. In extreme cases, the exhaust system becomes so blocked that the engine will not run.

Converter equipped trucks are delivered with the label Unleaded Fuel Only placed next to the fuel gauge on the instrument panel and next to the gas tank filler opening. In general, any unleaded fuel is suitable for use in these trucks as long as the gas has an octane rating of 87 or more. Octane ratings are posted on the gas pumps. However, in some cases, knocking may occur even though the recommended fuel is being used. The only practical solution for this is to switch to a slightly higher grade of unleaded fuel, or to switch brands of unleaded gasoline.

Diesel Engines

Diesel engined pick-ups require the use of diesel fuel. Two grades of diesel fuel are manufactured, #1 and #2, although #2 grade is generally the only grade available. Better fuel economy results from the use of #2 grade fuel. In some northern parts of the U.S., and in most parts of Canada, #1 grade fuel is available in winter, or a winterized blend of #2 grade is supplied in winter months. If #1 grade is available, it should be used whenever temperatures fall below 20°F (–7°C). Winterized #2 grade may also be used at these temperatures. However, unwinterized #2 grade should not be used below 20°F (–7°C). Cold temperatures cause unwinterized #2 grade to thicken (it actually gels), blocking the fuel lines and preventing the engine from running.

WARNING: *Do not use home heating oil or gasoline in the diesel pick-up. Do not attempt to thin unwinterized #2 diesel fuel with gasoling. Gasoline or home heating oil will damage the engine and void the manufacturer's warranty.*

Engine

OIL LEVEL CHECK

The engine oil should be checked on a regular basis, ideally at each fuel stop. If the truck is used for trailer towing or for heavy duty use, it would be safer to check it more often.

When checking the oil level it is best that the oil be at operating temperature, although checking the level immediately after stopping will give a false reading because all of the oil will not yet have drained back into the crankcase. Be sure that the truck is resting on a level surface, allowing time for the oil to drain back into the crankcase.

1. Open the hood and locate the dipstick. Remove it from the tube. The oil dipstick is located on the passenger's side of 6 cylinder engines and on the driver's side of V8s.

2. Wipe the dipstick with a clean rag.

3. Insert the dipstick fully into the tube, and remove it again. Hold the dipstick horizontally and read the oil level. The level should be between the FULL and ADD OIL marks. If the oil level is at or below the ADD OIL mark, oil

The oil level should show between the "ADD" and "FULL" marks on the dipstick

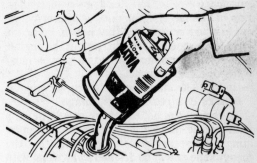

Add oil through the capped opening in the valve cover

should be added as necessary. Oil is added through the capped opening on the valve cover(s) on gasoline engines. Diesel engines have a capped oil fill tube at the front of the engine. See Oil and Fuel Recommendations for the proper viscosity oil to use.

4. Replace the dipstick and check the level after adding oil. Be careful not to overfill the crankcase. Approximately one quart of oil will raise the level from ADD to FULL.

OIL AND FILTER CHANGE

Engine oil should be changed according to the schedule in the Maintenance Interval Chart. Under conditions such as:

- Driving in dusty conditions,
- Continuous trailer pulling or RV use,
- Extensive or prolonged idling,
- Extensive short trip operation in freezing temperatures (when the engine is not thoroughly warmed-up),
- Frequent long runs at high speeds and high ambient temperatures, and
- Stop-and-go service such as delivery trucks,

Check engine crankcase oil level with the dipstick

The oil drain plug is located at the lowest point of the engine oil pan

the oil change interval and filter replacement interval should be cut in half. Operation of the engine in severe conditions such as a dust storm may require an immediate oil and filter change.

Chevrolet and GMC recommended changing both the oil and filter during the first oil change and the filter every other oil change thereafter. For the small price of an oil filter, it's cheap insurance to replace the filter at every oil change. One of the larger filter manufacturers points out in its advertisements that not changing the filter leaves one quart of dirty oil in the engine. This claim is true and should be kept in mind when changing your oil.

NOTE: *The oil filter on the diesel engines must be changed every oil change.*

To change the oil, the truck should be on a level surface, and the engine should be at operating temperature. This is to ensure that the foreign matter will be drained away along with the oil, and not left in the engine to form sludge. You should have available a container that will hold a minimum of 8 quarts of liquid, a wrench to fit the old drain plug, a spout for pouring in new oil, and a rag or two, which you will always need. If the filter is being replaced, you will also need a bank wrench or filter wrench to fit the end of the filter.

NOTE: *If the engine is equipped with an oil cooler, this will also have to be drained, using*

Use a strap wrench to loosen the oil filter; install the new filter by hand

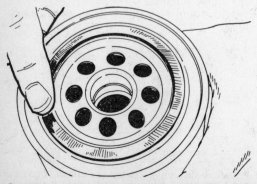

Coat the gasket on the new oil filter with a film of oil

the drain plug. Be sure to add enough oil to fill the cooler in addition to the engine.

1. Position the truck on a level surface and set the parking brake or block the wheels. Slide a drain pan under the oil drain plug.

2. From under the truck, loosen, but do not remove the oil drain plug. Cover your hand with a rag or glove and slowly unscrew the drain plug.

CAUTION: *The engine oil will be HOT. Keep your arms, face and hands clear of the oil as it drains out.*

3. Remove the plug and let the oil drain into the pan.

NOTE: *Do not drop the plug into the drain pan.*

4. When all of the oil has drained, clean off the drain plug and put it back into the hole. Remember to tighten the plug 20 ft.lb. (30 ft.lb. for diesel engines).

5. Loosen the filter with a band wrench or special oil filter cap wrench. On most Chevrolet engines, especially the V8s, the oil filter is next to the exhaust pipes. Stay clear of these, since even a passing contact will result in a painful burn.

CAUTION: *On trucks equipped with catalytic converters stay clear of the converter. The outside temperature of a hot catalytic converter can approach 1200 degrees F.*

6. Cover your hand with a rag, and spin the filter off by hand.

7. Coat the rubber gasket on a new filter with a light film of clean engine oil. Screw the filter onto the mounting stud and tighten according to the directions on the filter (usually hand tight one turn past the point where the gasket contacts the mounting base). Don't overtighten the filter.

8. Refill the engine with the specified amount of clean engine oil.

9. Run the engine for several minutes, checking the leaks. Check the level of the oil and add oil if necessary.

When you have finished this job, you will notice that you now possess four or five quarts of dirty oil. The best thing to do with it is to pour it into plastic jugs, such as milk or antifreeze containers. Then, if you are on good terms with your gas station man, he might let you pour it into his used oil container for recycling. Otherwise, the only thing to do with it is to put the containers into the trash.

Manual Transmission
FLUID RECOMMENDATIONS

The correct lubricant to use is SAE 80W-90 GL-5 Lubricant, or SAE 80W GL-5 for cold climates.

LEVEL CHECK

Check the lubricant level at the interval specified in the maintenance chart.

1. With the truck parked on a level surface, remove the filler plug from the side of the transmission case. Be careful not to take out the drain plug at the bottom.

2. If lubricant begins to trickle out of the hole, there is enough. If not, carefully insert a finger (watch out for sharp threads) and check that the level is up to the edge of the hole.

3. If not, add sufficient lubricant with a funnel and tube, or a squeeze bulb to bring it to the proper level.

4. Replace the plug and check for leaks.

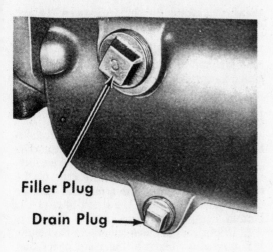

Filler Plug

Drain Plug →

DRAIN AND REFILL

No intervals are specified for changing the transmission lubricant, but it is a good idea on a used vehicle, one that has been worked hard, or one driven in deep water. The vehicle should be on a level surface and the lubricant should be at operating temperature.

1. Position the truck on a level surface.

2. Place a pan of sufficient capacity under the transmission drain plug.

3. Remove the upper (fill) plug to provide a vent opening.

4. Remove the lower (drain) plug and let the lubricant drain out. The 1976-80 Tremec top cover three speed is drained by removing the lower extension housing bolt.

5. Replace the drain plug.

6. Add lubricant with a suction gun or squeeze bulb. The correct lubricant is SAE 80W-90 GL-5 Gear Lubricant, or SAE 80W GL-5 for cold climates.

7. Reinstall the filler plug. Run the engine and check for leaks.

Automatic Transmissions

FLUID RECIMMENDATIONS

The correct fluid to use is DEXRON®II

LEVEL CHECK

Check the level of the fluid at the specified interval. The fluid level should be checked with the engine at normal operating temperature and running. If the truck has been running at high speed for a long period, in city traffic on a hot day, or pulling a trailer, let it cool down for about thirty minutes before checking the level.

1. Park on the level with the engine running and the shift lever in Park.

2. Remove the dipstick at the rear of the engine compartment. Cautiously feel the end of the dipstick with your fingers. Wipe it off and replace it, then pull it again and check the level of the fluid on the dipstick.

3. If the fluid felt cool, the level should be between the two dimples below ADD. If it was too hot to hold, the level should be between the ADD and FULL marks.

4. If the fluid is at or below the ADD mark, add fluid through the dipstick tube. One pint raises the level from ADD to FULL when the fluid is hot. The correct fluid to use is DEXRON®II. Be certain that the transmission is not overfilled; this will cause foaming, fluid loss, and slippage.

DRAIN AND REFILL

The fluid should be drained with the transmission warm. It is easier to change the fluid if the truck is raised somewhat from the ground, but this not always easy without a lift. The transmission must be level for it to drain properly.

1. Place a shallow pan underneath to catch the transmission fluid (about 5 pints). On earlier models, the transmission pan has a drain plug. Remove this and drain the fluid. For later models, loosen all the pan bolts, then pull one corner down to drain most of the fluid. If it sticks, VERY CAREFULLY pry the pan loose. You can buy aftermarket drain plug kits that makes this operation a bit less messy, once installed.

NOTE: *If the fluid removed smells burnt, se-*

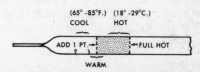

NOTE: DO NOT OVERFILL. It takes only one pint to raise level from ADD to FULL with a hot transmission.

Automatic transmission dipstick markings

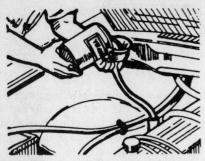

Add automatic transmission fluid through the automatic transmission dipstick tube, using a funnel

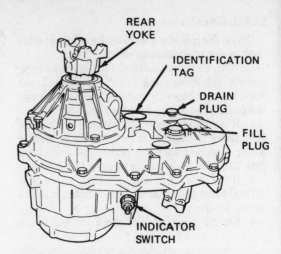

Model 208 Indicator Switch, Identification Tag, and Drain and Fill Plug Location

rious transmission troubles, probably due to overheating, should be suspected.

2. Remove the pan bolts and empty out the pan. On some models, there may not be much room to get at the screws at the front of the pan.

3. Clean the pan with solvent and allow it to air dry. If you use a rag to wipe it out, you risk leaving bits of lint and threads in the transmission.

4. Remove the filter or strainer retaining bolts. On the Turbo Hydra-Matic 400, there are two screws securing the filter or screen to the valve body. A reusable strainer may be found on some models. The strainer may be cleaned in solvent and air dried thoroughly. The filter and gasket must be replaced.

5. Install a new gasket and filter.

6. Install a new gasket on the pan, and tighten the bolts evenly to 12 foot pounds in a crisscross pattern.

7. Add DEXRON® or DEXRON®II transmission fluid through the dipstick tube. The correct amount is in the Capacities Chart. Do not overfill.

8. With the gearshift lever in PARK, start the engine and let it idle. Do not race the engine.

9. Move the gearshift lever through each position, holding the brakes. Return the lever to PARK, and check the fluid level with the engine idling. The level should be between the two dimples on the dipstick, about ¼" below the ADD mark. Add fluid, if necessary.

10. Check the fluid level after the truck has been driven enough to thoroughly warm up the transmission. Details are given under Fluid Level Checks earlier in the Chapter. If the transmission is overfilled, the excess must be drained off. Overfilling causes aerated fluid, resulting in transmission slippage and probable damage.

Transfer Case

FLUID RECOMMENDATIONS

Conventional transfer cases require SAE 80W or SAE 80W-90 GL-5 gear lubricant; full time systems use SAE 10W-30 or 10W-40 engine oil.

LEVEL CHECKS

Check the four wheel drive transfer case lubricant level every 4 months or 6,000 miles.

1. With the truck parked on a level surface, remove the filler plug from the rear of the transfer case (behind the transmission). Be careful not to take out the drain plug at the bottom.

2. If lubricant trickles out, there is enough. If not, carefully insert a finger and check that the level is up to the edge of the hole, EXCEPT in full time four wheel drive cases should be ½" below the hole.

Lubricant may be added, if necessary, with a funnel and tube, or a squeeze bulb.

DRAIN AND REFILL

Part Time Systems

No intervals are specified for changing transfer case lubricant, but it is a good idea for trucks that are worked hard or driven in deep water.

1. With the transfer case warmed up, park on a level surface.

2. Slide a pan of at least 6 pts. capacity under the case drain plug.

3. Remove the filler plug from the rear of the transfer case (behind the transmission). Remove the drain plug from the bottom.

4. Wipe the area clean and replace the drain plug.

5. Add lubricant with a suction gun or squeeze bulb. Conventional transfer cases require SAE 80W-90 GL-5 Gear Lubricant.

6. When the lubricant level is up to the bottom of the filler hole, replace the plug.

Full Time Four Wheel Drive

The full time system requires oil changes at regular intervals, according to the amount and type of work done by the unit. Trucks used for normal on-off road work should have the transfer case oil changed at 24,000 mile intervals. When used for heavy duty work, trailer towing, snowplowing, and the like, the interval should be halved to 12,000 miles. If the truck is exposed to extremely dusty or muddy conditions, the oil should be changed at 1,000 mile intervals.

The transfer case oil must be hot before changing. Drive the truck until the engine has reached normal operating temperature, and park on a level surface.

1. Slide a pan of at least 8 pts. capacity under the case drain plug.
2. Remove the filler plug.
3. Remove the lowest bolt from the front output shaft rear bearing retainer cover, and allow the lubricant to drain. Be careful; the oil will be hot. There may be a drain plug. If so, remove that instead.
4. Remove the six bolts on the left (driver's) side of the case which secure to P.T.O. (power take-off) cover. Remove this cover and allow the lubricant to drain out.
5. Remove the speedometer driven gear from the upper left rear corner of the case.
6. Use a suction gun to remove as much lubricant as possible from the case cover location and the speedometer gear location.
7. Install the speedometer driven gear, the P.T.O. cover, and the lowest bolt or drain plug.
8. Add approximately seven pints of oil through the filler plug opening. The proper oil to use is 10W-30 or 10W-40 engine oil.
9. Check the fluid level and add sufficient oil to raise the level to ½″ below the filler plug opening. Replace the plug, and wipe the surfaces of the case and skid plate to remove any excess oil. Drive the truck and check for leaks.

Drive Axle (Rear and/or Front)
FLUID RECOMMENDATIONS

Front axles use SAE 80W-90, GL-5 Gear Lubricant. Rear axles use SAE 80W-90 gear oil. Positraction axles must use special lubricant available from dealers. If the special fluid is not used, noise, uneven operation, and damage will result. There is also a Positraction additive used to cure noise and slippage. Positraction axles have an identifying tag, as well as a warning sticker near the jack or on the rear wheel well.

LEVEL CHECK

The fluid level in the front axle should be ½″ below the filler plug opening. The fluid level in

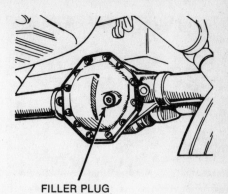

FILLER PLUG

The rear axle filler plug

the rear axle should be up to the bottom of the filler plug opening. Lubricant may be added with a suction gun or squeeze bulb.

1. Park on level ground.
2. Remove the filler plug from the differential housing cover.
3. If lubricant trickles out there is enough. If not, carefully insert a finger and check that the level is up to the bottom of the hole. Locking front hubs should be run in the LOCK position for at least 10 miles each month to assure proper lubrication to the front axle.

DRAIN AND REFILL

No intervals are specified for changing axle lubricant, but it is a good idea, especially if you have driven in water over the axle vents.

1. Park the vehicle on the level with the axles at normal operating temperature.
2. Place a pan of at least 6 pints capacity under the differential housing.
3. Remove the filler plug.
4. If you have a drain plug, remove it. If not, unbolt and remove the differential cover.
5. Replace the drain plug, or differential cover. Use a new gasket if the differential cover has been removed.

Cooling System
FLUID RECOMMENDATIONS

The proper coolant for your GM truck is a 50/50 mix of ethylene glycol antifreeze and water. Alcohol or methanol base coolants are not recommended. Antifreeze solutions should be used, even in summer, to prevent rust and to take advantage of the solution's higher boiling point compared to plain water. This is imperative on air conditioned trucks; the heater core can freeze if it isn't protected.

LEVEL CHECK

The coolant level should be checked at each fuel stop, ideally, to prevent the possibility of

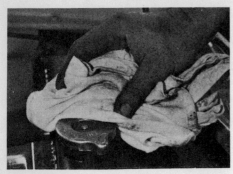

If you must remove the radiator cap when hot, cover the cap with a thick rag

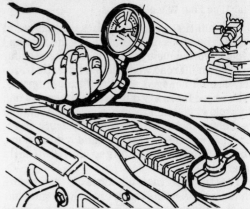

The system should be pressure tested once a year

Some radiator caps have levers to vent pressure before the cap is removed

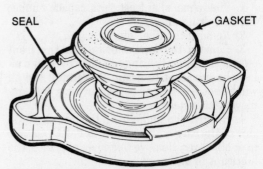

SEAL   GASKET

Check the radiator cap's rubber gasket and metal seal for deterioration at least once a year

Coolant protection can be checked with a simple float-type tester

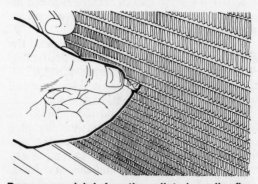

Remove any debris from the radiator's cooling fins

tem from freezing down to –20°F (–32°F in Canada). It is good for two full calendar years or 24,000 miles, whichever occurs first, provided that the proper concentration of coolant is maintained.

The 1973 and later cooling system differs slightly from those used on 1970-72 trucks. The 1973 and later system incorporates a plastic expansion tank connected to the radiator by a hose from the base of the radiator filler neck. The hot coolant level on 1973 and later trucks should be at the FULL HOT mark on the expansion tank and the cold coolant level should be at the FULL COLD mark on the tank. Do

overheating and serious engine damage. If not, it should at least be checked once each month.

The cooling system was filled at the factory with a high quality coolant solution that is good for year around operation and protects the sys-

not remove the radiator cap to check the coolant level on 1973 and later trucks. On 1970-72 trucks, the cold coolant level should be approximately 3″ below the bottom of the filler neck, and the hot level should be 1-1½″ below the bottom of the filler neck.

To check the coolant level:

1. On 1973 and later models, check the level on the see-through expansion tank. On earlier models it will be necessary to CAREFULLY remove the radiator cap.

CAUTION: *The radiator coolant is under pressure when hot. To avoid the danger of physical harm, coolant level should be checked or replenished only when the engine is cold. To remove the radiator cap when the engine is hot, first cover the cap with a thick rag, or wear a heavy glove for protection. Press down on the cap slightly and slowly turn it counterclockwise until it reaches the first stop. Allow all the pressure to vent (indicated when the hissing sound stops). When the pressure is released, press down on the cap and continue to rotate it counterclockwise. Some radiator caps have a lever for venting the pressure; lifting the lever will release the pressure, but you should still exercise extreme caution when removing the cap.*

2. Check the level and, if necessary, add coolant to the proper level. Use a 50/50 mix of ethylene glycol antifreeze and water. Alcohol or methanol base coolants are not recommended. Antifreeze solutions should be used, even in summer, to prevent rust and to take advantage of the solution's higher boiling point compared to plain water. This is imperative on air conditioned trucks; the heater core can freeze if it isn't protected. On 1974 and later models, coolant should be added through the coolant recovery tank, not the radiator filler neck.

CAUTION: *Never add large quantities of cold coolant to a hot engine. A cracked engine block may result.*

3. Replace the cap.

Each year the cooling system should be serviced as follows:

● Wash the radiator cap and filler neck with clean water.

● Check the coolant for proper level and freeze protection.

● Have the system pressure tested (15 psi).

If a replacement cap is installed, be sure that it conforms to the original specifications.

● Tighten the hose clamps and inspect all hoses. Replace hoses that are swollen, cracked or otherwise deteriorated.

● Clean the frontal area of the radiator core and the air conditioning condenser, if so equipped.

DRAINING, FLUSHING, CLEANING, TESTING THE COOLANT, COOLING SYSTEM AND REFILLING

The cooing system in your car accumulates some internal rust and corrosion in its normal operation. A simple method of keeping the system clean is known as flushing the system. It is performed by circulating a can of radiator flush through the system, and then draining and refilling the system with the normal coolant. Radiator flush is marketed by several different manufacturers, and is available in cans at auto departments, parts stores, and many hardware stores.

This operation should be performed every 30,000 miles or once a year.

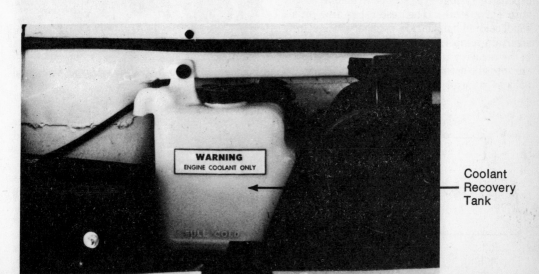

Typical coolant recovery tank

To flush the cooling system:

1. Drain the existing antifreeze and coolant. Open the radiator and engine drain petcocks (located near the bottom of the radiator and engine bloc, respectively), or disconnect the bottom radiator hose at the radiator outlet.

NOTE: *Before opening the radiator petcock, spray it with some penetrating oil. Be aware that if the engine has been run up to operating temperature, the coolant emptied will be HOT.*

2. Close the petcock or reconnect the lower hose and fill the system with water; hot water if the system has just been run.

3. Add a can of quality radiator flush to the radiator or recovery tank, following any special instructions on the can.

4. Idle the engine as long as specified on the can of flush, or until the upper radiator hose gets hot.

5. Drain the system again. There should be quite a bit of scale and rust in the drained water.

6. Repeat this process until the drained water is mostly clear.

7. Close all petcocks and connect all hoses.

8. Flush the coolant recovery reservoir with water and leave empty.

9. Determine the capacity of your car's cooling system (see Capacities specifications in this guide). Add a 50/50 mix of ethylene glycol antifreeze and water to provide the desired protection.

10. Run the engine to operating temperature, then stop the engine and check for leaks. Check the coolant level and top up if necessary.

11. Check the protection level of your antifreeze mix with an antifreeze tester (a small, inexpensive syringe-type device available at any auto parts store). The tester has five or six small colored balls inside, each of which signify a certain temperature rating. Insert the tester in the recovery tank and suck just enough coolant into the syringe to float as many individual balls as you can (without sucking in too much coolant and floating all the balls at once). A table supplied with the tester will explain how many floating balls equal protection down to a certain temperature (three floating balls might mean the coolant will protect your engine down to 5 degrees F, for example).

For problems with engine overheating, see Chapter 3.

Master Cylinder

FLUID RECOMMENDATIONS AND LEVEL CHECK

Chevrolet and GMC trucks are equipped with a dual braking system, allowing a vehicle to be brought to a safe stop in the event of failure in either the front or rear brakes. The dual master cylinder has two entirely separate reservoirs, one connected to the front brakes and the other connected to the rear brakes. In the event of failure in either portion, the remaining part is not affected.

1. Clean all of the dirt from around the cover of the master cylinder.

2. Be sure that the vehicle is resting on a level surface.

3. Carefully pry the clip from the top of the master cylinder to release the cover.

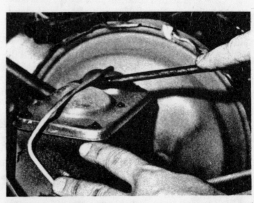

Pry the retaining bail from the top of the master cylinder

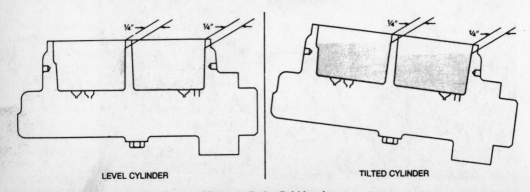

LEVEL CYLINDER   TILTED CYLINDER

Master cylinder fluid level

4. The fluid level should be approximately ⅛" from the top of the master cylinder. If not, add fluid until the level is correct. Only high quality brake fluids, such as General Motors Supreme No. 11 Hydraulic Brake Fluid, or fluids meeting DOT 3 specifications should be used.

NOTE: *It is normal for the fluid level to fall slightly as the disc brake pads wear, on 1971 and later trucks. However, if the level drops significantly between fluid level checks, or if the level is chronically low, the system should be examined for leakage.*

5. Install the cover of the master cylinder. On most models there is a rubber gasket under the cover, which fits into two slots on the cover. Be sure that this is seated properly.

6. Push the clip back into place and be sure that it seats in the groove on the top of the cover.

WARNING: *Brake fluid damages paint. It also absorbs moisture from the air; never leave a container or the master cylinder uncovered any longer than necessary. All parts in contact with the brake fluid (i.e. master cylinder, and its lid, hoses, plunger assemblies, etc.) must be kept clean, since any contamination of the brake fluid will adversely affect braking performance.*

Power Steering Pump
FLUID RECOMMENDATIONS AND LEVEL CHECK

The power steering pump is belt driven; it is located at the front of the engine. The fluid level is checked at the reservoir, located on the top of the pump. The reservoir is part of the belt-driven power steering pump at the front of the engine. To check the fluid level and/or add fluid:

1. Wipe off the cap and surrounding area, after stopping the engine with the wheels straight. On 1970-71 models, the wheels should be all the way to the left.

2. Remove the cap and attached dipstick.

3. Wipe the dipstick off with a clean, lint-free rag, replace the cap, and take a reading. If the fluid is hot, the level should be between HOT and COLD; if it is cold, it should be between COLD and ADD.

4. Either GM Power Steering Fluid or DEXRON®II Automatic Transmission Fluid may be used.

Steering Gear
FLUID RECOMMENDATIONS AND LEVEL CHECK

The steering gear is factory filled with a lubricant which does not require seasonal change. The housing should not be drained; no lubrication is required for the life of the gear.

The gear should be inspected for seal leakage when specified in the Maintenance chart. Look for solid grease, not an oily film. If a seal is replaced or the gear overhauled, it should be filled with Part No. 1051052 which meets GM Specification GM 4673M, or its equivalent. Do not use EP Chassis Lube to lubricate the gear and do not overfill.

Chassis Greasing

Water resistant EP chassis lubricant (grease) conforming to GM specification 6031-M should be used for all chassis grease points.

Every year or 7,500 miles the front suspension ball points, both upper and lower on each side of the truck, must be greased. Most trucks covered in this guide should be equipped with grease nipples on the ball joints, although some may have plugs which must be removed and nipples fitted.

WARNING: *Do not pump so much grease into the ball joint that excess grease squeezes out of the rubber boot. This destroys the watertight seal.*

Jack up the front end of the truck and safely support it with jackstands. Block the rear wheels and firmly apply the parking brake. If the truck has been parked in temperatures below 20°F for any length of time, park it in a heated garage for an hour or so until the ball joints loosen up enough to accept the grease.

Depending on which front wheel you work on first, turn the wheel and tire outward, either full-lock right or full-lock left. You now have the ends of the upper and lower suspension control arms in front of you; the grease nipples are visible pointing up (top ball joint) and down (lower ball joint) through the end of each control arm. If the nipples are not accessible

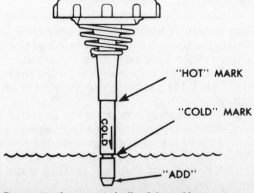

Power steering reservoir dipstick markings

"HOT" MARK

"COLD" MARK

COLD

"ADD"

enough, remove the wheel and tire. Wipe all dirt and crud from the nipples or from around the plugs (if installed). If plugs are on the truck, remove them and install grease nipples in the holes (nipples are available in various thread sizes at most auto parts stores). Using a hand operated, low pressure grease gun loaded with a quality chassis grease, grease the ball joint only until the rubber joint boot begins to swell out.

Steering Linkage

The steering linkage should be greased at the same interval as the ball joints. Grease nipples are installed on the steering tie rod ends on most models. Wipe all dirt and crud from around the nipples at each tie rod end. Using a hand operated, low pressure grease gun loaded with a suitable chassis grease, grease the linkage until the old grease begins to squeeze out around the tie rod ends. Wipe off the nipples and any excess grease. Also grease the nipples on the steering idler arms.

Parking Brake Linkage

Use chassis grease on the parking brake cable where it contacts the cable guides, levers and linkage.

Automatic Transmission Linkage

Apply a small amount of clean engine oil to the kickdown and shift linkage points at 7,500 mile intervals.

Body Lubrication

Hood Latch And Hinges

Clean the latch surfaces and apply clean engine oil to the latch pilot bolts and the spring anchor. Also lubricate the hood hinges with engine oil. Use a chassis grease to lubricate all the pivot points in the latch release mechanism.

Door Hinges

The gas tank filler door and truck doors should be wiped clean and lubricated with clean engine oil once a year. The door lock cylinders and latch mechanisms should be lubricated periodically with a few drops of graphite lock lubricant or a few shots of silicone spray.

Wheel Bearings

Before handling the bearings, there are a few things that you should remember to do and not to do.

Remember to DO the following:

- Remove all outside dirt from the housing before exposing the bearing.
- Treat a used bearing as gently as you would a new one.

- Work with clean tools in clean surroundings.
- Use clean, dry canvas gloves, or at least clean, dry hands.
- Clean solvents and flushing fluids are a must.
- Use clean paper when laying out the bearings to dry.
- Protect disassembled bearings from rust and dirt. Cover them up.
- Use clean rags to wipe bearings.
- Keep the bearings in oil-proof paper when they are to be stored or are not in use.
- Clean the inside of the housing before replacing the bearing.

Do NOT do the following:

- Don't work in dirty surroundings.
- Don't use dirty, chipped or damaged tools.
- Try not to work on wooden work benches or use wooden mallets.
- Don't handle bearings with dirty or moist hands.
- Do not use gasoline for cleaning; use a safe solvent.
- Do not spin-dry bearings with compressed air. They will be damaged.
- Do not spin dirty bearings.
- Avoid using cotton waste or dirty cloths to wipe bearings.
- Try not to scratch or nick bearing surfaces.
- Do not allow the bearing to come in contact with dirt or rust at any time.

2-Wheel Drive

1. Remove the wheel, tire assembly, and the brake drum or brake caliper. See Chapter 9 for details.

2. Remove the hub and disc as an assembly. Remove the caliper mounting bolts and insert a block between the brake pads as the caliper is removed. Remove the caliper and wire it out of the way.

3. Pry off the grease cap, remove the cotter pin, spindle nut, and washer, and then remove the hub. Be careful that you do not drop the wheel bearings.

4. Remove the outer roller bearing assembly from the hub. The inner bearing assembly will remain the the hub and may be removed after prying out the inner seal. Discard this seal.

5. Clean all parts in solvent and allow to air dry. Check the parts for excessive wear or damage.

6. If the bearing cups are worn or scored, they must be replaced. Using a hammer and a drift, remove the bearing cups from the hub. When installing new cups, make sure that they are not cocked, and that they are fully seated against the hub shoulder.

7. Pack both wheel bearings using high melt-

ing point wheel bearing grease. Ordinary grease will melt, and ruin the pads. High temperature grease provides an extra margin of protection. Place a healthy glob of grease in the palm of one hand and force the edge of the bearing into it so that the grease fills the bearing. Do this until the whole bearing is packed. Grease packing tools are available to make this job a lot less messy. There are also tools which make it possible to grease the inner bearing without removing it or the disc from the spindle.

8. Place the inner bearing in the hub and install a new inner seal, making sure that the seal flange faces the bearing cup.

9. Carefully install the wheel hub over the spindle.

10. Using your hands, firmly press the outer bearing into the hub. Install the spindle washer and nut.

11. To adjust the bearings on 1970-71 models, tighten the adjusting nut to 15 ft.lb. while rotating the hub. Back the nut off one flat ($\frac{1}{6}$ turn) and insert a new cotter pin. If the nut and spindle hole do not align, back the nut off slightly. There should be 0.001-0.008" end play in the bearing. This can be measured with a dial indicator, if you wish. Install the dust cap, wheel, and tire.

12. To adjust the bearings on 1972 through 1984 models, spin the wheel hub by hand and tighten the nut until it is just snug (12 ft.lb.). Back off the nut until it is loose, then tighten it finger tight. Loosen the nut until either hole in the spindle lines up with a slot in the nut, and insert a new cotter pin. There should be 0.001-0.008" end play in the bearing through 1973, and 0.001-0.005" 1974 and later. This can be measured with a dial indicator, if you wish. Replace the dust cap, wheel, and tire.

Four Wheel Drive

Refer to Chapter 7 (4 x 4s) for removal, installation, adjustment and repacking procedures.

TRAILER TOWING

General Recommendations

Your car was primarily designed to carry passengers and cargo. It is important to remember that towing a trailer will place additional loads on your vehicle's engine, drive train, steering, braking and other systems. However, if you find it necessary to tow a trailer, using the proper equipment is a must.

Local laws may require specific equipment such as trailer brakes or fender mounted mirrors. Check your local laws.

Trailer Weight

The weight of the trailer is the most important factor. A good weight-to-horsepower ratio is about 35:1, 35 lbs. of GCW (Gross Combined Weight) for every horsepower your engine develops. Multiply the engine's rated horsepower by 35 and subtract the weight of the car passengers and luggage. The result is the approximate ideal maximum weight you should tow, although a a numerically higher axle ratio can help compensate for heavier weight.

Hitch Weight

Figure the hitch weight to select a proper hitch. Hitch weight is usually 9-11% of the trailer gross weight and should be measured with the trailer loaded. Hitches fall into three types: those that mount on the frame and rear bumper or the bolt-on or weld-on distribution type used for larger trailers. Axle mounted or clamp-on bumper hitches should never be used.

Check the gross weight rating of your trailer. Tongue weight is usually figured as 10% of gross trailer weight. Therefore, a trailer with a maximum gross weight of 2,000 lb. will have a maximum tongue weight of 200 lb. Class I trailers fall into this category. Class II trailers are those with a gross weight rating of 2,000-3,500 lb., while Class III trailers fall into the 3,500-6,000 lb. category. Class IV trailers are those over 6,000 lb. and are for use with fifth wheel trucks, only.

When you've determined the hitch that you'll need, follow the manufacturer's installation instructions, exactly, especially when it comes to fastener torques. The hitch will subjected to a lot of stress and good hitches come with hardened bolts. Never substitute an inferior bolt for a hardened bolt.

Cooling

ENGINE

One of the most common, if not THE most common, problems associated with trailer towing is engine overheating.

If you have a standard cooling system, without an expansion tank, you'll definitely need to get an aftermarket expansion tank kit, preferably one with at least a 2 quart capacity. These kits are easily installed on the radiator's overflow hose, and come with a pressure cap designed for expansion tanks.

Another helpful accessory is a Flex Fan. These fan are large diameter units are designed to provide more airflow at low speeds, with blades that have deeply cupped surfaces. The blades then flex, or flatten out, at high speed, when less cooling air is needed. These fans are far lighter in weight than stock fans, requiring less horsepower to drive them. Also, they are far quieter than stock fans.

If you do decide to replace your stock fan with a flex fan, note that if your car has a fan clutch, a spacer between the flex fan and water pump hub will be needed.

Aftermarket engine oil coolers are helpful for prolonging engine oil life and reducing overall engine temperatures. Both of these factors increase engine life.

While not absolutely necessary in towing Class I and some Class II trailers, they are recommended for heavier Class II and all Class III towing.

Engine oil cooler systems consist of an adapter, screwed on in place of the oil filter, a remote filter mounting and a multi-tube, finned heat exchanger, which is mounted in front of the radiator or air conditioning condenser.

TRANSMISSION

An automatic transmission is usually recommended for trailer towing. Modern automatics have proven reliable and, of course, easy to operate, in trailer towing.

The increased load of a trailer, however, causes an increase in the temperature of the automatic transmission fluid. Heat is the worst enemy of an automatic transmission. As the temperature of the fluid increases, the life of the fluid decreases.

It is essential, therefore, that you install an automatic transmission cooler.

The cooler, which consists of a multi-tube, finned heat exchanger, is usually installed in front of the radiator or air conditioning compressor, and hooked inline with the transmission cooler tank inlet line. Follow the cooler manufacturer's installation instructions.

Select a cooler of at least adequate capacity, based upon the combined gross weights of the car and trailer.

Cooler manufacturers recommend that you use an aftermarket cooler in addition to, and not instead of, the present cooling tank in your radiator. If you do want to use it in place of the radiator cooling tank, get a cooler at least two sizes larger than normally necessary.

NOTE: *A transmission cooler can, sometimes, cause slow or harsh shifting in the transmission during cold weather, until the fluid has a chance to come up to normal operating temperature. Some coolers can be purchased with or retrofitted with a temperature bypass valve which will allow fluid flow through the cooler only when the fluid has reached operating temperature, or above.*

Handling A Trailer

Towing a trailer with ease and safety requires a certain amount of experience. It's a good idea to learn the feel of a trailer by practicing turning, stopping and backing in an open area such as an empty parking lot.

PUSHING AND TOWING

Pushing

Chevrolet and GMC trucks with manual transmissions can be push started.

To push start, make sure that both bumpers are in reasonable alignment. Turn the ignition key to ON and engage High ear. Depress the clutch pedal. When a speed of about 10 mph is reached, slightly depress the gas pedal and slowly release the clutch. The engine should start.

Automatic transmission equipped trucks cannot be started by pushing.

Towing

Two Wheel Drive

Chevrolet and GMC trucks can be towed on all four wheels (flat towed) at speeds of less than 35 mph for distances less than 50 miles, providing that the axle, driveline and engine/transmission are operable. The transmission should be in Neutral, the engine should be off, the steering column unlocked, and the parking brake released.

Do not attach chains to the bumpers or bracketing. All attachments must be made to the structural members. Safety chains should be used. It should also be remembered that power steering and brake assists will not be working with the engine off.

The rear wheels must be raised off the ground or the driveshaft disconnected when the transmission is not operating properly, or when speeds of over 35 mph will be used or when towing more than 50 miles.

CAUTION: *If a truck is towed on its front wheels only, the steering wheel must be secured with the wheels in a straight ahead position.*

Four Wheel Drive

Details for towing procedures are given in the Towing Four Wheel Drive Chart.

Remember that the power steering and power brakes will not have their power assist with the engine off. The only safe way to tow is with a tow bar. The steering column must be unlocked and the parking brake released. Attach-

Four Wheel Drive Towing Chart

FRONT WHEELS OFF THE GROUND	
FULL TIME (4 X 4) **AUTOMATIC TRANSMISSION**	**PART TIME (4 X 4)** **MANUAL TRANSMISSION**
1. TRANSFER CASE IN NEUTRAL 2. TRANSMISSION IN PARK 3. MAXIMUM SPEED 35 MPH 4. MAXIMUM DISTANCE 50 MILES NOTE: For distances over 50 miles, disconnect rear propshaft at rear axle carrier and secure in safe position.	1. TRANSFER CASE IN 2 H 2. TRANSMISSION IN NEUTRAL 3. MAXIMUM SPEED 35 MPH 4. MAXIMUM DISTANCE 50 MILES NOTE: For distances over 50 miles, disconnect the rear propshaft at rear axle carrier and secure in safe position.
REAR WHEELS OFF THE GROUND	
CAUTION: When towing a vehicle in this position, the steering wheel should be secured to keep the front wheels in a straight ahead position.	
FULL TIME (4 X 4)	**PART TIME (4 X 4)**
1. TRANSFER CASE IN NEUTRAL 2. TRANSMISSION IN PARK 3. MAXIMUM SPEED 35 MPH 4. MAXIMUM DISTANCE 50 MILES NOTE: For distances over 50 miles, disconnect front propshaft at front axle carrier and secure in safe position.	1. TRANSFER CASE IN 2 H 2. TRANSMISSION IN NEUTRAL 3. MAXIMUM SPEED 35 MPH 4. MAXIMUM DISTANCE 50 MILES NOTE: For distances over 50 miles, disconnect the front propshaft at front axle carrier and secure in safe position.
ALL FOUR WHEELS ON GROUND	
FULL TIME (4 X 4)	**PART TIME (4 X 4)**
1. TRANSFER CASE IN NEUTRAL 2. TRANSMISSION IN PARK NOTE: Do not exceed speed as per State laws for towing vehicles.	1. TRANSFER CASE IN 2 H 2. TRANSMISSION IN NEUTRAL 3. MAXIMUM SPEED 35 MPH 4. MAXIMUM DISTANCE 50 MILES NOTE: For speeds or distances greater than above, both propshafts must be disconnected at the axle carrier end and secured in a safe position. It is recommended that both propshafts be removed and stored in the vehicle. NOTE: Do not exceed speeds as per State laws for towing vehicles.

ments should be made to the frame and to the bumper or its brackets. Safety chains are also required.

NOTE: *When towing a full time four wheel drive manual transmission truck with all four wheels on the ground, the transfer case must be in Neutral and the transmission in high gear. There is no speed restriction.*

JUMP STARTING

All Except Diesels

The following procedure is recommended by the manufacturer. Be sure that the booster battery is 12 volt with negative ground.

CAUTION: *Do not attempt this procedure on a frozen battery; it will probably explode. Do not attempt it on a sealed Delco Freedom battery showing a light color in the charge indicator. Be certain to observe correct polarity connections. Failure to do so will result in almost immediate alternator and regulator destruction. Never allow the jumper cable ends to touch each other.*

1. Position the vehicles so that they are not touching. Set the parking brake and place automatic transmissions in Park and manual transmissions in Neutral. Turn off the lights, heater and other electrical loads.

2. Remove the vent caps from both the booster and discharged battery. Lay a cloth over the open vent cells of each battery. This isn't necessary on batteries equipped with sponge type flame arrestor caps, and it isn't possible on sealed batteries.

Diesels

JUMP-STARTING A DUAL BATTERY DIESEL

All GM V8 diesels are equipped with two 12 volt batteries. The batteries are connected in parallel circuit (positive terminal to positive terminal, negative terminal to negative terminal). Hooking the batteries up in parallel circuit increases battery cranking power without increasing total battery voltage output (12 volts). On the other hand, hooking two 12 volt batteries up in a series circuit (positive terminal to negative terminal, positive terminal to negative terminal) increases total battery output to 24 volts (12 volts + 12 volts).

CAUTION: *NEVER hook the batteries up in a series circuit or the entire electrical system will go up in smoke.*

In the event that a dual battery diesel must be jump started, use the following procedure.

1. Open the hood and locate the batteries. On GM diesels, the manufacturer usually suggests using the battery on the driver's side of the car to make the connection.

2. Position the donor car so that the jumper cables will reach from its battery (must be 12 volt, negative ground) to the appropriate battery in the diesel. Do not allow the cars to touch.

3. Shut off all electrical equipment on both vehicles. Turn off the engine of the donor car, set the parking brakes on both vehicles and block the wheels. Also, make sure both vehicles are in Neutral (manual transmission models) or Park (automatic transmission models).

4. Using the jumper cables, connect the posi-

JUMP STARTING A DEAD BATTERY

The chemical reaction in a battery produces explosive hydrogen gas. This is the safe way to jump start a dead battery, reducing the chances of an accidental spark that could cause an explosion.

Jump Starting Precautions

1. Be sure both batteries are of the same voltage.
2. Be sure both batteries are of the same polarity (have the same grounded terminal).
3. Be sure the vehicles are not touching.
4. Be sure the vent cap holes are not obstructed.
5. Do not smoke or allow sparks around the battery.
6. In cold weather, check for frozen electrolyte in the battery. Do not jump start a frozen battery.
7. Do not allow electrolyte on your skin or clothing.
8. Be sure the electrolyte is not frozen.
CAUTION: *Make certain that the ignition key, in the vehicle with the dead battery, is in the OFF position. Connecting cables to vehicles with on-board computers will result in computer destruction if the key is not in the OFF position.*

Jump Starting Procedure

1. Determine voltages of the two batteries; they must be the same.
2. Bring the starting vehicle close (they must not touch) so that the batteries can be reached easily.
3. Turn off all accessories and both engines. Put both cars in Neutral or Park and set the handbrake.
4. Cover the cell caps with a rag—do not cover terminals.
5. If the terminals on the run-down battery are heavily corroded, clean them.
6. Identify the positive and negative posts on both batteries and connect the cables in the order shown.
7. Start the engine of the starting vehicle and run it at fast idle. Try to start the car with the dead battery. Crank it for no more than 10 seconds at a time and let it cool off for 20 seconds in between tries.
8. If it doesn't start in 3 tries, there is something else wrong.
9. Disconnect the cables in the reverse order.
10. Replace the cell covers and dispose of the rags.

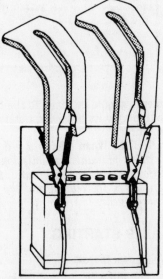

Side terminal batteries occasionally pose a problem when connecting jumper cables. There frequently isn't enough room to clamp the cables without touching sheet metal. Side terminal adaptors are available to alleviate this problem and should be removed after use.

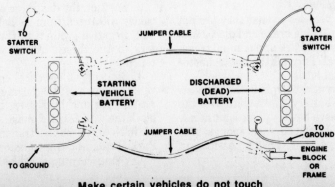

TO STARTER SWITCH

JUMPER CABLE

TO STARTER SWITCH

STARTING VEHICLE BATTERY

DISCHARGED (DEAD) BATTERY

TO GROUND

JUMPER CABLE

TO GROUND

ENGINE BLOCK OR FRAME

Make certain vehicles do not touch

This hook-up for negative ground cars only

tive (+) terminal of the donor car battery to the positive terminal of one (not both) of the diesel batteries.

5. Using the second jumper cable, connect the negative (–) terminal of the donor battery to a solid, stationary, metallic point on the diesel (alternator bracket, engine block, etc.) Be very careful to keep the jumper cables away from moving parts (cooling fan, alternator belt, etc.) on both vehicles.

6. Start the engine of the donor car and run it at moderate speed.

7. Start the engine of the diesel.

8. When the diesel starts, disconnect the battery cables in the reverse order of attachment.

JACKING

CAUTION: *To reduce the risk of personal injury, follow all jacking and stowage instructions. Use the jack only for lifting the vehicle during wheel change. Never get beneath the vehicle, start or run the engine while the vehicle is supported by the jack. Always secure and restow spare or flat tire and all jacking equipment.*

1. Park on a level surface and firmly set parking brake.

2. Turn on hazard warning flasher. (If necessary).

3. Set automatic transmission in **PARK** (manual transmission in **REVERSE**).

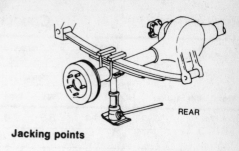

Jacking points

front jacking point

4. Block front and rear of tire at corner diagonally opposite to one being raised.

5. Remove jacking tools from stowage area.

6. Raise jack until lift head engages lower control arm (front location 2 wheel drive) or axle (front location 4 wheel drive/rear location 2 or 4 wheel drive).

7. Raise vehicle by rotating jack handle clockwise.

8. Make sure vehicle is supported properly, with jackstands, before starting any repairs.

Capacities

Year	Engine Displacement (cu in.)	Engine Crankcase (qts)		Transmission (pts)			Drive Axle		Fuel Tank (gals)	Transfer Case (pts)	Cooling System (qts)		
		With Filter	Without Filter	Manual 3-spd	4-spd	Auto (Refill)	Front	Rear			w/o A/C	w/A/C	HD
1970	250	5	4	1.75①	8.0	②	5	③	21.5	5	12.5	—	—
	292	6	5	1.75①	8.0	②	5	③	21.5	5	12.5	13.0	13.5
	307	5	4	1.75①	8.0	②	5	③	21.5	5	17.5	18.5	18.0
	350	5	4	1.75①	8.0	②	5	③	21.5	5	17.0	18.5	18.5
	396	5	4	1.75①	8.0	②	5	③	21.5	5	24.0	—	24.5
1971–72	250	5	4	3.5	7.0	②	5	③	20.2④	5	12.2	12.9	12.9
	292	6	5	3.5	7.0	②	5	③	20.2④	5	12.6	13.3	13.3
	307	5	4	3.5	7.0	②	5	③	20.2④	5	16.0	16.0	16.0
	350	5	4	3.5	7.0	②	5	③	20.2④	5	16.2	17.7	17.7
	402	5	4	3.5	7.0	②	5	③	20.2④	5	23.2	24.7	24.7

Capacities (cont.)

Year	Engine Displacement (cu in.)	Engine Crankcase (qts) With Filter	Engine Crankcase (qts) Without Filter	Transmission (pts) Manual 3-spd	Transmission (pts) Manual 4-spd	Transmission (pts) Auto (Refill)	Drive Axle Front	Drive Axle Rear	Fuel Tank (gals)	Transfer Case (pts)	Cooling System (qts) w/o A/C	Cooling System (qts) w/A/C	Cooling System (qts) HD
1973–74	250	5	4	3.5	7.0	②	5	⑥	20 ⑩	5 ⑤	12.2	12.5	12.5
	292	6	5	3.5	7.0	②	5	⑥	20 ⑩	5 ⑤	12.6	13.3	13.3
	307	5	4	3.5	7.0	②	5	⑥	20 ⑩	5 ⑤	16.0	16.0	16.0
	350, 400	5	4	3.5	7.0	②	5	⑥	20 ⑩	5 ⑤	16.2	17.7	17.7
	454	5	4	3.5	7.0	②	5	⑥	20 ⑩	5 ⑤	18.5	21.0	21.0
1975	250	5	4	3.2 ⑦	8.3	②	5	⑥	20 ⑩	5 ⑤	14.8	15.4	14.8
	292	6	5	3.2 ⑦	8.3	②	5	⑥	20 ⑩	5 ⑤	14.8	15.6	14.8
	350	5	4	3.2 ⑦	8.3	②	5	⑥	20 ⑩	5 ⑤	17.6	18.0	18.0
	400	5	4	3.2 ⑦	8.3	②	5	⑥	20 ⑩	5 ⑤	19.6	20.4	20.4
	454	5	4	3.2 ⑦	8.3	②	5	⑥	20 ⑩	5 ⑤	24.8	24.8	24.8
1976–80	250	5	4	3.2 ⑦	8.0	②	5 ⑧	⑥	20 ⑩	5 ⑤	15.0	15.6	15.0
	292	6	5	3.2 ⑦	8.0	②	5 ⑧	⑥	20 ⑩	5 ⑤	14.8	15.4	14.8
	305	5	4	3.2 ⑦	8.0	②	5 ⑧	⑥	20 ⑩	5 ⑤	17.6	18.0	18.0
	350	5	4	3.2 ⑦	8.0	②	5 ⑧	⑥	20 ⑩	5 ⑤	17.6	18.0	18.0
	350 Diesel	7	6	—	—	5.0	—	⑥	20 ⑩	—	18.0	18.0	18.0
	400	5	4	3.2 ⑦	8.0	②	5 ⑧	⑥	20 ⑩	5 ⑤	20.4	20.4	20.4
	454	7	6	3.2 ⑦	8.0	②	5 ⑧	⑥	20 ⑩	5 ⑤	24.4 ⑨	24.7	24.7
1981	250	5	4	3	8	6	5	⑥	20 ⑩	5	15	15	15
	292	6	5	3	8	6	5	⑥	20 ⑩	5	15	15	15
	305	5	4	3	8	6	5	⑥	20 ⑩	5	17.5	17.5	17.5
	350	5	4	3	8	6	5	⑥	20 ⑩	5	17.5	17.5	17.5
	350 Diesel	7	—	3	8	6	5	⑥	20 ⑩	5	17.5	18	18
	400	5	4	3	8	6	5	⑥	20 ⑩	5	18	19	20
	454	7	6	3	8	6	5	⑥	20 ⑩	5	23	23	24
1982–84	250	5	4	3	8	⑭	5	⑥	⑬	5 ⑫	15.5	15.5	15.5
	292	6	5	3	8	⑭	5	⑥	⑬	5 ⑫	15.5	15.5	15.5
	305	5	4	3	8	⑭	5	⑥	⑬	5 ⑫	17.5	17.5	17.5
	350	5	4	3	8	⑭	5	⑥	⑬	5 ⑫	17.5	17.5	17.5
	379 Diesel	7	—	3	8	⑭	5	⑥	⑬	5 ⑫	24.5	24.5	24.5
	454	7	6	3	8	⑭	5	⑥	⑬	5 ⑫	23	23	24
1985–86	250	5	4	3	8	6.3	⑮	⑥	⑬	5 ⑫	10.9	10.9	10.9
	262	5	5	—	8	⑭	5	⑥	22	5 ⑫	14	14	14
	292	6	5	3	8	⑭	⑮	⑥	⑬	5 ⑫	15.5	16.0	—

Capacities (cont.)

Year	Engine Displacement (cu in.)	Engine Crankcase (qts)		Transmission (pts)			Drive Axle		Fuel Tank (gals)	Transfer Case (pts)	Cooling System (qts)		
		With Filter	Without Filter	Manual		Auto (Refill)	Front	Rear			w/o A/C	w/A/C	HD
				3-spd	4-spd								
1985–86	305	5	4	3	8	⑭	⑮	6	⑭	5⑫	17.5	18	—
	350	7	6	3	8	⑭	⑮	6	⑬	5⑫	23	24.5	—
	Diesel	7	⑯	3	8	⑭	5	6	⑬	5⑫	25	25	—
	454	7	6	3	8	⑭	5	6	⑬	5⑫	23	23	24
1987	262	5	5	3	—	⑭	⑰	6	⑱	⑲	10.9	10.9	—
	305	5	4	3	8	⑭	⑰	6	⑱	⑲	17.0	17.0	—
	350	5	4	3	8	⑭	⑰	6	⑱	⑲	17.0	17.0	—
	454	7	6	3	8	⑭	⑰	6	⑱	⑲	24.5	24.5	—
	Diesel	7	7	3	8	⑭	⑰	6	⑱	⑲	25.5	25.5	—

① Heavy-duty 3-speed—3.5 pts
② Powerglide—4.0 pts
  Turbo Hydra-Matic 350—5.0 pts
  Turbo Hydra-Matic 400—7.5 pts
③ 3,300 and 3,500 lb. Chevrolet axles—4.5 pts
  5,200 and 7,200 lb. Chevrolet axles—6.5 pts
  5,500 lb. Dana axles—6.0 pts
  11,000 lb. Chevrolet axles—14.0 pts
④ 20 Series—21.0 gals
⑤ Full-time 4 wd—8 pts
⑥ 8½ in. ring gear—4.2 pts
  8⅞ in. ring gear (Chevrolet)—4.5 pts (3.5 pts 1977–82)
  9¾ in. ring gear (Dana) 6.0 pts.
  10½ in. ring gear (Chevrolet)—6½ pts
  10½ in. ring gear (Dana)—7.2 pts
  12½ in. ring gear (Chevrolet)—26.8 pts
⑦ Tremec 3-spd—4.0 pts
  Muncie 3-spd—3.0 pts
⑧ 8½ in. ring gear—4.25 pts (1977–80)
⑨ 22.8—1979–80
⑩ 16.0 gal—short wheelbase models
⑪ Not used
⑫ 10 pts on 208 transfer cases
⑬ Short bed w/single tank: 16 gal., 32 gal. w/dual tanks
  Long bed w/single tank: 20 gal. Long bed w/dual tanks under 8600 GVWR 32 gal.
  Long bed w/dual tanks over 8600 GVWR 40 gal.
  All diesel w/dual tanks 40 gal.
⑭ Turbo Hydra-Matic 350—6 pts
  Turbo Hydra-Matic 400—7 pts 1985 only 9 pts.
  Turbo Hydra-Matic 700R4—10 pts
⑮ K10-20: 2 Quarts, K30: 3 Quarts
⑯ Oil Filter should be changed at EVERY OIL CHANGE
⑰ V15/10, V25/20—5.2 qts.
  V35/30—3.0 qts.
⑱ Suburban, gas: 25 gal.
          Diesel: 27 gal.
  Pick-up, Shortbed—16 gal.
          Longbed—20 gal.
⑲ V15/10, V25/20—10.4 pts
  V35/30—5.0 pts

Maintenance Intervals

See text for procedures concerning regular maintenance.

NOTE: *Heavy-duty operation (trailer towing, prolonged idling, severe stop-and-start driving) should be accompanied by a 50% increase in maintenance. Cut the interval in half for these conditions. Figures given are maintenance intervals when service should be performed.*

Maintenance	1970	1971–74	1975–1987
Air Cleaner (Check and Clean) Paper element ①	24,000 mi (replace)	24,000 mi (replace)	30,000 mi (replace) ⑥
PCV Valve (Replace)	12 mo/12,000 mi	12 mo/12,000 mi	12 mo/15,000 mi ⑦ ⑧
Evaporative Canister Replace filter	—	12 mo/12,000 mi	24 mo/30,000 mi ⑧
Engine Oil Check Replace	Each fuel stop 4 mo/6,000 mi	Each fuel stop 4 mo/6,000 mi	Each fuel stop 6 mo/7,500 mi ⑨ ⑬ ⑭
Engine Oil Filter (Replace)	At 1st oil change; then every 2nd	At 1st oil change; then every 2nd	At 1st oil change; then every 2nd ⑬
Fuel Filter Replace ⑮	12,000 mi	12,000 mi	12 mo/15,000 mi ⑥ ⑫
Powerglide Transmission Fluid Check Replace	6,000 mi 24,000 mi ⑤	6,000 mi 24,000 mi	—
Turbo Hydra-Matic Fluid & Filter Check fluid Change fluid Replace filter	6,000 mi 24,000 mi 24,000 mi	6,000 mi 24,000 mi 24,000 mi	Each oil change 30,000 mi 30,000 ⑧ ⑩
Manual transmission (All) Check lubricant Add lubricant	6,000 mi As necessary	4 mo/6,000 mi As necessary	6 mo/7,500 mi ⑨ As necessary
Battery Lubricate terminal felt washer Clean terminals Check electrolyte level	6,000 mi ④ 6,000 mi Twice monthly	— As necessary Twice monthly	As necessary Twice monthly
Coolant Level	Each fuel stop	Each fuel stop	Each fuel stop
Front Wheel Bearings Lubricate	30,000 mi	30,000 mi ③	30,000 mi ⑧ ⑪
Front and Rear Axle Lube Check Replace	6,000 mi 24,000 mi	6,000 mi 24,000 mi	6 mo/7,500 mi ⑨ 1st 15,000 mi w/Posi-traction
Brake Fluid (Master Cylinder) Check fluid level Add fluid	6,000 mi As necessary	6,000 mi As necessary	6 mo/7,500 mi ⑨ As necessary
Manual Steering Gear Lubricant Check level Add lubricant	36,000 mi ② As necessary ②	36,000 mi ② ②	30,000 mi ②
Power Steering Reservoir Check fluid level Add fluid	At each oil change As necessary	At each oil change As necessary	6 mo/7,500 mi As necessary
Rotate Tires	6,000 mi	6,000 mi	Radial—1st 7,500 mi, then every 15,000 mi Bias Belted—every 7,500 mi
Chassis Lubrication	See Chassis Lubrication charts	See Chassis Lubrication charts	See Chassis Lubrication charts
Drive Belts Check and adjust (as necessary)	6,000 mi	6,000 mi	6 mo/7,500 mi

Maintenance Intervals

See text for procedures concerning regular maintenance.

NOTE: *Heavy-duty operation (trailer towing, prolonged idling, severe stop-and-start driving) should be accompanied by a 50% increase in maintenance. Cut the interval in half for these conditions. Figures given are maintenance intervals when service should be performed.*

Maintenance	1970	1971–74	1975–1987
Transfer Case			
Check	4 mo/6,000 mi	4 mo/6,000 mi	4 mo/6,000 mi
Add	As necessary	As necessary	As necessary
Driveshaft Centering Ball			
Lubricate (4WD only)	6,000 mi	6,000 mi	7,500 mi ⑨

—Not applicable

mi—Miles

mo—Months

① Paper element air cleaners should be rotated 180° each time they are checked

② From 1970 on, no lubrication of the manual steering gear is recommended. The gear should be inspected for leaks at the seal (lubricant leaks, not filmy oil leaks). Seasonal change of the lubricant is not required and the housing should not be drained.

③ 24,000 miles in 1972–74

④ May be equipped with a felt terminal washer

⑤ 20 Series—every 12,000 miles

⑥ 12,000 mi in heavy duty emissions vehicles (C 10 or C-1500 over 6000 lbs. GVW; all K models)

⑦ 24 mo/30,000 mi 1976–86

⑧ 24,000 mi in heavy duty emission vehicles

⑨ 4 mo/6,000 mi in heavy duty emissions vehicles

⑩ 60,000 mi 1976–78, 100,000 mi 1979–86 light duty emissions vehicles

⑪ 12,000 mi in four wheel drive vehicles

⑫ 24 mo/24,000 mi in California 350 and 400 engines through 1977; 12,000 mi on 1979–86 heavy duty emissions vehicles

⑬ Change at 3,000 mile intervals for 350 Diesel; 6,000 miles for 1981 and later models

⑭ Change at 5,000 mile intervals for 379 (6.2L) Diesel; or every 2,500 miles when operating under extreme temperatures, extended high speed or idle conditions, or frequent trailer towing.

⑮ Figures include diesel fuel filters

Engine Performance and Tune-Up

T2

TUNE-UP PROCEDURES

In order to extract the full measure of performance and economy from your engine it is essential that it be properly tuned at regular intervals. A regular tune-up will keep your vehicle's engine running smoothly and will prevent the annoying minor breakdowns and poor performance associated with an untuned engine.

Neither tune-up nor troubleshooting can be considered, independently since each has a direct relationship with each other.

It is advisable to follow a definite and thorough tune-up procedure. Tune-up consists of three separate steps: Analysis, the process of determining whether normal wear is responsible for performance loss, and whether parts require replacement or service; parts replacement or service; and adjustment, where engine adjustments are performed.

The manufacturer's recommended interval for tune-ups is every 12,000 miles or 12 months, whichever comes first for 1970-74, and 22,500 miles or 18 months for 1975-87, except for heavy duty emission models, which use the 12 mo/12,000 mi schedule in all years. These intervals should be shortened if the truck is subjected to severe operating conditions such as trailer pulling or off-road driving, or if starting and running problems are noticed. It is assumed that the routine maintenance described in Chapter 1 has been kept up, as this will have an effect on the results of the tune-up. All the applicable tune-up steps should be followed, as each adjustment complements the effects of the others. If the tune-up (emission control) sticker in the engine compartment disagrees with the information presented in the Tune-up Specifications chart in this chapter, the sticker figures must be followed. The sticker information reflects running changes made by the manufacturer during production. The light duty sticker is usually found on the underhood sheet metal above the grille. The heavy duty sticker is usually on top of the air cleaner.

Diesel engines do not require tune-ups per se, as there is no ignition system.

Troubleshooting is a logical sequence of procedures designed to locate a particular cause of trouble. Troubleshooting Charts in this book can be found at the end of each chapter and are general in nature (applicable to most vehicles), yet specific enough to locate the problem.

It is advisable to read the entire chapter before beginning a tune-up, although those who are more familiar with tune-up procedures may wish to go directly to the instructions.

Spark Plugs

A typical spark plug consists of a metal shell surrounding a ceramic insulator. A metal electrode extends downward through the center of the insulator and protrudes a small distance. Located at the end of the plug and attached to the side of the outer metal shell is the side electrode. The side electrode bends in at a 90° angle so that its tip is even with, and parallel to, the tip of the center electrode. The distance between these two electrodes (measured in thousandths of an inch) is called the spark plug gap. The spark plug in no way produces a spark but merely provides a gap across which the current can arc. The coil produces anywhere from 20,000 to 40,000 volts which travels to the distributor where it is distributed through the spark plug wires to the spark plugs. The current passes along the center electrode and jumps the gap to the side electrode, and, in do doing, ignites the air/fuel mixture in the combustion chamber.

Rough idle, hard starting, frequent engine miss at high speeds and physical deterioration are all indications that the plugs should be replaced.

The electrode end of a spark plug is a good in-

Gasoline Engine Tune-Up Specifications

Year	Engine Displacement (cu in.)	Spark Plugs Type	Gap (in.)	Distributor Point Dwell (deg)	Point Gap (in.) ▲	Ignition Timing (deg) MT	AT	Fuel Pump Pressure (psi)	Compression Pressure (psi) ●	Idle Speed (rpm)* MT	AT	Valve Clearance (in.) Ex	In
1970	250	R46T	0.035	31–34	0.019	TDC	4B	3.5–4.5	130	See Text	See Text	Hyd	Hyd
	292	R46T	0.035	31–34	0.019	TDC	4B	3.5–4.5	130	See Text	See Text	Hyd	Hyd
	307	R44	0.035	28–32	0.019	2B	8B	5.0–6.5	150	See Text	See Text	Hyd	Hyd
	350 (2 bbl)	R43	0.035	28–32	0.019	4B	—	7.0–8.5	150	See Text	See Text	Hyd	Hyd
	350 (4 bbl)	R43	0.035	28–32	0.019	TDC	4B	7.0–8.5	150	See Text	See Text	Hyd	Hyd
	396	R43T	0.035	28–32	0.019	4B	—	7.0–8.5	150	See Text	See Text	Hyd	Hyd
1971	250	R46TS	0.035	31–34	0.019	4B	4B	3.5–4.5	130	550	500	Hyd	Hyd
	292	R44T	0.035	31–34	0.019	4B	4B	3.5–4.5	130	550	500	Hyd	Hyd
	307 (200 HP)	R45TS	0.035	28–32	0.019	4B	8B	5.0–6.5	150	600	550	Hyd	Hyd
	307 (215 HP)	R45TS	0.035	28–32	0.019	4B	4B	7.0–8.5	150	550	500	Hyd	Hyd
	350	R44TS	0.035	28–32	0.019	4B	8B	7.0–8.5	150	600	550	Hyd	Hyd
	402	R44TS	0.035	28–32	0.019	8B	8B	7.0–8.5	150	600	600	Hyd	Hyd
1972	250	R46T	0.035	31–34	0.019	4B	4B	3.5–4.5	130	600	600	Hyd	Hyd
	292	R44T	0.035	31–34	0.019	4B	4B	3.5–4.5	130	700	600	Hyd	Hyd
	307	R44T	0.035	28–32	0.019	4B	8B ①	5.0–6.5	150	700	700	Hyd	Hyd
	350	R44T	0.035	28–32	0.019	4B	8B	7.0–8.5	150	900②	600	Hyd	Hyd
	402	R44T	0.035	28–32	0.019	8B	8B	7.0–8.5	150	800	600	Hyd	Hyd
1973	250 (LD)	R46T	0.035	31–34	0.019	6B	6B	3.5–4.5	130	750	600	Hyd	Hyd
	250 (HD)	R46T	0.035	31–34	0.019	4B	4B	3.5–4.5	130	700	600	Hyd	Hyd
	292 (Fed)	R44T	0.035	31–34	0.019	4B	4B	3.5–4.5	130	700	700	Hyd	Hyd
	292 (Calif)	R44T	0.035	31–34	0.019	8B	8B	3.5–4.5	130	700	700	Hyd	Hyd
	307 (LD)	R44T	0.035	28–32	0.019	4B	8B	5.0–6.5	150	900	600	Hyd	Hyd

Gasoline Engine Tune-Up Specifications (cont.)

Year	Engine Displacement (cu in.)	Spark Plugs Type	Gap (in.)	Distributor Point Dwell (deg)	Point Gap (in.) ▲	Ignition Timing (deg) MT	AT	Fuel Pump Pressure (psi)	Compression Pressure (psi) ●	Idle Speed (rpm)* MT	AT	Valve Clearance (in.) Ex	In
1973	307 (HD)	R44T	0.035	28–32	0.019	TDC	TDC	5.0–6.5	150	600	600	Hyd	Hyd
	350 (LD)	R44T	0.035	28–32	0.019	8B	12B	7.0–8.5	150	900	600	Hyd	Hyd
	350 (HD)	R44T	0.035	28–32	0.019	4B	4B	7.0–8.5	150	600	600	Hyd	Hyd
	454 (LD)	R44T	0.035	28–32	0.019	10B	10B	7.0–8.5	150	900	600	Hyd	Hyd
	454 (HD)	R44T	0.035	28–32	0.019	③	④	7.0–8.5	150	700	700	Hyd	Hyd
1974	250 (LD, Fed)	R46T	0.035	31–34	0.019	8B	8B	3.5–4.5	130	850	600	Hyd	Hyd
	250 (LD, Calif)	R46T	0.035	31–34	0.019	8B	—	3.5–4.5	130	850	—	Hyd	Hyd
	250 (HD)	R44T	0.035	31–34	0.019	6B	6B	3.5–4.5	130	600	600	Hyd	Hyd
	292 (HD)	R44T	0.035	31–34	0.019	8B	8B	3.5–4.5	130	600	600	Hyd	Hyd
	350 (2 bbl)	R44T	0.035	29–31	0.019	4B	8B	7.0–8.5	150	900	600	Hyd	Hyd
	350 (4 bbl, Calif)	R44T	0.035	29–31	0.019	4B	8B	7.0–8.5	150	900	600	Hyd	Hyd
	350 (4 bbl, Fed)	R44T	0.035	29–31	0.019	6B	12B	7.0–8.5	150	900	600	Hyd	Hyd
	350 (4 bbl, HD)	R44T	0.035	29–31	0.019	8B	8B	7.0–8.5	150	700	700	Hyd	Hyd
	454 (LD)	R44T	0.035	29–31	0.019	10B	10B	7.0–8.5	150	800	600	Hyd	Hyd
	454 (LD)	R44T	0.035	29–31	0.019	8B	8B	7.0–8.5	150	700	700	Hyd	Hyd
1975	250	R46TX	0.060	—	—	10B	10B	3.5–4.5	130	900	550	Hyd	Hyd
	292 (HD)	R44TX	0.060	—	—	8B	8B	3.5–4.5	130	600	600	Hyd	Hyd
	350 (2 bbl)	R44TX	0.060	—	—	—	6B	7.0–8.5	150	—	600	Hyd	Hyd
	350 (4 bbl)	R44TX	0.060	—	—	6B	6B	7.0–8.5	150	800	600	Hyd	Hyd
	350 (HD, Fed)	R44TX	0.060	—	—	8B	8B	7.0–8.5	150	600	600	Hyd	Hyd
	350 (HD, Calif)	R44TX	0.060	—	—	2B	2B	7.0–8.5	150	700	700	Hyd	Hyd
	400 (HD, Fed)	R44TX	0.060	—	—	4B	4B	7.0–8.5	150	700	700	Hyd	Hyd

Year	Engine	Spark Plug	Gap										
1976	400 (HD, Calif)	R44TX	0.060	—	—	2B	7.0–8.5	150	700	700	Hyd	Hyd
	454 (LD)	R44TX	0.060	—	—	16B	7.0–8.5	150	—	650	Hyd	Hyd
	454 (HD, Fed)	R44TX	0.060	—	8B	8B	7.0–8.5	150	700	700	Hyd	Hyd
	454 (HD, Calif)	R44TX	0.060	—¦	8B	8B	7.0–8.5	150	600	600	Hyd	Hyd
	250	R46TS	0.035	—	10B	10B	3.5–4.5	130	900	550	Hyd	Hyd
	250 (Calif)	R46TS	0.035	—	6B	10B	3.5–4.5	130	1000	600	Hyd	Hyd
	250 (HD)	R46T	0.035	—	6B	6B	3.5–4.5	130	600	600(N)	Hyd	Hyd
	292 (HD)	R44T	0.035	—	8B	8B	3.5–4.5	130	600	600(N)	Hyd	Hyd
	350	R45TS	0.045	—	2B	6B	7–8.5	150	800	600	Hyd	Hyd
	350 (4 bbl)	R45TS	0.045	—	8B	8B	7–8.5	150	800	600	Hyd	Hyd
	350 (4 bbl Calif)	R45TS	0.045	—	6B	6B	7–8.5	150	800	600	Hyd	Hyd
	350 (HD)	R44TX	0.060	—	8B	8B	7–8.5	150	600	600(N)	Hyd	Hyd
	350 (HD Calif)	R44TX	0.060	—	2B	2B	7–8.5	150	700	700(N)	Hyd	Hyd
	400 (HD)	R44TX	0.060	—	4B	4B	7–8.5	150	—	700(N)	Hyd	Hyd
	400 (HD Calif)	R44TX	0.060	—	2B	2B	7–8.5	150	—	700(N)	Hyd	Hyd
	454 (w/cat)	R45TS	0.045	—	12B	12B	7–8.5	150	—	600	Hyd	Hyd
	454 (w/o cat)	R45TS	0.045	—	8B	8B	7–8.5	150	—	600	Hyd	Hyd
	454 (HD)	R44T	0.045	—	8B	8B	7–8.5	150	700	700(N)	Hyd	Hyd
1977	250	R46TS	0.035	—	8B	12B	3.5–4.5	130	750	550	Hyd	Hyd
	250 (High Alt)	R46TS	0.035	—	8B	12B	3.5–4.5	130	750	600	Hyd	Hyd
	250 (Calif)	R46TS	0.035	—	6B	10B	3.5–4.5	130	850	600	Hyd	Hyd
	250 (HD)	R46T	0.035	—	6B	6B	3.5–4.5	130	600	600(N)	Hyd	Hyd
	292	R44T	0.035	—	8B	8B	3.5–4.5	130	600	600(N)	Hyd	Hyd
	305	R45TS	0.045	—	8B	8B	7–8.5	150	600	500	Hyd	Hyd
	305 (HD)	R44T	0.045	—	6B	6B	7–8.5	150	700	700(N)	Hyd	Hyd
	350	R45TS	0.045	—	8B	8B	7–8.5	150	700	500	Hyd	Hyd
	350 (High Alt)	R45TS	0.045	—	—	6B	7–8.5	150	—	600	Hyd	Hyd
	350 (Calif)	R45TS	0.045	—	6B	6B	7–8.5	150	700	500	Hyd	Hyd

Gasoline Engine Tune-Up Specifications (cont.)

Year	Engine Displacement (cu in.)	Spark Plugs Type	Gap (in.)	Distributor Point Dwell (deg)	Point Gap (in.)	Ignition Timing (deg) MT	AT	Fuel Pump Pressure (psi)	Compression Pressure (psi)	Idle Speed (rpm) MT	AT	Valve Clearance (in.) Ex	In
1977	350 (HD)	R44T	0.045	—	—	8B	8B	7–8.5	150	700	700(N)	Hyd	Hyd
	350 (HD Calif)	R44TX	0.060	—	—	2B	2B	7–8.5	150	700	700(N)	Hyd	Hyd
	400 (HD)	R44T	0.045	—	—	—	4B	7–8.5	150	—	700(N)	Hyd	Hyd
	400 (HD Calif)	R44T	0.045	—	—	—	2B	7–8.5	150	—	700(N)	Hyd	Hyd
	454	R45TS	0.045	—	—	—	4B	7–8.5	150	—	600	Hyd	Hyd
	454 (HD)	R44T	0.045	—	—	8B	8B	7–8.5	150	700	700(N)	Hyd	Hyd
1978	250 (LD Fed)	R46TS	0.035	—	—	8B	8B	4.5–6.0	130	750	550	Hyd	Hyd
	250 (LD Calif)	R46TS	0.035	—	—	8B	8B	4.5–6.0	130	750	750	Hyd	Hyd
	250 (LD High Alt)	R46TS	0.035	—	—	8B	12B	4.5–6.0	130	750	600	Hyd	Hyd
	250 (HD)	R46T	0.035	—	—	6B	6B	4.5–6.0	130	600	600(N)	Hyd	Hyd
	292 (HD)	R44T	0.035	—	—	8B	8B	4.5–6.0	130	600	600(N)	Hyd	Hyd
	305 (LD)	R45TS	0.045	—	—	4B	4B	7.5–9.0	150	600	500	Hyd	Hyd
	305 (HD)	R44T	0.045	—	—	6B	6B	7.5–9.0	150	700	700(N)	Hyd	Hyd
	350 (LD)	R45TS	0.045	—	—	8B	8B	7.5–9.0	150	600 ⑤	500	Hyd	Hyd
	350 (HD Fed)	R44T	0.045	—	—	8B	8B	7.5–9.0	150	700	700(N)	Hyd	Hyd
	350 (HD Calif)	R44TX	0.060	—	—	2B	2B	7.5–9.0	150	700	700(N)	Hyd	Hyd
	400 (LD)	R45TS	0.045	—	—	—	4B	7.5–9.0	150	—	500	Hyd	Hyd
	400 (HD Fed)	R44T	0.045	—	—	—	4B	7.5–9.0	150	—	700(N)	Hyd	Hyd
	400 (HD Calif)	R44T	0.045	—	—	—	2B	7.5–9.0	150	—	700(N)	Hyd	Hyd
	454 (LD Fed)	R45TS	0.045	—	—	—	8B	7.5–9.0 ⑥	150	—	550	Hyd	Hyd
	454 (LD Calif)	R45TS	0.045	—	—	—	8B	7.5–9.0 ⑥	150	—	700(N)	Hyd	Hyd
	454 (HD)	R44T	0.045	—	—	8B	8B	7.5–9.0 ⑥	150	700	700(N)	Hyd	Hyd

Year	Engine	Spark Plug	Gap									
1979	250 (LD Fed)	R46TS	0.035	—	10B	10B	4.5–6.0	130	750	600	Hyd	Hyd
	250 ⑦	R46TS	0.035	—	6B	8B	4.5–6.0	130	750	600	Hyd	Hyd
	292	R44T	0.035	—	8B	8B	4.5–6.0	130	700	700	Hyd	Hyd
	305	R45TS	0.045	—	6B	6B	7.5–9.0	150	600	500	Hyd	Hyd
	350 (LD)	R45TS	0.045	—	8B	8B	7.5–9.0	150	700	500	Hyd	Hyd
	350 (HD)	R44T	0.045	—	4B	4B	7.5–9.0	150	700	700(N)	Hyd	Hyd
	400	R45TS	0.045	—	—	4B	7.5–9.0	150	—	500	Hyd	Hyd
	454 (LD)	R45TS	0.045	—	8B	8B	7.5–9.0⑥	150	700	500	Hyd	Hyd
	454 (HD)	R44T	0.045	—	—	4B	7.5–9.0⑥	150	—	700(N)	Hyd	Hyd
1980	250 (LD Fed)	R46TS	0.035	—	10B	10B	4.5–6.0	130	750	650	Hyd	Hyd
	250 (LD Calif)	R46TS	0.035	—	10B	10B	4.5–6.0	130	750	600	Hyd	Hyd
	250 ⑦	R46TS	0.035	—	—	8B	4.5–6.0	130	—	600	Hyd	Hyd
	292	R44T	0.035	—	8B	8B	4.5–6.0	130	700	700(N)	Hyd	Hyd
	305	R45TS	0.045	—	8B	8B	7.5–9.0	150	600	500	Hyd	Hyd
	350 (LD)	R45TS	0.045	—	8B	8B	7.5–9.0	150	700	500	Hyd	Hyd
	350 (HD Fed)	R44T	0.045	—	4B	4B	7.5–9.0	150	700	700(N)	Hyd	Hyd
	350 (HD Calif)	R44T	0.045	—	6B	6B	7.5–9.0	150	700	700(N)	Hyd	Hyd
	400 (HD Fed)	R44T	0.045	—	—	4B	7.5–9.0	150	—	700(N)	Hyd	Hyd
	400 (HD Calif)	R44T	0.045	—	—	6B	7.5–9.0	150	—	700(N)	Hyd	Hyd
	454	R44T	0.045	—	4B	4B	7.5–9.0⑥	150	700	700(N)	Hyd	Hyd
1981	250 (Fed)	R45TS	0.035	—	10B	10B	4.5–6.0	130	750	650	Hyd	Hyd
	250 (Calif)	R46TS	0.035	—	10B	10B	4.5–6.0	130	750	650	Hyd	Hyd
	292	R44T	0.035	—	8B	8B	4.5–6.0	130	700	700(N)	Hyd	Hyd
	305 2 bbl	R45TS	0.045	—	8B	8B	7.5–9.0	150	600	500	Hyd	Hyd
	305 4 bbl	R45TS	0.045	—	4B	4B⑧	7.5–9.0	150	700	500	Hyd	Hyd
	350 (LD)	R45TS	0.045	—	8B	8B⑧	7.5–9.0	150	700	500	Hyd	Hyd
	350 (HD-Fed)	R44T	0.045	—	4B	4B	7.5–9.0	150	700	700(N)	Hyd	Hyd

Gasoline Engine Tune-Up Specifications (cont.)

Year	Engine Displacement (cu in.)	Spark Plugs Type	Spark Plugs Gap (in.)	Distributor Point Dwell (deg)	Distributor Point Gap (in.) ▲	Ignition Timing (deg) MT	Ignition Timing (deg) AT	Fuel Pump Pressure (psi)	Compression Pressure (psi) ●	Idle Speed (rpm)* MT	Idle Speed (rpm)* AT	Valve Clearance (in.) Ex	Valve Clearance (in.) In
1981	350 (HD Calif)	R44T	0.045	—	—	6B	6B	7.5–9.0	150	700	700(N)	Hyd	Hyd
	454	R44T	0.045	—	—	4B	4B	7.5–9.0	150	700	700(N)	Hyd	Hyd
1982	6-250	①	①	Electronic		①	①	4–6	—	①	①	Hydraulic	②
	6-292	R44T	.035	Electronic		8B	① ③	4–6	—	700	700	Hydraulic	②
	8-305	R45TS	.045	Electronic		①	①	7–9	—	①	①	Hydraulic	②
	8-350	R44T	.045	Electronic		4B	① ④	7–9	—	700 ⑤	700 ⑤	Hydraulic	②
1983	6-250	R45TS	.045	Electronic		①	①	4–6	—	①	①	Hydraulic	②
	6-292	R44T	.035	Electronic		①	①	4–6	—	700	700	Hydraulic	②
	8-305	R45TS	.045	Electronic		①	①	7–9	—	①	①	Hydraulic	②
	8-350	R45TS ⑦	.045	Electronic		①	①	7–9	—	700 ⑤	700 ⑤	Hydraulic	②
1984–86	6-250	R45TS	.045	Electronic		8	8	4–6	—	8 ⑤	8 ⑤	Hydraulic	②
	6-262	R43CTS	0.40	Electronic		0	0	—	—	①	①	Hydraulic	②
	6-292	R44T	.035	Electronic		8	8	4–6	—	①	①	Hydraulic	②
	8-305	R45TS	.045	Electronic		4	4	7–9	—	①	①	Hydraulic	②

Year	Engine	Spark Plug	Gap	Ignition							Valve Clearance
	8-350	R45TS	.045	Electronic	4	4	7–9	—	①	①	Hydraulic ②
	8-454	R44T	.045	Electronic	4	4	8.0	—	700	700	Hydraulic ②
1987	6-262	R43CTS	.040	Electronic	0	0	—	—	①	①	Hydraulic ②
	8-305	R45TS	.045	Electronic	4	4	40–47 ⑨	—	①	①	Hydraulic ②
	8-350	R45TS	.045	Electronic	4	4	34–46 ⑨	—	①	①	Hydraulic ②
	8-454	R44T	.045	Electronic	4	4	34–46 ⑨	—	①	①	Hydraulic ②

NOTE: See the underhood emission control sticker before making any adjustments. Sticker values must be used if they disagree with the specifications listed in the chart. Check for high or low altitude specifications before adjusting idle speed or timing.

▲ 0.016 in. for used points
● Maximum variation among cylinders—20 psi
B Before Top Dead Center
LD Light-duty
HD Heavy-duty
Fed Federal (49 states)
Calif California only
MT Manual transmission
AT Automatic transmission
N Neutral
NA Not available
— Not applicable
* Automatic transmission idle speed set in Drive unless otherwise indicated

Part numbers in this chart are not recommendations by Chilton for any product by brand name.
Cat catalytic converter
Hyd Hydraulic Lifters

① See underhood sticker
② One turn down from zero lash
③ With distributor vacuum hose disconnected and marked.
④ Non governed California engines—2 BTDC
⑤ With A/C on if equipped
⑥ With A/C off if equipped
⑦ R44T on heavy duty engines
⑧ California; 6B, Calif. w/emission label code AAD.8B
⑨ Carburetted: 5.0

Diesel Engine Tune-Up Specifications

Year	Engine No. Cyl Displacement (cu in.)	Fuel Pump Pressure (psi)	Compression (lbs.)	Intake Valve Opens (deg)	Idle Speed (rpm) ●
1978–79	8-350	5.5–6.5	275 min.	16	650/675
1980	8-350	5.5–6.5	275 min.	16	750/600
1981	8-350	5.5–6.5	275 min.	16	575 ①
1982–87	8-379	5.5–6.5 ②	275 min.	NA	575/550 ③

NOTE: The underhood specifications sticker often reflects tune-up specifications changes made in production. Sticker figures must be used if they disagree with those in this chart.
● Where two idle speed figures appear separately by a slash, the first is for manual trans, the second is for auto trans.
① In drive: Calif. 600 rpm
② Transfer pump pressure given—injector opening pressure for used injector—1500 psi
③ '82 slow idle speed. '82 fast idle: 700 rpm. '83–'84 slow idle: 650 rpm; fast idle: 800 rpm
NA—Not available

dicator of the internal condition of your engine. If a spark plug is fouled, causing the engine to misfire, the problem will have to be found and corrected. Often, reading the plugs will lead you to the cause of the problem. Spark plug conditions and probable causes are listed in the color insert section.

NOTE: *A small amount of light tan or rust red colored deposits at the electrode end of the plug is normal. These plugs need not be renewed unless they are severely worn.*

SPARK PLUG HEAT RANGE

Spark plug heat range is the ability of the plug to dissipate heat. The longer the insulator (or the farther it extends into the engine), the hotter the plug will operate; the shorter the insulator the cooler it will operate. A plug that absorbs little heat and remains too cool will quickly accumulate deposits of oil and carbon since it is not hot enough to burn them off. This leads to plug fouling and consequently to misfiring. A plug that absorbs too much heat will have no deposits, but, due to the excessive heat, the electrodes will burn away quickly and in some instances, pre-ignition may result. Pre-ignition takes place when plug tips get so hot that they glow sufficiently to ignite the fuel/air mixture before the actual spark occurs. This early ignition will usually cause a pinging during low speeds and heavy loads.

The general rule of thumb for choosing the correct heat range when picking a spark plug is: if most of your driving is long distance, high speed travel, use a colder plug; if most of your driving is stop and go, use a hotter plug. Original equipment plugs are compromise plugs, but most people never have occasion to change their

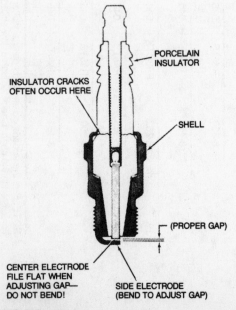

Spark plug heat range showing different electrode lengths. "Colder" plug (shorter electrode) is on left

COLD   HOT

PORCELAIN INSULATOR

INSULATOR CRACKS OFTEN OCCUR HERE

SHELL

(PROPER GAP)

CENTER ELECTRODE FILE FLAT WHEN ADJUSTING GAP— DO NOT BEND!

SIDE ELECTRODE (BEND TO ADJUST GAP)

Spark plug cutaway

Troubleshooting Engine Performance

Problem	Cause	Solution
Hard starting (engine cranks normally)	• Binding linkage, choke valve or choke piston	• Repair as necessary
	• Restricted choke vacuum diaphragm	• Clean passages
	• Improper fuel level	• Adjust float level
	• Dirty, worn or faulty needle valve and seat	• Repair as necessary
	• Float sticking	• Repair as necessary
	• Faulty fuel pump	• Replace fuel pump
	• Incorrect choke cover adjustment	• Adjust choke cover
	• Inadequate choke unloader adjustment	• Adjust choke unloader
	• Faulty ignition coil	• Test and replace as necessary
	• Improper spark plug gap	• Adjust gap
	• Incorrect ignition timing	• Adjust timing
	• Incorrect valve timing	• Check valve timing; repair as necessary
Rough idle or stalling	• Incorrect curb or fast idle speed	• Adjust curb or fast idle speed
	• Incorrect ignition timing	• Adjust timing to specification
	• Improper feedback system operation	• Refer to Chapter 4
	• Improper fast idle cam adjustment	• Adjust fast idle cam
	• Faulty EGR valve operation	• Test EGR system and replace as necessary
	• Faulty PCV valve air flow	• Test PCV valve and replace as necessary
	• Choke binding	• Locate and eliminate binding condition
	• Faulty TAC vacuum motor or valve	• Repair as necessary
	• Air leak into manifold vacuum	• Inspect manifold vacuum connections and repair as necessary
	• Improper fuel level	• Adjust fuel level
	• Faulty distributor rotor or cap	• Replace rotor or cap
	• Improperly seated valves	• Test cylinder compression, repair as necessary
	• Incorrect ignition wiring	• Inspect wiring and correct as necessary
	• Faulty ignition coil	• Test coil and replace as necessary
	• Restricted air vent or idle passages	• Clean passages
	• Restricted air cleaner	• Clean or replace air cleaner filler element
	• Faulty choke vacuum diaphragm	• Repair as necessary
Faulty low-speed operation	• Restricted idle transfer slots	• Clean transfer slots
	• Restricted idle air vents and passages	• Clean air vents and passages
	• Restricted air cleaner	• Clean or replace air cleaner filter element
	• Improper fuel level	• Adjust fuel level
	• Faulty spark plugs	• Clean or replace spark plugs
	• Dirty, corroded, or loose ignition secondary circuit wire connections	• Clean or tighten secondary circuit wire connections
	• Improper feedback system operation	• Refer to Chapter 4
	• Faulty ignition coil high voltage wire	• Replace ignition coil high voltage wire
	• Faulty distributor cap	• Replace cap
Faulty acceleration	• Improper accelerator pump stroke	• Adjust accelerator pump stroke
	• Incorrect ignition timing	• Adjust timing
	• Inoperative pump discharge check ball or needle	• Clean or replace as necessary
	• Worn or damaged pump diaphragm or piston	• Replace diaphragm or piston

Troubleshooting Engine Performance (cont.)

Problem	Cause	Solution
Faulty acceleration (cont.)	• Leaking carburetor main body cover gasket	• Replace gasket
	• Engine cold and choke set too lean	• Adjust choke cover
	• Improper metering rod adjustment (BBD Model carburetor)	• Adjust metering rod
	• Faulty spark plug(s)	• Clean or replace spark plug(s)
	• Improperly seated valves	• Test cylinder compression, repair as necessary
	• Faulty ignition coil	• Test coil and replace as necessary
	• Improper feedback system operation	• Refer to Chapter 4
Faulty high speed operation	• Incorrect ignition timing	• Adjust timing
	• Faulty distributor centrifugal advance mechanism	• Check centrifugal advance mechanism and repair as necessary
	• Faulty distributor vacuum advance mechanism	• Check vacuum advance mechanism and repair as necessary
	• Low fuel pump volume	• Replace fuel pump
	• Wrong spark plug air gap or wrong plug	• Adjust air gap or install correct plug
	• Faulty choke operation	• Adjust choke cover
	• Partially restricted exhaust manifold, exhaust pipe, catalytic converter, muffler, or tailpipe	• Eliminate restriction
	• Restricted vacuum passages	• Clean passages
	• Improper size or restricted main jet	• Clean or replace as necessary
	• Restricted air cleaner	• Clean or replace filter element as necessary
	• Faulty distributor rotor or cap	• Replace rotor or cap
	• Faulty ignition coil	• Test coil and replace as necessary
	• Improperly seated valve(s)	• Test cylinder compression, repair as necessary
	• Faulty valve spring(s)	• Inspect and test valve spring tension, replace as necessary
	• Incorrect valve timing	• Check valve timing and repair as necessary
	• Intake manifold restricted	• Remove restriction or replace manifold
	• Worn distributor shaft	• Replace shaft
	• Improper feedback system operation	• Refer to Chapter 4
Misfire at all speeds	• Faulty spark plug(s)	• Clean or replace spark plug(s)
	• Faulty spark plug wire(s)	• Replace as necessary
	• Faulty distributor cap or rotor	• Replace cap or rotor
	• Faulty ignition coil	• Test coil and replace as necessary
	• Primary ignition circuit shorted or open intermittently	• Troubleshoot primary circuit and repair as necessary
	• Improperly seated valve(s)	• Test cylinder compression, repair as necessary
	• Faulty hydraulic tappet(s)	• Clean or replace tappet(s)
	• Improper feedback system operation	• Refer to Chapter 4
	• Faulty valve spring(s)	• Inspect and test valve spring tension, repair as necessary
	• Worn camshaft lobes	• Replace camshaft
	• Air leak into manifold	• Check manifold vacuum and repair as necessary
	• Improper carburetor adjustment	• Adjust carburetor
	• Fuel pump volume or pressure low	• Replace fuel pump
	• Blown cylinder head gasket	• Replace gasket
	• Intake or exhaust manifold passage(s) restricted	• Pass chain through passage(s) and repair as necessary
	• Incorrect trigger wheel installed in distributor	• Install correct trigger wheel

Troubleshooting Engine Performance (cont.)

Problem	Cause	Solution
Power not up to normal	• Incorrect ignition timing	• Adjust timing
	• Faulty distributor rotor	• Replace rotor
	• Trigger wheel loose on shaft	• Reposition or replace trigger wheel
	• Incorrect spark plug gap	• Adjust gap
	• Faulty fuel pump	• Replace fuel pump
	• Incorrect valve timing	• Check valve timing and repair as necessary
	• Faulty ignition coil	• Test coil and replace as necessary
	• Faulty ignition wires	• Test wires and replace as necessary
	• Improperly seated valves	• Test cylinder compression and repair as necessary
	• Blown cylinder head gasket	• Replace gasket
	• Leaking piston rings	• Test compression and repair as necessary
	• Worn distributor shaft	• Replace shaft
	• Improper feedback system operation	• Refer to Chapter 4
Intake backfire	• Improper ignition timing	• Adjust timing
	• Faulty accelerator pump discharge	• Repair as necessary
	• Defective EGR CTO valve	• Replace EGR CTO valve
	• Defective TAC vacuum motor or valve	• Repair as necessary
	• Lean air/fuel mixture	• Check float level or manifold vacuum for air leak. Remove sediment from bowl
Exhaust backfire	• Air leak into manifold vacuum	• Check manifold vacuum and repair as necessary
	• Faulty air injection diverter valve	• Test diverter valve and replace as necessary
	• Exhaust leak	• Locate and eliminate leak
Ping or spark knock	• Incorrect ignition timing	• Adjust timing
	• Distributor centrifugal or vacuum advance malfunction	• Inspect advance mechanism and repair as necessary
	• Excessive combustion chamber deposits	• Remove with combustion chamber cleaner
	• Air leak into manifold vacuum	• Check manifold vacuum and repair as necessary
	• Excessively high compression	• Test compression and repair as necessary
	• Fuel octane rating excessively low	• Try alternate fuel source
	• Sharp edges in combustion chamber	• Grind smooth
	• EGR valve not functioning properly	• Test EGR system and replace as necessary
Surging (at cruising to top speeds)	• Low carburetor fuel level	• Adjust fuel level
	• Low fuel pump pressure or volume	• Replace fuel pump
	• Metering rod(s) not adjusted properly (BBD Model Carburetor)	• Adjust metering rod
	• Improper PCV valve air flow	• Test PCV valve and replace as necessary
	• Air leak into manifold vacuum	• Check manifold vacuum and repair as necessary
	• Incorrect spark advance	• Test and replace as necessary
	• Restricted main jet(s)	• Clean main jet(s)
	• Undersize main jet(s)	• Replace main jet(s)
	• Restricted air vents	• Clean air vents
	• Restricted fuel filter	• Replace fuel filter
	• Restricted air cleaner	• Clean or replace air cleaner filter element
	• EGR valve not functioning properly	• Test EGR system and replace as necessary
	• Improper feedback system operation	• Refer to Chapter 4

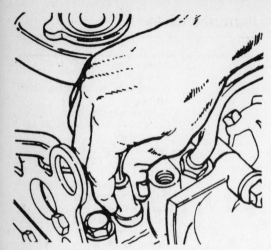

Pull on the spark plug boot, not on the wire

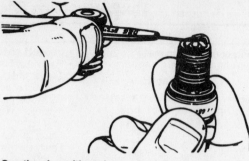

Gap the plug with a wire gauge; a flat gauge will give an inaccurate reading

plugs from the factory recommended heat range.

REPLACING SPARK PLUGS

A set of spark plugs usually requires replacement after about 20,000 to 30,000 miles, depending on your style of driving. In normal operation, plug gap increases about 0.001″ for every 1,000-2,500 miles. As the gap increases, the plug's voltage requirement also increases. It requires a greater voltage to jump the wider gap and about two to three times as much voltage to fire a plug at high speeds than at idle.

When you're removing spark plugs, you should work on one at a time. Don't start by removing the plug wires all at once, because un-

Bend the side electrode to adjust the gap. Never bend the center electrode

less you number them, they may become mixed up. Take a minute before you begin and number the wires with tape. The best location for numbering is near where the wires come out of the cap.

REMOVAL AND INSTALLATION

1. Before removing the spark plugs, number the plug wires so that the correct wire goes on the plug when replaced. This can be done with pieces of adhesive tape.

2. Next, clean the area around the plugs by brushing or blowing with compressed air. You can also loosen the plugs a few turns and crank the engine to blow the dirt away.

3. Disconnect the plug wires by twisting and pulling on the rubber cap, not on the wire. On H.E.I. systems, twist the plug caps ½ turn in either direction to break the seal before removing the wire. Never remove the wires from H.E.I. systems when the engine is running. Severe shock could result.

4. Remove each plug with a rubber insert spark plug socket, ⅝″ for tapered seat plugs (designated with a letter T), $^{13}/_{16}$″ for the rest. The tapered seat plugs are used in some engines

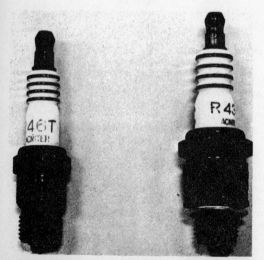

$^{13}/_{16}$ in. plug on right; ⅝ in. plug on left. ⅝ in. plug needs no gasket

in 1970 and all engines thereafter. Make sure that the socket is all the way down on the plug to prevent it from slipping and cracking the porcelain insulator. On some V8s the plugs are more accessible from under the truck.

5. After removing each plug, evaluate its condition. A spark plug's useful life is about 12,000 miles (optimistically 22,500 with H.E.I.). Thus, it would make sense to replace a plug if it has been in service that long. If the plug is to be replaced, refer to the Tune-up Specifications chart for the proper spark plug type.

The letter codes on the General Motors original equipment type plugs are read this way:
- R resistor
- S extended tip
- T tapered seat
- X wide gap

The numbers indicate heat range; hotter running plugs have higher numbers.

6. If the plugs are to be reused, file the center and side electrodes flat with a fine, flat points file. Heavy or baked on deposits can be carefully scraped off with a small knife blade or the scraper tool on a combination spark plug tool. Check the gap between the electrodes with a round wire spark plug gapping gauge. Do not use a flat feeler gauge; it will give an inaccurate reading. If the gap is not as specified, use the bending tool on the spark plug gap gauge to bend the outside electrode. Be careful not to bend the electrode too far or too often, because excessive bending may cause the electrode to break off and fall into the combustion chamber. This would require removing the cylinder head to reach the broken piece, and could also result in cylinder wall, piston ring, or valve damage.

WARNING: *Never bend the center electrode of the spark plug. This will break the insulator.*

7. Clean the plug threads with a wire brush. Lubricate the threads with a drop of oil.

8. Screw the plugs in finger tight, and then tighten them with the spark plug socket. Be very careful not to overtighten them. Just snug them in. If a torque wrench is available, torque them to 15 ft.lb. for plug designations with a T, 25 ft.lb. for all the rest.

9. Reinstall the wires. If, by chance, you have forgotten to number the plug wires, refer to the Firing Order illustrations in this Chapter.

NOTE: *On 1975-77 6-cylinder engines with HEI, the coil is not integral with the distributor cap. It is important that the coil wires be properly routed on these engines. On 6-250s, the coil wire goes in the wire loom clip above the plug wires. On 6-292s, the coil wire goes in the clip below the plug wires.*

SPARK PLUG WIRES

Visually inspect the spark plug cables for burns, cuts, or breaks in the insulation. Check the spark plug boots and the nipples on the distributor cap and coil. Replace any damaged wiring. If no physical damage is obvious, the wires can be checked with an ohmmeter for excessive resistance.

When installing a new set of spark plug cables, replace the cables one at a time so there will be no mixup. Start by replacing the longest cable first. Install the boot firmly over the spark plug. Route the wire exactly the same as the original. Insert the nipple firmly into the tower on the distributor cap. Repeat the process for each cable.

FIRING ORDERS

To avoid possible confusion remove and tag spark plug wires one at a time, for replacement.

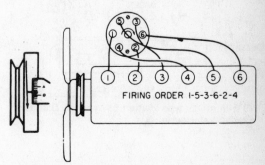

FIRING ORDER 1-5-3-6-2-4

Six-cylinder firing order. Distributor rotation—clockwise

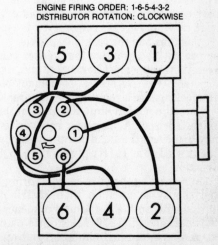

ENGINE FIRING ORDER: 1-6-5-4-3-2
DISTRIBUTOR ROTATION: CLOCKWISE

V6-262 firing order

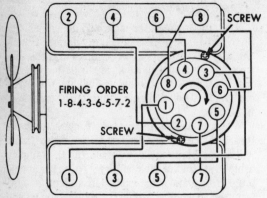

FIRING ORDER
1-8-4-3-6-5-7-2

V8 with electronic ignition firing order. Distributor rotation—clockwise

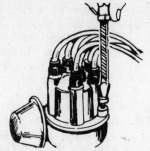

The six cylinder distributor cap is retained by two captive screws

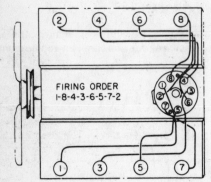

FIRING ORDER
1-8-4-3-6-5-7-2

V8 with points-type ignition firing order. Distributor rotation—clockwise

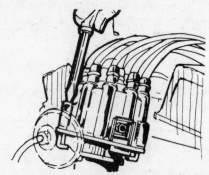

The eight cylinder distributor cap has latches

Breaker Points and Condenser

REMOVAL AND REPLACEMENT

1970-74

The usual procedure is to replace the condenser each time the point set is replaced. Although this is not always necessary, it is easy to do at this time and the cost is negligible. Every time you adjust or replace the breaker points, the ignition timing must be checked and, if necessary, adjusted. No special equipment other than a feeler gauge is required for point replacement or adjustment, but a dwell meter is strongly advised. A magnetic screwdriver is handy to prevent the small points and condenser screws from falling down into the distributor.

Point sets using the push-in type wiring terminal should be used on those distributors equipped with an R.F.I. (Radio Frequency Interference) shield (1970-74). Points using a lockscrew-type terminal may short out due to contact between the shield and the screw.

1. Push down on the spring loaded V8 distributor cap retaining screws and give them a half turn to release. Unscrew the 6-cylinder cap retaining screws. Remove the cap. You might have to unclip or detach some or all of the plug wires to remove the cap. If so, number the wires and the cap before removal.

2. Clean the cap inside and out with a clean rag. Check for cracks and carbon paths. A carbon path shows up as a dark line, usually from one of the cap sockets or inside terminals to a ground. Check the condition of the carbon button inside the center of the cap and the inside terminals. Replace the cap as necessary. Carbon paths usually cannot be successfully scraped off. It is better to replace the cap.

3. Pull the 6-cylinder rotor up and off the shaft. Remove the two screws and lift the round V8 rotor off. There is less danger of losing the screws if you just back them out all the way and lift them off with the rotor. Clean off the metal outer tip if it is burned or corroded. Don't file it. Replace the rotor as necessary or if one came with your tune-up kit.

4. Remove the radio frequency interference shield if your distributor has one. Watch out for those little screws!

5. Pull off the two wire terminals from the point assembly. One wire comes from the condenser and the other comes from within the distributor. The terminals are usually held in place by spring tension only. There might be a clamp screw securing the terminals on some

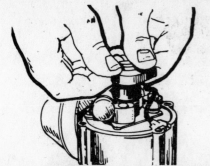

Pull the six cylinder rotor straight up to remove

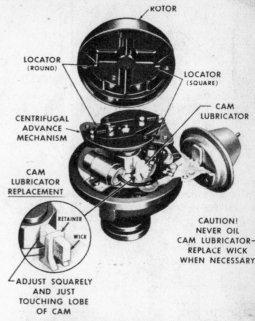

CAUTION!
NEVER OIL
CAM LUBRICATOR—
REPLACE WICK
WHEN NECESSARY

ADJUST SQUARELY
AND JUST
TOUCHING LOBE
OF CAM

Typical V8 points-type distributor

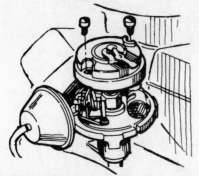

The eight cylinder rotor is held on by two screws

older versions. There is also available a one-piece point/condenser assembly for V8s. The radio frequency interference shield isn't needed with this set. Loosen the point set holddown screw(s). Be very careful not to drop any of these little screws inside the distributor. If this

happens, the distributor will probably have to be removed to get at the screw. If the holddown screw is lost elsewhere, it must be replaced with one that is no longer than the original to avoid interference with the distributor workings. Remove the point set, even if it is to be reused.

6. If the points are to be reused, clean them with a few strokes of a special point file. This is done with the points removed to prevent tiny

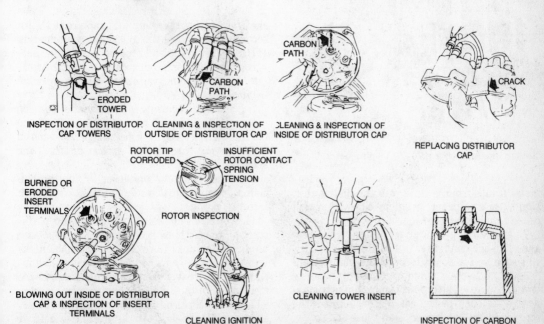

Areas to check on the distributor, rotor, cap and coil

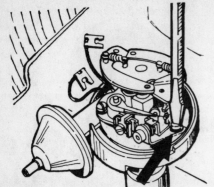

The points are retained by screws; use a magnetic screwdriver to avoid losing them

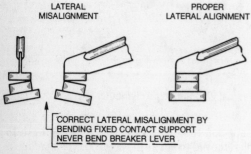

LATERAL MISALIGNMENT

PROPER LATERAL ALIGNMENT

CORRECT LATERAL MISALIGNMENT BY BENDING FIXED CONTACT SUPPORT NEVER BEND BREAKER LEVER

Breaker point alignment

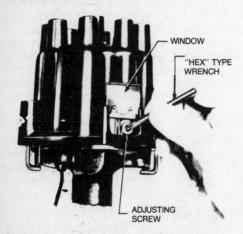

WINDOW

"HEX" TYPE WRENCH

ADJUSTING SCREW

Setting the dwell on a 1970–74 V8 distributor

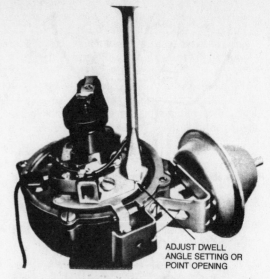

ADJUST DWELL ANGLE SETTING OR POINT OPENING

Adjusting the point gap (and therefore the dwell) on a six-cylinder distributor

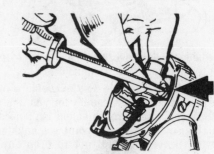

The condenser is also retained by a screw

metal filings from getting into the distributor. Don't use sandpaper or emery cloth; they will cause rapid point burning.

7. Loosen the condenser holddown screw and slide the condenser out of the clamp. This will save you a struggle with the clamp, condenser, and screw when you install the new one. If you have the type of clamp that is permanently fastened to the condenser, remove the screw and the condenser. Don't lose the screw.

8. Inspect the distributor cam lubricator. If you have the round king, turn it around on its shaft at the first tune-up and replace it at the second. If you have the long kind, switch ends at the first tune-up and replace it at the second. NOTE: *Don't oil or grease the lubricator. The foam is impregnated with a special lubricant.*

If you didn't get any lubricator at all, or if it looks like someone took it off, don't worry. You don't really need it. Just rub a matchhead size dab of grease on the cam lobes.

9. Install the new condenser. If you left the clamp in place, just slide the new condenser into the clamp.

10. Replace the point set and tighten the screws on a V8. Leave the screw slightly loose on a six. Replace the two wire terminals, making sure that the wires don't interfere with anything. Some V8 distributors have a ground wire that must go under one of the screws.

11. Check that the contacts meet squarely. If they don't bend the tab supporting the fixed contact.

NOTE: *If you are installing preset points on*

a V8, go ahead to step 16. If they are preset, it will say so on the package. It would be a good idea to make a quick check on point gap, anyway. Sometimes those preset points aren't.

12. Turn the engine until a high point on the cam that opens the points contacts the rubbing block on the point arm. You can turn the engine by hand if you can get a wrench on the crankshaft pulley nut, or you can grasp the fan belt and turn the engine with the spark plugs removed.

CAUTION: *If you try turning the engine by hand, be very careful not to get your fingers pinched in the pulleys.*

On a manual transmission you can push it forward in High gear. Another alternative is to bump the starter switch or use a remote starter switch.

13. On a 6-cylinder, there is a screwdriver slot near the contacts. Insert a screwdriver and lever the points open or closed until they appear to be at about the gap specified in the Tune-Up Specifications. On a V8, simply insert a ⅛" Allen wrench into the adjustment screw and turn. The wrench sometimes comes with a tune-up kit.

14. Insert the correct size feeler gauge and adjust the gap until you can push the gauge in and

The points have a locating tab which fits into a hole in the breaker plate

out between the contacts with a slight drag, but without disturbing the point arm. This operation takes a bit of experience to obtain the correct feel. Check by trying the gauges 0.001-0.002" larger and smaller than the setting size. The larger one should disturb the point arm, while the smaller one should not drag at all. Tighten the 6-cylinder point set holddown screw. Recheck the gap, because it often changes when the screw is tightened.

15. After all the point adjustments are complete, pull a white business card through (between) the contacts to remove any traces of oil. Oil will cause rapid contact burning.

NOTE: *You can adjust 6-cylinder dwell at this point, if you wish. Refer to Step 18.*

16. Replace the radio frequency interference shield, if any. You don't need it if you are installing the one-piece point/condenser set. Push the rotor firmly down into place. It will only go on one way. Tighten the V8 rotor screws. If the rotor is not installed properly, it will break when the starter is operated.

17. Replace the distributor cap.

18. If a dwell meter is available, check the dwell. The dwell meter hookup is shown in the Troubleshooting Section.

NOTE: *This hookup may not apply to electronic, capacitive discharge, or other special ignition systems. Some dwell meters won't work at all with such systems.*

Dwell can be checked with the engine running or cranking. Decrease dwell by increasing the point gap; increase by decreasing the gap. Dwell angle is simply the number of degrees of distributor shaft rotation during which the points stay closed. Theoretically, if the point gap is correct, the dwell should also be correct. Adjustment with a dwell meter produces more exact, consistent results since it is a dynamic adjustment. If dwell varies more than 3 degrees from idle speed to 1,750 engine rpm, the distributor is worn.

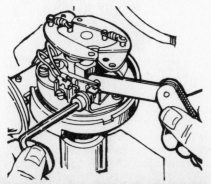

V8 point gap is adjusted with an Allen wrench

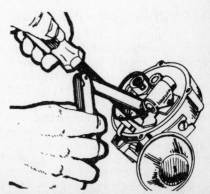

Six cylinder point gap is adjusted with a screwdriver

DWELL ADJUSTMENT

1970-74

1. To adjust dwell on a six, trial and error point adjustments are required. On a V8, simply open the metal window on the distributor and insert a ⅛″ Allen wrench. Turn until the meter shows the correct reading. Be sure to snap the window closed.

2. An approximate dwell adjustment can be made without a meter on a V8. Turn the adjusting screw clockwise until the engine begins to misfire, they turn it out ½ turn.

3. If the engine won't start, check:

a. That all the spark plug wires are in place.

b. That the rotor has been installed.

c. That the two (or three) wires inside the distributor are connected.

d. That the points open and close when the engine turns.

e. That the gap is correct and the holddown screw (on a six) is tight.

4. After the first 200 miles or so on a new set of points, the point gap often closes up due to initial rubbing block wear. For best performance, recheck the dwell (or gap) at this time. This quick initial wear is the reason why the factory recommends 0.003″ more gap on new points.

5. Since changing the gap affects the ignition timing, the timing should be checked and adjusted as necessary after each point replacement or adjustment.

1975 and Later

These engines use the breakerless HEI (High Energy Ignition) system. Since there is no mechanical contact, there is no wear or need for periodic service. There is an item in the distributor that resembles a condenser; it is a radio interference suppression capacitor which requires no service.

High Energy Ignition (HEI) System

The General Motors HEI system is a pulse-triggered, transistor controlled, inductive discharge ignition system. Except on inline 6-cylinder models 1975-77, the entire HEI system is contained within the distributor cap. Inline 6-cylinder engines 1975-77 have an external coil. Otherwise, the systems are the same.

The distributor, in addition to housing the mechanical and vacuum advance mechanisms, contains the ignition coil (except on some inline 6-cylinder engines), the electronic control module, and the magnetic triggering device. The magnetic pick-up assembly contains a permanent magnet, a pole piece with internal teeth, and a pick-up coil (not be be confused with the ignition coil).

In the HEI system, as in other electronic ignition systems, the breaker points have been replaced with an electronic switch—a transistor—which is located within the control module. This switching transistor performs the same function the points did in a conventional ignition system; it simply turns coil primary current on and off at the correct time. Essentially then, electronic and conventional ignition systems operate on the same principle.

The module which houses the switching transistor is controlled (turned on and off) by a magnetically generated impulse induced in the pick-up coil. When the teeth of the rotating timer align with the teeth of the pole piece, the induced voltage in the pick-up coil signals the electronic module to open the coil primary circuit. The primary current then decreases, and a high voltage is induced in the ignition coil secondary windings which is then directed through the rotor and spark plug wires to fire the spark plugs.

In essence then, the pick-up coil module system simply replaces the conventional breaker points and condenser. The condenser found within the distributor is for radio suppression purposes only and has nothing to do with the ignition process. The module automatically controls the dwell period, increasing it with increasing engine speed. Since dwell is automatically controlled, it cannot be adjusted. The module itself is non-adjustable and non-repairable and must be replaced if found defective.

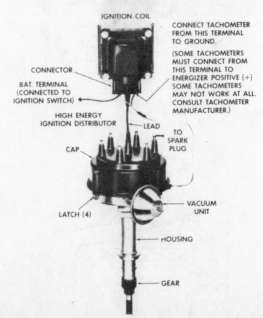

Six-cylinder HEI distributor, 1975–77. 1978 and later models have the coil in the distributor cap

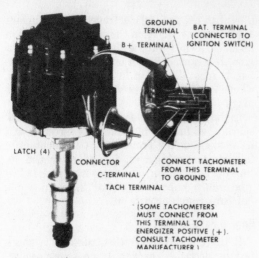

GROUND TERMINAL

BAT. TERMINAL (CONNECTED TO IGNITION SWITCH)

B + TERMINAL

LATCH (4)

CONNECTOR

C-TERMINAL

TACH TERMINAL

CONNECT TACHOMETER FROM THIS TERMINAL TO GROUND.

(SOME TACHOMETERS MUST CONNECT FROM THIS TERMINAL TO ENERGIZER POSITIVE (+). CONSULT TACHOMETER MANUFACTURER)

V8 HEI distributor

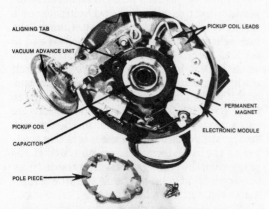

ALIGNING TAB

VACUUM ADVANCE UNIT

PICKUP COIL LEADS

PICKUP COIL

CAPACITOR

POLE PIECE

PERMANENT MAGNET

ELECTRONIC MODULE

Internal components of the HEI distributor; later models have slightly different connectors at the module, but the wiring is the same

HEI SYSTEM PRECAUTIONS

Before going on to troubleshooting, it might be a good idea to take note of the following precautions:

Timing Light Use

Inductive pick-up timing lights are the best kind to use with HEI. Timing lights which connect between the spark plug wire occasionally (not always) give false readings.

Spark Plug Wires

The plug wires used with HEI systems are of a different construction than conventional wires. When replacing them, make sure you get the correct wires, since conventional wires won't carry the voltage. Also handle them carefully to avoid cracking or splitting them and never pierce them.

Tachometer Use

Not all tachometers will operate or indicate correctly when used on a HEI system. While some tachometers may give a reading, this does not necessarily mean the reading is correct. In addition, some tachometers hook up differently from others. If you can't figure out whether or not your tachometer will work on your truck, check with the tachometer manufacturer. Dwell readings have no significance at all.

HEI System Testers

Instruments designed specifically for testing HEI systems are available from several tool manufacturers. Some of these will even test the module itself. However, the test given in the following section will require only an ohmmeter and a voltmeter.

SPRING

SEAL

COIL

CAP

VACUUM UNIT

HOUSING

GEAR

WASHER

COVER

CONNECTOR

ROTOR

V8 HEI distributor components

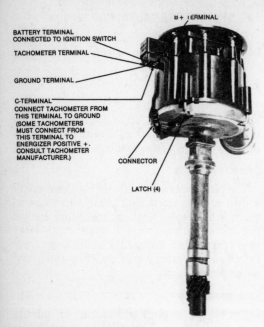

BATTERY TERMINAL
CONNECTED TO IGNITION SWITCH

TACHOMETER TERMINAL

GROUND TERMINAL

C-TERMINAL
CONNECT TACHOMETER FROM
THIS TERMINAL TO GROUND
(SOME TACHOMETERS
MUST CONNECT FROM
THIS TERMINAL TO
ENERGIZER POSITIVE +.
CONSULT TACHOMETER
MANUFACTURER.)

B+ TERMINAL

CONNECTOR

LATCH (4)

HEI distributor connections

TROUBLESHOOTING THE HEI SYSTEM

The symptoms of a defective component within the HEI system are exactly the same as those you would encounter in a conventional system.

Some of these symptoms are:
- Hard or no Starting
- Rough Idle
- Fuel Poor Economy
- Engine misses under load or while accelerating

If you suspect a problem in the ignition system, there are certain preliminary checks which you should carry out before you begin to check the electronic portions of the system. First, it is extremely important to make sure the vehicle battery is in a good state of charge. A defective or poorly charged battery will cause the various components of the ignition system to read incorrectly when they are being tested. Second, make sure all wiring connections are clean and tight, not only at the battery, but also at the distributor cap, ignition coil, and at the electronic control module.

Since the only change between electronic and conventional ignition systems is in the distributor component area, it is imperative to check the secondary ignition circuit first. If the secondary circuit checks out properly, then the engine condition is probably not the fault of the ignition system. To check the secondary ignition system, perform a simple spark test. Remove one of the plug wires and insert some sort of extension in the plug socket. An old spark

plug with the ground electrode removed makes a good extension. Hold the wire and extension about ¼″ away from the block and crank the engine. If a normal spark occurs, then the problem is most likely not in the ignition system. Check for fuel system problems, or fouled spark plugs.

If, however, there is no spark or a weak spark, then further ignition system testing will have to be done. Troubleshooting techniques fall into two categories, depending on the nature of the problem. The categories are (1) Engine cranks, but won't start or (2) Engine runs, but runs rough or cuts out.

Engine Fails to Start

If the engine won't start, perform a spark test as described earlier. If no spark occurs, check for the presence of normal battery voltage at the battery (BAT) terminal in the distributor cap. The ignition switch must be in the **on** position for this test. Either a voltmeter or a test light may be used for this test. Connect the test light wire to ground and the probe end to the BAT terminal at the distributor. If the light comes on, you have voltage to the distributor. If the light fails to come on, this indicates an open circuit in the ignition primary wiring leading to the distributor. In this case, you will have to check wiring continuity back to the ignition switch using a test light. If there is battery voltage at the BAT terminal, but no spark at the plugs, then the problem lies within the distributor assembly. Go on to the distributor components test section.

Engine Runs, but Runs Rough or Cuts Out

1. Make sure the plug wires are in good shape first. There should be no obvious cracks or breaks. You can check the plug wires with an ohmmeter, but do not pierce the wires with a probe. Check the chart for the correct plug wire resistance.

HEI Plug Wire Resistance Chart

Wire Length	Minimum	Maximum
0–15 inches	3000 ohms	10,000 ohms
15–25 inches	4000 ohms	15,000 ohms
25–35 inches	6000 ohms	20,000 ohms
Over 35 inches		25,000 ohms

2. If the plug wires are OK, remove the cap assembly, and check for moisture, cracks, chips, or carbon tracks, or any other high voltage leaks or failures. Replace the cap if you find any defects. Make sure the timer wheel rotates when the engine is cranked. If everything is all

right so far, go on to the distributor components test section.

Distributor Components Testing

If the trouble has been narrowed down to the units within the distributor, the following tests can help pinpoint the defective component. An ohmmeter with both high and low ranges should be used. These tests are made with the cap assembly removed and the battery wire disconnected.

1. Connect an ohmmeter between the TACH and BAT terminals in the distributor cap. The primary coil resistance should be less than one ohm (zero or nearly zero).

2. To check the coil secondary resistance, connect an ohmmeter between the rotor button and the BAT terminal. Then connect the ohmmeter between the ground terminal and the rotor button. The resistance in both cases should be between 6,000 and 30,000 ohms.

3. Replace the coil only if the readings in step one and two are infinite.

NOTE: *These resistance checks will not disclose shorted coil windings. This condition can be detected only with scope analysis or a suitably designed coil tester. If these instruments are unavailable, replace the coil with a known good coil as a final coil test.*

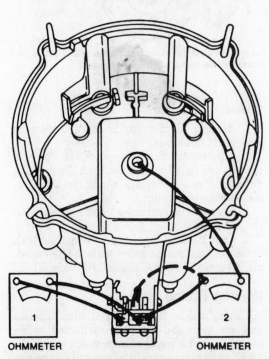

Checking coil resistance on the HEI system. Ohmmeter 1 shows the primary coil resistance connection. Ohmmeter 2 shows the secondary resistance connection. 1980 models shown, others similar

4. To test the pick-up coil, first disconnect the white and green module leads. Set the ohmmeter on the high scale and connect it between a ground and either the white or green lead. Any resistance measurement less than infinity requires replacement of the pick-up coil.

5. Pick-up coil continuity is tested by connecting the ohmmeter (on low range) between the white and green leads. Normal resistance is between 650 and 850 ohms, or 500 and 1500 ohms on 1977 and later models. Move the vacuum advance arm while performing this test. This will detect any break in coil continuity. Such a condition can cause intermittent misfiring. Replace the pick-up coil if the reading is outside the specified limits.

6. If no defects have been found at this time, and you still have a problem, then the module will have to be checked. If you do not have access to a module tester, the only possible alternative is a substitution test. If the module fails the substitution test, replace it.

COMPONENT REPLACEMENT

Integral Ignition Coil

1. Disconnect the feel and module wire terminal connectors from the distributor cap.

2. Remove the ignition set retainer.

3. Remove the 4 coil cover-to-distributor cap screws and coil cover.

4. Remove the 4 coil-to-distributor cap screws.

5. Using a blunt drift, press the coil wire spade terminals up out of distributor cap.

6. Lift the coil up out of the distributor cap.

7. Remove and clean the coil spring, rubber seal washer and coil cavity of the distributor cap.

8. Coat the rubber seal with a dielectric lubricant furnished in the replacement ignition coil package.

9. Reverse the above procedures to install.

Distributor Cap

1. Remove the feel and module wire terminal connectors from the distributor cap.

2. Remove the retainer and spark plug wires from the cap.

3. Depress and release the 4 distributor cap-to-housing retainers and lift off the cap assembly.

4. Remove the 4 coil cover screws and cover.

5. Using a finger or a blunt drift, push the spade terminals up out of the distributor cap.

6. Remove all 4 coil screws and lift the coil, coil spring and rubber seal washer out of the cap coil cavity.

7. Using a new distributor cap, reverse the above procedures to assemble, being sure to

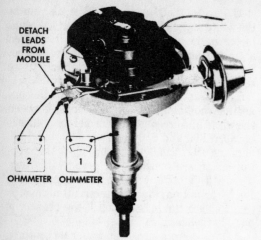

Checking the pick-up coil

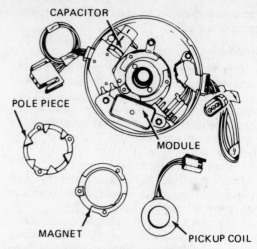

Pickup coil removed and disassembled

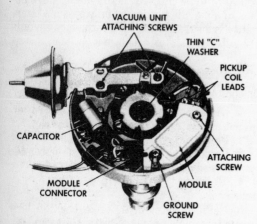

Distributor base and components

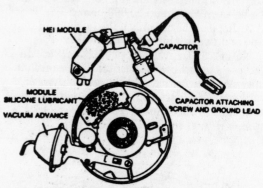

Be sure to coat the mating surfaces with silicone lubricant when replacing the HEI module

clean and lubricate the rubber seal washer with dielectric lubricant.

Rotor

1. Disconnect the feel and module wire connectors from the distributor.

2. Depress and release the 4 distributor cap to housing retainers and lift off the cap assembly.

3. Remove the two rotor attaching screws and rotor.

4. Reverse the above procedure to install.

Vacuum Advance

1. Remove the distributor cap and rotor as previously described.

2. Disconnect the vacuum hose from the vacuum advance unit.

3. Remove the two vacuum advance retaining screws, pull the advance unit outward, rotate and disengage the operating rod from its tang.

4. Reverse the above procedure to install.

Module

1. Remove the distributor cap and rotor as previously described.

2. Disconnect the harness connector and pick-up coil spade connectors from the module. Be careful not to damage the wires when removing the connector.

3. Remove the two screws and module from the distributor housing.

4. Coat the bottom of the new module with dielectric lubricant supplies with the new module. Reverse the above procedure to install.

Ignition Timing

Timing should be checked at each tune-up and any time the points are adjusted or replaced. It isn't likely to change much with HEI. The timing marks consist of a notch on the rim of the crankshaft pulley or vibration damper and a graduated scale attached to the engine front (timing) cover. A stroboscopic flash (dynamic) timing light must be used, as a static light is too inaccurate for emission controlled engines.

There are three basic types of timing light available. The first is a simple neon bulb with two wire connections. One wire connects to the spark plug terminal and the other plugs into the end of the spark plug wire for the No. 1 cylinder, thus connecting the light in series with the spark plug. This type of light is pretty dim and must be held very closely to the timing marks to be seen. Sometimes a dark corner has to be sought out to see the flash at all. This type of light is very inexpensive. The second type operates from the vehicle battery—two alligator clips connect to the battery terminals, while an adapter enables a third clip to be connected to the No. 1 spark plug and wire. This type is a bit more expensive, but it provides a nice bright flash that you can see even in bright sunlight. It is the type most often seen in professional shops. The third type replaces the battery power er source with 110 volt current.

Some timing lights have other features built into them, such as dwell meters or tachometers. These are convenient, in that they reduce the tangle of wires under the hood when you're working, but may duplicate the functions of tools you already have. One worthwhile feature, which is becoming more of a necessity with higher voltage ignition systems, is an inductive pickup. The inductive pickup clamps around the No. 1 spark plug wire, sensing the surges of high voltage electricity as they are sent to the plug. The advantage is that no mechanical connection is inserted between the wire and the plug, which eliminates false signals to the timing light. A timing light with an inductive pickup should be used on HEI systems.

To check and adjust the timing:

1. Warm up the engine to normal operating temperature. Stop the engine and connect the timing light to the No. 1 (left front on V8, front on six) spark plug wire. You can also use the No. 6 wire, if it is more convenient. Numbering is illustrated in this Chapter. Under no circumstances should the spark plug wire be pierced to hook up a timing light. Clean off the timing marks and mark the pulley or damper notch and timing scale with white chalk. The timing notch on the pulley or damper can be elusive. The best way to get it to an accessible position for marking is to bump the engine around using either the ignition key or a remote starter.

2. Disconnect and plug the vacuum line at the distributor. This is done to prevent any distributor vacuum advance. A short screw, pencil, or a golf tee can be used to plug the line.

3. Start the engine and adjust the idle speed to that specified in the Tune-Up Specifications

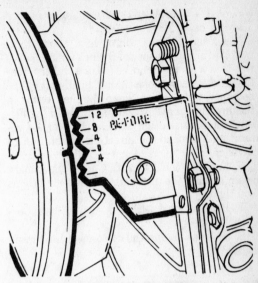

Timing marks (on pulley) and timing indicator on 1975 and later gasoline V8s

chart. With automatic transmission, set the specified idle speed in Park. It will be too high, since it is normally (in most cases) adjusted in Drive. However, it is safer to adjust the timing in Park and to reset the idle speed after all timing work is done. Some trucks require that the timing be set with the transmission in Neutral. Refer to the Tune-Up Specificationschart or the underhood sticker for details. You can disconnect the idle solenoid, if any, to get the speed down. Otherwise, adjust the idle speed screw. This is done to prevent any centrifugal (mechanical) advance.

The tachometer hookup for 1970-74 models is the same as the dwell meter hookup shown in the Tune-Up and Troubleshooting sections. On 1975-77 HEI systems, the tachometer connects to the TACH terminal on the distributor (V8) or on the coil (6-cylinder) and to a ground. For 1978 and later, all tachometer connections are to the TACH terminal. Some tachometers must connect to the TACH terminal and to the positive battery terminal. Some tachometers won't work with HEI.

WARNING: *Never ground the HEI TACH terminal; serious system damage will result.*

4. Aim the timing light at the pointer marks. Be careful not to touch the fan, because it may appear to be standing still. Keep the timing light wires clear of the fan, belts, and pulleys. If the pulley or damper notch isn't aligned with the proper timing mark (see the Tune-Up Specifications chart), the timing will have to be adjusted.

NOTE: *TDC or Top Dead Center corresponds to 0 degrees. B, or BTDC, or Before Top Dead Center may be shown as BEFORE.*

A, or ATDC, or After Top Dead Center may be shown as AFTER.

5. Loosen the distributor base clamp locknut. You can buy a special wrench which makes this task a lot easier on V8s. Turn the distributor slowly to adjust the timing, holding it by the body and not the cap. Turn the distributor in the direction of rotor rotation (found in the Firing Order illustration in this Chapter) to retard, and against the direction of rotation to advance.

6. Tighten the locknut. Check the timing again, in case the distributor moved slightly as you tighten it.

7. Replace the distributor vacuum line. Correct the idle speed.

8. Stop the engine and disconnect the timing light.

Diesel Injection Timing

8-350 and 8-379 cu. in. Diesels

For the engine to be properly timed, the marks on the top of the engine front cover (8-379) or injection pump adapter (8-350) must be aligned with the marks on the injection pump flange. The engine must be off when the timing is reset.

NOTE: *On 49 state 8-379s, the marks are scribe lines. On California 8-379s, the marks are half-circles.*

1. Loosen the three pump retaining nuts. If the marks are not aligned, adjustment is necessary.

2. Loosen the three pump retaining nuts. Special Tool #J-26987 is useful here on the 8-350.

3. Align the mark on the injection pump with the mark on the front cover (8-379) or adapter (8-350). Tighten the nuts to 30 ft.lb. on the 8-379, and 35 ft.lb. on the 8-350.

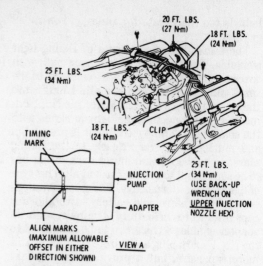

Injection pump timing marks location and alignment, 350 diesel shown

NOTE: *Use a ¾" open-end wrench on the nut at the front of the injection pump to aid in rotating the pump to align the marks.*

4. Adjust the throttle linkage if necessary.

Valve Lash

All engines covered in this guide are equipped with hydraulic valve lifters. Engines so equipped operate with zero clearance in the valve train; because of this the rocker arms are non-adjustable. The hydraulic lifters themselves do not require any adjustment as part of the normal tune-up, although they occasionally become noisy (especially on high mileage engines) and need to be replaced. In the event of cylinder head removal or any operation that requires disturbing or removing the rocker arms, the rocker arms have to be adjusted. Please refer to Chapter 3 for these procedures.

Carburetor Idle Speed And Mixture Adjustments

In most cases, the mixture screws have limiter caps, but in later years the mixture screws are concealed under staked in plugs. Idle mixture is adjustable only during carburetor overhaul, and requires the addition of propane as an artificial mixture enrichener. For these reasons, mixture adjustments are not covered here for affected models.

See the emission control label in the engine compartment for procedures and specifications not supplies here.

NOTE: *See Carburetor Identification in Chapter 6 for carburetor I.D. specifics.*

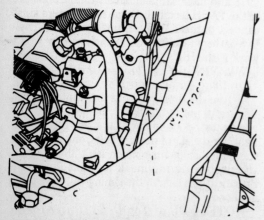

Diesel injection timing marks, 379 shown. Marks shown are in alignment

1970

On all vehicles, disconnect FUEL TANK line from the vapor canister. Remember to reconnect the line after setting the idle spped and mixture. The engine should be at operating temperature with the choke valve and air cleaner damper door fully open, ari conditioning OFF and park brake ON.

● 6-250 and 6-292 Engine, ½ ton models. Disconnect and plug the vacuum advance line. Turn the mixture screw in until it lightly contacts the seat, then back out 4 turns. Adjust the solenoid screw to obtain 800 rpm with manual transmission in drive. Adjust the mixture screw to obtain 750 rpm with manual transmission in Neutral or automatic in Drive. Electrically, disconnect the solenoid and set the carburetor idle speed screw to obtain 400 rpm and connect the solenoid. Reconnect the vacuum line.

● 6-292 Engine, ¾ and 1 ton Series: Disconnect and plug the distributor vacuum line. Turn the mixture screws in until they lightly contact the seats and back the screw(s) out 4 turns. On manual transmission models, adjust the carburetor idle speed screw to obtain 600 rpm in Neutral. Then adjust the mixture screw to obtain 550 rpm in Neutral. On automatic transmission models, adjust the solenoid screw to obtain 550 rpm with transmission in Drive. Adjust the mixture screw to obtain 500 rpm with transmission in Drive. Disconnect the solenoid and set the carburetor idle speed screw to obtain 400 rpm and connect the solenoid. Reconnect the distributor vacuum line on all models.

● 8-307 V8, ½ ton Series: Disconnect and plug the distributor vacuum line. Turn the mixture screws in until they lightly contact the seats then back them out 4 turns. Adjust the carburetor idle speed screw to obtain 800 rpm with manual transmission in Drive. Adjust the carburetor idle speed screw to obtain 800 rpm with manual transmission in Drive. Adjust the mixture screw to obtain 630 rpm with automatic transmission in Drive. Adjust the mixture screws in equally to obtain 700 rpm with manual transmission in Neutral or 600 rpm with automatic transmission in Drive. Disconnect the solenoid and set the carburetor idle speed screw to obtain 450 rpm and reconnect the solenoid. Reconnect the vacuum line.

● 8-307 V8, ¾ and 1 ton Series: Disconnect and plug the distributor vacuum line. Set the mixture screws for maximum idle rpm and adjust the idle speed screw to obtain 700 rpm with manual transmission in Neutral or 600 rpm with automatic transmission in Drive. Adjust the mixture screws equally to obtain a 200 rpm drop, then back the screws out ¼ turn. As nec-

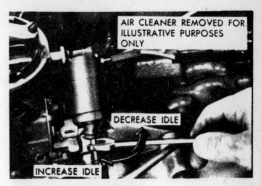

AIR CLEANER REMOVED FOR ILLUSTRATIVE PURPOSES ONLY

DECREASE IDLE

INCREASE IDLE

Adjusting the idle solenoid

essary, adjust the idle screw on manual transmission models to obtain 700 rpm with the transmission in Neutral. On automatic transmission models, adjust the solenoid screw to obtain 600 rpm with the transmission in Drive. Disconnect the solenoid electrically and set the carburetor idle screw to obtain 450 rpm and reconnect the solenoid. Reconnect the vacuum line.

● 8-350 V8, ½ ton Series: Disconnect and plug the distributor vacuum line. Turn the mixture screws in until they lightly contact the seats. Back the screws out 4 turns. Adjust the idle speed screw to obtain 650 rpm with manual transmission in Neutral or 550 rpm with automatic transmission in Drive. Adjust the mixture screws equally to obtain 600 rpm with manual transmission in Neutral or automatic transmission in Drive. Reconnect the vacuum advance line.

● 8-350 and 8-396 V8, ¾ and 1 ton Series: Disconnect and plug the distributor vacuum line. Turn the mixture screws in until they lightly contact the seats and back them out 4 turns. Adjust the carburetor idle speed screw to obtain 775 rpm (manual transmission in Neutral) or 630 rpm (automatic transmission in Drive). Adjust the mixture screws equally to obtain 700 rpm (manual transmission in Neutral) or 600 rpm (automatic transmission in Drive). Reconnect the vacuum line.

1971

The engine should be running at operating temperature, choke valve fully open, parking brake ON and drive wheels blocked.

● 6-250 and 6-292 Engines, ½ ton Series: Disconnect the FUEL TANK line from the evaporative canister. Disconnect the vacuum advance line and plug the vacuum source. Adjust the carburetor speed screw to obtain 550 rpm with manual transmission in Neutral or 550 rpm with automatic transmission in Drive. Do not adjust the solenoid screw.

CAUTION: *Use the CEC solenoid screw to*

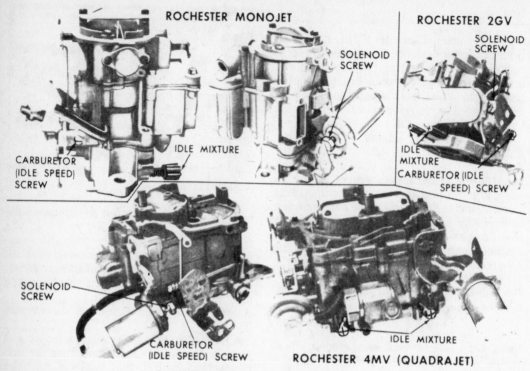

Idle speed and mixture screws, 1971

adjust the idle speed could result in a decrease in engine braking.

Reconnect the FUEL TANK line and the vacuum advance line.

• 8-307, ½ ton Series: Disconnect the FUEL TANK line from the evaporative canister. Disconnect the vacuum source opening. Adjust the carburetor speed screw to obtain 600 rpm with manual transmission in Neutral or 550 rpm with automatic transmission in Drive and air conditioner ON. Do not adjust the solenoid. See the previous Caution. Reconnect the FUEL TANK line and the vacuum advance line.

• 8-350 and 8-402, ½ ton Series: Disconnect the FUEL TANK line from the evaporative canister. Disconnect the vacuum advance line and plug the vacuum sourch opening. Turn the air conditioner OFF and adjust the carburetor speed screw to obtain 600 rpm with manual transmission in Neutral or 550 rpm (600 rpm on 8-402) with automatic transmission in Drive. Do not adjust the solenoid screw, or a decrease in engine breaking could result. Place the fast idle cam follower on the second step of the fast idle cam and turn the aid conditioner OFF. Adjust the fast idle to 1,350 rpm with manual transmission in Neutral or 1,500 rpm with automatic transmission in PARK. Reconnect the FUEL TANK and vacuum advance lines.

• 6-292 and 8-307, ¾ and 1 ton Series: Dis-

connect the vacuum advance line and plug the vacuum source opening. Turn the air conditioner ON. Turn the mixture screws in until they lightly contact the seats and back them out 4 turns. Adjust the carburetor speed screw to obtain 600 rpm with manual transmission in Neutral and 500 rpm with automatic in Drive. Reconnect the vacuum advance hose.

• 8-350 and 8-402, ¾ and 1 ton Series: Disconnect the distributor vacuum advance hose and plug the vacuum source opening. Turn the air conditioner off. Turn the mixture screws in until they contact the seats lightly. Back the screws out 4 turns. Adjust the carburetor speed screw to obtain 650 rpm with manual transmission in Neutral or 550 rpm with automatic transmission in Drive. Reconnect the vacuum advance hose.

1972

The engine should be at normal operating temperature on the choke valve fully open, parking brake ON and the drive wheels blocked. All carburetors are equipped with idle mixture limiter caps, which provide for only a small adjustment range. Normally, these should not be removed. However, if they are removed, the CO content of the exhaust should be checked to be sure that it meets Federal Emission Control limits.

• 6-250 and 6-292: Disconnect the FUEL

ROCHESTER CARBURETORS

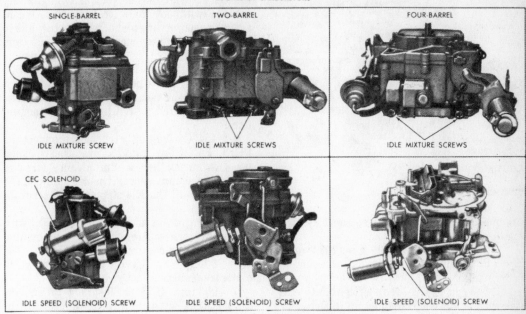

SINGLE-BARREL	TWO-BARREL	FOUR-BARREL
IDLE MIXTURE SCREW	IDLE MIXTURE SCREWS	IDLE MIXTURE SCREWS
CEC SOLENOID		
IDLE SPEED (SOLENOID) SCREW	IDLE SPEED (SOLENOID) SCREW	IDLE SPEED (SOLENOID) SCREW

Idle speed and mixture screws, 1972–75

TANK line from the vapor canister. Remember to reconnect it after making the adjustment. Disconnect the plug the vacuum line source. Adjust the idle stop solenoid to obtain 700 rpm with manual transmission in Neutral or 600 rpm with automatic transmission in Drive. Do not adjust the CEC solenoid screw.

CAUTION: *If the CEC solenoid screw is adjusted out of limits, a decrease in engine breaking may result.*

Reconnect the vacuum line.

• 8-307: Disconnect the FUEL TANK line from the vapor canister and remove and plug the vacuum line source. Adjust the idle stop solenoid screw to obtain 900 rpm (950 on California trucks) with manual transmission in Neutral or 600 rpm with automatic transmission in Drive. On trucks without TCS, adjust speed screw for 600 rpm with transmission in Neutral. With transmission in Park or Neutral, adjust the fast idle speed to obtain 1850 rpm. Reconnect the FUEL TANK line and the vacuum line.

• 8-350: Disconnect the FUEL TANK line and disconnect and plug the vacuum line. On vehicles with TCS, turn the air conditioner OFF and adjust the idle solenoid screw to obtain 800 rpm with manual transmission in Neutral or 600 rpm with automatic transmission in Drive. On vehicles without TCS, adjust the carburetor speed screw to obtain 600 rpm with transmission in Neutral. Place the fast idle cam, turn the air conditioner OFF and ad-

just the fast idle to 1,350 rpm with manual transmission in Neutral or automatic transmission in Drive. Reconnect the FUEL TANK and vacuum lines.

• 8-402: Disconnect the FUEL TANK line from the evaporative canister. Disconnect the vacuum advance hose and plug the vacuum source opening. On trucks with TCS, turn the air conditioning OFF and adjust the idle stop solenoid screw to obtain 750 rpm with manual transmission in Neutral or 600 rpm with automatic in Drive. On trucks without TCS, adjust the carburetor speed screw to obtain 600 rpm with transmission in Neutral. Place the fast idle cam follower on the second step of the fast idle cam, turn the air conditioner OFF and adjust the fast idle speed to 1,350 rpm with manual transmission in Neutral or 1,500 rpm with automatic transmission in Drive. Reconnect the FUEL TANK line and the vacuum advance line.

1973-75

Emission system requirements necessitate the division of trucks as follows:

• Light Duty: All ½ ton Series
• Heavy Duty: ¾ and 1 ton

All adjustments should be made with the engine at operating temperature, choke fully open, air conditioner OFF, parking brake ON and drive wheels blocked.

• 6-250: Disconnect the FUEL TANK line and the vacuum source opening. Plug the vacu-

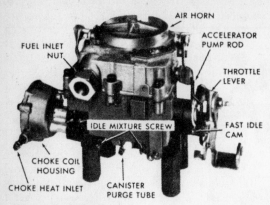

Rochester 2GC, 1975

um line. Adjust the idle stop solenoid by turning the hex nut to obtain:

700 rpm (1973) or 600 rpm (1974) on all heavy duty vehicles with manual transmission in Neutral;

600 rpm (1973-74) on all light duty vehicles with automatic transmission in Drive.

850 rpm (1974-75) on all light duty trucks with manual transmission.

CAUTION: *Do not adjust the CEC solenoid on 1973 vehicles or a decrease in engine braking may result.*

Place automatic transmissions in Park and manual transmission in Neutral and adjust the fast idle to 1800 rpm, on the top step of the fast idle cam.

Reconnect the FUEL TANK and vacuum lines.

● 6-292: Disconnect the vacuum advance line and plug the vacuum source opening. Adjust the idle stop solenoid screw to obtain 600 rpm on California (and all 1974-75) trucks or 700 rpm on all other trucks. Reconnect the vacuum advance line.

● 1973 8-307: On light duty vehicles, disconnect the FUEL TANK line from the vapor canister and plug the vacuum source opening. Adjust the idle stop solenoid to obtain 600 rpm with automatic transmission in Park or 900 rpm with manual transmission in Neutral. Disconnect the idle stop solenoid and adjust the low idle screw located inside the solenoid hex nut, to obtain 450 rpm in Neutral or Drive. Reconnect the idle stop solenoid, the FUEL TANK line, and the vacuum line.

● 8-350: On light duty vehicles, disconnect the FUEL TANK line from the vapor canister. Disconnect and plug the vacuum line. On heavy duty vehicles, adjust the carburetor idle speed screw to obtain 600 rpm with automatic transmission in Park or manual transmission in Neutral. On light duty vehicles, adjust the idle stop solenoid screw to obtain 600 rpm with automatic transmission in Drive or 900 rpm with

manual transmission in Neutral. On light duty vehicles with automatic transmission, reconnect the vacuum line and adjust the fast idle to 1600 rpm on the top step of the fast idle cam. On light duty vehicles with manual transmission, adjust the fast idle screw to obtain 1300 rpm with the screw on the top step of the fast idle cam and the vacuum line disconnected. Reconnect the FUEL TANK line and the vacuum line.

● 8-454: On light duty trucks, disconnect the FUEL TANK line from the evaporative canister. Disconnect the vacuum advance line and plug the vacuum source opening. Adjust the idle speed with the idle stop solenoid screw to obtain:

700 rpm on all heavy duty trucks with automatic transmission in Park and manual transmission in Neutral.

600 rpm on light duty trucks with automatic transmission in Drive.

900 rpm (1973) or 800 (1974-75) on light duty trucks with manual transmission in Neutral.

On light duty trucks with automatic transmission, reconnect the vacuum advance line. Adjust the fast idle screw to obtain 1,600 rpm with the screw on the top step of the fast idle cam.

On light duty trucks with manual transmission, adjust the fast idle screw to obtain 1,600 rpm (1973) or 1,500 rpm (1974-75) with the screw on the top step of the fast idle cam and the vacuum hose disconnected.

Reconnect the FUEL TANK line and the vacuum advance line.

Carburetor Idle Speed Adjustment

1976

All adjustments should be made with engine at normal operating temperature, air cleaner on, choke open, and air conditioning off, unless otherwise noted. Set the parking brake and block the rear wheels.

● 6-250 and 6-292 Engines: Disconnect and plug the carburetor and PCV hoses at the vapor canister on the 6-250. On heavy duty emissions 6-250s and all 6-292s, disconnect the FUEL TANK hose at the vapor canister. If the engine has a solenoid located between the carburetor and the distributor on the vacuum hose line, disconnect and plug the vacuum line. Otherwise, leave the vacuum hose connected. On heavy duty 6-250s and all 6-292s turn the air conditioning on, if so equipped. With manual transmissions in Neutral, 6-250 automatics in Drive, and heavy duty 6-250 and 6-292 automatics in Neutral, turn the solenoid body in or out to set the idle speed to specified rpm. Disconnect the electrical wire from the carburetor solenoid, and turn the air conditioner off. Turn the ⅛″ hex (Allen head) screw located in the end of the solenoid body to set the low idle to 425 rpm for 6-250s and 450 rpm for heavy duty 6-250s and 6-292s. Reconnect the electrical wire and any hoses that were disconnected.

• 8-350, 8-400, and 8-454 Engines: On California emissions engines, disconnect and plug the FUEL TANK hose at the vapor canister. On heavy duty emissions 8-350s and 8-400s, turn the air conditioning on. Place the automatic transmission in Drive, manuals in Neutral, unless otherwise noted in the Tune-Up Specifications chart. Adjust the carburetor idle speed to the specified rpm by turning the idle speed screw. Reconnect the FUEL TANK hose on California engines. On engines equipped with four barrel carburetors, place the transmission in Park for automatics, and leave manual transmission in Neutral. Disconnect and plug the vacuum hose at the EGR valve if so equipped. On 8-454 engines with electric chokes, disconnect and plug the vacuum hose to the front vacuum break unit located in front of the choke coil housing. Position the cam follower lever of the fast idle unit on the proper step on the cam, as specified on the underhood emissions sticker. Turn the fast idle screw to obtain the specified rpm on the sticker. Reconnect any hoses that were disconnected.

1977-78

All adjustments should be made with the engine at normal operating temperature, air cleaner on, choke open, and air conditioning off, unless otherwise noted. Set the parking brake and block the rear wheels. Automatics should be place in Drive, manuals in Neutral, except as noted in the Tune-Up Specifications chart.

• 6-250 and 6-292 Engines: Make certain that the fast idle follower is not on any of the steps marked H, 2, or L on the cam. It should be resting against the first step below L. Set the idle to specifications by turning the solenoid in or out. Do this with a wrench on the nut attached to the end of the solenoid body. Disconnect the electrical connector from the solenoid. The engine speed will drop. With a ⅛″ hex (Allen head) wrench, turn the screw located inside the nut attached to the solenoid body, and set the idle speed to 425 rpm for light duty emissions trucks, 450 rpm for heavy duty 6-250s and 6-292s.

Reconnect the solenoid wire and check idle speed.

• 8-305, 8-350, 8-400 and 8-454 Engines: Check the underhood emissions sticker to determine which hoses, if any, must be disconnected. On carburetors not equipped with a so-

lenoid: For two barrel carburetors, make sure that the idle speed screw is on the low (L) step of the fast idle cam. Then, for all engines except 1978 2-bbl models with a solenoid but without air conditioning: Turn the idle speed screw to adjust idle speed to the specification found in the Tune-Up Specifications chart or on the underhood emissions sticker.

On 1978 trucks with a two barrel carburetor which have a solenoid, but without air conditioning, open the throttle slightly to allow the solenoid plunger to extend. Turn the solenoid screw to adjust the curb idle to specification, as given in the chart or on the emission control sticker in the engine compartment. Then disconnect the electrical connector from the solenoid. The idle speed will drop. Turn the idle speed screw to set the slow engine idle to the figure given on the emission control sticker. Reconnect the solenoid and shut off the engine.

On carburetors equipped with a solenoid and air conditioning: Turn the idle speed screw to set the idle to specifications. Then, disconnect the air conditioner compressor electrical lead at the compressor, and turn the air conditioner on. Open the throttle slightly to allow the solenoid plunger to fully extend. Turn the solenoid screw and adjust to 650 rpm, except light duty emissions trucks with manual transmissions, which should be set to 700 rpm. Reconnect the air conditioner compressor lead.

1979 and Later

Idle mixture is not adjustable in these years, except for the heavy duty emission 292 6-cylinder equipped with the IME carburetor, and heavy duty emission V8s equipped with the four barrel M4MC.

All adjustments should be made with the engine at normal operating temperature, air cleaner on, choke open, and air conditioning off, unless otherwise noted. Set the parking brake and block the rear wheels. Automatic transmissions should be set in Drive, manuals in Neutral, unless otherwise noted in the procedures or in the Tune-Up Specifications chart, or on the emission control label.

• 6-250 Engine: Check the emission control label for any special insturctions. Open the throttle slightly to allow the solenoid plunger to extend. Turn the solenoid screw to adjust the curb idle to the figure given in the Tune-Up Specifications chart or on the emission control label. Disconnect the electrical connector from the solenoid. The idle speed will drop. Adjust the idle to the basic idle speed figure given on the emission control label by means of the idle speed screw. Connect the solenoid lead and shut off the engine.

• 6-292 Engine: See the procedure given for

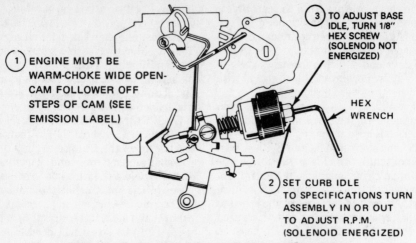

1. ENGINE MUST BE WARM-CHOKE WIDE OPEN-CAM FOLLOWER OFF STEPS OF CAM (SEE EMISSION LABEL)

3. TO ADJUST BASE IDLE, TURN 1/8" HEX SCREW (SOLENOID NOT ENERGIZED)

HEX WRENCH

2. SET CURB IDLE TO SPECIFICATIONS TURN ASSEMBLY IN OR OUT TO ADJUST R.P.M. (SOLENOID ENERGIZED)

Idle speed adjustment for 250 and 292 sixes, 1979 and later

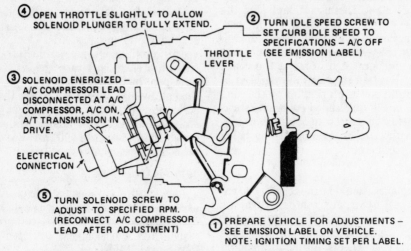

4. OPEN THROTTLE SLIGHTLY TO ALLOW SOLENOID PLUNGER TO FULLY EXTEND.

2. TURN IDLE SPEED SCREW TO SET CURB IDLE SPEED TO SPECIFICATIONS – A/C OFF (SEE EMISSION LABEL)

THROTTLE LEVER

3. SOLENOID ENERGIZED – A/C COMPRESSOR LEAD DISCONNECTED AT A/C COMPRESSOR, A/C ON, A/T TRANSMISSION IN DRIVE.

ELECTRICAL CONNECTION

5. TURN SOLENOID SCREW TO ADJUST TO SPECIFIED RPM. (RECONNECT A/C COMPRESSOR LEAD AFTER ADJUSTMENT)

1. PREPARE VEHICLE FOR ADJUSTMENTS – SEE EMISSION LABEL ON VEHICLE. NOTE: IGNITION TIMING SET PER LABEL.

Idle speed adjustment for V8 4-bbl. carburetors with solenoid, 1977

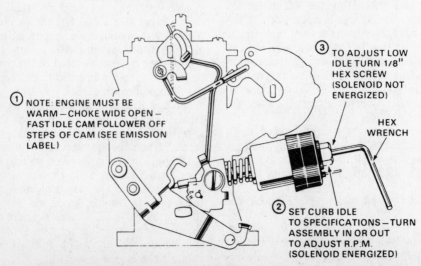

1. NOTE: ENGINE MUST BE WARM – CHOKE WIDE OPEN – FAST IDLE CAM FOLLOWER OFF STEPS OF CAM (SEE EMISSION LABEL)

3. TO ADJUST LOW IDLE TURN 1/8" HEX SCREW (SOLENOID NOT ENERGIZED)

HEX WRENCH

2. SET CURB IDLE TO SPECIFICATIONS – TURN ASSEMBLY IN OR OUT TO ADJUST R.P.M. (SOLENOID ENERGIZED)

1977 and later inline six cylinder idle speed adjustment, MV and ME-type 1-bbls,

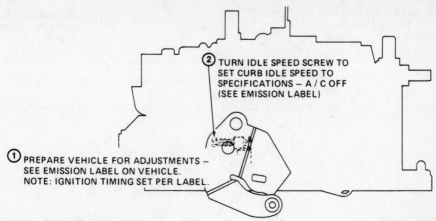

2 TURN IDLE SPEED SCREW TO SET CURB IDLE SPEED TO SPECIFICATIONS – A / C OFF (SEE EMISSION LABEL)

1 PREPARE VEHICLE FOR ADJUSTMENTS – SEE EMISSION LABEL ON VEHICLE. NOTE: IGNITION TIMING SET PER LABEL.

1979 and later 4 bbl adjustments without solenoid; 1978 4 bbl and 1979—81 V8 2 bbl (M2MC) models similar (© Chevrolet Motor Div.)

1977-78. Check the idle figures given against the emission control label in the engine compartment; the label figures must be used if different.

Idle mixture is adjustable on this carburetor (model 1ME):

1. Set the parking brake and block the rear wheels.

2. Remove the air cleaner but do not disconnect any of the hoses. Disconnect and plug the other hoses as directed on the emission control label.

3. The engine should be at normal operating temperature, choke open, and air conditioning off (if equipped). Connect an accurate tachometer to the engine.

4. Disconnect and plug the vacuum advance hose at the distributor and check the ignition timing. Correct as necessary. Reconnect the vacuum advance hose.

5. Carefully remove the limiter cap from the idle mixture screw. Lightly seat the screw, then back it out just enough to allow the engine to run.

6. Place the transmission in Neutral.

7. Back the mixture screw out 1/8 turn at a time until the maximum idle speed is obtained. Adjust the idle speed to the figure given on the emission control label by means of the idle speed screw. Repeat this step until you are certain that the maximum speed has been obtained with the mixture screw.

8. Turn the mixture screw in 1/8 turn at a time until the idle speed drops to the figure given on the emission control label.

9. Reset the idle speed to the figure given on the emission control label by means of the idle speed screw. Check and adjust the fast idle as directed on the emission control label. Reconnect any vacuum hoses removed in Step 2, in-

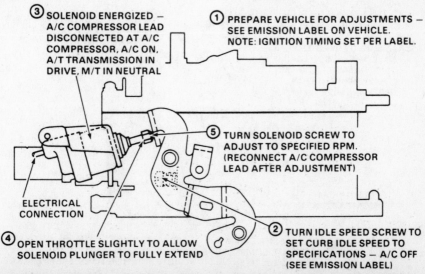

3 SOLENOID ENERGIZED – A/C COMPRESSOR LEAD DISCONNECTED AT A/C COMPRESSOR, A/C ON, A/T TRANSMISSION IN DRIVE, M/T IN NEUTRAL

1 PREPARE VEHICLE FOR ADJUSTMENTS – SEE EMISSION LABEL ON VEHICLE. NOTE: IGNITION TIMING SET PER LABEL.

5 TURN SOLENOID SCREW TO ADJUST TO SPECIFIED RPM. (RECONNECT A/C COMPRESSOR LEAD AFTER ADJUSTMENT)

ELECTRICAL CONNECTION

4 OPEN THROTTLE SLIGHTLY TO ALLOW SOLENOID PLUNGER TO FULLY EXTEND

2 TURN IDLE SPEED SCREW TO SET CURB IDLE SPEED TO SPECIFICATIONS – A/C OFF (SEE EMISSION LABEL)

1979 and later 4-bbl. adjustments with solenoid, 1978 4-bbl. and 1979 2-bbl. (M2MC) similar

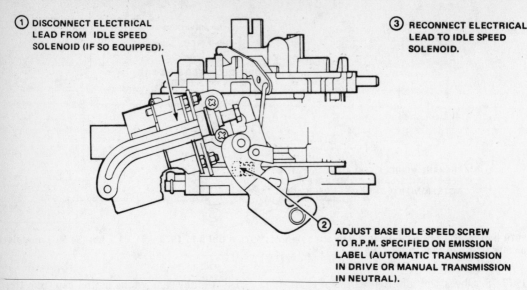

① DISCONNECT ELECTRICAL LEAD FROM IDLE SPEED SOLENOID (IF SO EQUIPPED).

③ RECONNECT ELECTRICAL LEAD TO IDLE SPEED SOLENOID.

② ADJUST BASE IDLE SPEED SCREW TO R.P.M. SPECIFIED ON EMISSION LABEL (AUTOMATIC TRANSMISSION IN DRIVE OR MANUAL TRANSMISSION IN NEUTRAL).

1980–81 V8 2-bbl. (M2MC) idle speed adjustment with solenoid

stall the air cleaner, and recheck the idle speed. Correct, if necessary, by means of the idle speed screw.

● 8-305 Engine: Check the emission control label in the engine compartment to determine which hoses, if any, must be disconnected. Make sure the idle speed screw is on the low (L) step of the fast idle cam. Turn the idle speed screw to adjust the idle speed to the figure given in the Tune-Up Specifications chart, or on the emission control label.

On carburetors equipped with a solenoid (air conditioned trucks): turn the idle speed screw to set the idle to specifications, as in the previous paragraph. Then, disconnect the air conditioner compressor electrical lead at the com-

pressor. Turn the air conditioning on. Open the throttle slightly to allow the solenoid plunger to fully extend. Turn the solenoid screw and adjust to 700 rpm with manual transmission (Neutral), or 600 rpm with automatic transmission (Drive). Reconnect the air conditioner electrical lead.

● 8-350, 8-400, and 8-454 Engines: The idle speed procedure is the same as given for 1977-78 models. Check the emission control label and the Tune-Up Specifications chart to determine the proper idle speeds.

Mixture is adjustable on heavy duty emissions V8s with the four barrel M4MC carburetor. This procedure will not work on light duty emissions trucks.

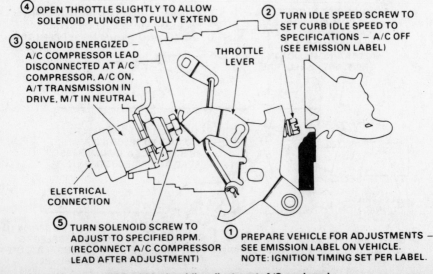

④ OPEN THROTTLE SLIGHTLY TO ALLOW SOLENOID PLUNGER TO FULLY EXTEND

③ SOLENOID ENERGIZED – A/C COMPRESSOR LEAD DISCONNECTED AT A/C COMPRESSOR, A/C ON, A/T TRANSMISSION IN DRIVE, M/T IN NEUTRAL

② TURN IDLE SPEED SCREW TO SET CURB IDLE SPEED TO SPECIFICATIONS – A/C OFF (SEE EMISSION LABEL)

THROTTLE LEVER

ELECTRICAL CONNECTION

⑤ TURN SOLENOID SCREW TO ADJUST TO SPECIFIED RPM. (RECONNECT A/C COMPRESSOR LEAD AFTER ADJUSTMENT)

① PREPARE VEHICLE FOR ADJUSTMENTS – SEE EMISSION LABEL ON VEHICLE. NOTE: IGNITION TIMING SET PER LABEL.

2GC 2-bbl. slow idle adjustment, A/C-equipped

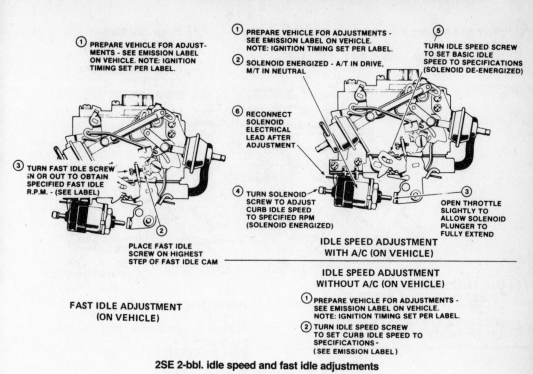

① PREPARE VEHICLE FOR ADJUST-
MENTS - SEE EMISSION LABEL
ON VEHICLE. NOTE: IGNITION
TIMING SET PER LABEL.

① PREPARE VEHICLE FOR ADJUSTMENTS -
SEE EMISSION LABEL ON VEHICLE.
NOTE: IGNITION TIMING SET PER LABEL.

⑤ TURN IDLE SPEED SCREW
TO SET BASIC IDLE
SPEED TO SPECIFICATIONS
(SOLENOID DE-ENERGIZED)

② SOLENOID ENERGIZED - A/T IN DRIVE,
M/T IN NEUTRAL

⑥ RECONNECT
SOLENOID
ELECTRICAL
LEAD AFTER
ADJUSTMENT

③ TURN FAST IDLE SCREW
iN OR OUT TO OBTAIN
SPECIFIED FAST IDLE
R.P.M. - (SEE LABEL)

④ TURN SOLENOID
SCREW TO ADJUST
CURB IDLE SPEED
TO SPECIFIED RPM
(SOLENOID ENERGIZED)

③ OPEN THROTTLE
SLIGHTLY TO
ALLOW SOLENOID
PLUNGER TO
FULLY EXTEND

PLACE FAST IDLE
SCREW ON HIGHEST
STEP OF FAST IDLE CAM

IDLE SPEED ADJUSTMENT
WITH A/C (ON VEHICLE)

IDLE SPEED ADJUSTMENT
WITHOUT A/C (ON VEHICLE)

FAST IDLE ADJUSTMENT
(ON VEHICLE)

① PREPARE VEHICLE FOR ADJUSTMENTS -
SEE EMISSION LABEL ON VEHICLE.
NOTE: IGNITION TIMING SET PER LABEL.

② TURN IDLE SPEED SCREW
TO SET CURB IDLE SPEED TO
SPECIFICATIONS
- (SEE EMISSION LABEL)

2SE 2-bbl. idle speed and fast idle adjustments

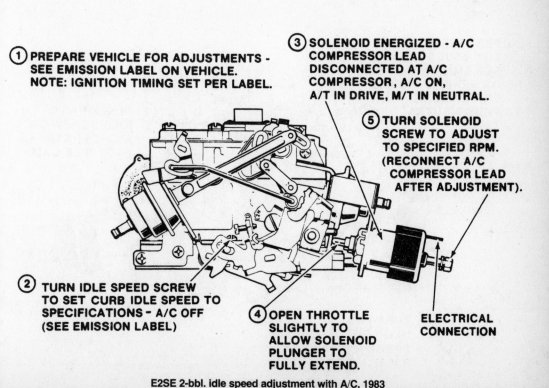

① **PREPARE VEHICLE FOR ADJUSTMENTS -
SEE EMISSION LABEL ON VEHICLE.
NOTE: IGNITION TIMING SET PER LABEL.**

③ **SOLENOID ENERGIZED - A/C
COMPRESSOR LEAD
DISCONNECTED AT A/C
COMPRESSOR , A/C ON,
A/T IN DRIVE, M/T IN NEUTRAL.**

⑤ **TURN SOLENOID
SCREW TO ADJUST
TO SPECIFIED RPM.
(RECONNECT A/C
COMPRESSOR LEAD
AFTER ADJUSTMENT).**

② **TURN IDLE SPEED SCREW
TO SET CURB IDLE SPEED TO
SPECIFICATIONS - A/C OFF
(SEE EMISSION LABEL)**

④ **OPEN THROTTLE
SLIGHTLY TO
ALLOW SOLENOID
PLUNGER TO
FULLY EXTEND.**

**ELECTRICAL
CONNECTION**

E2SE 2-bbl. idle speed adjustment with A/C, 1983

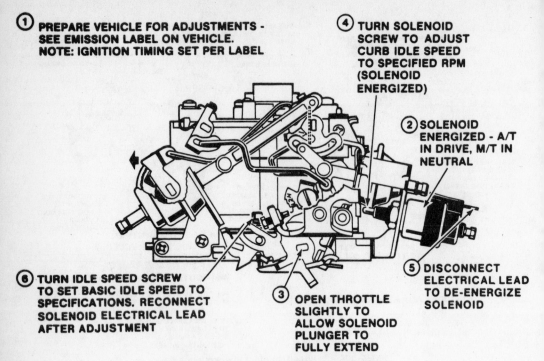

① PREPARE VEHICLE FOR ADJUSTMENTS - SEE EMISSION LABEL ON VEHICLE. NOTE: IGNITION TIMING SET PER LABEL

④ TURN SOLENOID SCREW TO ADJUST CURB IDLE SPEED TO SPECIFIED RPM (SOLENOID ENERGIZED)

② SOLENOID ENERGIZED - A/T IN DRIVE, M/T IN NEUTRAL

⑤ DISCONNECT ELECTRICAL LEAD TO DE-ENERGIZE SOLENOID

⑥ TURN IDLE SPEED SCREW TO SET BASIC IDLE SPEED TO SPECIFICATIONS. RECONNECT SOLENOID ELECTRICAL LEAD AFTER ADJUSTMENT

③ OPEN THROTTLE SLIGHTLY TO ALLOW SOLENOID PLUNGER TO FULLY EXTEND

E2SE 2-bbl. idle speed adjustment without A/C

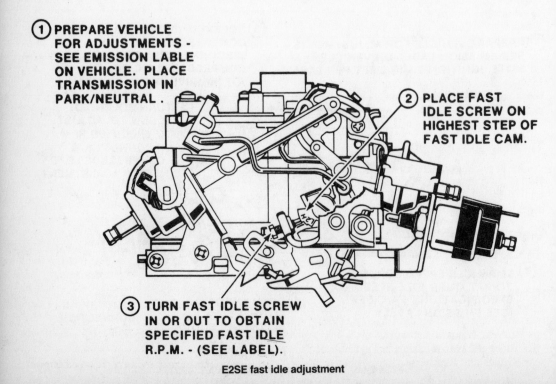

① PREPARE VEHICLE FOR ADJUSTMENTS - SEE EMISSION LABLE ON VEHICLE. PLACE TRANSMISSION IN PARK/NEUTRAL.

② PLACE FAST IDLE SCREW ON HIGHEST STEP OF FAST IDLE CAM.

③ TURN FAST IDLE SCREW IN OR OUT TO OBTAIN SPECIFIED FAST IDLE R.P.M. - (SEE LABEL).

E2SE fast idle adjustment

FAST IDLE ADJUSTMENT

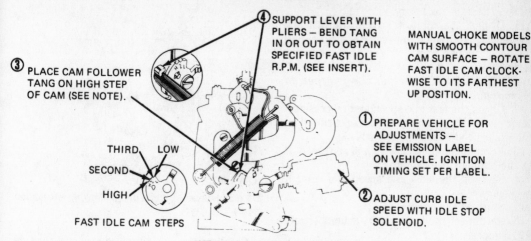

③ PLACE CAM FOLLOWER TANG ON HIGH STEP OF CAM (SEE NOTE).

④ SUPPORT LEVER WITH PLIERS – BEND TANG IN OR OUT TO OBTAIN SPECIFIED FAST IDLE R.P.M. (SEE INSERT).

MANUAL CHOKE MODELS WITH SMOOTH CONTOUR CAM SURFACE – ROTATE FAST IDLE CAM CLOCK-WISE TO ITS FARTHEST UP POSITION.

① PREPARE VEHICLE FOR ADJUSTMENTS – SEE EMISSION LABEL ON VEHICLE. IGNITION TIMING SET PER LABEL.

② ADJUST CURB IDLE SPEED WITH IDLE STOP SOLENOID.

THIRD   LOW
SECOND
HIGH

FAST IDLE CAM STEPS

1ME 1-bbl. fast idle adjustment

1. The engine must be at normal operating temperature, choke open, parking brake applied, and the transmission in Park or Neutral. Block the rear wheels and do not stand in front of the truck when making adjustments.

2. Remove the air cleaner. Connect a tachometer and a vacuum gauge to the engine.

3. Turn the idle mixture screws in lightly until they seat, then back them out two turns. Be careful not to tighten the mixture screw against its seat, or damage may result.

4. Adjust the idle speed screw to obtain the engine rpm figure specified on the emission control label.

5. Adjust the idle mixture screws equally to obtain the highest engine speed.

6. Repeat Steps 4 and 5 until the best idle is obtained.

7. Shut off the engine, remove the tachometer and vacuum gauge, and install the air cleaner.

Throttle Body Injection (TBI)

The throttle body injected vehicles are controlled by a computer which supplies the correct amount of fuel during all engine operating conditions; no adjustment is necessary.

Diesel Fuel Injection

IDLE SPEED ADJUSTMENT

8-350 V8 Diesel

A special tachometer with an RPM counter suitable for the 8-350 V8 diesel is necessary for this adjustment; a standard tach suitable for gasoline engines will not work.

1. Place the transmission in Park, block the rear wheels and firmly set the parking brake.

2. If necessary, adjust the throttle linkage as described in Chapter 6.

3. Start the engine and allow it to warm up for 10-15 minutes.

4. Shut off the engine and remove the air cleaner.

5. Clean off any grime from the timing probe holder on the front cover; also clean off the crankshaft balancer rim.

6. Install the magnetic probe end of the tachometer fully into the timing probe holder. Complete the remaining tachometer connections according to the tach manufacturer's instructions.

7. Disconnect the two-lead connector from the generator.

8. Make sure all electrical accessories are OFF.

NOTE: *At no time should either the steering wheel or the brake pedal be touched.*

9. Start the engine and place the transmission in Drive (after first making sure the parking brake is firmly applied).

10. Check the slow idle speed reading against

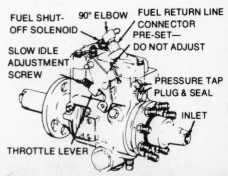

FUEL SHUT-OFF SOLENOID   90° ELBOW   FUEL RETURN LINE CONNECTOR PRE-SET— DO NOT ADJUST

SLOW IDLE ADJUSTMENT SCREW

PRESSURE TAP PLUG & SEAL

INLET

THROTTLE LEVER

350 diesel injection pump showing idle speed screws

the one printed on the underhood emissions sticker. Reset if necessary.

11. Unplug the connector from the fast idle cold advance (engine temperature) switch, and install a jumper wire between the connector terminals.

NOTE: *DO NOT allow the jumper to ground.*

12. Check the fast idle speed and reset if necessary according to the specification printed on the underhood emissions sticker.

13. Remove the jumper wire and reconnect it to the temperature switch.

14. Recheck the slow idle speed and reset if necessary.

15. Shut off the engine.

16. Reconnect the leads at the generator and A/C compressor.

17. Disconnect and remove the tachometer.

18. If the car is equipped with cruise control, adjust the servo throttle rod to minimum slack, then put the clip in the first free hole closest to the bell rank or throttle lever.

19. Install the air cleaner.

379 V8 Diesel

NOTE: *A special tachometer suitable for diesel engines must be used. A gasoline engine type tach will not work with the diesel engine.*

1. Set the parking brake and block the drive wheels.

2. Run the engine up to normal operating temperature. The air cleaner must be mounted and all accessories turned off.

3. Install the diesel tachometer as per the manufacturer's instructions.

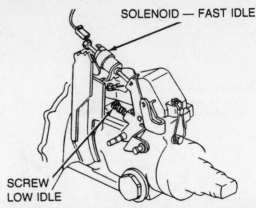

379 (6.2L) diesel injection pump showing idle adjustments

4. Adjust the low idle speed screw on the fuel injection pump to 650 rpm in Neutral or Park for both manual and automatic transmissions.

NOTE: *All idle speeds are to be set within 25 rpm of the specified values.*

5. Adjust the fast idle speed as follows:

a. Remove the connector from the fast idle solenoid. Use an insulated jumper wire from the battery positive terminal to the solenoid terminal to energize the solenoid.

b. Open the throttle momentarily to ensure that the fast idle solenoid plunger is energized and fully extended.

c. Adjust the extended plunger by turning the hex-head screw to an engine speed of 800 rpm in neutral.

d. Remove the jumper wire and reinstall the connector to the fast idle solenoid.

6. Disconnect and remove the tachometer.

ENGINE ELECTRICAL

Understanding the Engine Electrical System

The engine electrical system can be broken down into three separate and distinct systems:
1. The starting system.
2. The charging system.
3. The ignition system.

BATTERY AND STARTING SYSTEM

Basic Operating Principles

The battery is the first link in the chain of mechanisms which work together to provide cranking of the automobile engine. In most modern cars, the battery is a lead/acid electrochemical device consisting of six 2v subsections connected in series so the unit is capable of producing approximately 12v of electrical pressure. Each subsection, or cell, consists of a series of positive and negative plates held a short distance apart in a solution of sulfuric acid and water. The two types of plates are of dissimilar metals. This causes a chemical reaction to be set up, and it is this reaction which produces current flow from the battery when its positive and negative terminals are connected to an electrical appliance such as a lamp or motor. The continued transfer of electrons would eventually convert the sulfuric acid in the electrolyte to water, and make the two plates identical in chemical composition. As electrical energy is removed from the battery, its voltage output tends to drop. Thus, measuring battery voltage and battery electrolyte composition are two ways of checking the ability of the unit to supply power. During the starting of the engine, electrical energy is removed from the battery. However, if the charging circuit is in good condition and the operating conditions are normal, the power removed from the battery will be replaced by the generator (or alternator) which will force electrons back through the battery, reversing the normal flow, and restoring the battery to its original chemical state.

The battery and starting motor are linked by very heavy electrical cables designed to minimize resistance to the flow of current. Generally, the major power supply cable that leaves the battery goes directly to the starter, while other electrical system needs are supplied by a smaller cable. During starter operation, power flows from the battery to the starter and is grounded through the car's frame and the battery's negative ground strap.

The starting motor is a specially designed, direct current electric motor capable of producing a very great amount of power for its size. One thing that allows the motor to produce a great deal of power is its tremendous rotating speed. It drives the engine through a tiny pinion gear (attached to the starter's armature), which drives the very large flywheel ring gear at a greatly reduced speed. Another factor allowing it to produce so much power is that only intermittent operation is required of it. This, little allowance for air circulation is required, and the windings can be built into a very small space.

The starter solenoid is a magnetic device which employs the small current supplied by the starting switch circuit of the ignition switch. This magnetic action moves a plunger which mechanically engages the starter and electrically closes the heavy switch which connects it to the battery. The starting switch circuit consists of the starting switch contained within the ignition switch, a transmission neutral safety switch or clutch pedal switch, and the wiring necessary to connect these in series with the starter solenoid or relay.

A pinion, which is a small gear, is mounted to a one-way drive clutch. This clutch is splined to the starter armature shaft. When the ignition switch is moved to the **start** position, the solenoid plunger slides the pinion toward the flywheel ring gear via a collar and spring. If the teeth on the pinion and flywheel match properly, the pinion will engage the flywheel immediately. If the gear teeth butt one another, the spring will be compressed and will force the gears to mesh as soon as the starter turns far enough to allow them to do so. As the solenoid plunger reaches the end of its travel, it closes the contacts that connect the battery and starter and then the engine is cranked.

As soon as the engine starts, the flywheel ring gear begins turning fast enough to drive the pinion at an extremely high rate of speed. At this point, the one-way clutch begins allowing the pinion to spin faster than the starter shaft so that the starter will not operate at excessive speed. When the ignition switch is released from the starter position, the solenoid is de-energized, and a spring contained within the solenoid assembly pulls the gear out of mesh and interrupts the current flow to the starter.

Some starter employ a separate relay, mounted away from the starter, to switch the motor and solenoid current on and off. The relay thus replaces the solenoid electrical switch, buy does not eliminate the need for a solenoid mounted on the starter used to mechanically engage the starter drive gears. The relay is used to reduce the amount of current the starting switch must carry.

THE CHARGING SYSTEM

Basic Operating Principles

The automobile charging system provides electrical power for operation of the vehicle's ignition and starting systems and all the electrical accessories. The battery services as an electrical surge or storage tank, storing (in chemical form) the energy originally produced by the engine driven generator. The system also provides a means of regulating generator output to protect the battery from being overcharged and to avoid excessive voltage to the accessories.

The storage battery is a chemical device incorporating parallel lead plates in a tank containing a sulfuric acid/water solution. Adjacent plates are slightly dissimilar, and the chemical reaction of the two dissimilar plates produces electrical energy when the battery is connected to a load such as the starter motor. The chemical reaction is reversible, so that when the generator is producing a voltage (electrical pressure) greater than that produced by the battery, electricity is forced into the battery, and the battery is returned to its fully charged state.

The vehicle's generator is driven mechanically, through V-belts, by the engine crankshaft. It consists of two coils of fine wire, one stationary (the stator), and one movable (the rotor). The rotor may also be known as the armature, and consists of fine wire wrapped around an iron core which is mounted on a shaft. The electricity which flows through the two coils of wire (provided initially by the battery in some cases) creates an intense magnetic field around both rotor and stator, and the interaction between the two fields creates voltage, allowing the generator to power the accessories and charge the battery.

There are two types of generators: the earlier is the direct current (DC) type. The current produced by the DC generator is generated in the armature and carried off the spinning armature by stationary brushes contacting the commutator. The commutator is a series of smooth metal contact plates on the end of the armature. The commutator is a series of smooth metal contact plates on the end of the armature. The commutator plates, which are separated from one another by a very short gap, are connected to the armature circuits so that current will flow in one directions only in the wires carrying the generator output. The generator stator consists of two stationary coils of wire which draw some of the output current of the generator to form a powerful magnetic field and create the interaction of fields which generates the voltage. The generator field is wired in series with the regulator.

Newer automobiles use alternating current generators or alternators, because they are more efficient, can be rotated at higher speeds, and have fewer brush problems. In an alternator, the field rotates while all the current produced passes only through the stator winding. The brushes bear against continuous slip rings rather than a commutator. This causes the current produced to periodically reverse the direction of its flow. Diodes (electrical one-way switches) block the flow of current from traveling in the wrong direction. A series of diodes is wired together to permit the alternating flow of the stator to be converted to a pulsating, but unidirectional flow at the alternator output. The alternator's field is wired in series with the voltage regulator.

The regulator consists of several circuits. Each circuit has a core, or magnetic coil of wire, which operates a switch. Each switch is connected to ground through one or more resistors. The coil of wire responds directly to system voltage. When the voltage reaches the required level, the magnetic field created by the winding of wire closes the switch and inserts a resistance into the generator field circuit, thus reducing the output. The contacts of the switch cycle open and close many times each second to precisely control voltage.

While alternators are self-limiting as far as maximum current is concerned, DC generators employ a current regulating circuit which responds directly to the total amount of current flowing through the generator circuit rather than to the output voltage. The current regulator is similar to the voltage regulator except that all system current must flow through the energizing coil on its way to the various accessories.

Ignition Coil

TESTING, REMOVAL AND INSTALLATION

1. A 6-cylinder EST distributor with coil-in-cap is illustrated.
2. Detach wiring connector from cap, as shown.
3. Turn four latches and remove cap and coil assembly from lower housing.
4. Connect ohmmeter. Test 1.
5. Reading should be zero, or nearly zero. If not, replace coil. Step 8.
6. Connect ohmmeter both ways. Test 2. Use high scale. Replace coil only if both readings are infinite. Step 8.
7. If coil is good, go to Step 13.

8. Remove coil cover attaching screws and lift off cover.
9. Remove ignition coil attaching screws and lift coil with leads from cap.
10. Remove ignition coil arc seal.
11. Clean with soft cloth and inspect cap for defects. Replace, if needed.
12. Assemble new coil and cover to cap.
13. On all distributors, including distributors with Hall Effect Switch identified in Step 27, remove rotor and pickup coil leads from module.
14. Connect ohmmeter Test 1 and then Test 2.
15. If vacuum unit is used, connect vacuum source to vacuum unit. Replace unit if inoperative. Observe ohmmeter throughout vacuum range: flex leads by hand without vacuum to check for intermittent opens.
16. Test 1 should read infinite at all times. Test 2 should read steady at one value within 500-1,500Ω range.

NOTE: *Ohmmeter may deflect if operating vacuum unit causes teeth to align. This is not a defect.*

17. If pickup coil is defective, go to Step 18. If okay, go to Step 23.
18. Mark distributor shaft and gear so they can be reassembled in same position.
19. Drive out roll pin.
20. Remove gear and pull shaft assembly from distributor.
21. Remove three attaching screws and remove magnetic shield.

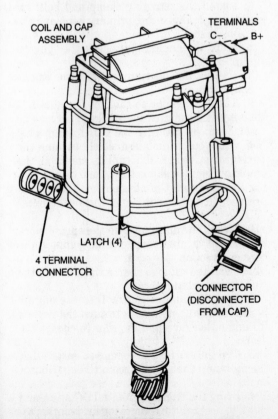

"COIL IN CAP" DISTRIBUTOR

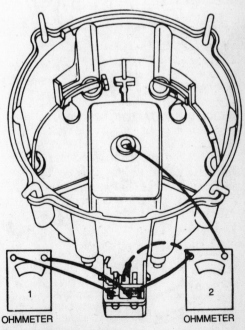

TESTING IGNITION COIL

22. Remove retaining ring and remove pick-up coil, magnet and pole piece.

23. Remove two module attaching screws, and capacitor attaching screw. Lift module, capacitor and harness assembly from base.

24. Disconnect wiring harness from module.

25. Check module with an approved module tester.

26. Install module, wiring harness, and capacitor assembly. Use silicone lubricant on housing under module.

27. The procedures previously covered, Steps 1-26, apply also to distributors with Hall Effect Switches.

Ignition Module
REMOVAL AND INSTALLATION

1. Remove distributor cap and rotor.

2. Remove two module attaching screws, and capacitor attaching screw. Lift module, capacitor and harness assembly from base.

3. Disconnect wiring harness from module.

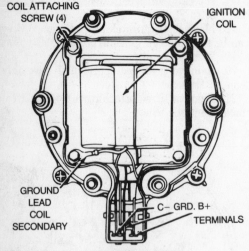

COIL ATTACHING SCREW (4)

IGNITION COIL

GROUND LEAD COIL SECONDARY

C– GRD. B+ TERMINALS

IGNITION COIL ATTACHING SCREWS

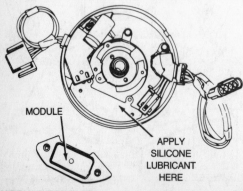

MODULE

APPLY SILICONE LUBRICANT HERE

MODULE REMOVED

4. Check module with approved module tester.

5. Install module, wiring harness, and capacitor assembly. Use silicone lubricant on housing under module.

Distributor
REMOVAL AND INSTALLATION
1970-74

1. Remove the distributor cap and position it out of the way.

2. Disconnect the primary coil wire and the vacuum advance line.

3. Scribe a mark on the distributor body and the engine block showing their relationship. Mark the distributor housing to show the direction in which the rotor is pointing. Note the positioning of the vacuum advance unit.

4. Remove the holddown bolt and clamp and remove the distributor.

To install the distributor with the engine undisturbed:

5. Reinsert the distributor into its opening, aligning the previously made marks on the housing and the engine block.

6. The rotor may have to be turned either way a slight amount to align the rotor-to-housing marks.

7. Install the retaining clamp and bolt. Install the distributor cap, primary wire, and the vacuum hose.

8. Start the engine and check the ignition timing.

To install the distributor with the engine disturbed:

9. Turn the engine so the No. 1 piston is at the top of its compression stroke. This may be determined by covering the No. 1 spark plug hole with your thumb and slowly turning the engine over. When the timing mark on the crankshaft pulley aligns with the 0 on the timing scale and your thumb is pushed out by compression, No. 1 piston is at top dead center (TDC).

10. Install the distributor to the engine block so that the vacuum advance unit points in the correct direction.

11. Turn the rotor so that it will point to the No. 1 terminal in the cap.

12. Install the distributor into the engine block. It may be necessary to turn the rotor a little in either direction in order to engage the gears.

13. Tap the starter a few times to ensure that the oil pump shaft is mated to the distributor shaft.

14. Bring the engine to No. 1 TDC again and check to see that the rotor is indeed pointing toward the No. 1 terminal of the cap.

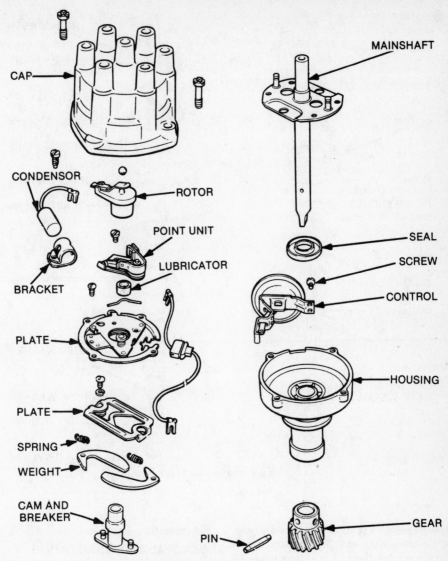

Six cylinder point-type distributor

15. After correct positioning is assured, turn the distributor housing so that the points are just opening. Tighten the retaining clamp.

16. Install the cap and primary wire. Check the ignition timing. Install the vacuum hose.

1975 and Later

1. Disconnect the wiring harness connectors at the side of the distributor cap.

2. Remove the distributor cap and lay it aside.

3. Disconnect the vacuum advance line.

4. Scribe a mark on the engine in line with the rotor and note the approximate position of the vacuum advance unit in relation to the engine.

5. Remove the distributor holddown clamp and nut.

6. Lift the distributor from the engine.

7. Installation is the same as for the standard (1970-74) distributor.

Alternator

Three basic alternators are used; the 5.5″ series ID Delcotron, the 6.2″ series 150 Delcotron and the integral regulator 10 SI Delcotron.

ALTERNATOR PRECAUTIONS

1. When installing a battery, ensure that the ground polarity of the battery, the alternator and the regulator are the same.

2. When connecting a jumper battery, be certain that the correct terminals are connected.

3. When charging, connect the correct charger leads to the battery terminals.

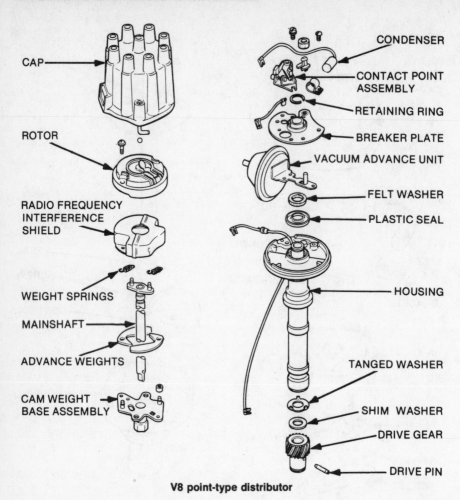

CAP

ROTOR

RADIO FREQUENCY INTERFERENCE SHIELD

WEIGHT SPRINGS

MAINSHAFT

ADVANCE WEIGHTS

CAM WEIGHT BASE ASSEMBLY

CONDENSER

CONTACT POINT ASSEMBLY

RETAINING RING

BREAKER PLATE

VACUUM ADVANCE UNIT

FELT WASHER

PLASTIC SEAL

HOUSING

TANGED WASHER

SHIM WASHER

DRIVE GEAR

DRIVE PIN

V8 point-type distributor

4. Never operate the alternator on an open circuit. Be sure that all connections in the charging circuit are tight.

5. Do not short across or ground any of the terminals on the alternator or regulator.

6. Never polarize an AC system.

REMOVAL AND INSTALLATION

1. Disconnect the battery ground cable.

2. Disconnect and tag all wiring to the alternator.

3. Remove the alternator brace bolt. If the truck is equipped with power steering, loosen the pump brace and mount nuts.

4. Remove the drive belt(s).

5. Support the alternator and remove the mounting bolts. Remove the alternator from the truck.

6. Installation is the reverse of removal. Adjust the belt(s) to have ¼-½" depression under thumb pressure on its longest run.

Regulator

REMOVAL AND INSTALLATION

1970-72

1. Disconnect the ground cable from the battery.

2. Disconnect the wiring harness from the regulator.

3. Remove the mounting screws and remove the regulator.

4. Make sure that the regulator base gasket is in place before installation.

5. Clean the attaching area for proper grounding.

6. Install the regulator. Do not overtighten the mounting screws, as this will cancel the cushioning effect of the rubber grommets.

VOLTAGE ADJUSTMENT

The standard voltage regulator from 1970-72 is a conventional double contact unit, although an optional transistorized regulator was avail-

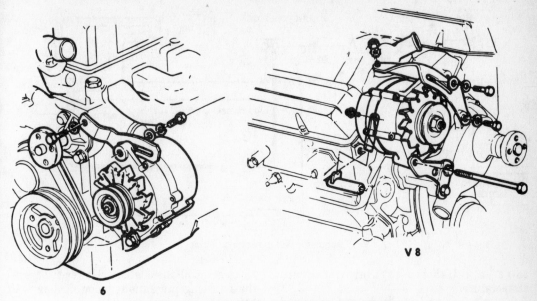

Typical alternator mounting, inline sixes and gasoline V8

able. Voltage adjustment procedures are the same for both types except for the point of adjustment. The double contact adjusting screw is located under the cover and the transistorized regulator is adjusted externally after removing an allen screw from the adjustment hole. On 1973 and later models, the 10 SI Delcotron is used which is equipped with an integral regulator that cannot be adjusted.

1. Insert a ¼Ω, 25 watt fixed resistor into the charging circuit at the horn relay junction block, between both leads and the terminal. Use a ½Ω, 25 watt resistor for 1971-72.

2. Install a voltmeter as shown in the figure.

3. Warm the engine by running it for several minutes at 1,500 rpm or more.

4. Cycle the voltage regulator by disconnecting and reconnecting the regulator connector.

5. Read the voltage on the voltmeter. If it is between 13.5 and 15.2, the regulator does not need adjustment or replacement. If the voltage is not within these limits, leave the engine running at 1,500 rpm.

6. Disconnect the four terminal connector and remove the regulator cover (except on transistorized regulators). Reconnect the four terminal connector and adjust the voltage to between 14.2 and 14.6 volts by turning the adjusting screw while observing the volt meter.

7. Disconnect the terminal, install the cover, and then reconnect the terminal.

8. Continue running the engine at 1,500 rpm

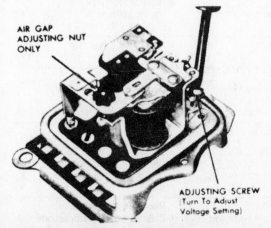

Conventional regulator voltage adjustment

Transistorized regulator voltage adjustments

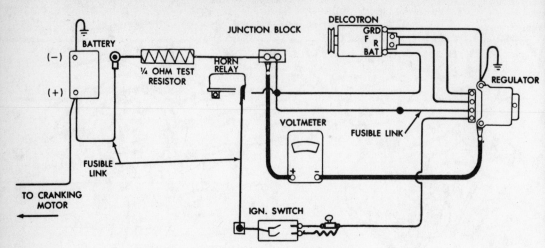

Regulator voltage setting circuit

to re-establish the regulator internal temperature.

9. Cycle the regulator by disconnecting and reconnecting the regulator connector. Check the voltage. If the voltage is between 13.5 and 15.2, the regulator is good.

WARNING: *Always disconnect the regulator before removing or installing the cover in order to prevent damage by short circuiting.*

Battery

Refer to Chapter 1 for battery maintenance. Battery installation and removal varies with the truck model and series, making it impossi-

ble to detail all installations. However, observe the following precautions when dealing with batteries:

1. Always disconnect the grounded (negative) terminal first and install it last to avoid short circuits and sparks. Special pullers are available to remove clamp-type battery terminals.

2. Be sure that the battery tray is clean and free of debris, so that the battery will seat squarely.

3. When installing batteries, tighten the holddown strap or clamp snugly, but not with such force that it cracks the cover or case.

4. Be sure that the cables are in good condi-

Troubleshooting Basic Charging System Problems

Problem	Cause	Solution
Noisy alternator	• Loose mountings • Loose drive pulley • Worn bearings • Brush noise • Internal circuits shorted (High pitched whine)	• Tighten mounting bolts • Tighten pulley • Replace alternator • Replace alternator • Replace alternator
Squeal when starting engine or accelerating	• Glazed or loose belt	• Replace or adjust belt
Indicator light remains on or ammeter indicates discharge (engine running)	• Broken fan belt • Broken or disconnected wires • Internal alternator problems • Defective voltage regulator	• Install belt • Repair or connect wiring • Replace alternator • Replace voltage regulator
Car light bulbs continually burn out—battery needs water continually	• Alternator/regulator overcharging	• Replace voltage regulator/alternator
Car lights flare on acceleration	• Battery low • Internal alternator/regulator problems	• Charge or replace battery • Replace alternator/regulator
Low voltage output (alternator light flickers continually or ammeter needle wanders)	• Loose or worn belt • Dirty or corroded connections • Internal alternator/regulator problems	• Replace or adjust belt • Clean or replace connections • Replace alternator or regulator

Alternator and Regulator Specifications

| Year | Alternator | | | Regulator |
	Part No. or Manufacturer	Field Current @ 12 V	Output (amps)	
'70–74	ID & 10 DN	1.5–3.2	37	13.8–14.8
	ID/10 DN	1.5–3.2	42	13.8–14.8
	ID/10 DN	1.5–3.2	55	13.8–14.8
	ID/10 DN	1.5–3.2	61	13.8–14.8
	ID/10 DN	1.5–3.2	63	13.8–14.8
	ID/10 DN	1.5–3.2	64	13.8–14.8
'70–'74	10 SI		37	14V ± .3V
	10 SI		42	14V ± .3V
	10 SI		55	14V ± .3V
	10 SI		61	14V ± .3V
	10 SI		63	14V ± .3V
	10 SI		80	14V ± .3V
'75–'77	1100497	4.4–4.9	37	①
	1100934	4.4–4.5	37	①
	1102394 1102483, 91 1102889	4.0–4.5	37	①
	1102346, 49, 82 1102485 1102841, 87 1100573	4.0–4.5	42	①
	1100560, 75 1102478, 79, 93	4.0–4.5	55	①
	1100597 1102347, 50, 83 1102480, 86, 90 1102886, 88	4.0–4.5	61	①
'78–'82	1102394 1102491 1102889	4.0–4.5	37	①
	1102485 1102841, 87	4.0–4.5	42	①
	1102480, 86 1102886, 88	4.0–4.5	61	①
	1101016, 28	4.0–4.5	80	①
'83–'86	1105185		37	①
	1100227		37	①
	1100204		37	①
	1100203		37	①
	1100207		66	①
	1100249		66	①
	1100275		66	①
	1100242		66	①
	1100208		66	①

Alternator and Regulator Specifications (cont.)

| Year | Alternator | | | Regulator |
	Part No. or Manufacturer	Field Current @ 12 V	Output (amps)	
'83–'86	1100241		66	①
	1100209		78	①
	1100273		78	①
	1100276		78	①
	1100217		78	①
	1100259		78	①
'87	1101241	4.2–5.0	94	①
	1101242	4.5–5.0	66	①
	1101240	4.2–5.0	94	①
	1105720	6.0–7.5	66	①
	1101243	4.2–5.0	66	①
	1101240	4.2–5.0	94	①
	1105720	6.0–7.5	105	①
	1105628	4.5–5.0	78	①
	1105632	4.5–5.0	66	①
	1105661	6.0–7.5	105	①
	1101244	4.0–5.0	66	①
	1101245	4.2–5.0	94	①

—Not available
NA Not applicable
① All alternators use integral regulators

tion and that the terminal clamps are clean and tight. Wire brushes are available to clean these items. Make sure that the ground cable is clean and tight at the engine block or frame. When installing cables, never hammer them in place. The terminals should be coated lightly with grease after installation to reduce corrosion.

5. Always check the battery polarity before installing cables. Reversed connections will destroy an alternator almost instantaneously.

Starter

No periodic lubrication of the starting motor or solenoid is required. Since the starting motor and brushes cannot be inspected without disassembling the unit, no service is required on these units.

REMOVAL AND INSTALLATION

The following is a general procedure for all trucks, and may vary slightly depending on model and series.

NOTE: *The starters on some engines require*

the addition of shims to provide proper clearance between the starter pinion gear and the flywheel. There shims are available in 0.015" sizes from Chevrolet dealers.

1. Disconnect the battery ground cable.
2. Raise and support the vehicle with jack stands.
3. Disconnect and tag all wires at the solenoid terminal.

NOTE: *1975 and later starters no longer have the R terminal. The High Energy Ignition System does not need a cable from solenoid to ignition coil.*

4. Reinstall all nuts as soon as they are removed, since the thread sizes are different.
5. Remove the front bracket from the starter and the two mounting bolts. On engines with a solenoid heat shield, remove the front bracket upper bolt and detach the bracket from the starter.
6. Remove the front bracket bolt or nut. Lower the starter front end first, and then remove the unit from the truck.
7. Reverse the removal procedures to install

the starter. Torque the two mounting bolts to 25-35 ft.lb.

SHIMMING THE STARTER

Starter noise during cranking and after the engine fires is often a result of too much or too little distance between the starter pinion gear and the flywheel. A high pitched whine during cranking (before the engine fires) can be caused by the pinion and flywheel being too far apart. Likewise, a whine after the engine starts (as the key is released) is often a result of the pinion-flywheel relationship being too close. In both cases flywheel damage can occur. Shims are available in 0.015″ sizes to properly adjust the starter on its mount. You will also need a flywheel turning tool, available at most auto parts stores or from any auto tool store or salesperson.

If your car's starter emits the above noises, follow the shimming procedure below:

1. Disconnect the negative battery cable.
2. Remove the flywheel inspection cover on the bottom of the bellhousing.
3. Using the flywheel turning tool, turn the flywheel and examine the flywheel teeth. If damage is evident, the flywheel should be replaced.
4. Insert a screwdriver into the small hole in the bottom of the starter and move the starter pinion and clutch assembly so the pinion and flywheel teeth mesh. If necessary, rotate the flywheel so that a pinion tooth is directly in the center of the two flywheel teeth and on the cen-

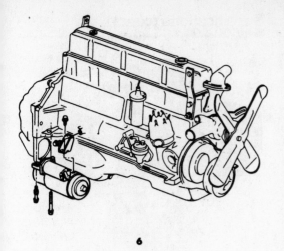
6

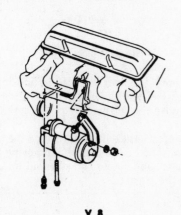
V 8

Typical starter mountings

1. Use shims as required
2. Shield

Starter Noise Diagnostic Procedure
1. Starter noise during cranking: remove 1–.015″ double shim or add single .015″ shim to *outer* bolt only.
2. High pitched whine after engine fires: add .015″ double shims until noise disappears.
See text for complete procedure.

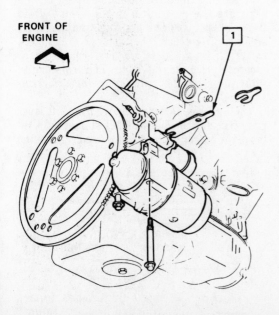

FRONT OF ENGINE

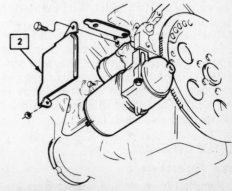

Shimming the starter motor; diesel 350 shown at right

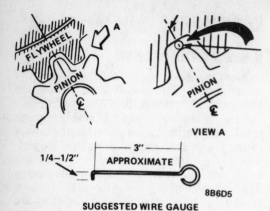

VIEW A

SUGGESTED WIRE GAUGE

8B6D5

Flywheel-to-pinion clearance check

A .015" SHIM WILL INCREASE THE
CLEARANCE APPROXIMATELY
.005". MORE THAN ONE SHIM
MAY BE REQUIRED.

Meshing starter teeth

terline of the two gears, as shown in the accompanying illustration.

5. Check the pinion-to-flywheel clearance by using a 0.020" wire gauge (a spark plug wire gauge may work here, or you can make your own). Make sure you center the pinion tooth between the flywheel teeth and the gauge—NOT in the corners, as you may get a false reading. If the clearance is under this minimum, shim the starter away from the flywheel by adding shim(s) one at a time to the starter mount. Check clearance after adding each shim.

6. If the clearance is a good deal over 0.020" (in the vicinity of 0.050" plus), shim the starter towards the flywheel. Broken or severely mangled flywheel teeth are also a good indicator that the clearance here is too great. Shimming the starter towards the flywheel is done by adding shims to the outboard starter mounting pad only. Check the clearance after each shim is added. A shim of 0.015" at this location will decrease the clearance about 0.010".

STARTER OVERHAUL

Solenoid Replacement

1. Remove the screw and washer from the field strap terminal.

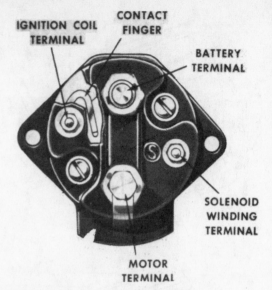

Starter solenoid terminals through 1974

2. Remove the two solenoid-to-housing retaining screws and the motor terminal bolt.

3. Remove the solenoid by twisting the unit 90 degrees.

4. To replace the solenoid, reverse the above procedure. Make sure the return spring is on the plunger, and rotate the solenoid unit into place on the starter.

Drive Replacement

1. Disconnect the field coil straps from the solenoid.

2. Remove the through-bolts (usually 2), and separate the commutator end frame, field frame assembly, drive housing, and armature assembly from each other.

NOTE: *On the diesel starters, remove the insulator from the end frame. The armature on the diesel starter remains in the drive end frame.*

3. On diesel starters, remove the shift lever pivot bolt. On the diesel 25 MT starter only, remove the center bearing screws and remove the

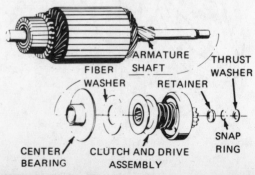

Starter drive assembly removed

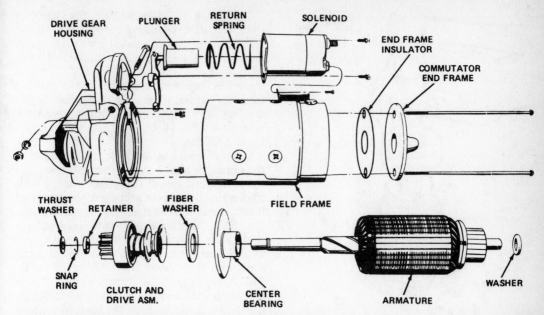

Exploded view of the 20MT starter motor used on the 350 diesel. Gasoline engine starters are almost identical; the only real difference is that they do not have the center bearing

drive gear housing from the armature shaft. The shift lever and plunger assembly will now fall away from the starter clutch.

4. Slide the two-piece thrust collar off the end of the armature shaft.

5. Slide a ⅝″ deep socket, piece of pipe or an old pinion onto the shaft so that the end of the pipe, socket, or pinion butts up against the edge of the pinion retainer.

6. Place the lower end of the armature securely on a soft surface, such as a wooden block or thick piece of foam rubber. Tap the end of the socket, pipe or pinion, driving the retainer towards the armature end of the snapring.

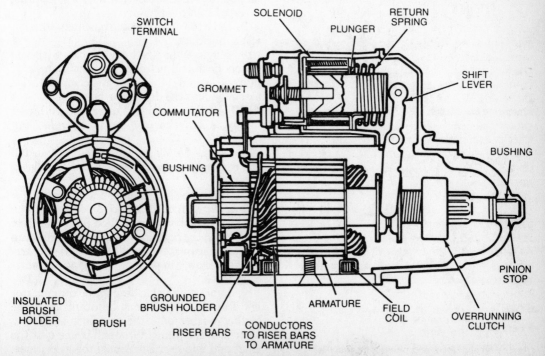

Cross-section of 10MT starter motor

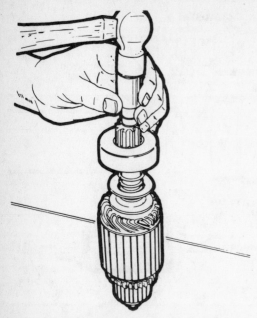

Use a piece of pipe or an old socket to drive the retainer toward the snap-ring

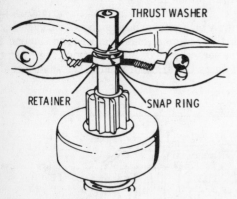

Snap-ring installation

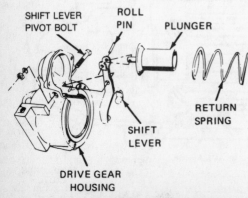

Removing shift lever and plunger from starter

7. Remove the snapring from the groove in the armature shaft with a pair of pliers. If the snapring is distorted, replace it with a new one during reassembly. Slide the retainer and starter drive from the shaft; on diesel starters, remove the fiber washer and the center bearing from the armature shaft. On gasoline engine starters, the shift lever and plunger may be disassembled at this time (if necessary) by removing the roll pin.

8. To reassemble, lubricate the drive end of the armature shaft with silicone lubricant. On diesel starters, install the center bearing with the bearing toward the armature winding, then install the fiber washer on the armature shaft.

9. Slide the starter drive onto the armature shaft with the pinion facing outward (away from the armature). Slide the retainer onto the shaft with the cupped surace facing outward.

10. Again support the armature on a soft surface, with the pinion on the upper end. Center the snapring on the top of the shaft (use a new ring if the old one was misshapen or damaged). Gently place a block of wood on top of the snapring so as not to move it from a centered position. Tap the wooden block with a hammer in order to force the snapring around the shaft. Slide the ring down into the snap groove.

11. Lay the armature down flat on your work surface. Slide the retainer close up onto the shaft and position it and the thrust collar next to the snapring. Using two pairs of pliers on opposite ends of the shaft, squeeze the thrust collar and the retainer together until the snapring is forced into the retainer.

12. Lube the drive housing bushing with a silicone lubricant.

13. Engage the shift lever yoke with the clutch. Position the front of the armature shaft into the bushing, then slide the complete drive assembly into the drive gear housing.

NOTE: *On non-diesel starters the shift lever may be installed in the drive gear housing first.*

14. On the 25 MT diesel starter only, install the center bearing screws and the shift lever pivot bolt, and tighten securely.

15. Apply a sealing compound approved for this application onto the drive housing, to the solenoid flange where the field frame contacts it. Position the field frame around the armature shaft and against the drive housing. Work carefully and slowly to prevent damaging the starter brushes.

16. Lubricate the bushing in the commutator end frame with a silicone lubricant, place the leather washer onto the armature shaft, and then slide the commutator end frame over the shaft and into position against the field frame.

Starter Specifications

Year	Identification	Starter ③			
			No Load Test		
		Volts	Amps ①	rpm	
'70–'75	1108744 1108788 ②	9	50–80	5500–10,500	
	1108747 1108780 ②	9	50–80	3500–6000	
	1108748 1108781 ②	9	65–90	7500–10,500	
	1108748 1108781 ②	9	65–90	7500–10,500	
'76	1108778 ②	9	50–80	5500–10,500	
	1108780 ②	⑨	50–80	3500–6000	
	1108781 ②	⑨	65–90	7500–10,500	
	1108781 ②	9	65–90	7500–10,500	
'77–'82	1108778 ②	9	50–80	5500–10,500	
	1187780 ②	9	50–80	3500–6000	
	1109056 ②	9	50–80	5500–10,500	
	1109052 ②	9	65–95	7500–10,500	
	1108776 ②	9	65–95	7500–10,500	
	1108776 ②	9	65–95	7500–10,500	
'83–'86	1109561	9	50–75	6000–11,900	
	1109535	9	45–70	7000–11,900	
	1998241	10	65–95	7500–10,500	
	1998244	10	60–85	6800–10,500	
	1998211	10	65–95	7500–10,500	
	1998396	10	70–110	6500–10,700	
	1998397	10	70–110	6500–10,700	
	1109563	10	120–210	9000–13,400	
'87	1113589	10	120–210	9000–13,400	
	1113590	10	120–210	9000–13,400	
	1998560	10	70–110	6500–10,700	
	1998561	10	70–110	6500–10,700	
	1998562	10	70–110	6500–11,070	
	1998565	10	70–110	6500–10,700	

① Solenoid included
② "R" terminal removed
③ Brush spring tension is 35 oz. for all starters. Lock test is not recommended.

On diesel starters, install the insulator and then the end frame onto the shaft. Line up the bolt holes, then install and tighten the through-bolts (make sure they pass through the bolt holes in the insulator).

17. Connect the field coil straps to the **motor** terminal of the solenoid.

NOTE: *If replacement of the starter drive fails to cure improper engagements of the starter pinion to the flywheel, there may be defective parts in the solenoid and/or shift lever. The best procedure is to take the assembly to a shop where a pinion clearance check can be made by energizing the solenoid on a test bench. If the pinion clearance check can be made by energizing the solenoid on a test*

Troubleshooting Basic Starting System Problems

Problem	Cause	Solution
Starter motor rotates engine slowly	• Battery charge low or battery defective	• Charge or replace battery
	• Defective circuit between battery and starter motor	• Clean and tighten, or replace cables
	• Low load current	• Bench-test starter motor. Inspect for worn brushes and weak brush springs.
	• High load current	• Bench-test starter motor. Check engine for friction, drag or coolant in cylinders. Check ring gear-to-pinion gear clearance.
Starter motor will not rotate engine	• Battery charge low or battery defective	• Charge or replace battery
	• Faulty solenoid	• Check solenoid ground. Repair or replace as necessary.
	• Damage drive pinion gear or ring gear	• Replace damaged gear(s)
	• Starter motor engagement weak	• Bench-test starter motor
	• Starter motor rotates slowly with high load current	• Inspect drive yoke pull-down and point gap, check for worn end bushings, check ring gear clearance
	• Engine seized	• Repair engine
Starter motor drive will not engage (solenoid known to be good)	• Defective contact point assembly	• Repair or replace contact point assembly
	• Inadequate contact point assembly ground	• Repair connection at ground screw
	• Defective hold-in coil	• Replace field winding assembly
Starter motor drive will not disengage	• Starter motor loose on flywheel housing	• Tighten mounting bolts
	• Worn drive end busing	• Replace bushing
	• Damaged ring gear teeth	• Replace ring gear or driveplate
	• Drive yoke return spring broken or missing	• Replace spring
Starter motor drive disengages prematurely	• Weak drive assembly thrust spring	• Replace drive mechanism
	• Hold-in coil defective	• Replace field winding assembly
Low load current	• Worn brushes	• Replace brushes
	• Weak brush springs	• Replace springs

bench. If the pinion clearance is incorrect, disassemble the solenoid and shift lever, inspect, and replace the worn parts.

Brush Replacement

1. Disassemble the starter by following steps 1 and 2 of the Drive Replacement procedure above.

2. Replace the brushes one at a time to avoid having to mark the wiring. For each brush: remove the brush holding screw; remove the old brush and position the new brush in the same direction (large end toward center of field frame), position the wire connector on top of the brush, line up the holes, and reinstall the screw. Make sure the screw is snug enough to ensure good contact.

3. Reassemble starter according to steps 8-17 above.

ENGINE MECHANICAL

Design

All Chevrolet and GMC truck engines, whether 6-cylinder or V8, are water-cooled, overhead valve powerplants. All engines use cast iron cylinder blocks and heads.

The 6-250 and 6-292 inline engines are all very similar in design although some 6-250s have an integral cylinder head and intake manifold beginning 1975. Crankshafts are supported in seven main bearings, with the thrust taken by No. 7. The camshaft is low in the block and driven by the crankshaft gear; no timing chain is used. Relatively long pushrods actuate the valve through ball jointed rocker arms.

The small block family of engines, which includes the 8-283, 8-305, 8-307, 8-327, 8-350, and 8-400 blocks, have all sprung from the basic design of the 1955 265 cu in. engine. It was this engine that introduced the ball joint rocker arm design which is now used by many car makers. This line of engines features a great deal of interchangeability, and later parts may be utilized on earlier engines for increased reliability and/or performance.

The Chevrolet built V6 262 cu. in. engine introduced in 1986 evolved from the small block V8 family of engines and share many of the same parts.

The 8-396, 8-402, and 8-454 engines are known as the Mark IV engines or big blocks. These engines feature unusual cylinder heads, in that the intake and exhaust valves are canted at the angle at which their respective port enters the cylinder. The big block cylinder heads use ball joint rockers similar to those on the small block engines.

Two V8 diesel engines have been available in the Chevrolet pick-ups since 1978. The first was the Oldsmobile built 8-350 engine which was derived from a gasoline engine of the same displacement. Internal engine components such as the crankshaft, main bearings, connecting rods, pistons, writs pins and piston rings all are heavier made to withstand the considerably higher pressures and stresses common to diesel engines.

Diesel ignition occurs because of heat developed in the combustion chamber during compression. This is the reason for the diesel's high compression ratio (22.5:1). Because the fuel ignites under compression, the need for spark plugs and high voltage ignition is eliminated.

A new V8 diesel of 379 cu. in (6.2L) was introduced for the pick-ups in 1982, superceding the 350. This engine is built by Chevrolet; GM's Detroit Diesel Division aided in much of the engine's design. The 379 is even stronger, component by component, than the 350. Designed "from the block up" as a diesel, it utilizes robust features such as four-bolt main bearing caps.

Engine Overhaul Tips

Most engine overhaul procedures are fairly standard. In addition to specific parts replacement procedures and complete specifications for your individual engine, this chapter also is a guide to accept rebuilding procedures. Examples of standard rebuilding practice are shown and should be used along with specific details concerning your particular engine.

Competent and accurate machine shop services will ensure maximum performance, reliability and engine life.

In most instances it is more profitable for the do-it-yourself mechanic to remove, clean and inspect the component, buy the necessary parts and deliver these to a shop for actual machine work.

On the other hand, much of the rebuilding work (crankshaft, block, bearings, piston rods, and other components) is well within the scope of the do-it-yourself mechanic.

TOOLS

The tools required for an engine overhaul or parts replacement will depend on the depth of your involvement. With a few exceptions, they will be the tools found in a mechanic's tool kit (see Chapter 1). More in-depth work will require any or all of the following:
- a dial indicator (reading in thousandths) mounted on a universal base
- micrometers and telescope gauges
- jaw and screw-type pullers
- scraper
- valve spring compressor
- ring groove cleaner
- piston ring expander and compressor
- ridge reamer
- cylinder hone or glaze breaker
- Plastigage®
- engine stand

The use of most of these tools is illustrated in this chapter. Many can be rented for a one-time use from a local parts jobber or tool supply house specializing in automotive work.

Occasionally, the use of special tools is called for. See the information on Special Tools and Safety Notice in the front of this book before substituting another tool.

INSPECTION TECHNIQUES

Procedures and specifications are given in this chapter for inspecting, cleaning and assessing the wear limits of most major components. Other procedures such as Magnaflux® and Zyglo® can be used to locate material flaws and stress cracks. Magnaflux® is a magnetic process applicable only to ferrous materials. The Zyglo® process coats the material with a fluorescent dye penetrant and can be used on any material Check for suspected surface cracks can be more readily made using spot check dye. The dye is sprayed onto the suspected area, wiped off and the area sprayed with a developer. Cracks will show up brightly.

OVERHAUL TIPS

Aluminum has become extremely popular for use in engines, due to its low weight. Observe the following precautions when handling aluminum parts:
- Never hot tank aluminum parts (the caustic hot tank solution will eat the aluminum.

- Remove all aluminum parts (identification tag, etc.) from engine parts prior to the tanking.
- Always coat threads lightly with engine oil or antiseize compounds before installation, to prevent seizure.
- Never overtorque bolts or spark plugs especially in aluminum threads.

Stripped threads in any component can be repaired using any of several commercial repair kits (Heli-Coil®, Microdot®, Keenserts®, etc.).

When assembling the engine, any parts that will be frictional contact must be prelubed to provide lubrication at initial start-up. Any product specifically formulated for this purpose can be used, but engine oil is not recommended as a prelube.

When semi-permanent (locked, but removable) installation of bolts or nuts is desired, threads should be cleaned and coated with Loctite® or other similar, commercial non-hardening sealant.

REPAIRING DAMAGED THREADS

Several methods of repairing damaged threads are available. Heli-Coil® (shown here), Keenserts® and Microdot® are among the most widely used. All involve basically the same principle – drilling out stripped threads, tapping the hole and installing a prewound insert – making welding, plugging and oversize fasteners unnecessary.

Two types of thread repair inserts are usually supplied: a standard type for most Inch Coarse, Inch Fine, Metric Course and Metric Fine thread sizes and a spark lug type to fit most spark plug port sizes. Consult the individual manufacturer's catalog to determine exact applications. Typical thread repair kits will contain a selection of prewound threaded inserts, a tap (corresponding to the outside diameter threads of the insert) and an installation tool. Spark plug inserts usually differ because they require a tap equipped with pilot threads and a

Standard thread repair insert (left) and spark plug thread insert (right)

Drill out the damaged threads with specified drill. Drill completely through the hole or to the bottom of a blind hole

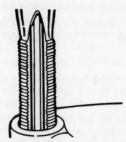

With the tap supplied, tap the hole to receive the thread insert. Keep the tap well oiled and back it out frequently to avoid clogging the threads

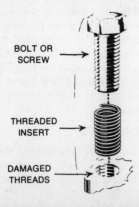

Damaged bolt holes can be repaired with thread repair inserts

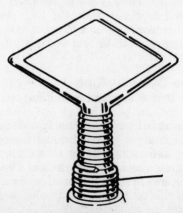

Screw the threaded insert onto the installation tool until the tang engages the slot. Screw the insert into the tapped hole until it is ¼–½ turn below the top surface. After installation break off the tang with a hammer and punch

combined reamer/tap section. Most manufacturers also supply blister-packed thread repair
inserts separately in addition to a master kit
containing a variety of taps and inserts plus installation tools.

Before effecting a repair to a threaded hole,
remove any snapped, broken or damaged bolts
or studs. Penetrating oil can be used to free frozen threads. The offending item can be removed with locking pliers or with a screw or
stud extractor. After the hole is clear, the
thread can be repaired, as shown in the series of
accompanying illustrations.

Checking Engine Compression

A noticeable lack of engine power, excessive
oil consumption and/or poor fuel mileage measured over an extended period are all indicators
of internal engine war. Worn piston rings,
scored or worn cylinder bores, blown head gaskets, sticking or burnt valves and worn valve
seats are all possible culprits here. A check of
each cylinder's compression will help you locate
the problems.

As mentioned in the Tools and Equipment
section of Chapter 1, a screw-in type compression gauge is more accurate that the type you
simply hold against the spark plug hole, although it takes slightly longer to use. It's worth
it to obtain a more accurate reading. Follow the
procedures below.

Gasoline Engines

1. Warm up the engine to normal operating
temperature.
2. Remove all the spark plugs.
3. Disconnect the high tension lead from the
ignition coil.
4. On fully open the throttle either by operating the carburetor throttle linkage by hand or
by having an assistant floor the accelerator
pedal.
5. Screw the compression gauge into the no.1
spark plug hole until the fitting is snug.
WARNING: *Be careful not to crossthread the
plug hole. On aluminum cylinder heads use
extra care, as the threads in these heads are
easily ruined.*
6. Ask an assistant to depress the accelerator
pedal fully on both carbureted and fuel injected
vehicles. Then, while you read the compression
gauge, ask the assistant to crank the engine two
or three times in short bursts using the ignition
switch.
7. Read the compression gauge at the end of
each series of cranks, and record the highest of
these readings. Repeat this procedure for each
of the engine's cylinders. Compare the highest
reading of each cylinder to the compression

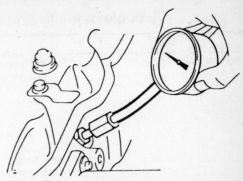

The screw-in type compression gauge is more
accurate

pressure specification in the Tune-Up Specifications chart in Chapter 2. The specs in this
chart are maximum values.

A cylinder's compression pressure is usually
acceptable if it is not less than 80% of maximum. The difference between any two cylinders should be no more than 12-14 pounds.

8. If a cylinder is unusually low, pour a table-
spoon of clean engine oil into the cylinder
through the spark plug hole and repeat the
compression test. If the compression comes up
after adding the oil, it appears that the cylinder's piston rings or bore are damaged or worn.
If the pressure remains low, the valves may not
be seating properly (a valve job is needed), or
the head gasket may be blown near that cylinder. If compression in any two adjacent cylinders is low, and if the addition of oil doesn't help
the compression, there is leakage past the head
gasket. Oil and coolant water in the combustion
chamber can result from this problem. There
may be evidence of water droplets on the engine
dipstick when a head gasket has blown.

Diesel Engines

Checking cylinder compression on diesel engines is basically the same procedure as on gasoline engines except for the following:

1. A special compression gauge adaptor suitable for diesel engines (because these engines
have much greater compression pressures)
must be used.

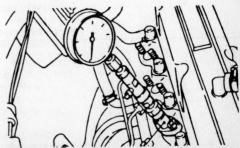

Diesel engines require a special compression
gauge adaptor

Troubleshooting Engine Mechanical Problems

Problem	Cause	Solution
External oil leaks	• Fuel pump gasket broken or improperly seated	• Replace gasket
	• Cylinder head cover RTV sealant broken or improperly seated	• Replace sealant; inspect cylinder head cover sealant flange and cylinder head sealant surface for distortion and cracks
	• Oil filler cap leaking or missing	• Replace cap
	• Oil filter gasket broken or improperly seated	• Replace oil filter
	• Oil pan side gasket broken, improperly seated or opening in RTV sealant	• Replace gasket or repair opening in sealant; inspect oil pan gasket flange for distortion
	• Oil pan front oil seal broken or improperly seated	• Replace seal; inspect timing case cover and oil pan seal flange for distortion
	• Oil pan rear oil seal broken or improperly seated	• Replace seal; inspect oil pan rear oil seal flange; inspect rear main bearing cap for cracks, plugged oil return channels, or distortion in seal groove
	• Timing case cover oil seal broken or improperly seated	• Replace seal
	• Excess oil pressure because of restricted PCV valve	• Replace PCV valve
	• Oil pan drain plug loose or has stripped threads	• Repair as necessary and tighten
	• Rear oil gallery plug loose	• Use appropriate sealant on gallery plug and tighten
	• Rear camshaft plug loose or improperly seated	• Seat camshaft plug or replace and seal, as necessary
	• Distributor base gasket damaged	• Replace gasket
Excessive oil consumption	• Oil level too high	• Drain oil to specified level
	• Oil with wrong viscosity being used	• Replace with specified oil
	• PCV valve stuck closed	• Replace PCV valve
	• Valve stem oil deflectors (or seals) are damaged, missing, or incorrect type	• Replace valve stem oil deflectors
	• Valve stems or valve guides worn	• Measure stem-to-guide clearance and repair as necessary
	• Poorly fitted or missing valve cover baffles	• Replace valve cover
	• Piston rings broken or missing	• Replace broken or missing rings
	• Scuffed piston	• Replace piston
	• Incorrect piston ring gap	• Measure ring gap, repair as necessary
	• Piston rings sticking or excessively loose in grooves	• Measure ring side clearance, repair as necessary
	• Compression rings installed upside down	• Repair as necessary
	• Cylinder walls worn, scored, or glazed	• Repair as necessary
	• Piston ring gaps not properly staggered	• Repair as necessary
	• Excessive main or connecting rod bearing clearance	• Measure bearing clearance, repair as necessary
No oil pressure	• Low oil level	• Add oil to correct level
	• Oil pressure gauge, warning lamp or sending unit inaccurate	• Replace oil pressure gauge or warning lamp
	• Oil pump malfunction	• Replace oil pump
	• Oil pressure relief valve sticking	• Remove and inspect oil pressure relief valve assembly
	• Oil passages on pressure side of pump obstructed	• Inspect oil passages for obstruction

Troubleshooting Engine Mechanical Problems (cont.)

Problem	Cause	Solution
No oil pressure (cont.)	• Oil pickup screen or tube obstructed	• Inspect oil pickup for obstruction
	• Loose oil inlet tube	• Tighten or seal inlet tube
Low oil pressure	• Low oil level	• Add oil to correct level
	• Inaccurate gauge, warning lamp or sending unit	• Replace oil pressure gauge or warning lamp
	• Oil excessively thin because of dilution, poor quality, or improper grade	• Drain and refill crankcase with recommended oil
	• Excessive oil temperature	• Correct cause of overheating engine
	• Oil pressure relief spring weak or sticking	• Remove and inspect oil pressure relief valve assembly
	• Oil inlet tube and screen assembly has restriction or air leak	• Remove and inspect oil inlet tube and screen assembly. (Fill inlet tube with lacquer thinner to locate leaks.)
	• Excessive oil pump clearance	• Measure clearances
	• Excessive main, rod, or camshaft bearing clearance	• Measure bearing clearances, repair as necessary
High oil pressure	• Improper oil viscosity	• Drain and refill crankcase with correct viscosity oil
	• Oil pressure gauge or sending unit inaccurate	• Replace oil pressure gauge
	• Oil pressure relief valve sticking closed	• Remove and inspect oil pressure relief valve assembly
Main bearing noise	• Insufficient oil supply	• Inspect for low oil level and low oil pressure
	• Main bearing clearance excessive	• Measure main bearing clearance, repair as necessary
	• Bearing insert missing	• Replace missing insert
	• Crankshaft end play excessive	• Measure end play, repair as necessary
	• Improperly tightened main bearing cap bolts	• Tighten bolts with specified torque
	• Loose flywheel or drive plate	• Tighten flywheel or drive plate attaching bolts
	• Loose or damaged vibration damper	• Repair as necessary
Connecting rod bearing noise	• Insufficient oil supply	• Inspect for low oil level and low oil pressure
	• Carbon build-up on piston	• Remove carbon from piston crown
	• Bearing clearance excessive or bearing missing	• Measure clearance, repair as necessary
	• Crankshaft connecting rod journal out-of-round	• Measure journal dimensions, repair or replace as necessary
	• Misaligned connecting rod or cap	• Repair as necessary
	• Connecting rod bolts tightened improperly	• Tighten bolts with specified torque
Piston noise	• Piston-to-cylinder wall clearance excessive (scuffed piston)	• Measure clearance and examine piston
	• Cylinder walls excessively tapered or out-of-round	• Measure cylinder wall dimensions, rebore cylinder
	• Piston ring broken	• Replace all rings on piston
	• Loose or seized piston pin	• Measure piston-to-pin clearance, repair as necessary
	• Connecting rods misaligned	• Measure rod alignment, straighten or replace
	• Piston ring side clearance excessively loose or tight	• Measure ring side clearance, repair as necessary
	• Carbon build-up on piston is excessive	• Remove carbon from piston

Troubleshooting Engine Mechanical Problems (cont.)

Problem	Cause	Solution
Valve actuating component noise	• Insufficient oil supply	• Check for: (a) Low oil level (b) Low oil pressure (c) Plugged push rods (d) Wrong hydraulic tappets (e) Restricted oil gallery (f) Excessive tappet to bore clearance
	• Push rods worn or bent	• Replace worn or bent push rods
	• Rocker arms or pivots worn	• Replace worn rocker arms or pivots
	• Foreign objects or chips in hydraulic tappets	• Clean tappets
	• Excessive tappet leak-down	• Replace valve tappet
	• Tappet face worn	• Replace tappet; inspect corresponding cam lobe for wear
	• Broken or cocked valve springs	• Properly seat cocked springs; replace broken springs
	• Stem-to-guide clearance excessive	• Measure stem-to-guide clearance, repair as required
	• Valve bent	• Replace valve
	• Loose rocker arms	• Tighten bolts with specified torque
	• Valve seat runout excessive	• Regrind valve seat/valves
	• Missing valve lock	• Install valve lock
	• Push rod rubbing or contacting cylinder head	• Remove cylinder head and remove obstruction in head
	• Excessive engine oil (four-cylinder engine)	• Correct oil level

Troubleshooting the Cooling System

Problem	Cause	Solution
High temperature gauge indication—overheating	• Coolant level low	• Replenish coolant
	• Fan belt loose	• Adjust fan belt tension
	• Radiator hose(s) collapsed	• Replace hose(s)
	• Radiator airflow blocked	• Remove restriction (bug screen, fog lamps, etc.)
	• Faulty radiator cap	• Replace radiator cap
	• Ignition timing incorrect	• Adjust ignition timing
	• Idle speed low	• Adjust idle speed
	• Air trapped in cooling system	• Purge air
	• Heavy traffic driving	• Operate at fast idle in neutral intermittently to cool engine
	• Incorrect cooling system component(s) installed	• Install proper component(s)
	• Faulty thermostat	• Replace thermostat
	• Water pump shaft broken or impeller loose	• Replace water pump
	• Radiator tubes clogged	• Flush radiator
	• Cooling system clogged	• Flush system
	• Casting flash in cooling passages	• Repair or replace as necessary. Flash may be visible by removing cooling system components or removing core plugs.
	• Brakes dragging	• Repair brakes
	• Excessive engine friction	• Repair engine
	• Antifreeze concentration over 68%	• Lower antifreeze concentration percentage
	• Missing air seals	• Replace air seals
	• Faulty gauge or sending unit	• Repair or replace faulty component
	• Loss of coolant flow caused by leakage or foaming	• Repair or replace leaking component, replace coolant
	• Viscous fan drive failed	• Replace unit

Troubleshooting the Cooling System (cont.)

Problem	Cause	Solution
Low temperature indication—undercooling	• Thermostat stuck open • Faulty gauge or sending unit	• Replace thermostat • Repair or replace faulty component
Coolant loss—boilover	• Overfilled cooling system • Quick shutdown after hard (hot) run • Air in system resulting in occasional "burping" of coolant • Insufficient antifreeze allowing coolant boiling point to be too low • Antifreeze deteriorated because of age or contamination • Leaks due to loose hose clamps, loose nuts, bolts, drain plugs, faulty hoses, or defective radiator • Faulty head gasket • Cracked head, manifold, or block • Faulty radiator cap	• Reduce coolant level to proper specification • Allow engine to run at fast idle prior to shutdown • Purge system • Add antifreeze to raise boiling point • Replace coolant • Pressure test system to locate source of leak(s) then repair as necessary • Replace head gasket • Replace as necessary • Replace cap
Coolant entry into crankcase or cylinder(s)	• Faulty head gasket • Crack in head, manifold or block	• Replace head gasket • Replace as necessary
Coolant recovery system inoperative	• Coolant level low • Leak in system • Pressure cap not tight or seal missing, or leaking • Pressure cap defective • Overflow tube clogged or leaking • Recovery bottle vent restricted	• Replenish coolant to FULL mark • Pressure test to isolate leak and repair as necessary • Repair as necessary • Replace cap • Repair as necessary • Remove restriction
Noise	• Fan contacting shroud • Loose water pump impeller • Glazed fan belt • Loose fan belt • Rough surface on drive pulley • Water pump bearing worn • Belt alignment	• Reposition shroud and inspect engine mounts • Replace pump • Apply silicone or replace belt • Adjust fan belt tension • Replace pulley • Remove belt to isolate. Replace pump. • Check pulley alignment. Repair as necessary.
No coolant flow through heater core	• Restricted return inlet in water pump • Heater hose collapsed or restricted • Restricted heater core • Restricted outlet in thermostat housing • Intake manifold bypass hole in cylinder head restricted • Faulty heater control valve • Intake manifold coolant passage restricted	• Remove restriction • Remove restriction or replace hose • Remove restriction or replace core • Remove flash or restriction • Remove restriction • Replace valve • Remove restriction or replace intake manifold

NOTE: *Immediately after shutdown, the engine enters a condition known as heat soak. This is caused by the cooling system being inoperative while engine temperature is still high. If coolant temperature rises above boiling point, expansion and pressure may push some coolant out of the radiator overflow tube. If this does not occur frequently it is considered normal.*

Troubleshooting the Serpentine Drive Belt

Problem	Cause	Solution
Tension sheeting fabric failure (woven fabric on outside circumference of belt has cracked or separated from body of belt)	· Grooved or backside idler pulley diameters are less than minimum recommended · Tension sheeting contacting (rubbing) stationary object · Excessive heat causing woven fabric to age · Tension sheeting splice has fractured	· Replace pulley(s) not conforming to specification · Correct rubbing condition · Replace belt · Replace belt
Noise (objectional squeal, squeak, or rumble is heard or felt while drive belt is in operation)	· Belt slippage · Bearing noise · Belt misalignment · Belt-to-pulley mismatch · Driven component inducing vibration · System resonant frequency inducing vibration	· Adjust belt · Locate and repair · Align belt/pulley(s) · Install correct belt · Locate defective driven component and repair · Vary belt tension within specifications. Replace belt.
Rib chunking (one or more ribs has separated from belt body)	· Foreign objects imbedded in pulley grooves · Installation damage · Drive loads in excess of design specifications · Insufficient internal belt adhesion	· Remove foreign objects from pulley grooves · Replace belt · Adjust belt tension · Replace belt
Rib or belt wear (belt ribs contact bottom of pulley grooves)	· Pulley(s) misaligned · Mismatch of belt and pulley groove widths · Abrasive environment · Rusted pulley(s) · Sharp or jagged pulley groove tips · Rubber deteriorated	· Align pulley(s) · Replace belt · Replace belt · Clean rust from pulley(s) · Replace pulley · Replace belt
Longitudinal belt cracking (cracks between two ribs)	· Belt has mistracked from pulley groove · Pulley groove tip has worn away rubber-to-tensile member	· Replace belt · Replace belt
Belt slips	· Belt slipping because of insufficient tension · Belt or pulley subjected to substance (belt dressing, oil, ethylene glycol) that has reduced friction · Driven component bearing failure · Belt glazed and hardened from heat and excessive slippage	· Adjust tension · Replace belt and clean pulleys · Replace faulty component bearing · Replace belt
"Groove jumping" (belt does not maintain correct position on pulley, or turns over and/or runs off pulleys)	· Insufficient belt tension · Pulley(s) not within design tolerance · Foreign object(s) in grooves · Excessive belt speed · Pulley misalignment · Belt-to-pulley profile mismatched · Belt cordline is distorted	· Adjust belt tension · Replace pulley(s) · Remove foreign objects from grooves · Avoid excessive engine acceleration · Align pulley(s) · Install correct belt · Replace belt
Belt broken (Note: identify and correct problem before replacement belt is installed)	· Excessive tension · Tensile members damaged during belt installation · Belt turnover · Severe pulley misalignment · Bracket, pulley, or bearing failure	· Replace belt and adjust tension to specification · Replace belt · Replace belt · Align pulley(s) · Replace defective component and belt

Troubleshooting the Serpentine Drive Belt (cont.)

Problem	Cause	Solution
Cord edge failure (tensile member exposed at edges of belt or separated from belt body)	• Excessive tension • Drive pulley misalignment • Belt contacting stationary object • Pulley irregularities • Improper pulley construction • Insufficient adhesion between tensile member and rubber matrix	• Adjust belt tension • Align pulley • Correct as necessary • Replace pulley • Replace pulley • Replace belt and adjust tension to specifications
Sporadic rib cracking (multiple cracks in belt ribs at random intervals)	• Ribbed pulley(s) diameter less than minimum specification • Backside bend flat pulley(s) diameter less than minimum • Excessive heat condition causing rubber to harden • Excessive belt thickness • Belt overcured • Excessive tension	• Replace pulley(s) • Replace pulley(s) • Correct heat condition as necessary • Replace belt • Replace belt • Adjust belt tension

2. Remove the injector tubes and remove the injectors from each cylinder.

WARNING: *Don't forget to remove the washer underneath each injector. Otherwise, it may get lost when the engine is cranked.*

3. When fitting the compression gauge adaptor to the cylinder head, make sure the bleeder of the gauge (if equipped) is closed.

4. When reinstalling the injector assemblies, install new washers underneath each injector.

Engine

REMOVAL AND INSTALLATION

The factory recommended procedure for engine removal is to remove the engine/transmission as a unit on two wheel drive models, except for the diesel. Only the engine should be removed on diesels and four wheel drive models.

1. Disconnect the negative battery terminal. On diesels, disconnect the negative cables at the batteries and ground wires at the inner fender panel.

2. Drain the cooling system.

CAUTION: *When draining the coolant, keep in mind that cats and dogs are attracted by the ethylene glycol antifreeze, and are quite likely to drink any that is left in an uncovered container or in puddles on the ground. This will prove fatal in sufficient quantity. Always drain the coolant into a sealable container. Coolant should be reused unless it is contaminated or several years old.*

3. Drain the engine oil.

4. Remove the air cleaner and ducts.

5. Scribe alignment marks around the hood hinges, and remove the hood.

6. Remove the radiator and hoses, and the fan shroud if so equipped.

7. Disconnect and label the wires at:
   a. Starter solenoid.
   b. Alternator.
   c. Temperature switch.
   d. Oil pressure switch.
   e. Transmission controlled spark solenoid.
   f. CEC solenoid.
   g. Coil.
   h. Neutral safety switch.

8. Disconnect:
   a. Accelerator linkage (hairpin at bellcrank, throttle and T.V. cables at intake manifold brackets on diesels.) Position away from the engine.
   b. Choke cable at carburetor (if so equipped).
   c. Release the fuel system pressure (see Chapter 1) and disconnect the fuel line to fuel pump.
   d. Heater hoses at engine.
   e. Air conditioning compressor with hoses attached. Do not remove the hoses from the air conditioning compressor. Remove it as a unit and set it aside. Its contents are under pressure, and can freeze body tissue on contact.
   f. Transmission dipstick and tube on automatic transmission models, except for diesel. Plug the tube hole.
   g. Oil dipstick and tube. Plug the hole.
   h. Vaccum lines.
   i. Oil pressure line to gauge, if so equipped.
   j. Parking brake cable.
   k. Power steering pump. This can be removed as a unit and set aside, without removing any of the hoses.
   l. Engine ground straps.
   m. Exhaust pipe (support if necessary).

9. Loosen and remove the fan belt, remove the fan blades and pulley. If you have the finned

General Engine Specifications

Year	Engine No. Cyl Displacement Cu In.	Fuel System	Advertised Horsepower @ rpm■	Advertised Torque @ rpm (ft. lbs.)■	Bore and Stroke (in.)	Advertised Compression Ratio	Oil Pressure @ 2000 rpm
1970	6-250	1 bbl	155 @ 4200	235 @ 1600	3.875 x 3.530	8.5:1	40
	6-292	1 bbl	170 @ 4000	275 @ 1600	3.875 x 4.120	8.0:1	40
	8-307	2 bbl	200 @ 4600	300 @ 2400	3.875 x 3.250	9.0:1	40
	8-350	2 bbl	215 @ 4400	320 @ 2400	4.000 x 3.480	8.0:1	40
	8-350	4 bbl	225 @ 4600	355 @ 3000	4.000 x 3.480	9.0:1	40
	8-396	4 bbl	310 @ 4800	400 @ 3200	4.125 x 3.760	9.0:1	40
1971	6-250	1 bbl	145 @ 4200	235 @ 1600	3.875 x 3.530	8.5:1	40
	6-292	1 bbl	165 @ 4000	270 @ 1600	3.875 x 4.120	8.0:1	40
	8-307	2 bbl	200 @ 4600	300 @ 2400	3.875 x 3.250	9.0:1	40
	8-307	2 bbl	215 @ 4800	305 @ 2800	3.875 x 3.250	8.5:1	40
	8-350	4 bbl	250 @ 4600	350 @ 3000	4.000 x 3.480	8.5:1	40
	8-402	4 bbl	300 @ 4800	400 @ 3200	4.125 x 3.760	8.5:1	40
1972	6-250	1 bbl	110 @ 3800	185 @ 1600	3.875 x 3.530	8.5:1	40
	6-292	1 bbl	125 @ 3600	225 @ 2400	3.875 x 4.120	8.0:1	40
	8-307	2 bbl	135 @ 4000	230 @ 2400	3.875 x 3.250	8.5:1	40
	8-350	4 bbl	175 @ 4000	290 @ 2400	4.000 x 3.480	8.5:1	40
	8-402	4 bbl	210 @ 4000	320 @ 2800	4.125 x 3.760	8.5:1	40
1973	6-250	1 bbl	100 @ 3800	175 @ 2000	3.875 x 3.530	8.25:1	40
	6-292	1 bbl	120 @ 3600	225 @ 2000	3.875 x 4.120	8.0:1	40
	8-307	2 bbl	115 @ 3600	205 @ 2000	3.875 x 3.250	8.5:1	40
	8-307	2 bbl	130 @ 4000	220 @ 2200	3.875 x 3.250	8.5:1	40
	8-350	4 bbl	155 @ 4000	255 @ 2400	4.000 x 3.480	8.5:1	40
	8-454	4 bbl	240 @ 4000	355 @ 2800	4.125 x 4.000	8.25:1	40
	8-454	4 bbl	250 @ 4000	365 @ 2800	4.125 x 4.000	8.25:1	40
1974	6-250	1 bbl	100 @ 3600	175 @ 1800	3.875 x 3.530	8.25:1	40
	6-292	1 bbl	120 @ 3600	215 @ 2000	3.875 x 4.120	8.0:1	40
	8-350	2 bbl	145 @ 3800	250 @ 2200	4.000 x 3.480	8.5:1	40
	8-350	4 bbl	160 @ 3800	250 @ 2400	4.000 x 3.480	8.5:1	40
	8-454	4 bbl	230 @ 4000	350 @ 2800	4.125 x 4.000	8.25:1	40
	8-454	4 bbl	245 @ 4000	365 @ 2800	4.125 x 4.000	8.25:1	40
1975	6-250	1 bbl	105 @ 3800	185 @ 1200	3.875 x 3.530	8.25:1	40
	6-292	1 bbl	120 @ 3600	213 @ 2000	3.875 x 4.120	8.0:1	40
	8-350	4 bbl	160 @ 3800	250 @ 2400	4.000 x 3.480	8.5:1	40
	8-400	4 bbl	175 @ 3600	290 @ 2800	4.125 x 3.750	8.5:1	40
	8-454	4 bbl	245 @ 4000	355 @ 3000 ①	4.125 x 4.000	8.25:1	40
1976	6-250	1 bbl	105 @ 3800	185 @ 1200	3.875 x 3.530	8.25:1	40–60
	6-250 HD	1 bbl	100 @ 3600	175 @ 1800	3.875 x 3.530	8.25:1	40–60
	6-292	1 bbl	120 @ 3600	215 @ 2000	3.870 x 4.120	8.0:1	40–60
	8-350	2 bbl	145 @ 3800	250 @ 2200	4.000 x 3.480	8.5:1	40

General Engine Specifications (cont.)

Year	Engine No. Cyl Displacement Cu In.	Fuel System	Advertised Horsepower @ rpm■	Advertised Torque @ rpm (ft. lbs.)■	Bore and Stroke (in.)	Advertised Compression Ratio	Oil Pressure @ 2000 rpm
1976	8-350	4 bbl	165 @ 3800	260 @ 2400 ②	4.000 x 3.480	8.5:1	40
	8-400	4 bbl	175 @ 3600	290 @ 2800	4.125 x 3.750	8.5:1	40
	8-454	4 bbl	245 @ 3800	365 @ 2800	4.251 x 4.000	8.25:1	40
	8-454 HD	4 bbl	240 @ 3800 ③	370 @ 2800 ④	4.251 x 4.000	8.15:1	40
1977	6-250	1 bbl	110 @ 3800	195 @ 1600	3.875 x 3.530	8.3:1	40–60
	6-250 HD	1 bbl	100 @ 3600	175 @ 1800	3.875 x 3.530	8.0:1	40–60
	6-292	1 bbl	120 @ 3600	215 @ 2000	3.870 x 4.120	8.0:1	40–60
	8-305 ⑤	2 bbl	145 @ 3800	245 @ 2200	3.740 x 3.480	8.5:1	40
	8-305 HD ⑤	2 bbl	140 @ 3800	235 @ 2000	3.740 x 3.480	8.5:1	40
	8-350	4 bbl	165 @ 3800	260 @ 2400 ②	4.000 x 3.480	8.5:1	40
	8-400	4 bbl	175 @ 3600	290 @ 2800	4.125 x 3.750	8.5:1	40
	8-454	4 bbl	245 @ 3800	365 @ 2800	4.251 x 4.000	8.25:1	40
	8-454 HD	4 bbl	240 @ 3800 ③	370 @ 2800 ④	4.251 x 4.000	8.15:1	40
1978	6-250 LD	1 bbl	115 @ 3800	195 @ 1600	3.870 x 3.530	8.0:1	40–60
	6-250 Calif	1 bbl	100 @ 3800	185 @ 1600	3.870 x 3.530	8.1:1	40–60
	6-250 HD	1 bbl	100 @ 3600	175 @ 1800	3.870 x 3.530	8.1:1	40–60
	6-292	1 bbl	120 @ 3600	215 @ 2000	3.870 x 4.120	8.0:1	40–60
	8-305	2 bbl	145 @ 3800	245 @ 2400	3.740 x 3.480	8.4:1	45
	8-350 LD	4 bbl	165 @ 3800	260 @ 2400	4.000 x 3.480	8.2:1	45
	8-350 HD	4 bbl	165 @ 3800	255 @ 2800	4.000 x 3.480	8.3:1	45
	8-350 Diesel	FI	120 @ 3600	220 @ 1600	4.057 x 3.385	22.5:1	35
	8-400	4 bbl	175 @ 3600	290 @ 2800	4.125 x 3.750	8.3:1	40
	8-400 Calif	4 bbl	165 @ 3600	290 @ 2000	4.125 x 3.750	8.2:1	40
	8-454 LD	4 bbl	205 @ 3600	335 @ 2800	4.250 x 4.000	8.0:1	40
	8-454 HD	4 bbl	240 @ 3800	370 @ 2800	4.250 x 4.000	7.9:1	40
	8-454 HD Calif	4 bbl	250 @ 3800	385 @ 2800	4.250 x 4.000	7.9:1	40
1979	6-250 LD	2 bbl	130 @ 3800	210 @ 2400	3.870 x 3.530	8.3:1	40–60
	6-250 Calif	2 bbl	125 @ 4000	205 @ 2000	3.870 x 3.530	8.3:1	40–60
	6-250 HD	2 bbl	130 @ 4000	205 @ 2000	3.870 x 3.530	8.3:1	40–60
	6-292	1 bbl	115 @ 3400	215 @ 1600	3.870 x 4.120	7.8:1	40–60
	8-305	2 bbl	140 @ 4000	240 @ 2000	3.740 x 3.480	8.4:1	45
	8-350 LD	4 bbl	165 @ 3600	270 @ 2000	4.000 x 3.480	8.2:1	45
	8-350 Hi Alt	4 bbl	155 @ 3600	260 @ 2000	4.000 x 3.480	8.2:1	45
	8-350 HD	4 bbl	165 @ 3800	255 @ 2800	4.000 x 3.480	8.3:1	45
	8-350 Diesel	FI	120 @ 3600	220 @ 1600	4.057 x 3.385	22.5:1	35
	8-400 HD	4 bbl	180 @ 3600	310 @ 2400	4.125 x 3.750	8.2:1	40
	8-454 LD	4 bbl	205 @ 3600	335 @ 2800	4.250 x 4.000	8.0:1	40
	8-454 HD	4 bbl	210 @ 3800	340 @ 2800	4.250 x 4.000	7.9:1	40

General Engine Specifications (cont.)

Year	Engine No. Cyl Displacement Cu In.	Fuel System	Advertised Horsepower @ rpm■	Advertised Torque @ rpm (ft. lbs.)■	Bore and Stroke (in.)	Advertised Compression Ratio	Oil Pressure @ 2000 rpm
1980	6-250	2 bbl	130 @ 4000	210 @ 2000	3.870 x 3.530	8.3:1	40–60
	6-250 Calif	2 bbl	130 @ 4000	205 @ 2000	3.870 x 3.530	8.3:1	40–60
	6-292	1 bbl	115 @ 3400	215 @ 1600	3.870 x 4.120	7.8:1	40–60
	8-305	2 bbl	135 @ 4200	235 @ 2400	3.740 x 3.480	8.5:1	45
	8-350 LD	4 bbl	175 @ 4000	275 @ 2400	4.000 x 3.480	8.2:1	45
	8-350 LD Calif	4 bbl	170 @ 4000	275 @ 2000	4.000 x 3.480	8.2:1	45
	8-350 HD	4 bbl	165 @ 3800	255 @ 2800	4.000 x 3.480	8.3:1	45
	8-350	Diesel	125 @ 3600	225 @ 1600	4.057 x 3.385	22.5:1	35
	8-400 HD	4 bbl	180 @ 3600	310 @ 2400	4.125 x 3.750	8.3:1	40
	8-454 HD	4 bbl	210 @ 3800	340 @ 2800	4.250 x 4.000	7.9:1	40
1981	6-250	2 bbl	130 @ 4000	210 @ 2000	3.870 x 3.530	8.3:1	40–60
	6-250 Calif	2 bbl	130 @ 4000	205 @ 2000	3.870 x 3.530	8.3:1	40–60
	6-292	1 bbl	115 @ 3400	215 @ 1600	3.870 x 4.120	7.8:1	40–60
	8-305	2 bbl	135 @ 4200	235 @ 2400	3.740 x 3.480	8.5:1	45
	8-305	4 bbl	155 @ 4400	252 @ 2400	3.740 x 3.480	9.2:1	45
	8-350 LD	4 bbl	175 @ 4000	275 @ 2000	4.000 x 3.480	8.2:1	45
	8-350 HD	4 bbl	165 @ 3800	255 @ 2800	4.000 x 3.480	8.3:1	45
	8-350	Diesel	125 @ 3600	225 @ 1600	4.057 x 3.385	22.5:1	35
	8-454	4 bbl	210 @ 3800	340 @ 2800	4.250 x 4.000	7.9:1	40
1982	6-250	2 bbl	130 @ 4000	210 @ 2000	3.870 x 3.530	8.3:1	40–60
	6-292	1 bbl	115 @ 3400	215 @ 1600	3.870 x 4.120	7.8:1	40–60
	8-305	4 bbl	140 @ 4200	240 @ 2400	3.740 x 3.480	8.5:1	45
	8-305	4 bbl	155 @ 4400	252 @ 2100	3.740 x 3.480	9.2:1	45
	8-350 LD	4 bbl	175 @ 4000	275 @ 2000	4.000 x 3.480	8.2:1	45
	8-350 HD	4 bbl	165 @ 3800	255 @ 2800	4.000 x 3.480	8.3:1	45
	8-379	Diesel	140 @ 3600	240 @ 2000	3.980 x 3.800	21.5:1	45
	8-454	4 bbl	210 @ 3800	340 @ 2800	4.250 x 4.000	7.9:1	40
1983–84	6-250	2 bbl	120 @ 4000	205 @ 2000	3.870 x 3.530	8.3:1	40–60
	6-292	1 bbl	115 @ 3600	215 @ 1600	3.870 x 4.120	7.8:1	40–60
	8-305 ⑥	4 bbl	160 @ 4400	235 @ 2000	3.740 x 3.480	8.5:1	45
	8-305 ⑦	4 bbl	155 @ 4000	245 @ 1600	3.740 x 3.480	9.2:1	45
	8-350 ⑥	4 bbl	165 @ 3800	275 @ 1600	4.000 x 3.480	8.2:1	45
	8-350 ⑦	4 bbl	155 @ 4000	240 @ 2800	4.000 x 3.480	8.2:1	45
	8-379	Diesel	140 @ 3600	240 @ 2000	3.980 x 3.800	21.5:1	45
	8-454	4 bbl	210 @ 3800	340 @ 2800	4.250 x 4.000	7.9:1	40
1985	6-250	4 bbl	115 @ 3600	200 @ 2000	4.000 x 4.000	9.3:1	40–60
	6-292	1 bbl	115 @ 3600	215 @ 1600	3.876 x 4.120	8.0:1	40–60
	8-305 ⑥	4 bbl	160 @ 4400	235 @ 2000	3.736 x 3.480	8.6:1	45

General Engine Specifications (cont.)

Year	Engine No. Cyl Displacement Cu In.	Fuel System	Advertised Horsepower @ rpm ■	Advertised Torque @ rpm (ft. lbs.) ■	Bore and Stroke (in.)	Advertised Compression Ratio	Oil Pressure @ 2000 rpm
1985	8-350 ⑦	4 bbl	155 @ 4000	240 @ 2800	4.000 x 3.480	8.3:1	45
	8-350 ⑥	4 bbl	165 @ 3800	275 @ 1600	4.000 x 3.480	8.2:1	45
	8-350 ⑦	4 bbl	155 @ 4000	240 @ 2800	4.000 x 3.480	8.3:1	45
	8-379	Diesel	130 @ 3600	240 @ 2000	3.980 x 3.800	21.5:1	45
	8-454	4 bbl	230 @ 3800	360 @ 2800	4.250 x 4.000	8.0:1	40
1986	6-292	1 bbl	115 @ 3400	215 @ 1600	3.870 x 4.120	8.0:1	50
	6-262	4 bbl	145 @ 4000	225 @ 2400	4.000 x 3.480	8.3:1	50
	8-305 ⑧	4 bbl	150 @ 3800	240 @ 2400	3.740 x 3.480	8.5:1	45
	8-305 ⑨	4 bbl	165 @ 4400	240 @ 2000	3.740 x 3.480	9.0:1	45
	8-350 ⑩	4 bbl	165 @ 3800	275 @ 1600	4.000 x 3.800	8.3:1	45
	8-350 ⑪	4 bbl	185 @ 4000	285 @ 2400	4.000 x 3.800	8.3:1	45
	8-454	4 bbl	240 @ 3800	375 @ 3200	4.250 x 4.000	8.0:1	40
1987	6-262	EFI	155 @ 4000	235 @ 2400	4.000 x 3.480	9.3:1	—
	8-305	EFI	170 @ 4400	250 @ 2400	3.740 x 3.480	9.0:1	—
	8-350	EFI ⑫	185 @ 4000	285 @ 2400	4.000 x 3.800	8.5:1	—
	8-454	EFI	240 @ 3800	375 @ 3200	4.250 x 4.000	8.0:1	—

■ Starting 1972, horsepower and torque are SAE net figures. They are measured at the rear of the transmission with all accessories installed and operating. Since the figures vary when a given engine is installed in different models, some are representative rather than exact.

① 375 @ 2800—Calif. ⑤ Not available in California ⑧ Eng. Code F ⑪ Eng. Code M
② 255 @ 2800 HD ⑥ 49-states ⑨ Eng. Code H ⑫ 195 @ 4000 for GVWR over 8500 lbs
③ 250 @ 3800—Calif. ⑦ California ⑩ Eng. Code L EFI Electronic Fuel Injection
④ 385 @ 2800—Calif.

Valve Specifications

Year	Engine No. Cyl Displacement (cu in.)	Seat Angle (deg)	Face Angle (deg)	Spring Test Pressure (lbs. @ in.)	Spring Installed Height (in.) ①	Stem to Guide Clearance (in.) Intake	Stem to Guide Clearance (in.) Exhaust	Stem Diameter (in.) Intake	Stem Diameter (in.) Exhaust
1970	6-250	46	45	186 @ 1.27	1 21/32	0.0010–0.0027	0.0015–0.0032	0.3414	0.3414
	6-292	46	45	180 @ 1.30	1 5/8	0.0010–0.0027	0.0015–0.0032	0.3414	0.3414
	8-307	46	45	200 @ 1.25	1 23/32	0.0010–0.0027	0.0010–0.0027	0.3414	0.3414
	8-350	46	45	200 @ 1.25	1 23/32	0.0010–0.0027	0.0010–0.0027	0.3414	0.3414
	8-396	46	45	220 @ 1.40	1 13/16	0.0017–0.0020	0.0019–0.0022	0.3414	0.3414
1971	6-250	46	45	186 @ 1.27	1 21/32	0.0010–0.0027	0.0015–0.0032	0.3414	0.3414
	6-292	46	45	180 @ 1.30	1 5/8	0.0010–0.0027	0.0015–0.0032	0.3414	0.3414
	8-307	46	45	200 @ 1.25	1 23/32	0.0010–0.0027	0.0010–0.0027	0.3414	0.3414
	8-350	46	45	200 @ 1.25	1 23/32	0.0010–0.0027	0.0010–0.0027	0.3414	0.3414
	8-402	46	45	240 @ 1.38	1 7/8	0.0010–0.0027	0.0012–0.0029	0.3414	0.3414
1972	6-250	46	45	186 @ 1.27	1 21/32	0.0010–0.0027	0.0015–0.0032	0.3414	0.3414
	6-292	46	45	180 @ 1.30	1 5/8	0.0010–0.0027	0.0015–0.0032	0.3414	0.3414

Valve Specifications (cont.)

Year	Engine No. Cyl Displacement (cu in.)	Seat Angle (deg)	Face Angle (deg)	Spring Test Pressure (lbs. @ in.)	Spring Installed Height (in.) ①	Stem to Guide Clearance (in.)		Stem Diameter (in.)	
						Intake	Exhaust	Intake	Exhaust
1972	8-307	46	45	200 @ 1.25	1²³⁄₃₂	0.0010–0.0027	0.0010–0.0027	0.3414	0.3414
	8-350	46	45	200 @ 1.25	1²³⁄₃₂	0.0010–0.0027	0.0010–0.0027	0.3414	0.3414
	8-402	46	46	240 @ 1.38	1⅞	0.0010–0.0027	0.0010–0.0029	0.3414	0.3414
1973	6-250	46	45	186 @ 1.27	1²¹⁄₃₂	0.0010–0.0027	0.0015–0.0032	0.3414	0.3414
	6-292	46	45	180 @ 1.30	1⅝	0.0010–0.0027	0.0015–0.0032	0.3414	0.3414
	8-307	46	45	200 @ 1.25	1⅝	0.0010–0.0027	0.0010–0.0027	0.3414	0.3414
	8-350	46	45	200 @ 1.25	1²³⁄₃₂	0.0010–0.0027	0.0010–0.0027	0.3414	0.3414
	8-454	46	45	300 @ 1.38	1⅞	0.0010–0.0027	0.0012–0.0029	0.3414	0.3414
1974	6-250	46	45	186 @ 1.27	1²¹⁄₃₂	0.0010–0.0027	0.0015–0.0032	0.3414	0.3414
	6-292	46	45	180 @ 1.30	1⅝	0.0010–0.0027	0.0015–0.0032	0.3414	0.3414
	8-350	46	45	200 @ 1.25	1²³⁄₃₂	0.0010–0.0027	0.0010–0.0027	0.3414	0.3414
	8-454	46	45	300 @ 1.38	1⅞	0.0010–0.0027	0.0012–0.0029	0.3414	0.3414
1975–80	6-250	46	45	186 @ 1.27 ②	1²¹⁄₃₂	0.0010–0.0027	0.0015–0.0032	0.3414	0.3414
	6-292	46	45 ⑤	180 @ 1.30 ⑥	1⅝ ⑦	0.0010–0.0027	0.0015–0.0032	0.3414	0.3414
	8-305	46	45	200 @ 1.25	③	0.0010–0.0027	0.0010–0.0027	0.3414	0.3414
	8-350	46	45	200 @ 1.25	③	0.0010–0.0027	0.0010–0.0027	0.3414	0.3414
	8-400	46	45	200 @ 1.25	③	0.0010–0.0027	0.0012–0.0029	0.3414	0.3414
	8-454	46	45	300 @ 1.38	1⅞	0.0010–0.0027	0.0012–0.0029	0.3719	0.3719
	8-350 Diesel	⑧	④	151 @ 1.30	1⁴³⁄₆₄	0.0010–0.0027	0.0015–0.0032	—	—
1981	6-250	46	45	175 @ 1.26	1.66	0.0010–0.0027	0.0015–0.0032	0.3414	0.3414
	6-292	46	46	175 @ 1.26	1.66	0.0010–0.0027	0.0015–0.0032	0.3414	0.3414
	8-305	46	45	200 @ 1.25 ⑨	1²³⁄₃₂ ⑩	0.0010–0.0027	0.0010–0.0027	0.3414	0.3414
	8-350	46	45	200 @ 1.25 ⑨	1²³⁄₃₂ ⑩	0.0010–0.0027	0.0010–0.0027	0.3414	0.3414
	8-350 Diesel	⑧	④	205 @ 1.30	—	0.0010–0.0027	0.0015–0.0032	—	—
	8-454	46	45	220 @ 1.40	1⁵¹⁄₆₄	0.0010–0.0027	0.0012–0.0029	0.3719	0.3719
1982–87	6-250	46	45	175 @ 1.26	1.66	0.0010–0.0027	0.0015–0.0032	0.3414	0.3414
	6-262	46	45	220 @ 1.25	1.70	0.0010–0.0027	0.0010–0.0027	0.3414	0.3414
	6-292	46	46	175 @ 1.26	1.66	0.0010–0.0027	0.0015–0.0032	0.3414	0.3414
	8-305	46	45	200 @ 1.25 ⑨	1²³⁄₃₂ ⑩	0.0010–0.0027	0.0010–0.0027	0.3414	0.3414
	8-350	46	45	200 @ 1.25 ⑨	1²³⁄₃₂ ⑩	0.0010–0.0027	0.0010–0.0027	0.3414	0.3414
	8-379 Diesel	46	45	740 @ 1.40	1¹³⁄₁₆	0.0010–0.0027	0.0010–0.0027	—	—
	8-454	46	45	220 @ 1.40	1⁵¹⁄₆₄	0.0010–0.0027	0.0012–0.0029	0.3719	0.3719

① ± ¹⁄₃₂ in.
② 172 @ 1.26 (1980)
③ Intake—1²³⁄₃₂
  Exhaust—1¹⁹⁄₃₂
④ Intake 44°
  Exhaust 30°
⑤ 1978–82: 46°
⑥ 185 @ 1.26 (1980)
⑦ 1978–82: 1²¹⁄₃₂
⑧ Intake 45°
  Exhaust 31°
⑨ 200 @ 1.16 exhaust
⑩ 1¹⁹⁄₃₂ exhaust

Camshaft Specifications
(All measurements in inches)

Year	Engine	Journal Diameter	Lobe Lift Intake	Lobe Lift Exhaust	Camshaft End Play
1970	6-250	1.8682–1.8692	.2217	.2217	—
	6-292	1.8682–1.8692	.2315	.2315	—
	8-307	1.8682–1.8692	.2600	.2733	—
	8-350	1.8682–1.8692	.2600	.2733	—
	8-396	1.9487–1.9497	.2343	.2343	—
1971	6-250	1.8682–1.8692	.2217	.2217	—
	6-292	1.8682–1.8692	.2315	.2315	—
	8-307	1.8682–1.8692	.2600	.2733	—
	8-350	1.8682–1.8692	.2600	.2733	—
	8-402	1.9487–1.9497	.2343	.2343	—
1972	6-250	1.8682–1.8692	.2217	.2217	—
	6-292	1.8682–1.8692	.2315	.2315	—
	8-307	1.8682–1.8692	.2600	.2733	—
	8-350	1.8682–1.8692	.2600	.2733	—
	8-402	1.9487–1.9497	.2343	.2343	—
1973	6-250	1.8682–1.8692	.2217	.2217	.001–.005
	6-292	1.8682–1.8692	.2315	.2315	.001–.005
	8-307	1.8682–1.8692	.2600	.2733	—
	8-350	1.8682–1.8692	.2600	.2733	—
	8-454	1.9482–1.9492	.2343	.2343	—
1974	6-250	1.8682–1.8692	.2217	.2217	.001–.005
	6-292	1.8682–1.8692	.2315	.2315	.001–.005
	8-350	1.8682–1.8692	.2600	.2733	—
	8-454	1.9482–1.9492	.2343	.2343	—
1975	6-250	1.8682–1.8692	.2217	.2217	—
	6-292	1.8682–1.8692	.2315	.2315	—
	8-350	1.8682–1.8692	.2600	.2733	—
	8-400	1.9482–1.9492	.2600	.2733	—
	8-454	1.9482–1.9492	.2590	.2590	—
1976	6-250	1.8682–1.8592	.2217	.2217	—
	6-292	1.8682–1.8692	.2315	.2315	—
	8-350	1.8682–1.8692	.2600	.2733	—
	8-400	1.9482–1.9492	.2600	.2733	—
	8-454	1.9482–1.9492	.2590	.2590	—
1977	6-250	1.8677–1.8697	.2217	.2217	.001–.005
	6-292	1.8677–1.8697	.2315	.2315	.001–.005
	8-305	1.8682–1.8692	.2485	.2485	—
	8-350	1.8682–1.8692	.2600	.2733	—
	8-400	1.9482–1.9492	.2600	.2733	—

Camshaft Specifications (cont.)

(All measurements in inches)

Year	Engine	Journal Diameter	Lobe Lift Intake	Lobe Lift Exhaust	Camshaft End Play
1977	8-454	1.9482–1.9492	.2343	.2343	—
1978	6-250	1.8677–1.8697	.2217	.2315	.003–.008
	6-292	1.8677–1.8697	.2217	.2315	.003–.008
	8-305	1.8682–1.8692	.2484	.2667	.004–.012
	8-350	1.8682–1.8692	.2600	.2733	.004–.012
	8-350 Diesel	—	—	—	.011–.077
	8-400	1.9482–1.9492	.2600	.2733	.004–.012
	8-454	1.9482–1.9492	.2343	.2343	.004–.012
1979	6-250	1.8677–1.8697	.2217	.2315	.003–.008
	6-292	1.8677–1.8697	.2217	.2315	.003–.008
	8-305	1.8682–1.8692	.2484	.2667	.004–.012
	8-350	1.8682–1.8692	.2600	.2733	.004–.012
	8-350 Diesel	—	—	—	—
	8-400	1.9482–1.9492	.2600	.2733	.004–.012
	8-454	1.9482–1.9492	.2343	.2343	.004–.012
1980	6-250	1.8677–1.8697	.2217	.2315	.003–.008
	6-292	1.8677–1.8697	.2315	.2315	.003–.008
	8-305	1.8682–1.8692	.2484	.2667	.004–.012
	8-350	1.8682–1.8692	.2600	.2733	.004–.012
	8-350 Diesel	①	—	—	.011–.077
	8-400	1.8682–1.8692	.2600	.2733	.004–.012
	8-454	1.9482–1.9492	.2343	.2530	—
1981	6-250	1.8677–1.8697	.2217	.2315	.003–.008
	6-292	1.8677–1.8697	.2315	.2315	.003–.008
	8-305	1.8682–1.8692	.2484	.2667	.004–.012
	8-350	1.8682–1.8692	.2600	.2733	.004–.012
	8-350 Diesel	①	—	—	.011–.077
	8-454	1.9482–1.9492	.2343	.2530	—
1982–87	6-250	1.8677–1.8697	.2217 ③	.2315	.003–.008
	6-292	1.8677–1.8697	.2315	.2315	.003–.008
	6-262	1.8682–1.8692	0.357	0.390	.004–0.012
	8-305	1.8682–1.8692	.2484	.2667	.004–.012
	8-350	1.8682–1.8692	.2600	.2733	.004–.012
	8-379 Diesel	②	.2808	.2808	—
	8-454	1.9482–1.9492	.2343	.2530	—

① 1. 2.0357–2.0365
  2. 2.0157–2.0165
  3. 1.9957–1.9965
  4. 1.9757–1.9765
  5. 1.9557–1.9565
② 2 #1,2,3,4: 2. 1663–2.1643
  #5: 2.0088–2.0068
③ .2315 Calif

Crankshaft and Connecting Rod Specifications

All measurements are given in in.

Year	Engine No. Cyl Displacement (cu in.)	Crankshaft				Connecting Rod		
		Main Brg Journal Dia.	Main Brg Oil Clearance	Shaft End-Play	Thrust on No.	Journal Diameter	Oil Clearance	Side Clearance
1970	6-250	2.2983–2.2993	.0003–.0029	.002–.006	7	1.999–2.000	.0007–.0027	.009–.014
	6-292	2.2983–2.2993	.0008–.0034	.002–.006	7	1.999–2.100	.0007–.0028	.009–.014
	8-307, 350	2.4484–2.4493 ②	.0008–.0020 ⑤	.002–.006	5	2.199–2.200	.0007–.0028	.008–.014
	8-396	⑥	⑦	.006–.010	5	2.199–2.200	.0009–.0025	.008–.014
1971	6-250	2.2983–2.2993	.0003–.0029	.002–.006	7	1.999–2.000	.0007–.0027	.009–.014
	6-292	2.2983–2.2993	.0008–.0034	.002–.006	7	2.099–2.100	.0007–.0027	.009–.014
	8-307, 350	2.4484–2.4493 ②	.0008–.0015 ⑤	.002–.006	5	2.199–2.200	.0007–.0028	.008–.014
	8-402	⑥	⑧	.006–.010	5	2.1985–2.1995	.0009–.0025	.013–.023
1972	6-250	2.2983–2.2993	.0003–.0029	.002–.006	7	1.999–2.000	.0007–.0027	.009–.014
	6-292	2.2983–2.2993	.0008–.0034	.002–.006	7	2.099–2.100	.0007–.0027	.009–.014
	8-307, 350	2.4484–2.4493 ②	.0008–.0020 ⑤	.002–.006	5	2.199–2.200	.0007–.0028	.008–.014
	8-402	⑥	⑧	.006–.010	5	2.1985–2.1995	.0009–.0025	.013–.023
1973–77	6-250	2.2983–2.2993	.0003–.0029	.002–.006	7	1.999–2.000	.0007–.0027	.006–.017
	6-292	2.2983–2.2993	.0008–.0034	.002–.006	7	2.099–2.100	.0007–.0027	.006–.017
	8-305, 307 350, 400	2.4484–2.4493 ②⑪	.0008–.0020 ⑤	.002–.006	5	2.199–2.200	.0013–.0035	.008–.014
	8-454	⑨	⑩	.006–.010	5	2.1985–2.1995	.0009–.0025	.013–.023
1978–81	6-250	2.2979–2.2994	Nos. 1–6 .0010–.0024 No. 7 .0016–.0035	.002–.006	7	1.999–2.000	.0010–.0026	.006–.017
	6-292	2.2979–2.2994	Nos. 1–6 .0010–.0024 No. 7 .0016–.0035	.002–.006	7	2.099–2.100	.0010–.0026	.006–.017

Crankshaft and Connecting Rod Specifications (cont.)

All measurements are given in in.

Year	Engine No. Cyl Displacement (cu in.)	Crankshaft Main Brg Journal Dia.	Main Brg Oil Clearance	Shaft End-Play	Thrust on No.	Connecting Rod Journal Diameter	Oil Clearance	Side Clearance
1978–81	8-305, 350, 400	⑪	.0008–.0020 ⑤	.002–.006	5	2.199–2.200 ⑫	.0013–.0035	.008–.014
	8-454	⑨	⑩	.006–.010	5	2.1985–2.1995	.0009–.0025	.013–.023
	8-350 Diesel	2.9993–3.0003	Nos. 1–4 .0005–.0021 No. 5 .0015–.0031	.0035–.0135	5	2.1238–2.1248	.0005–.0026	.006–.020
1982–87	6-250	2.2979–2.2994	Nos. 1–6 .0010–.0024 No. 7 .0016–.0035	.002–.006	7	1.999–2.000	.0010–.0026	.006–.017
	6-262	⑯	⑰	.0020–.0060	4	2.2487–2.2497	.0020–.0030	.0070–.0150
	6-292	2.2979–2.2994	Nos. 1–6 .0010–.0024 No. 7 .0016–.0035	.002–.006	7	2.099–2.100	.0010–.0026	.006–.017
	8-305 8-350	⑪	.0008–.0020 ⑤	.002–.006	5	2.0988–2.0998	.0013–.0035	.008–.014
	8-379 Diesel	⑭	⑮	.002–.007	5	2.398–2.399	—	.007–.024
	8-454	⑬	⑩	.006–.010	5	2.200–2.199	.009–.0025	.013–.023

② No. 5—2.4479–2.4488
⑤ Nos. 2-4—.0011–.0023 No. 5—.0017–.0033
⑥ Nos. 1-2—2.7487–2.7496 Nos. 3-4—2.7481–2.7490 No. 5—2.7478–2.7488
⑦ No. 1—.0007–.0019 Nos. 2-4—.0013–.0025 No. 5—.0024–.0040
⑧ No. 1—.0007–.0019

⑨ No. 1—2.7485–2.7494 Nos. 2-4—2.7481–2.7490 No. 5—2.7478–2.7488
⑩ Nos. 1-4—.0013–.0025 No. 5—.0024–.0040
⑪ 1977–1986: 305, 350—No. 1—2.4484–2.4493 Nos. 2-4—2.4481–2.4490 No. 5—2.4479–2.4488
⑫ 1978–80: 2.0988–2.0998

⑬ No. 5: 2.7476–2.7486
⑭ Nos. 1-4: 2.9494–2.9504 No. 5: 2.9492–2.9502
⑮ Nos. 1-4: .0018–.0032 No. 5: .0022–.0037
⑯ Front—2.4484–2.4493 Inter—2.4481–2.4490 Rear—2.4479–2.4488
⑰ Front—.0010–.0015 Inter—.0010–.0020

Ring Side Clearance—Compression Rings
(in.)

Year	Engine	Top Compression	Bottom Compression
1970–73	8-307	0.0012–0.0027	0.0012–0.0032
1970–84	6-250	0.0012–0.0027	0.0012–0.0032
1986–87	6-262	0.0012–0.0032	0.0012–0.0032
1970–86	6-292	0.0020–0.0040	0.0020–0.0040
1970–87	8-350	0.0012–0.0032	0.0012–0.0032
1975–80	8-400	0.0012–0.0032	0.0012–0.0032
1970	8-396	0.0012–0.0032	0.0012–0.0032
1971–72	8-402	0.0017–0.0032	0.0017–0.0032
1973–87	8-454	0.0017–0.0032	0.0017–0.0032
1977–87	8-305	0.0012–0.0032	0.0012–0.0032
1978–81	8-350 Diesel	0.0040–0.0060 ①	0.0018–0.0038
1982–87	8-379 Diesel	0.0030–0.0070	0.0015–0.0031

① .005–.007 (1980–82)

Ring Side Clearance—Oil Rings
(in.)

Year	Engine	Oil Control	Year	Engine	Oil Control
1970–73	6-250, 8-307	0.0000–0.0050	1973–87	8-454	0.0005–0.0065
1974–84	6-250	0.0000–0.0050	1975–80	8-400	0.002–0.007
1986–87	6-262	0.002–0.007	1977–87	8-305	0.002–0.007
1970–87	8-350	0.002–0.007	1978–81	8-350 Diesel	0.001–0.005
1970–86	6-292	0.0050–0.0055	1982–87	8-379 Diesel	0.0016–0.0038
1970	8-396	0.0012–0.0060			
1971–72	8-402	0.0005–0.0065			

Ring Gap
(in.)

Year	Engine	Top Compression	Bottom Compression	Oil Control
1970–86	6-250	0.010–0.020	0.010–0.020	0.015–0.055
1986–87	6-262	0.010–0.025	0.010–0.025	0.015–0.055
1970–86	6-292	0.010–0.020	0.010–0.020	0.015–0.055
1970–72	8-307	0.010–0.020	0.010–0.020	0.015–0.055
1970–87	8-350	0.010–0.020	0.013–0.025 ②	0.015–0.055
1975–80	8-400	0.010–0.020	0.010–0.025	0.010–0.035 ①
1970	8-396	0.010–0.020	0.010–0.020	0.010–0.030

Ring Gap (cont.)
(in.)

Year	Engine	Top Compression	Bottom Compression	Oil Control
1971–72	8-402	0.010–0.020	0.010–0.020	0.010–0.030
1973–86	8-454	0.010–0.020	0.010–0.020	0.010–0.030 ①
1977–87	8-305	0.010–0.020	0.010–0.025	0.015–0.055
1978–81	8-350 Diesel	0.015–0.025	0.015–0.025	0.015–0.055
1982–87	8-379 Diesel	0.0012–0.022	0.030–0.040	0.0098–0.0200

① 0.015–0.055—1977–87
② 0.010–0.025—1977–87

Piston Clearance

Year	Engine	Piston-to-Bore Production Clearance (in.)
1970	6-250	0.0005–0.0015
	6-292	0.0025–0.0031
	8-307	0.0005–0.0011
	8-350	0.0012–0.0022
	8-396	0.0018–0.0026
1971–72	6-250	0.0005–0.0015
	6-292	0.0025–0.0031
	8-307	0.0012–0.0018
	8-350	0.0007–0.0013
	8-402	0.0018–0.0026
1973	6-250	0.0005–0.0015
	6-292	0.0026–0.0036
	8-307	0.0012–0.0018
	8-350	0.0007–0.0013
	8-454	0.0018–0.0028
1974–76	6-250	0.0005–0.0015
	6-292	0.0026–0.0036
	8-350	0.0007–0.0013
	8-400	0.0014–0.0024
	8-454	0.0018–0.0028
1977–81	6-250	0.0005–0.0015 ①
	6-292	0.0026–0.0036
	8-305	0.0007–0.0017
	8-350	0.0007–0.0017
	8-350 (Diesel)	0.0050–0.0060 ②
	8-400	0.0014–0.0024
	8-454	0.0014–0.0024 ③
1982–86	6-250	0.0010–0.0020
	6-292	0.0026–0.0036
	8-305	0.0007–0.0017
	8-350	0.0007–0.0017
	8-379 (Diesel)	④
	8-454	0.0030–0.0040

① 0.0010–0.0020—1978–81
② Service clearance
③ .0030 .0040 (1980–81)
④ Bohn Pistons 1–6—0.089–0.115 mm
　　　　　　　7–8—0.102–0.128 mm
Zollner Pistons 1–6—0.112–0.138 mm
　　　　　　　　7–8—0.125–0.151 mm

aluminum viscous dirve fan clutch, keep it upright in its normal position. If the fluid leaks out, the unit will have to be replaced.

10. Remove the clutch cross-shaft.

11. Attach a lifting device to the engine. You may have to remove the carburetor. Take the engine weight off the engine mounts, and unbolt the mounts. On all models except the gas engined ½ and ¾ ton, support and disconnect the transmission. With automatic transmission, remove the torque converter underpan and starter, unbolt the converter from the flywheel, detach the throttle linkage and vacuum modulator line, and unbolt the engine from the transmission. Be certain that the converter does not fall out. With manual transmission, unbolt the clutch housing from the engine. Further details are in Chapter 7.

12. On two wheel drive models, remove the driveshaft. See details in Chapter 7. Either drain the transmission or plug the driveshaft opening. Disconnect the speedometer cable at the transmission. Disconnect the TCS switch wire, if so equipped. Disconnect the shift linkage or lever, or the clutch linkage. Disconnect the transmission cooler lines, if so equipped. If you have an automatic or a four speed transmission, the rear crossmember must be removed. With the three speed, unbolt the transmission from the crossmember. Raise the engine/transmission assembly and pull it forward.

13. On diesels, remove the three bolts, transmission, right side; disconnect the wires to the starter and remove the starter.

14. On four wheel drive, raise and pull the engine forward until it is free of the transmission. On diesels, slightly raise the transmission, remove the three left transmission to engine bolts, and remove the engine.

15. On all trucks, lift the engine out slowly, making certain as you go that all lines between

Torque Specifications
(ft. lbs.)

Engine No. Cyl Displacement (cu in.)	Cylinder Head Bolts	Rod Bearing Bolts	Main Bearing Bolts	Crankshaft Bolt ▲	Flywheel to Crankshaft Bolts	Manifold	
						Intake	Exhaust
6-250	95 ⑤	35	65	—	60	—	30 ①
6-262	65	45	75	70	75	36	⑱
6-292	95 ⑤	35	65	60 ⑥	110	38	30
8-305	65	45	70 ⑦	60 ⑧	60 ⑨	30 ⑩	20 ⑪
8-350	65	45	70 ⑦	60 ⑧	60 ⑨	30 ⑩	30 ⑪
8-350 Diesel	130 ②	42	120	200–310	60	40 ②	25
8-379 Diesel	100 ⑮	48	④	150 ⑯	65 ⑰	31	26
8-396	—	50	110	—	65	30	20
8-400	65	45	70	60	60	30	30
8-402	80	50	110	—	65	30	20
8-454	80 ⑫	50	110	65 ⑬	65	30	20 ⑭

▲ Front of crankshaft
① End bolts: 20 ft. lbs.
② Dip in oil.
③ ⁷/₁₆ in. bolts 70 ft. lbs.
④ inner: 110
   outer: 100
⑤ Left-hand front bolt: 85 ft. lbs.
⑥ 1986–87: 50 ft. lbs.
⑦ 1986–87: outer bolts on #2, 3, 4 caps—70 ft. lbs., all others 80 ft. lbs.
⑧ 1986–87: 70 ft. lbs.
⑨ 1986–87: 75 ft. lbs.
⑩ 1986–87: 36 ft. lbs.
⑪ 1986–87: Cast manifolds—two center bolts—26 ft. lbs.
                all others—20 ft. lbs.
   Tubular (stainless steel)—all bolts 26 ft. lbs.
⑫ 1986–87: 95 ft. lbs.
⑬ 1979–87: 85 ft. lbs.
⑭ 1986–87: stainless steel man.—40 ft. lbs.
   cast iron man.—18 ft. lbs.
⑮ 1985–87: 1st 20
         2nd 50
         3rd ¼ turn
⑯ 1986–87: 200 ft. lbs.
⑰ 1986–87: 30 ft. lbs.
⑱ Center two bolts: 26 ft. lbs.
   All others: 20 ft. lbs.

the engine and the truck have been disconnected.

Installation is as follows:

1. On four wheel drive and diesels, lower the engine into place and align it with the transmission. Push the engine back gently and turn the crankshaft until the manual transmission shaft and clutch engage. Bolt the transmission to the engine. With automatic transmission, align the converter with the flywheel, bolt the transmission to the engine, bolt the converter to the flywheel, replace the underpan and starter, and connect the throttle linkage and vacuum modulator line. See Chapter 7 for details.

2. On two wheel drive, lower the engine/transmission unit into place. Replace the rear crossmember if removed. Bolt the three speed transmission back to the crossmember. Replace the driveshaft.

3. Install the engine mounts.

4. Replace all transmission connections and the clutch cross-shaft. Replace the fan, pulley, and belts.

5. Replace all the items removed from the

engine earlier. Connect all the wires which were detached.

6. Replace the radiator and fan shroud, air cleaner, and battery or battery cables. Fill the cooling system and check the automatic transmission fuel level. Fill the crankcase with oil. Check for leaks.

Valve Cover(s)

REMOVAL AND INSTALLATION

All Engines

1. Remove air cleaner.
2. Disconnect and reposition as necessary any vacuum or PCV hoses that obstruct the valve covers.
3. On the left side, on some models, it may be necessary to remove the air conditioning compressor and lay to one side. (Do not disconnect the hoses).
4. Disconnect electrical wire(s) (spark plug, etc.) from the valve cover clips.
5. Unbolt and remove the valve cover(s).
NOTE: *Do not pry the covers off if they seem stuck. Instead, gently tap around each cover with a rubber mallet until the old gasket or sealer breaks loose.*
6. To install, use a new valve cover gasket or RTV (or any equivalent) sealer. If using sealer,

follow directions on the tube. Install valve cover and tighten cover bolts to 3 ft.lb.
7. Connect and reposition all vacuum and PCV hoses, and reconnect electrical and/or spark plug wires at the cover clips. Install the air cleaner.

Rocker Arms

REMOVAL AND INSTALLATION

Gasoline Engines

1. Remove the valve cover.
2. Remove the rocker arm flanged bolts, and remove the rocker pivots.
3. Remove the rocker arms.
NOTE: *Remove each set of rocker arms (one set per cylinder) as a unit.*
4. To install, position a set of rocker arms (for one cylinder) in the proper location.
NOTE: *Install the rocker arms for each cylinder only when the lifters are off the cam lobe and both valves are closed.*
5. Coat the replacement rocker arm and pivot with SAE 90 gear oil and install the pivots.
6. Install the flanged bolts and tighten alternately. Torque the bolts to 25 ft.lb.

8-350 Diesel

NOTE: *When the diesel engine rocker arms are removed or loosened, the lifters must be bled down to prevent oil pressure buildup inside each lifter, which could cause it to raise*

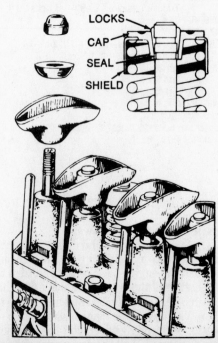

Six-cylinder rocker arm components—all gasoline V8s similar

Valve cover and rocker arm removal, gasoline V8 shown. Rocker arms are marked "L" and "R" for left and right

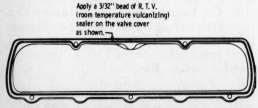

Apply sealer to all valve covers as shown. Always run the sealer bead on the inside edge of the bolt holes on the cover flange

up higher than normal and bring the valves within striking distance of the pistons.

1. Remove the valve cover.

2. Remove the rocker arm pivot bolts, the bridged pivot and rocker arms.

3. Remove each rocker set as a unit.

4. To install, lubricate the pivot wear point and position each set of rocker arms in its proper location. Do not tighten the pivot bolts for fear of bending the valves when the engine is turned.

5. The lifters can be bled down for 6-cylinders at once with the crankshaft in either of the following two positions:

a. For cylinders number 3,5,7,2,4 and 8, turn the crankshaft so the saw slot on the harmonic balancer is at 0 degrees on the timing indicator.

b. For cylinders 1,3,7,2,4 and 6, turn the crankshaft so the saw slot on the harmonic balancer is a 4 o'clock.

6. Tighten the rocker arm pivot bolts VERY SLOWLY to 28 ft.lb. It will take 45 minutes to completely bleed down the lifters in this position. If additional lifters must be bled, rotate the engine to the other position, tighten the rocker arm pivot bolts, and again wait 45 minutes before rotating the crankshaft. Excess torque here can bend the pushrods, so be careful!

7. Assemble the remaining components in the reverse of disassemble. The rocker covers do not use gaskets, but are sealed with a bead of RTV (Room Temperature Vulcanizing) silicone sealer.

8-379 (6.2L) Diesel

1. Remove the valve cover as previously explained.

2. The rocker assemblies on the 379 differ completely from those on the 350 diesel. The 379 arms are mounted on two short rocker

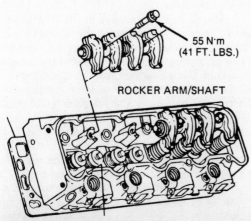

55 N·m
(41 FT. LBS.)

ROCKER ARM/SHAFT

6.2L diesel rocker shaft assemblies

shafts per cylinder head, with each shaft operating four rockers. Remove the two bolts which secure each rocker shaft assembly, and remove the shaft.

3. The rocker arms can be removed from the shaft by removing the cotter pin on the end of each shaft. The rocker arms and springs slide off.

4. To install, make sure first that the rocker arms and springs go back on the shafts in the exact order in which they were removed.

NOTE: *Always install new cotter pins on the rocker shaft ends.*

5. Install the rocker shaft assemblies, torquing the bolts to 41 ft.lb.

Valve Lash Adjustment

All engines described in this book use hydraulic lifters, which require no periodic adjustment. In the event of cylinder head removal or any operation that requires disturbing the rocker arms, the rocker arms will have to be adjusted.

1. Remove the rocker covers and gaskets.

2. Adjust the valves on inline 6-cylinder engines as follows:

a. Mark the distributor housing with a piece of chalk at the No. 1 and 6 plug wire positions. Remove the distributor cap with the plug wires attached.

b. Crank the engine until the distributor rotor points to the NO. 1 cylinder and the No. 1 piston is at TDC (both No. 1 cylinder valves closed). At this point, adjust the following valves:

- No. 1 Exhaust and Intake
- No. 2 Intake
- No. 3 Exhaust
- No. 4 Intake
- No. 5 Exhaust

c. Back out the adjusting nut until lash is felt at the pushrod, then turn the adjusting nut in until all lash is removed. This can be determined by checking pushrod end-play while turning the adjusting nut. When all play has been removed, turn the adjusting nut in 1 full turn.

d. Crank the engine until the distributor rotor points to the no. 6 cylinder and the no. 6 piston is at TDC (both No. 6 cylinder valves closed). The following valves can be adjusted:

- No. 2 Exhaust
- No. 3 Intake
- No. 4 Exhaust
- No. 5 Intake
- No. 6 Intake and Exhaust

3. Adjust the valves on V8 and V6 engines as follows:

a. Crank the engine until the mark on the

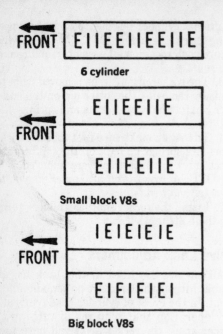

6 cylinder

Small block V8s

Big block V8s

Chevrolet intake(1) and exhaust(E) valve arrangements (except the V6 engine)

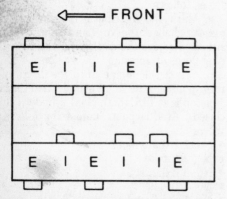

V6 262 valve arrangement (E-exhaust; I-intake)

damper aligns with the TDC or 0 degree mark on the timing tab and the engine is in the No. 1 firing position. This can be determined by placing the fingers on the No. 1 cylinder valves as the marks align. If the valves do not move, it is in the No. 1 firing position. If the valves move, it is in the No. 6 firing position (no. 4 on V6) and the crankcase should be rotated one more revolution to the No. 1 firing position.

b. With the engine in the No. 1 firing position, the following valves can be adjusted:
- V8: Exhaust 1, 3, 4, 8
- V8: Intake 1, 2, 5, 7
- V6: Exhaust 1, 5, 6
- V6: Intake 1, 2, 3

c. Back out the adjusting nut until lash is felt at the pushrod, then turn the adjusting nut in until all lash is removed. This can be determined by checking pushrod end-play while turning the adjusting nut. When all play has been removed, turn the adjusting nut in:
- ½-1¼ additional turn (flat lifter)
- ¾-1¼ additional turn (roller lifter V8)
- ¾ additional turn (roller lifter V6)

d. Crank the engine 1 full revolution until the marks are again in alignment. This is the No. 6 firing position (no. 4 on V6). The following valves can now be adjusted:
- V8: Exhaust 2, 5, 6, 7
- V8: Intake 3, 4, 6, 8
- V6: Exhaust 2, 3, 4
- V6: Intake 4, 5, 6

4. Reinstall the rocker arm covers using new gaskets or sealer.

5. Install the distributor cap and wire assembly.

6. Adjust the carburetor idle speed.

Thermostat

REMOVAL AND INSTALLATION

1. Drain the radiator until the level is below the thermostat level (below the level of the intake manifold).

CAUTION: *When draining the coolant, keep in mind that cats and dogs are attracted by the ethylene glycol antifreeze, and are quite likely to drink any that is left in an uncovered container or in puddles on the ground. This will prove fatal in sufficient quantity. Always drain the coolant into a sealable container. Coolant should be reused unless it is contaminated or several years old.*

2. Remove the water outlet elbow assembly from the engine. Remove the thermostat from inside the elbow.

3. Install new thermostat in the reverse order of removal, making sure the spring side is inserted into the elbow. Clean the gasket surfaces on the water outlet elbow and the intake manifold. Use a new gasket when installing the elbow to the manifold. On later models the thermostat housing may have been sealed with RTV sealant. If so, place a ⅛″ bead of RTV sealer all around the thermostat housing sealing surface on the intake manifold and install the housing while it is still wet. Refill the radiator to approximately 2½″ below the filler neck.

NOTE: *If the thermostat is equipped with a pin hole, be sure to install pin side facing upwards.*

Intake Manifold

REMOVAL AND INSTALLATION

Inline 6-Cylinder

1974 and earlier 250 and 292 6-cylinder engines use a combined intake and exhaust manifold, both of which are removed together. 1976 and later engines have an intake manifold which is cast integrally with the cylinder head and cannot be removed.

1. Remove the air cleaner assembly and air ducts.

2. Tag and disconnect the throttle linkage at the carburetor. Tag and disconnect the fuel line, vacuum lines, hoses, and electrical connections.

3. Disconnect the transmission downshift linkage (if equipped), and remove the PCV valve from the rocker cover. On models equipped with air injection, disconnect the air supply hose from the check valve on the air injection manifold.

4. Remove the carburetor, with spacer and heat shield (if equipped).

5. Spray the nuts and bolts connecting the exhaust manifold to the exhaust pipe with a rust penetrant, as these are usually quite difficult to remove. Unbolt the exhaust manifold from the pipe.

NOTE: *It may be necessary to remove the generator rear bracket and/or air conditioning compressor bracket on some models.*

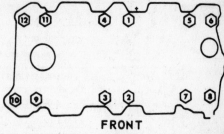

FRONT

305 and 350 V8 intake manifold bolt torque sequence

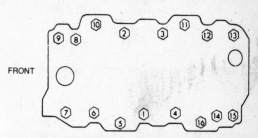

FRONT

396 and 454 intake manifold bolt torque sequence

6. Unbolt the manifold bolts and clamps, and remove the manifold assembly.

7. If you intend to separate the manifolds, remove the single bolt and two nuts at the center of the manifold assembly.

8. Installation is the reverse of removal. When assembling the manifolds, install the connecting bolts loosely first. Place the manifolds on a straight, flat surface and hold them

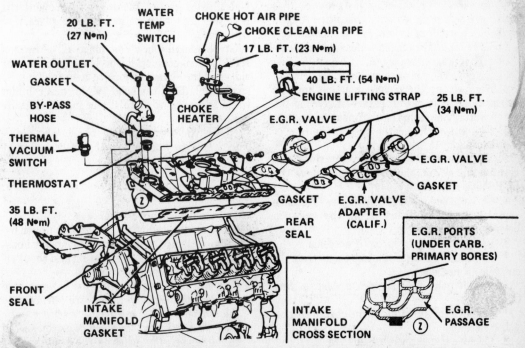

Typical gasoline V8 intake manifold installation showing related components

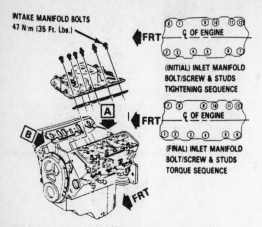

V6 engine intake manifold torque sequence

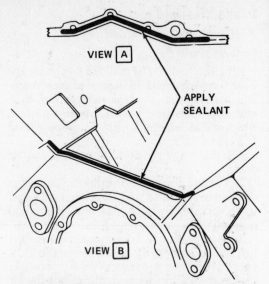

On small-blocks, run a ³⁄₁₆ in. bead of RTV sealer across the block and ½ in. up the sides of the block just prior to manifold installation

securely during tightening—this assures the proper mating of surfaces when the manifold assembly is fastened to the head. Stress cracking could occur if the manifolds are not assembled first in this manner. On all manifolds, always use new gaskets between the manifold and cylinder head.

V6 and V8 Except Diesel

1. Disconnect the negative battery cable.
2. Drain the cooling system.
CAUTION: *When draining the coolant, keep in mind that cats and dogs are attracted by the ethylene glycol antifreeze, and are quite likely to drink any that is left in an uncovered container or in puddles on the ground. This will prove fatal in sufficient quantity. Always drain the coolant into a sealable container. Coolant should be reused unless it is contaminated or several years old.*
3. Remove the air cleaner assembly.
4. Remove the thermostat housing and the bypass hose. It is not necessary to remove the top radiator hose from the thermostat housing.
5. Disconnect the heater hose at the rear of the manifold.
6. Disconnect all electrical connections and vacuum lines from the manifold. Remove the EGR valve if necessary.
7. On vehicles equipped with power brakes remove the vacuum line from the vacuum booster to the manifold.
8. Remove the distributor (if necessary).
9. Move the air conditioning compressor to one side, if necessary.
10. Relieve the fuel system pressure. See Chapter 1.
11. Remove the fuel line to the carburetor or TBI unit.
12. Remove the carburetor linkage.
13. Disconnect the electrical connections at the TBI unit.

14. Remove the carburetor or TBI unit, if necessary.
15. Remove the intake manifold bolts. Remove the manifold and the gaskets. Remember to reinstall the O-ring seal between the intake manifold and timing chain cover during assembly, if so equipped.
16. Reconnect all wires, hoses and linkage. Use plastic gasket retainers to prevent the manifold gasket from slipping out of place, if so equipped.
On the small block V8s, place a ³⁄₁₆″ bead of RTV type silicone sealer on the front and rear ridges of the cylinder block-to-manifold mating surfaces. Extend the bead ½″ up each cylinder head to seal and retain the manifold side gaskets.
NOTE: *Before installing the intake manifold, be sure that the gasket surfaces are thoroughly clean.*

8-350 Diesel

1. Remove the air cleaner.
2. Drain the radiator. Loosen the upper bypass hose clamp, remove the thermostat housing bolts, and remove the housing and the thermostat from the intake manifold.
CAUTION: *When draining the coolant, keep in mind that cats and dogs are attracted by the ethylene glycol antifreeze, and are quite likely to drink any that is left in an uncovered container or in puddles on the ground. This will prove fatal in sufficient quantity. Always drain the coolant into a sealable container.*

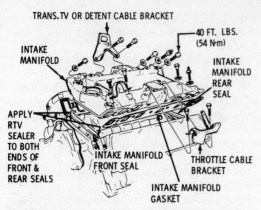

350 diesel intake manifold installation. Note sealer application

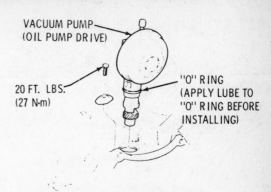

NOTICE: DO NOT OPERATE ENGINE WITHOUT VACUUM PUMP AS THIS IS THE DRIVE FOR THE ENGINE OIL PUMP AND ENGINE DAMAGE WOULD OCCUR.

Oil pump drive and vacuum pump, 350 diesel shown. 379 diesel pump simlar

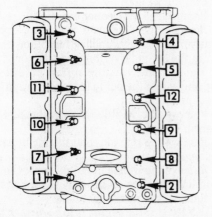

350 V8 diesel intake manifold torque sequence

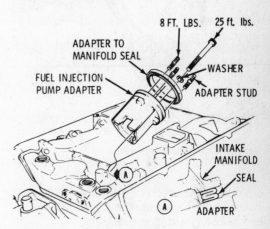

Adapter and seal details, 350 diesel

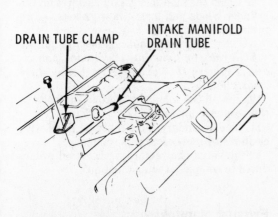

350 diesel intake manifold drain tube

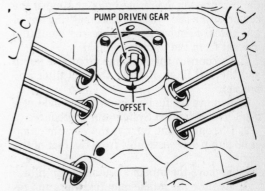

The index mark on the injection pump driven gear will be offset to the right when the No. 1 cylinder is at TDC

Coolant should be reused unless it is contaminated or several years old.

3. Remove the breather pipes from the rocker covers and the air crossover. Remove the air crossover.

4. Disconnect the throttle rod and the return spring. If equipped with cruise control, remove the servo.

5. Remove the hairpin clip at the bellcrank and disconnect the cables. Remove the throttle

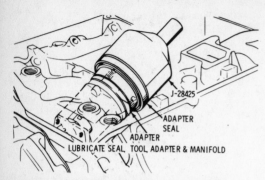

Adapter seal installation with the special tool

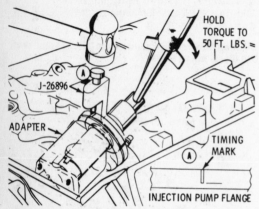

Adapter timing mark application

cable from the bracket on the manifold; position the cable away from the engine. Disconnect and label any wiring as necessary.

6. Remove the alternator bracket if necessary. If equipped with air conditioning, remove the compressor mounting bolts and move the compressor aside, without disconnecting any of the hoses. Remove the compressor mounting bracket from the intake manifold.

7. Disconnect the fuel line from the pump and the fuel filter. Remove the fuel filter and bracket.

8. Remove the fuel injection pump and lines. See Chapter 5, Fuel System, for procedures.

9. Disconnect and remove the vacuum pump or oil pump drive assembly from the rear of the engine.

10. Remove the intake manifold drain tube.

11. Remove the intake manifold bolts and remove the manifold. Remove the adapter seal. Remove the injection pump adapter.

12. Clean the mating surfaces of the cylinder heads and the intake manifold using a putty knife.

13. Coat both sides of the gasket surface that seal the intake manifold to the cylinder heads with G.M. sealer #1050026 or the equivalent. Position the intake manifold gaskets on the cyl-

inder heads. Install the end seals, making sure that the ends are positioned under the cylinder heads.

14. Carefully lower the intake manifold into place on the engine.

15. Clean the intake manifold bolts thoroughly, then dip them in clean engine oil. Install the bolts and tighten to 15 ft.lb. in the sequence shown. Next, tighten all the bolts to 30 ft.lb., in sequence, and finally tighten to 40 ft.lb. in sequence.

16. Install the intake manifold drain tube and clamp.

17. Install injection pump adapter. See Chapter 5. If a new adapter is not being used, skip steps 4 and 9.

8-379 (6.2L) Diesel

1. Disconnect both batteries.

2. Remove the air cleaner assembly.

3. Remove the crankcase ventilator tubes, and disconnect the secondary fuel filter lines. Remove the secondary filter and adaptor.

4. Loosen the vacuum pump holddown clamp and rotate the pump to gain access to the nearest manifold bolt.

5. Remove the EPR/EGR valve bracket, if equipped.

6. Remove the rear air conditioning bracket, if equipped.

7. Remove the intake manifold bolts; the infection line clips are retained by these bolts.

8. Remove the intake manifold.

WARNING: *If the engine is to be further serviced with the manifold removed, install protective covers over the intake ports.*

9. Clean the manifold gasket surfaces on the cylinder heads and install new gaskets before installing the manifold.

NOTE: *The gaskets have an opening for the EGR valve on light duty installations; an insert covers this opening on heavy duty installations.*

10. Install the manifold. Torque the bolts in the sequence illustrated.

11. The secondary filter must be filled with clean diesel fuel before it is reinstalled.

12. Reverse the remaining removal procedures to complete the installation.

Exhaust Manifold
REMOVAL AND INSTALLATION
Inline 6-Cylinder

NOTE: *1974 and earlier inline 6-cylinder exhaust manifold removal and installation procedures are covered under the Intake Manifold procedure (both manifolds are a unit).*

1975 and later inline six exhaust manifold torque sequence—engines with integral intake manifold/cylinder head

1975 and later inline 6-procedures are covered below.

1. Disconnect and remove the air cleaner assembly, including the carburetor preheat tube.

2. Disconnect the exhaust pipe at the exhaust manifold. You will probably have to use a liquid rust penetrant to free the bolts.

3. Remove the engine oil dipstick bracket bolt.

4. Liberally coat the manifold nuts with a rust penetrating lubricant. Remove the exhaust manifold bolts and remove the manifold.

5. To install, mount the manifold on the cylinder head and start all bolts.

6. Torque the bolts to specification using the torque sequence illustrated. Complete the installation by reversing the removal procedure.

Gasoline V6 and V8s

Tab locks are used on the front and rear pairs of bolts on each exhaust manifold. When removing the bolts, straighten the tabs from beneath the car using a suitable tool. When installing the tab locks, bend the tabs against the sides of the bolts, not over the top of the bolt.

1. Disconnect the negative battery cable.

2. Remove the air cleaner.

3. Remove the hot air shroud, (if so equipped).

4. Loosen the alternator and remove its lower bracket.

5. Jack up your car and support it with jack stands.

6. Disconnect the crossover pipe from both manifolds.

7. Lower the vehicle.

NOTE: *On models with air conditioning it may be necessary to remove the compressor, and tie it out of the way. Do not disconnect the compressor lines.*

6. Remove the manifold bolts and remove the manifold(s). Some models have lock tabs on the front and rear manifold bolts which must be removed before removing the bolts. These tabs can be bent with a drift pin.

7. Reverse the above to install. Torque the bolts to specifications and bend the tab washers over the heads of all bolts.

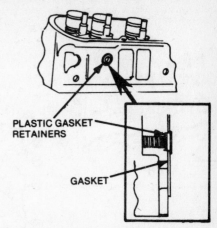

Plastic manifold gasket retainers, gasoline V8s

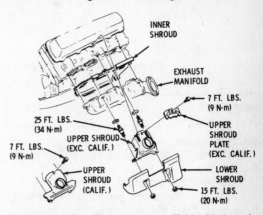

Typical gasoline V8 exhaust manifold with hot air shrouds

8-350 Diesel V8

LEFT SIDE

1. Remove the air cleaner and cover the air crossover with a protective plate, screen or cover.

2. Remove the lower generator bracket.

3. Jack up the truck and safely support it with jackstands.

4. Remove the exhaust pipe at the manifold flange.

5. Lower the truck.

6. Remove the exhaust manifold from above.

7. Reverse the above procedure to install. Torque the manifold nuts and bolts according to the illustration.

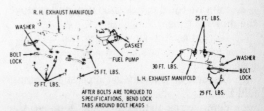

350 diesel exhaust manifold installation

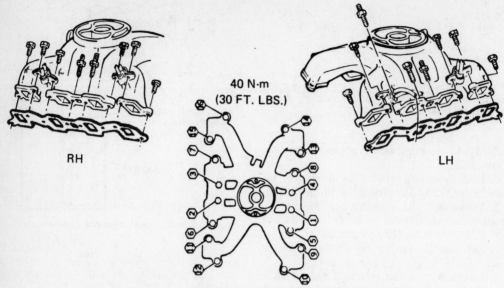

379 diesel intake manifold gasket mounting and bolt torque sequence

RIGHT SIDE

1. Jack up the truck and safely support it with jackstands.
2. Disconnect the exhaust pipe at the manifold flange.
3. Remove the manifold.
4. Reverse the above procedure to install, torquing the manifold bolts according to the accompanying illustration.

8-379 Diesel V8

RIGHT SIDE

1. Disconnect the batteries.
2. Jack up the truck and safely support it with jackstands.
3. Disconnect the exhaust pipe from the manifold flange and lower the truck.
4. Disconnect the glow plug wires.
5. Remove the air cleaner duct bracket.
6. Remove the glow plug wires.
7. Remove the manifold bolts and remove the manifold.
8. To install, reverse the above procedure and torque the bolts to 25 ft.lb.

LEFT SIDE

1. Disconnect the batteries.
2. Remove the dipstick tube nut, and remove the dipstick tube.
3. Disconnect the glow plug wires.
4. Jack up the truck and safely support it with jackstands.
5. Disconnect the exhaust pipe at the manifold flange.
6. Remove the manifold bolts. Remove the manifold from underneath the truck.

7. Reverse the above procedure to install. Start the manifold bolts while the truck is jacked up first. Torque the bolts to 25 ft.lb.

Radiator

All pick-up trucks are equipped with cross-flow type radiators.

REMOVAL AND INSTALLATION

1970-72

1. Drain the radiator and remove the hoses. CAUTION: *When draining the coolant, keep in mind that cats and dogs are attracted by the ethylene glycol antifreeze, and are quite likely to drink any that is left in an uncovered container or in puddles on the ground. This will prove fatal in sufficient quantity. Always drain the coolant into a sealable container. Coolant should be reused unless it is contaminated or several years old.*
2. Disconnect and plug the transmission cooler line (if equipped).
3. On 6-cylinder engines, remove the finger guard.
4. Remove the upper retainers with the fan shroud attached (V8 models) and rest the fan shroud over the engine.
5. Lift the radiator out of the lower retainers.
6. Installation is the reverse of removal. Fill the cooling system, check the automatic transmission fluid level and run the engine, checking for leaks.

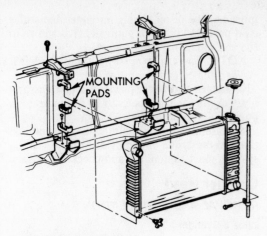

Typical radiator mounting

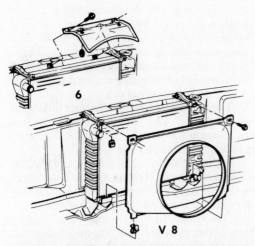

Typical radiator, shroud, and finger guard. The finger guard is usually found on trucks with six cylinder engines

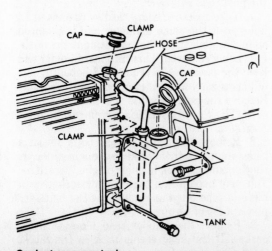

Coolant recovery tank

1973 and Later

1. Drain the radiator. On some 1973 models, you will have to siphon the coolant out of the filler neck or detach the lower radiator hose. 1974 and later models are equipped with a drain cock.

CAUTION: *When draining the coolant, keep in mind that cats and dogs are attracted by the ethylene glycol antifreeze, and are quite likely to drink any that is left in an uncovered container or in puddles on the ground. This will prove fatal in sufficient quantity. Always drain the coolant into a sealable container. Coolant should be reused unless it is contaminated or several years old.*

2. Disconnect the hoses and automatic transmission cooler line (if equipped). Plug the cooler lines. Diesels have transmission cooler and oil cooler lines.

3. Disconnect the coolant recovery system hose.

4. If the vehicle is equipped with a fan shroud, detach the shroud and hang it over the fan to provide clearance.

5. On 6-cylinder engines, remove the finger guard.

6. Remove the mounting panel from the radiator support and remove the upper mounting pads.

7. Lift the radiator up and out of the truck. Lift the shroud out if necessary.

8. Reverse the above to install. Fill the cooling system and check the automatic transmission fluid level, and run the engine, checking for leaks.

Water Pump

REMOVAL AND INSTALLATION

All Engines Except 379 (6.2L) Diesel

1. Drain the radiator and loosen the fan pulley bolts.

CAUTION: *When draining the coolant, keep in mind that cats and dogs are attracted by the ethylene glycol antifreeze, and are quite likely to drink any that is left in an uncovered container or in puddles on the ground. This will prove fatal in sufficient quantity. Always drain the coolant into a sealable container. Coolant should be reused unless it is contaminated or several years old.*

2. Disconnect the heater hose and radiator. Disconnect the lower radiator hose at the water pump.

3. Loosen the alternator swivel bolt and remove the fan belt. Remove the fan bolts, fan and pulley.

4. Remove the water pump attaching bolts and remove the pump and gasket from the en-

gine. On inline engines, remove the water pump straight out of the block to avoid damaging the impeller.

WARNING: *Do not store viscous drive (thermostatic) fan clutches in any other position than the normal installed position. They should be supported so that the clutch disc remains vertical; otherwise, silicone fluid may leak out.*

5. Check the water pump shaft bearings for end play or roughness in operation. Water pump bearings usually emit a squealing sound with the engine running when the bearings need to be replaced. Replace the pump with a rebuilt or new pump (usually on an exchange basis) if the bearings are not in good shape or have been noisy.

6. Installation is the reverse of removal. Clean the gasket surfaces and install new gaskets. Coat the gasket with sealer. A $5/16$"-24 x 1" guide stud installed in one hole of the fan will make installing the fan onto the hub easier. It can be removed after the other 3 bolts are started. Fill the cooling system and adjust the fan belt tension. Torque the pump retaining bolts to 15 ft. lbs.

8-379 Diesel

1. Disconnect the batteries.
2. Remove the fan and fan shroud.
3. Drain the radiator.

CAUTION: *When draining the coolant, keep in mind that cats and dogs are attracted by the ethylene glycol antifreeze, and are quite likely to drink any that is left in an uncovered container or in puddles on the ground. This will prove fatal in sufficient quantity. Always drain the coolant into a sealable container. Coolant should be reused unless it is contaminated or several years old.*

4. If the truck is equipped with air conditioning, remove the air conditioning hose bracket nuts.
5. Remove the oil fill tube.
6. Remove the generator pivot bolt and remove the generator belt.
7. Remove the generator lower bracket.
8. Remove the power steering belt. Remove the power steering belt and secure it out of the way.
9. Remove the air conditioning belt if equipped.
10. Disconnect the by-pass hose and the lower radiator hose.
11. Remove the water pump bolts. Remove the water pump plate and gasket and water pump. If the pump gasket is to be replaced, remove the plate attaching bolts to the water pump and remove (and replace) the gasket.
12. When installing the pump, the flanges

must be free of oil. Apply an anaerobic sealer (GM part #1052357 or equivalent) as shown in the accompanying illustration.

NOTE: *The sealer must be wet to the touch when the bolts are torqued.*

13. Attach the water pump and plate assembly. Torque the plate bolts to 18 ft. lbs. and the pump bolts to 35 ft. lbs.
14. Assemble the remaining components in the reverse order of removal. Fill the cooling system, start the engine and check for leaks.

Cylinder Head

REMOVAL AND INSTALLATION

Inline 6-Cylinder

1. Drain the cooling system and remove the air cleaner assembly. Disconnect the PCV hose.

CAUTION: *When draining the coolant, keep in mind that cats and dogs are attracted by the ethylene glycol antifreeze, and are quite likely to drink any that is left in an uncovered container or in puddles on the ground. This will prove fatal in sufficient quantity. Always drain the coolant into a sealable container. Coolant should be reused unless it is contaminated or several years old.*

2. Tag and disconnect the throttle linkage at the carburetor. Tag and disconnect the fuel line, vacuum lines, and any electrical connections at the carburetor.
3. Remove the top radiator hose, and the battery ground strap. Disconnect the wires from the temperature sending unit, leaving the harness clear of the clips on the rocker cover.
4. Disconnect the coil wires after tagging them, and remove the coil. Tag and disconnect the spark plug wires from the plugs.
5. Remove the intake and exhaust manifolds.
6. Remove the rocker arm cover. Back off the rocker arm nuts, and pivot the rocker arms so the pushrods will clear.
7. Take a piece of heavy cardboard and cut 12 holes in it the same diameter as the pushrod stem. Number the holes in relation to the pushrods being removed. This cardboard holder will keep the pushrods in order (and hopefully out of harms way) while they are out of the engine. Remove the pushrods one at a time.

NOTE: *Pushrods MUST be returned to their original locations.*

8. Remove the cylinder head bolts one at a time, and mark them or keep them in order, as they should go back in their original locations. You may need a flex bar on your socket, or a piece of pipe on your ratchet, as the bolts are under a lot of torque.
9. Remove the cylinder head, along with the gasket. If the head seems tuck to the block, gently tap around the edge of the head with a

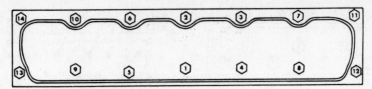

250 and 292 six cylinder head bolt torque sequence

rubber mallet until the joint breaks. NEVER pry between the head and block as you may gouge one or the other. Often it is necessary to carefully scrape the top of the engine block and the cylinder head to completely remove the gasket.

10. Clean the bottom of the head and top of block throughly before reinstalling the head. Place a new gasket over the dowel pin in the top of the block.

NOTE: *Different types of head gaskets are available. If you are using a steel/asbestos composition gasket, do not use gasket sealer.*

11. Lower the cylinder head carefully onto the block, over the dowel pins and gasket.

12. Coat the heads and threads of the cylinder head bolts with sealing compound, GM part No. 1052080 or equivalent, and install finger tight.

13. Tighten the heads bolts gradually in three stages, following the sequence illustrated, to the specification listed under Torque Specifications.

14. Install the pushrods in the exact location from which they were removed. Make sure they are seated in their lifter sockets.

15. Swing the rocker arms over into the correct position. Tighten the rocker arms until all pushrod play is taken up.

16. Install the manifold assembly, using new gaskets. Torque the manifold(s) to the specified torque.

17. Reverse the remainder of the removal procedure for installation. Adjust the valves, fol-lowing the procedure in this chapter. Use a new gasket or high temperature sealer when installing the rocker arm cover.

Gasoline V6 and V8s

1. Disconnect the negative battery cable.

2. Drain the coolant and save it if still fresh. CAUTION: *When draining the coolant, keep in mind that cats and dogs are attracted by the ethylene glycol antifreeze, and are quite likely to drink any that is left in an uncovered container or in puddles on the ground. This will prove fatal in sufficient quantity. Always drain the coolant into a sealable container. Coolant should be reused unless it is contaminated or several years old.*

3. Remove the air cleaner.

4. Remove the air conditioning compressor, but do not disconnect any air conditioning lines. Secure the compressor to one side.

5. Disconnect the AIR hose at the check valve.

6. Remove the intake manifold.

7. When removing the right cylinder head, loosen the alternator belt, disconnect the wiring and remove the alternator.

8. When removing the left cylinder head, re-move the dipstick, power steering pump and air pump if so equipped.

9. Label the spark plug wires and disconnect them.

10. Disconnect the exhaust manifold from the head being removed.

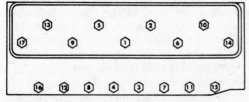

Small-block V8 cylinder head torque sequence

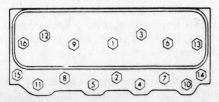

Big-block V8 torque sequence

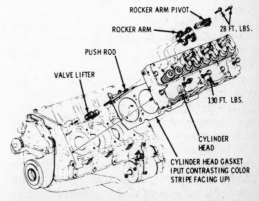

Typical Chevrolet gasoline V8 cylinder head instal-lation, all engines similar

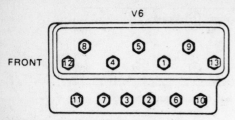

V6 262 Cylinder head torque sequence

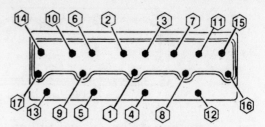

379 diesel cylinder head torque sequence

11. Remove the valve cover. Scribe the rocker arms with an identifying mark for reassembly; it is important that the rocker assembly is reinstalled in the same position as it was removed. Remove the rocker arm bolts, rocker arms and pivots.

12. Take a piece of heavy cardboard and cut 12 (V6), 16 holes (V8) (or half the number of holes if you are only removing one head) in it the same diameter as the pushrod stem. Number the holes in relation to the pushrods being removed. This cardboard holder will keep the pushrods in order (and hopefully out of harm's way) while they are out of the engine. Remove the pushrods.

NOTE: *Pushrods MUST be returned to their original locations.*

13. On models equipped with power brakes, it is necessary to disconnect the brake booster and turn it sideways to remove the No. 7 pushrod.

14. Remove the cylinder head bolts, and remove the cylinder head and gasket. If the head seems stuck to the block, gently tap around the edge of the head with a rubber mallet until the joint breaks.

15. Install the rocker arms and push rods in their original position. Adjust the valves as outlined earlier. New head gasket(s) should be used. On all engines, the head bolts should be dipped in clean oil before installing. Tighten all head bolts in sequence to the specified torque (see Torque Specifications chart in this chapter).

NOTE: *When installing the intake manifold remember to use new gaskets.*

Diesel Engines

1. Remove the intake manifold, using the procedure outlined above.

2. Remove the rocker arm cover(s), after removing any accessory brackets which interfere with cover removal.

3. Disconnect and label the glow plug wiring.

4. If the right cylinder head is being removed, remove the ground strap from the head.

5. On the 350, remove the rocker arms bolts, the bridged pivots, the rocker arms, and the pushrods, keeping all the parts in order so that they can be returned to their original positions. On the 379, remove the rocker shaft assemblies. It is a good practice to number or mark the parts to avoid interchanging them.

6. Remove the fuel return lines from the nozzles.

7. Remove the exhaust manifold(s), using the procedure outlined earlier in this chapter.

8. On the 8-350, remove the engine block drain plug on the side of the engine from which the cylinder head is being removed.

9. Remove the head bolts. Remove the cylinder head.

10. To install, first clean the mating surfaces thoroughly. Install new head gaskets on the engine block. DO NOT coat the gaskets with any sealer on the either engine. The gaskets have a special coating that eliminates the need for sealer. The use of sealer will interfere with this coating and cause leaks. Install the cylinder head onto the block.

11. Clean the head bolts thoroughly. On the 350, dip the bolts in clean engine oil and install them into the cylinder block until the heads of the bolts lightly contact the cylinder head. On the 379, the left rear head bolt must be installed into the head prior to head installation. Coat the threads of the 379 cylinder head bolts with sealing compound (GM part #1052080 or equivalent) before installation.

12. On the 350, tighten the bolts in the illustrated sequence to 100 ft.lb. When all the bolts have been tightened to this figure, begin the tightening sequence again, and torque all bolts to 130 ft.lb. On the 379, tighten each bolt gradually in the sequence shown until the final torque specified (100 ft.lb.) is met.

13. Install the engine block drain plugs on the 350, the exhaust manifolds, the fuel return lines, the glow plug wiring, and the ground strap for the right cylinder head.

14. Install the valve train assembly. Refer to the Diesel Engine Rocker Arm Replacement in this chapter for the valve lifter bleeding procedures.

15. Install the intake manifold.

16. Install the valve covers. These are sealed with RTV-type silicone sealer instead of a gasket. See the Valve Cover procedure for proper

sealer application. Install the cover to the head within 10 minutes, while the sealer is still wet.

CLEANING AND INSPECTION

Gasoline Engines

NOTE: *Any diesel cylinder head work should be handled by a reputable machine shop familiar with diesel engines. Disassembly, valve lapping, and assembly can be completed by following the gasoline engine procedures.*

Once the complete valve train has been removed from the cylinder head(s), the head itself can be inspected, cleaned and machined (if necessary). Set the head(s) on a clean work space, so the combustion chambers are facing up. Begin cleaning the chambers and ports with a hardwood chisel or other non-metallic tool (to avoid nicking or gouging the chamber, ports, and especially the valve seats). Chip away the major carbon deposits, then remove the remainder of carbon with a wire brush fitted to an electric drill.

Be sure that the carbon is actually removed, rather than just burnished. After decarbonizing is completed, take the head(s) to a machine shop and have the head hot tanked. In this process, the head is lowered into a hot chemical bath that very effectively cleans all grease, corrosion, and scale from all internal and external head surfaces. Also have the machinist check the valve seats and recut them if necessary. When you bring the clean head(s) home, place them on a clean surface. Completely clean the entire valve train with solvent.

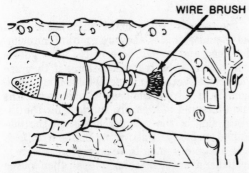

Use a wire brush and electric drill to remove carbon from the combustion chambers and exhaust ports

CHECKING FOR HEAD WARPAGE

Lay the head down with the combustion chambers facing up. Place a straightedge across the gasket surface of the head, both diagonally and straight across the center. Using a flat feeler gauge, determine the clearance at the center

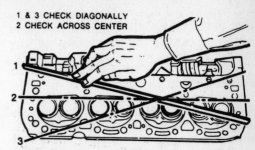

Check the cylinder head mating surface for warpage with a precision straight edge

of the straightedge. If warpage exceeds 0.003″ in a 6″ span, or 0.006″ over the total length, the cylinder head must be resurfaced (which is akin to planing a piece of wood). Resurfacing can be performed at most machine shops.

NOTE: *When resurfacing the cylinder head(s) of V8 engines, the intake manifold mounting position is altered, and must be corrected by machining a proportionate amount from the intake manifold flange.*

Valves and Springs

REMOVAL AND INSTALLATION

Cylinder Heads Removed

1. Remove the head(s), and place on a clean surface.

2. Using a suitable spring compressor (for pushrod type overhead valve engines), compress the valve spring and remove the valve spring cap key. Release the spring compressor and remove the valve spring and cap (and valve rotator on some engines).

NOTE: *Use care in removing the keys; they are easily lost.*

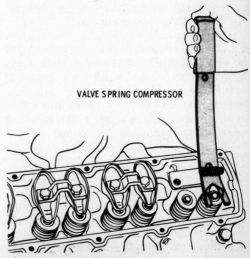

Removing the valve springs

3. Remove the valve seals from the intake valve guides. Throw these old seals away, as you'll be installing new seals during reassembly.

4. Slide the valves out of the head from the combustion chamber side.

5. Make a holder for the valves out of a piece of wood or cardboard, as outlined for the pushrods in gasoline engine Cylinder Head Removal. Make sure you number each hole in the cardboard to keep the valves in proper order. Slide the valves out of the head from the combustion chamber side; they MUST be installed as they were removed.

Cylinder Head(s) Installed

It is often not necessary to remove the cylinder head(s) in order to service the valve train. Such is the case when valve seals need to be replaced. Valve seals can be easily replaced with the head(s) on the engine; the only special equipment needed for this job are an air line adapter (sold in most auto parts stores), which screws a compressed air line into the spark plug hole of the cylinder on which you are working, and a valve spring compressor. A source of compressed air is needed, of course.

1. Remove the valve cover as previously detailed.

2. Remove the spark plug, rocker arm and push rod on the cylinder(s) to be serviced.

3. Install the air line adapter (GM tool #J-23590 or equivalent) into the spark plug hole. Turn on the air compressor to apply compressed air into the cylinder. This keeps the valves up in place.

NOTE: *Set the regulator of the air compressor at least 50 pounds to ensure adequate pressure.*

4. Using the valve spring compressor, compress the valve spring and remove the valve keys and keepers, the valve spring and damper.

5. Remove the valve stem seal.

6. To reassemble, oil the valve stem and new seal. Install a new seal over the valve stem. Set the spring, damper and keeper in place. Compress the spring. Coat the keys with grease to hold them onto the valve stem and install the keys, making sure they are seated fully in the keeper. Reinstall the valve cover after adjusting the valves, as outlined in this chapter.

INSPECTION

Inspect the valve faces and seats (in the head) for pits, burned spots and other evidence of poor seating. If a valve face is in such bad shape that the head of the valve must be ground in order to true up the face, discard the valve because the sharp edge will run too hot. The correct angle for valve faces is 45 degrees. We recommend the refacing be done at a reputable machine shop.

Check the valve stem for scoring and burned spots. If not noticeably scored or damaged, clean the valve stem with solvent to remove all gum and varnish. Clean the valve guides using solvent and an expanding wire type valve guide cleaner. If you have access to a dial indicator for measuring valve stem-to-guide clearance, mount it so that the stem of the indicator is at 90 degrees to the valve stem, and as close to the valve guide as possible. Move the valve off its seat, and measure the valve guide-to-stem clearance by rocking the stem back and forth to actuate the dial indicator. Measure the valve stems using a micrometer, and compare to specifications to determine whether stem or guide wear is responsible for the excess clearance. If a dial indicator and micrometer are not available to you, take your cylinder head and valves to a reputable machine shop for inspection.

Some of the engines covered in this guide are equipped with valve rotators, which double as valve spring caps. In normal operation the rotators put a certain degree of wear on the tip of the valve stem; this wear appears as concentric rings on the stem tip. However, if the rotator is not working properly, the wear may appear as straight notches or **X** patterns across the valve stem tip. Whenever the valves are removed from the cylinder head, the tips should be inspected for improper pattern, which could indicate valve rotator problems. Valve stem tips will have to be ground flat if rotator patterns are severe.

Valve Guides

The engines covered in this guide use integral valve guides; that is, they are a part of the cylinder head and cannot be replaced. The guides can, however, be reamed oversize if they are found to be worn past an acceptable limit. Occasionally, a valve guide bore will be oversize as manufactured. These are marked on the inboard side of the cylinder heads on the machined surface just above the intake manifold.

If the guides must be reamed (this service is available at most machine shops), then valves with oversize stems must be fitted. Valves are usually available in 0.001″, 0.003″ and 0.005″ stem oversizes. Valve guides which are not excessively worn or distorted may, in some cases, be knurled rather than reamed. Knurling is a process in which the metal on the valve guide bore is displaced and raised, thereby reducing clearance. Knurling also provides excellent oil control. The option of knurling rather than reaming valve guides should be discussed with a reputable machinist or engine specialist.

Lapping the valves by hand

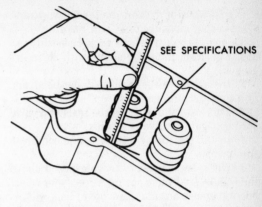

Check valve spring installed height

LAPPING THE VALVES

When valve faces and seats have been refaced and recut, or if they are determined to be in good condition, the valves must be lapped in to ensure efficient sealing when the valve closes against the seat.

1. Invert the cylinder head so that the combustion chambers are facing up.

2. Lightly lubricate the valve stems with clean oil, and coat the valve seats with valve grinding compound. Install the valves in the head as numbered.

3. Attach the suction cup of a valve lapping tool to a valve head. You'll probably have to moisten the cup to securely attach the tool to the valve.

4. Rotate the tool between the palms, changing position and lifting the tool often to prevent grooving. Lap the valve until a smooth, polished seat is evident (you may have to add a bit more compound after some lapping is done).

5. Remove the valve and tool, and remove ALL traces of grinding compound with solvent soaked rag, or rinse the head with solvent.

NOTE: *Valve lapping can also be done by fastening a suction cup to a piece of drill rod in a hand eggbeater type drill. Proceed as above, using the drill as a lapping tool. Due to the higher speeds involved when using the hand drill, care must be exercised to avoid grooving the seat. Lift the tool and change direction of rotation often.*

Valve Springs

HEIGHT AND PRESSURE CHECK

1. Place the valve spring on a flat, clean surface next to a square.

2. Measure the height of the spring, and rotate it against the edge of the square to measure distortion (out-of-roundness). If spring height

varies between springs by more than $\frac{1}{16}''$ or if the distortion exceeds $\frac{1}{16}''$ replace the spring.

A valve spring tester is needed to test spring test pressure, so the valve springs must usually be taken to a professional machine shop for this test. Spring pressure at the installed and compressed heights is checked, and a tolerance of plus or minus 5 lbs. is permissible on the springs covered in this guide.

VALVE INSTALLATION

NOTE: *For installing new valve stem seals without removing the cylinder head(s), see the procedure under Valves and Springs— Cylinder Head(s) Installed earlier in this chapter.*

New valve seals must be installed when the valve train is put back together. Certain seals slip over the valve stem and guide boss, while others require that the boss be machined. In some applications Teflon® guide seals are available. Check with a machinist and/or automotive parts store for a suggestion on the proper seals to use.

NOTE: *Remember that when installing valve seals, a small amount of oil must be able*

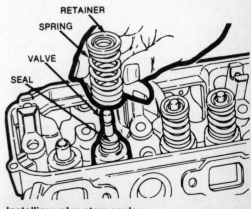

Installing valve stem seals

to pass the seal to lubricate the valve guides; otherwise, excessive wear will result.

To install the valves and rocker assembly.

1. Lubricate the valve stems with clean engine oil.

2. Install the valves in the cylinder head, one at a time, as numbered.

3. Lubricate and position the seals and valve springs, again a valve at a time.

4. Install the spring retainers, and compress the springs.

5. With the valve key groove exposed above the compressed valve spring, wipe some wheel bearing grease around the groove. This will retain the keys as you release the spring compressor.

6. Using needlenosed pliers (or your fingers), place the keys in the key grooves. The grease should hold the keys in place. Slowly release the spring compressor; the valve cap or rotator will raise up as the compressor is released, retaining the keys.

7. Install the rocker assembly, and install the cylinder head(s).

VALVE ADJUSTMENT

All gasoline and diesel engines in this guide use hydraulic valve lifters, which require no periodic maintenance or adjustment. However, in the event of cylinder head removal or any operation that requires disturbing or removing the rocker arms, the rocker arms have to be adjusted.

NOTE: *Please refer to the valve arrangement illustrations which appear earlier in this chapter.*

Inline 6-Cylinder
PRELIMINARY ADJUSTMENT

After rocker arm or cylinder head disassembly, proceed as follows:

1. Remove the valve cover if it is not already removed.

2. Remove the distributor cap and crank the engine until the rotor points at number one plug terminal in the cap. It is easier to do this if you mark the location of number one plug wire before you remove the cap. The points should be open (pre-1975) and timing marks should be aligned. (the 0 degree mark on the timing tab). Number one cylinder should now be at TDC.

3. With the number one cylinder of the six in this position, adjust: Intake valves 1,2,4, and exhaust valves 1,3,5 (numbered from the front of the engine). The adjustment is performed as follows: Turn the adjusting nut until all lash is removed from this particular valve train. This is determined by checking pushrod sideplay while turning the adjusting nut. When all play

has been removed, turn the adjusting nut one more turn. This will place the lifter plunger in the center of its travel.

4. Crank the engine over through one complete revolution until number six cylinder is in the firing (TDC, timing pointer at 0 degree) position. As this point, you can adjust the following valves on the 6-250: Intake valves 3,5, and 6; exhaust valves 2,4 and 6.

5. After the engine is running, readjust the valves following the procedure under Engine Running. Install the valve covers using new gaskets or sealer.

ENGINE RUNNING ADJUSTMENT

1. Run the engine until normal operating temperature is attained. Remove the valve cover. To prevent oil splashing, install oil deflector clips, which are available at auto supply stores.

2. With the engine at idle, back off the rocker arm nut until the rocker arm begins to clatter.

3. Slowly tighten the rocker arm nut until the clatter just stops. This is zero lash.

4. Tighten the nut another quarter turn and then wait about ten seconds until the engine is running smoothly. Tighten the nut another quarter turn and wait another ten seconds. Repeat the procedure until the nut has been turned down one full turn from zero lash.

NOTE: *Pausing ten seconds each time allows the lifter to adjust itself. Failing to pause might cause interference between the intake valve and the piston top causing internal damage and bent pushrods.*

5. Adjust the remaining valves in the same manner.

6. Replace the valve cover.

V6 and V8 Including 350 Diesel

NOTE: *After the 350 diesel valves are adjusted (following rocker arm or cylinder head removal and installation), the hydraulic lifters must be bled down. See the lifter bleeding procedure under Rocker Arm Removal and Installation — 350 Diesel earlier in this chapter.*

1. Remove the valve covers and crank the engine until the mark on the damper aligns with the TDC or 0 degree mark on the timing tab and the engine is in the No. 1 firing position. This can be determined by placing the fingers on the No. 1 cylinder valves as the marks align. If the valves do not move, it is in the No. 1 firing position. If the valves move, it is in the No. 6 firing position and the crankshaft should be rotated one more revolution to the No. 1 firing position.

2. With the engine in the No. 1 firing position, the following valves can be adjusted:

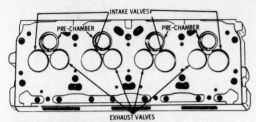

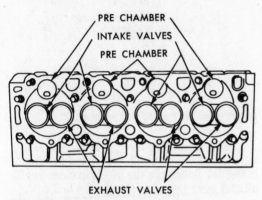

Diesel 350 V8 valve location

6.2L (379) diesel valve arrangement

- V8: Exhaust 1, 3, 4, 8
- V8: Intake 1, 2, 5, 7
- V6: Exhaust 1, 5, 6
- V6: Intake 1, 2, 3

NOTE: *Even numbered cylinders are on the right bank, odd numbered cylinders are on the left bank, when viewed from the rear of the engine.*

3. Back out the adjusting nut until lash is felt at the pushrod, then turn the adjusting nut in until all lash is removed. This can be determined by checking pushrod end-play while turning the adjusting nut. When all play has

been removed, turn the adjusting nut in 1 full turn to center the lifter plunger.

4. Crank the engine 1 full revolution until the marks are again in alignment. This is the No. 6 firing position (no. 4 on V6). The following valves can now be adjusted:

- V8: Exhaust 2, 5, 6, 7
- V8: Intake 3, 4, 6, 8
- V6: Exhaust 2, 3, 4
- V6: Intake 4, 5, 6

6. Install the valve covers using new gaskets or sealer as required.

Valve Lifters

REMOVAL AND INSTALLATION

Inline 6-Cylinder

1. Remove the rocker arm cover.

2. Loosen the rocker arm until you can rotate it away from the pushrod, giving clearance to the top of the pushrod.

3. Remove the pushrod. If you are replacing all of the lifters, it is wise to make a pushrod holder as mentioned under Cylinder Head Removal. This will help keep the pushrods in order, as they MUST go back in their original positions.

4. Remove the pushrod covers on the side of the block.

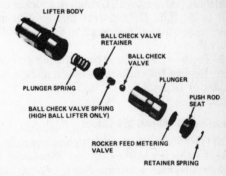

Valve lifter, exploded view

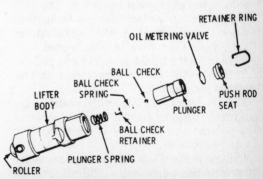

Roller lifter, all 379 and 1981 350 diesel engines. 1980 and earlier 350s have a conventional lifter

Typical valve adjustment, all except 6.2L diesel

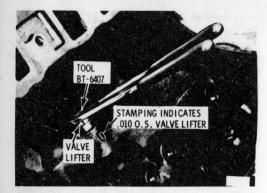

Removing hydraulic valve lifter

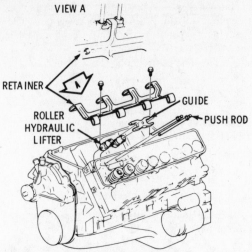

Diesel valve lifter guide and retainer

5. Remove the lifter(s). A hydraulic lifter removal tool (GM part #J-3049 or equivalent) is available at dealers and most parts stores, and is quite handy for this procedure.

6. Before installing new lifters, all sealer coating must be removed from the inside. This can be done with kerosene or carburetor cleaning solvent. Also, the new lifters must be primed before installation, as dry lifters will seize when the engine is started. Submerge the lifters in clean engine oil and work the lifter plunger up and down.

7. Install the lifter(s) and pushrod(s) into the cylinder block in their original positions.

8. Pivot the rocker arm back into its original position. With the lifter on the base circle of the camshaft (valve closed), tighten the rocker arm nut to 20 ft.lb. Do not over torque. You will have to rotate the crankshaft to do the individual valves.

9. Replace the pushrod covers using new gaskets. Replace the rocker arm cover, using a new gasket or sealer.

Gasoline V6, V8 and 350 Diesel

NOTE: *Valve lifters and pushrods should be kept in order so they can be reinstalled in their original position. Some engines will have both standard size and 0.010" oversize valve lifters as original equipment. The oversize lifters are etched with an* **O** *on their sides; the cylinder block will also be marked with an* **O** *if the oversize lifter is used.*

1. Remove the intake manifold and gasket.

2. Remove the valve covers, rocker arm assemblies and pushrods.

3. If the lifters are coated with varnish, apply carburetor cleaning solvent to the lifter body. The solvent should dissolve the varnish in about 10 minutes.

4. Remove the lifters. On diesels, remove the lifter retainer guide bolts, and remove the guides. A special tool for removing lifters is available, and is helpful for this procedure.

5. New lifter MUST be primed before installation, as dry lifters will seize when the engine is started. Submerge the lifters in clean engine oil and work the lifter plunger up and down.

6. Install the lifters and pushrods into the cylinder block in their original order. On diesels, install the lifter retainer guide.

7. Install the intake manifold gaskets and manifold.

8. Position the rocker arms, pivots and bolts on the cylinder head.

9. Install the valve covers, connect the spark plug wires and install the air cleaner.

8-379 Diesel

1. Remove the valve covers as previously detailed.

2. Remove the rocker shaft assemblies.

3. Remove the cylinder head(s).

4. Remove the guide clamps and guide plates. It may be necessary to use mechanical fingers to remove the guide plates.

5. Using GM tool #J-29834 or another suitable lifter removal tool and a magnet, remove the lifter(s) through the access in the block.

6. Coat the lifters with clean engine oil before installation. If installing new lifters, they must be primed first by working the lifter plunger while the lifter is submerged in clean kerosene or diesel fuel. Lifters that have not been primed will seize when the engine is started.

7. Install the lifters in their original positions in the block. A lifter installation tool can be fabricated out of welding rod or similar gauge wire and may help.

8. Install the lifter guide plate and guide plate clamp. The crankshaft must be turned two full rotations (720 degrees) after assembly

of the lifter guide plate clamp to insure free movement of the lifters in the guide plates.

9. Install the remainder of components in the reverse order of removal.

NOTE: *The pushrods must be installed with their painted ends facing UP.*

Oil Pan

REMOVAL AND INSTALLATION

Inline 6-Cylinder

1. Disconnect the negative battery cable. Raise the vehicle and support it safely. Drain the engine oil.

2. Remove the flywheel cover. Remove the starter assembly.

3. Remove the engine mount through bolts from the engine front mounts. Raise the engine enough to remove the oil pan.

4. Remove the oil pan retaining bolts. Remove the oil pan from the engine.

5. Installation is the reverse of the removal procedure. Use new gaskets or RTV sealant, as required. Torque the pan to front cover bolts to 45 in. lbs. Torque the 1/4 in. pan to block bolts to 80 in. lbs. and the 5/16 in. bolts to 165 in. lbs.

Gasoline V8 and V6 Engines

1. Disconnect the negative battery cable. Remove the air cleaner assembly, as required. Remove the distributor cap, if necessary.

2. Raise the vehicle and support it safely. Drain the engine oil. Remove the flywheel cover. Remove the starter assembly.

3. On some vehicles equipped with V6 engine, remove the strut rods at the flywheel cover, as necessary.

4. On 4wd vehicles with automatic transmission, remove the strut rods at the engine mounts.

5. On vehicles equipped with gauges, remove the oil pressure line from the side of the engine block to avoid damage when raising the engine. As necessary, remove the oil filter.

6. Properly raise the engine to gain clearance in order to remove the oil pan. Remove the oil pan retaining bolts. Remove the oil pan from the engine.

7. Installation is the reverse of the removal procedure. Use new gaskets or RTV sealant, as required. On the V6 engine torque the pan retaining bolts to 100 in. lbs. On the small block V8 engines torque the bolts to 100 in. lbs. and the nuts to 200 in. lbs. On some 350 engines so equipped, torque the oil pan baffle bolts to 26 ft. lbs. On the 454 V8 engine torque the pan to front cover to 70 in. lbs and the pan to block to 135 in. lbs.

Diesel Engines

1. Remove the vacuum pump and drive (with air conditioning) or the oil pump drive (without air conditioning).

2. Disconnect the batteries and remove the dipstick.

3. Remove the upper radiator support and fan shroud.

4. Raise and support the truck. Drain the oil.

5. Remove the flywheel cover.

6. Disconnect the exhaust and crossover pipes.

7. Remove the oil cooler lines at the filter base.

8. Remove the starter assembly. Support the engine with a jack.

9. Remove the engine mounts from the block.

10. Raise the front of the engine and remove the oil pan.

11. Installation is the reverse of removal. On the 8-379 diesel engine torque all but the rear two pan retaining bolts to 84 in. lbs and the two rear bolts to 17 ft. lbs. On the 8-350 diesel engine torque all pan retaining bolts to 10 ft. lbs.

Oil Pump

REMOVAL AND INSTALLATION

Gasoline and Diesel

The oil pump is mounted to the bottom of the block and is accessible only by removing the oil pan.

On all engines, including diesel, remove the oil pan, then unbolt and remove the oil pump and screen as an assembly. On the inline sixes, remove the flange mounting bolts and nut from the elongated number 6 main bearing cap bolt, then remove the pump.

To install, align the oil pump drive shaft on

DRIVE SHAFT EXTENSION

DRIVE SHAFT

OIL PUMP ATTACHING BOLTS TORQUE 35 FT. LBS.

PICK UP MUST BE SQUARE WITH MOUNTING SURFACE

Oil pump installation, typical

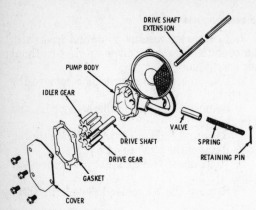

Oil pump exploded view

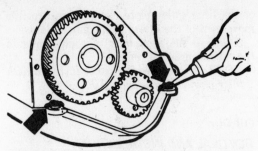

Applying sealer front cover mounting on the 250 in-line six

Oil pan front seal modification

the inline 6-cylinder engines to match with the distributor tang and position the pump flange over the distributor lower bushing. Install the pump mounting bolts. On V6 and V8 engines, insert the drive shaft extension through the opening in the main bearing cap until the shaft mates with the distributor drive gear. You may have to turn the drive shaft extension one way or the other to get the two to mesh. Position the pump on the cap and install the attaching bolts. Install the oil pans on all engines.

Timing Chain Cover and Front Oil Seal

REMOVAL AND INSTALLATION

Inline 6-Cylinder

1. Drain the engine coolant, remove the radiator hoses, and remove the radiator.

CAUTION: *When draining the coolant, keep in mind that cats and dogs are attracted by the ethylene glycol antifreeze, and are quite likely to drink any that is left in an uncovered container or in puddles on the ground. This will prove fatal in sufficient quantity. Always drain the coolant into a sealable container. Coolant should be reused unless it is contaminated or several years old.*

2. Remove the fan belt and any accessory belts. Remove the fan pulley.

3. A harmonic balancer puller is necessary to pull the balancer. Install the puller and remove the balancer.

4. Remove the two screws which attach the oil pan to the front cover. Remove the screws which attach the front cover to the block. Do not remove the cover yet.

5. Before the front cover is removed, it is necessary to cut the oil pan front seal. Pull the cover forward slightly.

6. Using a sharp knife or razor knife, cut the oil pan front seal flush with the cylinder block on both sides of the cover.

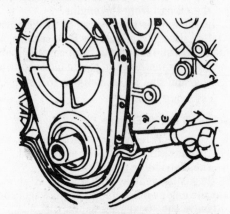

Cut the oil pan seal flush with the front of the block

Installing timing cover, inline six cylinder

7. Remove the front cover and the attached portion of oil pan front seal. Remove the front cover gasket from the block.

8. To install the front cover, first obtain an

oil pan front seal. Cut the tabs from the new seal.

9. Install the seal in the front cover, pressing the tips into the holes provided in the cover. Coat the mating area of the front cover with a room temperature vulcanizing (RTV) sealer first.

10. Coat the new front cover gasket with sealer and install it on the cover.

11. Apply a ⅛" bead of RTV sealer to the joint formed at the oil pan and cylinder block.

12. Install the front cover.

13. Install the harmonic balancer. Make sure the front cover seal is positioned evenly around the balancer. If you do not have access to a balancer installation tool (and you probably don't) you can either fabricate one using the illustration as a guide, or you can tap the balancer on using a brass or plastic mallet. If you use the last method, make sure the balancer goes on evenly.

14. The rest of the installation is in the reverse order of removal.

Gasoline V6 and V8s

1. Drain the cooling system.

CAUTION: *When draining the coolant, keep in mind that cats and dogs are attracted by the ethylene glycol antifreeze, and are quite likely to drink any that is left in an uncovered container or in puddles on the ground. This will prove fatal in sufficient quantity. Always drain the coolant into a sealable container. Coolant should be reused unless it is contaminated or several years old.*

2. Remove the crankshaft pulley and damper, using Tool J-23523 Damper Pulley remover and installer. Remove the water pump. Remove the screws holding the timing case cover to the block and remove the cover and gaskets.

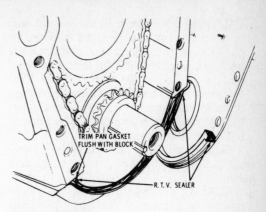

Sealer application

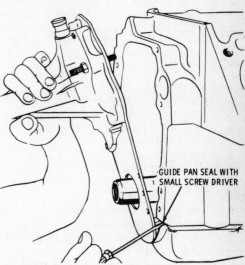

Guiding front cover into place. Be careful seal remains in place

3. Use a suitable tool to pry the old seal out of the front face of the cover.

4. Install the new seal so that the open end is toward the inside of the cover, using Tool J-35468 Seal installer.

NOTE: *Coat the lip of the new seal with oil prior to installation.*

5. Check that the timing chain oil slinger is in place against the crankshaft sprocket.

6. Apply sealer to the front cover as shown in the accompanying illustration. Install the cover carefully onto the locating dowels.

7. Tighten the attaching screws to 6-8 ft.lb.

8. Install the damper pulley using Tool J-23523 Damper Pulley installer and torque the retaining bolt to specifications. (See the Torque Specifications Chart).

8-350 Diesel

1. Drain the cooling system and disconnect the radiator hoses.

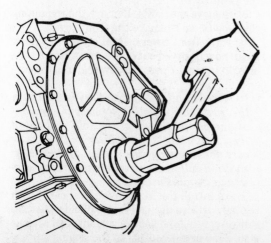

Seal installation with cover installed, V8s

CAUTION: *When draining the coolant, keep in mind that cats and dogs are attracted by the ethylene glycol antifreeze, and are quite likely to drink any that is left in an uncovered container or in puddles on the ground. This will prove fatal in sufficient quantity. Always drain the coolant into a sealable container. Coolant should be reused unless it is contaminated or several years old.*

2. Remove all belts, fan and pulley, crankshaft pulley and balancer, using a balancer puller.

WARNING: *The use of any other type of puller, such as a universal claw type which pulls on the outside of the hub, can destroy the balancer. The outside ring of the balancer is bonded in rubber to the hub. Pulling on the outside will break the bond. The timing mark is on the outside ring. If it is suspected that the bond is broken, check that the center of the keyway is 16 degrees from the center of the timing slot. In addition, there are chiseled aligning marks between the weight and the hub.*

3. Unbolt and remove the cover, timing indicator and water pump.

4. It may be necessary to grind a flat on the cover for gripping purposes.

5. Grind a chamfer on one end of each dowel pin.

6. Cut the excess material from the front end of the oil pan gasket on each side of the block.

7. Clean the block, oil pan and front cover mating surfaces with solvent.

8. Trim about ⅛″ off each end of a new front pan seal.

9. Install a new front cover gasket on the block and a new seal in the front cover.

10. Apply sealer to the gasket around the coolant holes.

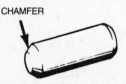

CHAMFER

Grinding chamfer o 350 diesel dowel pin

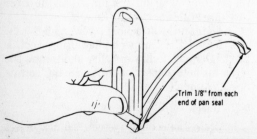

Trim 1/8″ from each end of pan seal

Trimming pan seal with razor blade

11. Apply sealer to the block at the junction of the pan and front cover.

12. Place the cover on the block and press down to compress the seal. Rotate the cover left and right and guide the pan seal into the cavity using a small screwdriver. Oil the bolt threads and install two bolts to hold the cover in place. Install both dowel pins (chamfered end first), then install the remaining front cover bolts.

13. Apply a lubricant, compatible with rubber, on the balancer seal surface.

14. Install the balancer and bolt. Torque the bolt to 200-300 ft.lb.

15. Install the other parts in the reverse order of removal.

379 Diesel

1. Drain the cooling system.

CAUTION: *When draining the coolant, keep in mind that cats and dogs are attracted by the ethylene glycol antifreeze, and are quite likely to drink any that is left in an uncovered container or in puddles on the ground. This will prove fatal in sufficient quantity. Always drain the coolant into a sealable container. Coolant should be reused unless it is contaminated or several years old.*

2. Remove the water pump as outlined elsewhere in this chapter.

3. Rotate the crankshaft to align the marks on the injection pump driven gear and the camshaft gear as shown in the illustration.

4. Scribe a mark aligning the injection pump flange and the front cover.

5. Remove the crankshaft pulley and torsional damper.

6. Remove the front cover-to-oil pan bolts (4).

7. Remove the two fuel return line clips.

8. Remove the injection pump drive gear. Remove the injection pump retaining nuts from the front cover.

9. Remove the baffle. Remove the remaining cover bolts, and remove the front cover.

10. If the front cover oil seal is to be replaced, it can now be pried out of the cover with a suitable prying tool. Press the new seal into the cover evenly.

NOTE: *The oil seal can also be replaced with the front cover installed. Remove the torsional damper first, then pry the old seal out of the cover using a suitable prying tool. Use care not to damage the surface of the crankshaft. Install the new seal evenly into the cover and install the damper.*

11. To install the front cover, first clean both sealing surfaces until all traces of old sealer are gone. Apply a 2mm bead of sealant (GM sealant #1052357 or equivalent) to the sealing surface as shown in the illustration. Apply a bead of

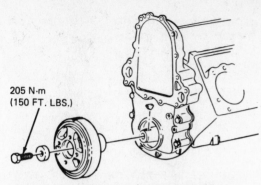

205 N·m
(150 FT. LBS.)

379 diesel crankshaft (torsional) damper. Note key

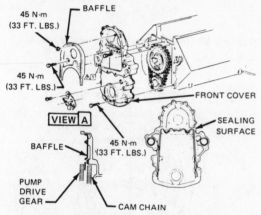

45 N·m
(33 FT. LBS.)

BAFFLE

45 N·m
(33 FT. LBS.)

FRONT COVER

VIEW A

45 N·m
(33 FT. LBS.)

SEALING
SURFACE

BAFFLE

PUMP
DRIVE
GEAR

CAM CHAIN

Front cover assembly showing sealer application, 379 diesel

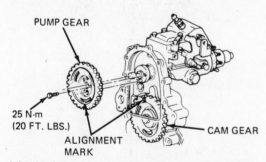

PUMP GEAR

25 N·m
(20 FT. LBS.)

ALIGNMENT
MARK

CAM GEAR

Injection pump and cam gear alignment, 379 diesel

RTV-type sealer to the bottom portion of the front cover which attaches to the oil pan. Install the front cover.

12. Install the baffle.

13. Install the injection pump, making sure the scribe marks on the pump and front cover are aligned.

14. Install the injection pump driven gear, making sure the marks on the cam gear and pump gear are aligned. Be sure the dowel pin and the three holes on the pump flange are also aligned.

15. Install the fuel line clips, the front cover-

to-oil pan bolts, and the torsional damper and crankshaft pulley. Torque the pan bolts to 4-7 ft.lb., and the damper bolt to 140-162 ft.lb.

Timing Gears
REMOVAL AND INSTALLATION
Inline 6-Cylinder

The camshaft in these engines is gear-driven, unlike the chain-driven cams in V8s. The removal of the timing gear requires removal of the camshaft.

1. After the cam is removed, place the camshaft and gear in an arbor press and remove the gear from the cam. Many well equipped machine shops have this piece of equipment if you need the gear pressed off.

2. Installation is in the reverse order of removal. The clearance between the camshaft and the thrust plate should be 0.001-0.005″ on both engines. If less than 0.0015″ clearance exists, the spacer ring should be replaced. If more than 0.005″ clearance, the thrust plate should be replaced.

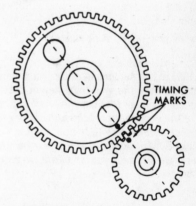

TIMING
MARKS

Inline six-cylinder timing gear alignment

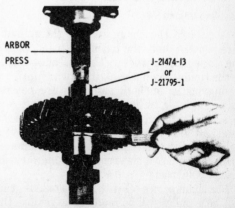

ARBOR
PRESS

J-21474-13
or
J-21795-1

Installing camshaft timing gear and checking thrust plate end clearances, inline sixes

Access holes in the inline six cylinder camshaft gear for the camshaft thrust plate screws

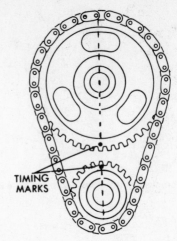

Gasoline V8 timing sprocket alignment, 1970–78

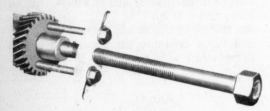

Crankshaft gear puller, inline sixes

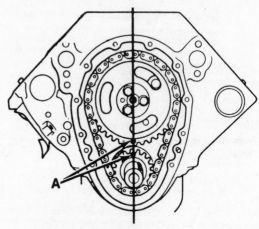

A. Align Marks as Shown

V6 262 timing sprocket alignment

WARNING: *The thrust plate must be positioned so that the Woodruff key in the shaft does not damage it when the shaft is pressed out of the gear. Support the hub of the gear or the gear will be seriously damaged.*

The 6-cylinder crankshaft gear may be removed with a gear puller while in place on the block.

Timing Chain And Sprockets
REMOVAL AND INSTALLATION
Gasoline V8 and V6

To replace the chain, remove the radiator core, water pump, the harmonic balancer and the crankcase front cover. This will allow access to the timing chain. Crank the engine until the timing marks on both sprockets are nearest each other and in line between the shaft centers. Then take out the three bolts that hold the camshaft gear to the camshaft. This gear is a light press fit on the camshaft and will come off easily. On others it may require a puller. It is located by a dowel.

The chain comes off with the camshaft gear.

A gear puller will be required to remove the crankshaft gear. Without disturbing the position of the engine, mount the new crankshaft

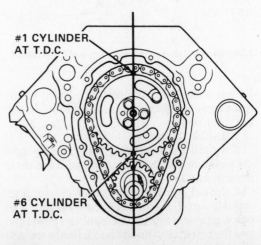

Timing sprocket alignment, 1979 and later gasoline V8s

Gasoline V8 crankshaft sprocket removal

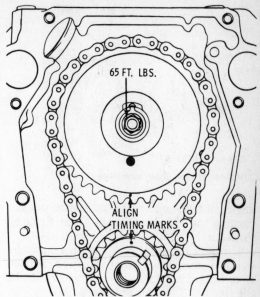

350 diesel timing sprocket alignment

gear on the shaft, and mount the chain over the camshaft gear. Arrange the camshaft gear in such a way that the timing marks will line up between the shaft centers and the camshaft locating dowel will enter the dowel hole in the cam sprocket.

Place the cam sprocket, with its chain mounted over it, in position on the front of the car and pull up with the three bolts that hold it to the camshaft. After the gears are in place, turn the engine two full revolutions to make certain that the timing marks are in correct alignment between the shaft centers.

NOTE: *When installing the timing chain, install the sprockets with the timing marks facing each other; this position is TDC of the No. 6 cyl. (V8) or No. 4 cyl. (V6). To locate the TDC of the No. 1 cyl., turn the crankshaft one full revolution, the camshaft timing mark will now be at the top of the sprocket.*

8-350 Diesel

1. Remove the crankshaft pulley, the harmonic balancer and the front cover as previously detailed.
2. Align the timing marks on the cam and crankshaft.
3. Remove the oil slinger and camshaft sprocket retaining nut.
4. Remove the crankshaft sprocket. The sprocket-to-crankshaft fit is such that a puller may be necessary. If possible, the crankshaft key should be removed before using the puller. If this is not possible, align the puller so that the fingers of the tool do not overlap the end of the key when the sprocket is removed. The keyway is machined only part way in the crankshaft sprocket, and breakage can occur if the sprocket is improperly removed.
5. Remove the timing chain and camshaft sprocket.
6. The fuel pump eccentric is behind the crankshaft sprocket, and may be removed if necessary.
7. Install the key in the crankshaft, if removed. Install the fuel pump eccentric, if removed.
8. Install the camshaft sprocket, crankshaft sprocket, and the timing chain together, with the timing marks aligned. Tighten the camshaft sprocket retaining bolt to 65 ft.lb.

NOTE: *When the two timing marks are in alignment and closest together, the No. 6 cylinder is at TDC. To obtain TDC for No. 1 cylinder, slowly rotate the crankshaft one full revolution. This will move the camshaft sprocket timing mark to the top. No. 1 cylinder will then be at TDC.*

9. Install the oil slinger.
10. The injection pump must be re-timed. Refer to Chapter 2.
11. Install the front cover, harmonic balancer, and the crankshaft pulley.

8-379 Diesel

1. Remove the front cover as previously detailed.
2. Remove the bolt and washer attaching the camshaft gear. Remove the injection pump gear.
3. Remove the camshaft sprocket, timing chain, and crankshaft sprocket as a unit.
4. To install, the cam sprocket, timing chain and crankshaft sprocket as a unit, aligning the timing marks on the sprockets as shown in the illustration.
5. Rotate the crankshaft 360 degrees so that the camshaft gear and the injection pump gear

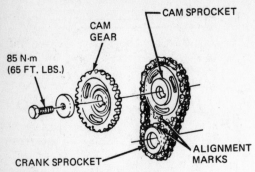

379 diesel timing chain assembly

Checking camshaft gear runout, inline six engines

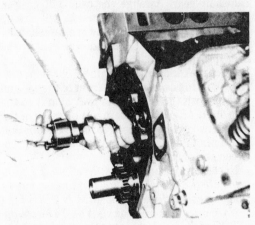

Removing camshaft. Slowly turn the cam as you remove it

are aligned as shown in the illustration (accompanying the 379 Diesel Front Cover Removal Procedure).

6. Install the front cover as previously detailed. The injection pump must be retimed since the timing chain assembly was removed. See Chapter 2 for this procedure.

Camshaft

REMOVAL AND INSTALLATION

Inline 6-Cylinder

1. Remove the grille. Remove the radiator hoses and remove the radiator.

2. Remove the timing gear cover.

3. Remove the valve cover and gasket, loosen all the rocker arm nuts, and pivot the rocker arms clear of the pushrods.

4. Remove the distributor and the fuel pump.

5. Remove the pushrods. Remove the coil and then remove the side cover. Remove the valve lifters.

6. Remove the two camshaft thrust plate retaining screws by working through the holes in the camshaft gear.

7. Remove the camshaft and gear assembly by pulling it out through the front of the block.

8. If either the camshaft or the camshaft gear is being renewed, the gear must be pressed off the camshaft. The replacement parts must be assembled in the same way. When placing the gear on the camshaft, press the gear onto the shaft until it bottoms against the gear spacer ring. The end clearance of the thrust plate should be 0.001-0.005".

9. Pre-lube the camshaft lobes with clean engine oil and then install the camshaft assembly in the engine. Be careful not to damage the bearings.

10. Turn the crankshaft and the camshaft gears so that the timing marks align. Push the camshaft into position and install and torque the thrust plate bolts to 7 ft.lb.

11. Check camshaft and crankshaft gear run-

out with a dial indicator. Camshaft gear runout should not exceed 0.004" and crankshaft gear run-out should not be above 0.003".

12. Using a dial indicator, check the backlash at several points between the camshaft and crankshaft gear teeth. Backlash should be 0.004-0.006".

13. Install the timing gear cover. Install the harmonic balancer.

14. Install the valve lifters and the pushrods. Install the side cover. Install the coil and the fuel pump.

15. Install the distributor and set the timing. Pivot the rocker arms over the pushrods and adjust the valves.

16. Install the radiator, hoses and grille.

Gasoline V6 and V8

1. Disconnect the negative battery cable.

2. Drain and remove the radiator.

CAUTION: *When draining the coolant, keep*

in mind that cats and dogs are attracted by the ethylene glycol antifreeze, and are quite likely to drink any that is left in an uncovered container or in puddles on the ground. This will prove fatal in sufficient quantity. Always drain the coolant into a sealable container. Coolant should be reused unless it is contaminated or several years old.

3. Disconnect the fuel line at the fuel pump. Remove the pump on 1978 and later models.
4. Disconnect the throttle cable and the air cleaner.
5. Remove the alternator belt, loosen the alternator bolts and move the alternator to one side.
6. Remove the power steering pump from its brackets and move it out of the way.
7. It may be necessary, on some models, to remove the air conditioning compressor from its brackets and move the compressor out of the way without disconnecting the lines.
8. Disconnect the hoses from the water pump.
9. Disconnect the electrical and vacuum connections.
10. Mark the distributor as to location in the block. Remove the distributor.
11. Raise the car and drain the oil pan.
12. Remove the exhaust crossover pipe and starter motor.
13. Disconnect the exhaust pipe at the manifold.
14. Remove the harmonic balancer and pulley.
15. Support the engine and remove the front motor mounts.
16. Remove the flywheel inspection cover.
17. Remove the engine oil pan.
18. Support the engine by placing wooden blocks between the exhaust manifolds and the front crossmember.
19. Remove the engine front cover.
20. Remove the valve covers.
21. Remove the intake manifold, oil filler pipe, and temperature sending switch.
22. Mark the lifters, pushrods, and rocker arms as to location so that they may be installed in the same position. Remove these parts.
23. If the car is equipped with air conditioning, discharge the air conditioning system (see Chapter 1) and remove the condenser.
24. Remove the fuel pump eccentric, camshaft gear, oil slinger, and timing chain. Remove the camshaft thrust plate (on front of camshaft) if equipped.
25. Carefully remove the camshaft from the engine.
26. Inspect the shaft for signs of excessive wear or damage.
27. Liberally coat camshaft and bearings with

heavy engine oil or engine assembly lubricant and insert the cam into the engine.
28. Align the timing marks on the camshaft and crankshaft gears. See Timing Chain Replacement for details.
29. Install the distributor using the locating marks made during removal. If any problems are encountered, see Distributor Installation.
30. Install the remainder of the parts in the reverse of above but pay attention to the following points:
   a. Install the timing indicator before installing the power steering pump bracket.
   b. Install the flywheel inspection cover after installing the starter.
   c. Replace the engine oil and radiator coolant.

8-350 Diesel

NOTE: *If equipped with air conditioning, the system must be discharged by an air conditioning specialist before the camshaft is removed. The condenser must also be removed from the car.*

Removal of the camshaft also requires removal of the injection pump drive and driven gears, removal of the intake manifold, disassembly of the valve lifters, and retiming of the injection pump.

1. Disconnect the negative battery cables.
2. Remove the intake manifold and gasket and the front and rear intake manifold seals. Refer to the intake manifold removal and installation procedure.
3. Remove the balancer pulley and the balancer. See Caution under diesel engine front cover removal and installation, above. Remove the engine front cover using the appropriate procedure.
4. Remove the valve covers. Remove the rocker arms, pushrods and valve lifters; see the procedure earlier in this section. Be sure to keep the parts in order so that they may be returned to their original positions.
5. Remove the camshaft sprocket retaining bolt, and remove the timing chain and sprockets, using the procedure outlined earlier.
6. Position the camshaft dowel pin at the 3 o'clock position.
7. Push the camshaft rearward and hold it there, being careful not to dislodge the oil gallery plug at the rear of the engine. Remove the fuel injection pump drive gear by sliding it from the camshaft while rocking the pump driven gear.
8. To remove the fuel injection pump driven gear, remove the pump adapter, the snapring, and remove the selective washer. Remove the driven gear and spring.
9. Remove the camshaft by sliding it out the

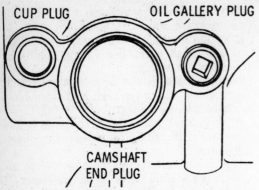

CUP PLUG   OIL GALLERY PLUG

CAMSHAFT END PLUG

Camshaft and oil gallery plugs at rear of block

front of the engine. Be extremely careful not to allow the cam lobes to contact any of the bearings, or the journals to dislodge the bearings during camshaft removal. Do not force the camshaft, or bearing damage will result.

10. If either the injection pump drive or driven gears are to be replaced, replace both gears.

11. Coat the camshaft and the cam bearings with a heavy weight engine oil, GM lubricant #1052365 or the equivalent.

12. Carefully slide the camshaft into position in the engine.

13. Fit the crankshaft and camshaft sprockets, aligning the timing marks as shown in the timing chain removal and installation procedure, above. Remove the sprockets without disturbing the timing.

14. Install the injection pump driven gear, spring, shim, and snapring. Check the gear end play. If the end play is not within 0.002-0.006″ on V8s through 1979, and 0.002-0.015″ on 1980 and later, replace the shim to obtain the specified clearance. Shims are available in 0.003″ increments, from 0.080″ to 0.115″.

15. Position the camshaft dowel pin at the 3 o'clock position. Align the zero marks on the pump drive gear and pump driven gear. Hold the camshaft in the rearward position and slide

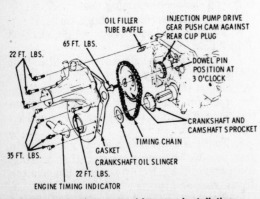

OIL FILLER TUBE BAFFLE

INJECTION PUMP DRIVE GEAR PUSH CAM AGAINST REAR CUP PLUG

65 FT. LBS.

22 FT. LBS.

DOWEL PIN POSITION AT 3 O'CLOCK

CRANKSHAFT AND CAMSHAFT SPROCKET

TIMING CHAIN

GASKET
CRANKSHAFT OIL SLINGER

35 FT. LBS.

22 FT. LBS.

ENGINE TIMING INDICATOR

350 diesel injection pump drive gear installation

the pump drive gear onto the camshaft. Install the camshaft bearing retainer.

16. Install the timing chain and sprockets, making sure the timing marks are aligned.

17. Install the lifters, pushrods and rocker arms. See Rocker Arm Replacement, Diesel Engine for lifter bleed down procedures. Failure to bleed down the lifters could bend valves when the engine is turned over.

18. Install the injection pump adapter and injection pump. See the appropriate sections under Fuel System above for procedures.

19. Install the remaining components in the reverse order of removal

8-379 Diesel

REMOVAL

1. Disconnect both batteries.

2. Jack up the truck and safely support it with jackstands.

3. Drain the cooling system, including the block.

CAUTION: *When draining the coolant, keep in mind that cats and dogs are attracted by the ethylene glycol antifreeze, and are quite likely to drink any that is left in an uncovered container or in puddles on the ground. This will prove fatal in sufficient quantity. Always drain the coolant into a sealable container. Coolant should be reused unless it is contaminated or several years old.*

4. Disconnect the exhaust pipes at the manifolds. Remove the fan shroud.

5. Lower the truck.

6. Remove the radiator and fan.

7. Remove the vacuum pump, and remove the intake manifold as previously detailed.

8. Remove the injection pump and lines as outlined in Chapter 5. Make sure you cap all injection lines to prevent dirt from entering the system, and tag the lines for later installation.

9. Remove the water pump.

10. Remove the injection pump drive gear.

11. Scribe a mark aligning the line on the injection pump flange to the front cover.

12. Remove the injection pump from the cover.

13. Remove the power steering pump and the generator and lay them aside.

14. If the truck is equipped with air conditioning, remove the compressor (with the lines attached) and position it out of the way.

CAUTION: *DO NOT disconnect the air conditioning lines unless you are familiar with this procedure. Refer to Chapter 1 "Air Conditioning".*

15. Remove the valve covers.

16. Remove the rocker shaft assemblies and pushrods. Place the pushrods in order in a rack (easily by punching holes in a piece of heavy

cardboard and numbering the holes) so that they can be installed in correct order.

17. Remove the thermostat housing and the crossover from the cylinder heads.

18. Remove the cylinder heads as previously detailed, with the exhaust manifolds attached.

19. Remove the valve lifter clamps, guide plates and valve lifters. Place these parts in a rack so they can be installed in the correct order.

20. Remove the front cover.

21. Remove the timing chain assembly.

22. Remove the fuel pump.

23. Remove the camshaft retainer plate.

24. If the truck is equipped with air conditioning, remove the air conditioning condenser mounting bolts. Have an assistant help in lifting the condenser out of the way.

25. Remove the camshaft by carefully sliding it out of the block.

INSTALLATION

Whenever a new camshaft is installed, GM recommends replacing all the valve lifters, as well as the oil filter. The engine oil must be changed. These measures will help ensure proper wear characteristics of the new camshaft.

1. Coat the camshaft lobes with Molykote or an equivalent lube. Liberally lube the camshaft journals with clean engine oil and install the camshaft carefully.

2. Install the camshaft retainer plate and torque the bolts to 20 ft.lb.

3. Install the fuel pump.

4. Install the timing chain assembly as previously detailed.

5. Install the front cover as previously detailed.

6. Install the valve lifters, guide plates and clamps, and rotate the crankshaft as previously outlined so that the lifters are free to travel.

7. Install the cylinder heads.

8. Install the pushrods in their original order. Install the rocker shaft assemblies, then install the valve covers.

9. Install the injection pump to the front cover, making sure the lines on the pump and the scribe line on the front cover are aligned.

10. Install the injection pump driven gear, making sure the gears are aligned. Re-time the injection pump.

11. Install the remaining engine components in the reverse order of removal. Make the necessary adjustments (drive belts, etc.) and refill the cooling system.

CAMSHAFT INSPECTION

Completely clean the camshaft with solvent, paying special attention to cleaning the oil holes. Visually inspect the cam lobes and bearing journals for excessive wear. If a lobe is questionable, have the cam checked at a reputable machine shop; if a journal or lobe is worn, the camshaft must be reground or replaced. Also have the camshaft checked for straightness on a dial indicator.

NOTE: *If a cam journal is worn, there is a good chance that the bushings are worn.*

Camshaft Bearings

REMOVAL AND INSTALLATION

If excessive camshaft wear is found, or if the engine is being completely rebuilt, the camshaft bearings should be replaced.

NOTE: *The front and rear bearings should be removed last, and installed first. Those bearings act as guides for the other bearings and pilot.*

1. Drive the camshaft rear plug from the block.

2. Assemble the removal puller with its shoulder on the bearing to be removed. Gradually tighten the puller nut until the bearing is removed.

3. Remove the remaining bearings, leaving the front and rear for last. To remove these, reverse the position of the puller, so as to pull the bearings towards the center of the block. Leave the tool in this position, pilot the new front and rear bearings on the installer, and pull them into position.

4. Return the puller to its original position and pull the remaining bearings into position.

NOTE: *You must make sure that the oil holes of the bearings and block align when installing the bearings. If they don't align, the camshaft will not get proper lubrication and may seize or at least be seriously damaged. To check for correct oil hole alignment, use a piece of brass rod with a 90 degree bend in the*

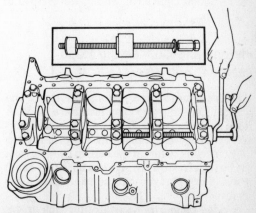

Camshaft bearing removal and installation tool

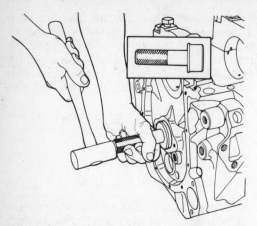

Installing front cam bearing on 379 diesel. Bearing tool is illustrated inset. Method is similar on other engines

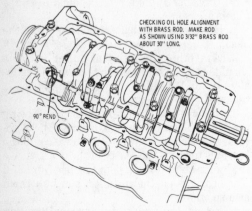

CHECKING OIL HOLE ALIGNMENT WITH BRASS ROD. MAKE ROD AS SHOWN USING 3/32" BRASS ROD ABOUT 30" LONG.

90° BEND

Make this simple tool to check camshaft bearing oil hole alignment

end as shown in the illustration. Check all oil hole openings; the wire must enter each hole, or the hole is not properly aligned.

5. Replace the camshaft rear plug, and stake it into position. On the 379 diesel, coat the outer diameter of the new plug with GM sealant #1052080 or equivalent, and install it flush to $\frac{1}{32}$" deep.

Pistons and Connecting Rods

REMOVAL AND INSTALLATION

Before removing the pistons, the top of the cylinder bore must be examined for a ridge. A ridge at the top of the bore is the result of normal cylinder wear, caused by the piston rings only traveling so far up the bore in the course of the piston stroke. The ridge can be felt by hand; it must be removed before the pistons are removed.

A ridge reamer is necessary for this operation. Place the piston at the bottom of its

stroke, and cover it with a rag. Cut the ridge away with the ridge reamer, using extreme care to avoid cutting too deeply. Remove the rag, and remove the cuttings that remain on the piston with a magnet and a rag soaked in clean oil.

Make sure the piston top and cylinder bore are absolutely clean before moving the piston.

1. Remove intake manifold and cylinder head or heads.
2. Remove oil pan.
3. Remove oil pump assembly if necessary.
4. Matchmark the connecting rod cap to the connecting rod with a scribe; each cap must be reinstalled on its proper rod in the proper direction. Remove the connecting rod bearing cap and the rod bearing. Number the top of each piston with silver paint or a felt-tip pen for later assembly.
5. Cut lengths of ⅜" diameter hose to use as rod bolt guides. Install the hose over the threads of the rod bolts, to prevent the bolt threads from damaging the crankshaft journals and cylinder walls when the piston is removed.
6. Squirt some clean engine oil onto the cylinder wall from above, until the wall is coated.

Carefully push the piston and rod assembly up and out of the cylinder by tapping on the bottom of the connecting rod with a wooden hammer handle.

7. Place the rod bearing and cap back on the connecting rod, and install the nuts temporarily. Using a number stamp or punch, stamp the cylinder number on the side of the connecting rod and cap; this will help keep the proper piston and rod assembly on the proper cylinder.

NOTE: On V6 engines, starting at the front the cylinders are numbered 2-4-6 on the right bank and 1-3-5 on the left. On all V8s, starting at the front the right bank cylinders are 2-4-6-8 and the left bank 1-3-5-7.

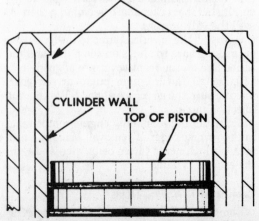

RIDGE CAUSED BY CYLINDER WEAR

CYLINDER WALL

TOP OF PISTON

Ridge formed by piston rings at the top of their travel

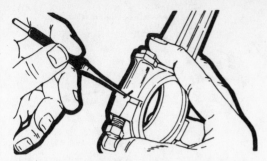

Match the connecting rods to their caps with a scribe mark

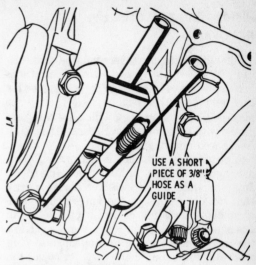

USE A SHORT PIECE OF 3/8" HOSE AS A GUIDE

Connecting rod bolt guide

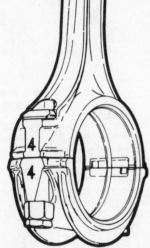

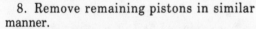

Match the connecting rods to their cylinders with a number stamp

8. Remove remaining pistons in similar manner.

On all gasoline engines, the notch on the piston will face the front of the engine for assembly. The chamfered corners of the bearing caps should face toward the front of the left bank and toward the rear of the right bank, and the boss on the connecting rod should face toward the front of the engine for the right bank and to the rear of the engine on the left bank.

On the 350 diesel, install each piston and rod in its respective cylinder bore so the valve depression in the top of the piston is towards the inner side of the engine. On the forward half of the engine (cylinders 1,2,3,4) the large valve depression goes to the front. On the rear half, the large valve depression goes to the rear. On the 379 diesel, install the piston and rod assemblies with the rod bearing tang slots on the side opposite the camshaft.

On various engines, the piston compression rings are marked with a dimple, a letter **T**, a letter **O**, **GM** or the word **TOP** to identify the side of the ring which must face toward the top of the piston.

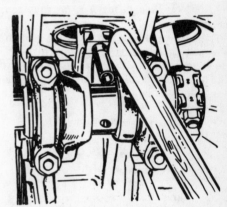

Push the piston and rod out with a hammer handle

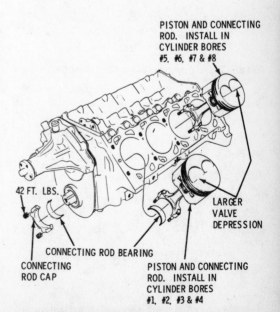

PISTON AND CONNECTING ROD. INSTALL IN CYLINDER BORES #5, #6, #7 & #8

LARGER VALVE DEPRESSION

42 FT. LBS.

CONNECTING ROD BEARING

CONNECTING ROD CAP

PISTON AND CONNECTING ROD. INSTALL IN CYLINDER BORES #1, #2, #3 & #4

350 diesel piston positioning

Piston Ring and Wrist Pin

REMOVAL

Some of the engines covered in this guide utilize pistons with pressed-in wrist pins; these must be removed by a special press designed for this purpose. Other pistons have their wrist pins secured by snaprings, which are easily removed with snapring pliers. Separate the piston from the connecting rod.

A piston ring expander is necessary for removing piston rings without damaging them; any other method (screwdriver blades, pliers, etc.) usually results in the rings being bent, scratched or distorted, or the piston itself being damaged. When the rings are removed, clean the ring grooves using an appropriate ring groove cleaning tool, using care not to cut too deeply. Thoroughly clean all carbon and varnish from the piston with solvent.

WARNING: *Do not use a wire brush or caustic solvent (acids, etc.) on pistons.*

Inspect the pistons for scuffing, scoring, cracks, pitting, or excessive ring groove wear. If these are evident, the piston must be replaced.

The piston should also be checked in relation to the cylinder diameter. Using a telescoping

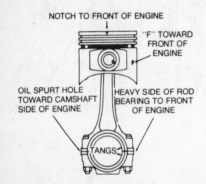

250 and 292 six cylinder piston and rod positioning

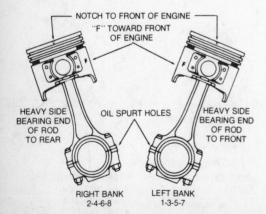

Small-block V8 piston and rod positioning, V6 similar

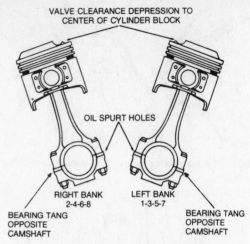

Big-block (Mark IV) V8 piston and rod positioning

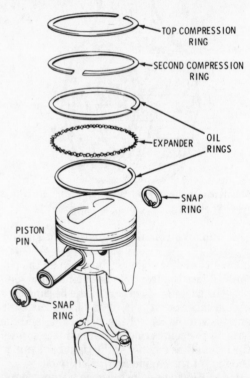

Piston ring and wrist pin assembly, 350 diesel shown. Gas engines similar

gauge and micrometer, or a dial gauge, measure the cylinder bore diameter perpendicular (90 degree) to the piston pin, 2½″ below the cylinder block deck (surface where the block mates with the heads). Then, with the micrometer, measure the piston perpendicular to its wrist pin on the shirt. The difference between the two measurements is the piston clearance. If the clearance is within specifications or slightly below (after the cylinders have been bored or honed), finish honing is all that is necessary. If

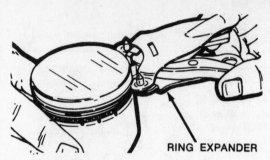

RING EXPANDER

Remove the piston rings

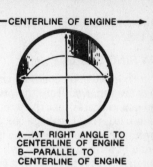

←——CENTERLINE OF ENGINE——→

A—AT RIGHT ANGLE TO
CENTERLINE OF ENGINE
B—PARALLEL TO
CENTERLINE OF ENGINE

Cylinder bore measuring points

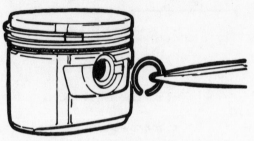

Install the piston lock-rings, if used

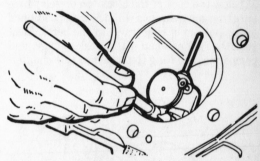

Measuring cylinder bore with a dial gauge

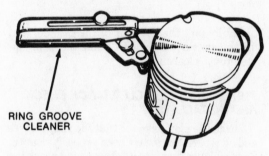

RING GROOVE
CLEANER

Clean the piston ring grooves using a ring groove cleaner

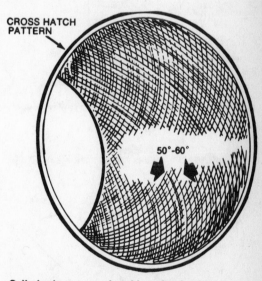

CROSS HATCH
PATTERN

50°-60°

Cylinder bore cross-hatching after honing

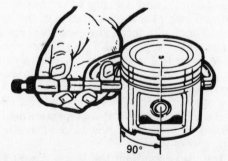

90°

Measuring the piston prior to fitting

the clearance is excessive, try to obtain a slightly larger piston to bring clearance to within specifications. If this is not possible, obtain the first oversize piston and hone (or if necessary, bore) the cylinder to size. Generally, if the cylinder bore is tapered 0.005″ or more or is out-of-round 0.003″ or more it is advisable to rebore for the smallest possible oversize piston and rings.

After measuring, mark pistons with a felt-tip pen for reference and for assembly.

NOTE: *Cylinder honing and/or boring should be performed by a reputable, professional mechanic with the proper equipment. In some cases, clean-up honing can be done with the cylinder block in the car, but most excessive honing and all cylinder boring must be done with the block stripped and removed from the car.*

PISTON RING END GAP

Piston ring end gap should be checked while the rings are removed from the pistons. Incorrect end gap indicates that the wrong size rings are being used; ring breakage could occur.

Compress the piston rings to be used in a cylinder, one at a time, into that cylinder. Squirt clean oil into the cylinder, so that the rings and the top 2″ of cylinder wall are coated. Using an inverted piston, press the rings approximately 1″ below the deck of the block (on diesels, measure ring gap clearance with the ring positioned at the bottom of ring travel in the bore). Measure the ring end gap with a feeler gauge, and compare to the Ring Gap chart in this chapter.

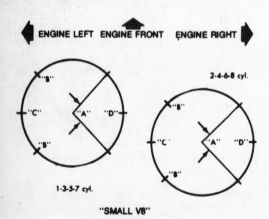

Checking piston ring end gap with a feeler gauge

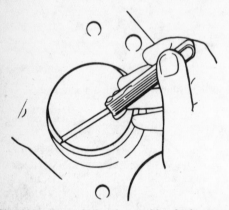

"A" OIL RING SPACER GAP
(Tang in Hole or Slot within Arc)

"B" OIL RING RAIL GAPS

"C" 2ND COMPRESSION RING CAP

"D" TOP COMPRESSION RING GAP

Ring gap location—all gasoline engines. Inline sixes same on all cylinders also

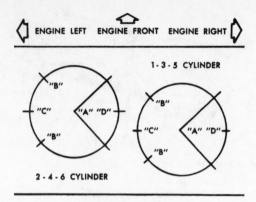

"A" OIL RING SPACER GAP
(Tang in Hole or Slot within Arc)

"B" OIL RING RAIL GAPS

"C" 2ND COMPRESSION RING GAP

"D" TOP COMPRESSION RING GAP

V6 262 ring gap location

Carefully pull the ring out of the cylinder and file the ends squarely with a fine file to obtain the proper clearance.

PISTON RING SIDE CLEARANCE CHECK AND INSTALLATION

Check the pistons to see that the ring grooves and oil return holes have been properly cleaned. Slide a piston ring into its groove, and check the side clearance with a feeler gauge. On gasoline engines, make sure you insert the gauge between the ring and its lower land (lower edge of the groove), because any wear that occurs forms a step at the inner portion of the lower land. On diesels, insert the gauge between the ring and the upper land. If the piston grooves have worn to the extent that relatively high steps exist on the lower land, the piston should be replaced, because these will interfere with the operation of the new rings and ring clearances will be excessive. Piston rings are not furnished in oversize widths to compensate for ring groove wear.

Install the rings on the piston, lowest ring first, using a piston ring expander. There is a high risk of breaking or distorting the rings, or scratching the piston, if the rings are installed by hand or other means.

Position the rings on the piston as illustrated; spacing of the various piston ring gaps is crucial to proper oil retention and even cylinder wear. When installing new rings, refer to the in-

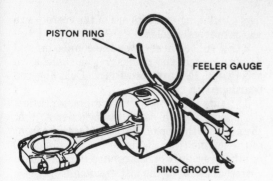

Checking piston ring side clearance

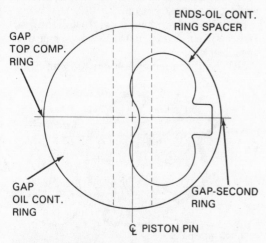

379 diesel piston ring gap positioning

stallation diagram furnished with the new parts.

Connecting Rod Bearings

Connecting rod bearings for the engines covered in this guide consist of two halves or shells which are interchangeable in the rod and cap. When the shells are placed in position, the ends extend slightly beyond the rod and cap surfaces so that when the rod bolts are torqued the shells will be clamped tightly in place to insure positive seating and to prevent turning. A tang holds the shells in place.

NOTE: *The ends of the bearing shells must never be filed flush with the mating surface of the rod and cap.*

If a rod bearing becomes noisy or is worn so that its clearance on the crank journal is sloppy, a new bearing of the correct undersize must be selected and installed since there is a provision for adjustment.

WARNING: *Under no circumstances should the rod end or cap be filed to adjust the bear-*

ing clearance, nor should shims of any kind be used.

Inspect the rod bearings while the rod assemblies are out of the engine. If the shells are scored or show flaking, they should be replaced. If they are in good shape check for proper clearance on the crank journal (see below). Any scoring or ridges on the crank journal means the crankshaft must be replaced, or reground and fitted with undersized bearings.

CHECKING BEARING CLEARANCE AND REPLACING BEARINGS

NOTE: *Make sure connecting rods and their caps are kept together, and that the caps are installed in the proper direction.*

Replacement bearings are available in standard size, and in undersizes for reground crankshafts. Connecting rod-to-crankshaft bearing clearance is checked using Plastigage® at either the top or bottom of each crank journal. The Plastigage® has a range of 0.001-0.003".

1. Remove the rod cap with the bearing shell. Completely clean the bearing shell and the crank journal, and blow any oil from the oil hole in the crankshaft; Plastigage® is soluble in oil.

2. Place a piece of Plastigage® lengthwise along the bottom center of the lower bearing shell, then install the cap with shell and torque the bolt or nuts to specification. DO NOT turn the crankshaft with Plastigage® in the bearing.

3. Remove the bearing cap with the shell. The flattened Plastigage® will be found sticking to either the bearing shell or crank journal. Do not remove it yet.

4. Use the scale printed on the Plastigage® envelope to measure the flattened material at its widest point. The number within the scale which most closely corresponds to the width of the Plastigage® indicates bearing clearance in thousandths of an inch.

5. Check the specifications chart in this chapter for the desired clearance. It is advisable to install a new bearing if clearance exceeds 0.003"; however, if the bearing is in good condition and is not being checked because of bearing noise, bearing replacement is not necessary.

6. If you are installing new bearings, try a standard size, then each undersize in order until one is found that is within the specified limits when checked for clearance with Plastigage®. Each undersize shell has its size stamped on it.

7. When the proper size shell is found, clean off the Plastigage®, oil the bearing thoroughly, reinstall the cap with its shell and torque the rod bolt nuts to specification.

NOTE: *With the proper bearing selected and the nuts torqued, it should be possible to move*

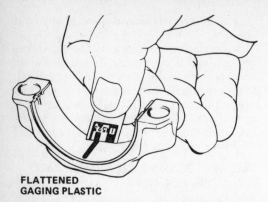

FLATTENED
GAGING PLASTIC

Checking rod bearing clearance with Plastigage®
or equivalent

TANG

GM M400

8943

UNDERSIZE STAMP
IN THOUSANDS

Undersize marks are stamped on the bearing shells.
Tangs fit in the notches in the rod and cap

the connecting rod back and forth freely on
the crank journal as allowed by the specified
connecting rod end clearance. If the rod cannot be moved, either the rod bearing is too far
undersize or the rod is misaligned.

Piston and Connecting Rod
ASSEMBLY AND INSTALLATION

Install the connecting rod to the piston, making sure piston installation notches and any
marks on the rod are in proper relation to one
another. Lubricate the wrist pin with clean engine oil, and install the pin into the rod and piston assembly, either by hand or by using a wrist
pin press as required. Install snaprings if
equipped, and rotate them in their grooves to
make sure they are seated. To install the piston
and connecting rod assembly:

1. Make sure connecting rod big-end bear-

ings (including end cap) are of the correct size
and properly installed.

2. Fit rubber hoses over the connecting rod
bolts to protect the crankshaft journals, as in
the Piston Removal procedure. Coat the rod
bearings with clean oil.

3. Using the proper ring compressor, insert
the piston assembly into the cylinder so that
the notch in the top of the piston faces the front
of the engine (this assumes that the dimple(s)
or other markings on the connecting rods are in
correct relation to the piston notch(es).

4. From beneath the engine, coat each crank
journal with clean oil. Pull the connecting rod,
with the bearing shell in place, into position
against the crank journal.

5. Remove the rubber hoses. Install the bearing cap and cap nuts and torque to
specification.

NOTE: *When more than one rod and piston*

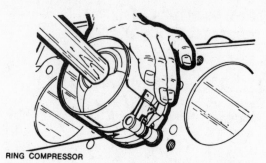

RING COMPRESSOR

Using a wooden hammer handle, tap the piston
down through the ring compressor and into the cylinder

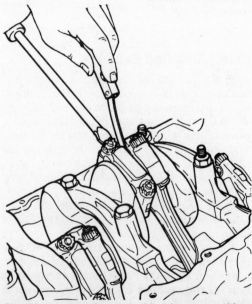

Checking connecting rod side clearance with a
feeler gauge. Use a small pry bar to carefully spread
the connecting rods

assembly is being installed, the connecting rod cap attaching nuts should only be tightened enough to keep each rod in position until all have been installed. This will ease the installation of the remaining piston assemblies.

6. Check the clearance between the sides of the connecting rods and the crankshaft using a feeler gauge. Spread the rods slightly with a screwdriver to insert the gauge. If clearance is below the minimum tolerance, the rod may be machined to provide adequate clearance. If clearance is excessive, substitute an unworn rod, and recheck. If clearance is still outside specifications, the crankshaft must be welded and reground, or replaced.

7. Replace the oil pump if removed and the oil pan.

8. Install the cylinder head(s) and intake manifold.

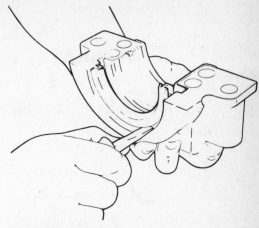

Remove the seal half from the bearing cap without scratching the cap

Rear Main Oil Seal

REMOVAL AND INSTALLATION

Inline 6-Cylinder

The rear main bearing oil seal, both halves, can be removed without removal of the crankshaft. Always replace the upper and lower halves together.

1. Remove the oil pan.
2. Remove the rear main bearing cap.
3. Remove the old oil seal from its groove in the cap, prying from the bottom using a small screwdriver.
4. Coat a new seal half completely with clean engine oil, and insert it into the bearing cap groove. Keep oil off of the parting line surface, as this surface is treated with glue. Gradually push the seal with a hammer handle until the seal is rolled into place.
5. To remove the upper half of the old seal, use a small hammer and a soft, blunt punch to tap one end of the oil seal out until it protrudes far enough to be removed with needlenosed pliers. Push the new seal into place with the lip toward the front of the engine.
6. Install the bearing cap and torque the bolts to a loose fit – do not final torque. With the cap fitted loosely, move the crankshaft first to the rear and then to the front with a rubber mallet. This will properly position the thrust bearing. Torque the bearing cap to a final torque of 65 ft.lb. Install the oil pan.

All V6 and V8 Gasoline Engines Through 1985

1. Refer to the Oil Pan Removal and Installation procedures in this section and remove the oil pan.
2. Remove the oil pump and the rear main bearing cap.

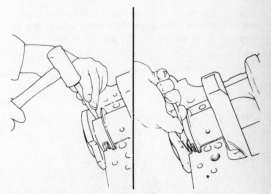

Removing the upper seal half from the block

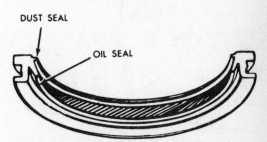

DUST SEAL

OIL SEAL

Typical rear main seal half, bearing cap side

3. Using a small pry bar, pry the oil seal from the rear main bearing cap.
4. Using a small hammer and a brass pin punch, drive the top half of the oil seal from the rear main bearing. Drive it out far enough, so it may be removed with a pair of pliers.
5. Using a non-abrasive cleaner, clean the rear main bearing cap and the crankshaft.
6. Fabricate an oil seal installation tool from 0.004″ shim stock, shape the end to ½″ long by $\frac{11}{64}$″ wide.
7. Coat the new oil seal with engine oil; DO NOT coat the ends of the seal.

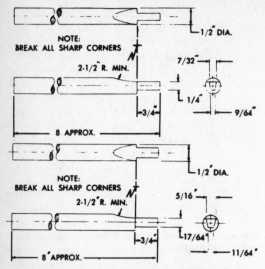

NOTE:
BREAK ALL SHARP CORNERS
2-1/2" R. MIN.
1/2" DIA.
7/32"
1/4"
9/64"
3/4"
8" APPROX.

NOTE:
BREAK ALL SHARP CORNERS
2-1/2" R. MIN.
1/2" DIA.
5/16"
17/64"
3/4"
11/64"
8" APPROX.

Make a rear main bearing seal packing tool from a wooden dowel. The upper tool dimensions are for engines up to 400 cu. in.; the bottom is for 454s

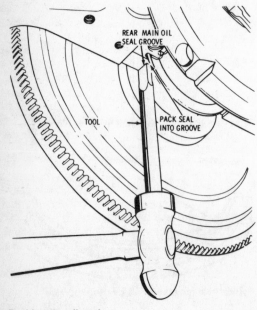

REAR MAIN OIL SEAL GROOVE

TOOL

PACK SEAL INTO GROOVE

Packing the oil seal

8. Position the fabricated tool between the crankshaft and the seal seat in the cylinder case.

9. Position the new half seal between the crankshaft and the top of the tool, so that the seal bead contacts the tip of the tool.

NOTE: *Make sure that the seal lip is positioned toward the front of the engine.*

10. Using the fabricated tool as a shoe horn, to protect the seal's bead from the sharp edge of the seal seat surface in the cylinder case, roll the seal around the crankshaft. when the seal's ends are flush with the engine block, remove the installation.

11. Using the same manner of installation, install the lower half onto the lower half of the rear main bearing cap.

12. Apply sealant to the cap-to-case mating surfaces and install the lower rear main bearing half to the engine; keep the sealant off of the seal's mating line.

13. Install the rear main bearing cap bolts and torque to 10-12 ft.lb. Using a lead hammer, tap the crankshaft forward and rearward, to line up the thrust surfaces. Torque the main bearing bolts to 70-85 ft.lb. (V6 and V8) or 60-75 ft.lb. (inline 6-cylinder) and reverse the removal procedures. Refill the crankcase.

All V8 and V6 Gasoline Engines 1986-88 (One Piece Seal)

1. Remove the transmission from the vehicle.

2. Using the notches provided in the rear seal retainer, pry out the seal using the proper tool.

NOTE: *Care should be taken when removing the seal so as not to nick the crankshaft sealing surface.*

3. Before installation lubricate the new seal with clean engine oil.

4. Install the seal on tool J-3561 or equivalent. Thread the tool into the rear of the crankshaft. Tighten the screws snugly, this is to insure that the seal will be installed squarely over the crankshaft. Tighten the tool wing nut until it bottoms.

5. Remove the tool from the crankshaft.

6. Install the transmission.

One Piece Seal Retainer and Gasket (1986-87)

REMOVAL AND INSTALLATION

1. Remove the transmission from the vehicle.

2. Remove the oil pan bolts. Lower the oil pan.

3. Remove the retainer and seal assembly.

4. Remove the gasket.

NOTE: *Whenever the retainer is removed a new retainer gasket and rear main seal must be installed.*

5. Installation is the reverse of the removal procedure. Once the oil pan has been installed the new rear main oil seal can be installed.

8-350 and 8-379 Diesel

The crankshaft need not be removed to replace the rear main bearing upper oil seal. The lower seal is installed in the bearing cap.

1. Drain the crankcase oil and remove the oil pan and rear main bearing cap.

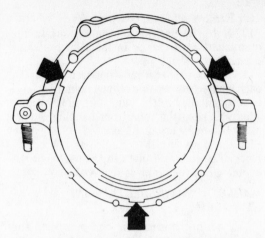

Rear main seal removal notches, 1986–87 V6 and V8

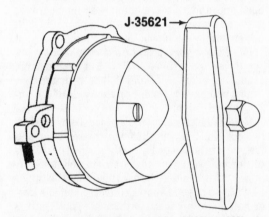

J-35621 →

Rear main seal installation, 1986–87 V6 and V8

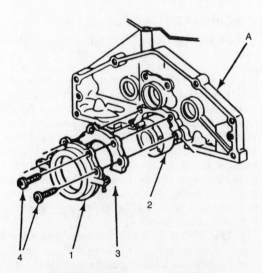

A. Rear of block   3. Gasket
1. Seal retainer   4. Screw
2. Crankshaft

Rear main seal retainer installation, 1986–87 V6 and V8

2. Using a special main seal tool or a tool that can be made from a dowel (see illustration), drive the upper seal into its groove on each side until it is tightly packed. This is usually $\frac{1}{4}$-$\frac{3}{4}$".

3. Measure the amount the seal was driven up on one side; add $\frac{1}{16}$", then cut this length from the old seal that was removed from the main bearing cap. Use a single-edge razor blade. Measure the amount the seal was driven up on the other side, add $\frac{1}{16}$" and cut another length from the old seal. Use the man bearing cap as a holding fixture when cutting the seal as illustrated. Carefully trim protruding seal.

4. Work these two pieces of seal up into the cylinder block on each side with two nailsets or small screwdrivers. Using the packing tool again, pack these pieces into the block, then trim them flush with a razor blade or hobby knife as shown. Do not scratch the bearing surface with the razor.

NOTE: *It may help to use a bit of oil on the short pieces of the rope seal when packing it into the block.*

5. Apply Loctite® #496 sealer or equivalent to the rear main bearing cap and install the rope seal. Cut the ends of the seal flush with the cap.

6. Check to see if the rear main cap with the new seal will seat properly on the block. Place a piece of Plastigage® on the rear main journal, install the cap and torque to 70 ft.lb. Remove the cap and check the Plastigage® against specifications. If out of specs, recheck the ends of the seal for fraying that may be preventing the cap from seating properly.

7. Make sure all traces of Plastigage® are removed from the crankshaft journal. Apply a thin film of sealer (GM part #1052357 or equivalent) to the bearing cap. Keep the sealant off of both the seal and bearing.

8. Just before assembly, apply a light coat of clean engine oil on the crankshaft surface that will contact the seal.

9. Install the bearing cap and torque the bolts to specifications.

10. Install the oil pump and oil pan.

Crankshaft and Main Bearings

CRANKSHAFT REMOVAL

1. Drain the engine oil and remove the engine from the car. Mount the engine on a work stand in a suitable working area. Invert the engine, so the oil pan is facing up.

2. Remove the engine front (timing) cover.

3. Remove the timing chain and gears.

4. Remove the oil pan.

5. Remove the oil pump.

6. Stamp the cylinder number on the machined surfaces of the bolt bosses of the con-

necting rods and caps for identification when reinstalling. If the pistons are to be removed eventually from the connecting rod, mark the cylinder number on the pistons with silver paint or felt-tip pen for proper cylinder identification and cap-to-rod location.

7. Remove the connecting rod caps. Install lengths of rubber hose on each of the connecting rod bolts, to protect the crank journals when the crank is removed.

8. Mark the main bearing caps with a number punch or punch so that they can be reinstalled in their original positions.

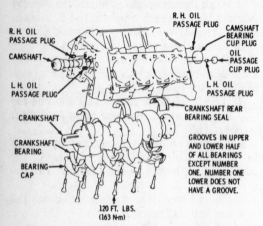

350 diesel crankshaft, exploded view. Gasoline V8 engines and 6.2L (379) diesel similar configuration

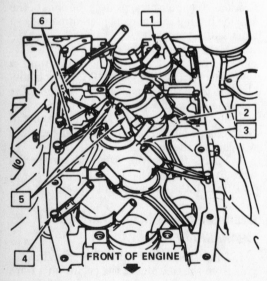

1. Rubber hose
2. #4 rod
3. #3 rod
4. Oil pan bolt
5. Note overlap of adjacent rods
6. Rubber bands

Crankshaft removal showing hose lengths on rod bolts

9. Remove all main bearing caps.

10. Note the position of the keyway in the crankshaft so it can be installed in the same position.

11. Install rubber bands between a bolt on each connecting rod and oil pan bolts that have been reinstalled in the block (see illustration). This will keep the rods from banging on the block when the crank is removed.

12. Carefully lift the crankshaft out of the block. The rods will pivot to the center of the engine when the crank is removed.

MAIN BEARING INSPECTION AND REPLACEMENT

Life connecting rod big-end bearings, the crankshaft main bearings are shell-type inserts that do not utilize shims and cannot be adjusted. The bearings are available in various standard and undersizes; if main bearing clearance is found to be too sloppy, a new bearing (both upper and lower halves) is required.

NOTE: *Factory undersized crankshafts are marked, sometimes with a* **9** *and/or a large spot of light green paint; the bearing caps also will have the paint on each side of the undersized journal.*

Generally, the lower half of the bearing shell (except No. 1 bearing) shows greater wear and fatigue. If the lower half only shows the effects of normal wear (no heavy scoring or discoloration), it can usually be assumed that the upper half is also in good shape; conversely, if the lower half is heavily worn or damaged, both halves should be replaced. Never replace one bearing half without replacing the other.

CHECKING CLEARANCE

Main bearing clearance can be checked both with the crankshaft in the car and with the engine out of the car. If the engine block is still in the car, the crankshaft should be supported both front and rear (by the damper and to remove clearance from the upper bearing.) Total clearance can then be measured between the lower bearing and journal. If the block has been removed from the car, and is inverted, the crank will rest on the upper bearings and the total clearance can be measured between the lower bearing and journal. Clearance is checked in the same manner as the connecting rod bearings, with Plastigage®.

NOTE: *Crankshaft bearing caps and bearing shells should NEVER be filed flush with the cap-to-block mating surface to adjust for wear in the old bearings. Always install new bearings.*

1. If the crankshaft has been removed, install it (block removed from car). If the block is still in the car, remove the oil pan and oil pump.

Starting with the rear bearing cap, remove the cap and wipe all oil from the crank journal and bearing cap.

2. Place a strip of Plastigage® the full width of the bearing (parallel to the crankshaft), on the journal.

WARNING: *Do not rotate the crankshaft while the gauging material is between the bearing and the journal.*

3. Install the bearing cap and evenly torque the cap bolts to specification.

4. Remove the bearing cap. The flattened Plastigage® will be sticking to either the bearing shell or the crank journal.

5. Use the graduated scale on the Plastigage® envelope to measure the material at its widest point.

NOTE: *If the flattened Plastigage® tapers towards the middle or ends, there is a difference in clearance indicating the bearing or journal has a taper, low spot or other irregularity. If this is indicated, measure the crank journal with a micrometer.*

6. If bearing clearance is within specifications, the bearing insert is in good shape. Replace the insert if the clearance is not within specifications. Always replace both upper and lower inserts as a unit.

7. Standard, 0.001″ or 0.002″ undersize bearings should produce the proper clearance. If these sizes still produce too sloppy a fit, the crankshaft must be reground for use with the next undersize bearing. Recheck all clearances after installing new bearings.

8. Replace the rest of the bearings in the same manner. After all bearings have been checked, rotate the crankshaft to make sure there is no excessive drag. When checking the No. 1 main bearing, loosen the accessory drive belts (engine in car) to prevent a tapered reading with the Plastigage®.

Main Bearing Replacement

ENGINE OUT OF CAR

1. Remove and inspect the crankshaft.

2. Remove the main bearings from the bearing saddles in the cylinder block and main bearing caps.

3. Coat the bearing surfaces of the new, correct size main bearings with clean engine oil and install them in the bearing saddles in the block and in the main bearing caps.

4. Install the crankshaft. See Crankshaft Installation.

ENGINE IN CAR

1. With the oil pan, oil pump and spark plugs removed, remove the cap from the main bearing needing replacement and remove the bearing from the cap.

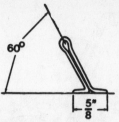

Home-made bearing roll-out pin

Roll-out pin installed for removing upper half of main bearing

2. Make a bearing roll-out pin, using a bent cotter pin as shown in the illustration. Install the end of the pin in the oil hole in the crankshaft journal.

3. Rotate the crankshaft clockwise as viewed from the front of the engine. This will roll the upper bearing out of the block.

4. Lube the new upper bearing with clean engine oil and insert the plain (un-notched) end between the crankshaft and the indented or notched side of the block. Roll the bearing into place, making sure that the oil holes are aligned. Remove the roll pin from the oil hole.

5. Lube the new lower bearing and install the main bearing cap. Install the main bearing cap, making sure it is positioned in proper direction with the matchmarks in alignment.

6. Torque the main bearing cap bolts to specification.

NOTE: *See Crankshaft Installation for thrust bearing alignment.*

CRANKSHAFT END PLAY AND INSTALLATION

When main bearing clearance has been checked, bearings examined and/or replaced,

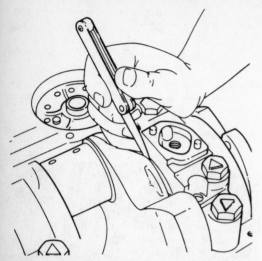

Measuring crankshaft end play at the front of the rear main bearing

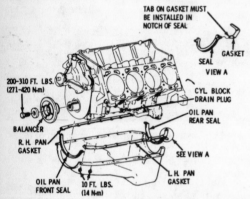

TAB ON GASKET MUST BE INSTALLED IN NOTCH OF SEAL

GASKET

SEAL

VIEW A

200-310 FT. LBS. (271-420 N·m)

CYL BLOCK DRAIN PLUG

OIL PAN REAR SEAL

BALANCER

R. H. PAN GASKET

SEE VIEW A

L. H. PAN GASKET

OIL PAN FRONT SEAL

10 FT. LBS. (14 N·m)

Oil pan installation; gaskets and seals may differ among engines

the crankshaft can be installed. Thoroughly clean the upper and lower bearing surfaces, and lube them with clean engine oil. Install the crankshaft and main bearing caps.

Dip all main bearing cap bolts in clean oil, and torque all main bearing caps, excluding the thrust bearing cap, to specifications (see the Crankshaft and Connecting Rod chart in this chapter to determine which bearing is the thrust bearing). Tighten the thrust bearing, pry the crankshaft the extent of its axial travel several times, holding the last movement toward the front of the engine. Add thrust washers if required for proper alignment. Torque the thrust bearing cap to specifications.

To check crankshaft end-play, pry the crankshaft to the extreme rear of its axial travel, then to the extreme front of its travel. Using a feeler gauge, measure the end-play at the front of the rear main bearing. End play may also be measured at the thrust bearing. Install a new rear main bearing oil seal in the cylinder block and main bearing cap. Continue to reassemble the engine.

Flywheel and Ring Gear
REMOVAL AND INSTALLATION

The ring gear is an integral part of the flywheel and is not replaceable.

1. Remove the transmission.
2. Remove the six bolts attaching the flywheel to the crankshaft flange. Remove the flywheel.
3. Inspect the flywheel for cracks, and inspect the ring gear for burrs or worn teeth. Replace the flywheel if any damage is apparent. Remove burrs with a mill file.
4. Install the flywheel. The flywheel will only attach to the crankshaft in one position, as the bolt holes are unevenly spaced. Install the bolts and torque to specification.

EXHAUST SYSTEM

CAUTION: *Never work on your truck's exhaust when it has just been used. The exhaust system reaches extremely high temperatures and can cause severe burns. Always allow the truck to cool completely before attempting any exhaust repair. The exhaust system is sus-*

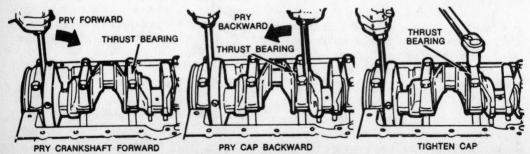

PRY FORWARD

THRUST BEARING

PRY CRANKSHAFT FORWARD

PRY BACKWARD

THRUST BEARING

PRY CAP BACKWARD

THRUST BEARING

TIGHTEN CAP

Aligning the crankshaft thrust bearing

pended by hangers attached to the frame members.

Annoying rattles and noise vibrations in the Exhaust System are usually caused by misalignment of parts. When aligning the system, leave all bolts or nuts loose until all parts are properly aligned, then tighten, working from front to rear.

When replacing a muffler, the tailpipe(s) should also be replaced.

Sealer such as 1051249, or equivalent, should be used at all clamped joint connections.

WARNING: *When jacking or lifting vehicle from frame side rails, be certain lift pads do not contact catalytic converter as damage to converter will result.*

Catalytic Converter

The catalytic converter is an emission control device added to a gasoline engine light duty emission exhaust system to reduce hydrocarbon and carbon monoxide pollutants from the exhaust gas stream. The catalyst in the converter is not serviceable. THE CATALYTIC CONVERTER REQUIRES THE USE OF UNLEADED FUEL ONLY.

Periodic maintenance of the exhaust system is not required; however, if the vehicle is raised for other service; it is advisable to check the general condition of the catalytic converter, pipes and muffler(s).

EXHAUST SYSTEM REMOVAL

Manifolds

The exhaust manifold studs have to be heated, in most cases, before they can be removed. If the studs are badly rusted, there is a large possibility that they will break off inside the manifold. If this happens, the studs will have to be drilled out of the manifold, and the manifold retapped. Due to the cost of the equipment necessary to perform this procedure, it is recommended that it be done by a qualified mechanic.

Exhaust and Y-Pipe

Two studs hold the exhaust pipe to the manifold on four and inline 6-cylinder engines. Four studs hold the Y-pipe on V6 and V8 models. A good quality lubricant, such as Liquid Wrench, should be applied to the studs before attempting to remove the nuts. Use a wire brush to remove some of the rust on the studs, this will make removing the nuts earlier. If the nuts are frozen to the studs, they will have to be heated to be removed. Before applying heat to the studs, make sure that you have removed the lubricant completely from the studs and nuts, as some lubricants are highly flammable. If the studs appear to be badly worn, and will probably break if the necessary force to free the nuts is applied, refer servicing to a qualified mechanic.

Catalytic Converter

The catalytic converter is connected to the exhaust or Y-pipe and the muffler by a muffler clamp. After removing the clamps, it may be necessary to use a hammer and chisel to separate the converter from the exhaust or Y-pipe and the muffler. Be careful not to damage any parts of the exhaust system that do not need to be replaced. Replace all clamps, nuts, bolts and

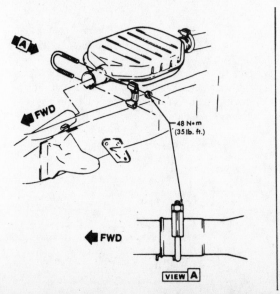

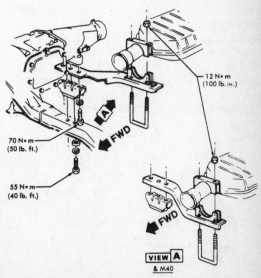

Catalytic converter installation, 1978–87 shown

straps. You do not want your new exhaust system to fall on the ground due to a worn clamp.

Muffler

The muffler is attached to the catalytic converter by a muffler clamp, to the frame by two muffler hangers and to the tail pipe by a muffler clamp. After removing the clamps and hangers, it may be necessary to use a hammer and chisel to separate the muffler from the tail pipe.

Tail Pipe

The tail pipe is removed by loosening the nuts on the hanger that secure the pipe to the frame.

INSTALLATION

Exhaust System Sealer is to be applied to all slip joints before assembly.

When installing exhaust parts, make sure there is sufficient clearance between the hot exhaust parts and pipes and hoses that would be adversely affected by excessive heat.

Check complete exhaust system and nearby body areas and trunk lid for broken, damaged, missing, or mispositioned parts, open seams, holes, loose connections, or other deterioration which could permit exhaust fumes to seep into the passenger compartment. Any damaged areas must be corrected immediately. To help insure continued integrity, when replacing the muffler, resonator or pipes rearward of the muffler due to wear out, all parts rearward and including the muffler should be replaced.

When aligning the system, leave all bolts or nuts loose until all parts are properly aligned, then tighten, working from front to rear.

WARNING: *If any mispositioning, incorrect assembly, or failure of components in the area of the brake system pipes, hoses, or cylinders is observed, be sure to check for any brake damage that may have resulted from such a condition and correct as required. Make sure that exhaust system components have adequate clearance from the floor pan to avoid possible overheating of the floor pan and possible damage to the passenger compartment carpets.*

When jacking or lifting vehicle from frame side rails, be certain lift pads do not contact catalytic converter as damage to converter will result.

Emission Controls

GASOLINE ENGINE EMISSION CONTROLS

The emission control devices required in Chevrolet and GMC pick-ups are determined by weight classification. Light duty emission models use the same controls as cars. These are all 1970-74 trucks; all 1975-78 two wheel drive trucks under 6,000 lbs. Gross Vehicle Weight; all 1979 trucks under 8,500 lbs. GVW; and all 1980 trucks under 8,600 lbs. GVW. Heavy duty models use fewer emission controls and include all four wheel drive trucks, 1970-74; all trucks over 6,000 lbs. GVW, 1975-78; all trucks over 8,500 lbs. GVW, 1979; and all trucks over 8,600 lbs. GVW, 1980 and later.

The CEC (Combined Emission Control) and TCS (Transmission Controlled Spark) have been used since 1970 and basically do not allow distributor vacuum advance in Low gear.

In 1973, the EGR (Exhaust Gas Recirculation) system was developed in response to more stringent Federal exhaust emission standards regarding NOx (oxides of nitrogen). Oxides of nitrogen are formed at higher combustion chamber temperatures and increase with higher temperatures. The EGR system is designed to reduce combustion temperature thereby reducing the formation of NOx.

In addition to controlling the engine emissions, the ECS (Evaporative Control System) is designed to control fuel vapors that escape from the fuel tank through evaporation. When the fuel vapors combine with the atmosphere and sunlight they form photochemical smog. This system seals the fuel tank to retain vapors in a charcoal canister. The canister is purged and the vapors burned during engine operation.

In 1975, a catalytic converter was added to the emission control system on some light duty models, and its use has slowly spread through the line in succeeding years. Through catalytic action (that is, causing a chemical reaction without taking part in the reaction itself) the platinum and palladium coated beads in the converter oxidize unburnt hydrocarbons (HC) and carbon monoxide (CO) into carbon dioxide (CO_2) and water (H_2O). The converter itself is a muffler shaped device installed in the exhaust system of the truck. Converter equipped trucks require the use of unleaded fuel.

With emission level maintenance standards getting stricter on state and Federal levels, proper testing and service of each system becomes more important. Much confusion results from the variety and combinations of systems used in any year. The following sections are devoted to the description and service of each separate system.

Positive Crankcase Ventilation

This system draws crankcase vapors that are formed through normal combustion into the intake manifold and subsequently into the combustion chambers to be burned. Fresh air is introduced to the crankcase by way of a hose connected to the carburetor air cleaner. Manifold vacuum is used to draw the vapors from the crankcase through a PCV valve and into the intake manifold.

SERVICE

The PCV system should be inspected as stated in the Maintenance Interval chart in Chapter 1. Other than checking and replacing the PCV valve and associated hoses, there is no other service required.

1. Remove the PCV valve from the intake manifold or valve cover.
2. Allow the engine to idle.
3. Place your thumb over the end of the valve to check for vacuum. If there is no vacuum at the valve, check for plugged hoses or valve.
4. Remove the valve and shake it. If it rattles the valve is still good, if not, replace it.

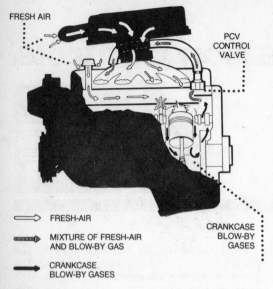

FRESH AIR

PCV CONTROL VALVE

⇨ FRESH-AIR

▭▭▭▭ MIXTURE OF FRESH-AIR AND BLOW-BY GAS

➤ CRANKCASE BLOW-BY GASES

CRANKCASE BLOW-BY GASES

PCV system

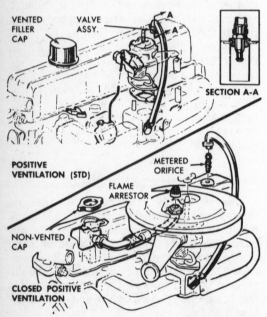

VENTED FILLER CAP

VALVE ASSY.

A

SECTION A-A

POSITIVE VENTILATION (STD)

METERED ORIFICE

FLAME ARRESTOR

NON-VENTED CAP

CLOSED POSITIVE VENTILATION

Closed and positive PCV systems, 6-cylinder shown

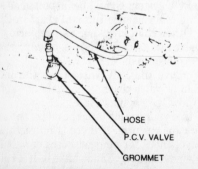

HOSE

P.C.V. VALVE

GROMMET

V8 PCV valve location

5. After installation of a PCV valve or hoses adjust the idle if necessary.

Air Injector Reactor (A.I.R.)

The AIR system injects compressed air into the exhaust system, near enough to the exhaust valves to continue the burning of the normally unburned segment of the exhaust gases. To do this it employs an air injection pump and a system of hoses, valves, tubes, etc., necessary to carry the compressed air from the pump to the exhaust manifolds. Carburetors and distributors for AIR engines have specific modifications to adapt them to the air injection system. These components should not be interchanged with those intended for use on engines that do not have the system.

A diverter valve is used to prevent backfiring. The valve senses sudden increases in manifold vacuum and ceases the injection of air during fuel-rich periods. During coasting, this valve diverts the entire air flow through a muffler and during high engine speeds, expels it through a relief valve. Check valves in the system prevent exhaust gases from entering the pump.

TESTING

Check Valve

To test the check valve, disconnect the hose at the diverter valve. Blow into the hose and suck on it. Air should flow only into the engine.

Diverter Valve

Pull off the vacuum line to the top of the valve with the engine running. There should be vacuum in the line. Replace the line. No air should be escaping with the engine running at a steady idle. Open and quickly close the throttle. A blast of air should come out of the valve muffler for at least one second. If the valve must be replaced, use a new gasket at the valve mounting on the pump and torque the bolts to 85 in.lb.

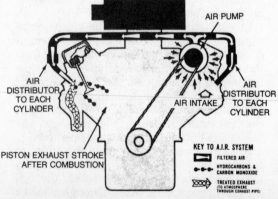

AIR PUMP

AIR DISTRIBUTOR TO EACH CYLINDER

AIR INTAKE

AIR DISTRIBUTOR TO EACH CYLINDER

PISTON EXHAUST STROKE AFTER COMBUSTION

KEY TO A.I.R. SYSTEM
▭ FILTERED AIR
●◗● HYDROCARBONS & CARBON MONOXIDE
▩▩▩ TREATED EXHAUST (TO ATMOSPHERE THROUGH EXHAUST PIPE)

AIR system operation

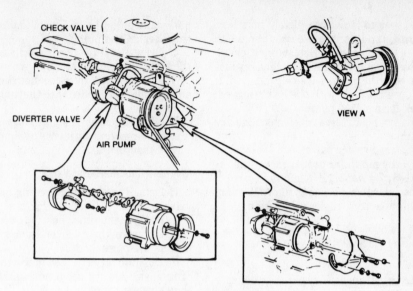

Inline six air pump mounting

Air Pump

Disconnect the hose from the diverter valve. Start the engine and accelerate it to about 1,500 rpm. The airflows should increase as the engine is accelerated. If no airflow is noted or it remains constant, check the following:

1. Drive belt tension.

2. Listen for a leaking pressure relief valve. If it is defective, replace the whole relief/diverter valve.

3. Foreign matter in pump filter openings. If the pump is defective or excessively noisy, it must be replaced.

SERVICE

The AIR system's effectiveness depends on correct engine idle speed, ignition timing, and dwell. These settings should be strictly adhered to and checked frequently. All hoses and fittings should be inspected for condition and tightness of connections. Check the drive belt for wear and tension every 12 months or 12,000 miles (4 months/6,000 miles 1974-75). If, after completion of a tune-up and/or individual inspection of components, a malfunction still exists, the vehicle should be serviced by qualified mechanics.

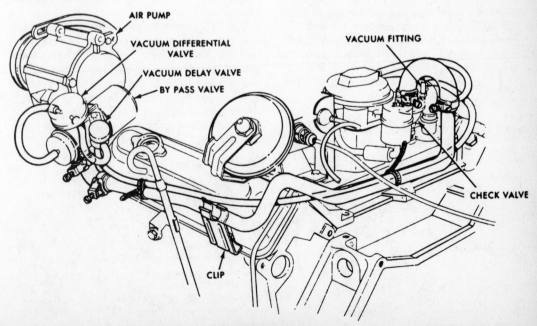

Air pump system, V8

The AIR system is not completely noiseless. Under normal conditions, noise rises in pitch as engine speed increases. To determine if excessive noise is the fault of the AIR system, operate the engine with the pump drive belt removed. If the noise does not exist with the belt removed:

1. Check for a seized pump.
2. Check hoses, tubes and connections for leaks or kinks.
3. Check the diverter valve.
4. Check the pump for proper mounting.

WARNING: *Do not oil AIR pump.*

If no irregularities exist and the AIR pump noise is still excessive, replace the pump.

COMPONENT REMOVAL

Air Pump

WARNING: *Do not pry on the pump housing or clamp the pump in a vise: the housing is soft and may become distorted.*

1. Disconnect the air hoses at the pump.
2. Hold the pump pulley from turning and loosen the pulley bolts.
3. Loosen the pump mounting bolt and adjustment bracket bolt. Remove the drive belt.
4. Remove the mounting bolts, and then remove the pump.
5. Install the pump using a reverse of the removal procedure.

Pump Filter

1. Remove the drive belt and pump pulley.
2. Using needlenosed pliers, pull the fan from the pump hub.

WARNING: *Use care to prevent any dirt or fragments from entering the air intake hole. DO NOT insert a screwdriver between the pump and the filter, and do not attempt to remove the metal hub. It is seldom possible to remove the filter without destroying it.*

3. To install a new filter, draw it on with the pulley and pulley bolts. Do not hammer or press the filter on the pump.

4. Draw the filter down evenly by torquing the bolts alternately. Make sure the outer edge of the filter slips into the housing. A slight amount of interference with the housing bore is normal.

NOTE: *The new filter may squeal initially until the sealing lip on the pump outer diameter has worn in.*

Diverter (Anti-afterburn) Valve

1. Detach the vacuum sensing line from the valve.
2. Remove the other hose(s) from the valve.
3. Unfasten the diverter valve from the elbow or the pump body.

Installation is performed in the reverse order of removal. Always use a new gasket. Tighten the valve securing bolts to 85 in.lb.

Air Management System

The Air Management System is used on 1980 and later models, to provide additional oxygen to continue the combustion process after the exhaust gases heave the combustion chamber; much the same as the AIR system described earlier in this chapter. Air is injected into either the exhaust port(s), the exhaust manifold(s) or the catalytic converter by an engine driven air pump. The system is in operation at all times and will bypass air only momentarily during deceleration and at high speeds. The bypass function is performed by the Air Management Valve, while the check valve protects the air pump by preventing any backflow of exhaust gases.

The AIR system helps to reduce HC and CO content in the exhaust gases by injecting air into the exhaust ports during cold engine operation. This air injection also helps the catalytic converter to reach the proper temperature quicker during warm-up. When the engine is warm (closed loop), the AIR system injects air into the beds of a three-way converter to lower the HC and CO content in the exhaust.

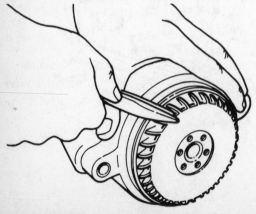

AIR filter removal

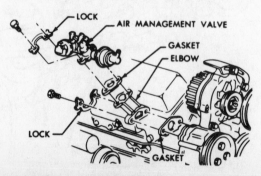

LOCK — AIR MANAGEMENT VALVE — GASKET — ELBOW — LOCK — GASKET

Air management system—typical

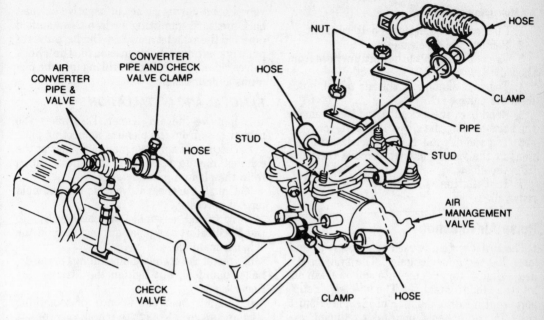

Check valve and hoses—1981 and later air management system

The Air Management System utilizes the following components:

1. An engine driven air pump.
2. Air management valves (Air Control and Air Switching).
3. Air flow and control hoses.
4. Check valves.
5. A dual-bed, three-way catalytic converter.

The belt driven, vane-type air pump is located at the front of the engine and supplies clean air to the system for purposes already stated. When the engine is cold, the Electronic Control Module (ECM) energizes an air control solenoid. This allows air to flow to the air switching valve. The air switching valve is then energized to direct air into the exhaust ports.

When the engine is warm, the ECM de-energizes the air switching valve, thus directing the air between the beds of the catalytic converter. This then provides additional oxygen for the oxidizing catalyst in the second bed to decrease HC and CO levels, while at the same time keeping oxygen levels low in the first bed, enabling the reducing catalyst to effectively decrease the levels of NOx.

If the air control valve detects a rapid increase in manifold vacuum (deceleration), certain operating modes (wide open throttle, etc.) or if the ECM self-diagnostic system detects any problems in the system, air is diverted to the air cleaner or directly into the atmosphere.

The primary purpose of the ECM's divert mode is to prevent backfiring. Throttle closure at the beginning of deceleration will temporar-

ily create air/dual mixtures which are too rich to burn completely. These mixtures will become burnable when they reach the exhaust if they are combined with injection air. The next firing of the engine will ignite the mixture causing an exhaust backfire. Momentary diverting of the injection air from the exhaust prevents this.

The Air Management System check valves and hoses should be checked periodically for any leaks, cracks or deterioration.

REMOVAL AND INSTALLATION

Air Pump

1. Remove the valves and/or adapter at the air pump.
2. Loosen the air pump adjustment bolt and remove the drive belt.
3. Unscrew the three mounting bolts and then remove the pump pulley.
4. Unscrew the pump mounting bolts and then remove the pump.
5. Installation is in the reverse order of removal. Be sure to adjust the drive belt tension after installing it.

Check Valve

1. Release the clamp and disconnect the air hoses from the valve.
2. Unscrew the check valve from the air injection pipe.
3. Installation is in the reverse order of removal.

Air Management Valve

1. Disconnect the negative battery cable.
2. Remove the air cleaner.
3. Tag and disconnect the vacuum hose from the valve.
4. Tag and disconnect the air outlet hoses from the valve.
5. Bend back the lock tabs and then remove the bolts holding the elbow to the valve.
6. Tag and disconnect any electrical connections at the valve and then remove the valve from the elbow.
7. Installation is in the reverse order of removal.

Pulse Air Injection

The PAIR system is used on some 1979 and later 250 6-cylinder engines. The system utilizes exhaust system pulses to siphon fresh air into the exhaust manifold. The injected air supports continued combustion of the hot exhaust gases in the exhaust manifold, reducing exhaust emissions.

Air is drawn into the PAIR plenums through a hose connected to the air cleaner case. There are two plenums, mounted on the rocker arm cover. The air passes through a check valve (there are four check valves—two at each plenum), then through a manifold pipe to the exhaust manifold. All manifold pipes are the same length, to prevent uneven pulsation. The check valves open during pulses of negative exhaust back pressure, admitting air into the manifold pipe and the exhaust manifold. During pulses of positive exhaust back pressure, the check valves close, preventing backfiring into the plenums and air cleaner.

REMOVAL AND INSTALLATION

1. Remove the air cleaner. Disconnect the rubber hose from the plenum connecting pipe.
2. Disconnect the four manifold pipes at the exhaust manifold. Remove the check valves from the plenum grommets.
3. Unbolt the check valve from the manifold pipe, if necessary.
4. To install, assemble the check valves to the pipes before the pipes are installed on the exhaust manifold.
5. Install the manifold pipe fillings to the exhaust manifold, but tighten the fittings only finger tight.
6. Use a 1″ open end wrench, or something similar, as a lever to align the check valve on the **A** pipe assemblies (see the illustration) with the plenum grommet. Use the palm of your hand to press the check valve into the grommet. A rubber lubricant can be used to ease assembly.
7. Repeat this operation on the **B** pipe assembly.
8. After all the check valves have been installed in the rubber grommets, tighten the manifold pipe-to-exhaust manifold fittings to

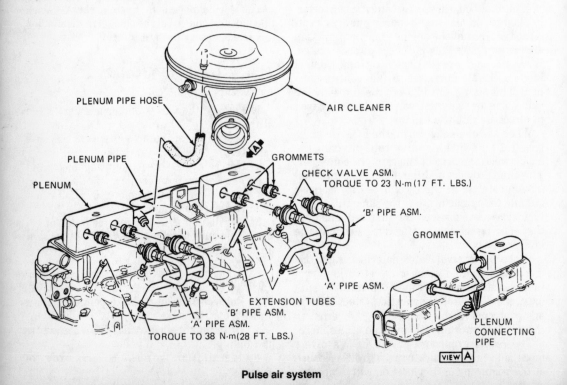

Pulse air system

28 ft.lb. Connect the rubber hose to the plenum pipe and install the air cleaner.

Controlled Combustion System

The CCS system is a combination of systems and calibrations. Many of these are not visible or serviceable, but are designed into the engine. Originally the system was comprised of special carburetion and distributor settings, higher engine operating temperatures and a thermostatically controlled air cleaner. In later years, the thermostatically controller air cleaner was used independently of the other settings on some engines. Likewise, some engines used the special settings without Thermac. In 1970, the TCS system was incorporated and the entire system was renamed CEC in 1971. The name reverted to TCS in 1972. In 1973, EGR was also added to the system.

The various systems, TCS, CEC and EGR are all part of the Controlled Combustion System.

SERVICE

Refer to the TCS, CEC or EGR Sections for maintenance and service (if applicable). In addition be sure that the ignition timing, dwell and carburetor settings are correct.

Thermostatic Air Cleaner

The thermostatic air cleaner (Thermac) is on all gasoline engines. This system uses a damper assembly in the air cleaner inlet, controlled by a vacuum motor to mix preheated and cold air entering the air cleaner. This is necessary to maintain a controlled air temperature into the carburetor. The vacuum motor is controlled by a temperature sensor in the air cleaner. The preheating of the air cleaner inlet air allows leaner carburetor and choke settings, which result in lower emissions, while maintaining good driveability.

SERVICE

1. Either start with a cold engine or remove the air cleaner from the engine for at least half an hour. While cooling the air cleaner, leave the engine compartment hood open.

2. Tape a thermometer, of known accuracy, to the inside of the air cleaner so that it is near the temperature sensor unit. Install the air cleaner on the engine but do not fasten its securing nut.

3. Start the engine. With the engine cold and the outside temperature less than 90°F., the door should be in the HEAT ON position (closed to outside air).

NOTE: *Due to the position of the air cleaner on some trucks, a mirror may be necessary when observing the position of the air door.*

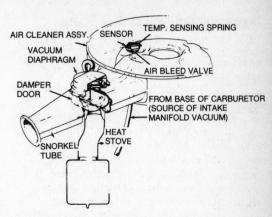

Thermostatically-controlled air cleaner case

4. Operate the throttle lever rapidly to ½-¾ of its opening and release it. The air door should open to allow outside air to enter and then close again.

5. Allow the engine to warm up to normal temperature. Watch the door. When it opens to the outside air, remove the cover from the air cleaner. The temperature should be over 90°F and no more than 130°F; 115°F is about normal. If the door does not work within these temperature ranges, or fails to work at all, check for linkage or door binding.

If binding is not present and the air door is not working, proceed with the vacuum tests, given below. If these indicate no faults in the vacuum motor and the door is not working, the temperature sensor is defective and must be replaced.

Vacuum Motor Test

NOTE: *Be sure that the vacuum hose which runs between the temperature switch and the vacuum motor is not pinched by the retaining clip under the air cleaner. This could prevent the air door from closing.*

1. Check all of the vacuum lines and fittings for leaks. Correct any leaks. If none are found, proceed with the test.

2. Remove the hose which runs from the sensor to the vacuum motor. Run a hose directly from the manifold vacuum source to the vacuum motor.

3. If the motor closes the air door, it is functioning properly and the temperature sensor is defective.

4. If the motor does not close the door and no binding is present in its operation, the vacuum motor is defective and must be replaced.

NOTE: *If an alternate vacuum source is applied to the motor, insert a vacuum gauge in the line by using a T-fitting. Apply at least 9 in.Hg of vacuum in order to operate the motor.*

Transmission Controlled Spark

Introduced in 1970, this system controls exhaust emissions by eliminating vacuum advance in the lower forward gears.

The 1970 system consists of a transmission switch, solenoid vacuum switch, time delay relay, and a thermostatic water temperature switch. The solenoid vacuum switch is de-energized in the lower gears via the transmission switch and closes off distributor vacuum. The two-way transmission switch is activated by the shifter shaft on manual transmissions, and by oil pressure on automatic transmissions. The switch energizes the solenoid in High gear, the plunger extends and uncovers the vacuum port, and the distributor receives full vacuum. The temperature switch overrides the system, until the engine temperature reaches 82°F. This allows vacuum advance in all gears, thereby preventing stalling after starting. A time delay relay opens fifteen seconds after the ignition is switched on. Full vacuum advance during this delay eliminated the possibility of stalling.

The 1971 system is similar, except that the vacuum solenoid (now called a Combination Emissions Control solenoid) serves two functions. One function is to control distributor vacuum; the added function is to act as a deceleration throttle stop in High gear. This cuts down on emissions when the vehicle is coming to a stop in High gear. Two throttle settings are necessary; one for curb idle and one for emission control on coast. Both settings are described in the tune-up section.

The 1972 6-cylinder system is similar to that used in 1971, except that an idle stop solenoid has been added to the system and the name is changed back to TCS. In the energized position, the solenoid maintains engine speed at a predetermined fast idle. When de-energized the solenoid allows the throttle plates to close beyond the normal idle position; thus cutting off the air supply and preventing engine run-on. The 6-cylinder is the only 1972 engine with a CEC valve, which serves the same deceleration function as in 1971. The time delay relay now delays full vacuum twenty seconds after the transmission is shifted into High gear. 1972 V8 engines use a vacuum advance solenoid similar to that used in 1970. The solenoid controls distributor vacuum advance and performs no throttle positioning function. The idle stop solenoid used on V8s operates in the same manner as the one on 6-cylinder engines. All air conditioned cars have an additional anti-diesel (run-on) solenoid which engages the compressor clutch for three seconds after the ignition is switched off.

The 1973 TCS system on the 6-cylinder engine is identical to that on 1972 six, except for recalibration of the temperature switch. The system used on small block 1973 engines changed slightly from 1972. In place of the CEC solenoid on the 6, the V8 continues to use a vacuum advance solenoid. The other differences are: the upshift delay relay, previously located under the instrument panel has been done away with; a 20 second time delay relay identical to the one on 6-cylinder engines is now used; small block V8s use manifold vacuum with TCS and ported vacuum without TCS.

The 6-cylinder TCS system was revised for 1974-75 by replacing the CEC solenoid with a vacuum advance solenoid. Otherwise the system remains the same as 1973.

TESTING

If there is a TCS system malfunction, first connect a vacuum gauge in the hose between the solenoid valve and the distributor vacuum unit. Drive the vehicle or raise it on a frame lift and observe the vacuum gauge. If full vacuum is available in all gears, check for the following:

1. Blown fuse.
2. Disconnected wire at solenoid operated vacuum valve.
3. Disconnected wire at transmission switch.
4. Temperature override switch energized due to low engine temperature.
5. Solenoid failure.

If no vacuum is available in any gear, check the following:

1. Solenoid valve vacuum lines switched.
2. Clogged solenoid vacuum valve.
3. Distributor or manifold vacuum lines leaking or disconnected.
4. Transmission switch or wire grounded.

Test for individual components are as follows:

Idle Stop Solenoid

This unit may be checked simply by observing it while an assistant switches the ignition on and off. It should extend further with the current switched on. The unit is not repairable.

Solenoid Vacuum Valve

Check that proper manifold vacuum is available. Connect the vacuum gauge in the line between the solenoid valve and the distributor. Apply 12 volts to the solenoid. If vacuum is still not available, the valve is defective, either mechanically or electrically. The unit is not repairable. If the valve is satisfactory, check the relay next.

Relay

1. With the engine at normal operating temperature and the ignition on, ground the solenoid vacuum valve terminal with the black lead.

The solenoid should energize (no vacuum) if the relay is satisfactory.

2. With the solenoid energized as in Step 1, connect a jumper from the relay terminal with the green/white stripe lead to ground. The solenoid should de-energize (vacuum available) if the relay is satisfactory.

3. If the relay worked properly in Steps 1 and 2, check the temperature switch. The relay unit is not repairable.

Temperature Switch

The vacuum valve solenoid should be de-energized (vacuum available) with the engine cold. If it is not, ground the green/white stripe wire from the switch. If the solenoid now de-energizes, replace the switch. If the switch was satisfactory, check the transmission switch.

Transmission Switch

With the engine at normal operating temperature and the transmission in one of the no-vacuum gears, the vacuum valve solenoid should be energized (no vacuum). If not, remove and ground the switch electrical lead. If the solenoid energizes, replace the switch.

Evaporation Control System

Introduced on California vehicles in 1970, and nationwide in 1971, this system reduces the amount of escaping gasoline vapors. Float bowl emissions are controlled by internal carburetor modifications. Redesigned bowl vents, reduced bowl capacity, heat shields, and improved intake manifold-to-carburetor insulation serve to reduce vapor loss into the atmosphere. The venting of fuel tank vapors into the air has been stopped. Fuel vapors are now directed through lines to a canister containing an activated charcoal filter. Unburned vapors are trapped here until the engine is started. When the engine is running, the canister is purged by air drawn in by manifold vacuum. The air and fuel vapors are directed into the engine to be burned.

SERVICE

Replace the filter in the engine compartment canister as specified in the Maintenance Intervals Chart in Chapter 1. If the fuel tank cap requires replacement, ensure that the new cap is the correct part for your truck.

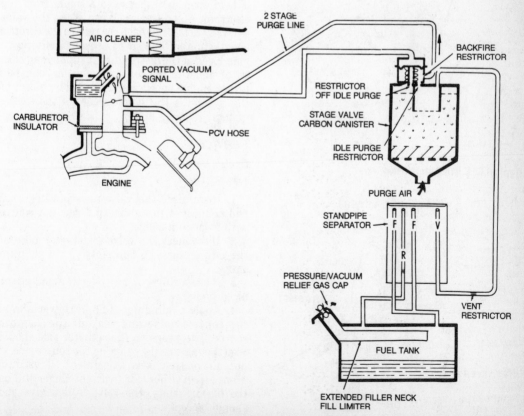

Evaporation Control System (ECS)

Early Fuel Evaporation

The 6-cylinder and 1975 Mark IV (big block) V8 EFE systems consist of an EFE valve mounted at the flange of the exhaust manifold, and actuator, a thermal vacuum switch (TVS) and a vacuum solenoid. The TVS is located on the right hand side of the engine forward of the oil pressure switch on 6-cylinder engines and directly above the oil filter on the Mark IV V8. The TVS is normally closed and sensitive to oil temperature.

The small block V8 and 1976 and later Mark IV EFE system consists of an EFE valve at the flange of the exhaust manifold, an actuator, and a thermal vacuum switch. The TVS is located in the coolant outlet housing and directly controls vacuum.

In both systems, manifold vacuum is applied to the actuator, which in turn, closes the EFE valve. This routes hot exhaust gases to the base of the carburetor. When coolant or oil temperatures reach a set limit, vacuum is denied to the actuator allowing an internal spring to return

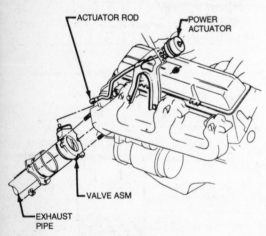

Typical EFE valve installation

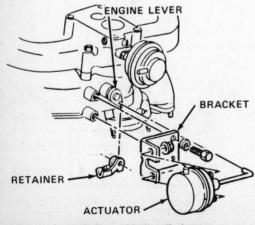

EFE valve, installation, 250 six cylinder

the actuator to its normal position, opening the EFE valve.

Throttle Return Control

Two different throttle return control systems are used. The first is used from 1975 to 1978. It consists of a control valve and a throttle lever actuator. When the truck is coasting against the engine, the control valve is open to allow vacuum to operate the throttle lever actuator. The throttle lever actuator then pushes the throttle lever slightly open reducing the HC (hydrocarbon) emission level during coasting. When manifold vacuum drops below a predetermined level, the control valve closes, the throttle lever retracts, and the throttle lever closes to the idle position.

The second TRC system is used in 1979 and later. It consists of a throttle lever actuator, a solenoid vacuum control valve, and an electronic speed sensor. The throttle lever actuator, mounted on the carburetor, opens the primary throttle plates a preset amount, above normal engine idle speed in response to a signal from the solenoid vacuum control valve. The valve, mounted at the left rear of the engine above the intake manifold on the 6-cylinder, or on the thermostat housing mounting stud on the V8, is held open in response to a signal from the electronic speed sensor. When open, the valve allows a vacuum signal to be sent to the throttle lever actuator. The speed sensor monitors engine speed at the distributor. It supplies an electrical signal to the solenoid valve, as long as a preset engine speed is exceeded. The object of this system is the same as that of the earlier system.

SERVICE

Control Valve

1975-76

1. Disconnect the valve-to-carburetor hose and connect it to an external vacuum source with a vacuum gauge.

2. Disconnect the valve-to-actuator hose at the connector and connect it to a vacuum gauge.

3. Place a finger firmly over the end of the bleed fitting.

4. Apply a minimum of 23 in.Hg vacuum to the control valve and seal off the vacuum source. The gauge on the actuator side should read the same as the gauge on the source side. If not, the valve needs adjustment. If vacuum drops off on either side (with the finger still on the bleed fitting), the valve is defective and should be replaced.

5. With a minimum of 23 in.Hg vacuum in

THROTTLE RETURN CONTROL SYSTEM

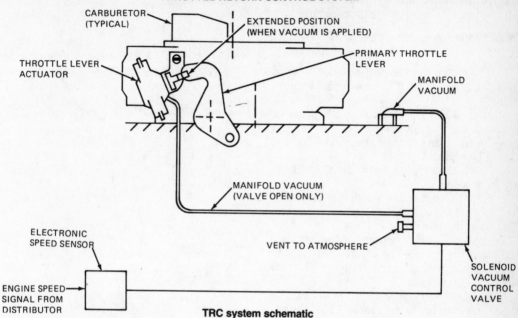

TRC system schematic

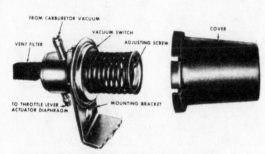

Throttle return control valve through 1978

the valve, remove the finger from the bleed fitting. The vacuum level in the actuator side will drop to zero and the reading on the source side will drop to a value that will be the value set point. If the value is not within ½ in.Hg vacuum of the specified valve set point, adjust the valve.

6. Gently pry off the plastic cover.

7. Turn the adjusting screw in (clockwise) to

TRS Control Valve Set Points

Engine	Set Point (in. Hg)
292	22.5
305	22.5
350	21.5
400	21.5
454 (1975–76)	21.0
454 (1977–78)	23.0

TRC Speed

Engine	Setting (rpm)
292	1600
305	1600
350	1500
400	1500
454 (1975–76)	1400
454 (1977–78)	1500

raise the set point or out (counterclockwise) to lower the set point.

8. Recheck the valve set point.

9. If necessary, repeat the adjustment until the valve set point is attained ± ½ in.Hg vacuum.

1977-78

1. Disconnect the valve-to-carburetor hose at the carburetor. Connect the hose to an external vacuum source, with an accurate vacuum gauge connected into the line near the valve.

2. Apply a minimum of 25 in.Hg of vacuum to the control valve vacuum supply fitting while sealing off the vacuum supply between the gauge and the vacuum source. The vacuum gauge will indicate the set point valve of the valve.

3. If the gauge reading is not within 0.5 in.Hg of the specified value (see the chart), the valve must be adjusted. If the trapped vacuum drops off faster than 0.1 in.Hg per second, the valve is leaking and must be replaced.

4. To adjust the valve set point, follow Steps 6-9 of the 1975-76 adjustment procedure.

Throttle Valve

1975-78

1. Disconnect the valve-to-actuator hose at the valve and connect it to an external vacuum source.

2. Apply 20 in.Hg vacuum to the actuator and seal the vacuum source. If the vacuum gauge reading drops, the valve is leaking and should be replaced.

3. Check the throttle lever, shaft, and linkage for freedom of operation.

4. Start the engine and warm it to operating temperature.

5. Note the idle rpm.

6. Apply 20 in.Hg vacuum to the actuator and manually operate the throttle. Allow it to close against the extended actuator plunger. Note the engine rpm.

7. Release and reapply 20 in.Hg vacuum to the actuator and note the rpm at which the engine speed increases (do not assist the actuator).

8. If the engine speed obtained in Step 7 is not within 150 rpm of that obtained in Step 6, then the actuator may be binding. If the binding cannot be corrected, replace the actuator.

9. Release the vacuum from the actuator and the engine speed should return to within 50 rpm of the speed noted in Steps 4 and 5.

To adjust the actuator:

10. Turn the screw on the actuator plunger until the specified TRC speed range is obtained.

Throttle Lever Actuator

1979 AND LATER

The checking procedure is the same as for earlier years. Follow Steps 1-9 of the Throttle Valve procedure. Adjustment procedures are covered in the carburetor adjustments section, later is this chapter.

TRC SYSTEM CHECK

1979 and Later

1. Connect a tachometer to the distributor TACH terminal. Start the engine and raise the engine speed to 1890 rpm. The throttle lever actuator on the carburetor should extend.

2. Reduce the engine speed to 1700 rpm. The lever actuator should retract.

3. If the actuator operates outside of the speed limits, the speed switch is faulty and must be replaced. It cannot be adjusted.

4. If the actuator does not operate at all:

a. Check the voltage at the vacuum solenoid and the speed switch with a voltmeter. Connect the negative probe of the voltmeter

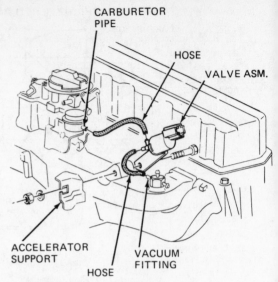

TRC valve assembly—inline six

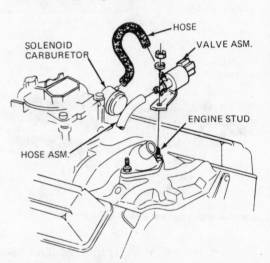

TRC valve assembly—V8s

to the engine ground and the positive probe to the voltage source wire on the component. The positive probe can be inserted on the connector body at the wire side; it is not necessary to unplug the connector. Voltage should be 12 to 14 volts in both cases.

b. If the correct voltage is present at one component but not the other, the engine wiring harness is faulty.

c. If voltage is not present at all, check the engine harness connections at the distributor and the bulkhead connector and repair as necessary.

d. If the correct voltage is present at both components, check the solenoid operation: ground the solenoid-to-speed switch connecting wire terminal at the solenoid connector with a jumper wire. This should cause the throttle lever actuator to extend, with the engine running.

e. If the lever actuator does not extend, remove the hose from the solenoid side port which connects to the actuator hose. Check the port for obstructions or blockage. If the port is not plugged, replace the solenoid.

f. If the actuator extends in Step d, ground the solenoid-to-speed switch wire terminal at the switch. If the actuator does not extend, the wire between the speed switch and the solenoid is open and must be repaired. If the actuator does extend, check the speed switch ground wire for a ground; it should read zero volts with the engine running. Check the speed switch-to-distributor wire for a proper connection. If the ground and distributor wires are properly connected and the actuator still does not extend when the engine speed is above 1890 rpm, replace the speed switch.

5. If the actuator is extended at all speeds:

a. Remove the connector from the vacuum solenoid.

b. If the actuator remains extended, check the solenoid side port orifice for blockage. If plugged, clear and reconnect the system and recheck. If the actuator is still extended, remove the solenoid connector; if the actuator does not retreat, replace the vacuum solenoid.

c. If the actuator retracts with the solenoid connector off, reconnect it and remove the speed switch connector. If the actuator retracts, the problem is in the speed switch, which should be replaced. If the actuator

does not retract, the solenoid-to-speed switch wire is shorted to ground in the wiring harness. Repair the short.

Oxygen Sensor

1983 and Later

The oxygen sensor is a spark plug-shaped device that is screwed into the exhaust manifold on V8s and into the exhaust pipe on inline sixes. It monitors the oxygen content of the exhaust gases and sends as voltage signal to the Electronic Control Module (ECM). The ECM monitors this voltage and, depending on the value of the received signal, issues a command to the mixture control solenoid on the carburetor to adjust for rich or lean conditions.

The proper operation of the oxygen sensor depends upon four basic conditions:

1. Good electrical connections—since the sensor generates low currents, good clean electrical connections at the sensor are a must.

2. Outside air supply—air must circulate to the internal portion of the sensor. When servicing the sensor, do not restrict the air passages.

3. Proper operating temperatures—The ECM will not recognize the sensor's signals until the sensor reaches approximately 600°F.

4. Non-leaded fuel—the use of leaded gasoline will damage the sensor very quickly.

WARNING: *No attempt should be made to measure the output voltage of the sensor. The current drain of any conventional voltmeter would be enough to permanently damage the sensor. No jumpers, test leads, or other electrical connections should ever be made to the*

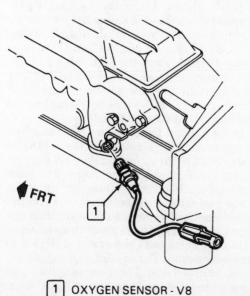

⬆ **FRT**

1 OXYGEN SENSOR - V8

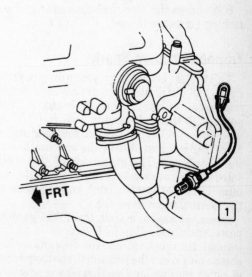

⬆ **FRT**

1 OXYGEN SENSOR - L6

Oxygen sensor locations, V6 similar to V8

sensor. Use these tools ONLY on the ECM side of the harness connector AFTER the oxygen sensor has been disconnected.

REMOVAL AND INSTALLATION

WARNING: *The sensor uses a permanently attached pigtail and connector. This pigtail should not be removed from the sensor. Damage or removal of the pigtail or connector could affect the proper operation of the sensor. Keep the electrical connector and louvered end of the sensor clean and free of grease. NEVER use cleaning solvents of any type on the sensor.*

The oxygen sensor may be difficult to remove when the temperature of the engine is below 120°F. Excessive force may damage the threads in the exhaust manifold or exhaust pipe.

1. Disconnect the electrical connector and any attaching hardware.
2. Remove the sensor.
3. Coat the threads of the sensor with a GM anti-seize compound (#5613695) before installation. New sensors are pre-coated with this compound.

WARNING: *The GM anti-seize compound is NOT a conventional anti-seize paste. The use of a regular paste may electrically insulate the sensor, rendering it useless. The threads MUST be coated with the proper electrically conductive anti-seize compound.*

4. Install the sensor and torque to 30 ft.lb. Use care in making sure the silicone boot is in the correct position to avoid melting it during operation.
5. Connect the electrical connector and attaching hardware if used.

Trapped Vacuum Spark

This system is used to prevent a drop in vacuum to the distributor vacuum advance during cold engine operation, when the engine is accelerating. A thermal vacuum switch (TVS) is used to sense engine coolant temperature. A check valve is installed in the vacuum line to the distributor. The other side of the check valve has two connections: one to manifold vacuum (at the carburetor base), and the other to the thermal vacuum switch.

When the engine is cold, the TVSA vacuum ports are closed. Manifold vacuum is routed through the check valve to the distributor. The check valve keeps the vacuum to the distributor at a high vacuum level, so that when the engine is accelerated, the vacuum to the distributor does not drop. This results in a constant spark advance.

When the engine temperature reaches a pre-

determined value, the TVS ports open to allow manifold vacuum to the distributor, and the check valve operates only as a connector.

Exhaust Gas Recirculation

The EGR system and valve were introduced in 1973. Its purpose is to control oxides of nitrogen which are formed during the peak combustion temperatures. The end products of combustion are relatively inert gases derived from the exhaust gases which are directed into the EGR valve to help lower peak combustion temperatures.

The EGR valve contains a vacuum diaphragm operated by manifold vacuum. The vacuum signal port is located in the carburetor body and is exposed to engine vacuum in the off/idle, part-throttle, and wide open throttle operation. In 1974, a thermo-delay switch was added to delay operation of the valve during engine warm-up, when NOx levels are already at a minimum.

There are actually three types of EGR systems: Vacuum Modulated, Positive Exhaust Backpressure Modulated, and Negative Exhaust Backpressure Modulated. The principle of all the systems is the same; the only difference is in the method used to control how far the EGR valve opens.

In the Vacuum Modulated system, which is used on all trucks through 1976, and some models thereafter, the amount of exhaust gas admitted into the intake manifold depends on a ported vacuum signal. A ported vacuum signal is one taken from the carburetor above the throttle plates. Thus, the vacuum signal (amount of vacuum) is dependent on how far the throttle plates are opened. When the throttle is closed (idle or deceleration) there is no vacuum signal. Thus, the EGR valve is closed, and no exhaust gas enters the intake manifold. As the throttle is opened, a vacuum is produced, which opens the EGR valve, admitting exhaust gas into the intake manifold.

In the Exhaust Backpressure Modulated system, a transducer is installed in the EGR valve body, reacting to either positive or negative backpressure, depending on design. The vacuum used is still ported vacuum, but the transducer uses exhaust gas backpressure to control an air bleed within the valve to modify this vacuum signal. Backpressure valves are used on all light duty emissions California and High Altitude engines in 1976 and 1978, and on most engines, 1979 and later. The choice of either a positive or negative backpressure valve is determined by measurement of the engine's normal backpressure output. Negative valves are used on engines with relatively low backpressure;

positive valves are used on engines with relatively high backpressure. The choice of valve usage is made at the factory, and is nothing for the backyard mechanic to worry about; however, if the valve is replaced, it is important to install the same type as the original. The difference between the three valves (ported, positive, or negative) can be determined by the shape of the diaphragm plate; your Chevrolet or GMC dealer will be able to match the old valve to a new one.

On 6-cylinder engines, the EGR valve is located on the intake manifold adjacent to the carburetor. On small block V8 engines, the valve is located on the right rear side of the intake manifold adjacent to the rocker arm cover. Mark IV V8 EGR valves are located in the left front corner of the intake manifold in front of the carburetor.

SERVICE

The EGR valve is not serviceable, except for replacement. To check the ported vacuum signal valve, proceed as follows:

1. Connect a tachometer to the engine.
2. With the engine running at normal operating temperature, with the choke valve fully open, set the engine rpm at 2,000. The transmission should be in Park (automatic) or Neutral (manual) with the parking brake on and the wheels blocked.
3. Disconnect the vacuum hose at the valve. Make sure that vacuum is available at the valve and look at the tachometer to see if the engine speed increases. If it does, a malfunction of the valve is indicated.
4. If necessary, replace the valve.

A back pressure EGR valve is used on all light duty emissions California and High Altitude 6-cylinder and V8 engines in 1977 and 1978, and most 1979 and later models.

The system can be tested as follows:

1. Remove air cleaner so that the EGR valve diaphragm movement can be observed. The choke secondary vacuum break TVS can be unclipped and removed from the air cleaner body, rather than removing hoses.
2. Plug the intake manifold air cleaner vacuum fitting. Connect as tachometer.
3. Start the engine and warm to operating temperature. Open the throttle part way and release. Watch or feel the EGR diaphragm for movement. The valve should open slightly when the throttle is opened and close when it is released.
4. Remove the EGR hose from the EGR valve and plug the hose. Place the carburetor cam follower on the second step of the fast idle cam and note the speed.
5. Attach a vacuum hose between the air

cleaner vacuum fitting and the EGR valve. Note the speed change. The speed should drop at least 200 rpm with automatic transmissions, or at least 150 with manuals.

If the EGR valve does not meet the criteria specified in these tests, it must be replaced.

DIESEL ENGINE EMISSIONS CONTROLS

Crankcase Ventilation

A Crankcase Depression Regulator Valve (CDRV) is used to regulate (meter) the flow of crankcase gases back into the engine to be burned. the CDRV is designed to limit vacuum in the crankcase as the gases are drawn from the valve covers through the CDRV and into the intake manifold (air crossover).

Fresh air enters the engine through the combination filter, check valve and oil fill cap. The fresh air mixes with blow-by gases and enters both valve covers. The gases pass through a filter installed on the valve covers and are drawn into connecting tubing.

Intake manifold vacuum acts against a spring loaded diaphragm to control the flow of crankcase gases. Higher intake vacuum levels pull the diaphragm closer to the top of the outlet tube. This reduces the amount of gases being drawn from the crankcase and decreases the vacuum level in the crankcase. As the intake vacuum decreases, the spring pushes the diaphragm away from the top of the outlet tube al-

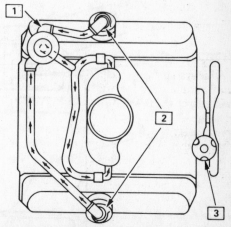

CRANKCASE VENTILATION SYSTEM SCHEMATIC
V-TYPE DIESEL ENGINE
WITH DEPRESSION REGULATOR VALVE

1. Crankcase depression regulator
2. Ventilation filter
3. Breather cap

Diesel crankcase ventilation system flow, 350 shown

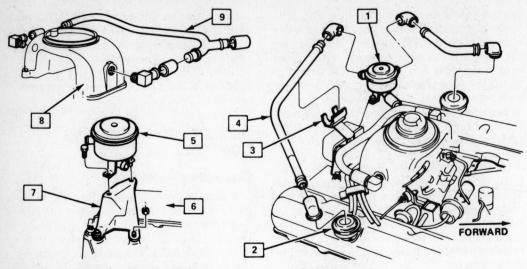

1. Crankcase depression regulator (CDR)
2. Ventilation filter
3. Brace clip
4. Ventilation pipes
5. Crankcase depression regulator (CDR)
6. L.H. valve cover
7. Bracket
8. Air crossover
9. Air crossover to regulator valve pipe

Crankcase ventilation system components, diesels

lowing more gases to flow to the intake manifold.

WARNING: *Do not allow any solvent to come in contact with the diaphragm of the Crankcase Depression Regulator Valve because the diaphragm will fail.*

Exhaust Gas Recirculation (EGR)

To lower the formation of nitrogen oxides (NOx) in the exhaust, it is necessary to reduce combustion temperatures. This is done in the diesel, as in the gasoline engine, by introducing

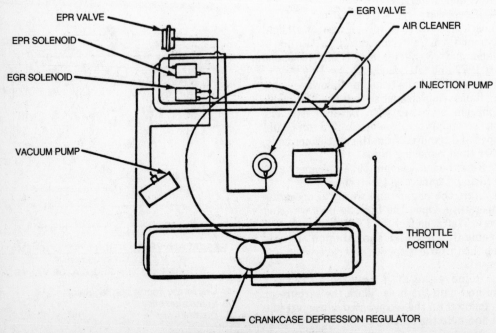

379 diesel emissions components

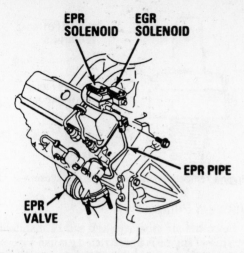

Exhaust Pressure Regulator valve and solenoid, 379 diesels

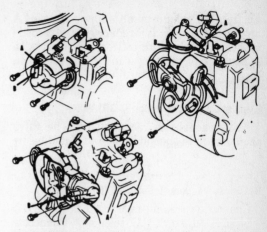

Diesel vacuum regulator valve (VRV), mounted to injection pump

exhaust gases into the cylinders through the EGR valve.

On the 379 diesel, an Exhaust Pressure Regulator (EPR) valve and solenoid operate in conjunction with the EGR valve. The EPR valve's job is to increase exhaust backpressure in order to increase EGR flow (to reduce nitrous oxide emissions). The EPR valve is usually open, and the solenoid is normally closed. When energized by the **B+** wire from the Throttle Position Switch (TPS), the solenoid opens, allowing vac-

uum to the EPR valve, closing it. This occurs at idle. As the throttle is opened, at a calibrated throttle angle, the TPS de-energizes the EPR solenoid, cutting off vacuum to the EPR valve, closing the valve.

FUNCTIONAL TESTS OF COMPONENTS

Vacuum Regulator Valve (VRV)

The Vacuum Regulator Valve is attached to the side of the injection pump and regulates vacuum in proportion to throttle angle. Vacu-

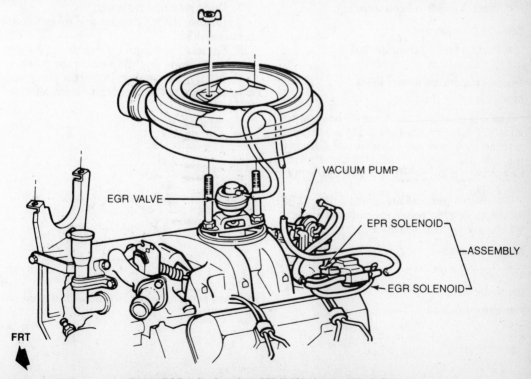

Diesel EGR valve location; 379 (6.2L) shown, 350 similar

um from the vacuum pump is supplied to port **A** and vacuum at port **B** is reduced as the throttle is opened. At closed throttle, the vacuum is 15 in.Hg; at half throttle, 6 in.Hg; at wide open throttle there is zero vacuum.

Exhaust Gas Recirculation (EGR) Valve

Apply vacuum to vacuum port. The valve should be fully open at 10.5″ and closed below 6″.

Response Vacuum Reducer (RVR)

Connect a vacuum gauge to the port marked "To EGR valve or T.C.C. solenoid." Connect a hand operated vacuum pump to the VRV port. Draw a 50.66 kPa (15 in.Hg) vacuum on the pump and the reading on the vacuum gauge should be lower than the vacuum pump reading as follows:
- 0.75″ Except High Altitude
- 2.50″ High Altitude

Torque converter Clutch Operated Solenoid

When the torque converter clutch is engaged, an electrical signal energizes the solenoid allowing ports 1 and 2 to be interconnected. When the solenoid is not energized, port 1 is closed and ports 2 and 3 are interconnected.

Solenoid Energized
- Ports 1 and 3 are connected.

Solenoid De-energized
- Ports 2 and 3 are connected.

Engine Temperature Sensor (ETS)
OPERATION

The engine temperature sensor has two terminals. Twelve volts are applied to one terminal and the wire from the other terminal leads to the fast idle solenoid and Housing Pressure Cold Advance solenoid that is part of the injection pump.

The switch contacts are closed below 125°F. At the calibration point, the contacts are open which turns off the solenoids.

Above Calibration
- Open Circuit.

Below Calibration
- Closed Circuit.

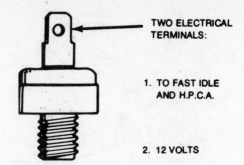

TWO ELECTRICAL TERMINALS:

1. TO FAST IDLE AND H.P.C.A.

2. 12 VOLTS

Engine Temperature Sensor (ETS), 350 diesel

Vacuum Pump

Since the air crossover and intake manifold in a diesel engine is unrestricted (unlike a gasoline engine which has throttle plates creating a venturi effect) there is no vacuum source. To provide vacuum, a vacuum pump is mounted in the location occupied by the distributor in a gasoline engine. This pump supplies the air conditioning servos, the cruise control servos, and the transmission vacuum modulator where required.

The pump is a diaphragm type which needs no maintenance. It is driven by a drive gear on its lower end which meshes with gear teeth on the end of the engine's camshaft.

REMOVAL AND INSTALLATION

350 and 379 Diesels

1. Disconnect the batteries.
2. Remove the air cleaner, and cover the intake manifold.
3. Remove the vacuum pump clamp, disconnect the vacuum line and remove the pump.
4. Install a new gasket. Install the pump and reverse the removal procedures for installation.

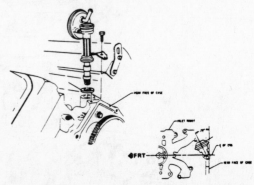

Vacuum pump mounting, 379 diesel. 350 diesel engine similar

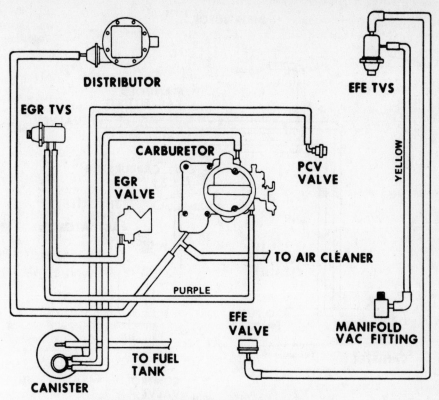

DISTRIBUTOR

EGR TVS

CARBURETOR

EFE TVS

EGR VALVE

PCV VALVE

YELLOW

TO AIR CLEANER

PURPLE

EFE VALVE

MANIFOLD VAC FITTING

TO FUEL TANK

CANISTER

Vacuum hose schematic-6-250, LD emissions-1977

DISTRIBUTOR

PCV VALVE

MANIFOLD VAC FITTING

TO AIR CLEANER

Vacuum hose schematic-6-250/292, HD emissions, except Calif.-1977

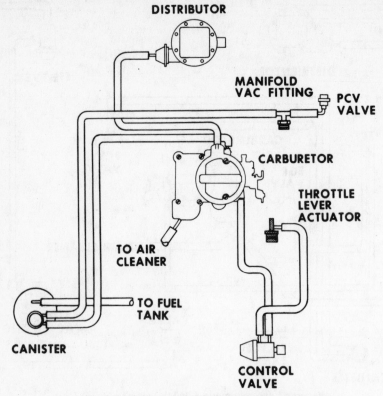

Vacuum hose schematic-6-292, HD emissions, Calif.-1977

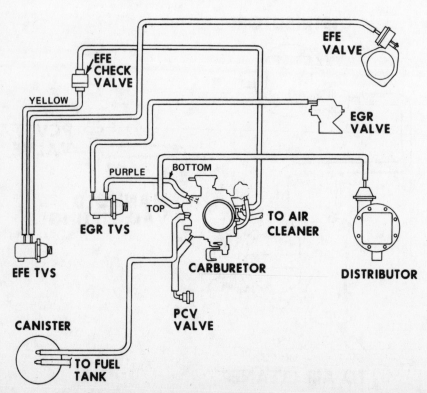

Vacuum hose schematic-8-305, low altitude, LD emissions-1977

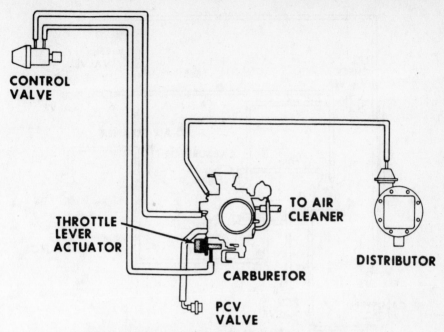

Vacuum hose schematic-8-305, HD emissions-1977

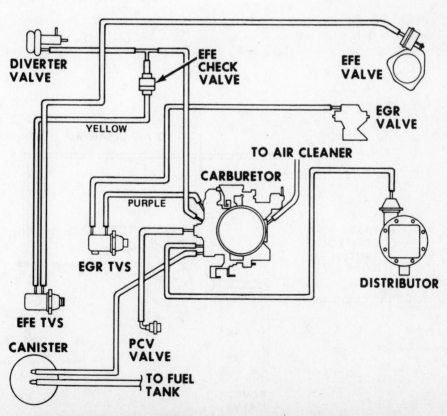

Vacuum hose schematic-8-350, high altitude & Calif., LD emissions-1977

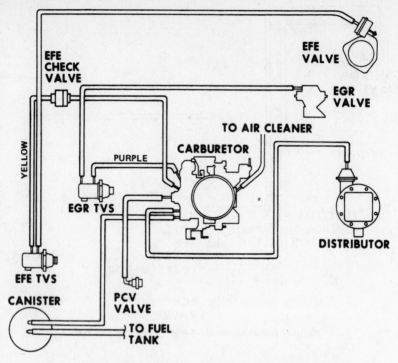

Vacuum hose schematic-8-350, low altitude, LD emissions-1977

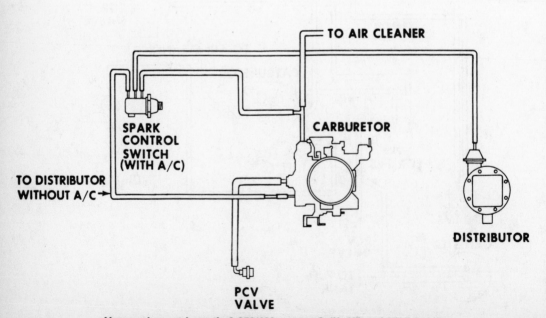

Vacuum hose schematic-8-350/400, except Calif., HD emissions-1977

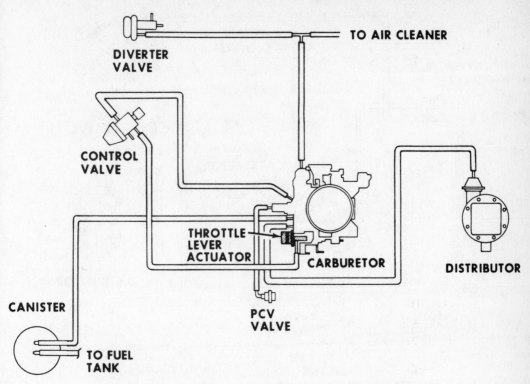

Vacuum hose schematic-8-350/400, Calif., HD emissions-1977

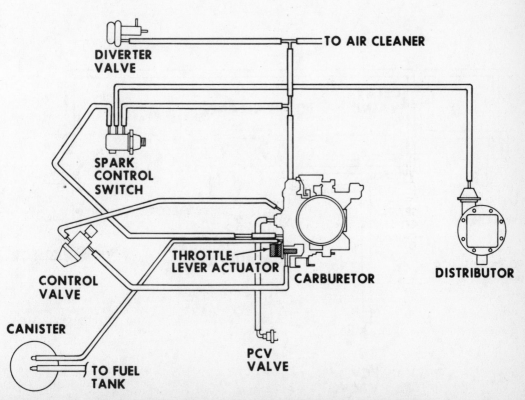

Vacuum hose schematic-8-400, with A/C, Calif., HD emissions-1977

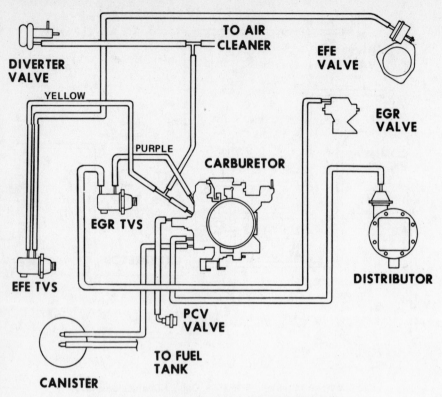

DIVERTER
VALVE

YELLOW

PURPLE

TO AIR
CLEANER

EFE
VALVE

EGR
VALVE

CARBURETOR

EGR TVS

DISTRIBUTOR

EFE TVS

PCV
VALVE

TO FUEL
TANK

CANISTER

Vacuum hose schematic-8-454, LD emissions-1977

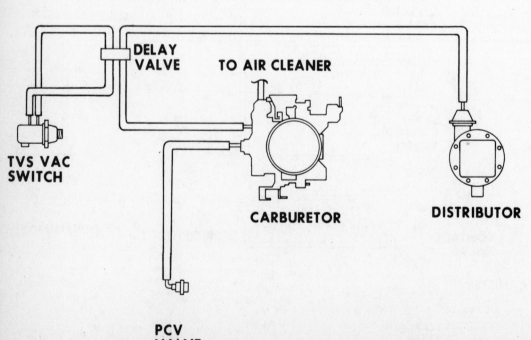

DELAY
VALVE

TO AIR CLEANER

TVS VAC
SWITCH

CARBURETOR

DISTRIBUTOR

PCV
VALVE

Vacuum hose schematic-8-454, HD emissions, except Calif.-1977

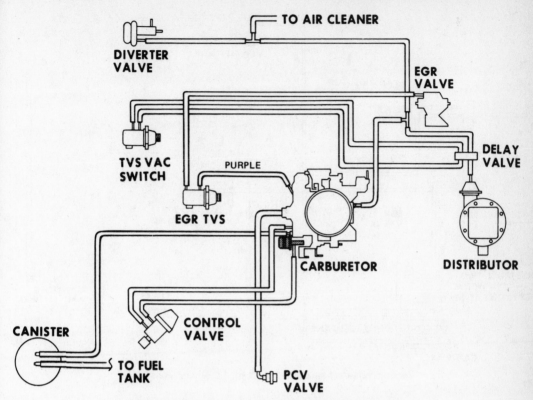

Vacuum hose schematic-8-454, HD emissions, Calif.-1977

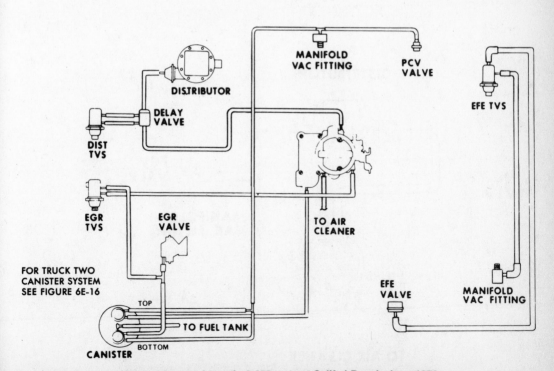

Vacuum hose schematic-6-250, except Calif., LD emissions-1978

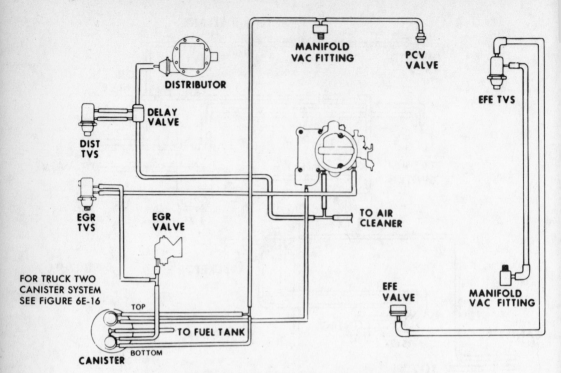

Vacuum hose schematic-6-250, Calif., LD emissions-1978

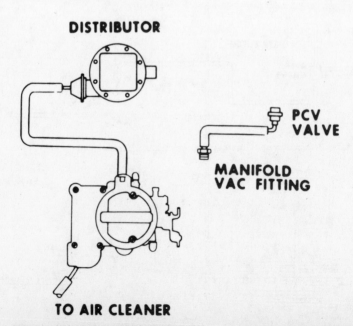

Vacuum hose schematic-6-250/292, HD emissions, except Calif.-1978

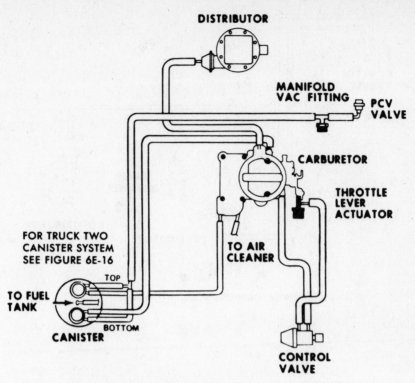

Vacuum hose schematic-6-292, HD emissions, Calif.-1978

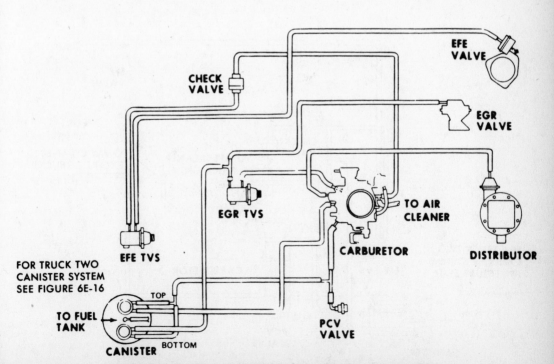

Vacuum hose schematic-8-305, low altitude, LD emissions-1978

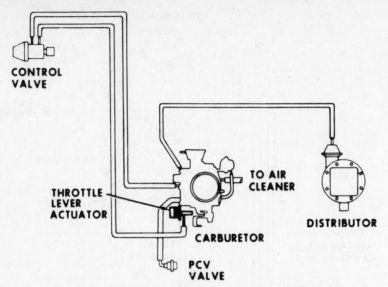

Vacuum hose schematic-8-305, HD emissions-1978

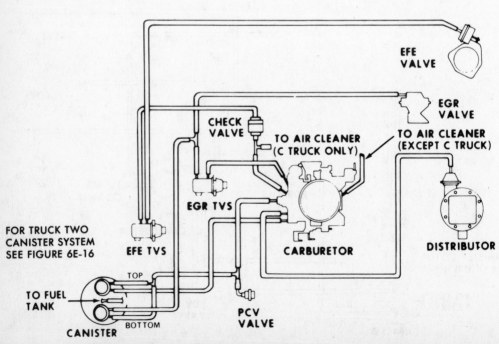

Vacuum hose schematic-8-350, low altitude, LD emissions-1978

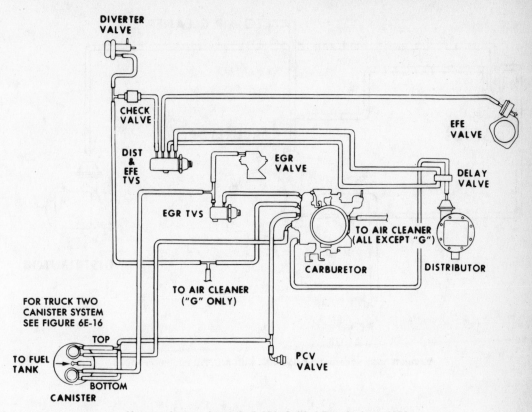

Vacuum hose schematic-8-350, Calif., LD emissions-1978

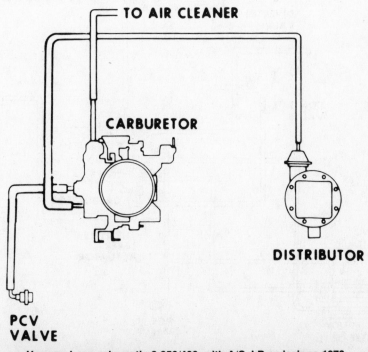

Vacuum hose schematic-8-350/400, with A/C, LD emissions-1978

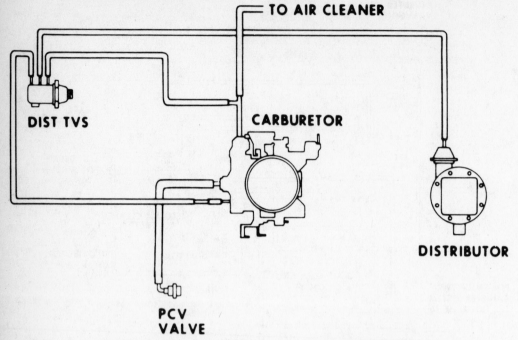

Vacuum hose schematic-8-350/400, with A/C, HD emissions-1978

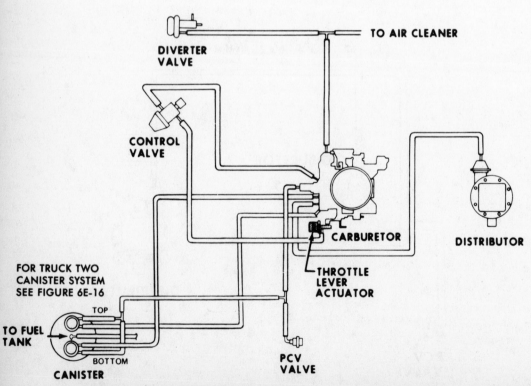

Vacuum hose schematic-8-350/400, Calif., with A/C, LD emissions-1978

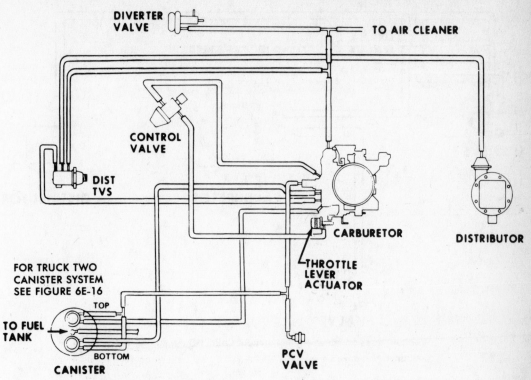

Vacuum hose schematic-8-350/400, Calif., with A/C, HD emissions-1978

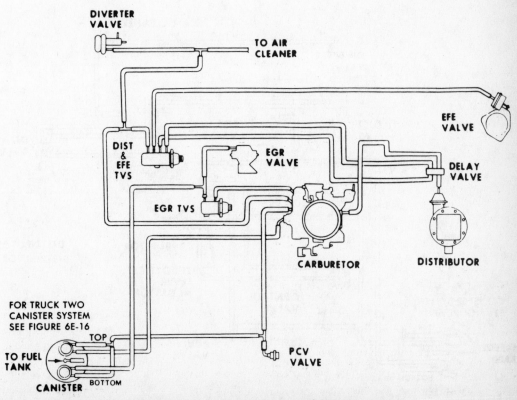

Vacuum hose schematic-8-454, LD emissions-1978

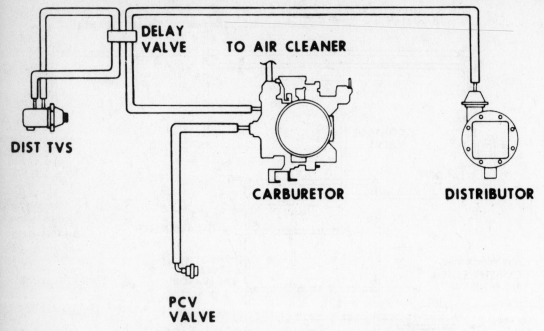

DIST TVS

DELAY VALVE

TO AIR CLEANER

CARBURETOR

DISTRIBUTOR

PCV VALVE

Vacuum hose schematic-8-454, except Calif., HD emissions-1978

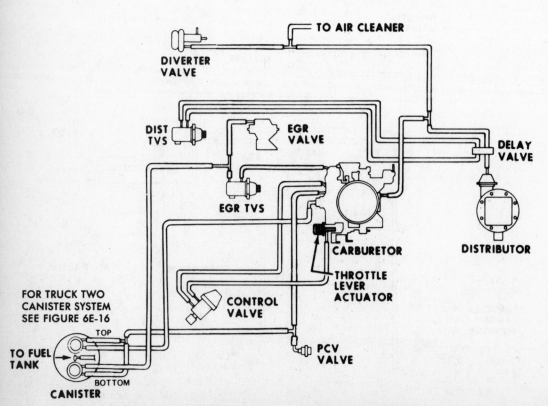

DIVERTER VALVE

TO AIR CLEANER

DIST TVS

EGR VALVE

DELAY VALVE

EGR TVS

CARBURETOR

DISTRIBUTOR

THROTTLE LEVER ACTUATOR

FOR TRUCK TWO CANISTER SYSTEM SEE FIGURE 6E-16

CONTROL VALVE

TOP

TO FUEL TANK

PCV VALVE

BOTTOM

CANISTER

Vacuum hose schematic-8-454, Calif., HD emissions-1978

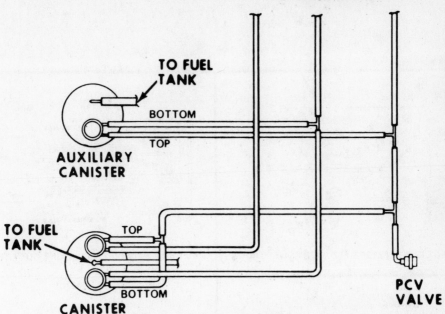

Vacuum hose schematic-truck two canister system-1978

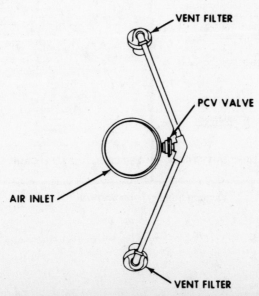

Vacuum hose schematic-8-350 diesel, LD emissions-1978

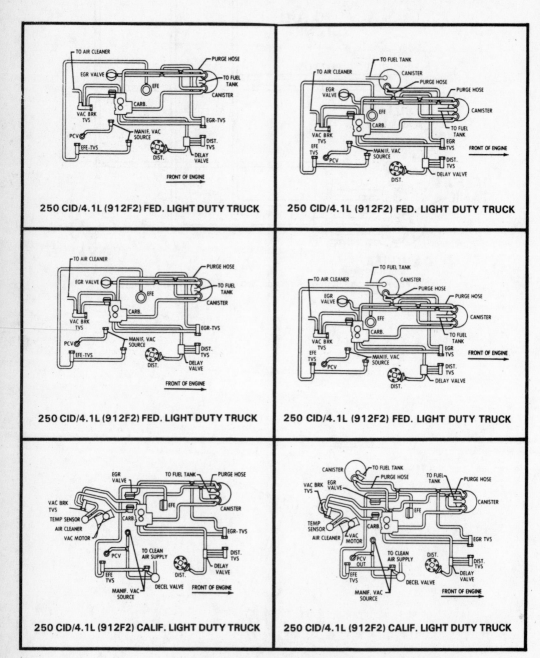

250 CID/4.1L (912F2) FED. LIGHT DUTY TRUCK

250 CID/4.1L (912F2) FED. LIGHT DUTY TRUCK

250 CID/4.1L (912F2) FED. LIGHT DUTY TRUCK

250 CID/4.1L (912F2) FED. LIGHT DUTY TRUCK

250 CID/4.1L (912F2) CALIF. LIGHT DUTY TRUCK

250 CID/4.1L (912F2) CALIF. LIGHT DUTY TRUCK

Vacuum hose schematic-1979

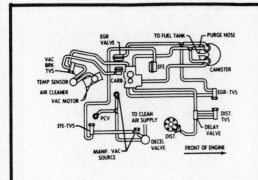

250 CID/4.1L (912F2) CALIF. LIGHT DUTY TRUCK

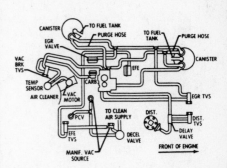

250 CID/4.1L (912F2) CALIF. LIGHT DUTY TRUCK

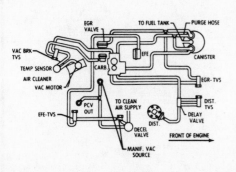

250 CID/4.1L (912F2) CALIF. LIGHT DUTY TRUCK

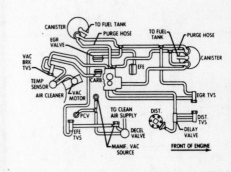

250 CID/4.1L (912F2) CALIF. LIGHT DUTY TRUCK

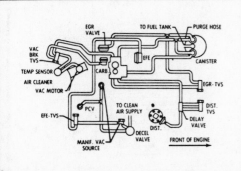

250 CID/4.1L (912F2) CALIF. LIGHT DUTY TRUCK

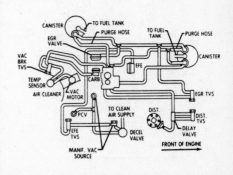

250 CID/4.1L (912F2) CALIF. LIGHT DUTY TRUCK

Vacuum hose schematic-1979

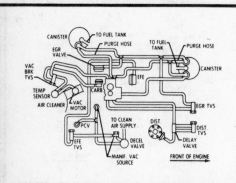

250 CID/4.1L (912F2) CALIF. LIGHT DUTY TRUCK

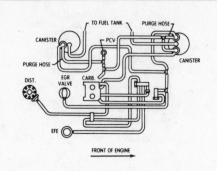

305 CID/5.0L (912Y2) FED. LIGHT DUTY TRUCK

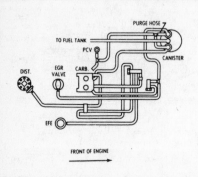

305 CID/5.0L (912Y2) FED. LIGHT DUTY TRUCK

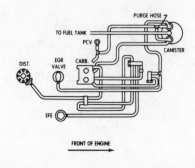

305 CID/5.0L (912Y2) FED. LIGHT DUTY TRUCK

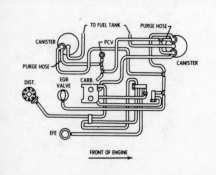

305 CID/5.0L (912Y2) FED. LIGHT DUTY TRUCK

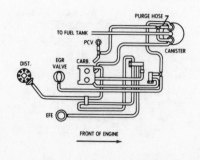

305 CID/5.0L (912Y2) FED. LIGHT DUTY TRUCK

Vacuum hose schematic-1979

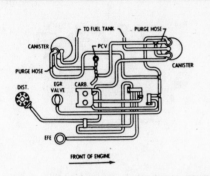

305 CID/5.0L (912Y2) FED. LIGHT DUTY TRUCK

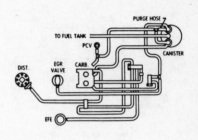

305 CID/5.0L (912Y2) FED. LIGHT DUTY TRUCK

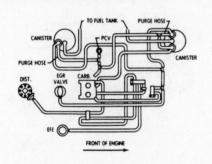

305 CID/5.0L (912Y2) FED. LIGHT DUTY TRUCK

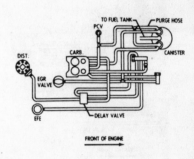

350 CID/5.7L (912K4B) FED. LIGHT DUTY TRUCK

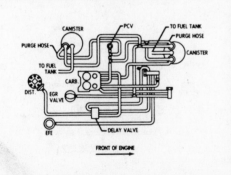

350 CID/5.7L (912K4B) FED. LIGHT DUTY TRUCK

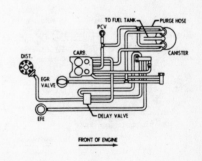

350 CID/5.7L (912K4B) FED. LIGHT DUTY TRUCK

Vacuum hose schematic-1979

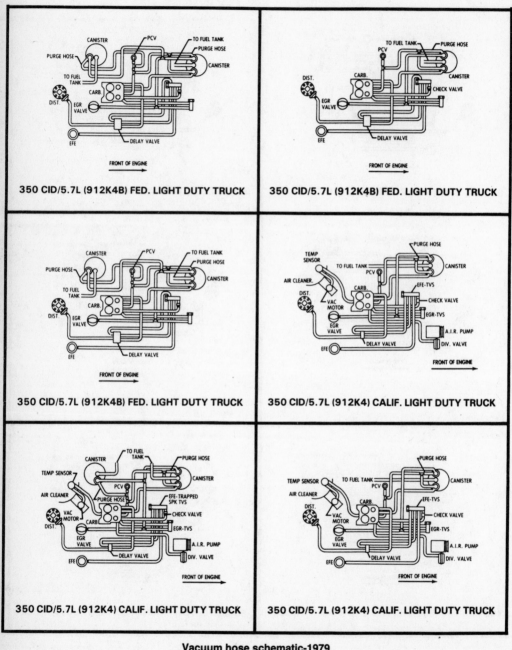

350 CID/5.7L (912K4B) FED. LIGHT DUTY TRUCK

350 CID/5.7L (912K4B) FED. LIGHT DUTY TRUCK

350 CID/5.7L (912K4B) FED. LIGHT DUTY TRUCK

350 CID/5.7L (912K4) CALIF. LIGHT DUTY TRUCK

350 CID/5.7L (912K4) CALIF. LIGHT DUTY TRUCK

350 CID/5.7L (912K4) CALIF. LIGHT DUTY TRUCK

Vacuum hose schematic-1979

EMISSION HOSE ROUTING

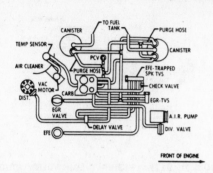

350 CID/5.7L (912K4) CALIF. LIGHT DUTY TRUCK

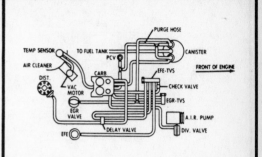

350 CID/5.7L (912K4) CALIF. LIGHT DUTY TRUCK

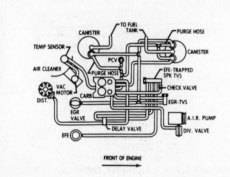

350 CID/5.7L (912K4) CALIF. LIGHT DUTY TRUCK

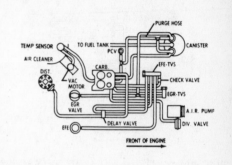

350 CID/5.7L (912K4) CALIF. LIGHT DUTY TRUCK

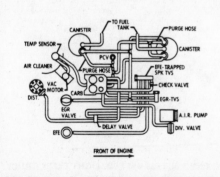

350 CID/5.7L (912K4) CALIF. LIGHT DUTY TRUCK

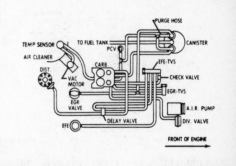

350 CID/5.7L (912K4) CALIF. LIGHT DUTY TRUCK

Vacuum hose schematic-1979

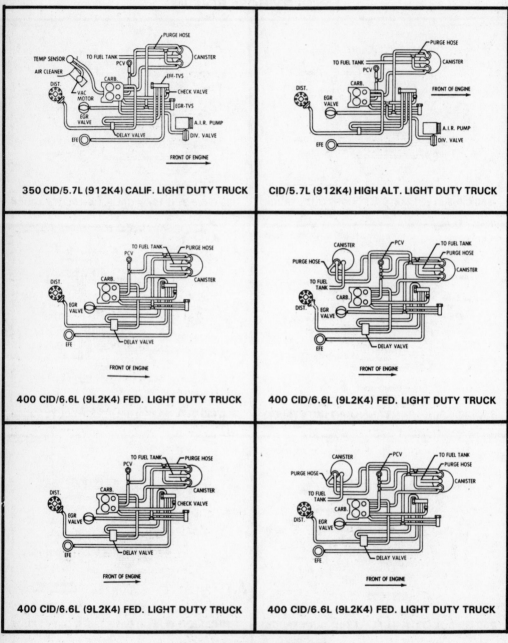

350 CID/5.7L (912K4) CALIF. LIGHT DUTY TRUCK

CID/5.7L (912K4) HIGH ALT. LIGHT DUTY TRUCK

400 CID/6.6L (9L2K4) FED. LIGHT DUTY TRUCK

400 CID/6.6L (9L2K4) FED. LIGHT DUTY TRUCK

400 CID/6.6L (9L2K4) FED. LIGHT DUTY TRUCK

400 CID/6.6L (9L2K4) FED. LIGHT DUTY TRUCK

Vacuum hose schematic-1979

EMISSION HOSE ROUTING

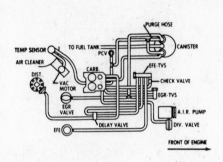

400 CID/6.6L (912K4) CALIF. LIGHT DUTY TRUCK

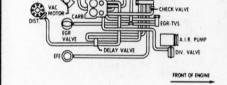

400 CID/6.6L (912K4) CALIF. LIGHT DUTY TRUCK

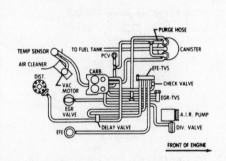

400 CID/6.6L (912K4) CALIF. LIGHT DUTY TRUCK

400 CID/6.6L (912K4) CALIF. LIGHT DUTY TRUCK

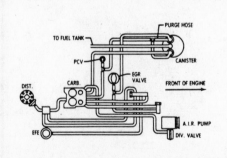

454 CID/7.4L (912R4) FED. LIGHT DUTY TRUCK

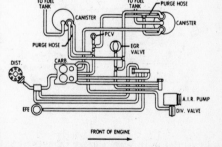

454 CID/7.4L (912R4) FED. LIGHT DUTY TRUCK

Vacuum hose schematic-1979

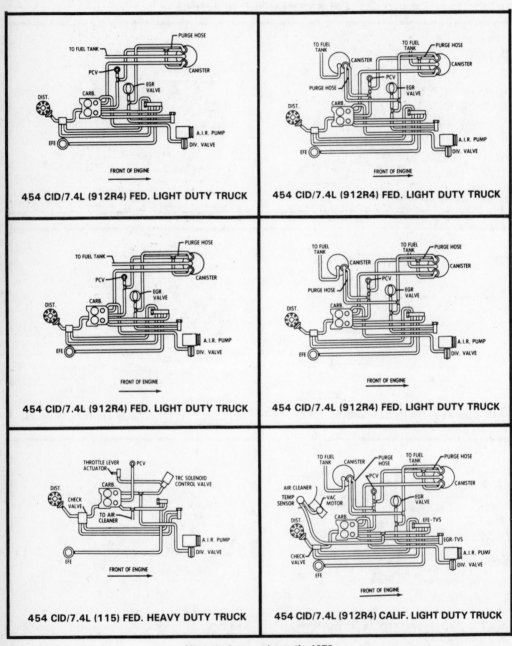

454 CID/7.4L (912R4) FED. LIGHT DUTY TRUCK

454 CID/7.4L (912R4) FED. LIGHT DUTY TRUCK

454 CID/7.4L (912R4) FED. LIGHT DUTY TRUCK

454 CID/7.4L (912R4) FED. LIGHT DUTY TRUCK

454 CID/7.4L (115) FED. HEAVY DUTY TRUCK

454 CID/7.4L (912R4) CALIF. LIGHT DUTY TRUCK

Vacuum hose schematic-1979

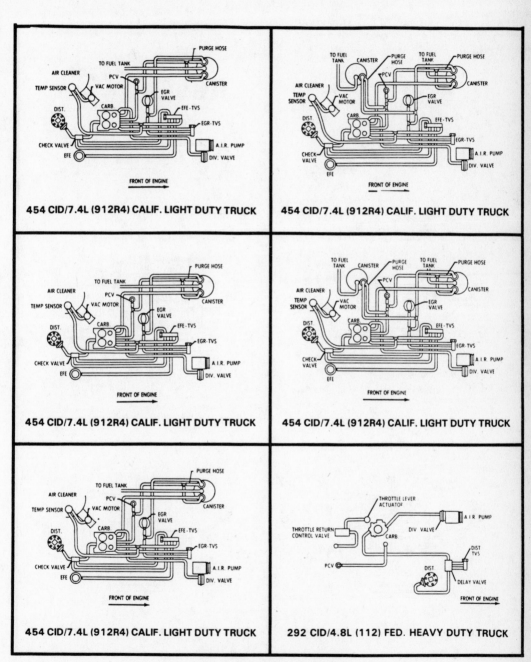

454 CID/7.4L (912R4) CALIF. LIGHT DUTY TRUCK

454 CID/7.4L (912R4) CALIF. LIGHT DUTY TRUCK

454 CID/7.4L (912R4) CALIF. LIGHT DUTY TRUCK

454 CID/7.4L (912R4) CALIF. LIGHT DUTY TRUCK

454 CID/7.4L (912R4) CALIF. LIGHT DUTY TRUCK

292 CID/4.8L (112) FED. HEAVY DUTY TRUCK

Vacuum hose schematic-1979

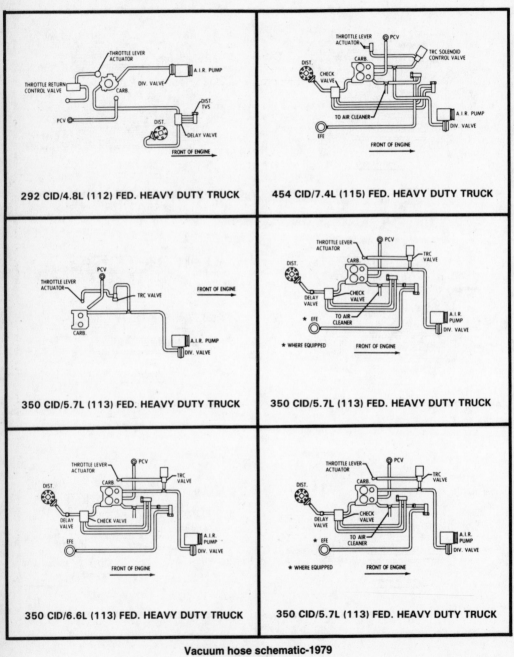

292 CID/4.8L (112) FED. HEAVY DUTY TRUCK

454 CID/7.4L (115) FED. HEAVY DUTY TRUCK

350 CID/5.7L (113) FED. HEAVY DUTY TRUCK

350 CID/5.7L (113) FED. HEAVY DUTY TRUCK

350 CID/6.6L (113) FED. HEAVY DUTY TRUCK

350 CID/5.7L (113) FED. HEAVY DUTY TRUCK

Vacuum hose schematic-1979

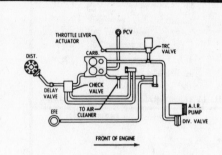

400 CID/6.6L (113) FED. HEAVY DUTY TRUCK

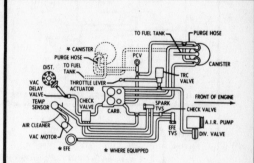

350 CID/5.7L (113) CALIF. HEAVY DUTY TRUCK

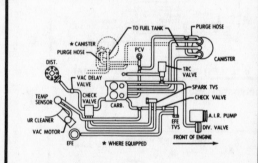

400 CID/6.6L (113) CALIF. HEAVY DUTY TRUCK

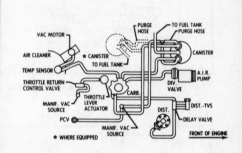

292 CID/4.8L (112) CALIF. HEAVY DUTY TRUCK

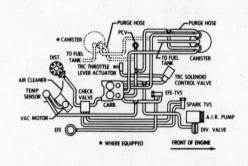

454 CID/7.4L (115) CALIF. HEAVY DUTY TRUCK

Vacuum hose schematic-1979

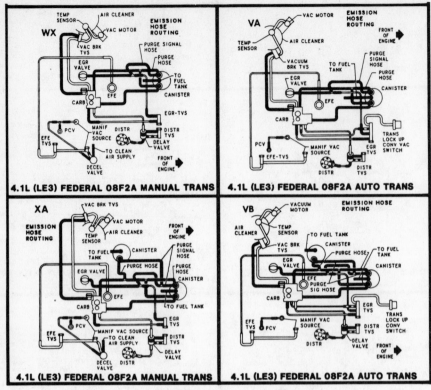

Vacuum hose schematic-1980

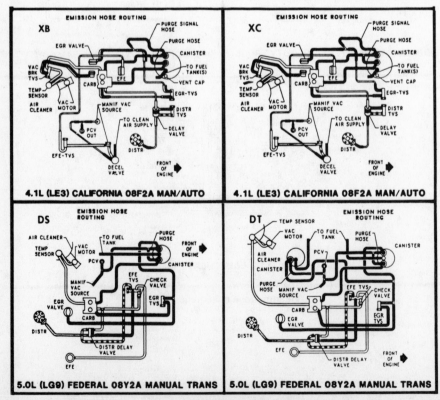

Vacuum hose schematic-1980

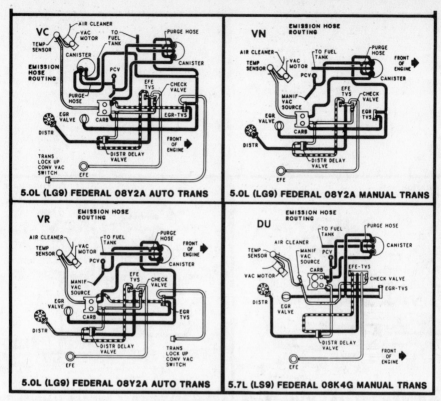

Vacuum hose schematic-1980

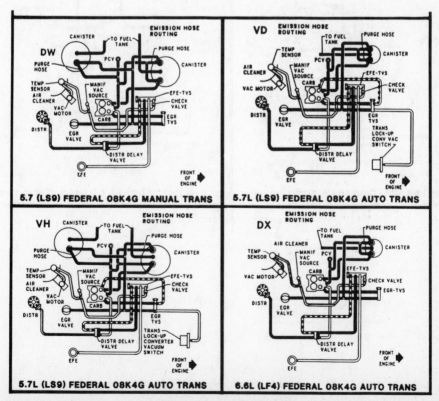

Vacuum hose schematic-1980

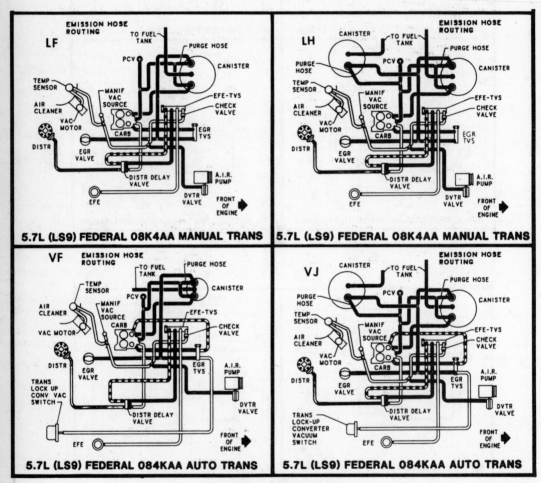

Vacuum hose schematic-1980

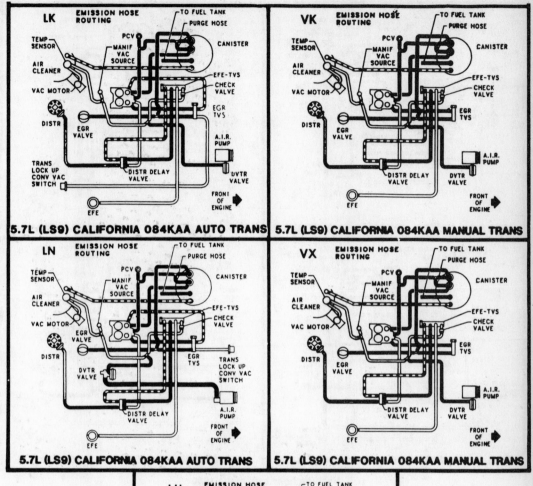

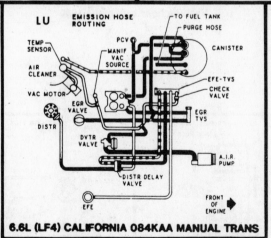

Vacuum hose schematic-1980

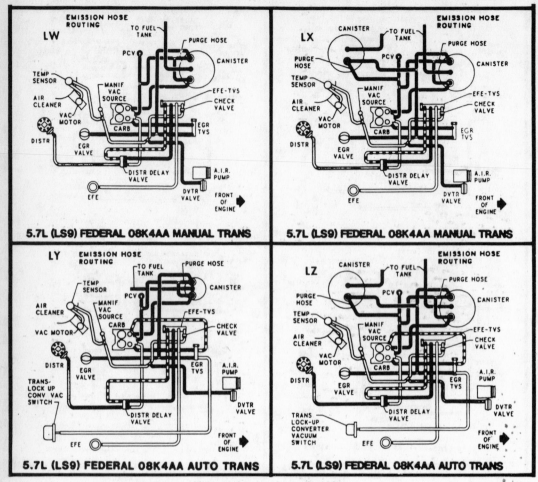

Vacuum hose schematic-1980

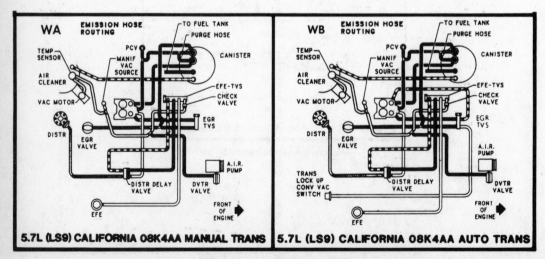

Vacuum hose schematic-1980

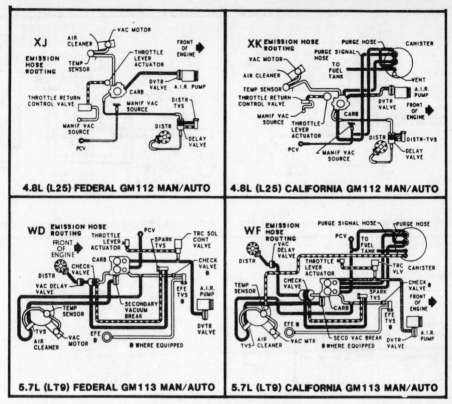

Vacuum hose schematic-1980

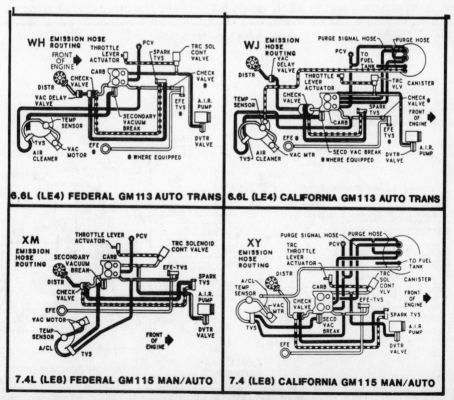

Vacuum hose schematic-1980

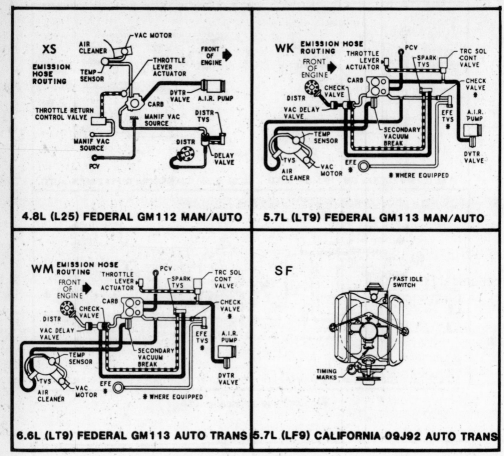

Vacuum hose schematic-1980

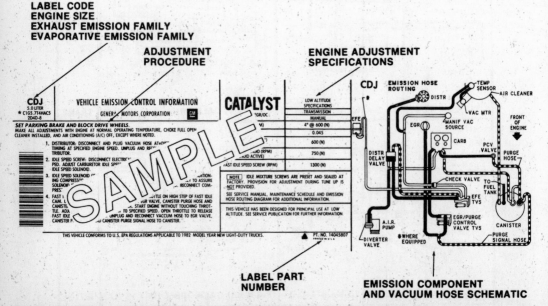

The Vehicle Emission Control Information label, located under the hood, shows the vacuum hose schematic on 1981 and later vehicles

Fuel System

5

CARBURETED FUEL SYSTEM

Mechanical Fuel Pump

The fuel pump is a single action AC diaphragm type. All fuel pumps used on inline and V8 engines in trucks are diaphragm type and because of design are serviced by replacement only. No adjustments or repairs are possible.

The pump is operated by an eccentric on the camshaft on gasoline engines. On six cylinder engines, the eccentric acts directly on the pump rocker arm. On V8 engines, a pushrod between the camshaft eccentric and the fuel pump operates the pump rocker arm.

Some trucks have a fuel pump which has a metering outlet for a vapor return system; any vapor which forms is returned to the fuel tank along with hot fuel through a separate line. This greatly reduces any possibility of vapor lock by keeping cool fuel from the tank constantly circulating through the fuel pump.

TESTING THE FUEL PUMP

Fuel pumps should always be tested on the vehicle. The larger line between the pump and tank is the suction side of the system and the smaller line, between the pump and carburetor is the pressure side. A leak in the pressure side would be apparent because of dripping fuel. A leak in the suction side is usually only apparent because of a reduced volume of fuel delivered to the pressure side.

1. Tighten any loose line connections and look for any kinks or restrictions.

2. Disconnect the fuel line at the carburetor. Disconnect the distributor-to-coil primary wire. Place a container at the end of the fuel line and crank the engine a few revolutions. If little or no fuel flows from the line, either the fuel pump is inoperative or the line is plugged. Blow through the lines with compressed air and try the test again. Reconnect the line.

3. If fuel flows in good volume, check the fuel pump pressure to be sure.

4. Attach a pressure gauge to the pressure side of the fuel line. On trucks equipped with a vapor return system, squeeze off the return hose.

5. Run the engine at idle and note the reading on the gauge. Stop the engine and compare the reading with the specifications listed in the Tune-Up Specifications chart. If the pump is operating properly, the pressure will be as specified and will be constant at idle speed. If pressure varies sporadically or is too high or low, the pump should be replaced.

6. Remove the pressure gauge.

The following flow test can also be performed:

1. Disconnect fuel line from carburetor. Run fuel line into a suitable measuring container.

2. Run the engine at idle until there is one pint of fuel in the container. One pint should be pumped in 30 seconds or less.

3. If flow is below minimum, check for a restriction in the line.

The only way to check fuel pump pressure is by connecting an accurate pressure gauge to the fuel line at the carburetor level. Never replace a fuel pump without performing this simple test. If the engine seems to be starving out, check the ignition system first. Also check for a plugged fuel filter or a restricted fuel line before replacing the pump.

REMOVAL AND INSTALLATION

NOTE: *When you connect the fuel pump outlet fitting, always use two wrenches to avoid damaging the pump.*

1. Disconnect the fuel intake and outlet lines at the pump and plug the pump intake line.

2. On small block V8 engines, remove the upper bolt from the right front mounting boss. Insert a long bolt ($\frac{3}{8}$"-16 x 2") in this hole to hold the fuel pump pushrod.

Troubleshooting Basic Fuel System Problems

Problem	Cause	Solution
Engine cranks, but won't start (or is hard to start) when cold	• Empty fuel tank • Incorrect starting procedure • Defective fuel pump • No fuel in carburetor • Clogged fuel filter • Engine flooded • Defective choke	• Check for fuel in tank • Follow correct procedure • Check pump output • Check for fuel in the carburetor • Replace fuel filter • Wait 15 minutes; try again • Check choke plate
Engine cranks, but is hard to start (or does not start) when hot— (presence of fuel is assumed)	• Defective choke	• Check choke plate
Rough idle or engine runs rough	• Dirt or moisture in fuel • Clogged air filter • Faulty fuel pump	• Replace fuel filter • Replace air filter • Check fuel pump output
Engine stalls or hesitates on acceleration	• Dirt or moisture in the fuel • Dirty carburetor • Defective fuel pump • Incorrect float level, defective accelerator pump	• Replace fuel filter • Clean the carburetor • Check fuel pump output • Check carburetor
Poor gas mileage	• Clogged air filter • Dirty carburetor • Defective choke, faulty carburetor adjustment	• Replace air filter • Clean carburetor • Check carburetor
Engine is flooded (won't start accompanied by smell of raw fuel)	• Improperly adjusted choke or carburetor	• Wait 15 minutes and try again, without pumping gas pedal • If it won't start, check carburetor

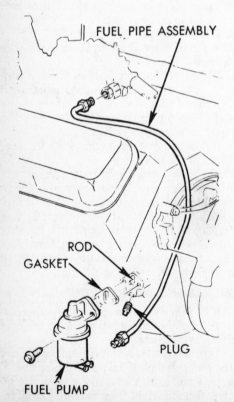

FUEL PIPE ASSEMBLY

ROD

GASKET

PLUG

FUEL PUMP

Big-block (Mark IV) fuel pump installation; other engines similar

3. Remove the two pump mounting bolts and lockwashers; remove the pump and its gasket.

4. If the rocker arm pushrod is to be removed from V8s, remove the two adapter bolts and lockwashers and remove the adapter and its gasket from small blocks and remove the pipe plug and pushrod from 454 cu. in. engines.

5. Install the fuel pump with a new gasket reversing the removal procedure. Coat the mating surfaces with sealer.

6. Connect the fuel lines and check for leaks.

Carburetor

REMOVAL AND INSTALLATION

1. Remove the air cleaner and its gasket.

2. Disconnect the fuel and vacuum lines from the carburetor.

3. Disconnect the choke coil rod or heated air line tube.

4. Disconnect the throttle linkage.

5. On automatic transmission trucks, disconnect the throttle valve linkage.

6. Remove the CEC valve vacuum hose and electrical connector.

7. Remove the idle stop electrical wiring from the idle stop solenoid, if so equipped.

8. Remove the carburetor attaching nuts and/or bolts, gasket or insulator, and remove the carburetor.

9. Install the carburetor using a reverse of the removal procedure. Use a new gasket and fill the float bowl with gasoline to east starting the engine.

IDENTIFICATION

Carburetor identification numbers will generally be found in the following locations:

• MV, ME: Stamped on the vertical portion of the float bowl, adjacent to the fuel inlet nut.

• GV, GC: Stamped on the flat section of the float bowl next to the fuel inlet nut.

• E2SE, 2SE: Stamped on the vertical surface of the float bowl adjacent to the vacuum tube.

• M2MC: Stamped on the vertical surface of the left rear corner of the float bowl.

• E4ME, 4MV, M4MC, M4ME: Stamped on the vertical section of the float bowl, near the secondary throttle lever.

OVERHAUL

Efficient carburetion depends greatly on careful cleaning and inspection during overhaul, since dirt, gum, water, or varnish in or on the carburetor parts are often responsible for poor performance.

Overhaul your carburetor in a clean, dust free area. Carefully disassemble the carburetor, referring often to the exploded views and directions packaged with the rebuilding kit. Keep all similar and look-alike parts segregated during disassembly and cleaning to avoid accidental interchange during assembly. Make a note of all jet sizes.

When the carburetor is disassemble, wash all parts (except diaphragms, electric choke units, pump plunger, and any other plastic, leather, fiber, or rubber parts) in clean carburetor solvent. Do not leave parts in the solvent any longer than is necessary to sufficiently loosen the deposits. Excessive cleaning may remove the special finish from the float bowl and choke valve bodies, leaving these parts unfit for service. Rinse all parts in clean solvent, and blow them dry with compressed air or allow them to air dry. Wipe clean all cork, plastic, leather, and fiber parts with a clean, lint-free cloth.

Blow out all passages and jets with compressed air and be sure that there are no restrictions or blockages. Never use wire or similar tools to clean jets, fuel passages, or air bleeds. Clean all jets and valves separately to avoid accidental interchange.

Check all parts for wear or damage. If wear or damage is found, replace the defective parts. Especially check the following:

1. Check the float needle and seat for wear. If wear is found, replace the complete assembly.

2. Check the float hinge pin for wear and the float(s) for dents or distortion. Replace the float if fuel has leaked into it.

3. Check the throttle and choke shaft bores for wear or an out-of-round condition. Damage or wear to the throttle arm, shaft, or shaft bore will often require replacement of the throttle body. These parts require a close tolerance of it; wear may allow air leakage, which could affect starting and idling.

NOTE: *Throttle shafts and bushings are not included in overhaul kits. They can be purchased separately.*

4. Inspect the idle mixture adjusting needles for burrs or grooves. Any such condition requires replacement of the needle, since you will not be able to obtain a satisfactory idle.

5. Test the accelerator pump check valves. They should pass air one way but not the other. Test for proper seating by blowing and sucking on the valve. Replace the valve as necessary. If the valve is satisfactory, wash the valve again to remove breath moisture.

6. Check the bowl cover for warped surfaces with a straightedge.

7. Closely inspect the valves and seats for wear and damage, replacing as necessary.

8. After the carburetor is assembled, check the choke valve for freedom of operation.

Carburetor overhaul kits are recommended for each overhaul. These kits contain all gaskets and new parts to replace those which deteriorate most rapidly. Failure to replace all parts supplies with the kit (especially gaskets) can result in poor performance later.

Some carburetor manufacturers supply overhaul kits of three basic types: minor repair; major repair; and gasket kits.

After cleaning and checking all components, reassemble the carburetor, using new parts and referring to the exploded view. When reassembling, make sure that all screws and jets are tight in their seats, but do not overtighten as the tips will be distorted. Tighten all screws gradually, in rotation. Do not tighten needle valves into their seats; uneven jetting will result. Always use new gaskets. Be sure to adjust the float level when reassembling.

PRELIMINARY CHECKS (ALL CARBURETORS)

The following should be observed before attempting any adjustments.

1. Run the engine to normal operating temperature.

2. Check the torque of all carburetor mounting nuts. Also check the intake manifold-to-cylinder head bolts. If air is leaking at any of these points, you will not get a proper adjustment.

3. Check the manifold heat control valve (if used) to be sure that it is free.

4. Check and adjust the choke as necessary.

5. Adjust the idle speed and mixture. If any adjustments are performed that might possibly change the idle speed or mixture, adjust the idle and mixture again when you are finished.

Carburetor Adjustments

ROCHESTER MV (1970-74)

Fast Idle

NOTE: *The fast idle adjustment must be made with the transmission in Neutral.*

1. Position the fast idle lever on the high step of the fast idle cam.

2. Be sure that the choke is properly adjusted and in the wide open position with the engine warm. Disconnect the vacuum advance on 1974 manual transmission models.

3. Bend the fast idle lever until the specified speed is obtained.

Choke Rod (Fast Idle Cam)

NOTE: *Adjust the fast idle before making choke rod adjustments.*

1. Place the fast idle cam follower on the second step of the fast idle cam and hold it firmly against the rise to the high step.

2. Rotate the choke valve in the direction of a closed choke by applying force to the choke coil lever.

3. Bend the choke rod, to give the specified opening between the lower edge of the choke valve and the inside air horn wall.

NOTE: *Measurement must be made at the center of the choke valve.*

Choke Vacuum Break

The adjustment of the vacuum break diaphragm unit insures correct choke valve opening after engine starting.

1. Remove the air cleaner on vehicles with Thermac air cleaner; plug the sensor's vacuum take off port.

2. Using an external vacuum source, apply vacuum to the vacuum break diaphragm until the plunger is fully seated.

3. When the plunger is seated, push the choke valve toward the closed position.

4. Holding the choke valve in this position, place the specified gauge between the lower end of the choke valve and the air horn wall.

5. If the measurement is not correct, bend the vacuum break rod.

Choke Unloader

1. Apply pressure to the choke valve and hold it in the closed position.

2. Open the throttle valve to the wide open position.

3. Check the dimension between the lower edge of the choke plate and the air horn wall; if adjustment is needed, bend the unloader tang on the throttle lever to adjust to specification.

Choke Coil Rod

1. Disconnect the coil rod from the upper choke lever and hold the choke valve closed.

2. Push down on the coil rod to the end of its travel.

3. The top of the rod should be even with the bottom hole in the choke lever.

4. To make adjustments, bend the rod as needed.

Float

1. Hold the float retainer in place and the float arm against the top of the float needle by pushing down on the float arm at the outer end toward the float bowl casting.

2. Using an adjustable T-scale, measure the distance from the toe of the float to the float bowl gasket surface.

NOTE: *The float bowl gasket should be removed and the gauge held on the index point on the float for accurate measurement.*

3. Adjust the float level by bending the float arm up or down at the float arm junction.

Metering Rod

1. Hold the throttle valve wide-open and push down on the metering rod against spring tension, then remove the rod from the main metering jet.

2. In order to check adjustment, the slow idle screw must be backed out and the fast idle cam rotated so that the fast idle cam follower does not contact the steps on the cam.

3. With the throttle valve closed, push down on the power piston until it contacts its stop.

4. With the power piston depressed, swing the metering rod holder over the flat surface of the bowl casting next to the carburetor bore.

5. Insert a specified size drill between the bowl casting sealing bead and the lower surface of the metering rod holder. The drill should slide smoothly between both surfaces.

6. If adjustment is needed, carefully bend the metering rod holder up or down. After adjustment, reinstall the metering rod.

C.E.C. Solenoid Adjustment

Do not set the C.E.C. valve to the idle rpm. This adjustment should only be made after replacement of the solenoid, carburetor overhaul, or after the throttle body is replaced.

1. With the engine running, and transmission in Neutral (manual or Drive (Automatic), air conditioner OFF, distributor vacuum hose removed and plugged, and fuel tank vapor hose

disconnected, manually extend the C.E.C. valve plunger to contact the throttle lever.

2. Adjust the plunger length to obtain the C.E.C. valve rpm.

3. Reconnect the vapor hose and vacuum hose.

ROCHESTER MV (1975-76), ME (1977 AND LATER)

Fast Idle

1. Check and adjust the idle speed.

2. With the engine at normal operating temperature, air cleaner ON, EGR valve signal line disconnected and plugged and the air conditioning OFF, connect a tachometer.

3. Disconnect the vacuum advance hose at the distributor and plug the line.

4. With the transmission in Neutral, start the engine and set the fast idle cam follower on the high step of the cam.

5. Bend the tank in or out to obtain the fast idle speed.

Fast Idle Cam

1. Check and adjust the fast idle speed.

2. Set the fast idle cam follower on the second step of the cam.

3. Apply force to the choke coil rod and hold the choke valve toward the closed position.

4. Measure the clearance between the lower edge of the choke valve and the inside of the air horn wall. For 1976-77, insert the gauge between the upper edge of the choke valve and the inside of the air horn wall.

5. Bend the cam to choke rod to obtain clearance.

Choke Unloader

1. Hold the choke valve down by applying light force to the choke coil lever.

2. Open the throttle valve to wide open.

3. Measure the clearance between the upper edge of the choke valve and the air horn wall. Measure at the lower edge of the choke valve on 1978 and later models only.

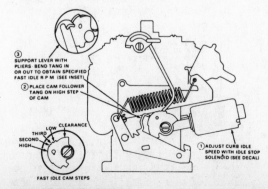

MV fast idle adjustment

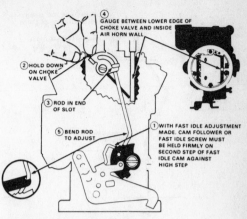

MV fast idle cam adjustment

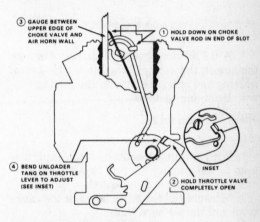

MV choke unloader adjuster

4. If adjustment is necessary, bend the tang on the throttle lever.

Choke Coil Rod

1975

1. Pull the rod up to the end of its travel to completely close the choke valve.

2. The bottom of the rod should be even with the top of the lever.

3. If adjustment is necessary, bend the rod.

1976

1. Disconnect the upper end of the choke coil rod at the choke valve.

2. Completely close the choke valve.

3. Push up on the choke coil rod to its end of travel.

4. Bottom of rod should be even with the top of the lever.

5. Bend the rod for adjustment.

6. Connect rod to choke valve.

1977 AND LATER

1. Place the cam follower on the high step of the cam.

2. Hold the choke valve completely closed.

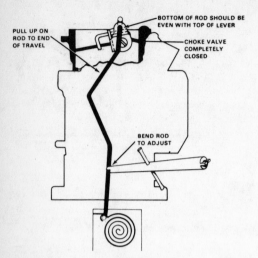

PULL UP ON ROD TO END OF TRAVEL

BOTTOM OF ROD SHOULD BE EVEN WITH TOP OF LEVER

CHOKE VALVE COMPLETELY CLOSED

BEND ROD TO ADJUST

MV choke coil rod adjustment—1975

3. A 0.120" plug gauge must pass through the hole in the lever attached to the choke coil housing and enter the hole in the casting.

4. Bend link to adjust.

Primary Vacuum Break

1975

1. With an outside vacuum source, apply vacuum to the primary vacuum break diaphragm until the plunger is fully seated.

2. Measure the clearance between the choke valve and the air horn wall.

3. Bend the vacuum break rod to adjust the clearance. Be sure that there is no binding or interference.

1976 AND LATER

1. Place cam follower on high step of cam.

2. Plug purge bleed hole with masking tape over vacuum break and cover. Not all 1977 and later models will have this hole.

3. Using an outside vacuum source, apply vacuum to primary vacuum break diaphragm until the plunger is fully seated.

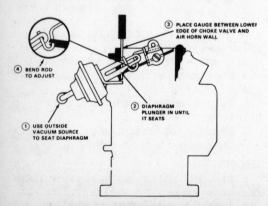

④ BEND ROD TO ADJUST

③ PLACE GAUGE BETWEEN LOWER EDGE OF CHOKE VALVE AND AIR HORN WALL

② DIAPHRAGM PLUNGER IN UNTIL IT SEATS

① USE OUTSIDE VACUUM SOURCE TO SEAT DIAPHRAGM

MV primary vacuum break adjustment—1975

4. Push up on choke coil lever rod in the end of the slot. Push down on the choke valve for 1978 and later.

5. Insert a specified gauge between the upper edge of the choke valve and the air horn wall. Measure at the lower edge of the choke valve, 1978 and later only.

6. Bend vacuum break rod for adjustment.

7. After adjustment, check for binding or interference. Remove tape.

Auxiliary Vacuum Break (1975-76 Only)

1. With an outside vacuum source, apply vacuum to the auxiliary vacuum break diaphragm until the plunger is seated.

2. Place the cam follower on the high step of the fast idle cam.

3. Measure the clearance between the upper edge of the choke valve and the air horn wall. Bend the link between the vacuum break and the choke valve to adjust.

Metering Rod Adjustment—1977 and Later

1. Remove metering rod by holding throttle valve wide open. Push downward on metering rod against spring tension, then slide metering rod out of slot in holder and remove from main metering jet.

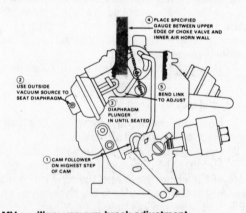

④ PLACE SPECIFIED GAUGE BETWEEN UPPER EDGE OF CHOKE VALVE AND INNER AIR HORN WALL

② USE OUTSIDE VACUUM SOURCE TO SEAT DIAPHRAGM

③ DIAPHRAGM PLUNGER IN UNTIL SEATED

⑤ BEND LINK TO ADJUST

① CAM FOLLOWER ON HIGHEST STEP OF CAM

MV auxiliary vacuum break adjustment

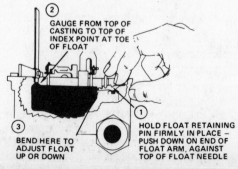

② GAUGE FROM TOP OF CASTING TO TOP OF INDEX POINT AT TOE OF FLOAT

① HOLD FLOAT RETAINING PIN FIRMLY IN PLACE – PUSH DOWN ON END OF FLOAT ARM, AGAINST TOP OF FLOAT NEEDLE

③ BEND HERE TO ADJUST FLOAT UP OR DOWN

MV and ME float level adjustment

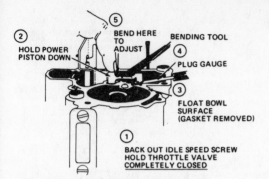

MV metering rod adjustment—1975–76

2. Back out idle stop solenoid-hold throttle valve completely closed.

3. Hold power piston down and swing metering rod holder over flat surface (gasket removed) of bowl casting next to carburetor bore.

4. Insert specified gauge.

5. Bend the metering rod holder as necessary.

ROCHESTER 2GV (1970-74)

These procedures are for both the 1¼" and 1½" models. Where there are differences these are noted. The 1½" model has larger throttle bores and an additional fuel feed circuit to make it suitable for use on the 350 V8.

Fast Idle Cam

1. Turn the idle screw onto the second step of the fast idle cam.

2. Hold the choke valve toward the closed position and check the clearance between the upper edge of the choke valve and the air horn wall.

3. If this measurement varies from specifications, bend the tang on the choke lever.

Choke Vacuum Break

1. Apply vacuum to the diaphragm to fully seat the plunger.

2. Push the choke valve in toward the closed position and hold it there.

3. Check the distance between the lower edge of the choke valve and the air horn wall.

4. If this dimension is not within specifications, bend the vacuum break rod to adjust.

Choke Unloader

1. Hold the throttle valves wide-open and use a rubber band to hold the choke valve toward the closed position.

2. Measure the distance between the upper edge of the choke valve and the air horn wall.

3. If this measurement is not within specifications, bend the unloader tang on the throttle lever to correct it.

Choke Coil Rod

1. Hold the choke valve completely open.

2. With the choke coil rod disconnected from the upper lever, push downward on the end of the rod to the end of its travel.

3. With the rod pushed fully downward, the bottom of the rod should be even with the bottom of the slotted hole in the lever.

4. To adjust the lever, bend the lever as needed.

Accelerator Pump Rod

1. Back the idle stop screw out and close the throttle valves in their bores.

2. Measure the distance from the top of the air horn to the top of the pump rod.

3. Bend the pump rod at a lower angle to correct this dimension.

Float Level

Invert the air horn, and with the gasket in place and the needle seated, measure the level as follows:

- On nitrophyl floats, measure from the air horn gasket to the lip on the toe of the float.
- On brass floats, measure from the air horn gasket to the lower edge of the float seam.
- Bend the float tang to adjust the level.

Float Drop

Holding the air horn right side up, measure float drop as follows:

- On nitrophyl floats, measure from the air horn gasket to the lop at the toe of the float.
- On brass floats, measure from the air horn gasket to the bottom of the float.
- Bend the float tang to adjust either type float.

ROCHESTER 2GC (1975-78)

Pump Rod

1. Back out the idle speed adjusting screw.

2. Hold the throttle valve completely closed.

3. Measure the distance from the top of the air horn ring to the top of the pump rod.

4. If necessary, bend the pump rod to adjust.

Fast Idle Cam

1. Turn the idle speed screw in until it contacts the low step of the fast idle cam. Then turn the screw in one full turn.

2. Place the idle speed screw on the second step of the fast idle cam against the highest step.

3. Measure the clearance between the upper edge of the choke valve and the air horn wall.

4. Bend the choke lever tang to adjust.

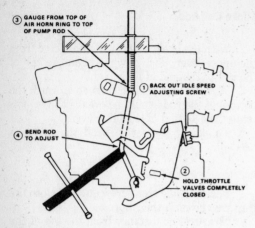

2GC pump rod adjustment

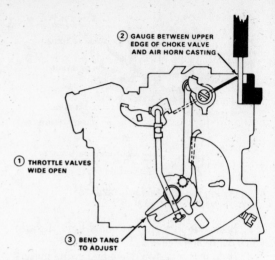

2GC choke unloader adjustment

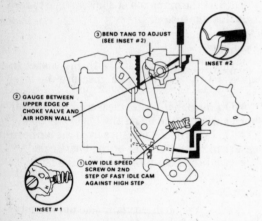

2GC fast idle cam adjustment

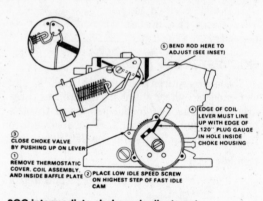

2GC intermediate choke rod adjustment

Choke Unloader

1. With the throttle valves wide open, place the choke valve in the closed position.

2. Measure the clearance between the upper edge of the choke valve and the air horn casting.

3. Bend the throttle lever tang to adjust.

Intermediate Choke Rod

1. Remove the thermostatic cover coil, gasket, and inside baffle plate.

2. Place the idle screw on the high step of the fast idle cam.

3. Close the choke valve by pushing up on the intermediate choke lever.

4. The edge of the choke lever inside the choke housing must align with the edge of the plug gauge.

5. Bend the intermediate choke lever to adjust.

6. Replace the cover and set as in the following adjustment.

Automatic Choke Coil

1. Place the idle screw on the high step of the fast idle cam.

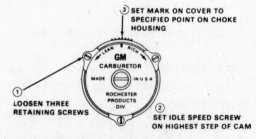

2GC automatic choke coil adjustment

2. Loosen the thermostatic choke coil cover retaining screws.

3. Rotate the choke cover against coil tension until the choke valve begins to close. Continue rotating it until the index mark aligns with the specified point on the choke housing. On models with slotted coil pick-up lever, make sure coil tang is installed in slot in lever. This will have to be checked with the choke coil cover removed.

4. Tighten the choke cover retaining screws.

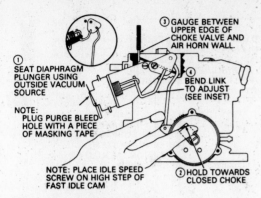

2GC vacuum break adjustment

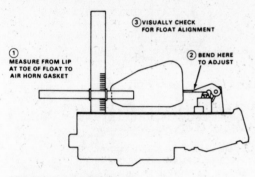

2GC float level adjustment

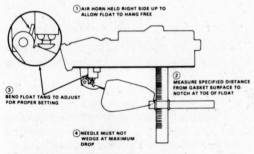

2GC float drop adjustment

Vacuum Break

1. Disconnect the vacuum hose. Using an outside vacuum source, seat the vacuum diaphragm.

2. Cover the vacuum break bleed hole with a small piece of tape so that the diaphragm will be held inward.

3. Place the idle speed screw on the high step of the fast idle cam.

4. 1975-76: Remove the thermostatic coil and cover; hold the choke coil lever inside the choke coil housing towards the closed choke position.

1977-78: Pull out the stem from the vacuum diaphragm to the vacuum break rod until seated.

5. Measure the clearance between the upper edge of the choke valve and the air horn wall.

6. Bend the vacuum break rod to adjust.

7. After adjustment, remove the piece of tape and reconnect the vacuum hose.

ROCHESTER 2SE (1979 AND LATER)

Float Adjustment

1. Remove the air horn from the throttle body.

2. Use your fingers to hold the retainer in place, and to push the float down into light contact with the needle.

3. Measure the distance from the toe of the float (furthest from the hinge) to the top of the carburetor (gasket removed).

4. To adjust, remove the float and gently bend the arm to specification. After adjustment, check the float alignment in the chamber.

Pump Adjustment

1. With the throttle closed and the fast idle screw off the steps of the fast idle cam, measure the distance from the air horn casting to the top of the pump stem.

2. To adjust, remove the retaining screw and washer and remove the pump lever. Bend the end of the lever to correct the stem height. Do not twist the lever or bend it sideways.

3. Install the lever, washer and screw and check the adjustment. When correct, open and close the throttle a few times to check the linkage movement and alignment.

NOTE: *1981 and later models do not require this adjustment.*

Fast Idle Adjustment

1. Set the ignition timing and curb idle speed, and disconnect and plug hoses as directed on the emission control decal.

2. Place the fast idle screw on the highest step of the cam.

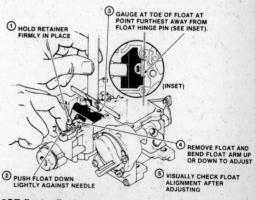

2SE float adjustment

> **NOTE:**
> THE PUMP ADJUSTMENT SHOULD NOT BE CHANGED FROM ORIGINAL FACTORY SETTING UNLESS GAUGING SHOWS OUT OF SPECIFICATION. THE PUMP LEVER IS MADE FROM HEAVY DUTY, HARDENED STEEL MAKING BENDING DIFFICULT. DO NOT REMOVE PUMP LEVER FOR BENDING UNLESS ABSOLUTELY NECESSARY.

② GAUGE FROM AIR HORN CASTING SURFACE TO TOP OF PUMP STEM. DIMENSION SHOULD BE AS SPECIFIED.

① THROTTLE VALVES COMPLETELY CLOSED. MAKE SURE FAST IDLE SCREW IS OFF STEPS OF FAST IDLE CAM.

③ IF NECESSARY TO ADJUST, REMOVE PUMP LEVER RETAINING SCREW AND WASHER AND REMOVE PUMP LEVER BY ROTATING LEVER TO REMOVE FROM PUMP ROD. PLACE LEVER IN A VISE, PROTECTING LEVER FROM DAMAGE, AND BEND END OF LEVER (NEAREST NECKED DOWN SECTION).

⑤ OPEN AND CLOSE THROTTLE VALVES CHECKING LINKAGE FOR FREEDOM OF MOVEMENT AND OBSERVING PUMP LEVER ALIGNMENT.

NOTE: DO NOT BEND LEVER IN A SIDEWAYS OR TWISTING MOTION.

④ REINSTALL PUMP LEVER, WASHER AND RETAINING SCREW. RECHECK PUMP ADJUSTMENT ① AND ②. TIGHTEN RETAINING SCREW SECURELY AFTER THE PUMP ADJUSTMENT IS CORRECT.

2SE pump adjustment

3. Start the engine and adjust the engine speed to specification with the fast idle screw.

Choke Coil Lever Adjustment

1. Remove the three retaining screws and remove the choke cover and coil. On models with a riveted choke cover, drill out the three rivets and remove the cover and choke coil.

NOTE: *A choke stat cover retainer kit is required for reassembly.*

2. Place the fast idle screw on the high step on the cam.

3. Close the choke by pushing in on the intermediate choke lever. The intermediate choke lever is behind the choke vacuum diaphragm.

4. Insert a drill or gauge of the specified size (.085) into the hole in the choke housing. The choke lever in the housing should be up against the side of the gauge.

5. If the lever does not just touch the gauge, bend the intermediate choke rod to adjust.

Fast Idle Cam (Choke Rod) Adjustment

NOTE: *A special angle gauge should be used.*

1. Adjust the choke coil lever and fast idle first.

2. Rotate the degree scale until it is zeroed.

3. Close the choke and install the degree scale onto the choke plate. Center the leveling bubble.

4. Rotate the scale so that the specified degree is opposite the scale pointer.

5. Place the fast idle screw on the second step of the cam (against the high step). Close the choke by pushing in the intermediate lever.

6. Push on the vacuum break lever in the direction of opening choke until the lever is against the rear tang on the choke lever.

7. Bend the fast idle cam rod at the "U" to adjust angle to specifications.

Air Valve Rod Adjustment

1. Seat the vacuum diaphragm with an outside vacuum source. Tape over the purge bleed hole if present.

2. Close the air valve.

3. Insert the specified gauge between the rod and the end of the slot in the air valve.

4. Bend the rod to adjust the clearance.

Primary Side Vacuum Break Adjustment

1. Follow Steps 1-4 of the Fast Idle Cam Adjustment.

2. Seat the choke vacuum diaphragm with an outside vacuum source.

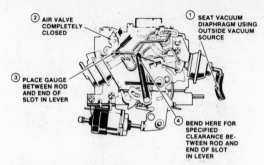

2SE air valve rod adjustment

3. Push in on the intermediate choke lever to close the choke valve, and hold closed during adjustment.

4. Adjust by bending the vacuum break rod until the bubble in centered.

Secondary Vacuum Break Adjustment

1. Follow Steps 1-4 of the Fast Idle Cam Adjustment.

2. Seat the choke vacuum diaphragm with an outside vacuum source.

3. Push in on the intermediate choke level to close the choke valve, and hold closed during adjustment. Make sure the plunger spring is compressed and seated, if present.

4. Bend the vacuum break rod at the "U" next to the diaphragm until the bubble is centered.

Electric Choke Setting

This procedure is only for those carburetors with choke covers retained by screws. Riveted choke covers are preset and nonadjustable.

1. Loosen the three retaining screws.

2. Place the fast idle screw on the high step of the cam.

3. Rotate the choke cover to align the cover mark with the specified housing mark.

Choke Unloader Adjustment

1. Follow Steps 1-4 of the Fast Idle Cam Adjustment.

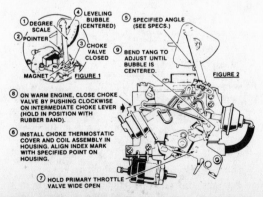

2SE unloader adjustment

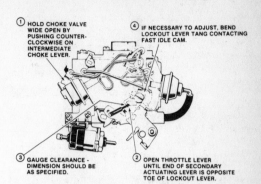

2SE secondary lockout adjustment

2. Install the choke cover and coil, if removed, aligning the marks on the housing and cover as specified.

3. Hold the primary throttle wide open.

4. If the engine is warm, close the choke valve by pushing in on the intermediate choke lever.

5. Bend the unloader tang until the bubble is centered.

Secondary Lockout Adjustment

1. Pull the choke wide open by pushing out on the intermediate choke lever.

2. Open the throttle until the end of the secondary actuating lever is opposite the toe of the lockout lever.

3. Gauge clearance between the lockout lever and secondary lever should be as specified.

4. To adjust, bend the lockout lever where it contacts the fast idle cam.

ROCHESTER M2MC M2ME (1979 AND LATER)

Float Adjustment

NOTE: *The M2ME carburetor is the same as the M2MC except that the choke is now electrically operated.*

1. Remove the air horn from the throttle body.

2. Use your fingers to hold the retainer in place, and to push the float down into light contact with the needle.

3. Gauge from the top of the casting to the top of the float, at a point $3/16''$ back from the end of the toe of the float (gasket removed).

4. To adjust, remove the float and gently bend the arm to specification. After adjustment, check the float alignment in the chamber.

Fast Idle Speed

1. Place the fast idle lever on the high step of the fast idle cam.

2. Turn the fast idle screw out until the throttle valves are closed.

3. Turn the screw in to contact the lever,

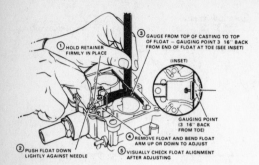

M2MC float adjustment

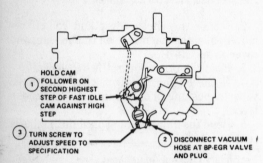

M2MC fast idle adjustment on the bench

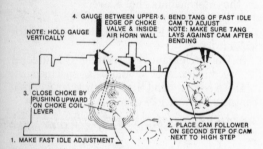

M2MC fast idle cam adjustment

then turn it in two more turns. Check this preliminary setting against the sticker figure.

Fast Idle Cam Adjustment

1. Adjust the fast idle speed.
2. Place the cam follower lever on the second step of the fast idle cam, holding it firmly against the rise of the high step.
3. Close the choke valve by pushing upward on the choke coil lever inside the choke housing.
4. Gauge between the upper edge of the choke valve and the inside of the air horn wall.
5. Bend the tang on the fast idle cam to adjust.

Pump Adjustment

1. With the fast idle cam follower off the steps of the fast idle cam, back out the idle speed screw until the throttle valves are completely closed.

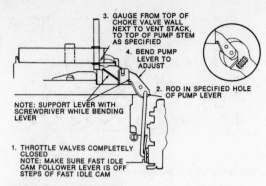

M2MC pump adjustment

2. Place the pump rod in the proper hole of the lever.
3. Measure from the top of the choke valve wall, next to the vent stack, to the top of the pump stem.
4. Bend the pump lever to adjust.

Choke Coil Lever Adjustment

1. Remove the choke cover and thermostatic coil from the choke housing.
2. Push up on the coil tang (counterclockwise) until the choke valve is closed. The top of the choke rod should be at the bottom of the slot in the choke valve lever. Place the fast idle cam follower on the high step of the cam.
3. Insert a 0.120″ plug gauge in the hole in the choke housing.
4. The lower edge of the choke coil lever should just contact the side of the plug gauge.
5. Bend the choke rod to adjust.

Front Vacuum Break Adjustment

1. Seat the choke vacuum diaphragm, using an outside vacuum source. If there is an air bleed hole on the diaphragm, tape it over.
2. Remove the choke cover and coil. Rotate the inside coil lever counterclockwise.
3. Check that the specified gap is present between the top of the choke valve and the air horn wall.
4. Turn the vacuum break adjusting screw to adjust.

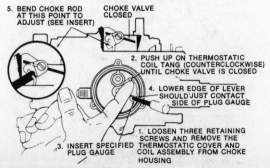

M2MC choke coil lever adjustment

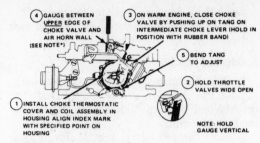

M2MC unloader adjustment

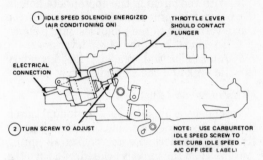

M2MC A/C idle speed-up solenoid adjustment

Automatic Choke Coil Adjustment

1. Place the cam follower on the highest step of the fast idle cam.

2. Loosen the three choke cover retaining screws.

3. Rotate the cover and coil assembly counterclockwise until the choke valve just closes.

4. Align the mark on the choke cover with the specified mark on the housing. Make sure the slot in the lever is engaged with the coil tang. Tighten the cover retaining screws.

Unloader Adjustment

1. With the choke valve completely closed, hold the throttle valves wide open.

2. Measure between the upper edge of the choke valve and the air horn wall.

3. Bend the tang on the fast idle lever to obtain the proper measurement.

Air Conditioning Idle Speed-Up Solenoid Adjustment

1. With the engine at normal operating temperature and automatic transmissions in drive, manual transmissions in neutral, adjust the curb idle to specifications by means of the idle speed screw (air conditioning off).

2. Turn the air conditioning on and disconnect the compressor clutch electrical lead at the connector. The solenoid should be energized.

3. Open the throttle slightly to allow the solenoid plunger to fully extend.

4. Turn the solenoid screw (plunger) to adjust the engine idle to the specified rpm. See your underhood specifications sticker for proper idle speed.

ROCHESTER 4MV (1970-78)

Fast Idle

1. Position the fast idle lever on the high step of the fast idle cam.

2. Be sure that the choke is wide-open and the engine warm. On 1974 models, with manual transmission, disconnect the vacuum advance. On 1976 California 454s and all 1977-78 models, disconnect and plug vacuum hose at EGR valve.

3. Turn the fast idle screw to gain the proper fast idle rpm.

Choke Rod (Fast Idle Cam)

1. Place the cam follower on the second step of the fast idle cam.

2. Close the choke valve by exerting counterclockwise pressure on the external choke lever.

3. Insert a gauge of the proper size between the lower edge of the choke valve and the inside air horn wall. For 1976-78, measure between the upper edge of the choke valve and the inside air horn wall.

4. To adjust, bend the choke rod.

Vacuum Break

1. Fully seat the vacuum break diaphragm using an outside vacuum source.

2. Open the throttle valve enough to allow the fast idle cam follower to clear the fast idle cam.

3. The end of the vacuum break rod should be at the outer end of the slot in the vacuum break diaphragm plunger.

4. The specified clearance should register from the lower end of the choke valve to the inside air horn wall. For 1976-78, measure between the upper edge of the choke valve to the inside air horn wall.

5. If the clearance is not correct, bend the vacuum break line at the point shown in the illustration.

Secondary Vacuum Break (1970-75 Only)

1. Using an outside vacuum source, seat the auxiliary vacuum break diaphragm plunger.

2. Rotate the choke lever in the closed position until the spring-loaded diaphragm plunger is fully extended.

3. Holding the choke valve closed, check the distance between the lower edge of the choke valve and the air horn wall.

4. To adjust to specifications, bend the vacuum break link.

Choke Unloader

1. Push up on the vacuum break lever and fully open the throttle valves. (1976-78: push up or down to close choke).
2. Measure the distance from the lower edge of the choke valve to the air horn wall (1976-78: measure from the upper edge of choke valve).
3. To adjust, bend the tang on the fast idle lever.

Choke Coil Rod

Before making this adjustment, check choke mechanism for free operation. Any binding caused by gum on shaft or linkage should be cleaned off. Do not oil linkage.
1. Close the choke valve by rotating the choke coil lever counterclockwise.
2. Disconnect the thermostatic coil rod from the upper lever.
3. Push down on the rod until it contacts the bracket of the coil.
4. The rod must fit in the notch of the upper lever.
5. If it does not, it must be bent on the curved portion just below the upper lever.

Secondary Closing Adjustment

This adjustment assures proper closing of the secondary throttle plates.
1. Set the slow idle as per instructions in Chapter 2. Make sure that the fast idle cam follower is not resting on the fast idle cam. The choke valve should be wide open.
2. There should be the specified clearance between the secondary throttle actuating rod and the front of the slot on the secondary throttle lever with the closing tang on the throttle lever resting against the actuating lever.
3. Bend the tang on the primary throttle actuating rod to adjust.

Secondary Opening Adjustment

1. Open the primary throttle valves until the actuating link contacts the upper tang on the secondary lever.
2. With two point linkage, the bottom of the link should be in the center of the secondary lever slot.
3. With three point linkage, there should be the specified clearance between the link and the middle tang.
4. Bend the upper tang on the secondary lever to adjust as necessary.

Float Level

With the air horn assembly upside down, measure the distance from the air horn gasket surface (gasket removed) to the top of the float at the toe.

NOTE: *Make sure that the retaining pin is*

firmly held in place and that the tang of the float is firmly against the needle and seat assembly.

Accelerator Pump

1. Close the primary throttle valves by backing out the slow idle screw and making sure that the fast idle cam follower is off the steps of the fast idle cam.
2. Bend the secondary throttle closing tang away from the primary throttle lever, if necessary.
3. With the pump in the appropriate hole in the pump lever, measure from the top of the choke valve wall to the top of the pump stem.
4. To adjust, bend the pump lever.
5. After adjusting, readjust the secondary throttle tank and the slow idle screw.

Air Valve Spring Adjustment

To adjust the air valve spring windup, loosen the allen head lockscrew and turn the adjusting screw counterclockwise to remove all spring tension. Hold the air valve closed, and turn the adjusting screw clockwise the specified number of turns after the torsion spring contacts the pin on the shaft. Hold the adjusting screw in this position and tighten the lockscrew.

Secondary Lockout Adjustment

For 1970-75, see the illustration in this section. For 1976-78, refer to the secondary throttle lock-out adjustment in the next section.

ROCHESTER M4MC AND M4MCA (1975) M4MC AND M4ME (1976-1978)

NOTE: *The illustrations in this section apply to all M4MC, M4MCA, and M4ME carburetors unless otherwise indicated.*

Pump Rod

1. Take the fast idle cam follower off the fast idle cam steps.
2. Back out the idle speed screw until the throttle valves are completely closed.
3. Be sure that the secondary actuating rod is not preventing the throttle from closing completely. If the primary throttle valves do not close completely, bend the secondary closing tang out of position, then readjust later.
4. Place the pump rod in the specified hole in the lever.
5. Measure the clearance from the top of the choke valve wall, next to the vent stack, and the top of the pump stem.
6. To adjust the dimension, support the pump lever and bend the pump lever.
7. Adjust the idle speed.
8. If necessary, readjust the secondary actuating rod.

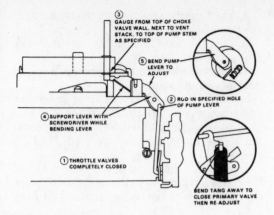

M4MC and M4ME pump rod adjustment

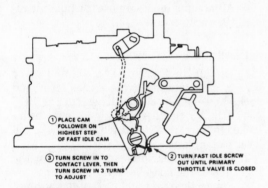

M4MC and M4ME fast idle adjustment

Fast Idle – 1975-77

NOTE: *This procedure is to be used only when the carburetor is off the truck, as a means of roughly setting the fast idle speed before the carburetor is reinstalled. For normal adjustment of fast idle speed, refer to the idle adjustment section in Chapter 2.*

1. Hold the cam follower on the high step of the fast idle cam.

2. Turn the fast idle screw out until the primary throttle valves are closed (1975), or until it pulls away from the fast idle cam follower (1976-77).

3. Turn the fast idle screw in to contact the lever, then turn the screw in three turns.

4. Recheck the fast idle speed.

Choke Coil Lever

1. Loosen the three retaining screws and remove the cover and coil assembly from the choke housing. On the 1978 and later models, also place the fast idle cam follower on the high step of the cam.

2. Push up on the thermostatic coil tang (counterclockwise) until the choke valve closes.

3. Insert the specified gauge into the hole in the choke housing.

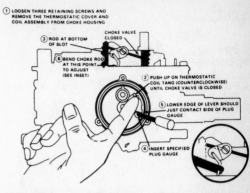

M4ME/M4MC choke coil lever adjustment-through 1978

4. The lower edge of the choke coil lever should just contact the side of the gauge.

5. Bend the choke rod to adjust.

Choke Rod

The choke coil lever adjustment must be made before making the following adjustment. The thermostatic cover and coil will remain off for this adjustment.

1. Adjust the fast idle.

2. Place the cam follower on the second step of the fast idle cam firmly against the rise of the high step.

3. Close the choke valve by pushing up on the choke coil lever inside the choke housing.

4. Measure the clearance between the upper edge of the choke valve and the inside of the air horn wall.

5. Bend the tang on the fast idle cam to adjust the clearance. Be sure that the tang lies against the cam after bending it.

6. Recheck the fast idle.

Air Valve Dashpot

1. Seat the front vacuum diaphragm using an outside vacuum source. Plug the purge bleed hole with masking tape on models where used. Remove tape after making adjustment.

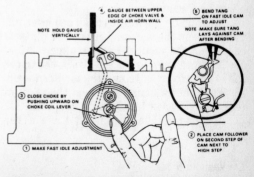

M4ME/M4MC choke rod-fast idle cam adjustment-through 1978

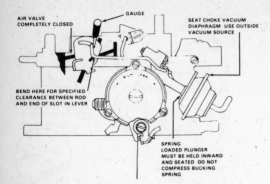

M4ME/M4MC pump adjustment-1979 and later-through 1978

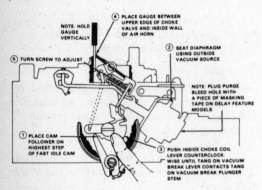

M4ME/M4MC vacuum break adjustment information-through 1978

2. The air valves must be completely closed.

3. Measure the clearance between the air valve dashpot and the end of the slop in the air valve lever.

4. Bend the air valve dashpot rod to adjust the clearance.

Front Vacuum Break

1. Remove the thermostatic cover and coil assembly from the choke housing.

2. Place the cam follower on the high step of the fast idle cam.

3. Seat the front vacuum diaphragm using an outside vacuum source.

4. Push up on the inside choke coil lever until the tang on the vacuum break lever contacts the tang on the vacuum break plunger.

5. Measure the clearance between the upper edge of the choke valve and the air horn wall.

6. Turn the adjusting screw on the vacuum break plunger lever to adjust.

7. Reconnect the vacuum hose after adjustment.

Rear Vacuum Break

1. Remove the thermostatic cover and coil assembly from the choke housing.

2. Place the cam follower on the high step of the fast idle cam.

3. Plug the bleed hose in the vacuum break unit cover with tape.

4. Seat the rear vacuum diaphragm using an outside vacuum source.

5. Push up the choke coil lever inside the choke housing toward the closed position. Diaphragm should be pulled out until seated, bucking spring compressed (where used) on 1976 and later.

6. With the choke rod in the bottom slot of the choke lever, measure the clearance between the upper edge of the choke valve and air horn wall.

7. Bend the vacuum break rod if necessary to adjust.

8. After adjustment, remove the tape and install the vacuum hose.

Automatic Choke Coil, M4MC

1. Install the thermostatic coil and cover with a gasket between the choke cover and choke housing. On all models except the 1976 454 cu. in. V8, the thermostatic coil must be installed in the slot in the inside of the choke coil lever pick-up arm.

2. Place the fast idle cam follower on the high step of the fast idle cam.

3. Rotate the cover and coil assembly counterclockwise until the choke valve just closes.

4. Align the index point on the cover with the specified mark on the choke housing.

5. Tighten the retaining screws.

Automatic Choke Coil, M4ME

1. Install the electric choke assembly in choke housing, making sure coil tang contacts bottom side of inside choke coil lever pick-up arm.

2. Place fast idle cam follower on high step of cam.

3. Rotate cover and coil assembly counterclockwise until choke valve just closes.

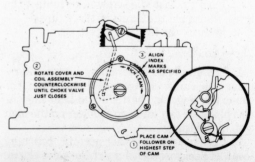

M4ME/M4MC choke coil lever adjustment-through 1978

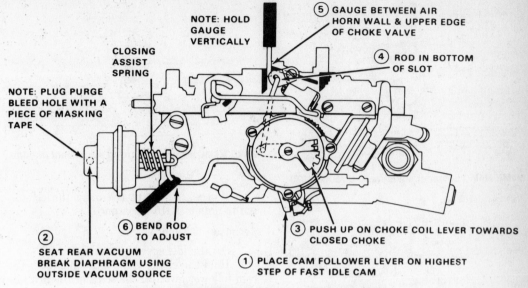

NOTE: HOLD GAUGE VERTICALLY

⑤ GAUGE BETWEEN AIR HORN WALL & UPPER EDGE OF CHOKE VALVE

CLOSING ASSIST SPRING

④ ROD IN BOTTOM OF SLOT

NOTE: PLUG PURGE BLEED HOLE WITH A PIECE OF MASKING TAPE

⑥ BEND ROD TO ADJUST

② SEAT REAR VACUUM BREAK DIAPHRAGM USING OUTSIDE VACUUM SOURCE

③ PUSH UP ON CHOKE COIL LEVER TOWARDS CLOSED CHOKE

① PLACE CAM FOLLOWER LEVER ON HIGHEST STEP OF FAST IDLE CAM

(ALL EXCEPT 454 ENGINE)

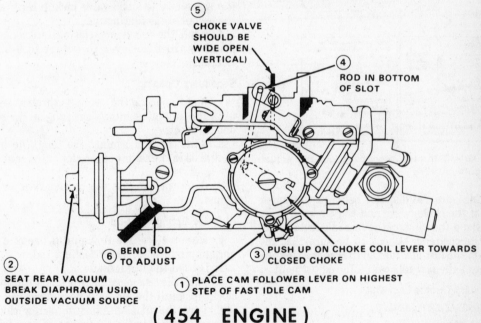

⑤ CHOKE VALVE SHOULD BE WIDE OPEN (VERTICAL)

④ ROD IN BOTTOM OF SLOT

⑥ BEND ROD TO ADJUST

② SEAT REAR VACUUM BREAK DIAPHRAGM USING OUTSIDE VACUUM SOURCE

③ PUSH UP ON CHOKE COIL LEVER TOWARDS CLOSED CHOKE

① PLACE CAM FOLLOWER LEVER ON HIGHEST STEP OF FAST IDLE CAM

(454 ENGINE)

M4MC and M4MCA rear vacuum break adjustment. Refer to the upper illustration for 1976–78 M4ME

4. Align index point on cover with specified mark on housing.

5. Install cover retainers and screws.

NOTE: *Ground contact for the electric choke is provided by a metal plate located at the rear of the choke assembly. Do not install a choke cover gasket between the electric choke assembly and the choke housing. Do not immerse the electric choke assembly in any cleaning solution. Severe damage can result.*

Unloader

1. Perform Step 1 of the appropriate automatic choke coil procedure.

2. Hold the throttle valves wide open with the choke valve completely closed. On a warm engine, close the choke valve by pushing on the tang of the intermediate choke lever which contacts the fast idle cam. A rubber band will hold it in position.

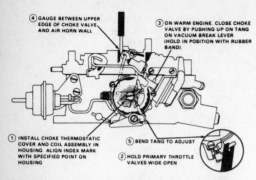

④ GAUGE BETWEEN UPPER EDGE OF CHOKE VALVE AND AIR HORN WALL

③ ON WARM ENGINE, CLOSE CHOKE VALVE BY PUSHING UP ON TANG ON VACUUM BREAK LEVER (HOLD IN POSITION WITH RUBBER BAND)

① INSTALL CHOKE THERMOSTAT COVER AND COIL ASSEMBLY IN HOUSING. ALIGN INDEX MARK WITH SPECIFIED POINT ON HOUSING

⑤ BEND TANG TO ADJUST

② HOLD PRIMARY THROTTLE VALVES WIDE OPEN

M4ME/M4MC unloader adjustment-through 1978

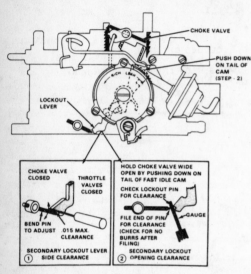

CHOKE VALVE

PUSH DOWN ON TAIL OF CAM (STEP · 2)

LOCKOUT LEVER

CHOKE VALVE CLOSED / THROTTLE VALVES CLOSED

BEND PIN TO ADJUST .015 MAX. CLEARANCE

SECONDARY LOCKOUT LEVER ① SIDE CLEARANCE

HOLD CHOKE VALVE WIDE OPEN BY PUSHING DOWN ON TAIL OF FAST IDLE CAM. CHECK LOCKOUT PIN FOR CLEARANCE

FILE END OF PIN FOR CLEARANCE (CHECK FOR NO BURRS AFTER FILING)

GAUGE

SECONDARY LOCKOUT ② OPENING CLEARANCE

M4ME/M4MC throttle secondary lock-out adjustment-through 1978

3. Measure the distance between the upper edge of the choke valve and the air horn wall.

4. Bend the tang on the fast idle lever to adjust the clearance. Check to be sure that the tang on the fast idle cam lever is contacting the center of the fast idle cam after adjustment.

Secondary Throttle Lock-Out

SECONDARY LEVER CLEARANCE

1. Hold the choke valve and secondary throttle valves closed.

2. Measure the clearance between the lockout pin and the lock-out lever.

3. If necessary, bend the lock-out pin to adjust to 0.015″.

OPENING CLEARANCE

4. Hold the choke valve wide open by pushing down on the fast idle cam.

5. Hold the secondary throttle valves slightly open.

6. Measure the clearance between the end of the lock-out pin and the toe of the lock-out lever.

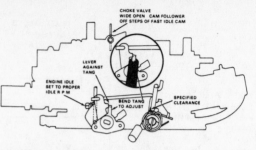

CHOKE VALVE WIDE OPEN · CAM FOLLOWER OFF STEPS OF FAST IDLE CAM

LEVER AGAINST TANG

ENGINE IDLE SET TO PROPER IDLE R P M

BEND TANG TO ADJUST

SPECIFIED CLEARANCE

M4ME/M4MC secondary closing adjustment-through 1978

7. If necessary, file off the end of the lock-out pin to obtain 0.015″. clearance.

Secondary Closing

1. Set the idle speed to specification.

2. Hold the choke valve wide open with the cam follower lever off the steps of the fast idle cam.

3. Measure the clearance between the slot in the secondary throttle valve pickup lever and the secondary actuating rod.

4. Bend the secondary closing tang on the primary throttle lever to adjust to 0.020″ clearance.

Secondary Opening

1. Lightly, crack the primary throttle lever until the link just contacts the tang on the secondary lever.

2. With the link against the tang, the link should be in the center of the slot in the secondary lever.

3. Bend the tang on the secondary lever to adjust.

Air Valve Spring Wind-Up

1. Remove the front vacuum break diaphragm and the air valve dashpot rod.

2. Loosen the lockscrew.

3. Turn the tension adjusting screw counterclockwise until the air valve opens partway.

4. Turn the tension adjusting screw clockwise while tapping lightly on the casting with the handle of a screwdriver.

5. When the air valve just closes, turn the tension adjusting screw clockwise the specified number of turns after the spring contacts the pin.

6. Tighten the lockscrew and install the diaphragm and dashpot rod.

Deceleration Throttle Stop

1. Adjust the idle speed.

2. Push the hex end of the throttle stop plunger in (toward the throttle lever) until the plunger stem hits the stop inside the diaphragm.

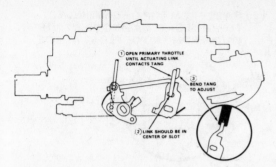

M4ME/M4MC secondary opening adjustment-through 1978

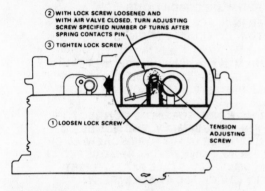

M4ME/M4MC air valve spring wind-up adjustment-through 1978

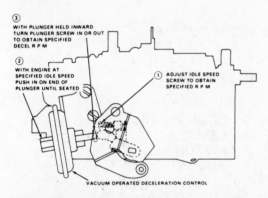

M4ME/M4MC deceleration throttle stop adjustment-through 1978

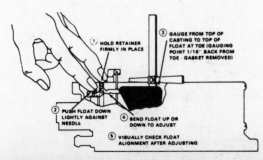

M4ME/M4MC float level adjustment-through 1978

3. With the plunger against the stop, turn the plunger adjusting screw in or out to obtain the specified deceleration rpm.

ROCHESTER M4ME/M4MC (1979 AND LATER)

For carburetor adjustments for the 1979-87 M4ME/M4MC Rochester carburetor, please refer to the following illustrations.

ROCHESTER E2SE 2-bbl

The model E2SE, introduced on Chevrolet pick-up trucks in 1983, is designed as part of the GM Computer Command Control System (C3). An electrically operated mixture control solenoid differentiates the E2SE from the conventional 2SE series.

A plunger in the end of the above mentioned solenoid is submerged in fuel in the fuel chamber of the float bowl. The plunger is controlled, or pulsed, by electrical signals received from the Electronic Control Module (ECM). The solenoid system is used to control the air/fuel mixture in the primary bore of the carburetor.

The mode E2SE also has a Throttle Position Sensor (TPS) mounted in the float bowl and is used to signal the ECM as throttle position changes occur. As throttle position changes, a tang on the pump lever moves the TPS plunger, modifying an electrical signal to the ECM. This modifying an electrical signal to the ECM. This signal is used in conjunction with signals from various other engine sensors by the ECM to control various engine operating modes.

Float Adjustment

1. Remove the air horn from the throttle body.
2. Use your fingers to hold the retainer in place, and to push the float down into light contact with the needle.
3. Measure the distance from the toe of the float (furthest from the hinge) to the top of the carburetor (gasket removed).
4. To adjust, remove the float and gently bend the arm to specification. After adjustment, check the float alignment in the chamber.

Pump Adjustment

1. With the throttle closed and the fast idle screw off the steps of the fast idle cam, measure the distance from the air horn casting to the top of the pump stem.
2. To adjust, remove the retaining screw and washer and remove the pump lever. Bend the end of the lever to correct the stem height. Do not twist the lever or bend it sideways.

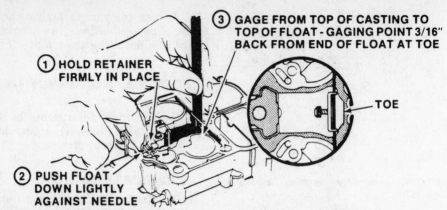

③ GAGE FROM TOP OF CASTING TO TOP OF FLOAT - GAGING POINT 3/16" BACK FROM END OF FLOAT AT TOE

① HOLD RETAINER FIRMLY IN PLACE

TOE

② PUSH FLOAT DOWN LIGHTLY AGAINST NEEDLE

④ IF FLOAT LEVEL VARIES OVER ±1/16" FROM SPECIFICATIONS, FOR LEVEL TOO HIGH, HOLD RETAINER IN PLACE AND PUSH DOWN ON CENTER OF FLOAT PONTOON TO OBTAIN CORRECT SETTING. FOR LEVEL TOO LOW,

A   IF M4M OR M2M CARBURETOR, REMOVE POWER PISTON, METERING RODS, PLASTIC FILLER BLOCK. REMOVE FLOAT, BEND FLOAT ARM UPWARD TO ADJUST. REINSTALL PARTS. VISUALLY CHECK FLOAT ALIGNMENT.

B   IF E4M OR E2M REMOVE METERING RODS, SOLENOID CONNECTOR SCREW. COUNT, AND RECORD FOR REASSEMBLY, THE NUMBER OF TURNS NEEDED TO LIGHTLY BOTTOM LEAN MIXTURE SCREW. BACK OUT AND REMOVE SCREW, SOLENOID, CONNECTOR. REMOVE FLOAT AND FLOAT ARM UPWARD TO ADJUST. REINSTALL PARTS, RESET LEAN MIXTURE SCREW. VISUALLY CHECK FLOAT ALIGNMENT.

M4ME/M4MC float adjustment-1979 and later

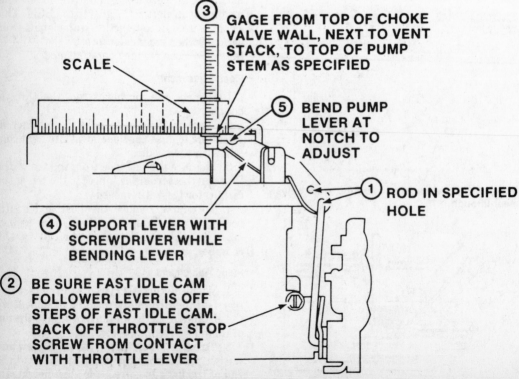

③ GAGE FROM TOP OF CHOKE VALVE WALL, NEXT TO VENT STACK, TO TOP OF PUMP STEM AS SPECIFIED

SCALE

⑤ BEND PUMP LEVER AT NOTCH TO ADJUST

① ROD IN SPECIFIED HOLE

④ SUPPORT LEVER WITH SCREWDRIVER WHILE BENDING LEVER

② BE SURE FAST IDLE CAM FOLLOWER LEVER IS OFF STEPS OF FAST IDLE CAM. BACK OFF THROTTLE STOP SCREW FROM CONTACT WITH THROTTLE LEVER

M4ME/M4MC pump adjustment-1979 and later

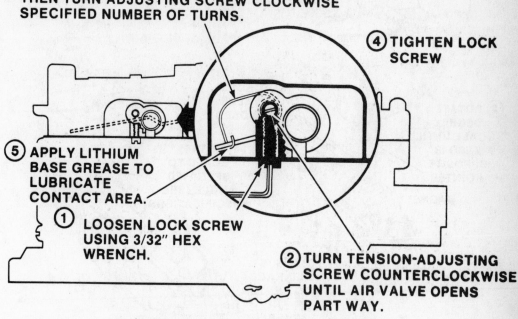

③ TURN TENSION-ADJUSTING SCREW CLOCKWISE UNTIL AIR VALVE JUST CLOSES. THEN TURN ADJUSTING SCREW CLOCKWISE SPECIFIED NUMBER OF TURNS.

④ TIGHTEN LOCK SCREW

⑤ APPLY LITHIUM BASE GREASE TO LUBRICATE CONTACT AREA.

① LOOSEN LOCK SCREW USING 3/32″ HEX WRENCH.

② TURN TENSION-ADJUSTING SCREW COUNTERCLOCKWISE UNTIL AIR VALVE OPENS PART WAY.

M4ME/M4MC air valve spring adjustment-1979 and later

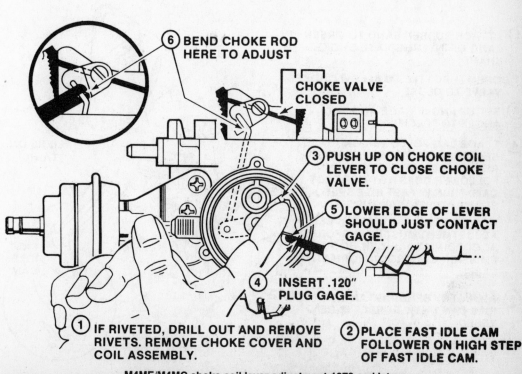

⑥ BEND CHOKE ROD HERE TO ADJUST

CHOKE VALVE CLOSED

③ PUSH UP ON CHOKE COIL LEVER TO CLOSE CHOKE VALVE.

⑤ LOWER EDGE OF LEVER SHOULD JUST CONTACT GAGE.

④ INSERT .120″ PLUG GAGE.

① IF RIVETED, DRILL OUT AND REMOVE RIVETS. REMOVE CHOKE COVER AND COIL ASSEMBLY.

② PLACE FAST IDLE CAM FOLLOWER ON HIGH STEP OF FAST IDLE CAM.

M4ME/M4MC choke coil lever adjustment-1979 and later

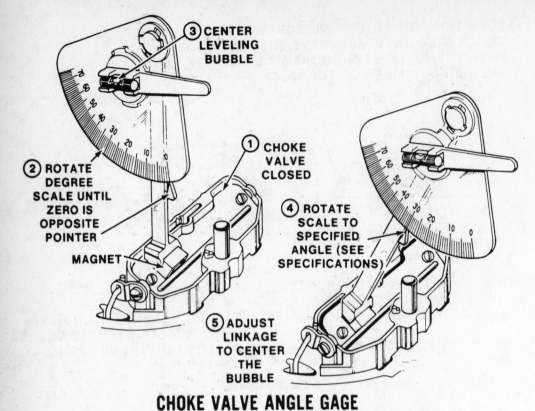

CHOKE VALVE ANGLE GAGE
TOOL J-26701 OR BT-7704

M4ME/M4MC choke valve angle gauge adjustment-1979 and later

① ATTACH RUBBER BAND TO GREEN TANG OF INTERMEDIATE CHOKE SHAFT

② OPEN THROTTLE TO ALLOW CHOKE VALVE TO CLOSE

③ SET UP ANGLE GAGE AND SET ANGLE TO SPECIFICATIONS

④ PLACE CAM FOLLOWER ON SECOND STEP OF CAM, AGAINST RISE OF HIGH STEP. IF CAM FOLLOWER DOES NOT CONTACT CAM, TURN IN FAST IDLE SPEED SCREW ADDITIONAL TURN(S).

NOTICE: FINAL FAST IDLE SPEED ADJUSTMENT MUST BE PERFORMED ACCORDING TO UNDER-HOOD EMISSION CONTROL INFORMATION LABEL.

⑤ ADJUST BY BENDING TANG OF FAST IDLE CAM UNTIL BUBBLE IS CENTERED.

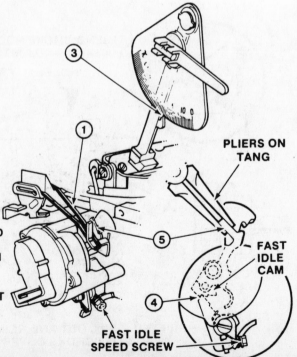

M4ME/M4MC choke rod-fast idle cam adjustment-1979 and later

PLUGGING AIR BLEED HOLES

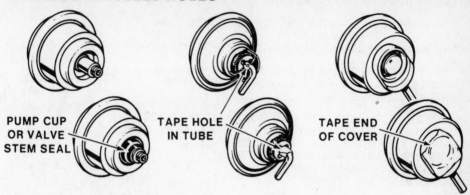

PUMP CUP
OR VALVE
STEM SEAL

TAPE HOLE
IN TUBE

TAPE END
OF COVER

BUCKING SPRINGS

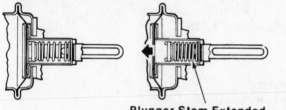

Plunger Stem Extended
(Spring Compressed)

PLUNGER BUCKING SPRING

Spring
Seated

LEAF TYPE BUCKING SPRING

M4ME/M4MC vacuum break adjustment information-1979 and later

(1) ATTACH RUBBER BAND TO GREEN TANG OF INTERMEDIATE CHOKE SHAFT

(2) OPEN THROTTLE TO ALLOW CHOKE VALVE TO CLOSE

(3) SET UP ANGLE GAGE AND SET TO SPECIFICATION

(4) RETRACT VACUUM BREAK PLUNGER USING VACUUM SOURCE, AT LEAST 18" HG. PLUG AIR BLEED HOLES WHERE APPLICABLE

ON QUADRAJETS, AIR VALVE ROD MUST NOT RESTRICT PLUNGER FROM RETRACTING FULLY. IF NECESSARY, BEND ROD (SEE ARROW) TO PERMIT FULL PLUNGER TRAVEL. FINAL ROD CLEARANCE MUST BE SET AFTER VACUUM BREAK SETTING HAS BEEN MADE.

(5) WITH AT LEAST 18" HG STILL APPLIED, ADJUST SCREW TO CENTER BUBBLE

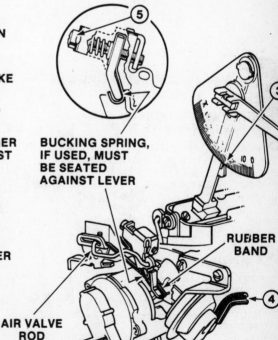

BUCKING SPRING,
IF USED, MUST
BE SEATED
AGAINST LEVER

RUBBER
BAND

AIR VALVE
ROD

M4ME/M4MC front vacuum break adjustment-1979 and later

① ATTACH RUBBER BAND TO GREEN TANG OF INTERMEDIATE CHOKE SHAFT.

② OPEN THROTTLE TO ALLOW CHOKE VALVE TO CLOSE.

③ SET UP ANGLE GAGE AND SET ANGLE TO SPECIFICATION.

④ RETRACT VACUUM BREAK PLUNGER, USING VACUUM SOURCE, AT LEAST 18" HG. PLUG AIR BLEED HOLES WHERE APPLICABLE.

④A ON QUADRAJETS, AIR VALVE ROD MUST NOT RESTRICT PLUNGER FROM RETRACTING FULLY. IF NECESSARY, BEND ROD HERE TO PERMIT FULL PLUNGER TRAVEL. WHERE APPLICABLE, PLUNGER STEM MUST BE EXTENDED FULLY TO COMPRESS PLUNGER BUCKING SPRING.

⑤ TO CENTER BUBBLE, EITHER:
A. ADJUST WITH 1/8" HEX WRENCH (VACUUM STILL APPLIED)

   -OR-

B. SUPPORT AT "S" AND BEND VACUUM BREAK ROD (VACUUM STILL APPLIED)

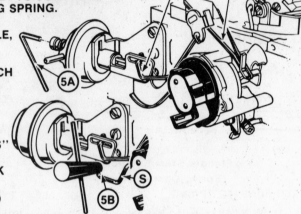

M4ME/M4MC rear vacuum break adjustment-1979 and later

③ .025" PLUG GAGE BETWEEN ROD AND END OF SLOT

② AIR VALVE CLOSED COMPLETELY

① USE VACUUM SOURCE, AT LEAST 18" HG, TO SEAT VACUUM BREAK PLUNGER. PLUG AIR BLEED HOLES WHERE APPLICABLE.

④ BEND ROD HERE TO ADJUST GAGE CLEARANCE TO .025", WITH VACUUM AT LEAST 18" HG.

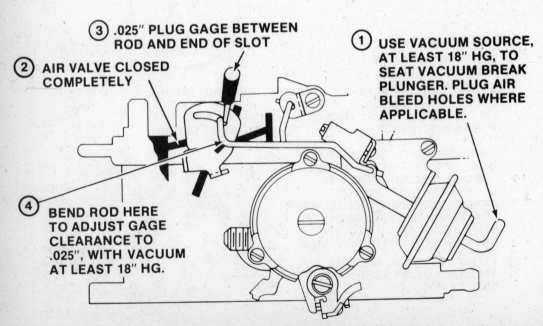

M4ME/M4MC air valve rod adjustment (front)-1979 and later

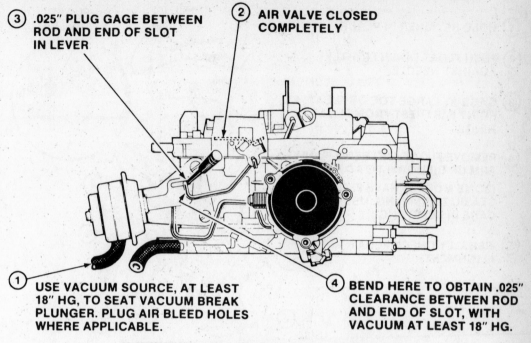

③ .025" PLUG GAGE BETWEEN ROD AND END OF SLOT IN LEVER

② AIR VALVE CLOSED COMPLETELY

① USE VACUUM SOURCE, AT LEAST 18" HG, TO SEAT VACUUM BREAK PLUNGER. PLUG AIR BLEED HOLES WHERE APPLICABLE.

④ BEND HERE TO OBTAIN .025" CLEARANCE BETWEEN ROD AND END OF SLOT, WITH VACUUM AT LEAST 18" HG.

M4ME/M4MC air valve rod adjustment (rear)-1979 and later

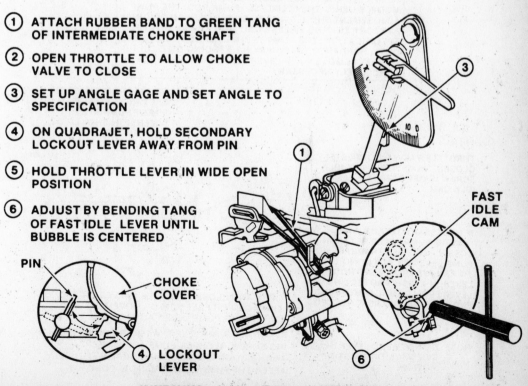

① ATTACH RUBBER BAND TO GREEN TANG OF INTERMEDIATE CHOKE SHAFT

② OPEN THROTTLE TO ALLOW CHOKE VALVE TO CLOSE

③ SET UP ANGLE GAGE AND SET ANGLE TO SPECIFICATION

④ ON QUADRAJET, HOLD SECONDARY LOCKOUT LEVER AWAY FROM PIN

⑤ HOLD THROTTLE LEVER IN WIDE OPEN POSITION

⑥ ADJUST BY BENDING TANG OF FAST IDLE LEVER UNTIL BUBBLE IS CENTERED

PIN

CHOKE COVER

④ LOCKOUT LEVER

FAST IDLE CAM

M4ME/M4MC unloader adjustment—1979 and later

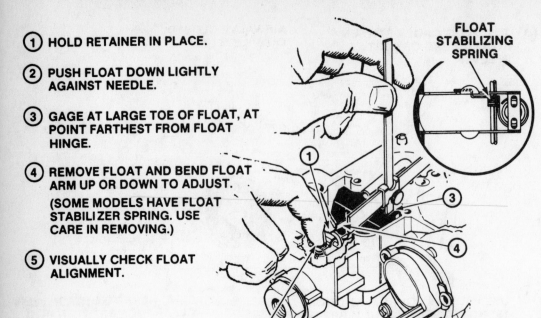

① HOLD RETAINER IN PLACE.

② PUSH FLOAT DOWN LIGHTLY AGAINST NEEDLE.

③ GAGE AT LARGE TOE OF FLOAT, AT POINT FARTHEST FROM FLOAT HINGE.

④ REMOVE FLOAT AND BEND FLOAT ARM UP OR DOWN TO ADJUST.

(SOME MODELS HAVE FLOAT STABILIZER SPRING. USE CARE IN REMOVING.)

⑤ VISUALLY CHECK FLOAT ALIGNMENT.

FLOAT STABILIZING SPRING

E2SE 2-bbl. float adjustment

NOTE: ON MODELS USING A CLIP TO RETAIN PUMP ROD IN PUMP LEVER, NO PUMP ADJUSTMENT IS REQUIRED. ON MODELS USING THE "CLIPLESS" PUMP ROD, THE PUMP ADJUSTMENT SHOULD NOT BE CHANGED FROM ORIGINAL FACTORY SETTING UNLESS GAUGING SHOWS OUT OF SPECIFICATION. THE PUMP LEVER IS MADE FROM HEAVY DUTY, HARDENED STEEL MAKING BENDING DIFFICULT. DO NOT REMOVE PUMP LEVER FOR BENDING UNLESS ABSOLUTELY NECESSARY.

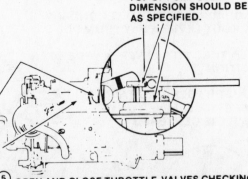

① THROTTLE VALVES COMPLETELY CLOSED. MAKE SURE FAST IDLE SCREW IS OFF STEPS OF FAST IDLE CAM.

③ IF NECESSARY TO ADJUST, REMOVE PUMP LEVER RETAINING SCREW AND WASHER AND REMOVE PUMP LEVER BY ROTATING LEVER TO REMOVE FROM PUMP ROD. PLACE LEVER IN A VISE, PROTECTING LEVER FROM DAMAGE, AND BEND END OF LEVER (NEAREST NECKED DOWN SECTION).

NOTE: DO NOT BEND LEVER IN A SIDEWAYS OR TWISTING MOTION.

② GAUGE FROM AIR HORN CASTING SURFACE TO TOP OF PUMP STEM. DIMENSION SHOULD BE AS SPECIFIED.

⑤ OPEN AND CLOSE THROTTLE VALVES CHECKING LINKAGE FOR FREEDOM OF MOVEMENT AND OBSERVING PUMP LEVER ALIGNMENT.

④ REINSTALL PUMP LEVER, WASHER AND RETAINING SCREW. RECHECK PUMP ADJUSTMENT ① AND ②. TIGHTEN RETAINING SCREW SECURELY AFTER THE PUMP ADJUSTMENT IS CORRECT.

E2SE 2-bbl. pump adjustment

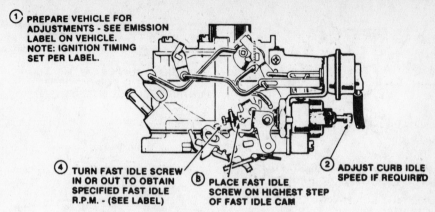

① PREPARE VEHICLE FOR ADJUSTMENTS - SEE EMISSION LABEL ON VEHICLE. NOTE: IGNITION TIMING SET PER LABEL.

④ TURN FAST IDLE SCREW IN OR OUT TO OBTAIN SPECIFIED FAST IDLE R.P.M. - (SEE LABEL)

③ PLACE FAST IDLE SCREW ON HIGHEST STEP OF FAST IDLE CAM

② ADJUST CURB IDLE SPEED IF REQUIRED

Fast idle adjustment, E2SE 2-bbl.

3. Install the lever, washer and screw and check the adjustment. When correct, open and close the throttle a few times to check the linkage movement and alignment.

NOTE: *No pump adjustment is required on 1981 and later models.*

Fast Idle Adjustment

1. Set the ignition timing and curb idle speed, and disconnect and plug hoses as directed on the emission control decal.

2. Place the fast idle screw on the highest step of the cam.

3. Start the engine and adjust the engine speed to specification with the fast idle screw.

Choke Coil Lever Adjustment

1. Remove the three retaining screws and remove the choke cover and coil. On models with a riveted choke cover, drill out the three rivets and remove the cover and choke coil.

NOTE: *A choke stat cover retainer kit is required for reassembly.*

2. Place the fast idle screw on the high step of the cam.

3. Close the choke by pushing in on the intermediate choke lever. On front wheel drive models, the intermediate choke lever is behind the choke vacuum diaphragm.

4. Insert a drill or gauge of the specified size into the hole in the choke housing. The choke lever in the housing should be up against the side of the gauge.

5. If the lever does not just touch the gauge, bend the intermediate choke rod to adjust.

Air Valve Rod Adjustment

Refer to the accompanying illustration for this procedure.

Primary Side Vacuum Break Adjustment

Refer to the illustration for this procedure.

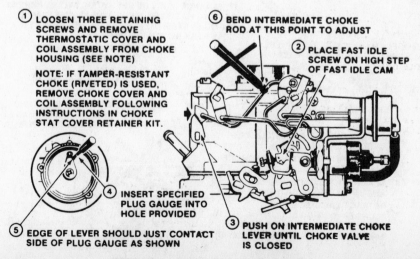

① LOOSEN THREE RETAINING SCREWS AND REMOVE THERMOSTATIC COVER AND COIL ASSEMBLY FROM CHOKE HOUSING (SEE NOTE)

NOTE: IF TAMPER-RESISTANT CHOKE (RIVETED) IS USED, REMOVE CHOKE COVER AND COIL ASSEMBLY FOLLOWING INSTRUCTIONS IN CHOKE STAT COVER RETAINER KIT.

⑥ BEND INTERMEDIATE CHOKE ROD AT THIS POINT TO ADJUST

② PLACE FAST IDLE SCREW ON HIGH STEP OF FAST IDLE CAM

④ INSERT SPECIFIED PLUG GAUGE INTO HOLE PROVIDED

⑤ EDGE OF LEVER SHOULD JUST CONTACT SIDE OF PLUG GAUGE AS SHOWN

③ PUSH ON INTERMEDIATE CHOKE LEVER UNTIL CHOKE VALVE IS CLOSED

E2SE 2-bbl. choke coil lever adjustment

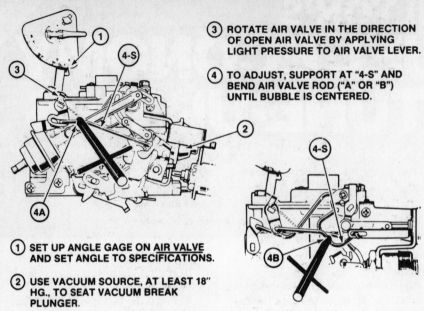

③ **ROTATE AIR VALVE IN THE DIRECTION OF OPEN AIR VALVE BY APPLYING LIGHT PRESSURE TO AIR VALVE LEVER.**

④ **TO ADJUST, SUPPORT AT "4-S" AND BEND AIR VALVE ROD ("A" OR "B") UNTIL BUBBLE IS CENTERED.**

① **SET UP ANGLE GAGE ON AIR VALVE AND SET ANGLE TO SPECIFICATIONS.**

② **USE VACUUM SOURCE, AT LEAST 18" HG., TO SEAT VACUUM BREAK PLUNGER.**

Air valve rod adjustment, 2-bbl. E2SE

Electric Choke Setting

This procedure is only for those carburetors with choke covers retained by screws. Riveted choke covers are preset and nonadjustable.

1. Loosen the three retaining screws.
2. Place the fast idle screw on the high step of the cam.
3. Rotate the choke cover to align the cover mark with the specified housing mark.

Choke Unloader Adjustment

Refer to the accompanying illustrations for this procedure.

ROCHESTER E4ME AND E4MC QUADRAJET 4-bbl

These 4-bbl carburetors feature an electrically operated mixture control solenoid, and are designed as part of the GM Computer Com-

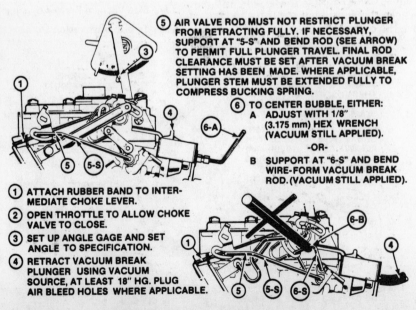

⑤ **AIR VALVE ROD MUST NOT RESTRICT PLUNGER FROM RETRACTING FULLY. IF NECESSARY, SUPPORT AT "5-S" AND BEND ROD (SEE ARROW) TO PERMIT FULL PLUNGER TRAVEL. FINAL ROD CLEARANCE MUST BE SET AFTER VACUUM BREAK SETTING HAS BEEN MADE. WHERE APPLICABLE, PLUNGER STEM MUST BE EXTENDED FULLY TO COMPRESS BUCKING SPRING.**

⑥ **TO CENTER BUBBLE, EITHER:**
A **ADJUST WITH 1/8" (3.175 mm) HEX WRENCH (VACUUM STILL APPLIED).**

-OR-

B **SUPPORT AT "6-S" AND BEND WIRE-FORM VACUUM BREAK ROD. (VACUUM STILL APPLIED).**

① **ATTACH RUBBER BAND TO INTERMEDIATE CHOKE LEVER.**

② **OPEN THROTTLE TO ALLOW CHOKE VALVE TO CLOSE.**

③ **SET UP ANGLE GAGE AND SET ANGLE TO SPECIFICATION.**

④ **RETRACT VACUUM BREAK PLUNGER USING VACUUM SOURCE, AT LEAST 18" HG. PLUG AIR BLEED HOLES WHERE APPLICABLE.**

E2SE primary vacuum break adjustment

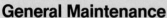

CHILTON'S
FUEL ECONOMY & TUNE-UP TIPS

Tune-up • Spark Plug Diagnosis • Emission Controls

Fuel System • Cooling System • Tires and Wheels

General Maintenance

55 WAYS TO IMPROVE FUEL ECONOMY

CHILTON'S FUEL ECONOMY & TUNE-UP TIPS

Fuel economy is important to everyone, no matter what kind of vehicle you drive. The maintenance-minded motorist can save both money and fuel using these tips and the periodic maintenance and tune-up procedures in this Repair and Tune-Up Guide.

There are more than 130,000,000 cars and trucks registered for private use in the United States. Each travels an average of 10-12,000 miles per year, and, and in total they consume close to 70 billion gallons of fuel each year. This represents nearly ⅔ of the oil imported by the United States each year. The Federal government's goal is to reduce consumption 10% by 1985. A variety of methods are either already in use or under serious consideration, and they all affect you driving and the cars you will drive. In addition to "down-sizing", the auto industry is using or investigating the use of electronic fuel delivery, electronic engine controls and alternative engines for use in smaller and lighter vehicles, among other alternatives to meet the federally mandated Corporate Average Fuel Economy (CAFE) of 27.5 mpg by 1985. The government, for its part, is considering rationing, mandatory driving curtailments and tax increases on motor vehicle fuel in an effort to reduce consumption. The government's goal of a 10% reduction could be realized — and further government regulation avoided — if every private vehicle could use just 1 less gallon of fuel per week.

How Much Can You Save?

Tests have proven that almost anyone can make at least a 10% reduction in fuel consumption through regular maintenance and tune-ups. When a major manufacturer of spark plugs sur-

TUNE-UP

1. Check the cylinder compression to be sure the engine will really benefit from a tune-up and that it is capable of producing good fuel economy. A tune-up will be wasted on an engine in poor mechanical condition.

2. Replace spark plugs regularly. New spark plugs alone can increase fuel economy 3%.

3. Be sure the spark plugs are the correct type (heat range) for your vehicle. See the Tune-Up Specifications.

Heat range refers to the spark plug's ability to conduct heat away from the firing end. It must conduct the heat away in an even pattern to avoid becoming a source of pre-ignition, yet it must also operate hot enough to burn off conductive deposits that could cause misfiring.

The heat range is usually indicated by a number on the spark plug, part of the manufacturer's designation for each individual spark plug. The numbers in bold-face indicate the heat range in each manufacturer's identification system.

Manufacturer	Typical Designation
AC	R **45** TS
Bosch (old)	WA **145** T30
Bosch (new)	HR **8** Y
Champion	RBL **15** Y
Fram/Autolite	4**15**
Mopar	P-**62** PR
Motorcraft	BRF-**42**
NGK	BP **5** ES-15
Nippondenso	W **16** EP
Prestolite	14GR **5** 2A

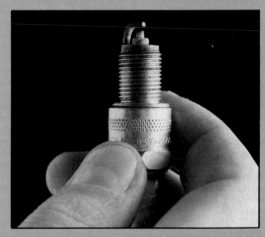

Periodically, check the spark plugs to be sure they are firing efficiently. They are excellent indicators of the internal condition of your engine.

On AC, Bosch (new), Champion, Fram/Autolite, Mopar, Motorcraft and Prestolite, a higher number indicates a hotter plug. On Bosch (old), NGK and Nippondenso, a higher number indicates a colder plug.

4. Make sure the spark plugs are properly gapped. See the Tune-Up Specifications in this book.

5. Be sure the spark plugs are firing efficiently. The illustrations on the next 2 pages show you how to "read" the firing end of the spark plug.

6. Check the ignition timing and set it to specifications. Tests show that almost all cars have incorrect ignition timing by more than 2°.

veyed over 6,000 cars nationwide, they found that a tune-up, on cars that needed one, increased fuel economy over 11%. Replacing worn plugs alone, accounted for a 3% increase. The same test also revealed that 8 out of every 10 vehicles will have some maintenance deficiency that will directly affect fuel economy, emissions or performance. Most of this mileage-robbing neglect could be prevented with regular maintenance.

Modern engines require that all of the functioning systems operate properly for maximum efficiency. A malfunction anywhere wastes fuel. You can keep your vehicle running as efficiently and economically as possible, by being aware of your vehicle's operating and performance characteristics. If your vehicle suddenly develops performance or fuel economy problems it could be due to one or more of the following:

PROBLEM	POSSIBLE CAUSE
Engine Idles Rough	Ignition timing, idle mixture, vacuum leak or something amiss in the emission control system.
Hesitates on Acceleration	Dirty carburetor or fuel filter, improper accelerator pump setting, ignition timing or fouled spark plugs.
Starts Hard or Fails to Start	Worn spark plugs, improperly set automatic choke, ice (or water) in fuel system.
Stalls Frequently	Automatic choke improperly adjusted and possible dirty air filter or fuel filter.
Performs Sluggishly	Worn spark plugs, dirty fuel or air filter, ignition timing or automatic choke out of adjustment.

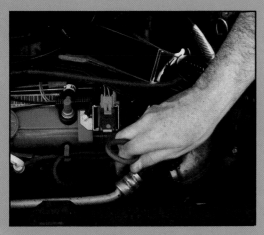

Check spark plug wires on conventional point type ignition for cracks by bending them in a loop around your finger.

Be sure that spark plug wires leading to adjacent cylinders do not run too close together. (Photo courtesy Champion Spark Plug Co.)

7. If your vehicle does not have electronic ignition, check the points, rotor and cap as specified.

8. Check the spark plug wires (used with conventional point-type ignitions) for cracks and burned or broken insulation by bending them in a loop around your finger. Cracked wires decrease fuel efficiency by failing to deliver full voltage to the spark plugs. One misfiring spark plug can cost you as much as 2 mpg.

9. Check the routing of the plug wires. Misfiring can be the result of spark plug leads to adjacent cylinders running parallel to each other and too close together. One wire tends to pick up voltage from the other causing it to fire "out of time".

10. Check all electrical and ignition circuits for voltage drop and resistance.

11. Check the distributor mechanical and/or vacuum advance mechanisms for proper functioning. The vacuum advance can be checked by twisting the distributor plate in the opposite direction of rotation. It should spring back when released.

12. Check and adjust the valve clearance on engines with mechanical lifters. The clearance should be slightly loose rather than too tight.

SPARK PLUG DIAGNOSIS

Normal

APPEARANCE: This plug is typical of one operating normally. The insulator nose varies from a light tan to grayish color with slight electrode wear. The presence of slight deposits is normal on used plugs and will have no adverse effect on engine performance. The spark plug heat range is correct for the engine and the engine is running normally.

CAUSE: Properly running engine.

RECOMMENDATION: Before reinstalling this plug, the electrodes should be cleaned and filed square. Set the gap to specifications. If the plug has been in service for more than 10-12,000 miles, the entire set should probably be replaced with a fresh set of the same heat range.

Oil Deposits

APPEARANCE: The firing end of the plug is covered with a wet, oily coating.

CAUSE: The problem is poor oil control. On high mileage engines, oil is leaking past the rings or valve guides into the combustion chamber. A common cause is also a plugged PCV valve, and a ruptured fuel pump diaphragm can also cause this condition. Oil fouled plugs such as these are often found in new or recently overhauled engines, before normal oil control is achieved, and can be cleaned and reinstalled.

RECOMMENDATION: A hotter spark plug may temporarily relieve the problem, but the engine is probably in need of work.

Incorrect Heat Range

APPEARANCE: The effects of high temperature on a spark plug are indicated by clean white, often blistered insulator. This can also be accompanied by excessive wear of the electrode, and the absence of deposits.

CAUSE: Check for the correct spark plug heat range. A plug which is too hot for the engine can result in overheating. A car operated mostly at high speeds can require a colder plug. Also check ignition timing, cooling system level, fuel mixture and leaking intake manifold.

RECOMMENDATION: If all ignition and engine adjustments are known to be correct, and no other malfunction exists, install spark plugs one heat range colder.

Photos Courtesy Fram Corporation

Carbon Deposits

APPEARANCE: Carbon fouling is easily identified by the presence of dry, soft, black, sooty deposits.

CAUSE: Changing the heat range can often lead to carbon fouling, as can prolonged slow, stop-and-start driving. If the heat range is correct, carbon fouling can be attributed to a rich fuel mixture, sticking choke, clogged air cleaner, worn breaker points, retarded timing or low compression. If only one or two plugs are carbon fouled, check for corroded or cracked wires on the affected plugs. Also look for cracks in the distributor cap between the towers of affected cylinders.

RECOMMENDATION: After the problem is corrected, these plugs can be cleaned and reinstalled if not worn severely.

MMT Fouled

APPEARANCE: Spark plugs fouled by MMT (Methycyclopentadienyl Maganese Tricarbonyl) have reddish, rusty appearance on the insulator and side electrode.

CAUSE: MMT is an anti-knock additive in gasoline used to replace lead. During the combustion process, the MMT leaves a reddish deposit on the insulator and side electrode.

RECOMMENDATION: No engine malfunction is indicated and the deposits will not affect plug performance any more than lead deposits (see Ash Deposits). MMT fouled plugs can be cleaned, regapped and reinstalled.

High Speed Glazing

APPEARANCE: Glazing appears as shiny coating on the plug, either yellow or tan in color.

CAUSE: During hard, fast acceleration, plug temperatures rise suddenly. Deposits from normal combustion have no chance to fluff-off; instead, they melt on the insulator forming an electrically conductive coating which causes misfiring.

RECOMMENDATION: Glazed plugs are not easily cleaned. They should be replaced with a fresh set of plugs of the correct heat range. If the condition recurs, using plugs with a heat range one step colder may cure the problem.

Ash (Lead) Deposits

APPEARANCE: Ash deposits are characterized by light brown or white colored deposits crusted on the side or center electrodes. In some cases it may give the plug a rusty appearance.

CAUSE: Ash deposits are normally derived from oil or fuel additives burned during normal combustion. Normally they are harmless, though excessive amounts can cause misfiring. If deposits are excessive in short mileage, the valve guides may be worn.

RECOMMENDATION: Ash-fouled plugs can be cleaned, gapped and reinstalled.

Detonation

APPEARANCE: Detonation is usually characterized by a broken plug insulator.

CAUSE: A portion of the fuel charge will begin to burn spontaneously, from the increased heat following ignition. The explosion that results applies extreme pressure to engine components, frequently damaging spark plugs and pistons.

Detonation can result by over-advanced ignition timing, inferior gasoline (low octane) lean air/fuel mixture, poor carburetion, engine lugging or an increase in compression ratio due to combustion chamber deposits or engine modification.

RECOMMENDATION: Replace the plugs after correcting the problem.

Photos Courtesy Champion Spark Plug Co.

EMISSION CONTROLS

13. Be aware of the general condition of the emission control system. It contributes to reduced pollution and should be serviced regularly to maintain efficient engine operation.

14. Check all vacuum lines for dried, cracked or brittle conditions. Something as simple as a leaking vacuum hose can cause poor performance and loss of economy.

15. Avoid tampering with the emission control system. Attempting to improve fuel econ-

FUEL SYSTEM

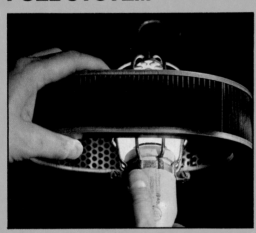

Check the air filter with a light behind it. If you can see light through the filter it can be reused.

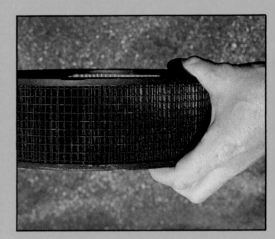

Extremely clogged filters should be discarded and replaced with a new one.

18. Replace the air filter regularly. A dirty air filter richens the air/fuel mixture and can increase fuel consumption as much as 10%. Tests show that 1/3 of all vehicles have air filters in need of replacement.

19. Replace the fuel filter at least as often as recommended.

20. Set the idle speed and carburetor mixture to specifications.

21. Check the automatic choke. A sticking or malfunctioning choke wastes gas.

22. During the summer months, adjust the automatic choke for a leaner mixture which will produce faster engine warm-ups.

COOLING SYSTEM

29. Be sure all accessory drive belts are in good condition. Check for cracks or wear.

30. Adjust all accessory drive belts to proper tension.

31. Check all hoses for swollen areas, worn spots, or loose clamps.

32. Check coolant level in the radiator or expansion tank.

33. Be sure the thermostat is operating properly. A stuck thermostat delays engine warm-up and a cold engine uses nearly twice as much fuel as a warm engine.

34. Drain and replace the engine coolant at least as often as recommended. Rust and scale

TIRES & WHEELS

38. Check the tire pressure often with a pencil type gauge. Tests by a major tire manufacturer show that 90% of all vehicles have at least 1 tire improperly inflated. Better mileage can be achieved by over-inflating tires, but never exceed the maximum inflation pressure on the side of the tire.

39. If possible, install radial tires. Radial tires deliver as much as 1/2 mpg more than bias belted tires.

40. Avoid installing super-wide tires. They only create extra rolling resistance and decrease fuel mileage. Stick to the manufacturer's recommendations.

41. Have the wheels properly balanced.

omy by tampering with emission controls is more likely to worsen fuel economy than improve it. Emission control changes on modern engines are not readily reversible.

16. Clean (or replace) the EGR valve and lines as recommended.

17. Be sure that all vacuum lines and hoses are reconnected properly after working under the hood. An unconnected or misrouted vacuum line can wreak havoc with engine performance.

23. Check for fuel leaks at the carburetor, fuel pump, fuel lines and fuel tank. Be sure all lines and connections are tight.

24. Periodically check the tightness of the carburetor and intake manifold attaching nuts and bolts. These are a common place for vacuum leaks to occur.

25. Clean the carburetor periodically and lubricate the linkage.

26. The condition of the tailpipe can be an excellent indicator of proper engine combustion. After a long drive at highway speeds, the inside of the tailpipe should be a light grey in color. Black or soot on the insides indicates an overly rich mixture.

27. Check the fuel pump pressure. The fuel pump may be supplying more fuel than the engine needs.

28. Use the proper grade of gasoline for your engine. Don't try to compensate for knocking or "pinging" by advancing the ignition timing. This practice will only increase plug temperature and the chances of detonation or pre-ignition with relatively little performance gain.

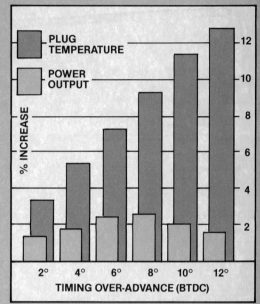

Increasing ignition timing past the specified setting results in a drastic increase in spark plug temperature with increased chance of detonation or preignition. Performance increase is considerably less. (Photo courtesy Champion Spark Plug Co.)

that form in the engine should be flushed out to allow the engine to operate at peak efficiency.

35. Clean the radiator of debris that can decrease cooling efficiency.

36. Install a flex-type or electric cooling fan, if you don't have a clutch type fan. Flex fans use curved plastic blades to push more air at low speeds when more cooling is needed; at high speeds the blades flatten out for less resistance. Electric fans only run when the engine temperature reaches a predetermined level.

37. Check the radiator cap for a worn or cracked gasket. If the cap does not seal properly, the cooling system will not function properly.

42. Be sure the front end is correctly aligned. A misaligned front end actually has wheels going in differed directions. The increased drag can reduce fuel economy by .3 mpg.

43. Correctly adjust the wheel bearings. Wheel bearings that are adjusted too tight increase rolling resistance.

Check tire pressures regularly with a reliable pocket type gauge. Be sure to check the pressure on a cold tire.

GENERAL MAINTENANCE

Check the fluid levels (particularly engine oil) on a regular basis. Be sure to check the oil for grit, water or other contamination.

A vacuum gauge is another excellent indicator o internal engine condition and can also be installed i the dash as a mileage indicator.

44. Periodically check the fluid levels in the engine, power steering pump, master cylinder, automatic transmission and drive axle.

45. Change the oil at the recommended interval and change the filter at every oil change. Dirty oil is thick and causes extra friction between moving parts, cutting efficiency and increasing wear. A worn engine requires more frequent tune-ups and gets progressively worse fuel economy. In general, use the lightest viscosity oil for the driving conditions you will encounter.

46. Use the recommended viscosity fluids in the transmission and axle.

47. Be sure the battery is fully charged for fast starts. A slow starting engine wastes fuel.

48. Be sure battery terminals are clean and tight.

49. Check the battery electrolyte level and add distilled water if necessary.

50. Check the exhaust system for crushed pipes, blockages and leaks.

51. Adjust the brakes. Dragging brakes o brakes that are not releasing create increased drag on the engine.

52. Install a vacuum gauge or miles-per gallon gauge. These gauges visually indicate engine vacuum in the intake manifold. High vacuum = good mileage and low vacuum = poorer mileage. The gauge can also be an ex cellent indicator of internal engine conditions.

53. Be sure the clutch is properly adjusted. A slipping clutch wastes fuel.

54. Check and periodically lubricate the hea control valve in the exhaust manifold. A sticking or inoperative valve prevents engine warm-up and wastes gas.

55. Keep accurate records to check fue economy over a period of time. A sudden drop in fuel economy may signal a need for tune-up or other maintenance.

① **ATTACH RUBBER BAND TO INTER-MEDIATE CHOKE LEVER.**

② **OPEN THROTTLE TO ALLOW CHOKE VALVE TO CLOSE.**

③ **SET UP ANGLE GAGE AND SET ANGLE TO SPECIFICATIONS.**

④ **HOLD THROTTLE LEVER IN WIDE OPEN POSITION.**

⑤ **PUSH ON CHOKE SHAFT LEVER TO OPEN CHOKE VALVE AND TO MAKE CONTACT WITH BLACK CLOSING TANG.**

⑥ **ADJUST BY BENDING TANG UNTIL BUBBLE IS CENTERED.**

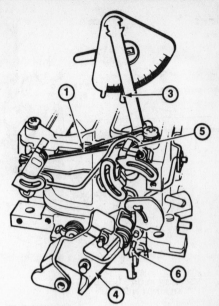

E2SE choke unloader adjustment

mand Control (C3) system. As with the E2SE 2-bbl, the electric mixture control solenoid is mounted in the float bowl, and is used to control the air/fuel mixture in the primary bores of the carburetor. The plunger in the solenoid is controlled, or pulsed, by electrical signals received from the Electronic Control Module.

An Idle Speed Control (ISC) assembly, monitored by the ECM, controls engine idle speed. The curb (base) idle is programmed into the ECM and is not adjustable. When the throttle lever is resting against the ISC plunger, the ISC acts as a dashpot on throttle closing. An Idle Speed Solenoid or Idle Load Compensator is used on some models to position the primary throttle valve, providing engine idle speed requirements.

On E4MC models, an Idle Load Compensator (ILC) mounted on the float bowl is used to control curb idle speeds. The ILC used manifold vacuum to sense changes in engine load (the A/C compressor clutch engaged, for example) and compensates by adjusting throttle angle for the curb idle speed. The ILC uses a spring loaded vacuum-sensitive diaphragm whose plunger either extends (vacuum decrease) or retracts (vacuum increase) to adjust throttle angle for curb idle speeds. Both the ISC and ILC are factory adjusted.

Float Level

With the air horn assembly removed, measure the distance from the air horn gasket surface (gasket removed) to the top of the float at the toe ($\frac{1}{16}$″ back from the toe).

NOTE: *Make sure the retaining pin is firmly held in place and that the tang of the float is lightly held against the needle and seat assembly.*

Remove the float and bend the float arm to adjust except on carburetors used with the computer controlled systems (E4MC and E4ME). For those carburetors, if the float level is too high, hold the retainer firmly in place and push down on the center of the float to adjust. If the float level is too low on models with the computer controlled system, lift out the metering rods. Remove the solenoid connector screw. Turn the lean mixture solenoid screw in clockwise, counting and recording the exact number of turns until the screw is lightly bottomed in the bowl. Then turn the screw out clockwise and remove. Lift out the solenoid and connector. Remove the float and bend the arm up to adjust. Install the parts, turning the mixture solenoid screw in until it is lightly bottomed, then unscrewing it the exact number of turns counted earlier.

Accelerator Pump

The accelerator pump is not adjustable on computer controlled carburetors (E4MC and E4ME).

1. Close the primary throttle valves by backing out the slow idle screw and making sure that the fast idle cam follower is off the steps of the fast idle cam.

2. Bend the secondary throttle closing tang away from the primary throttle lever, if neces-

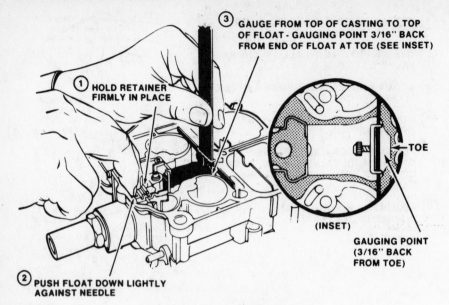

③ **GAUGE FROM TOP OF CASTING TO TOP OF FLOAT - GAUGING POINT 3/16" BACK FROM END OF FLOAT AT TOE (SEE INSET)**

① **HOLD RETAINER FIRMLY IN PLACE**

← **TOE**

(INSET)

GAUGING POINT (3/16" BACK FROM TOE)

② **PUSH FLOAT DOWN LIGHTLY AGAINST NEEDLE**

E4ME/MC float level adjustment

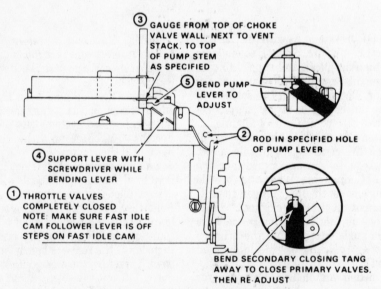

③ **GAUGE FROM TOP OF CHOKE VALVE WALL, NEXT TO VENT STACK, TO TOP OF PUMP STEM AS SPECIFIED**

⑤ **BEND PUMP LEVER TO ADJUST**

② **ROD IN SPECIFIED HOLE OF PUMP LEVER**

④ **SUPPORT LEVER WITH SCREWDRIVER WHILE BENDING LEVER**

① **THROTTLE VALVES COMPLETELY CLOSED NOTE: MAKE SURE FAST IDLE CAM FOLLOWER LEVER IS OFF STEPS ON FAST IDLE CAM**

BEND SECONDARY CLOSING TANG AWAY TO CLOSE PRIMARY VALVES, THEN RE-ADJUST

Accelerator pump adjustment, E4ME/MC 4-bbl.

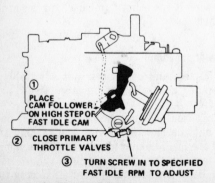

① **PLACE CAM FOLLOWER ON HIGH STEP OF FAST IDLE CAM**

② **CLOSE PRIMARY THROTTLE VALVES**

③ **TURN SCREW IN TO SPECIFIED FAST IDLE RPM TO ADJUST**

Fast idle adjustment, E4ME/MC

sary, to insure that the primary throttle valves are fully closed.

3. With the pump in the appropriate hole in the pump lever, measure from the top of the choke valve wall to the top of the pump stem.

4. To adjust, bend the pump lever.

5. After adjusting, readjust the secondary throttle tang and the slow idle screw.

GASOLINE FUEL INJECTION SYSTEM

CAUTION: *The 220 TBI Unit introduced in 1986 has a bleed in the pressure regulator to*

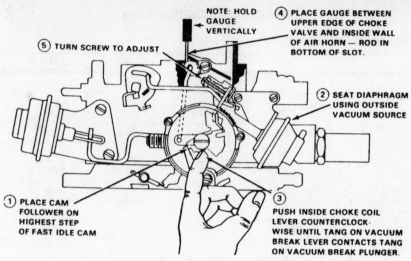

NOTE: HOLD GAUGE VERTICALLY

⑤ TURN SCREW TO ADJUST

④ PLACE GAUGE BETWEEN UPPER EDGE OF CHOKE VALVE AND INSIDE WALL OF AIR HORN — ROD IN BOTTOM OF SLOT.

② SEAT DIAPHRAGM USING OUTSIDE VACUUM SOURCE

① PLACE CAM FOLLOWER ON HIGHEST STEP OF FAST IDLE CAM

③ PUSH INSIDE CHOKE COIL LEVER COUNTERCLOCK-WISE UNTIL TANG ON VACUUM BREAK LEVER CONTACTS TANG ON VACUUM BREAK PLUNGER.

E4ME/MC front vacuum break adjustment

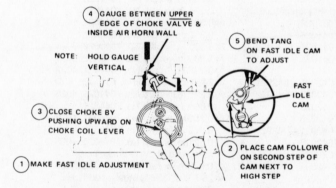

④ GAUGE BETWEEN UPPER EDGE OF CHOKE VALVE & INSIDE AIR HORN WALL

⑤ BEND TANG ON FAST IDLE CAM TO ADJUST

NOTE: HOLD GAUGE VERTICAL

FAST IDLE CAM

③ CLOSE CHOKE BY PUSHING UPWARD ON CHOKE COIL LEVER

① MAKE FAST IDLE ADJUSTMENT

② PLACE CAM FOLLOWER ON SECOND STEP OF CAM NEXT TO HIGH STEP

Choke rod (fast idle cam) adjustment—E4ME/MC

① ATTACH RUBBER BAND TO GREEN TANG OF INTERMEDIATE CHOKE SHAFT.

② OPEN THROTTLE TO ALLOW CHOKE VALVE TO CLOSE.

③ SET UP ANGLE GAGE AND SET ANGLE TO SPECIFICATION.

④ RETRACT VACUUM BREAK PLUNGER, USING VACUUM SOURCE, AT LEAST 18" HG. PLUG AIR BLEED HOLES WHERE APPLICABLE.

④A ON QUADRAJETS, AIR VALVE ROD MUST NOT RESTRICT PLUNGER FROM RETRACTING FULLY. IF NECESSARY, BEND ROD HERE TO PERMIT FULL PLUNGER TRAVEL. WHERE APPLICABLE, PLUNGER STEM MUST BE EXTENDED FULLY TO COMPRESS PLUNGER BUCKING SPRING.

⑤ TO CENTER BUBBLE, EITHER:
A. ADJUST WITH 1/8" HEX WRENCH (VACUUM STILL APPLIED)

-OR-

B. SUPPORT AT "S" AND BEND VACUUM BREAK ROD (VACUUM STILL APPLIED)

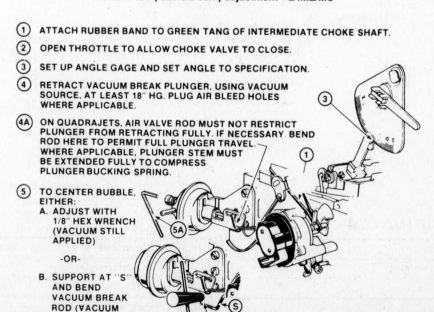

E4ME/MC rear vacuum break adjustment

Carburetor Specifications

ROCHESTER MV (1970–74)

	1970	1971	1972	1973	1974
Float Level (in.)	¼	¼	¼	¼	¼ ⑮
Fast idle					
Mechanical (in.)	0.100	0.100	—	—	—
Running (rpm)	2400	2400	2400	2400	1800 ⑯
Choke Rod (in.)	0.180 ①	0.180 ④	⑦	⑪	.0245 ⑰
Vacuum Break (in.)	0.260 ②	0.350 ⑤	0.190 ⑧	0.430 ⑫	0.300 ⑱
Choke Unloader (in.)	0.350	0.350	0.500	0.600 ⑬	0.500 ⑲
Thermostat Choke Rod (in.)	③	—	—	—	—
Metering Rod (in.)	0.070	0.070 ⑥	0.070 ⑨	0.070 ⑭	0.080 ⑳
CEC Valve (rpm)	NA	㉑	⑩	⑩	—

—Not applicable
① W/292 cu in. engine—0.275 in.
② W/292 cu in. engine—0.350 in.
③ Bottom of the rod even with top of hole
④ 0.300 in. w/carb No. 7021022
  0.275 in. w/carb No. 7041026
⑤ 0.230 in. w/carb No. 7041021
  0.260 in. w/carb No. 7041025
⑥ 0.080 in. w/carb No. 7041021
⑦ 0.150 in. w/carb No. 7042021, 7042921
  0.125 in. w/carb No. 7042022, 7042922
  0.180 in. w/carb No. 7042025
  0.275 in. w/carb No. 7042026
⑧ 0.225 in. w/carb No. 7042021, 7042921
  0.260 in. w/carb No. 7042025
  0.350 in. w/carb No. 7042026
⑨ 0.076 in. w/carb No. 7042991
  0.078 in. w/carb No. 7042021
  0.079 in. w/carb No. 7042022
⑩ 250 cu in. only—1000 (manual/Neutral)
          —650 (automatic/Drive)

⑪ 0.245 in. w/carb No. 7043022
  0.275 in. w/carb No. 7043021
  0.350 in. w/carb No. 7043025
  0.375 in. w/carb No. 7043026
⑫ 0.300 in. w/carb No. 7043022
  0.350 in. w/carb No. 7043021
⑬ 0.500 in. w/carb No. 7043022, 3021
⑭ 0.080 in. w/carb No. 7043022, 3021
⑮ 0.295 in. w/carb No. 7044021, 4022, 4321
⑯ 2400 rpm w/carb No. 7044025, 4026
⑰ 0.275 in. w/carb No. 7044021, 4026
  0.300 in. w/carb No. 7044321
⑱ 0.350 in. w/carb No. 7044021, 4026
  0.375 in. w/carb No. 7044321
⑲ 0.521 in. w/carb No. 7044025, 4026
  measured at top of choke blade
⑳ 0.070 in. w/carb No. 7044025, 4026
㉑ 250, 292, 307 Manual—1000 rpm
  350V8 Manual—900 rpm
  402V8 Manual—850 rpm
  250, 292 Automatic—750
  350, 307V8 Automatic—650
  402V8 Automatic—650

ROCHESTER MV (1975)

Float Level (in.)	¹¹⁄₃₂	Primary Vacuum Break (in.)	0.300 ②
Metering Rod (in.)	0.080	Auxiliary Vacuum Break (in.)	③
Choke Rod (in.)	①	Choke Unloader (in.)	0.325 ④

① 0.245 w/carb No. 7045004, 302, 304
  0.260 in. w/carb No. 7045002
  0.275 in. w/carb No. 7045003, 005, 303, 305
② 0.350 in. w/carb No. 7045005, 303, 305

③ 0.150 in. w/carb No. 7045004, 302
  0.170 in. w/carb No. 7045303
  0.290 in. w/carb No. 7045002, 003, 005, 304, 305
④ 0.275 in. w/carb No. 7045302, 303

Carburetor Specifications (cont.)

ROCHESTER MV (1976)

Carburetor Number	Float Level (in.)	Metering Rod (in.)	Choke Rod (Fast Idle Cam) (in.)	Primary Vacuum Break (in.)	Auxiliary Vacuum Break (in.)	Choke Unloader (in.)
17056002	11/32	0.080	0.130	0.165	0.265	0.335
6003	11/32	0.080	0.145	0.180	W.O.	0.335
6302	11/32	0.080	0.155	0.190	W.O.	0.325
6303	11/32	0.080	0.180	0.225	W.O.	0.325
6004	11/32	0.080	0.130	0.165	0.265	0.335
6006	1/4	0.080	0.130	0.165	—	0.270
6007	1/4	0.070	0.130	0.165	—	0.275
6008, 6009, 6308, 6309	1/4	0.070	0.150	0.190	—	0.275

ROCHESTER ME (1977)

Carburetor Number	Float Level (in.)	Metering Rod (in.)	Choke Rod (Fast Idle Cam) (in.)	Primary Vacuum Break (in.)	Auxiliary Vacuum Break (in.)	Choke Unloader (in.)
17057001	3/8	0.080	0.125	0.150	—	0.325
7002, 7004, 7101, 7302	3/8	0.080	0.110	0.135	—	0.325
7005	3/8	0.080	0.125	0.180	—	0.325
7006, 7007	5/16	0.070	0.150	0.180	—	0.275
7008, 7009, 7308, 7309	5/16	0.065	0.150	0.180	—	0.275
7303	3/8	0.090	0.125	0.150	—	0.325

ROCHESTER ME (1978)

Carburetor Number	Float Level (in.)	Metering Rod (in.)	Choke Rod (Fast Idle Cam) (in.)	Primary Vacuum Break (in.)	Auxiliary Vacuum Break (in.)	Choke Unloader (in.)
17058008, 8009, 8308, 8309, 8358, 8359	5/16	0.065	0.275	0.275	—	0.520
8006, 8007	5/16	0.070	0.275	0.275	—	0.520
8310, 8312, 8320, 8322	5/16	0.080	0.190	0.250	—	0.600
8311, 8313, 8323	5/16	0.100	0.190	0.250	—	0.600
8021, 8022, 8024, 8081, 8082, 8084	5/16	—	0.200	0.250	—	0.450

ROCHESTER ME (1979)

Carburetor Number	Float Level (in.)	Metering Rod (in.)	Choke Rod (Fast Idle Cam) (in.)	Primary Vacuum Break (in.)	Auxiliary Vacuum Break (in.)	Choke Unloader (in.)
17059009, 9309, 9359	5/16	0.065	0.275	0.400	—	0.521

Carburetor Specifications (cont.)

ROCHESTER ME (1980–86)

Carburetor Number	Float Level (in.)	Metering Rod (in.)	Choke Rod (Fast Idle Cam) (in.)	Primary Vacuum Break (in.)	Auxiliary Vacuum Break (in.)	Choke Unloader (in.)
17080009, 0309, 0359, 1309	11/32	0.090	0.275	0.400	—	0.520
17085009						
17084329						
17085009						
1009, 1329,						
17085036						
17085044						

ROCHESTER 2GV, 2GC

	(2GV) 1970	(2GV) 1971	(2GV) 1972	(2GV) 1973	(2GV) 1974	(2GC) 1975	(2GC) 1976	(2GC) 1977–78
Float Level (in.)	23/32 ⑦	21/32 ①	21/32 ㉒	21/32 ⑬	19/32	21/32	21/32	19/32
Float Drop (in.)	1¾	1¾ ②	19/32	19/32	19/32	31/32	19/32	19/32
Pump Rod (in.)	—	13/64 ③	15/16 ㉓	15/16 ⑭	19/32 ⑱	1⅝	1 11/16	1 21/32
Choke Rod (in.) (Fast Idle Cam)	0.060	0.040 ④	0.040 ⑩	0.150 ⑮	0.200 ⑲	0.400	0.260	0.260
Vacuum Break (in.)	0.140 ⑧	0.080 ⑤	0.080 ⑪	0.080 ⑯	0.140 ⑳	0.130	0.130	0.130 ㉕㉖
Choke Unloader (in.)	0.215	0.215 ⑥	0.210 ㉔	0.215 ⑰	0.250 ㉑	0.350	0.325	0.325
Thermostatic Choke Rod	⑨	—	—	—	—	—	—	—
CEC Valve (rpm)	⑫	⑫	—	—	—	—	—	—
Fast Idle (rpm)	2200– 2400	—	1850 (1¼) 2200 (1½)	1600	1600	—	—	—

① 23/32 in. w/carb No. 7041138, 139
② 1¼ in. w/carb No. 7041138, 139
③ 15/32 in. w/carb No. 7041138, 139
④ 0.100 in. w/carb No. 7041138, 139
⑤ 0.170 in. w/carb No. 7041138
　0.180 in. w/carb No. 7041139
⑥ 0.325 in. w/carb No. 7041138, 139
⑦ 27/32 in. w/carb No. 7040108
⑧ 0.130 in. w/carb No. 7040108
⑨ Bottom of rod even with top of hole
⑩ 0.075 in. w/carb No. 7042824, 825
　0.100 in. w/carb No. 7042108
⑪ 0.110 in. w/carb No. 7042824, 825
　0.170 in. w/carb No. 7042108
⑫ 1000 w/Manual
　650 w/Automatic

⑬ 25/32 in. w/carb No. 7043108
⑭ 17/16 in. w/carb No. 7043108
⑮ 0.200 in. w/carb No. 7043108
⑯ 0.140 in. w/carb No. 7043108
⑰ 0.250 in. w/carb No. 7043108
⑱ 13/16 in. w/carb No. 7044114
⑲ 0.245 in. w/carb No. 7044114
⑳ 0.130 in. w/carb No. 7044114
㉑ 0.325 in. w/carb No. 7044114
㉒ 25/32 in. w/carb No. 7042108
㉓ 1½ in. w/carb No. 7042108
㉔ 0.325 in. w/carb No. 7042108
㉕ Below 22,500 mi
　0.160 above 22,500 mi
㉖ 0.190 in. w/carb No. 17056137
—Not applicable

NOTE: 2 versions of the 2GV are available: 1½ in. diameter and 1¼ in. diameter venturi.

Carburetor Specifications (cont.)

ROCHESTER 2SE (1979–82)

Carburetor Identification	Float Level (in.)	Pump Rod (in.)	Fast Idle (rpm)	Choke Coil Lever (in.)	Fast Idle Cam (deg./in.)	Air Valve Rod (in.)	Primary Vacuum Break (deg./in.)	Secondary Vacuum Break (deg./in.)	Choke Unloader (deg./in.)	Secondary Lockout (in.)
17059640	1/8	9/16	2000	0.085	17/.090	0.040	20/.110	37/.234	49/.341	.011–.040
17059641	1/8	9/16	1800	0.085	17/.090	0.040	23.5/.132	37/.234	49/.341	.011–.040
17059643	1/8	9/16	1800	0.085	17/.090	0.040	23.5/.132	37/.234	49/.341	.011–.040
17059740	1/8	9/16	2000	0.085	17/.090	0.040	20/.110	37/.234	49/.341	.011–.040
17059741	1/8	9/16	2100	0.085	17/.090	0.040	20/.110	37/.234	49/.341	.011–.040
17058764	1/8	9/16	2100	0.085	17/.090	0.040	20/.110	37/.234	49/.341	.011–.040
17059765	1/8	9/16	2100	0.085	17/.090	0.040	23.5/.132	37/.234	49/.341	.011–.040
17059767	1/8	9/16	2100	0.085	17/.090	0.040	23.5/.132	37/.234	49/.341	.011–.040
17080621	1/8	9/16	2000	0.085	17/.090	0.010	22/.123	35/.220	41/.269	.011–.040
17080622	1/8	9/16	2200	0.085	17/.090	0.010	22/.123	35/.220	41/.269	.011–.040
17080623	1/8	9/16	2000	0.085	17/.090	0.010	22/.123	35/.220	41/.269	.011–.040
17080626	1/8	9/16	2200	0.085	17/.090	0.010	22/.123	35/.220	41/.269	.011–.040
17080720	1/8	9/16	2200	0.085	17/.090	0.010	20/.110	35/.220	41/.269	.011–.040
17080721	1/8	9/16	2000	0.085	17/.090	0.010	23.5/.132	35/.220	41/.269	.011–.040
17080722	1/8	9/16	2200	0.085	17/.090	0.010	20/.110	35/.220	41/.269	.011–.040
17080723	1/8	9/16	2000	0.085	17/.090	0.010	23.5/.132	35/.220	41/.269	.011–.040
17081621	3/16	5/8	①	—	15/.077	②	26/.149	38/.243	38/.243	—
17081622	3/16	5/8	①	—	15/.077	②	26/.149	38/.243	38/.243	—
17081623	3/16	5/8	①	—	15/.077	②	26/.149	38/.243	38/.243	—
17081624	3/16	5/8	①	—	15/.077	②	26/.149	38/.243	38/.243	—
17081625	3/16	5/8	①	—	15/.077	②	26/.149	38/.243	38/.243	—
17081626	3/16	5/8	①	—	15/.077	②	26/.149	38/.243	38/.243	—
17081627	3/16	5/8	①	—	15/.077	②	26/.149	38/.243	38/.243	—
17081629	3/16	5/8	①	—	15/.077	②	24/.136	34/.211	41/.269	—
17081630	3/16	5/8	①	—	15/.077	②	26/.149	38/.243	38/.243	—
17081633	3/16	5/8	①	—	15/.077	②	26/.149	38/.243	38/.243	—
17081720	3/16	5/8	①	—	15/.077	②	30/.179	37/.234	41/.269	—
17081721	3/16	5/8	①	—	15/.077	②	30/.179	37/.234	41/.269	—
17081725	3/16	5/8	①	—	15/.077	②	30/.179	37/.234	41/.269	—
17081726	3/16	5/8	①	—	15/.077	②	30/.179	37/.234	41/.269	—
17081727	3/16	5/8	①	—	15/.077	②	30/.179	37/.234	41/.269	—

① See underhood specifications sticker
② 1° all carburetors

Carburetor Specifications (cont.)

ROCHESTER M2MC (1979–81)

Carburetor Identification	Float Level (in.)	Choke Rod (in.)	Choke Unloader (in.)	Front Vacuum Break (in.)	Pump Rod (in.)	Choke Coil Lever (in.)	Automatic Choke (notches)
All 1979	15/32	0.243	0.243	0.171	13/32 ①	0.120	1 Lean
All 1980	7/16	0.243	0.243	0.171	9/32 ①	0.120	②
All 1981	13/32	0.243	0.243	0.142	5/16	—	—

① Inner hole
② Riveted cover; replacement kits contain setting instructions

ROCHESTER 4MV

	1970	1971	1972	1973	1974	1975
Float Level (in.)	1/4	1/4 ④	⑥	⑨	⑫	⑯
Accelerator Pump (in.)	5/16	5/16	3/8	13/32	13/32	0.275
Fast Idle (rpm)	2400	2400	⑦	1600	1600 ⑬	1600
Choke Rod (in.)	0.100	0.100	0.100	0.430	0.430	0.430
Choke Vacuum Break (in.)	0.245 ①	0.260	0.215 ⑧	0.215 ⑩	0.215 ⑭	⑰
Choke Unloader (in.)	0.450	0.450	0.450	0.450	0.450	0.450
Thermostatic Choke Rod Setting	②	②	—	—	—	—
Air Valve Spring (in.)	7/16 ③	—	—	1/2 ⑪	7/8 ⑮	⑱
Air Valve Dashpot	0.020	0.020	0.020	—	—	0.015
CEC Valve (rpm)	—	⑤	—	—	—	—

—Not applicable
① 0.275 in. w/carb No. 7040511 and manual trans
　　　　　No. 7040509 and manual trans
② Top of rod should be even with bottom of hole
③ 13/16 in. w/all 396 cu in. V8
④ 11/32 in. w/carb No. 7041209
⑤ 350 V8 w/manual trans—900 rpm
　402 V8 w/manual trans—850 rpm
　350 V8 w/automatic trans—650 rpm
　402 V8 w/automatic trans—650 rpm
⑥ 1/4 in. w/carb No. 7042206, 218
　3/16 in. w/carb No. 7042208, 210, 211, 910, 911
　11/32 in. w/carb No. 7042207, 219
⑦ 1350—Manual transmission
　1500—Automatic transmission
⑧ 0.250 in. w/carb No. 7042206, 207, 218, 219
⑨ 7/32 in. w/carb No. 7043202, 203
　5/16 in. w/carb No. 7043208, 215
　1/4 in. w/carb No. 7043200, 216, 207, 507
⑩ 0.250 in. w/carb No. 7043200, 216
　0.275 in. w/carb No. 7043507
⑪ 11/16 in. w/carb No. 7043200, 216, 207, 507

⑫ 1/4 in. w/carb No. 7044202, 502, 203, 503, 218, 518, 219, 519
　11/32 in. w/carb No. 7044213, 513
　0.675 in. w/carb No. 7044212, 217, 512, 517, 500, 520
⑬ 1700 rpm in. w/carb No. 7044212, 217, 512, 517
⑭ 0.220 in. w/carb No. 7044223, 227
　0.230 in. w/carb No. 7044212, 217, 512, 517
　0.250 in. w/carb No. 7044500, 520
⑮ 7/16 in. w/carb No. 7044223, 227, 212, 217, 512, 517, 500, 520
⑯ 3/8 in. w/carb No. 7045212
　11/32 in. w/carb No. 7045213, 229, 583, 589
　15/32 in. w/carb No. 7045229
⑰ 0.225 in. w/carb No. 7045212
　0.210 in. w/carb No. 7045213
　0.200 in. w/carb No. 7045229
　0.230 in. w/carb No. 7045583, 589
⑱ 7/16 in. w/carb No. 7045212
　7/8 in. w/carb No. 7045213, 583
　3/4 in. w/carb No. 7045229, 589

Carburetor Specifications (cont.)

ROCHESTER 4MV (1976)

Carburetor Number	Float Level (in.)	Vacuum Break (in.)	Air Valve Spring Windup (in.)
7045231	11/32	0.145	7/8
7045229	11/32	0.138	3/4
7045583	11/32	0.155	7/8
7045588	11/32	0.155	3/4
17056212	3/8	0.155	7/16

ROCHESTER 4MV (1977)

Carburetor Number	Float Level (in.)	Vacuum Break (in.)	Air Valve Spring Windup (in.)
7045583	11/32	0.120	7/8
17056212	3/8	0.120	7/16
17057213	11/32	0.115	7/8

NOTE: Pump Rod: 9/32 in. in all applications
Air Valve Dashpot: 0.015 in. in all applications
Choke Unloader: 0.295 in. except 17057213: 0.205 in.
Choke Rod (Fash Idle Cam): 0.290 in. except 17057213: 0.220 in.

ROCHESTER M4MC, M4MCA (1975)

Carburetor Number	Float Level (in.)	Choke Rod (Fast Idle Cam) (in.)	Front Vacuum Break (in.)	Rear Vacuum Break (in.)	Choke Unloader (in.)	Choke Setting
7045202, 203	15/32	0.300	0.180	0.170	0.325	*
7045220	17/32	0.300	0.200	0.550	0.325	*
7045512	17/32	0.300	0.180	0.550	0.325	*

ROCHESTER M4MC (1976)

Carburetor Number	Float Level (in.)	Choke Rod (Fast Idle Cam) (in.)	Front Vacuum Break (in.)	Rear Vacuum Break (in.)	Choke Unloader (in.)	Choke Setting
17056208, 508	**	0.325	0.185	—	0.325	2 NL
17056209	**	0.325	0.185	—	0.325	3 NL
17056509	**	0.325	0.185	—	0.325	1 NL
17056512	7/16	0.325	0.185	—	0.275	Index

ROCHESTER M4MC (1977)

Carburetor Number	Float Level (in.)	Choke Rod (Fast Idle Cam) (in.)	Front Vacuum Break (in.)	Rear Vacuum Break (in.)	Choke Unloader (in.)	Choke Setting
17057202, 204	15/32	0.325	0.160	—	0.280	2 NL
17057209	7/16	0.325	0.160	—	0.325	3 NL
17057229	11/32	0.285	0.160	—	0.280	2 NL
17057502, 504	15/32	0.325	0.165	—	0.280	2 NL
17057503	15/32	0.325	0.165	—	0.280	1 NL
17057512	7/16	0.285	0.165	—	0.240	Index
17057529	11/32	0.285	0.175	—	0.280	2 NL
17057582, 584	15/32	0.385	0.180	—	0.280	2 NL

ROCHESTER M4ME (1976–77)

Carburetor Number	Float Level (in.)	Choke Rod (Fast Idle Cam) (in.)	Front Vacuum Break (in.)	Rear Vacuum Break (in.)	Choke Unloader (in.)	Choke Setting
17056221	7/16	0.300	—	0.160	0.325	2 NR
17057221	3/8	0.385	—	0.160	0.280	2 Notches Counter-clockwise

Inner Pump Rod Setting: 0.275 in.—1975; 9/32 in.—1976; 9/32 in.—1977 except: 17057582, 584: 3/8 in. Outer Pump Rod only
Choke Coil Lever: 0.120 in. all years
Air Valve Dashpot: 0.015 in. all years
Air Valve Spring Windup: 7/8 in. all years except:

7045220, 512: 9/16 in. 1975 only
NL: Notches Lean
NR: Notches Rich
* Choke valve setting is at the top of the valve
** Needle seat with groove at upper edge: 5/16 in. Need seat without groove at upper edge: 7/16 in.

Carburetor Specifications (cont.)

ROCHESTER M4MC, 4MV (1978)

Float Adjustment: (in.)	
17058212, 8218, 8219, 8222, 8525	7/16
8500, 8501, 8520, 8521	3/8
8512	13/32
All others	15/32

Pump Adjustment: (in.)	
17058509, 8510, 8586, 8558	11/32 Outer
All others	9/32 Inner

Choke Coil: (in.)	
All	0.120

Choke Setting	
17058512	Index
8201, 8219, 8500, 8501, 8520, 8521	3 NL
8218, 8222, 8509, 8510, 8586, 8588	2 NL
All others	1 NL

Air Valve Spring Windup:	
17058525	3/4 turn
All others	7/8 turn

ROCHESTER M4MC (1979)

Float Adjustment: (in.)	
17059212	7/16
512	13/32
520, 521	3/8
All others	15/32

Pump Adjustment: (in.)	
17059212, 213, 215, 229, 510, 512, 513, 515, 520, 521, 529	3/32 Inner
377, 378, 527, 528	9/32 Outer
All others	13/32 Inner

Choke Coil Lever: (in.)	
All	0.120

Choke Rod: (in.)	
17059213, 215, 229, 513, 515, 529	0.234
All others	0.314

Air Valve Rod: (in.)	
All	0.015

Unloader Adjustment: (in.)	
17059212, 213, 215, 229, 512, 513, 515, 529	0.260
All others	0.277

Front Vacuum Break: (in.)	
17059213, 215, 229, 513, 515, 529	0.129
212, 512	0.136
501, 520, 521	0.164
509, 510, 586, 588	0.179

Rear Vacuum Break: (in.)	
17059363, 366, 368, 377, 378, 503, 506, 508, 527, 528	0.149
All others	0.129

Carburetor Specifications (cont.)

ROCHESTER M4MC, (1979)

Air Valve Spring: (turns)	
17059212, 512	¾
213, 215, 229, 513, 515, 529	1
All others	⅞

Choke Setting:	
17059061, 201	Index
509, 510, 586, 588	2 Lean
520, 521, 501	3 Lean
212, 213, 215, 229, 512, 513, 515, 529	1 Rich
All others	1 Lean

ROCHESTER M4MC (1980)

Float Adjustment: (in.)	
17080213, 215, 513, 515, 229, 529	⅜
All others	15/32

Pump Adjustment: (in.)	
All	9/32 Inner

Choke Coil Lever (in.)	
All	0.120

Choke Rod: (in.)	
17080213, 215, 513, 515, 229, 529	0.234
All others	0.314

Air Valve Rod: (in.)	
All	0.015

Unloader Adjustment: (in.)	
17080212, 213, 215, 512, 513, 515, 229, 529	0.260
All others	0.277

Front Vacuum Break: (in.)	
17080212, 512	0.136
All others	0.129

Rear Vacuum Break: (in.)	
17080290, 291, 292, 503, 506, 508	0.149
212, 213, 215, 512, 513, 515, 229, 529	0.179
All others	0.129

Air Valve Spring: (turns)	
17080212, 512	¾
213, 215, 513, 515, 229, 529	1
All others	⅞

Choke Setting:
All models have a riveted choke cover; replacement kits contain setting instructions.

NOTE: *All other adjustments require special angle gauge.*

Carburetor Specifications (cont.)

ROCHESTER M4MC–M4ME (1981–82)

Carburetor Identification	Float Adjustment: (in.)	Pump Adjustment: (in.)	Choke Rod: (in.)	Air Valve Rod: (in.)	Unloader Adjustment: (in.)	Front Vacuum Break: (in.)	Rear Vacuum Break (in.)	Air Valve Spring: (turns)	Choke Setting:
17080212	⅜	9/32	.314	.025	.260	.136	.179	¾	①
17080213	⅜	9/32	.234	.025	.260	.129	.179	1	①
17080215	⅜	9/32	.234	.025	.260	.129	.179	1	①
17080298	⅜	9/32	.234	.025	.260	.129	.179	1	①
17080507	⅜	9/32	.234	.025	.260	.129	.179	1	①
17080512	⅜	9/32	.314	.025	.260	.136	.179	¾	①
17080513	⅜	9/32	.234	.025	.260	.129	.179	¾	①
17081200	15/32	9/32	.314	.025	.277	.136	.129	⅞	①
17081201	15/32	9/32	.314	.025	.277	.129	.129	⅞	①
17081205	15/32	9/32	.314	.025	.277	.129	.129	⅞	①
17081206	15/32	9/32	.314	.025	.277	.129	.129	⅞	①
17081220	15/32	9/32	.314	.025	.277	.129	.129	⅞	①
17081226	15/32	9/32	.314	.025	.277	.136	.129	⅞	①
17081227	15/32	9/32	.314	.025	.277	.136	.129	⅞	①
17081290	13/32	9/32	.314	.025	.277	.129	.136	⅞	①
17081291	13/32	9/32	.314	.025	.277	.129	.136	⅞	①
17081292	13/32	9/32	.314	.025	.277	.129	.136	⅞	①
17081506	13/32	9/32	.314	.025	.227	.129	.227	⅞	①
17081508	13/32	9/32	.314	.025	.227	.129	.227	⅞	①
17081524	13/32	5/16	.314	.025	.243	.142	.227	⅞	①
17081526	13/32	5/16	.314	.025	.243	.142	.227	⅞	①

① All models have a riveted choke cover; replacement kit contains setting instructions.

ROCHESTER E2SE (1983–84)

Carburetor Identification	Float Level (in.)	Air Valve Spring (turns)	Fast Idle (rpm)	Choke Coil Lever (in.)	Fast Idle Cam (deg./in.)	Air Valve Rod (deg.)	Primary Vacuum Break (deg./in.)	Secondary Vacuum Break (deg./in.)	Choke Unloader (deg./in.)
17083430	11/32	1	①	.085	15/.077	1	26/.149	38/.243	42/.277
17083431	11/32	1	①	.085	15/.077	1	26/.149	38/.243	42/.277
17083434	11/32	1	①	.085	15/.077	1	26/.149	38/.243	42/.277
17083435	11/32	1	①	.085	15/.077	1	26/.149	38/.243	42/.277

① See Underhood Specifications Sticker

Carburetor Specifications (cont.)

ROCHESTER E4ME (1983–84)

Carburetor Number	Float Level (in.)	Choke Rod (Fast Idle Cam) (deg./in.)	Front Vacuum Break (deg./in.)	Rear Vacuum Break (deg./in.)	Air Valve Spring (turns)	Choke Unloader (deg./in.)
17083202	11/32	20/.110	—	27/.157	7/8	38/.243
17083203	11/32	38/.243	—	27/.157	7/8	38/.243
17083204	11/32	20/.110	—	27/.157	7/8	38/.243
17083207	11/32	38/.243	—	27/.157	7/8	38/.243
17083216	11/32	20/.110	—	27/.157	7/8	38/.243
17083218	11/32	20/.110	—	27/.157	7/8	38/.243
17083236	11/32	20/.110	—	27/.157	7/8	38/.243
17083506	7/16	20/.110	27/.157	36/.227	7/8	36/.227
17083508	7/16	20/.110	27/.157	36/.227	7/8	36/.227
17083524	7/16	20/.110	25/.142	36/.227	7/8	36/.227
17083526	7/16	20/.110	25/.142	36/.227	7/8	36/.227

ROCHESTER M4MC–M4ME (1985)

Carburetor Identification	Float Adjustment: (in.)	Pump Adjustment: (in.)	Choke Rod: (deg)	Air Valve Rod: (in.)	Unloader Adjustment: (deg)	Front Vacuum Break: (deg)	Rear Vacuum Break: (deg)	Air Valve Spring: (turns)	Choke Setting:
17080212	12/32	9/32	46°	.025	40°	24°	30°	3/4	①
17080213	12/32	9/32	37°	.025	40°	23°	30°	1	①
17080298	12/32	9/32	37°	.025	40°	23°	30°	1	①
17082213	12/32	9/32	37°	.025	40°	23°	30°	1	①
17083298	12/32	9/32	37°	.025	40°	23°	30°	1	①
17084500	12/32	9/32	37°	.025	40°	23°	30°	1	①
17084501	12/32	9/32	37°	.025	40°	23°	30°	1	①
17084502	12/32	9/32	46°	.025	40°	24°	30°	7/8	①
17085000	12/32	9/32	46°	.025	40°	24°	30°	7/8	①
17085001	12/32	9/32	46°	.025	40°	23°	30°	1	①
17085003	13/32	9/32	46°	.025	35°	23°	—	7/8	①
17085004	13/32	9/32	46°	.025	35°	23°	—	7/8	①
17085205	13/32	9/32	20°	.025	39°	26°	38°	7/8	①
17085206	13/32	9/32	46°	.025	39°	—	26°	7/8	①
17085208	13/32	9/32	20°	.025	39°	26°	38°	7/8	①
17085209	13/32	3/8	20°	.025	39°	26°	36°	7/8	①
17085210	13/32	9/32	20°	.025	39°	26°	38°	7/8	①
17085211	13/32	3/8	20°	.025	39°	26°	36°	7/8	①
17085212	13/32	9/32	46°	.025	35°	23°	—	7/8	①
17085213	13/32	9/32	46°	.025	35°	23°	—	7/8	①

Carburetor Specifications (cont.)

ROCHESTER M4MC–M4ME (1985)

Carburetor Identification	Float Adjustment: (in.)	Pump Adjustment: (in.)	Choke Rod: (deg)	Air Valve Rod: (in.)	Unloader Adjustment: (deg)	Front Vacuum Break: (deg)	Rear Vacuum Break: (deg)	Air Valve Spring: (turns)	Choke Setting:
17085215	13/32	9/32	46°	.025	32°	—	26°	7/8	①
17085216	13/32	9/32	20°	.025	39°	26°	38°	7/8	①
17085217	13/32	9/32	20°	.025	39°	26°	36°	1/2	①
17085219	13/32	9/32	20°	.025	39°	26°	36°	1/2	①
17085220	13/32	3/8	20°	.025	32°	—	26°	7/8	①
17085221	13/32	3/8	20°	.025	32°	—	26°	7/8	①
17085222	13/32	9/32	20°	.025	39°	26°	36°	1/2	①
17085223	13/32	3/8	20°	.025	39°	26°	36°	1/2	①
17085224	13/32	9/32	20°	.025	39°	26°	36°	1/2	①
17085225	13/32	3/8	20°	.025	39°	26°	36°	1/2	①
17085226	13/32	9/32	20°	.025	32°	—	24°	7/8	①
17085227	13/32	9/32	20°	.025	32°	—	24°	7/8	①
17085228	13/32	9/32	46°	.025	39°	—	24°	7/8	①
17085229	13/32	9/32	46°	.025	39°	—	24°	7/8	①
17085230	13/32	9/32	20°	.025	32°	—	26°	7/8	①
17085231	13/32	9/32	20°	.025	32°	—	26°	7/8	①
17085235	13/32	9/32	46°	.025	39°	—	26°	7/8	①
17085238	13/32	3/8	20°	.025	32°	—	26°	7/8	①
17085239	13/32	3/8	20°	.025	32°	—	26°	7/8	①
17085290	13/32	9/32	46°	.025	39°	—	24°	7/8	①
17085291	13/32	3/8	46°	.025	39°	—	26°	7/8	①
17085292	13/32	9/32	46°	.025	39°	—	24°	7/8	①
17085293	13/32	3/8	46°	.025	39°	—	26°	7/8	①
17085294	13/32	9/32	46°	.025	39°	—	26°	7/8	①
17085298	13/32	9/32	46°	.025	39°	—	26°	7/8	①

relieve pressure any time the engine is turned off, however a small amount of fuel may be released when the fuel line is disconnected. As a precaution, cover the fuel line with a cloth and dispose of properly.

Electric Fuel Pump

REMOVAL AND INSTALLATION

1. With the engine turned OFF, relieve the fuel pressure at the pressure regulator. See Warning above.

2. Disconnect the negative battery cable.

3. Raise and support the rear of the vehicle on jackstands.

4. Drain the fuel tank, then remove it.

5. Using a hammer and a drift punch, drive the fuel lever sending device and pump assembly locking ring (located on top of the fuel tank) counterclockwise, Lift the assembly from the tank and remove the pump from the fuel lever sending device.

6. Pull the pump up into the attaching hose while pulling it outward away from the bottom support. Be careful not to damage the rubber insulator and strainer during removal. After

Carburetor Specifications (cont.)

Rochester Model M4MC/M4ME Quadrajet Chevolet/GMC

(All measurements in inches or degrees)

Year	Carburetor Number	Float Level	Pump Rod Hole	Pump Rod Setting	Choke Rod ① Setting	Air Valve Rod	Vacuum Break Front	Vacuum Break Rear	Air Valve Turns	Choke Unloader
1986–87	17080201	15/32	Inner	9/32	46°	.025	—		23°	7/8	42°
	17080205	15/32	Inner	9/32	46°	.025	—		23°	7/8	42°
	17080206	15/32	Inner	9/32	46°	.025	—		23°	7/8	42°
	17080213	3/8	Inner	9/32	37°	.025	23°		30°	1	40°
	17080290	15/32	Inner	9/32	46°	.025	—		26°	7/8	42°
	17080291	15/32	Inner	9/32	46°	.025	—		26°	7/8	42°
	17080292	15/32	Inner	9/32	46°	.025	—		26°	7/8	42°
	17080298	3/8	Inner	9/32	37°	.025	23°		30°	1	40°
	17080507	3/8	Inner	9/32	37°	.025	23°		30°	1	40°
	17080513	3/8	Inner	9/32	37°	.025	23°		30°	1	40°
	17082213	9/32	Inner	9/32	37°	.025	23°		30°	1	40°
	17083234	13/32	Inner	9/32	46°	.025	—		26°	7/8	39°
	17083235	13/32	Inner	9/32	46°	.025	—		26°	7/8	39°
	17083290	13/32	Inner	9/32	46°	.025	—		24°	7/8	39°
	17083291	13/32	Inner	9/32	46°	.025	—		24°	7/8	39°
	17083292	13/32	Inner	9/32	46°	.025	—		24°	7/8	39°
	17083293	13/32	Inner	9/32	46°	.025	—		24°	7/8	39°
	17083298	3/8	Inner	9/32	37°	.025	23°		30°	1	40°
	17083507	3/8	Inner	9/32	37°	.025	23°		30°	1	40°

the pump assembly is clear of the bottom support, pull it out of the rubber connector.

7. To install, reverse the removal procedures.

Testing

1. Secure two sections of 3/8″ x 10″ (steel tubing), with a double-flare on one end of each section.

2. Install a flare nut on each section of tubing, then connect each of the sections into the flare nut-to-flare nut adapter, while care included in the Gage Adapter tool No. J-29658-82.

3. Attach the pipe and the adapter assembly to the Gage tool No. J-29658.

4. Raise and support the vehicle on jackstands.

5. Remove the air cleaner and plug the THERMAC vacuum port on the TBI.

6. Disconnect the fuel feed hose between the fuel tank and the filter, then secure the other ends of the 3/8″ tubing into the fuel hoses with hose clamps.

7. Start the engine, check for leaks and observe the fuel pressure, it should be 9-13 psi.

8. Depressurize the fuel system, remove the testing tool, remove the plug from the THERMAC vacuum port, reconnect the fuel line, start the engine and check for fuel leaks.

Throttle Body
REMOVAL AND INSTALLATION

1. Release the fuel pressure at the pressure regulator (see Warning above).

2. Disconnect the THERMAC hose from the engine fitting and remove the air cleaner.

3. Disconnect the electrical connectors at the idle air control, throttle position sensor and the injector.

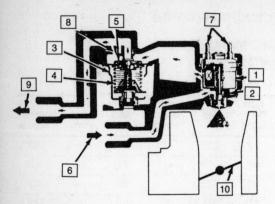

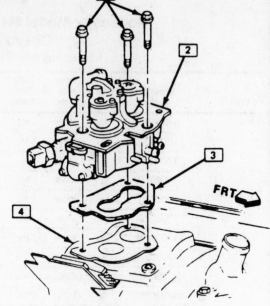

1. Fuel injector
2. Inlet filter
3. Pressure regulator
4. Spring
5. Diaphragm assembly
6. Fuel from pump
7. Injector electrical terminals
8. Constant bleed
9. Fuel return to tank
10. Throttle valve

Cross-sectional view of the TBI 220 operation

4. Disconnect the throttle linkage, return spring and cruise control (if equipped).

5. Disconnect the throttle body vacuum hoses, the fuel supply and fuel return lines.

6. Disconnect the bolts securing the throttle body, then remove it.

7. To install, reverse the removal procedures. Replace the manifold gaskets and O-rings.

1. Bolt-tighten to 16 N·m (12 ft. lbs.)
2. TBI unit
3. Gasket
4. Engine inlet manifold

Throttle body installation-V8 305, 350 engine

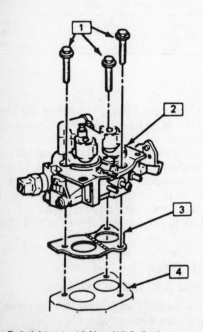

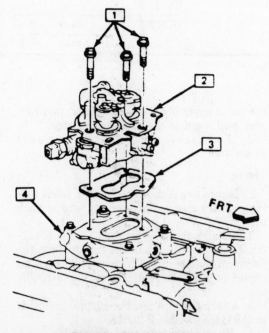

1. Bolt-tighten to 16 N·m (12 ft. lbs.)
2. TBI unit
3. Gasket (must be installed with stripe facing up)
4. Engine intake manifold

Throttle body installation-V6 262 engine engine

1. Bolt-tighten to 16 N.m (12 ft. lbs.)
2. TBI unit
3. Gasket
4. Heater

Throttle body installation-V8 454 engine

Injector
REPLACEMENT

WARNING: *When removing the injectors, be careful not to damage the electrical connector pins (on top of the injector), the injector fuel filter and the nozzle. The fuel injector is serviced as a complete assembly ONLY. The injector is an electrical component and should not be immersed in any kind of cleaner.*

1. Remove the air cleaner. Relieve the fuel pressure (see Warning above).
2. At the injector connector, squeeze the two tabs together and pull straight up.
3. Remove the fuel meter cover and leave the cover gasket in place.
4. Using a small pry bar or tool No. J-26868, carefully lift the injector until it is free from the fuel meter body.
5. Remove the small O-ring from the nozzle end of the injector. Carefully rotate the injector's fuel filter back and forth to remove it from the base of the injector.
6. Discard the fuel meter cover gasket.

7. Remove the large O-ring and back-up washer from the top of the counterbore of the fuel meter body injector cavity.
8. To install, lubricate the O-rings with automatic transmission fluid and reverse the removal procedures.

Fuel Meter Cover
REPLACEMENT

1. Remove the air cleaner.
2. Disconnect the electrical connector from the fuel injector.
3. Remove the fuel meter-to-fuel meter body screws and lockwashers.

NOTE: *When removing the fuel meter cover screws note the location of the two short screws.*

4. Remove the fuel meter cover and discard the gasket.
5. To install, use a new gasket and reverse the removal procedures.

Idle Air Control Valve

NOTE: *All engines except the 454 use a thread type IAC valve. The 454 is equipped with a flange type IAC valve which is attached with screws.*

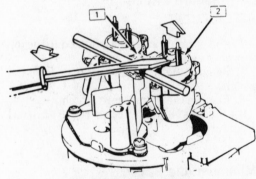

1. Fuel meter cover gasket
2. Removing fuel injector

Removing the fuel injector-TBI 220

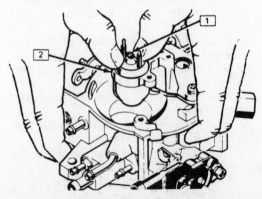

1. Fuel injector
2. Fuel meter body

Installing the fuel injector-TBI 220

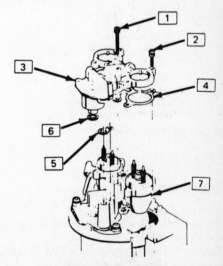

1. Attaching screw-long
2. Attaching screw-short
3. Fuel meter cover assembly
4. Cover gasket
5. Outlet gasket
6. Dust seal
7. Fuel meter body assembly

Replacing the fuel meter cover-TBI 220

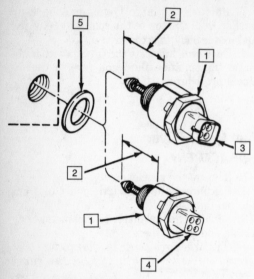

1. Idle air control valve
2. Less than 28mm (1-⅛ in.)
3. Type I (with collar)
4. Type II (without collar)
5. Gasket (part of IAC valve service kit)

Thread type IAC valves-TBI 220

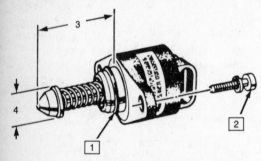

1. O-ring
2. Screw and washer assy.
3. Distance of pintle extension
4. Diameter of pintle

Flange type IAC valve-TBI 220

REPLACEMENT

1. Remove the air cleaner.
2. Disconnect the electrical connector from the idle air control valve.
3. On the threaded type, use a 1¼" (32mm) wrench or tool J-33031, remove the idle air control valve.
4. On the 454 engine, remove the retaining screws and remove the IAC valve.
   WARNING: *Before install a new idle air control valve, measure the distance that the valve extends (from the motor housing to the end of the cone); the distance should be no greater*

than 1⅛" (28mm). If it extends too far, damage will occur to the valve when it is installed.
4. To adjust the threaded type without a collar compress the valve retaining spring, while turning the valve "in". On all others, exert firm pressure, with slight side to side movement, on the pintle to retract it.
5. To complete the installation, use a new gasket and reverse the removal procedures. Start the engine and allow it to reach operating temperature.
NOTE: *The ECM will reset the idle speed when the vehicle is driven at 30 mph.*

Fuel Pump Relay
REPLACEMENT

The fuel pump relay is located in the engine compartment. Other than checking for loose electrical connections, the only service necessary is to replace the relay.

Oil Pressure Switch
REPLACEMENT

The oil pressure switch is mounted to the top rear of the engine.
1. Remove the electrical connector from the switch.
2. Remove the oil pressure switch.
3. To install, reverse the removal procedures.

Minimum Idle Speed
ADJUSTMENT

Only if parts of the throttle body have been replaced should this procedure be performed; the engine should be at operating temperature.
1. Ground the diagnostic lead of the IAC motor.
2. Turn the ignition ON, DO NOT start the engine and wait for 30 seconds.
3. With the ignition ON, disconnect the electrical connector from the IAC motor.
4. Remove the ground from the diagnostic lead and start the engine.
5. Adjust the idle set screw to 500-600 rpm with the transmission in Drive.
6. Turn the ignition OFF and reconnect the electrical to the IAC motor.
7. Adjust the Throttle Position Sensor (TPS) to 0.450-0.600 volts.
8. Recheck the setting.
9. Start the engine and inspect for proper idle operation.

DIESEL FUEL SYSTEM

Injection Pump Fuel Lines

REMOVAL AND INSTALLATION

379 cu. in.

NOTE: *When the fuel lines are to be removed, clean all the fuel line fittings thoroughly before loosening. Immediately cap the lines, nozzles and pump fittings to maintain cleanliness.*

1. Disconnect both batteries.
2. Disconnect the air cleaner bracket at the valve cover.
3. Remove the crankcase ventilator bracket and move it aside.
4. Disconnect the secondary filter lines.
5. Remove the secondary filter adapter.
6. Loosen the vacuum pump holddown clamp and rotate the pump in order to gain access to the intake manifold bolt. Remove the intake manifold bolts. The injection line clips are retained by the same bolts.
7. Remove the intake manifold. Install a protective cover (GM part #J-29664-1 or equivalent) so no foreign material falls into the engine.

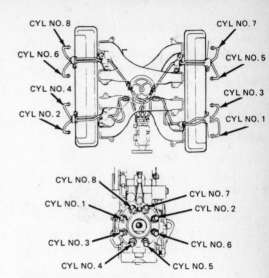

Fuel line connections, 379 diesel

8. Remove the injection line clips at the loom brackets.
9. Remove the injection lines at the nozzles and cover the nozzles with protective caps.
10. Remove the injection lines at the pump and tag the lines for later installation.

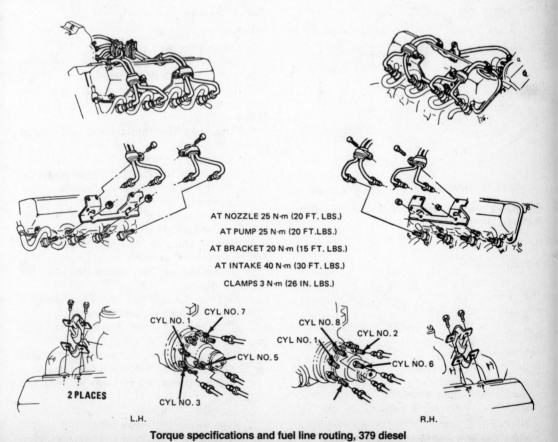

AT NOZZLE 25 N·m (20 FT. LBS.)

AT PUMP 25 N·m (20 FT.LBS.)

AT BRACKET 20 N·m (15 FT. LBS.)

AT INTAKE 40 N·m (30 FT. LBS.)

CLAMPS 3 N·m (26 IN. LBS.)

Torque specifications and fuel line routing, 379 diesel

11. Remove the fuel line from the injection pump.

12. Install all components in the reverse order of removal. Follow the illustrations for injection line connection.

Fuel Injectors
REMOVAL AND INSTALLATION
350 cu. in.

1. Remove the fuel return line from the injector.

2. Remove the nozzle holddown clamp and spacer using tool J-26952.

3. Cap the high pressure line and nozzle tip. WARNING: *The nozzle tip is highly suscep-*

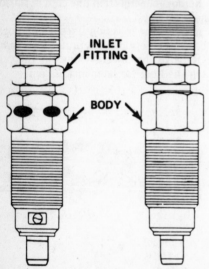

INLET FITTING TO BODY TORQUE
DIESEL EQUIPMENT – 45 FT. LBS. (60 N·m)
C.A.V. LUCAS – 25 FT. LBS. (34 N·m)

INLET FITTING

BODY

DIESEL EQUIPMENT   C.A.V. LUCAS

350 diesel injection nozzles. Note visual differences between manufacturers

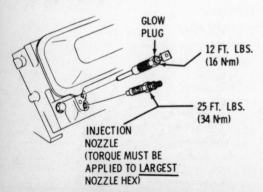

GLOW PLUG

12 FT. LBS. (16 N·m)

25 FT. LBS. (34 N·m)

INJECTION NOZZLE
(TORQUE MUST BE APPLIED TO LARGEST NOZZLE HEX)

Injector and glow plug installation, 350 diesel

tible to damage and must be protected at all times.

3. If an old injector is to be reinstalled, a new compression seal and carbon stop seal must be installed after removal of the used seals.

4. Remove the caps and install the injector spacer and clamp. Torque to 25 ft.lb.

5. Replace return line, start the engine and check for leaks.

379 cu. in.

1. Disconnect the truck's batteries.

2. Disconnect the fuel line clip, and remove the fuel return hose.

3. Remove the fuel injection line as previously detailed.

4. Using GM special tool #J-29873, remove the injector. Always remove the injector by turning the 30mm hex portion of the injector; turning the round portion will damage the injector. Always cap the injector and fuel lines when disconnected, to prevent contamination.

5. Install the injector with new gasket and torque to 50 ft.lb. Connect the injection line and torque the nut to 20 ft.lb. Install the fuel return hose, fuel line clips; and connect the batteries.

Fuel Injection Pump
REMOVAL AND INSTALLATION
350 cu. in.

1. Remove the air cleaner.

2. Remove the filters and pipes from the valve covers and air crossover.

3. Remove the air crossover and cap and intake manifold with screened covers (tool J-26996-1).

4. Disconnect the throttle rod and return spring.

5. Remove the bellcrank.

6. Remove the throttle and transmission cables from the intake manifold brackets.

7. Disconnect the fuel lines from the filter and remove the filter.

8. Disconnect the fuel inlet line at the pump.

9. Remove the rear A/C compressor brace and remove the fuel line.

10. Disconnect the fuel return line from the injection pump.

11. Remove the clamps and pull the fuel return lines from each injection nozzle.

12. Using two wrenches, disconnect the high pressure lines at the nozzles.

13. Remove the three injection pump retaining nuts with tool J-26987 or its equivalent.

14. Remove the pump and cap all lines and nozzles.

To install:

15. Remove the protective caps.

16. Line up the offset tang on the pump drive-

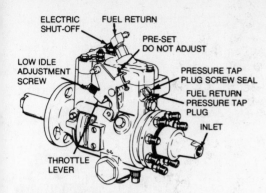

350 diesel injection pump

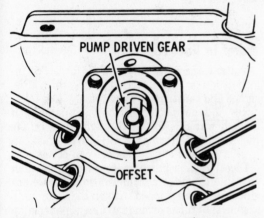

Offset on 350 diesel injection pump driven gear

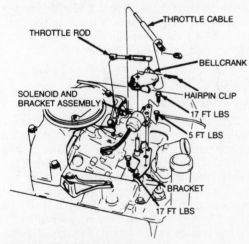

350 diesel throttle assembly

shaft with the pump driven gear and install the pump.

17. Install, but do not tighten the pump retaining nuts.

18. Connect the high pressure lines at the nozzles.

19. Using two wrenches, torque the high pressure line nuts to 25 ft.lb.

20. Connect the fuel return lines to the nozzles and pump.

21. Align the timing mark on the injection pump with the line on the timing mark adaptor and torque the mounting nuts to 35 ft.lb.

NOTE: *A ¾" open end wrench on the boss at the front of the injection pump will aid in rotating the pump to align the marks.*

22. Adjust the throttle rod:

a. remove the clip from the cruise control rod and remove the rod from the bellcrank.

b. loosen the locknut on the throttle rod a few turns, then shorten the rod several turns.

c. rotate the bellcrank to the full throttle stop, then lengthen the throttle rod until the injection pump lever contacts the injection pump full throttle stop, then release the bellcrank.

d. tighten the throttle rod locknut.

23. Install the fuel inlet line between the transfer pump and the filter.

24. Install the rear A/C compressor brace.

25. Install the bellcrank and clip.

26. Connect the throttle rod and return spring.

27. Adjust the transmission cable:

a. push the snap-lock to the disengaged position.

b. rotate the injection pump lever to the full throttle stop and hold it there.

c. push in the snap-lock until it is flush.

d. release the injection pump lever.

28. Start the engine and check for fuel leaks.

29. Remove the screened covers and install the air crossover.

30. Install the tubes in the air flow control valve in the air crossover and install the ventilation filters in the valve covers.

31. Install the air cleaner.

32. Start the engine and allow it to run for two minutes. Stop the engine, let it stand for two minutes, then restart. This permits the air to bleed off within the pump.

379 cu. in.

1. Disconnect both batteries.

2. Remove the fan and fan shroud.

3. Remove the intake manifold as described in Chapter 3.

4. Remove the fuel lines as described in this chapter.

5. Disconnect the alternator cable at the injection pump, and the detent cable (see illustration) where applicable.

6. Tag and disconnect the necessary wires and hoses at the injection pump.

7. Disconnect the fuel return line at the top of the injection pump.

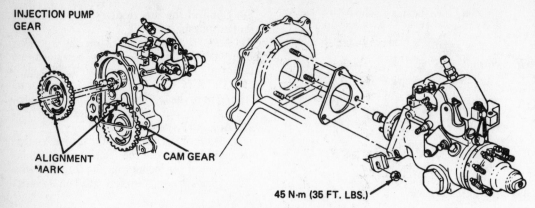

INJECTION PUMP GEAR

ALIGNMENT MARK

CAM GEAR

45 N·m (35 FT. LBS.)

379 diesel injection pump mounting

8. Disconnect the fuel feed line at the injection pump.

9. Remove the air conditioning hose retainer bracket if equipped with A/C.

10. Remove the oil fill tube, including the crankcase depression valve vent hose assembly.

11. Remove the grommet.

12. Scribe or paint a match mark on the front cover and on the injection pump flange.

13. The crankshaft must be rotated in order to gain access to the injection pump drive gear bolts through the oil filler neck hole.

14. Remove the injection pump-to-front cover attaching nuts. Remove the pump and cap all open lines and nozzles.

INSTALLATION

1. Replace the gasket. This is important.

2. Align the locating pin on the pump hub with the slot in the injection pump dirven gear. At the same time, align the timing marks.

3. Attach the injection pump to the front cover, aligning the timing marks before torquing the nuts to 30 ft.lb.

4. Install the drive gear to injection pump bolts, torquing the bolts to 20 ft.lb.

5. Install the remaining components in the reverse order of removal. Torque the fuel feed line at the injection pump to 20 ft.lb. Start the engine and check for leaks.

Fuel Supply Pump
REMOVAL AND INSTALLATION

The diesel fuel supply pump is serviced in the same manner as the fuel pump on the gasoline engines.

Fuel Filter

See Diesel Fuel Filter in Chapter 1 for service procedures.

Water In Fuel (DieseL)

Water is the worst enemy of the diesel fuel injection system. The injection pump, which is designed and constructed to extremely close tolerances, and the injectors can be easily damaged if enough water is forced through them in the fuel. Engine performance will also be drastically affected, and engine damage can occur.

Diesel fuel is much more susceptible than gasoline to water contamination. Diesel engined cars are equipped with an indicator lamp system that turns on an instrument panel lamp if water is detected in the fuel tank. The lamp will come on for 2 to 5 seconds each time the ignition is turned on, assuring the driver the lamp is working. If there is water in the fuel, the light will come back on after a 15 to 20 second off delay, and then remain on.

Purging The Fuel Tank
350 cu. in. Diesels

Trucks which have a Water in Fuel light may have the water removed from the tank with a siphon pump. The pump hose should be hooked up to the ¼" fuel return hose (the smaller of the two hoses) above the rear axle or under the hood near the fuel pump. Siphoning should continue until all water is removed from the tank. Use a clear plastic hose or observe the filter bowl on the siphon pump (if equipped) to determine when clear fuel begins to flow. Be sure to remove the cap on the fuel tank while purging. Replace the cap when finished. Discard the fuel filter and replace with a new filter.

379 cu. in. Diesels

The 379 (6.2L) diesel equipped trucks also have a water-in-fuel warning system. The fuel tank is equipped with a filter which screens out the water and lets it lay in the bottom of the

ANTI-WATER MEASURES
(CHASSIS INSTALLED)

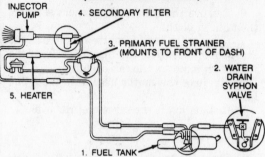

379 diesel-equipped pickups have this anti-water system built into the fuel system. Siphoning valve is located either at mid-frame, or to the rear of the fuel tank, depending on model

tank below the fuel pickup. When the water level reaches a point where it could be drawn into the system, a warning light flashes in the cab. A built-in siphoning system, starting at the fuel tank and going to the rear spring hanger on some models, and at the midway point of the right frame rail on other models permits you to attach a hose at the shut-off and siphon out the water.

If it becomes necessary to drain water from the fuel tank, also check the primary fuel filter for water. This procedure is covered under Diesel Fuel Filter in Chapter 1.

Injection Timing Adjustment

350 Cu. In.

For the engine to be properly timed, the lines on the top of the injection pump adapter and the flange of the injection pump must be aligned.

1. The engine must be off for resetting the timing.
2. Loosen the three pump retaining nuts with tool J-26987, an injection pump intake manifold wrench, or its equivalent.
3. Align the mark on the injection pump with the marks on the adapter and tighten the nuts. Torque to 35 ft.lb. Use a ¾" open-end wrench on the boss at the front of the injection pump to aid in rotating the pump to align the marks.
4. Adjust the throttle rod. See step 22, Fuel Injection Pump Removal and Installation.

CHECKING

For the engine to be properly timed, the marks on the top of the engine front cover and the injection pump flange must be aligned. The engine must be off when the timing is reset. On 49 states models, align the scribe marks. On California models, align the half-circles.

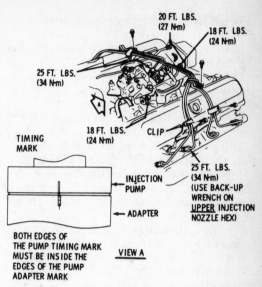

350 diesel timing marks and injection pump lines

ADJUSTING

If the marks mentioned above are not aligned, adjustment is necessary. Loosen the three pump retaining nuts. Align the mark on the injection pump with the mark on the front cover, and tighten the nuts to 30 ft.lb. Adjust the throttle rod (see step 22, Fuel Injection Pump Removal and Installation).

Fuel Tank

DRAINING

CAUTION: *Disconnect the battery before beginning the draining operation.*

If the vehicle is not equipped with a drain

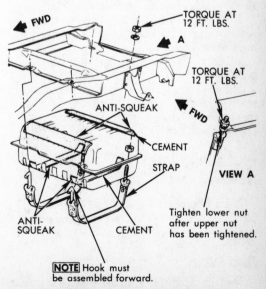

NOTE Hook must be assembled forward.

Fuel tank installation, typical of most models

plug, use the following procedure to remove the gasoline.

1. Using a 10 foot piece of ⅜″ hose cut a flap slip 18″ from one end.

2. Install a pipe nipple, of slightly larger diameter than the hose, into the opposite end of the hose.

3. Install the nipple end of the hose into the fuel tank with the natural curve of the hose pointing downward. Keep feeding the hose in until the nipple hits the bottom of the tank.

4. Place the other end of the hose in a suitable container and insert an air hose pointing it in the downward direction of the slit and inject air into the line.

NOTE: *If the vehicle is to be stored, always drain the gasoline from the complete fuel system including the carburetor, fuel pump, fuel lines, and tank.*

REMOVAL AND INSTALLATION

Cab-Mounted Tanks

1. Remove the seat back holddown bolts and tilt the seat back forward.

2. If equipped, remove the tank cover.

3. Drain the tank.

4. Disconnect the fuel line, meter wire, and ground wire.

5. Remove the lug wrench and lug wrench mount.

6. Remove the bolts and fasteners securing the tank in place.

7. Remove the tank from the cab, and at the same time, disengage the filler neck from the rubber grommet in the cab opening.

8. Remove the meter assembly from the tank.

9. Installation is the reverse of removal.

All Other Tanks

1. Drain the tank.

2. Jack up your vehicle and support it with jack stands.

3. Remove the clamp on the filler neck and the vent tube hose.

4. Remove the gauge hose which is attached to the frame.

5. While supporting the tank securely, remove the support straps.

6. Lower the tank until the gauge wiring can be removed.

7. Remove the tank.

8. Install the unit by reversing the removal procedure. Make certain that the anti-squeak material is replaced during installation.

9. Lower the vehicle.

Chassis Electrical

UNDERSTANDING AND TROUBLESHOOTING ELECTRICAL SYSTEMS

At the rate which both import and domestic manufacturers are incorporating electronic control systems into their production lines, it won't be long before every new vehicle is equipped with one or more on-board computer, like the unit installed on your truck. These electronic components (with no moving parts) should theoretically last the life of the vehicle, provided nothing external happens to damage the circuits or memory chips.

While it is true that electronic components should never wear out, in the real world malfunctions do occur. It is also true that any computer-based system is extremely sensitive to electrical voltages and cannot tolerate careless or haphazard testing or service procedures. An inexperienced individual can literally do major damage looking for a minor problem by using the wrong kind of test equipment or connecting test leads or connectors with the ignition switch ON. When selecting test equipment, make sure the manufacturers instructions state that the tester is compatible with whatever type of electronic control system is being serviced. Read all instructions carefully and double check all test points before installing probes or making any test connections.

The following section outlines basic diagnosis techniques for dealing with computerized automotive control systems. Along with a general explanation of the various types of test equipment available to aid in servicing modern electronic automotive systems, basic repair techniques for wiring harnesses and connectors is given. Read the basic information before attempting any repairs or testing on any computerized system, to provide the background of information necessary to avoid the most common and obvious mistakes that can cost both time and money. Although the replacement and testing procedures are simple in themselves, the systems are not, and unless one has a thorough understanding of all components and their function within a particular computerized control system, the logical test sequence these systems demand cannot be followed. Minor malfunctions can make a big difference, so it is important to know how each component affects the operation of the overall electronic system to find the ultimate cause of a problem without replacing good components unnecessarily. It is not enough to use the correct test equipment; the test equipment must be used correctly.

Safety Precautions

CAUTION: *Whenever working on or around any computer based microprocessor control system, always observe these general precautions to prevent the possibility of personal injury or damage to electronic components.*

• Never install or remove battery cables with the key ON or the engine running. Jumper cables should be connected with the key OFF to avoid power surges that can damage electronic control units. Engines equipped with computer controlled systems should avoid both giving and getting jump starts due to the possibility of serious damage to components from arcing in the engine compartment when connections are made with the ignition ON.

• Always remove the battery cables before charging the battery. Never use a high output charger on an installed battery or attempt to use any type of "hot shot" (24 volt) starting aid.

• Exercise care when inserting test probes into connectors to insure good connections without damaging the connector or spreading the pins. Always probe connectors from the rear (wire) side, NOT the pin side, to avoid accidental shorting of terminals during test procedures.

• Never remove or attach wiring harness connectors with the ignition switch ON, especially to an electronic control unit.

• Do not drop any components during service procedures and never apply 12 volts directly to any component (like a solenoid or relay) unless instructed specifically to do so. Some component electrical windings are designed to safely handle only 4 or 5 volts and can be destroyed in seconds if 12 volts are applied directly to the connector.

• Remove the electronic control unit if the vehicle is to be placed in an environment where temperatures exceed approximately 176°F (80°C), such as a paint spray booth or when arc or gas welding near the control unit location in the car.

ORGANIZED TROUBLESHOOTING

When diagnosing a specific problem, organized troubleshooting is a must. The complexity of a modern automobile demands that you approach any problem in a logical, organized manner. There are certain troubleshooting techniques that are standard:

1. Establish when the problem occurs. Does the problem appear only under certain conditions? Were there any noises, odors, or other unusual symptoms?

2. Isolate the problem area. To do this, make some simple tests and observations; then eliminate the systems that are working properly. Check for obvious problems such as broken wires, dirty connections or split or disconnected vacuum hoses. Always check the obvious before assuming something complicated is the cause.

3. Test for problems systematically to determine the cause once the problem area is isolated. Are all the components functioning properly? Is there power going to electrical switches and motors? Is there vacuum at vacuum switches and/or actuators? Is there a mechanical problem such as bent linkage or loose mounting screws? Doing careful, systematic checks will often turn up most causes on the first inspection without wasting time checking components that have little or no relationship to the problem.

4. Test all repairs after the work is done to make sure that the problem is fixed. Some causes can be traced to more than one component, so a careful verification of repair work is important to pick up additional malfunctions that may cause a problem to reappear or a different problem to arise. A blown fuse, for example, is a simple problem that may require more than another fuse to repair. If you don't look

for a problem that caused a fuse to blow, for example, a shorted wire may go undetected.

Experience has shown that most problems tend to be the result of a fairly simple and obvious cause, such as loose or corroded connectors or air leaks in the intake system; making careful inspection of components during testing essential to quick and accurate troubleshooting. Special, hand held computerized testers designed specifically for diagnosing the EEC-IV system are available from a variety of aftermarket sources, as well as from the vehicle manufacturer, but care should be taken that any test equipment being used is designed to diagnose that particular computer controlled system accurately without damaging the control unit (ECU) or components being tested.

NOTE: *Pinpointing the exact cause of trouble in an electrical system can sometimes only be accomplished by the use of special test equipment. The following describes commonly used test equipment and explains how to put it to best use in diagnosis. In addition to the information covered below, the manufacturer's instructions booklet provided with the tester should be read and clearly understood before attempting any test procedures.*

TEST EQUIPMENT

Jumper Wires

Jumper wires are simple, yet extremely valuable, pieces of test equipment. Jumper wires are merely wires that are used to bypass sections of a circuit. The simplest type of jumper wire is merely a length of multistrand wire with an alligator clip at each end. Jumper wires are usually fabricated from lengths of standard automotive wire and whatever type of connector (alligator clip, spade connector or pin connector) that is required for the particular vehicle being tested. The well equipped tool box will have several different styles of jumper wires in several different lengths. Some jumper wires are made with three or more terminals coming from a common splice for special purpose testing. In cramped, hard-to-reach areas it is advisable to have insulated boots over the jumper wire terminals in order to prevent accidental grounding, sparks, and possible fire, especially when testing fuel system components.

Jumper wires are used primarily to locate open electrical circuits, on either the ground (–) side of the circuit or on the hot (+) side. If an electrical component fails to operate, connect the jumper wire between the component and a good ground. If the component operates only with the jumper installed, the ground circuit is open. If the ground circuit is good, but the component does not operate, the circuit between the power feed and component is open. You can sometimes connect the jumper wire directly from the battery to the hot terminal of the component, but first make sure the component uses 12 volts in operation. Some electrical components, such as fuel injectors, are designed to operate on about 4 volts and running 12 volts directly to the injector terminals can burn out the wiring. By inserting an inline fuseholder between a set of test leads, a fused jumper wire can be used for bypassing open circuits. Use a 5 amp fuse to provide protection against voltage spikes. When in doubt, use a voltmeter to check the voltage input to the component and measure how much voltage is being applied normally. By moving the jumper wire successively back from the lamp toward the power source, you can isolate the area of the circuit where the open is located. When the component stops functioning, or the power is cut off, the open is in the segment of wire between the jumper and the point previously tested.

CAUTION: *Never use jumpers made from wire that is of lighter gauge than used in the circuit under test. If the jumper wire is of too small gauge, it may overheat and possibly melt. Never use jumpers to bypass high resistance loads (such as motors) in a circuit. Bypassing resistances, in effect, creates a short circuit which may, in turn, cause damage and fire. Never use a jumper for anything other than temporary bypassing of components in a circuit.*

12 Volt Test Light

The 12 volt test light is used to check circuits and components while electrical current is flowing through them. It is used for voltage and ground tests. Twelve volt test lights come in different styles but all have three main parts; a ground clip, a probe, and a light. The most commonly used 12 volt test lights have pick-type probes. To use a 12 volt test light, connect the ground clip to a good ground and probe wherever necessary with the pick. The pick should be sharp so that it can penetrate wire insulation to make contact with the wire, without making a large hole in the insulation. The wrap-around light is handy in hard to reach areas or where it is difficult to support a wire to push a probe pick into it. To use the wrap around light, hook the wire to probed with the hook and pull the trigger. A small pick will be forced through the wire insulation into the wire core.

CAUTION: *Do not use a test light to probe electronic ignition spark plug or coil wires. Never use a pick-type test light to probe wiring on computer controlled systems unless specifically instructed to do so. Any wire insulation that is pierced by the test light probe should be taped and sealed with silicone after testing.*

Like the jumper wire, the 12 volt test light is used to isolate opens in circuits. But, whereas the jumper wire is used to bypass the open to operate the load, the 12 volt test light is used to locate the presence of voltage in a circuit. If the test light glows, you know that there is power up to that point; if the 12 volt test light does not glow when its probe is inserted into the wire or connector, you know that there is an open circuit (no power). Move the test light in successive steps back toward the power source until the light in the handle does glow. When it does glow, the open is between the probe and point previously probed.

NOTE: *The test light does not detect that 12 volts (or any particular amount of voltage) is present; it only detects that some voltage is present. It is advisable before using the test light to touch its terminals across the battery posts to make sure the light is operating properly.*

Self-Powered Test Light

The self-powered test light usually contains a 1.5 volt penlight battery. One type of self-powered test light is similar in design to the 12 volt test light. This type has both the battery and the light in the handle and pick-type probe tip. The second type has the light toward the open tip, so that the light illuminates the contact point. The self-powered test light is dual purpose piece of test equipment. It can be used to test for either open or short circuits when power is isolated from the circuit (continuity test). A powered test light should not be used on any computer controlled system or component unless specifically instructed to do so. Many engine sensors can be destroyed by even this small amount of voltage applied directly to the terminals.

Open Circuit Testing

To use the self-powered test light to check for open circuits, first isolate the circuit from the vehicle's 12 volt power source by disconnecting the battery or wiring harness connector. Connect the test light ground clip to a good ground and probe sections of the circuit sequentially with the test light. (start from either end of the circuit). If the light is out, the open is between the probe and the circuit ground. If the light is on, the open is between the probe and end of the circuit toward the power source.

Short Circuit Testing

By isolating the circuit both from power and from ground, and using a self-powered test light, you can check for shorts to ground in the circuit. Isolate the circuit from power and ground. Connect the test light ground clip to a good ground and probe any easy-to-reach test point in the circuit. If the light comes on, there is a short somewhere in the circuit. To isolate the short, probe a test point at either end of the isolated circuit (the light should be on). Leave the test light probe connected and open connectors, switches, remove parts, etc., sequentially, until the light goes out. When the light goes out, the short is between the last circuit component opened and the previous circuit opened.

NOTE: *The 1.5 volt battery in the test light does not provide much current. A weak battery may not provide enough power to illuminate the test light even when a complete circuit is made (especially if there are high resistances in the circuit). Always make sure that the test battery is strong. To check the battery, briefly touch the ground clip to the probe; if the light glows brightly the battery is strong enough for testing. Never use a self-powered test light to perform checks for opens or shorts when power is applied to the electrical system under test. The 12 volt vehicle power will quickly burn out the 1.5 volt light bulb in the test light.*

Voltmeter

A voltmeter is used to measure voltage at any point in a circuit, or to measure the voltage drop across any part of a circuit. It can also be used to check continuity in a wire or circuit by indicating current flow from one end to the other. Voltmeters usually have various scales on the meter dial and a selector switch to allow the selection of different voltages. The voltmeter has a positive and a negative lead. To avoid damage to the meter, always connect the negative lead to the negative (–) side of circuit (to ground or nearest the ground side of the circuit) and connect the positive lead to the positive (+) side of the circuit (to the power source or the nearest power source). Note that the negative voltmeter lead will always be black and that the positive voltmeter will always be some color other than black (usually red). Depending on how the voltmeter is connected into the circuit, it has several uses.

A voltmeter can be connected either in parallel or in series with a circuit and it has a very high resistance to current flow. When connected in parallel, only a small amount of current will flow through the voltmeter current path; the rest will flow through the normal circuit current path and the circuit will work normally. When the voltmeter is connected in series with a circuit, only a small amount of current can flow through the circuit. The circuit will not

work properly, but the voltmeter reading will show if the circuit is complete or not.

Available Voltage Measurement

Set the voltmeter selector switch to the 20V position and connect the meter negative lead to the negative post of the battery. Connect the positive meter lead to the positive post of the battery and turn the ignition switch ON to provide a load. Read the voltage on the meter or digital display. A well charged battery should register over 12 volts. If the meter reads below 11.5 volts, the battery power may be insufficient to operate the electrical system properly. This test determines voltage available from the battery and should be the first step in any electrical trouble diagnosis procedure. Many electrical problems, especially on computer controlled systems, can be caused by a low state of charge in the battery. Excessive corrosion at the battery cable terminals can cause a poor contact that will prevent proper charging and full battery current flow.

Normal battery voltage is 12 volts when fully charged. When the battery is supplying current to one or more circuits it is said to be "under load". When everything is off the electrical system is under a "no-load" condition. A fully charged battery may show about 12.5 volts at no load; will drop to 12 volts under medium load; and will drop even lower under heavy load. If the battery is partially discharged the voltage decrease under heavy load may be excessive, even though the battery shows 12 volts or more at no load. When allowed to discharge further, the battery's available voltage under load will decrease more severely. For this reason, it is important that the battery be fully charged during all testing procedures to avoid errors in diagnosis and incorrect test results.

Voltage Drop

When current flows through a resistance, the voltage beyond the resistance is reduced (the larger the current, the greater the reduction in voltage). When no current is flowing, there is no voltage drop because there is no current flow. All points in the circuit which are connected to the power source are at the same voltage as the power source. The total voltage drop always equals the total source voltage. In a long circuit with many connectors, a series of small, unwanted voltage drops due to corrosion at the connectors can add up to a total loss of voltage which impairs the operation of the normal loads in the circuit.

INDIRECT COMPUTATION OF VOLTAGE DROPS

1. Set the voltmeter selector switch to the 20 volt position.

2. Connect the meter negative lead to a good ground.

3. Probe all resistances in the circuit with the positive meter lead.

4. Operate the circuit in all modes and observe the voltage readings.

DIRECT MEASUREMENT OF VOLTAGE DROPS

1. Set the voltmeter switch to the 20 volt position.

2. Connect the voltmeter negative lead to the ground side of the resistance load to be measured.

3. Connect the positive lead to the positive side of the resistance or load to be measured.

4. Read the voltage drop directly on the 20 volt scale.

Too high a voltage indicates too high a resistance. If, for example, a blower motor runs too slowly, you can determine if there is too high a resistance in the resistor pack. By taking voltage drop readings in all parts of the circuit, you can isolate the problem. Too low a voltage drop indicates too low a resistance. If, for example, a blower motor runs too fast in the MED and/or LOW position, the problem can be isolated in the resistor pack by taking voltage drop readings in all parts of the circuit to locate a possibly shorted resistor. The maximum allowable voltage drop under load is critical, especially if there is more than one high resistance problem in a circuit because all voltage drops are cumulative. A small drop is normal due to the resistance of the conductors.

HIGH RESISTANCE TESTING

1. Set the voltmeter selector switch to the 4 volt position.

2. Connect the voltmeter positive lead to the positive post of the battery.

3. Turn on the headlights and heater blower to provide a load.

4. Probe various points in the circuit with the negative voltmeter lead.

5. Read the voltage drop on the 4 volt scale. Some average maximum allowable voltage drops are:

FUSE PANEL – 7 volts
IGNITION SWITCH – 5volts
HEADLIGHT SWITCH – 7 volts
IGNITION COIL (+) – 5 volts
ANY OTHER LOAD – 1.3 volts
NOTE: *Voltage drops are all measured while a load is operating; without current flow, there will be no voltage drop.*

Ohmmeter

The ohmmeter is designed to read resistance (ohms) in a circuit or component. Although there are several different styles of ohmmeters, all will usually have a selector switch which permits the measurement of different ranges of resistance (usually the selector switch allows the multiplication of the meter reading by 10, 100, 1000, and 10,000). A calibration knob allows the meter to be set at zero for accurate measurement. Since all ohmmeters are powered by an internal battery (usually 9 volts), the ohmmeter can be used as a self-powered test light. When the ohmmeter is connected, current from the ohmmeter flows through the circuit or component being tested. Since the ohmmeter's internal resistance and voltage are known values, the amount of current flow through the meter depends on the resistance of the circuit or component being tested.

The ohmmeter can be used to perform continuity test for opens or shorts (either by observation of the meter needle or as a self-powered test light), and to read actual resistance in a circuit. It should be noted that the ohmmeter is used to check the resistance of a component or wire while there is no voltage applied to the circuit. Current flow from an outside voltage source (such as the vehicle battery) can damage the ohmmeter, so the circuit or component should be isolated from the vehicle electrical system before any testing is done. Since the ohmmeter uses its own voltage source, either lead can be connected to any test point.

NOTE: *When checking diodes or other solid state components, the ohmmeter leads can only be connected one way in order to measure current flow in a single direction. Make sure the positive (+) and negative (–) terminal connections are as described in the test procedures to verify the one-way diode operation.*

In using the meter for making continuity checks, do not be concerned with the actual resistance readings. Zero resistance, or any resistance readings, indicate continuity in the circuit. Infinite resistance indicates an open in the circuit. A high resistance reading where there should be none indicates a problem in the circuit. Checks for short circuits are made in the same manner as checks for open circuits except that the circuit must be isolated from both power and normal ground. Infinite resistance indicates no continuity to ground, while zero resistance indicates a dead short to ground.

RESISTANCE MEASUREMENT

The batteries in an ohmmeter will weaken with age and temperature, so the ohmmeter must be calibrated or "zeroed" before taking measurements. To zero the meter, place the selector switch in its lowest range and touch the two ohmmeter leads together. Turn the calibration knob until the meter needle is exactly on zero.

NOTE: *All analog (needle) type ohmmeters must be zeroed before use, but some digital ohmmeter models are automatically calibrated when the switch is turned on. Self-calibrating digital ohmmeters do not have an adjusting knob, but its a good idea to check for a zero readout before use by touching the leads together. All computer controlled systems require the use of a digital ohmmeter with at least 10 meagohms impedance for testing. Before any test procedures are attempted, make sure the ohmmeter used is compatible with the electrical system or damage to the onboard computer could result.*

To measure resistance, first isolate the circuit from the vehicle power source by disconnecting the battery cables or the harness connector. Make sure the key is OFF when disconnecting any components or the battery. Where necessary, also isolate at least one side of the circuit to be checked to avoid reading parallel resistances. Parallel circuit resistances will always give a lower reading than the actual resistance of either of the branches. When measuring the resistance of parallel circuits, the total resistance will always be lower than the smallest resistance in the circuit. Connect the meter leads to both sides of the circuit (wire or component) and read the actual measured ohms on the meter scale. Make sure the selector switch is set to the proper ohm scale for the circuit being tested to avoid misreading the ohmmeter test value.

CAUTION: *Never use an ohmmeter with power applied to the circuit. Like the self-powered test light, the ohmmeter is designed to operate on its own power supply. The normal 12 volt automotive electrical system current could damage the meter.*

Ammeters

An ammeter measures the amount of current flowing through a circuit in units called amperes or amps. Amperes are units of electron flow which indicate how fast the electrons are flowing through the circuit. Since Ohms Law dictates that current flow in a circuit is equal to the circuit voltage divided by the total circuit resistance, increasing voltage also increases the current level (amps). Likewise, any decrease in resistance will increase the amount of amps in a circuit. At normal operating voltage, most circuits have a characteristic amount of amperes, called "current draw" which can be measured using an ammeter. By referring to a specified current draw rating, measuring the amperes, and comparing the two values, one can determine what is happening within the circuit to aid in diagnosis. An open circuit, for example, will not allow any current to flow so the ammeter reading will be zero. More current flows through a heavily loaded circuit or when the charging system is operating.

An ammeter is always connected in series with the circuit being tested. All of the current that normally flows through the circuit must also flow through the ammeter; if there is any other path for the current to follow, the ammeter reading will not be accurate. The ammeter itself has very little resistance to current flow and therefore will not affect the circuit, but it will measure current draw only when the circuit is closed and electricity is flowing. Excessive current draw can blow fuses and drain the battery, while a reduced current draw can cause motors to run slowly, lights to dim and other components to not operate properly. The ammeter can help diagnose these conditions by locating the cause of the high or low reading.

Multimeters

Different combinations of test meters can be built into a single unit designed for specific tests. Some of the more common combination test devices are known as Volt/Amp testers, Tach/Dwell meters, or Digital Multimeters. The Volt/Amp tester is used for charging system, starting system or battery tests and consists of a voltmeter, an ammeter and a variable resistance carbon pile. The voltmeter will usually have at least two ranges for use with 6, 12 and 24 volt systems. The ammeter also has more than one range for testing various levels of battery loads and starter current draw and the carbon pile can be adjusted to offer different amounts of resistance. The Volt/Amp tester has heavy leads to carry large amounts of current and many later models have an inductive ammeter pickup that clamps around the wire to simplify test connections. On some models, the ammeter also has a zero-center scale to allow testing of charging and starting systems without switching leads or polarity. A digital multimeter is a voltmeter, ammeter and ohmmeter combined in an instrument which gives a digital readout. These are often used when testing solid state circuits because of their high input impedance (usually 10 megohms or more).

The tach/dwell meter combines a tachometer and a dwell (cam angle) meter and is a specialized kind of voltmeter. The tachometer scale is marked to show engine speed in rpm and the dwell scale is marked to show degrees of distributor shaft rotation. In most electronic ignition systems, dwell is determined by the control unit, but the dwell meter can also be used to check the duty cycle (operation) of some electronic engine control systems. Some tach/dwell meters are powered by an internal battery, while others take their power from the car battery in use. The battery powered testers usually require calibration much like an ohmmeter before testing.

Special Test Equipment

A variety of diagnostic tools are available to help troubleshoot and repair computerized engine control systems. The most sophisticated of these devices are the console type engine analyzers that usually occupy a garage service bay, but there are several types of aftermarket electronic testers available that will allow quick circuit tests of the engine control system by plugging directly into a special connector located in the engine compartment or under the dashboard. Several tool and equipment manufacturers offer simple, hand held testers that measure various circuit voltage levels on command to check all system components for proper operation. Although these testers usually cost about $300-$500, consider that the average computer control unit (or ECM) can cost just as much and the money saved by not replacing perfectly good sensors or components in an attempt to correct a problem could justify the purchase price of a special diagnostic tester the first time it's used.

These computerized testers can allow quick and easy test measurements while the engine is operating or while the car is being driven. In addition, the on-board computer memory can be read to access any stored trouble codes; in effect allowing the computer to tell you where it hurts and aid trouble diagnosis by pinpointing exactly which circuit or component is malfunctioning. In the same manner, repairs can be tested to make sure the problem has been corrected. The biggest advantage these special testers have is their relatively easy hookups that minimize or eliminate the chances of making the wrong connections and getting false voltage readings or damaging the computer accidentally.

NOTE: *It should be remembered that these testers check voltage levels in circuits; they don't detect mechanical problems or failed components if the circuit voltage falls within the preprogrammed limits stored in the tester PROM unit. Also, most of the hand held testes are designed to work only on one or two systems made by a specific manufacturer.*

A variety of aftermarket testers are available to help diagnose different computerized control systems. Owatonna Tool Company (OTC), for example, markets a device called the OTC Monitor which plugs directly into the assembly line diagnostic link (ALDL). The OTC tester makes diagnosis a simple matter of pressing the correct buttons and, by changing the internal PROM or inserting a different diagnosis cartridge, it will work on any model from full size to subcompact, over a wide range of years. An adapter is supplied with the tester to allow connection to all types of ALDL links, regardless of the number of pin terminals used. By inserting an updated PROM into the OTC tester, it can be easily updated to diagnose any new modifications of computerized control systems.

Wiring Harnesses

The average automobile contains about ½ mile of wiring, with hundreds of individual connections. To protect the many wires from damage and to keep them from becoming a confusing tangle, they are organized into bundles, enclosed in plastic or taped together and called wire harnesses. Different wiring harnesses serve different parts of the vehicle. Individual wires are color coded to help trace them through a harness where sections are hidden from view.

A loose or corroded connection or a replacement wire that is too small for the circuit will add extra resistance and an additional voltage drop to the circuit. A ten percent voltage drop can result in slow or erratic motor operation, for example, even though the circuit is complete. Automotive wiring or circuit conductors can be in any one of three forms:

1. Single strand wire
2. Multistrand wire
3. Printed circuitry

Single strand wire has a solid metal core and is usually used inside such components as alternators, motors, relays and other devices. Multistrand wire has a core made of many small strands of wire twisted together into a single conductor. Most of the wiring in an automotive electrical system is made up of multistrand wire, either as a single conductor or grouped together in a harness. All wiring is color coded on the insulator, either as a solid color or as a colored wire with an identification stripe. A printed circuit is a thin film of copper or other conductor that is printed on an insulator backing. Occasionally, a printed circuit is sandwiched between two sheets of plastic for more protection and flexibility. A complete printed circuit, consisting of conductors, insulating material and connectors for lamps or other components is called a printed circuit board. Printed circuitry is used in place of individual wires or harnesses in places where space is limited, such as behind instrument panels.

Wire Gauge

Since computer controlled automotive electrical systems are very sensitive to changes in resistance, the selection of properly sized wires is critical when systems are repaired. The wire gauge number is an expression of the cross section area of the conductor. The most common system for expressing wire size is the American Wire Gauge (AWG) system.

Wire cross section area is measured in circular mils. A mil is $\frac{1}{1000}''$ (0.001"); a circular mil is the area of a circle one mil in diameter. For example, a conductor $\frac{1}{4}''$ in diameter is 0.250 in. or 250 mils. The circular mil cross section area of the wire is 250 squared (250^2) or 62,500 circular mils. Imported car models usually use metric wire gauge designations, which is simply the cross section area of the conductor in square millimeters (mm^2).

Gauge numbers are assigned to conductors of various cross section areas. As gauge number increases, area decreases and the conductor becomes smaller. A 5 gauge conductor is smaller than a 1 gauge conductor and a 10 gauge is smaller than a 5 gauge. As the cross section area of a conductor decreases, resistance increases and so does the gauge number. A conductor with a higher gauge number will carry less current than a conductor with a lower gauge number.

NOTE: *Gauge wire size refers to the size of the conductor, not the size of the complete wire. It is possible to have two wires of the same gauge with different diameters because one may have thicker insulation than the other.*

12 volt automotive electrical systems generally use 10, 12, 14, 16 and 18 gauge wire. Main power distribution circuits and larger accessories usually use 10 and 12 gauge wire. Battery cables are usually 4 or 6 gauge, although 1 and 2 gauge wires are occasionally used. Wire length must also be considered when making repairs to a circuit. As conductor length increases, so does resistance. An 18 gauge wire, for example, can carry a 10 amp load for 10 feet without excessive voltage drop; however if a 15 foot wire is required for the same 10 amp load, it must be a 16 gauge wire.

An electrical schematic shows the electrical current paths when a circuit is operating properly. It is essential to understand how a circuit works before trying to figure out why it doesn't. Schematics break the entire electrical system down into individual circuits and show only one particular circuit. In a schematic, no attempt is made to represent wiring and components as they physically appear on the vehicle; switches and other components are shown as simply as possible. Face views of harness connectors show the cavity or terminal locations in all multi-pin connectors to help locate test points.

If you need to backprobe a connector while it is on the component, the order of the terminals must be mentally reversed. The wire color code can help in this situation, as well as a keyway, lock tab or other reference mark.

NOTE: *Wiring diagrams are not included in this book. As trucks have become more complex and available with longer option lists, wiring diagrams have grown in size and complexity. It has become almost impossible to provide a readable reproduction of a wiring diagram in a book this size. Information on ordering wiring diagrams from the vehicle manufacturer can be found in the owner's manual.*

WIRING REPAIR

Soldering is a quick, efficient method of joining metals permanently. Everyone who has the occasion to make wiring repairs should know how to solder. Electrical connections that are soldered are far less likely to come apart and will conduct electricity much better than connections that are only "pig-tailed" together. The most popular (and preferred) method of soldering is with an electrical soldering gun. Soldering irons are available in many sizes and wattage ratings. Irons with higher wattage ratings deliver higher temperatures and recover lost heat faster. A small soldering iron rated for no more than 50 watts is recommended, especially on electrical systems where excess heat can damage the components being soldered.

There are three ingredients necessary for successful soldering; proper flux, good solder and sufficient heat. A soldering flux is necessary to clean the metal of tarnish, prepare it for soldering and to enable the solder to spread into tiny crevices. When soldering, always use a resin flux or resin core solder which is non-corrosive and will not attract moisture once the job is finished. Other types of flux (acid core) will leave a residue that will attract moisture and cause the wires to corrode. Tin is a unique metal with a low melting point. In a molten state, it dissolves and alloys easily with many metals. Solder is made by mixing tin with lead. The most common proportions are 40/60, 50/50 and 60/40, with the percentage of tin listed first. Low priced solders usually contain less tin, making them very difficult for a beginner to use because more heat is required to melt the solder. A common solder is 40/60 which is well suited for all-around general use, but 60/40 melts easier, has more tin for a better joint and is preferred for electrical work.

Soldering Techniques

Successful soldering requires that the metals to be joined be heated to a temperature that will melt the solder—usually 360–460°F (182–238°C). Contrary to popular belief, the purpose of the soldering iron is not to melt the solder itself, but to heat the parts being soldered to a temperature high enough to melt the solder when it is touched to the work. Melting flux-cored solder on the soldering iron will usually destroy the effectiveness of the flux.

NOTE: *Soldering tips are made of copper for good heat conductivity, but must be "tinned" regularly for quick transference of heat to the project and to prevent the solder from sticking to the iron. To "tin" the iron, simply heat it and touch the flux-cored solder to the tip; the solder will flow over the hot tip. Wipe the excess off with a clean rag, but be careful as the iron will be hot.*

After some use, the tip may become pitted. If so, simply dress the tip smooth with a smooth file and "tin" the tip again. An old saying holds that "metals well cleaned are half soldered." Flux-cored solder will remove oxides but rust, bits of insulation and oil or grease must be removed with a wire brush or emery cloth. For maximum strength in soldered parts, the joint must start off clean and tight. Weak joints will result in gaps too wide for the solder to bridge.

If a separate soldering flux is used, it should be brushed or swabbed on only those areas that are to be soldered. Most solders contain a core of flux and separate fluxing is unnecessary. Hold the work to be soldered firmly. It is best to solder on a wooden board, because a metal vise will only rob the piece to be soldered of heat and make it difficult to melt the solder. Hold the soldering tip with the broadest face against the work to be soldered. Apply solder under the tip close to the work, using enough solder to give a heavy film between the iron and the piece being soldered, while moving slowly and making sure the solder melts properly. Keep the work level or the solder will run to the lowest part and favor the thicker parts, because these require more heat to melt the solder. If the soldering tip overheats (the solder coating on the face of the tip burns up), it should be retinned. Once the soldering is completed, let the soldered joint stand until cool. Tape and seal all soldered wire splices after the repair has cooled.

Wire Harness and Connectors

The on-board computer (ECM) wire harness electrically connects the control unit to the various solenoids, switches and sensors used by the control system. Most connectors in the engine compartment or otherwise exposed to the elements are protected against moisture and dirt which could create oxidation and deposits on the terminals. This protection is important because of the very low voltage and current levels used by the computer and sensors. All connectors have a lock which secures the male and fe-male terminals together, with a secondary lock holding the seal and terminal into the connector. Both terminal locks must be released when disconnecting ECM connectors.

These special connectors are weather-proof and all repairs require the use of a special terminal and the tool required to service it. This tool is used to remove the pin and sleeve terminals. If removal is attempted with an ordinary pick, there is a good chance that the terminal will be bent or deformed. Unlike standard blade type terminals, these terminals cannot be straightened once they are bent. Make certain that the connectors are properly seated and all of the sealing rings in place when connecting leads. On some models, a hinge-type flap provides a backup or secondary locking feature for the terminals. Most secondary locks are used to improve the connector reliability by retaining the terminals if the small terminal lock tangs are not positioned properly.

Molded-on connectors require complete replacement of the connection. This means splicing a new connector assembly into the harness. All splices in on-board computer systems should be soldered to insure proper contact. Use care when probing the connections or replacing terminals in them as it is possible to short between opposite terminals. If this happens to the wrong terminal pair, it is possible to damage certain components. Always use jumper wires between connectors for circuit checking and never probe through weather-proof seals.

Open circuits are often difficult to locate by sight because corrosion or terminal misalignment are hidden by the connectors. Merely wiggling a connector on a sensor or in the wiring harness may correct the open circuit condition. This should always be considered when an open circuit or a failed sensor is indicated. Intermittent problems may also be caused by oxidized or loose connections. When using a circuit tester for diagnosis, always probe connections from the wire side. Be careful not to damage sealed connectors with test probes.

All wiring harnesses should be replaced with identical parts, using the same gauge wire and connectors. When signal wires are spliced into a harness, use wire with high temperature insulation only. With the low voltage and current levels found in the system, it is important that the best possible connection at all wire splices be made by soldering the splices together. It is seldom necessary to replace a complete harness. If replacement is necessary, pay close attention to insure proper harness routing. Secure the harness with suitable plastic wire clamps to prevent vibrations from causing the harness to wear in spots or contact any hot components.

NOTE: *Weatherproof connectors cannot be replaced with standard connectors. Instructions are provided with replacement connector and terminal packages. Some wire harnesses have mounting indicators (usually pieces of colored tape) to mark where the harness is to be secured.*

In making wiring repairs, it's important that you always replace damaged wires with wires that are the same gauge as the wire being replaced. The heavier the wire, the smaller the gauge number. Wires are color-coded to aid in identification and whenever possible the same color coded wire should be used for replacement. A wire stripping and crimping tool is necessary to install solderless terminal connectors. Test all crimps by pulling on the wires; it should not be possible to pull the wires out of a good crimp.

Wires which are open, exposed or otherwise damaged are repaired by simple splicing. Where possible, if the wiring harness is accessible and the damaged place in the wire can be located, it is best to open the harness and check for all possible damage. In an inaccessible harness, the wire must be bypassed with a new insert, usually taped to the outside of the old harness.

When replacing fusible links, be sure to use fusible link wire, NOT ordinary automotive wire. Make sure the fusible segment is of the same gauge and construction as the one being replaced and double the stripped end when crimping the terminal connector for a good contact. The melted (open) fusible link segment of the wiring harness should be cut off as close to the harness as possible, then a new segment spliced in as described. In the case of a damaged fusible link that feeds two harness wires, the harness connections should be replaced with two fusible link wires so that each circuit will have its own separate protection.

NOTE: *Most of the problems caused in the wiring harness are due to bad ground connections. Always check all vehicle ground connections for corrosion or looseness before performing any power feed checks to eliminate the chance of a bad ground affecting the circuit.*

Repairing Hard Shell Connectors

Unlike molded connectors, the terminal contacts in hard shell connectors can be replaced. Weatherproof hard-shell connectors with the leads molded into the shell have non-replaceable terminal ends. Replacement usually involves the use of a special terminal removal tool that depress the locking tangs (barbs) on the connector terminal and allow the connector to be removed from the rear of the shell. The connector shell should be replaced if it shows any evidence of burning, melting, cracks, or breaks. Replace individual terminals that are burnt, corroded, distorted or loose.

NOTE: *The insulation crimp must be tight to prevent the insulation from sliding back on the wire when the wire is pulled. The insulation must be visibly compressed under the crimp tabs, and the ends of the crimp should be turned in for a firm grip on the insulation.*

The wire crimp must be made with all wire strands inside the crimp. The terminal must be fully compressed on the wire strands with the ends of the crimp tabs turned in to make a firm grip on the wire. Check all connections with an ohmmeter to insure a good contact. There should be no measurable resistance between the wire and the terminal when connected.

Mechanical Test Equipment

Vacuum Gauge

Most gauges are graduated in inches of mercury (in.Hg), although a device called a manometer reads vacuum in inches of water (in. H_2O). The normal vacuum reading usually varies between 18 and 22 in.Hg at sea level. To test engine vacuum, the vacuum gauge must be connected to a source of manifold vacuum. Many engines have a plug in the intake manifold which can be removed and replaced with an adapter fitting. Connect the vacuum gauge to the fitting with a suitable rubber hose or, if no manifold plug is available, connect the vacuum gauge to any device using manifold vacuum, such as EGR valves, etc. The vacuum gauge can be used to determine if enough vacuum is reaching a component to allow its actuation.

Hand Vacuum Pump

Small, hand-held vacuum pumps come in a variety of designs. Most have a built-in vacuum gauge and allow the component to be tested without removing it from the vehicle. Operate the pump lever or plunger to apply the correct amount of vacuum required for the test specified in the diagnosis routines. The level of vacuum in inches of Mercury (in.Hg) is indicated on the pump gauge. For some testing, an additional vacuum gauge may be necessary.

Intake manifold vacuum is used to operate various systems and devices on late model vehicles. To correctly diagnose and solve problems in vacuum control systems, a vacuum source is necessary for testing. In some cases, vacuum can be taken from the intake manifold when the engine is running, but vacuum is normally provided by a hand vacuum pump. These hand vacuum pumps have a built-in vacuum gauge that allow testing while the device is still at-

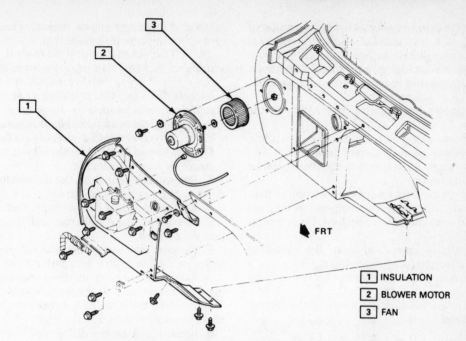

1	INSULATION
2	BLOWER MOTOR
3	FAN

Blower motor assembly. Later models have the insulator shield

tached to the component. For some tests, an additional vacuum gauge may be necessary.

HEATER AND AIR CONDITIONER

Blower

REMOVAL AND INSTALLATION

1. Disconnect the negative battery terminal, open the hood, and securely support it.

2. On 1970-72 models, scribe the hood and fender location of the right hood hinge. Remove the hinge.

3. Mark the position of the blower motor in relation to its case. Remove the electrical connection at the motor.

4. Remove the blower attaching screws and remove the assembly. Pry gently on the flange if the sealer sticks.

5. The blower wheel can be removed from the motor shaft by removing the nut at the center.

6. Installation is the reverse of removal. Apply a bead of sealer to the mounting flange before installation.

Heater Core

REMOVAL AND INSTALLATION

1970-72 Without Air Conditioning

1. Drain the cooling system and disconnect the negative battery terminal.

CAUTION: *When draining the coolant, keep in mind that cats and dogs are attracted by the ethylene glycol antifreeze, and are quite*

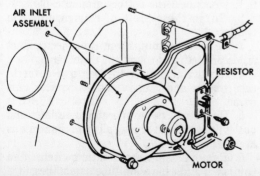

Heater blower assembly, 1973 and later

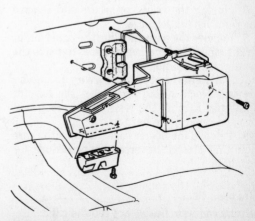

Heater distributor, 1973 and later

likely to drink any that is left in an uncovered container or in puddles on the ground. This will prove fatal in sufficient quantity. Always drain the coolant into a sealable container. Coolant should be reused unless it is contaminated or several years old.

2. Remove the electrical connection at the blower.

3. Remove the heater hoses at the core tubes.

4. Remove the right front fender skirt. Remove enough screws so that the fender can be moved outward.

5. Working from under the instrument panel, remove the seal on the temperature door cable and disconnect the cable from the temperature door.

6. Pull the case away from the mounting studs after removing the retaining bolts.

7. Remove the core retainers and remove the core.

8. The installation procedure is the reverse of removal.

1970-72 With Factory Installed Air Conditioning

NOTE: *Models with dealer installed air conditioning use the same procedure as those without air conditioning.*

1. Drain the coolant. Disconnect the battery ground cable.

CAUTION: *When draining the coolant, keep in mind that cats and dogs are attracted by the ethylene glycol antifreeze, and are quite likely to drink any that is left in an uncovered container or in puddles on the ground. This will prove fatal in sufficient quantity. Always drain the coolant into a sealable container. Coolant should be reused unless it is contaminated or several years old.*

2. Detach the heater hoses from the core tubes at the firewall.

3. Remove the stud nuts on the engine side of the firewall.

4. Remove the glove box.

5. Unplug the relay connector and remove the right ball outlet hose.

6. Remove the screw holding the panel outlet air distributor to the heater case. Remove the heater case retaining screws.

7. Pull the heater case away from the firewall; reach in and disconnect the resistor connector. Remove the resistor harness grommet and remove the harness.

8. Remove the heater case. Remove the core mounting straps. Reverse the procedure for installation.

1973 and Later

1. Disconnect the battery ground cable.

2. Disconnect the heater hoses at the core

tubes and drain the engine coolant. Plug the core tubes to prevent spillage.

CAUTION: *When draining the coolant, keep in mind that cats and dogs are attracted by the ethylene glycol antifreeze, and are quite likely to drink any that is left in an uncovered container or in puddles on the ground. This will prove fatal in sufficient quantity. Always drain the coolant into a sealable container. Coolant should be reused unless it is contaminated or several years old.*

3. Remove the nuts from the distributor air ducts in the engine compartment.

4. Remove the glove compartment and door.

5. Disconnect the Air-Defrost and Temperature door cables.

6. Remove the floor outlet and remove the defroster duct-to-heater distributor screw.

7. Remove the heater distributor-to-instrument panel screws. Pull the assembly rearward to gain access to the wiring harness and disconnect the wires attached to the unit.

8. Remove the heater distributor from the truck.

9. Remove the heater core retaining straps and remove the core from the truck.

10. Installation is the reverse of removal. Be sure that the core-to-core and case-to-dash panel sealer is intact. Fill the cooling system and check for leaks.

Control Head
REMOVAL AND INSTALLATION

1. Disconnect the negative battery cable.

2. Remove the radio.

3. Remove the instrument panel bezel.

4. Disconnect the control head from the dash.

5. Lower the control head from the dash, without kinking the cable, and disconnect the cable, vacuum harness and electrical harness.

6. Reverse the above to install.

Evaporator Core
REMOVAL AND INSTALLATION

1. Disconnect the battery ground cable.

2. Purge the system of refrigerant. See Chapter 1.

3. Remove the nuts from the selector duct studs projecting through the dash panel.

4. Remove the cover to dash and cover to case screws and remove the evaporator case cover.

5. Disconnect the evaporator core inlet and outlet lines and cap or plug all open connections at once.

6. Remove the thermostatic switch (if so equipped) and expansion tube assemblies.

7. Remove the evaporator core.

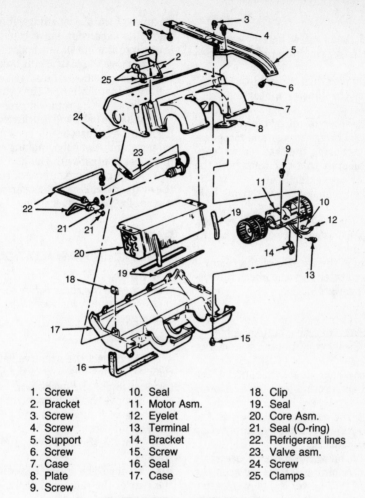

1. Screw
2. Bracket
3. Screw
4. Screw
5. Support
6. Screw
7. Case
8. Plate
9. Screw
10. Seal
11. Motor Asm.
12. Eyelet
13. Terminal
14. Bracket
15. Screw
16. Seal
17. Case
18. Clip
19. Seal
20. Core Asm.
21. Seal (O-ring)
22. Refrigerant lines
23. Valve asm.
24. Screw
25. Clamps

Auxiliary A/C system-Suburban

8. When installing remember the following:

a. Use new O-rings, coated with clean refrigerant oil, when connecting refrigerant lines.

b. Be sure the cover to case and dash panel sealer is intact before installing the cover.

c. Add three ounces of clean refrigerant oil to a new evaporator core.

d. Evacuate and charge the system following the precautions outlined in Chapter

Suburban Auxiliary Air Conditioning System

REMOVAL AND INSTALLATION

Overhead Duct

1. Disconnect the negative battery cable.
2. Disconnect the condensation drain tube from the rear duct.
3. Remove the screws securing the duct to the roof panel. Remove the rear header bracket.

4. Remove the duct assembly.

5. Installation is the reverse of the removal procedure.

Blower Motor Assembly

1. Disconnect the negative battery cable.
2. Remove the rear duct assembly.
3. Disconnect the blower motor lead wire and the motor ground strap.
4. Remove the lower to upper blower/evaporator case screws. Lower the lower case and motor assembly. Before removing the case assembly screws, support the case to prevent damage to the motor or case.
5. Remove the motor retaining strap and remove the motor and wheels. The wheels can be removed from the motor shaft.
6. Installation is the reverse of the removal procedure. Be sure the blower wheels rotate freely and no binding exists.

Expansion Valve

1. Disconnect the negative battery cable.
2. Discharge the air conditioning system. See Chapter 1.
3. Remove the rear duct assembly.
4. Disconnect the blower motor lead and ground wires.
5. Remove the loser to upper blower/evaporator case screws. Lower the case and motor assembly. Before removing the case screws, support the case assembly to avoid damage to the motor/evaporator case assembly.
6. Remove the expansion valve sensing bulb clamps.
7. Disconnect the valve inlet and outlet lines. Remove the expansion valve assembly. Cap the openings immediately.
8. Installation is the reverse of the removal procedure. Evacuate, charge and check the system for proper operation.

Evaporator Core

1. Disconnect the negative battery cable.
2. Discharge the air conditioning system. See Chapter 1.
3. Remove the rear duct. Disconnect the power lead and the ground lead to the blower motor.
4. Disconnect the refrigerant lines at the rear of the blower/evaporator assembly. Cap the openings immediately.
5. Support the blower/evaporator assembly and remove the retaining screws between the case and the roof rail. Lower the blower/evaporator assembly and place it on a work area away from the vehicle.
6. Remove the lower to upper case screws and remove the lower case assembly. Remove the support to upper case screws and remove the upper case from the evaporator core.
7. Remove the expansion valve inlet and out-

let lines. Cap the openings immediately. Remove the expansion valve capillary tube from the evaporator outlet line and remove the valve.
8. Remove the plastic pins holding the screen to the core. Remove the screen.
9. The installation of the evaporator core is the reverse of the removal procedure. New O-rings must be used and lubricated with fresh refrigerant oil. Install the sensing bulb to the evaporator outlet tube, making sure the tube is in proper contact with the line.
10. Add three fluid ounces of refrigerant oil to the evaporator. Evacuate, charge and check the system for proper operation.

RADIO

REMOVAL AND INSTALLATION

WARNING: *Make certain that the speaker is attached to the radio before the unit is turned ON. If it is not, the output transistors will be damaged.*

1970-72

1. Disconnect the negative battery cable and remove the flex hoses from the heater distributor duct under the dashboard.
2. Remove the heater control head by removing the attaching screws and pushing the unit back and down.
3. Remove the ash tray and the ash tray retainer.
4. Remove the electrical connections from the rear of the radio and also the front attaching screws and knobs.
5. Remove the mounting screw on the side of the radio chassis. Push the radio back and up before slipping it down and out of the instrument panel.
6. To install the radio, reverse the removal procedure.

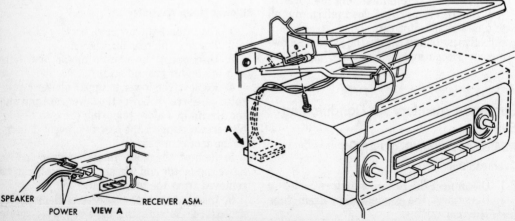

Radio installation, 1972–72

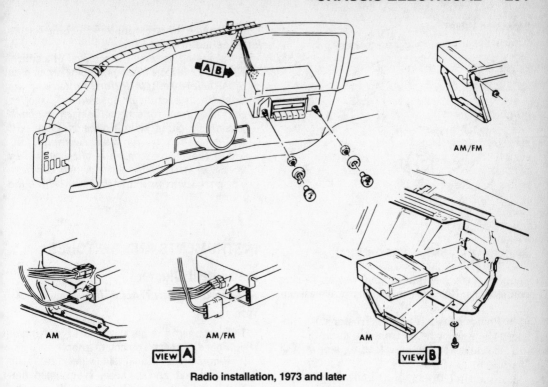

Radio installation, 1973 and later

1973 and Later

1. Remove the negative battery cable and the control knobs and the bezels from the radio control shafts.

2. On the AM radios, remove the support bracket stud nut and its lockwasher.

3. On AM/FM radios, remove the support bracket-to-instrument panel screws.

4. Lifting the rear edge of the radio, push the radio forward until the control shafts clear the instrument panel then lower the radio far enough so that the electrical connections can be disconnected.

5. Remove the power lead, speaker, and antenna wires and then pull out the unit.

6. Installation is the reverse of removal.

WINDSHIELD WIPERS

Motor

REMOVAL AND INSTALLATION

1970-72

1. Disconnect the battery ground cable. Be sure the wipers are in the parked position.

2. Remove the wiper arms and blades.

3. Remove the plenum chamber grille.

4. Disconnect wiper drive rods from crank arm; remove crank arm nut and arm from motor shaft.

5. Working under the instrument panel, dis-

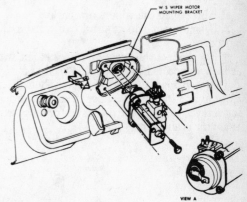

Wiper installation, 1970–72

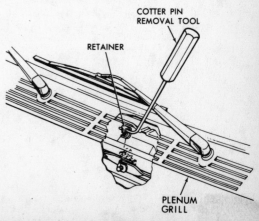

Removing the 1970–72 drive rod retainer

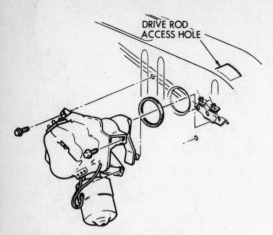

DRIVE ROD
ACCESS HOLE

Wiper motor installation, 1973 and later

connect the wiper motor and washer wiring connections. Remove the parking brake assembly if it is in the way.

6. Remove the left hand defroster hose. Remove the washer hoses from the pump.

7. Remove the motor attaching screws and the motor.

8. To install, reverse the removal procedure.

1973 and Later

1. Make sure the wipers are parked.

2. Disconnect the ground cable from the battery.

3. Disconnect the wiring harness at the wiper motor and the hoses from the washer pump.

4. Reach down through the access hole in the plenum and loosen the wiper drive rod attaching screws. Remove the drive rod from the wiper motor crank arm.

5. Remove the wiper motor attaching screws and the motor assembly.

6. To install, reverse the removal procedure.

NOTE: *Lubricate the wiper motor crank arm pivot before reinstallation. Failure of the washers to operate or to shut off is often caused by grease or dirt on the electromagnetic contacts. Simply unplug the wire and pull off the plastic cover for access. Likewise, failure of the wipers to park is often caused by grease or dirt on the park switch contacts. The park switch is under the cover behind the pump.*

INSTRUMENTS AND SWITCHES

Instrument Cluster

REMOVAL AND INSTALLATION

1970-72

1. Disconnect the negative battery terminal. If equipped, remove the choke knob.

2. Remove the windshield wiper knob, the light switch rod, and the bezel. If equipped, disconnect and plug the oil pressure line to the gauge.

3. Disconnect the speedometer cable and the chassis wiring harness which is located at the rear of the instrument panel. Protect the mast jacket with a rag or other covering so that it doesn't become scratched.

4. Remove the cluster retaining screws and remove the cluster.

5. To install the cluster, reverse the removal procedure.

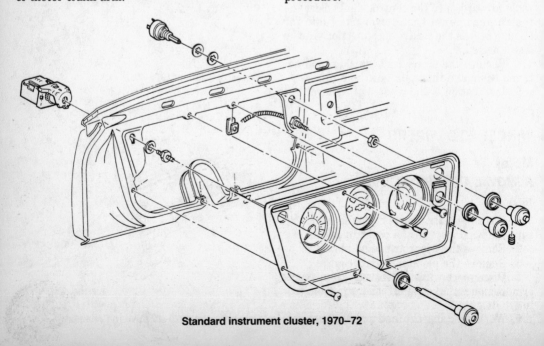

Standard instrument cluster, 1970–72

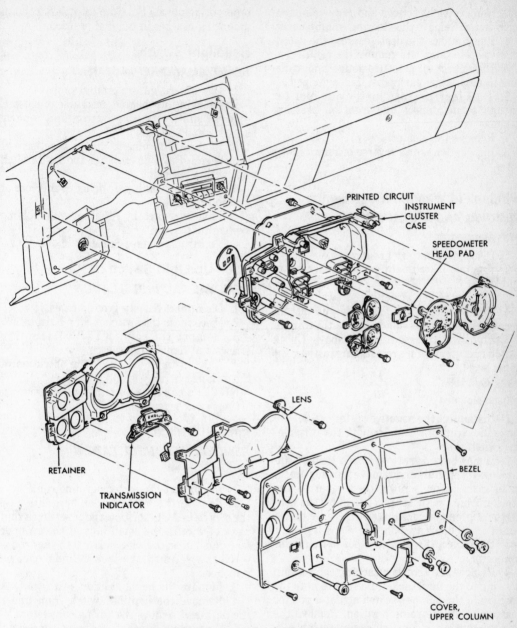

PRINTED CIRCUIT
INSTRUMENT
CLUSTER
CASE

SPEEDOMETER
HEAD PAD

LENS

RETAINER

TRANSMISSION
INDICATOR

BEZEL

COVER,
UPPER COLUMN

1973–76 instrument cluster; 1977 and later similar

1973-76

1. Remove the negative battery cable.
2. Remove the steering column cover and the cluster bezel.
3. Remove the knob from the clock (if equipped).
4. Remove the lens retaining screws and the lens.
5. Remove the transmission gear indicator (PRNDL) and the cluster retainer.
6. Disconnect the speedometer cable by depressing the spring clip and pulling the cable

out of the speedometer head. Disconnect and plug the oil pressure line, if so equipped.
7. Disconnect the cluster wiring harness and remove the cluster retaining screws and pull out the cluster.
8. To install the cluster, reverse the removal procedure.

1977 and Later

1. Disconnect the battery ground cable.
2. Remove the headlamp switch control knob and radio control knobs.

3. Remove eight screws and remove instrument bezel. Remove the steering column cover.

4. Reach under the dash, depress the speedometer cable tang, and remove the cable.

5. Disconnect oil pressure gauge line at fitting in engine compartment, if so equipped.

6. Pull instrument cluster out just far enough to disconnect line from oil pressure gauge.

7. Remove the cluster.

8. Installation is the reverse of removal.

Windshield Washer/Wiper Switch
REMOVAL AND REPLACEMENT
Dash Mounted

1. Disconnect battery ground cable.

2. Remove instrument panel bezel screws and bezel.

3. Remove switch attaching screws.

4. Pull out on switch assembly and disconnect electrical harness and remove the switch.

5. To install, reverse Steps 1-4 above. Check switch operation before reinstalling instrument panel bezel.

Column Mounted

1. Disconnect the negative battery cable. Remove the steering wheel. Remove the turn signal switch.

2. It may be necessary to loosen the two column mounting nuts and remove the four bracket to mast jacket screws, then separate the bracket from the mast jacket to allow the connector clip on the ignition switch to be pulled out of the column assembly.

3. Disconnect the washer/wiper switch lower connector.

4. Remove the screws attaching the column housing to the mast jacket. Be sure to note the position of the dimmer switch actuator rod for reassembly in the same position. Remove the column housing and switch as an assembly.

NOTE: *Some tilt columns have a removable plastic cover on the column housing. This provides access to the wiper switch without removing the entire column housing.*

5. Turn the assembly upside down and use a drift to remove the pivot pin from the washer/wiper switch. Remove the switch.

6. Place the switch into position in the housing, then install the pivot pin.

7. Position the housing onto the mast jacket and attach by installing the screws. Install the dimmer switch actuator rod in the same position as noted earlier. Check switch operation.

8. Reconnect lower end of switch assembly.

9. Install remaining components in reverse order of removal. Be sure to attach column mounting bracket in original position.

Headlight Switch
REMOVAL AND REPLACEMENT

1. Disconnect battery ground cable.

2. Reaching up behind instrument cluster, depress shaft retaining button and remove switch knob and rod.

3. Remove instrument cluster bezel screws on left end. Pull out on bezel and hold switch nut with a wrench.

4. Disconnect multiple wiring connectors at switch terminals.

5. Remove switch by rotating while holding switch nut.

6. To install, reverse Steps 1-5 above.

Back-Up Light Switch
REMOVAL AND INSTALLATION

1. Disconnect battery ground cable.

2. Disconnect the switch wiring harness.

3. Remove the column switch mounting screws and remove the switch.

4. After installation, check the operation of the switch.

NOTE: *Transmission mounted back-up light switches are found in Chapter 7.*

Ignition Switch
REMOVAL AND INSTALLATION
1970-72

1. Disconnect the battery ground cable.

2. Remove the lock cylinder by positioning the switch in **ACC** position and inserting a thin piece of wire in the small hole in the cylinder face. Push in on the wire and turn the key counterclockwise until the lock cylinder can be removed.

3. Remove the metal ignition switch nut.

4. Remove the ignition switch from under the dash and remove the wiring connector.

5. To remove the theft-resistant connector, the switch must be removed from under the dash. Use a small screwdriver, unsnap the locking tangs on the connector, and unplug the connector.

6. Installation is the reverse of removal.

Speedometer Cable
REMOVAL AND INSTALLATION
1970 and Later

1. Disconnect the negative battery terminal.

2. Disconnect the cable from the back of the speedometer.

3. Remove the old core by pulling it out at the speedometer end. If the core is broken, it

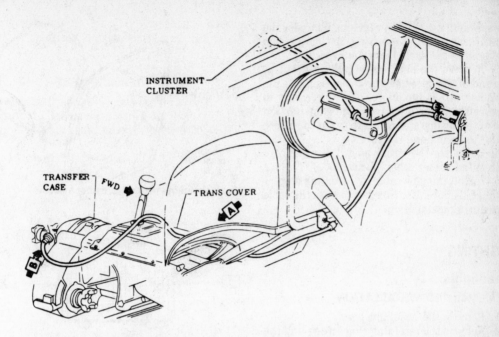

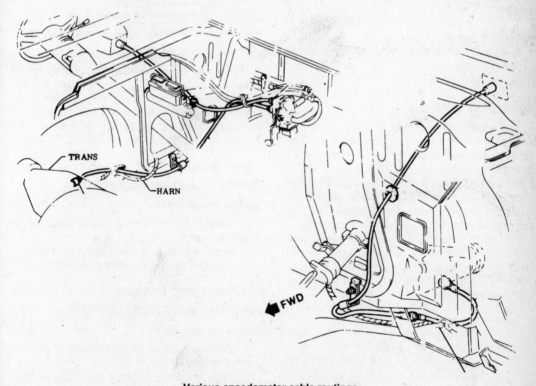

Various speedometer cable routings

will be necessary to remove the broken half from the transmission end of the cable.

4. Lubricate the entire length of the core before installation.

5. Installation is the reverse of removal.

Speedometer Cable Core
REPLACEMENT

1. Disconnect the battery ground cable.

2. Disconnect the speedometer cable from

the speedometer head by reaching up under the instrument panel, depressing the spring clip and pulling the cable from the head.

3. Remove the old core by pulling it out at the end of the speedometer cable casing. If the old cable core is broken it will be necessary to remove the lower piece from the transmission end of the casing. It is also important to replace both the casing and the core.

4. Lubricate the entire length of cable core with speedometer cable lubricant.

5. Install the new cable by reversing steps 1 through 3 above. Use care not to kink the cable core during installation.

LIGHTING

Headlights

REMOVAL AND INSTALLATION

1. Remove the headlight bezel.
2. Remove the retaining ring screws and the retaining ring. Do not disturb the adjusting screws.
3. Unplug the headlight from the electrical connector and remove it.
4. Installation is the reverse of removal.

NOTE: *The number molded into the lens face must be at the top.*

HEADLIGHT AIMING

The headlights must be properly aimed to provide the best, safest road illumination. The lights should be checked for proper aim, and adjusted if necessary, after installing a new sealed beam unit or if the front end sheet metal has been replaced. Certain state and local authorities have requirements for headlight aiming and you should check these before adjusting.

The truck's fuel tank should be about half full when adjusting the headlights. Tires should be properly inflated, and if a heavy load is carried in the pick-up bed, it should remain there.

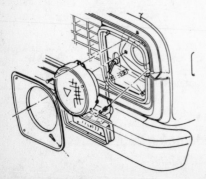

Typical headlight mounting, 170-72; later models similar

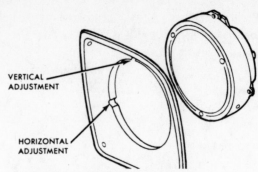

VERTICAL ADJUSTMENT

HORIZONTAL ADJUSTMENT

Headlight adjustment slots, earlier models

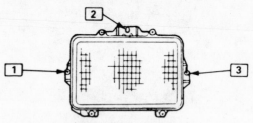

1. Horizontal adj. screw-RH
2. Vertical adj. screw
3. Horizontal adj. screw-LH

Headlight aiming. Round headlight models similar

Horizontal and vertical aiming of each sealed beam unit is provided by two adjusting screws, which move the mounting ring in the body against the tension of the coil spring. There is no adjustment for focus; this is done during headlight manufacturing.

Parking Lamp Bulb

REMOVAL AND REPLACEMENT

Models through 1985

1. Remove lens retaining screws and remove lens from the housing.
2. Replace bulb and check lamp operation.
3. Install lens and retaining screws.

Parking Lamp Housing

REMOVAL AND REPLACEMENT

Models through 1985

1. Remove parking lamp lens screws and remove the lens.
2. Remove lamp housing retaining screws and pull housing forward.
3. Disconnect parking lamp wiring harness from housing by rotating bulb socket counterclockwise.
4. Connect wiring harness to new housing by inserting bulb socket into housing and rotation clockwise.
5. Install bulb if removed during disassembly. Install lens and retaining screws.

Front Parking Lamp Assembly
REMOVAL AND INSTALLATION

1986-87 W/Two Lamp Option

1. Disconnect the negative battery cable.
2. Remove the four bezel retaining screws and remove the bezel.
3. Remove the three parking lamp retaining screws, disconnect the electrical connector and remove the parking lamp.
4. Reverse the above to replace.

1986–87 W/Four Lamp Option

1. Remove the radiator grille.
2. Disconnect the electrical connector from the parking lamp assembly.
3. Remove the two nuts at the top of the housing and lift it up from the radiator grille.
4. Reverse the above to install.

Front Side Marker Lamp Bulb and/or Housing
REMOVAL AND REPLACEMENT

All Models through 1985

1. For housing replacement follow procedure for the right side bulb replacement below.
   a. Left Side: Raise hood.
   b. Right Side: Remove lamp assembly retaining screws and pull outward on assembly.
2. Twist wiring harness socket 90 degrees counterclockwise and remove harness and bulb from housing.
3. Replace bulb and check lamp operation.
4. Insert bulb into housing, press in on harness socket and twist 90 degrees clockwise. Check that socket is securely attached.
5. Left Side: Lower hood.
6. Right Side: Install housing in opening and install retaining screws.

1986-87

1. Remove the two screws and remove the side marker lamp.
2. Remove the bulb from the lamp.
3. Reverse the above to install.

Rear Side Marker Lamp Bulb and/or Housing
REMOVAL AND REPLACEMENT

Stepside Models

Same as Right Front Side Marker Lamp Bulb and/or Housing Replacement—All Vehicles.

Fleetside Models

1. Remove lens-to-housing four screws.
2. Replace bulb and check operation.
3. Position lens and install four attaching screws.

Tail, Stop and Backup Lamp Bulbs
REMOVAL AND REPLACEMENT

1. Remove lens to housing attaching screws.
2. Replace bulb and check operation.
3. Position lens and install attaching screws.

Tail, Stop and Backup Lamp Housing
REMOVAL AND REPLACEMENT

1. Remove lens to housing attaching screws.
2. Remove bulbs from sockets.
3. Remove housing attaching screws.
4. Rotate wiring harness sockets counterclockwise and remove housing.
5. To install, reverse Steps 1-4 above.

Directional Signal Lamps

Directional signal lamps are an integral part of parking and tail lamp assemblies. Refer to the applicable lamp or bulb replacement procedures covered previously.

TRAILER WIRING

Wiring the truck for towing is fairly easy. There are a number of good wiring kits available and these should be used, rather than trying to design your own. All trailers will need brake lights and turn signals as well as tail lights and side marker lights. Most states require extra marker lights for overly wide trailers. Also, most states have recently required back-up lights for trailers, and most trailer manufacturers have been building trailers with back-up lights for several years.

Additionally, some Class I, most Class II and just about all Class III trailers will have electric brakes.

Add to this number an accessories wire, to operate trailer internal equipment or to charge the trailer's battery, and you can have as many as seven wires in the harness.

Determine the equipment on your trailer and buy the wiring kit necessary. The kit will contain all the wires needed, plus a plug adapter set which included the female plug, mounted on the bumper or hitch, and the male plug, wired into, or plugged into the trailer harness.

When installing the kit, follow the manufacturer's instructions. The color coding of the wires is standard throughout the industry.

One point to note, some domestic vehicles, and most imported vehicles, have separate turn signals. On most domestic vehicles, the brake lights and rear turn signals operate with the same bulb. For those vehicles with separate turn signals, you can purchase an isolation unit so that the brake lights won't blink whenever the turn signals are operated, or, you can go to your local electronics supply house and buy four diodes to wire in series with the brake and turn signal bulbs. Diodes will isolate the brake and turn signals. The choice is yours. The isolation units are simple and quick to install, but far more expensive than the diodes. The diodes, however, require more work to install properly, since they require the cutting of each bulb's wire and soldering in place of the diode.

One final point, the best kits are those with a spring loaded cover on the vehicle mounted socket. This cover prevents dirt and moisture from corroding the terminals. Never let the vehicle socket hang loosely. Always mount it securely to the bumper or hitch.

NOTE: *For more information on towing a trailer please refer to Chapter 1.*

CIRCUIT PROTECTION

Fusible Links

In addition to circuit breakers and fuses, the wiring harness incorporates fusible links to protect the wiring. Links are used rather than a fuse, in wiring circuits that are not normally fused, such as the ignition circuit. Fusible links are color coded red in the charging and load circuits to match the color of the circuits they protect. Each link is four gauges smaller than the cable it protects, and is marked on the insulation with the gauge size because the insulation makes it appear heavier than it really is.

The engine compartment wiring harness has

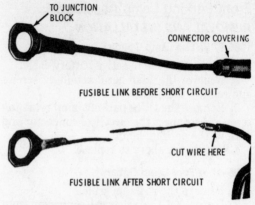

FUSIBLE LINK BEFORE SHORT CIRCUIT

FUSIBLE LINK AFTER SHORT CIRCUIT

Fusible links work like a fuse

several fusible links. The same size wire with a special hypalon insulation must be used when replacing a fusible link.

The links are located in the following areas:

1. A molded splice at the starter solenoid **Bat** terminal, a 14 gauge red wire.

2. A 16 gauge red fusible link at the junction block to protect the unfused wiring of 12 gauge or larger wire. This link stops at the bulkhead connector.

3. The alternator warning light and field circuitry is protected by a 20 gauge red wire fusible link used in the battery feed to voltage regular #3 terminal. The link is installed as a molded splice in the circuit at the junction block.

4. The ammeter circuit is protected by two 20 gauge fusible links installed as molded

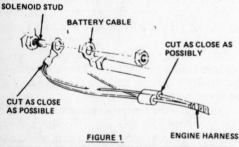

FIGURE 1
REMOVE BATTERY CABLE & FUSIBLE LINK FROM STARTER SOLENOID AND CUT OFF DEFECTIVE WIRE AS SHOWN TWO PLACES.

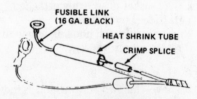

FIGURE 2
STRIP INSULATION FROM WIRE ENDS. PLACE HEAT SHRINK TUBE OVER REPLACEMENT LINK. INSERT WIRE ENDS INTO CRIMP SPLICE AS SHOWN. NOTE: PUSH WIRES IN FAR ENOUGH TO ENGAGE WIRE ENDS.

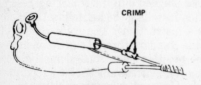

FIGURE 3
CRIMP SPLICE WITH CRIMPING TOOL TWO PLACES TO BIND BOTH WIRES.

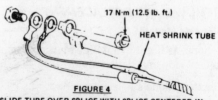

FIGURE 4
SLIDE TUBE OVER SPLICE WITH SPLICE CENTERED IN TUBE. APPLY LOW TEMPERATURE HEAT TO SHRINK TUBE AROUND WIRES & SPLICE. REASSEMBLE LINKS & BATTERY CABLE.

Fusible link repair

splices in the circuit at the junction block and battery to starter circuit.

FUSIBLE LINK REPAIR

1. Determine the circuit that is damaged.
2. Disconnect the negative battery terminal.
3. Cut the damaged fuse link from the harness and discard it.
4. Identify and procure the proper fuse link and butt connectors.
5. Strip the wire about ½″ on each end.
6. Connect the fusible link and crimp the butt connectors making sure that the wires are secure.
7. Solder each connection with resin core solder, and wrap the connections with plastic electrical tape.
8. Reinstall the wire in the harness.
9. Connect the negative battery terminal and test the system for proper operation.

Circuit Breakers

A circuit breaker is an electrical switch which breaks the circuit in case of an overload. All models have a circuit breaker in the headlight switch to protect the headlight and parking light systems. An overload may cause the lamps to flicker or flash on and off, or in some cases, to remain off. 1974 and later windshield wiper motors are protected by a circuit breaker at the motor.

Fuses and Flashers

Fuses are located in the junction box below the instrument panel to the left of the steering column. The turn signal flasher and the hazard/warning flasher also plug into the fuse block. Each fuse receptacle is marked as to the circuit it protects and the correct amperage of the fuse. Inline fuses are also used on the following circuits: 1970-75, ammeter; auxiliary heater and air conditioning 1973-74; and underhood lamp and air conditioning 1975 and later.

NOTE: *A special heavy duty turn signal flasher is required to properly operate the turn signals when a trailer's lights are connected to the system.*

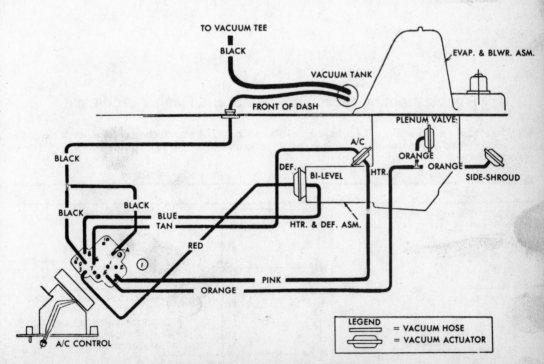

Air conditioning vacuum schematic-1976–85

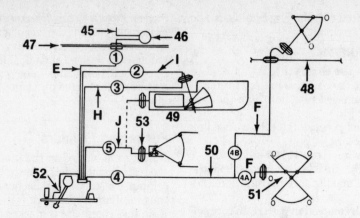

Connection	Port No.	Select Lever Valve Operation Chart						
		Off	Max A/C	Norm A/C	Bi-Level	Vent	Heat	Defrost
Source	1	← Vac →						
A/C Mode	2	Vent	Vacuum	← Vent →				
Heater/Mode	3	Vent	Optional	Optional	Vent	Optional	Vent	Vacuum
OSA/REC	4	Vacuum	Vent	Vent	Vent	Vent	Vacuum	Vacuum
Defroster	5	Vent	Vacuum	Vacuum	Vent	Vacuum	Vent	Vent
Ports 6,7,8 and 9 not used (sealed on vacuum hose assembly)								

1. Vacuum source-engine
2. Vacuum tank (gas)
3. Cowl
4. Plenum valve
5. Mode door

6. Defroster door
7. Recirculator door
8. Actuator
E. Vacuum line-gary (source)

F. Vacuum line-orange (defroster)
H. Vacuum line-dark blue (heat)
I. Vacuum line-tan (A/C)
J. Vacuum line-black (defroster)

Air conditioning vacuum schematic-1986–87

Troubleshooting Basic Turn Signal and Flasher Problems

Most problems in the turn signals or flasher system, can be reduced to defective flashers or bulbs, which are easily replaced. Occasionally, problems in the turn signals are traced to the switch in the steering column, which will require professional service.

F = Front   R = Rear   ● = Lights off   o = Lights on

Problem		Solution
Turn signals light, but do not flash	(F)---(F) / (R)---(R)	• Replace the flasher
No turn signals light on either side	(F)---(F) / (R)---(R)	• Check the fuse. Replace if defective. • Check the flasher by substitution • Check for open circuit, short circuit or poor ground

Troubleshooting Basic Turn Signal and Flasher Problems (cont.)

Most problems in the turn signals or flasher system can be reduced to defective flashers or bulbs, which are easily replaced. Occasionally, problems in the turn signals are traced to the switch in the steering column, which will require professional service.

F = Front   R = Rear   ● = Lights off   ○ = Lights on

Problem		Solution
Both turn signals on one side don't work		• Check for bad bulbs • Check for bad ground in both housings
One turn signal light on one side doesn't work	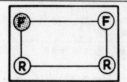	• Check and/or replace bulb • Check for corrosion in socket. Clean contacts. • Check for poor ground at socket
Turn signal flashes too fast or too slow	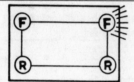	• Check any bulb on the side flashing too fast. A heavy-duty bulb is probably installed in place of a regular bulb. • Check the bulb flashing too slow. A standard bulb was probably installed in place of a heavy-duty bulb. • Check for loose connections or corrosion at the bulb socket
Indicator lights don't work in either direction		• Check if the turn signals are working • Check the dash indicator lights • Check the flasher by substitution
One indicator light doesn't light		• On systems with 1 dash indicator: See if the lights work on the same side. Often the filaments have been reversed in systems combining stoplights with taillights and turn signals. Check the flasher by substitution • On systems with 2 indicators: Check the bulbs on the same side Check the indicator light bulb Check the flasher by substitution

Troubleshooting Basic Lighting Problems

Problem	Cause	Solution
Lights		
One or more lights don't work, but others do	• Defective bulb(s) • Blown fuse(s) • Dirty fuse clips or light sockets • Poor ground circuit	• Replace bulb(s) • Replace fuse(s) • Clean connections • Run ground wire from light socket housing to car frame

Troubleshooting Basic Lighting Problems (cont.)

Problem	Cause	Solution
Lights burn out quickly	• Incorrect voltage regulator setting or defective regulator • Poor battery/alternator connections	• Replace voltage regulator • Check battery/alternator connections
Lights go dim	• Low/discharged battery • Alternator not charging • Corroded sockets or connections • Low voltage output	• Check battery • Check drive belt tension; repair or replace alternator • Clean bulb and socket contacts and connections • Replace voltage regulator
Lights flicker	• Loose connection • Poor ground • Circuit breaker operating (short circuit)	• Tighten all connections • Run ground wire from light housing to car frame • Check connections and look for bare wires
Lights "flare"—Some flare is normal on acceleration—if excessive, see "Lights Burn Out Quickly"	• High voltage setting	• Replace voltage regulator
Lights glare—approaching drivers are blinded	• Lights adjusted too high • Rear springs or shocks sagging • Rear tires soft	• Have headlights aimed • Check rear springs/shocks • Check/correct rear tire pressure
Turn Signals		
Turn signals don't work in either direction	• Blown fuse • Defective flasher • Loose connection	• Replace fuse • Replace flasher • Check/tighten all connections
Right (or left) turn signal only won't work	• Bulb burned out • Right (or left) indicator bulb burned out • Short circuit	• Replace bulb • Check/replace indicator bulb • Check/repair wiring
Flasher rate too slow or too fast	• Incorrect wattage bulb • Incorrect flasher	• Flasher bulb • Replace flasher (use a variable load flasher if you pull a trailer)
Indicator lights do not flash (burn steadily)	• Burned out bulb • Defective flasher	• Replace bulb • Replace flasher
Indicator lights do not light at all	• Burned out indicator bulb • Defective flasher	• Replace indicator bulb • Replace flasher

Troubleshooting Basic Dash Gauge Problems

Problem	Cause	Solution
Coolant Temperature Gauge		
Gauge reads erratically or not at all	• Loose or dirty connections • Defective sending unit • Defective gauge	• Clean/tighten connections • Bi-metal gauge: remove the wire from the sending unit. Ground the wire for an instant. If the gauge registers, replace the sending unit. • Magnetic gauge: disconnect the wire at the sending unit. With ignition ON gauge should register COLD. Ground the wire; gauge should register HOT.

Troubleshooting Basic Dash Gauge Problems (cont.)

Problem	Cause	Solution
Ammeter Gauge—Turn Headlights ON (do not start engine). Note reaction		
Ammeter shows charge Ammeter shows discharge Ammeter does not move	• Connections reversed on gauge • Ammeter is OK • Loose connections or faulty wiring • Defective gauge	• Reinstall connections • Nothing • Check/correct wiring • Replace gauge
Oil Pressure Gauge		
Gauge does not register or is inaccurate	• On mechanical gauge, Bourdon tube may be bent or kinked	• Check tube for kinks or bends preventing oil from reaching the gauge
	• Low oil pressure	• Remove sending unit. Idle the engine briefly. If no oil flows from sending unit hole, problem is in engine.
	• Defective gauge	• Remove the wire from the sending unit and ground it for an instant with the ignition ON. A good gauge will go to the top of the scale.
	• Defective wiring	• Check the wiring to the gauge. If it's OK and the gauge doesn't register when grounded, replace the gauge.
	• Defective sending unit	• If the wiring is OK and the gauge functions when grounded, replace the sending unit
All Gauges		
All gauges do not operate	• Blown fuse • Defective instrument regulator	• Replace fuse • Replace instrument voltage regulator
All gauges read low or erratically	• Defective or dirty instrument voltage regulator	• Clean contacts or replace
All gauges pegged	• Loss of ground between instrument voltage regulator and car • Defective instrument regulator	• Check ground • Replace regulator
Warning Lights		
Light(s) do not come on when ignition is ON, but engine is not started	• Defective bulb • Defective wire • Defective sending unit	• Replace bulb • Check wire from light to sending unit • Disconnect the wire from the sending unit and ground it. Replace the sending unit if the light comes on with the ignition ON.
Light comes on with engine running	• Problem in individual system • Defective sending unit	• Check system • Check sending unit (see above)

Troubleshooting the Heater

Problem	Cause	Solution
Blower motor will not turn at any speed	• Blown fuse • Loose connection • Defective ground • Faulty switch • Faulty motor • Faulty resistor	• Replace fuse • Inspect and tighten • Clean and tighten • Replace switch • Replace motor • Replace resistor
Blower motor turns at one speed only	• Faulty switch • Faulty resistor	• Replace switch • Replace resistor

Troubleshooting the Heater (cont.)

Problem	Cause	Solution
Blower motor turns but does not circulate air	· Intake blocked · Fan not secured to the motor shaft	· Clean intake · Tighten security
Heater will not heat	· Coolant does not reach proper temperature · Heater core blocked internally · Heater core air-bound · Blend-air door not in proper position	· Check and replace thermostat if necessary · Flush or replace core if necessary · Purge air from core · Adjust cable
Heater will not defrost	· Control cable adjustment incorrect · Defroster hose damaged	· Adjust control cable · Replace defroster hose

Troubleshooting Basic Windshield Wiper Problems

Problem	Cause	Solution
Electric Wipers		
Wipers do not operate— Wiper motor heats up or hums	· Internal motor defect · Bent or damaged linkage · Arms improperly installed on linking pivots	· Replace motor · Repair or replace linkage · Position linkage in park and reinstall wiper arms
Wipers do not operate— No current to motor	· Fuse or circuit breaker blown · Loose, open or broken wiring · Defective switch · Defective or corroded terminals · No ground circuit for motor or switch	· Replace fuse or circuit breaker · Repair wiring and connections · Replace switch · Replace or clean terminals · Repair ground circuits
Wipers do not operate— Motor runs	· Linkage disconnected or broken	· Connect wiper linkage or replace broken linkage
Vacuum Wipers		
Wipers do not operate	· Control switch or cable inoperative · Loss of engine vacuum to wiper motor (broken hoses, low engine vacuum, defective vacuum/fuel pump) · Linkage broken or disconnected · Defective wiper motor	· Repair or replace switch or cable · Check vacuum lines, engine vacuum and fuel pump · Repair linkage · Replace wiper motor
Wipers stop on engine acceleration	· Leaking vacuum hoses · Dry windshield · Oversize wiper blades · Defective vacuum/fuel pump	· Repair or replace hoses · Wet windshield with washers · Replace with proper size wiper blades · Replace pump

UNDERSTANDING THE MANUAL TRANSMISSION

Because of the way an internal combustion engine breathes, it can produce torque, or twisting force, only within a narrow speed range. Most modern, overhead valve engines must turn at about 2,500 rpm to produce their peak torque. By 4,500 rpm they are producing so little torque that continued increases in engine speed produce no power increases.

The torque peak on overhead camshaft engines is, generally, much higher, but much narrower.

The manual transmission and clutch are employed to vary the relationship between engine speed and the speed of the wheels so that adequate engine power can be produced under all circumstances. The clutch allows engine torque to be applied to the transmission input shaft gradually, due to mechanical slippage. The car can, consequently, be started smoothly from a full stop.

The transmission changes the ratio between the rotating speeds of the engine and the wheels by the use of gears. 4-speed or 5-speed transmissions are most common. The lower gears allow full engine power to be applied to the rear wheels during acceleration at low speeds.

The clutch drive plate is a thin disc, the center of which is splined to the transmission input shaft. Both sides of the disc are covered with a layer of material which is similar to brake lining and which is capable of allowing slippage without roughness or excessive noise.

The clutch cover is bolted to the engine flywheel and incorporates a diaphragm spring which provides the pressure to engage the clutch. The cover also houses the pressure plate. The driven disc is sandwiched between the pressure plate and the smooth surface of the flywheel when the clutch pedal is released,

thus forcing it to turn at the same speed as the engine crankshaft.

The transmission contains a mainshaft which passes all the way through the transmission, from the clutch to the driveshaft. This shaft is separated at one point, so that front and rear portions can turn at different speeds.

Power is transmitted by a countershaft in the lower gears and reverse. The gears of the countershaft mesh with gears on the mainshaft, allowing power to be carried from one to the other. All the countershaft gears are integral with that shaft, while several of the mainshaft gears can either rotate independently of the shaft or be locked to it. Shifting from one gear to the next causes one of the gears to be freed from rotating with the shaft and locks another to it. Gears are locked and unlocked by internal dog clutches which slide between the center of the gear and the shaft. The forward gears usually employ synchronizers; friction members which smoothly bring gear and shaft to the same speed before the toothed dog clutches are engaged.

The clutch is operating properly if:

1. It will stall the engine when released with the vehicle held stationary.

2. The shift lever can be moved freely between first and reverse gears when the vehicle is stationary and the clutch disengaged.

A clutch pedal free-play adjustment is incorporated in the linkage. If there is about 1-2" (25-50mm) of motion before the pedal begins to release the clutch, it is adjusted properly. Inadequate free-play wears all parts of the clutch releasing mechanisms and may cause slippage. Excessive free-play may cause inadequate release and hard shifting of gears.

Some clutches use a hydraulic system in place of mechanical linkage. If the clutch fails to release, fill the clutch master cylinder with fluid to the proper level and pump the clutch pedal to fill the system with fluid. Bleed the system in the same way as a brake system. If leaks are located, tighten loose connections or overhaul the master or slave cylinder as necessary.

MANUAL TRANSMISSION

Most 3-speed transmissions used are the very similar Saginaw and Muncie side cover units. These may be told apart by the shape of the side cover. The Saginaw has a single bolt centered at the top edge of the side cover, while the Muncie has two bolts along the top edge. Some 1976-80 models use the top cover Tremec 3-speed. All 3-speed transmissions use side mounted external linkage, with provision for linkage adjustment, and a column shift.

The Muncie CH465 with synchronized 2nd, 3rd and 4th gears is the standard 4-speed transmission for 1970 and later. The transmission is distinguished by its top cover and the absence of external linkage. In addition, the New Process 435CR close ratio 4-speed transmission was available on all ½ and ¾ ton models in 1970. It was also available in 1971 in those trucks, but only with the 8-350 engine. The 435CR is also a top cover unit, with no provision for linkage adjustment. 1981 and later models have a 4 speed overdrive transmission as an option. This unit uses external linkage which is adjustable.

LINKAGE ADJUSTMENT

Column Shift

1. Place the column lever in the neutral position.
2. Under the truck, loosen the shift rod clamps. These are at the bottom of the column

on 1970-72 models, and at the transmission for 1973 and later.
3. Make sure that the two levers on the transmission are in their center, neutral positions.
4. Install a $\frac{3}{16}$″ to $\frac{7}{32}$″ pin or drill bit through the alignment holes in the levers at the bottom of the steering column. This holds these levers in the neutral position.
5. Tighten the shift rod clamps.
6. Remove the pin and check the shifting operation.

Floor Shift

Place the shift lever in neutral. A 0.249-0.250″ gauge pin must fit freely through the shifter levers (see illustration) in the neutral position. A ¼″ or **D** size (0.249″) drill bit will work here. Adjust the linkage at the point shown until the gauge pin fits properly. Check adjustment by operating the shift lever through every gear shift combination.

Back-Up Light
REMOVAL AND INSTALLATION
Transmission Mounted

1. Disconnect the negative battery cable.
2. Raise the vehicle and support it safely.
3. Disconnect the electrical connector at the switch.
4. Remove the retaining screws.
5. After installation, check the operation of the switch.

Manual Transmission
REMOVAL AND INSTALLATION
2-Wheel Drive
3-SPEED AND 4-SPEED

1. Jack up your vehicle and support it with jackstands.
2. Drain the transmission.
3. Disconnect the speedometer cable, and back-up lamp wire at transmission.
4. Disconnect the shift control lever or shift control from the transmission. On 4-speeds. remove the gearshift lever by pressing down firmly on the slotted collar plate with a pair of channel lock pliers and rotating counterclockwise. Plug the opening to keep out dirt.
5. Remove driveshaft after making the position of the shaft to the flange.
6. Position a transmission jack or its equivalent under the transmission to support it.
7. Remove the crossmember. Visually inspect to see if other equipment, brackets or

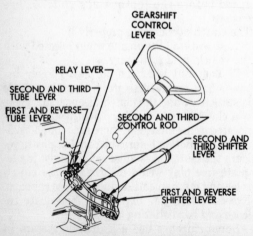

Three speed column shift controls, 1970–72

GEARSHIFT CONTROL LEVER

RELAY LEVER

SECOND AND THIRD TUBE LEVER

FIRST AND REVERSE TUBE LEVER

SECOND AND THIRD CONTROL ROD

SECOND AND THIRD SHIFTER LEVER

FIRST AND REVERSE SHIFTER LEVER

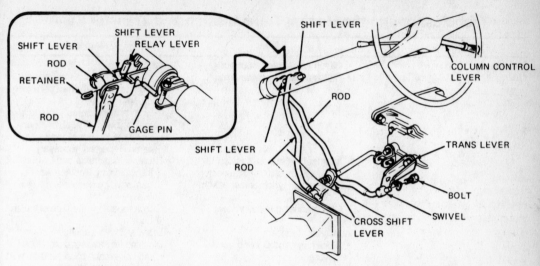

Three-speed column shift linkage adjustment. Note gage pin for aligning the shift levers

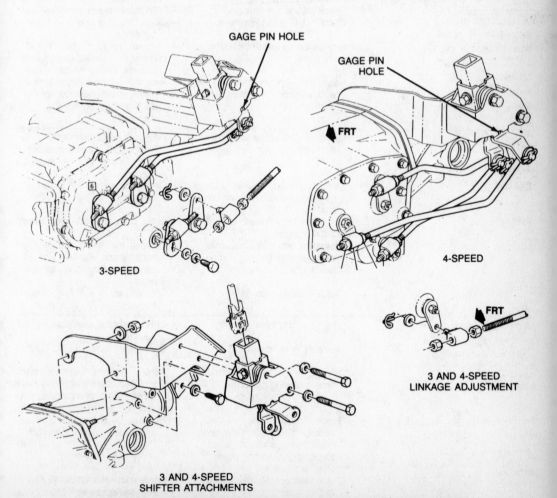

Three and four speed floor shift linkages, showing gage pin holes for adjustment

Troubleshooting the Manual Transmission and Transfer Case

Problem	Cause	Solution
Transmission shifts hard	• Clutch adjustment incorrect • Clutch linkage or cable binding • Shift rail binding	• Adjust clutch • Lubricate or repair as necessary • Check for mispositioned selector arm roll pin, loose cover bolts, worn shift rail bores, worn shift rail, distorted oil seal, or extension housing not aligned with case. Repair as necessary.
	• Internal bind in transmission caused by shift forks, selector plates, or synchronizer assemblies • Clutch housing misalignment • Incorrect lubricant • Block rings and/or cone seats worn	• Remove, dissemble and inspect transmission. Replace worn or damaged components as necessary. • Check runout at rear face of clutch housing • Drain and refill transmission • Blocking ring to gear clutch tooth face clearance must be 0.030 inch or greater. If clearance is correct it may still be necessary to inspect blocking rings and cone seats for excessive wear. Repair as necessary.
Gear clash when shifting from one gear to another	• Clutch adjustment incorrect • Clutch linkage or cable binding • Clutch housing misalignment • Lubricant level low or incorrect lubricant • Gearshift components, or synchronizer assemblies worn or damaged	• Adjust clutch • Lubricate or repair as necessary • Check runout at rear of clutch housing • Drain and refill transmission and check for lubricant leaks if level was low. Repair as necessary. • Remove, disassemble and inspect transmission. Replace worn or damaged components as necessary.
Transmission noisy	• Lubricant level low or incorrect lubricant • Clutch housing-to-engine, or transmission-to-clutch housing bolts loose • Dirt, chips, foreign material in transmission • Gearshift mechanism, transmission gears, or bearing components worn or damaged • Clutch housing misalignment	• Drain and refill transmission. If lubricant level was low, check for leaks and repair as necessary. • Check and correct bolt torque as necessary • Drain, flush, and refill transmission • Remove, disassemble and inspect transmission. Replace worn or damaged components as necessary. • Check runout at rear face of clutch housing
Jumps out of gear	• Clutch housing misalignment • Gearshift lever loose • Offset lever nylon insert worn or lever attaching nut loose • Gearshift mechanism, shift forks, selector plates, interlock plate, selector arm, shift rail, detent plugs, springs or shift cover worn or damaged • Clutch shaft or roller bearings worn or damaged	• Check runout at rear face of clutch housing • Check lever for worn fork. Tighten loose attaching bolts. • Remove gearshift lever and check for loose offset lever nut or worn insert. Repair or replace as necessary. • Remove, disassemble and inspect transmission cover assembly. Replace worn or damaged components as necessary. • Replace clutch shaft or roller bearings as necessary

Troubleshooting the Manual Transmission and Transfer Case (cont.)

Problem	Cause	Solution
Jumps out of gear (cont.)	• Gear teeth worn or tapered, synchronizer assemblies worn or damaged, excessive end play caused by worn thrust washers or output shaft gears • Pilot bushing worn	• Remove, disassemble, and inspect transmission. Replace worn or damaged components as necessary. • Replace pilot bushing
Will not shift into one gear	• Gearshift selector plates, interlock plate, or selector arm, worn, damaged, or incorrectly assembled • Shift rail detent plunger worn, spring broken, or plug loose • Gearshift lever worn or damaged • Synchronizer sleeves or hubs, damaged or worn	• Remove, disassemble, and inspect transmission cover assembly. Repair or replace components as necessary. • Tighten plug or replace worn or damaged components as necessary • Replace gearshift lever • Remove, disassemble and inspect transmission. Replace worn or damaged components.
Locked in one gear—cannot be shifted out	• Shift rail(s) worn or broken, shifter fork bent, setscrew loose, center detent plug missing or worn • Broken gear teeth on countershaft gear, clutch shaft, or reverse idler gear Gearshift lever broken or worn, shift mechanism in cover incorrectly assembled or broken, worn damaged gear train components	• Inspect and replace worn or damaged parts • Inspect and replace damaged part • Disassemble transmission. Replace damaged parts or assemble correctly.
Transfer case difficult to shift or will not shift into desired range	• Vehicle speed too great to permit shifting • If vehicle was operated for extended period in 4H mode on dry paved surface, driveline torque load may cause difficult shifting • Transfer case external shift linkage binding • Insufficient or incorrect lubricant • Internal components binding, worn, or damaged	• Stop vehicle and shift into desired range. Or reduce speed to 3–4 km/h (2–3 mph) before attempting to shift. • Stop vehicle, shift transmission to neutral, shift transfer case to 2H mode and operate vehicle in 2H on dry paved surfaces • Lubricate or repair or replace linkage, or tighten loose components as necessary • Drain and refill to edge of fill hole with SAE 85W-90 gear lubricant only • Disassemble unit and replace worn or damaged components as necessary
Transfer case noisy in all drive modes	• Insufficient or incorrect lubricant	• Drain and refill to edge of fill hole with SAE 85W-90 gear lubricant only. Check for leaks and repair if necessary. Note: If unit is still noisy after drain and refill, disassembly and inspection may be required to locate source of noise.
Noisy in—or jumps out of four wheel drive low range	• Transfer case not completely engaged in 4L position • Shift linkage loose or binding • Shift fork cracked, inserts worn, or fork is binding on shift rail	• Stop vehicle, shift transfer case in Neutral, then shift back into 4L position • Tighten, lubricate, or repair linkage as necessary • Disassemble unit and repair as necessary
Lubricant leaking from output shaft seals or from vent	• Transfer case overfilled • Vent closed or restricted	• Drain to correct level • Clear or replace vent if necessary

Troubleshooting the Manual Transmission and Transfer Case (cont.)

Problem	Cause	Solution
Lubricant leaking from output shaft seals or from vent (cont.)	• Output shaft seals damaged or installed incorrectly	• Replace seals. Be sure seal lip faces interior of case when installed. Also be sure yoke seal surfaces are not scored or nicked. Remove scores, nicks with fine sandpaper or replace yoke(s) if necessary.
Abnormal tire wear	• Extended operation on dry hard surface (paved) roads in 4H range	• Operate in 2H on hard surface (paved) roads

lines, must be removed to permit removal of transmission.

NOTE: *Mark position of crossmember when removing to prevent incorrect installation. The tapered surface should face the rear.*

8. Remove the flywheel housing underpan.

9. Remove the top two transmission to housing bolts and insert two guide pins.

NOTE: *The use of guide pins will not only support the transmission but will prevent damage to the clutch disc. Guide pins can be made by taking two bolts, the same as those just removed only longer, and cutting off the heads. Slot for a screwdriver. Be sure to support the clutch release bearing and support assembly during removal of the transmission. This will prevent the release from falling out of the flywheel housing.*

10. Remove two remaining bolts and slide transmission straight back from engine. Use care to keep the transmission drive gear straight in line with clutch disc hub.

11. Remove the transmission from beneath your vehicle.

12. When installing torque the mounting bolts to 55 ft.lb., through 1972, 75 ft.lb. 1973 and later.

Place transmission in gear and rotate transmission flange or output yoke to aid entry of main drive gear into disc's splines. Make sure clutch release bearing is in position.

WARNING: *Do not force the transmission into the clutch disc hub. Do not let the transmission hang unsupported in the splined portion of the clutch disc.*

4-Wheel Drive

3-SPEED

1. Jack up the vehicle and support it on jackstands. Remove the skid plate, if so equipped.

2. Drain the transmission and transfer case. Remove the speedometer cable and the TCS switch, if so equipped, from the side of the transmission.

3. Disconnect the driveshafts and secure them out of the way.

4. Remove the shifter lever by removing the pivot bolt to the adapter assembly. You can then push the shifter up out of the way.

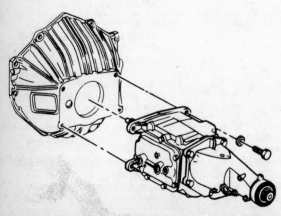

Transmission-to-bell housing mounting, manual transmissions

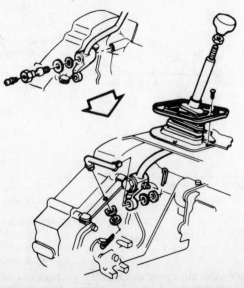

205-series transfer case linkage

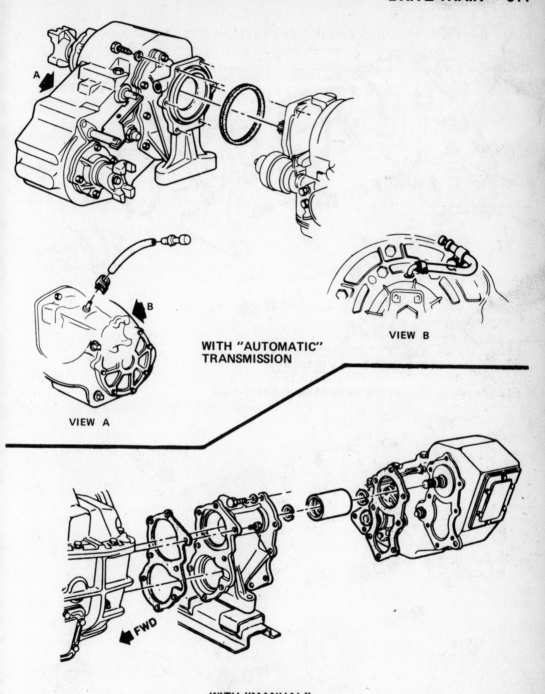

WITH "AUTOMATIC"
TRANSMISSION

VIEW A

VIEW B

WITH "MANUAL"
TRANSMISSION

Transfer case mounting, 205-series

5. On 1978 and later models, remove the bolts attaching the strut to the right side of the transfer case and the rear of the engine, and remove the strut.

6. While supporting the transfer case, remove the attaching bolts to the adapter.

7. Remove the transfer case securing bolts from the frame and lower and remove the transfer case. (The case is attached to the right side of the frame).

8. Disconnect the shift rods from the transmission.

9. While holding the rear of the engine with a jack, remove the adapter mounting bolts.

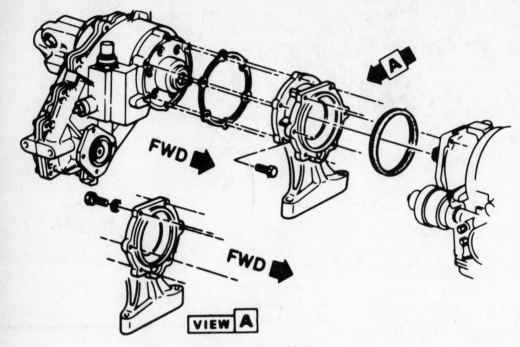

WITH AUTOMATIC TRANSMISSION

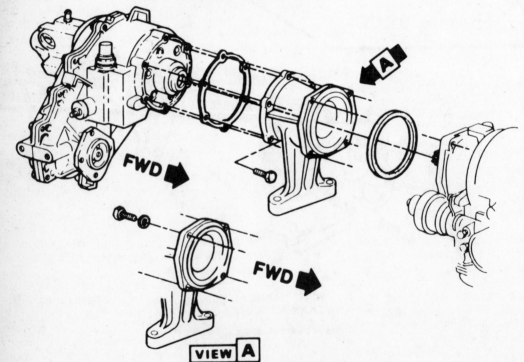

WITH MANUAL TRANSMISSION

208-series transfer case mounting

10. Remove the upper transmission bolts and insert two guide pins to keep the assembly aligned. See the two wheel drive procedure for details on making these.

11. Remove the flywheel pan and the lower transmission bolts.

12. Pull the transmission and the adapter straight back on the guide pins until the input shaft is free of the clutch disc.

13. The transmission and the adapter are removed as on assembly. The adapter can be separated once the assembly is out.

14. When installing, place the transmission in gear and turn the output shaft to align the clutch splines. Transmission bolt torque is 55 ft.lb. through 1972, and 75 ft.lb. for 1973 and later. See Transfer Case installation for adapter bolt torques.

4-SPEED

1. Remove the shifter boots and retainers.

2. Remove the transmission shift lever. See the two wheel drive procedure for details on removing the lever. It may be necessary to remove the center floor outlet from the heater to complete the next step. Remove the center console, if so equipped.

3. Remove the transmission cover after releasing the attaching screws. It will be necessary to rotate the cover 90 degrees to clear the transfer case shift lever.

4. Disconnect the transfer case shift lever link assembly and the lever from the adapter. Remove the skid plate, if any.

5. Remove the back-up light, the TCS switch, and the speedometer cable from the transmission.

6. Raise and support the truck with jackstands. Support the engine. Drain the transmission and the transfer case. Detach both driveshafts and secure them out of the way.

7. Remove the transmission-to-frame bolts. To do this, it will be necessary to open the locking tabs. Remove the transfer case-to-frame bracket bolts.

8. While supporting the transmission and transfer case, remove the crossmember bolts and the crossmember. It will be necessary to rotate the crossmember to remove it from the frame.

9. Remove the lower clutch housing cover.

NOTE: *On V8 engines it is necessary to remove the exhaust crossover pipe.*

10. Remove the transmission-to-clutch housing bolts. Remove the upper bolts first and install guide pins. See the two wheel drive procedure for details.

11. Slide the transmission back until the in-

put shaft clears the clutch assembly and then lower the unit.

12. The transfer case and transmission is installed as an assembly. Put the transmission in gear and turn the output shaft to align the clutch splines. Torque the transmission bolts to 55 ft.lb. through 1972, to 75 ft.lb. 1973 and later.

TRANSMISSION OVERHAUL

Saginaw 3-Speed (76mm)

TRANSMISSION CASE DISASSEMBLY

1. Remove the side cover assembly and the shift forks.

2. Remove the clutch gear bearing retainer.

3. Remove the clutch gear bearing-to-gear stem snapring. Pull the clutch gear outward until a screwdriver can be inserted between the bearing and the case. Remove the clutch gear bearing.

4. Remove the speedometer driven gear and the extension bolts.

5. Remove the Reverse idler shaft snapring.

6. Remove the mainshaft and the extension assembly through the rear of the case.

7. Remove the clutch gear and the 3rd speed blocking ring from inside the case. Remove the 14 roller bearings from the clutch gear.

8. Expand the snapring which retains the mainshaft rear bearing and remove the extension.

9. Using a dummy shaft, drive the countershaft and the key out through the rear of the case. Remove the gear, the two tanged thrust washers and the dummy shaft. Remove the bearing washer and the 27 roller bearings from each end of the countergear.

10. Using a long drift, drive the Reverse idler shaft and key through the rear of the case.

11. Remove the Reverse idler gear and the tanged steel thrust washer.

TRANSMISSION CASE ASSEMBLY

1. Using a dummy shaft, grease and load a row of 27 roller bearings and a thrust washer at each end of countergear.

2. Place the countergear assembly into the case from the rear. Place a tanged thrust washer (tang away from the gear) at each end. Install the countershaft and the key, making sure that the tangs align with the notches in the case.

3. Install the Reverse idler gear thrust washer, the gear and the shaft with a key from the rear of the case.

NOTE: *Be sure the thrust washer is between the gear and the rear of the case with the tang toward the notch in the case.*

4. Expand the snapring in the extension housing. Assemble the extension over the rear

1 Synchronizer retainer ring
2 Synchronizer blocking ring
3 Synchronizer assembly
4 Second speed gear
5 Main shaft
6 Synchronizer assembly
7 Gear assembly
8 Thrust washer
9 Retainer clip

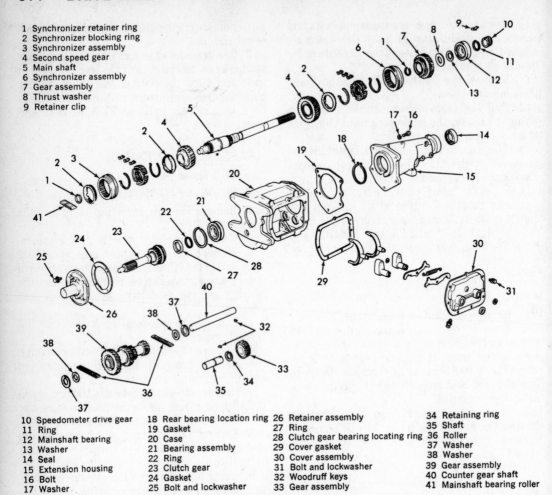

10 Speedometer drive gear	18 Rear bearing location ring	26 Retainer assembly	34 Retaining ring
11 Ring	19 Gasket	27 Ring	35 Shaft
12 Mainshaft bearing	20 Case	28 Clutch gear bearing locating ring	36 Roller
13 Washer	21 Bearing assembly	29 Cover gasket	37 Washer
14 Seal	22 Ring	30 Cover assembly	38 Washer
15 Extension housing	23 Clutch gear	31 Bolt and lockwasher	39 Gear assembly
16 Bolt	24 Gasket	32 Woodruff keys	40 Counter gear shaft
17 Washer	25 Bolt and lockwasher	33 Gear assembly	41 Mainshaft bearing roller

Exploded view-Saginaw 3-speed

of the mainshaft and onto the rear bearing. Seat the snapring in the rear bearing groove.

5. Install the 14 mainshaft pilot bearings into the clutch gear cavity. Assemble the 3rd speed blocking ring onto the clutch gear clutching surface with the teeth toward the gear.

6. Place the clutch gear, the pilot bearings and the 3rd speed blocking ring assembly over the front of the mainshaft assembly; be sure the blocking rings align with the keys in the 2nd/3rd synchronizer assembly.

7. Stick the extension gasket to the case with grease. Install the clutch gear, the mainshaft and the extension together; be sure the clutch gear engages the teeth of the countergear anti lash plate. Torque the extension bolts to 45 ft.lb.

8. Place the bearing over the stem of the clutch gear and into the front case bore. Install the front bearing to the clutch gear snapring.

9. Install the clutch gear bearing retainer and the gasket. The retainer oil return hole

must be at the bottom. Torque the retainer bolts to 10 ft.lb.

10. Install the Reverse idler gear shaft E-ring.

11. Shift the synchronizer sleeves to the Neutral positions. Install the cover, the gasket and the forks; aligning the forks with the synchronizer sleeve grooves. Torque the side cover bolts to 10 ft.lb.

12. Install the speedometer driven gear.

MAINSHAFT DISASSEMBLY

1. Remove the 2nd/3rd speed sliding clutch hub snapring from the mainshaft. Remove the clutch assembly, the 2nd speed blocking ring and the 2nd gear from front of the mainshaft.

2. Depress the speedometer drive gear retaining clip and remove the gear. Some units have a metal speedometer driver gear which must be pulled off.

3. Remove the rear bearing snapring.

4. Support the Reverse gear and press on the rear of the mainshaft. Remove the Reverse

gear, the thrust washer, the spring washer, the rear bearing and the snapring.

NOTE: *When pressing off the rear bearing, be careful not to cock the bearing on the shaft.*

5. Remove the 1st and Reverse sliding clutch hub snapring. Remove the clutch assembly, 1st speed blocking ring and the 1st gear; sometimes the synchronizer hub and gear must be pressed off.

MAINSHAFT ASSEMBLY

1. Turn the front of the mainshaft up.
2. Install the 2nd gear with the clutching teeth up; the rear face of the gear butts against the flange on the mainshaft.
3. Install a blocking ring with the clutching teeth down. The three blocking rings are the same.
4. Install the 2nd/3rd speed synchronizer assembly with the fork slot down; press it onto the mainshaft splines.

NOTE: *Both synchronizer assemblies are the same. Be sure that the blocking ring notches align with the synchronizer assembly keys.*

5. Install the synchronizer snapring; both synchronizer snaprings are the same.
6. Turn the rear of the shaft up, then install the 1st gear with the clutching teeth up; the front face of the gear butts against the flange on the mainshaft.
7. Install a blocking ring with the clutching teeth down.
8. Install the 1st/Reverse synchronizer assembly with the fork slot down, then press it onto the mainshaft splines; be sure the blocking ring notches align with the synchronizer assembly keys.
9. Install the snapring.
10. Install the Reverse gear with the clutching teeth down.
11. Install the steel Reverse gear thrust washer and the spring washer.
12. Press the rear ball bearing onto the shaft with the snapring slot down.
13. Install the snapring.
14. Install the speedometer drive gear and the retaining clip; press on the metal speedometer drive gear.

CLUTCH KEYS AND SPRINGS REPLACEMENT

The keys and the springs may be replaced if worn or broken, but the hubs and sleeves are matched pairs, they must be kept together.

1. Mark the hub and sleeve for reassembly.
2. Push the hub from the sleeve, then remove the keys and the springs.
3. Place the three keys and the two springs (one on each side of hub) in position, so the three keys are engaged by both springs; the

tanged ends of the springs should not be installed into the same key.

4. Slide the sleeve onto the hub by aligning the marks.

NOTE: *A groove around the outside of the synchronizer hub marks the end that must be opposite the fork slot in the sleeve when assembled.*

EXTENSION OIL SEAL AND BUSHING REPLACEMENT

1. Remove the seal.
2. Using the bushing removal and installation tool, drive the bushing into the extension housing.
3. Drive the new bushing in from the rear. Lubricate the inside of the bushing and the seal. Install a new oil seal with the extension seal installation tool or other suitable tool.

CLUTCH BEARING RETAINER OIL SEAL REPLACEMENT

1. Pry the old seal out.
2. Install the new seal using the seal installer. Seat the seal in the bore.

Muncie 3-Speed (83mm)

TRANSMISSION UNIT DISASSEMBLY

1. Remove side cover and shift forks.
2. Unbolt extension and rotate to line up groove in extension flange with reverse idler shaft. Drive reverse idler shaft and key out of case with a brass drift.
3. Move 2nd/3rd synchronizer sleeve forward. Remove extension housing and mainshaft assembly.
4. Remove reverse idler gear from case.
5. Remove 3rd speed blocker ring from clutch gear.
6. Expand snapring which holds mainshaft rear bearing. Tap gently on end of mainshaft to remove extension.
7. Remove clutch gear bearing retainer and gasket.
8. Remove snapring. Remove clutch gear from inside case by gently tapping on end of clutch gear.
9. Remove oil slinger and 16 mainshaft pilot bearings from clutch gear cavity.
10. Slip clutch gear bearing out front of case. Aid removal with a screwdriver between case and bearing outer snapring.
11. Drive countershaft and key out to rear.
12. Remove countergear and two tanged thrust washers.

MAINSHAFT DISASSEMBLY

1. Remove speedometer drive gear. Some speedometer drive gears, made of metal, must be pulled off.
2. Remove rear bearing snapring.
3. Support reverse gear. Press on rear of

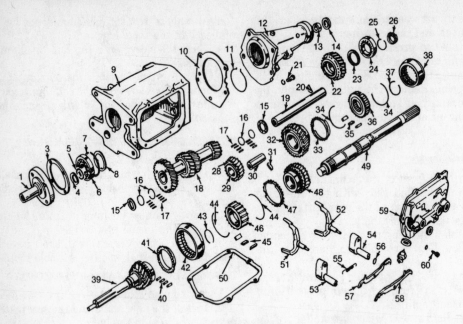

1. Bearing retainer	14. Oil seal	28. Reverse idler gear	40. Pilot bearings
2. Bolt and lock washer	15. Thrust washer	29. Reverse idler bushing	41. 3rd speed blocker ring
3. Gasket	16. Bearing washer	30. Reverse idler shaft	42. 2nd and 3rd
4. Oil seal	17. Needle bearings	31. Woodruff key	synchronizer collar
5. Snap-ring (bearing-to-	18. Countergear	32. 1st speed gear	43. Snap-ring
main drive gear)	19. Countershaft	33. 1st speed blocker ring	44. Synchronizer key
6. Main drive gear	20. Woodruff key	34. Synchronizer key	spring
bearing	21. Bolt (extension-to-	spring	45. Synchronizer keys
7. Snap-ring bearing	case)	35. Synchronizer keys	46. 2nd and 3rd
8. Oil slinger	22. Reverse gear	36. 1st and reverse	synchronizer hub
9. Case	23. Thrust washer	synchronizer hub	47. 2nd speed blocker
10. Gasket	24. Rear bearing	assembly	ring
11. Snap-ring (rear	25. Snap-ring	37. Snap-ring	48. 2nd speed gear
bearing-to-extension)	26. Speedometer drive	38. 1st and reverse	49. Mainshaft
12. Extension	gear	synchronizer collar	50. Gasket
13. Extension bushing	27. Retainer clip	39. Main drive gear	51. 2nd and 3rd shifter

fork
52. 1st and reverse shifter
fork
53. 2-3 shifter shaft
assembly
54. 1st and reverse shifter
shaft assembly
55. Spring
56. O-ring seal
57. 1st and reverse
detent cam
58. 2nd and 3rd detent
cam
59. Side cover
60. Bolt and lock washer

Exploded view-Muncie 3-speed (83mm)

mainshaft to remove reverse gear, thrust washer and rear bearing. Be careful not to cock the bearing on the shaft.

4. Remove 1st and reverse sliding clutch hub snapring.

5. Support 1st gear. Press on rear of mainshaft to remove clutch assembly, blocker ring and 1st gear.

6. Remove 2nd and 3rd speed sliding clutch hub snapring.

7. Support 2nd gear. Press on front of mainshaft to remove clutch assembly, 2nd speed blocker ring and 2nd gear from shaft.

CLEANING AND INSPECTION

For more detailed information, see the Cleaning and Inspection instructions at front of transmission section.

1. Wash all parts in solvent.
2. Allow them to air dry.

CLUTCH KEYS AND SPRINGS REPLACEMENT

Keys and springs may be replaced if worn or broken, but the hubs and sleeves must be kept together as originally assembled.

1. Mark hub and sleeve for reassembly.
2. Push hub from sleeve. Remove keys and springs.
3. Place three keys and two springs, one on each side of hub, so all three keys are engaged by both springs. The tanged end of the springs should not be installed into the same key.
4. Slide the sleeve onto the hub, aligning the marks.

EXTENSION OIL SEAL AND BUSHING REPLACEMENT

1. Remove seal.
2. Using bushing remover and installer, or other suitable tool, drive bushing into extension housing.
3. Drive new bushing in from rear. Lubricate inside of bushing and seal. Install new oil seal with extension seal installer or suitable tool.

CLUTCH BEARING RETAINER OIL SEAL REPLACEMENT

1. Pry old seal out.
2. Install new seal using seal installer or suitable tool. Seat seal in bore.

MAINSHAFT ASSEMBLY

1. Lift front of mainshaft.

2. Install 2nd gear with clutching teeth up; the rear face of the gear butts against the mainshaft flange.

3. Install a blocking ring with clutching teeth downward. All three blocking rings are the same.

4. Install 2nd and 3rd synchronizer assembly with fork slot down. Press it onto mainshaft splines. Both synchronizer assemblies are identical but are assembled differently. The 2nd/3rd speed hub and sleeve is assembled with the sleeve fork slot toward the thrust face of the hub; the 1st/reverse hub and sleeve, with the fork slot opposite the thrust face. Be sure that the blocker ring notches align with the synchronizer assembly keys.

5. Install synchronizer snapring. Both synchronizer snaprings are the same.

6. Turn rear of shaft up.

7. Install 1st gear with clutching teeth upward; the front face of the gear butts against the flange on the mainshaft.

8. Install a blocker ring with clutching teeth down.

9. Install 1st and reverse synchronizer assembly with fork slot down. Press it onto mainshaft splines. Be sure blocker ring notches align with synchronizer assembly keys and synchronizer sleeves face front of mainshaft.

10. Install snapring.

11. Install reverse gear with clutching teeth down.

12. Install steel reverse gear thrust washer with flats aligned.

13. Press rear ball bearing onto shaft with snapring slot down.

14. Install snapring.

15. Install speedometer drive gear and retaining clip.

TRANSMISSION UNIT ASSEMBLY

1. Place a row of 29 roller bearings, a bearing washer, a second row of 29 bearings and a 2nd bearing washer at each end of the countergear. Hold in place with grease.

2. Place countergear assembly through rear case opening with a tanged thrust washer, tang away from gear, at each end. Install countershaft and key from rear of case. Be sure that thrust washer tangs are aligned with notches in case.

3. Place reverse idler gear in case. Do not install reverse idler shaft yet. The reverse idler gear bushing may not be replaced separately, it must be replaced as a unit.

4. Expand snapring in extension. Assemble extension over mainshaft and onto rear bearing. Seat snap ring.

5. Load 16 mainshaft pilot bearings into clutch gear cavity. Assemble 3rd speed blocker ring onto clutch gear clutching surface with teeth toward gear.

6. Place clutch gear assembly, without front bearing, over front of mainshaft. Make sure that blocker ring notches align with keys in 2nd/3rd synchronizer assembly.

7. Stick gasket onto extension housing with grease. Assemble clutch gear, mainshaft and extension to case together. Make sure that clutch gear teeth engage teeth of countergear anti-lash plate.

8. Rotate extension housing. Install reverse idler shaft and key.

9. Torque extension bolts to 45 ft.lb.

10. Install oil slinger with inner lip facing forward. Install front bearing outer snapring and slide bearing into case bore.

11. Install snapring to clutch gear stem. Install bearing retainer and gasket and torque to 20 ft.lb. Retainer oil return hole must be at 6 o'clock.

12. Shift both synchronizer sleeves to neutral positions. Install side cover, inserting shifter forks in synchronizer sleeve grooves.

13. Torque side cover bolts to 20 ft.lb.

Tremec 3-Speed

TRANSMISSION DISASSEMBLY

1. Drain the lubricant by removing the lower extension housing bolt.

2. Remove the case cover and gasket.

3. Remove the long spring that holds the detent plug in the case and remove the detent plug with a small magnet.

4. Remove the extension housing and gasket.

5. Remove the front bearing retainer and gasket.

6. Remove the filler plug on the right side of the transmission case. Working through the plug opening, drive the roll pin out of the case and countershaft with a ¼" (6mm) punch.

7. Hold the countershaft gear with a hook. Install dummy shaft and push the countershaft out of the rear of the case. As the countershaft comes out, lower the gear cluster to the bottom of the case. Remove the countershaft.

8. Remove the snapring that holds the speedometer drive gear on the output shaft. Slip the gear off the shaft and remove the gear lock ball.

9. Remove the snapring that holds the output shaft bearing. Using a special bearing puller, remove the output shaft bearing.

10. Place both shift levers in the neutral (center) position.

11. Remove the set screw that holds the 1st/reverse shift fork to the shift rail. Slip the 1st/reverse shift rail out through the rear of the case.

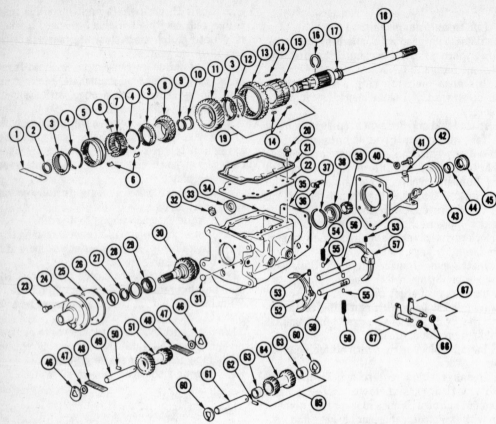

1. Mainshaft roller bearings
2. 2nd & 3rd synchronizer retaining ring
3. Synchronizer blocker rings
4. 2nd & 3rd synchronizer spring
5. 2nd & 3rd synchronizer sleeve
6. 2nd & 3rd synchronizer keys
7. 2nd & 3rd synchrinizer hub
8. Second speed gear
9. 1st speed gear retaining ring
10. 1st speed gear tabbed washer
11. 1st speed gear
12. Reverse synchronizer spring
13. 1st & reverse synchronizer sleeve & gear
14. Reverse synchronizer keys
15. 1st & reverse synchronizer hub
16. 1st & reverse synchronizer retaining ring
17. Rear bearing retaining ring
18. Transmission mainshaft
19. Reverse-synchronizer assembly
20. Access cover bolts
21. Access cover
22. Access cover gasket
23. Bearing Retainer-to case bolts
24. Bearing retainer-clutch gear
25. Gasket-clutch gear bearing retainer
26. Seal assembly-clutch gear bearing retainer
27. Clutch gear bearing retaining ring
28. Clutch gear bearing lock ring
29. Clutch gear bearing assembly
30. Clutch gear
31. Expansion plug
32. Filler plug
33. Transmission case magnet
34. Case

35. Extension housing to case gasket
36. Speedometer driver gear retaining clip
37. Transmission rear bearing lock ring
38. Mainshaft bearing assembly
39. Speedometer drive gear
40. Extension to case washer
41. Extension to case bolt
42. Transmission extension ventilator assembly
43. Extension housing assembly
44. Extension housing bushing
45. Extension housing oil seal assembly
46. Countergear thrust washer
47. Countergear spacer
48. Countergear rollet bearings
49. Countergear shaft
50. Countergear spring pin
51. Countergear
52. 2nd & 3rd shifter fork
53. Shift fork locking screw
54. 1st & 2nd shifter interlock spring
55. Shifter interlock pin
56. 1st & reverse shift rail
57. 1st & reverse shift fork
58. 2nd & 3rd shifter interlock spring
59. 2nd & 3rd shift rail
60. Reverse idler gear thrust washer
61. Reverse idler gear shaft
62. Spring pin idler gear shaft
63. Reverse idler gear bushing
64. Reverse idler gear
65. Reverse idler gear assembly
66. Seal transmission shifter
67. Transmission shifter shaft & lever assembly

Exploded view-Tremec

12. Move the 1st/reverse synchronizer forward as far as possible. Rotate the 1st/reverse shift fork upwards and lift it out of the case.

13. Place the 2nd/3rd shift fork in the 2nd position. Remove the set screw. Rotate the shift rail 90 degrees.

14. Lift the interlock plug out of the case with a magnet.

15. Remove the expansion plug from the 2nd/3rd shift rail by lightly tapping the end of the rail. Remove the 2nd/3rd shift rail.

16. Remove the 2nd/3rd shift rail detent plug and spring from detent bore.

17. Remove the input gear and shaft from the case.

18. Rotate the 2nd/3rd shift fork upwards and remove from case.

19. Using caution, lift the output shaft assembly out through top of case.

20. Lift the reverse idler gear and thrust washers out of case. Remove the countershaft gear, thrust washer and dummy shaft from case.

21. Remove the snapring from the front of the output shaft. Slip the synchronizer and 2nd gear off shaft.

22. Remove the 2nd snapring from output shaft and remove the thrust washer, 1st gear and blocking ring.

23. Remove the 3rd snapring from the output shaft. The 1st/reverse synchronizer hub is a press fit on the output shaft. Remove the synchronizer hub with an arbor press.

WARNING: *Do not attempt to remove or install the synchronizer hub by prying or hammering.*

SHIFT LEVERS & SEALS

1. Remove shift levers from the shafts. Slip the levers out of case. Discard shaft sealing O-rings.

2. Lubricate and install new O-rings on shift shafts.

3. Install the shift shafts in the case and secure shift levers.

INPUT SHAFT BEARINGS

1. Remove the snapring securing the input shaft bearing. Using an arbor press, remove the bearing.

2. Press the input shaft bearing onto shaft using correct tool.

SYNCHRONIZERS

1. Scribe alignment marks on synchronizer hubs before disassembly. Remove each synchronizer hub from the synchronizer sleeves.

2. Separate the inserts and insert springs from the hubs.

CAUTION: *Do not mix parts from the separate synchronizer assemblies.*

3. Install the insert spring in the hub of the 1st/reverse synchronizer. Be sure that the spring covers all the insert grooves. Start the hub on the sleeve making certain that the scribed marks are properly aligned. Place the 3 inserts in the hub, small ends on the inside. Slide the sleeve and reverse gear onto hub.

4. Install 1 insert spring into a groove on the 2nd/3rd synchronizer hub. Be sure that all 3 insert slots are covered. Align the scribed marks on the hub and sleeve and start the hub into the sleeve. Position the 3 inserts on the top of the retaining spring and push the assembly together. Install the remaining retainer spring so that the spring ends cover the same slots as the 1st spring. Do not stagger the springs. Place a synchronizer blocking ring on the ends of the synchronizer sleeve.

COUNTERSHAFT GEAR BEARINGS

1. Remove the dummy shaft, needle bearings and bearing retainers from the countershaft gear.

2. Coat the bore in each end of the countershaft gear with grease.

3. Hold the dummy shaft in the gear and install the needle bearings in the case.

4. Place the countershaft gear, dummy shaft, and needle bearings in the case.

5. Place the case in a vertical position. Align the gear bore and the thrust washers with the bores in the case and install the countershaft.

6. Place the case in a horizontal position. Check the countershaft gear end play with a feeler gauge. Clearance should be between 0.004-0.018″ (0.10-0.45mm). If clearance does not come within specifications, replace the thrust washers.

7. Install the dummy shaft in the countershaft gear and leave the gear at the bottom of the transmission case.

TRANSMISSION ASSEMBLY

1. Cover the reverse idler gear thrust surfaces in the case with a thin film of lubricant, and install the 2 thrust washers in the case.

2. Install the reverse idler gear and shaft in the case. Align the case bore and thrust washers with gear bore and install the reverse idler shaft.

3. Measure the reverse idler gear end play with a feeler gauge. Clearance should be between 0.004-0.018″ (0.10-0.45mm). If end play is not within specifications, replace the thrust washers. If clearance is correct, leave the reverse idler gear in case.

4. Lubricate the output shaft splines and machined surfaces with transmission oil.

5. The 1st/reverse synchronizer hub is a press fit on the output shaft. Hub must be installed in an arbor press. Install the synchronizer hub with the teeth end of the gear facing towards the rear of the shaft.

WARNING: *Do not attempt to install the 1st/reverse synchronizer with a hammer.*

6. Place the blocking ring on the tapered surface of the 1st gear.

7. Slide the 1st gear on the output shaft with the blocking ring toward the rear of the shaft. Rotate the gear as necessary to engage the 3 notches in the blocking ring with the synchronizer inserts. Install the thrust washer and snapring.

8. Slide the blocking ring onto the tapered surface of the 2nd gear. Slide the 2nd gear with blocking ring and the 2nd/3rd synchronizer on the mainshaft. Be sure that the tapered surface of 2nd gear is facing the front of the shaft and that the notches in the blocking ring engage the synchronizer inserts. Install the snapring and secure assembly.

9. Cover the core of the input shaft with a thin coat of grease.

WARNING: *A thick film of grease will plug lubricant holes and cause damage to bearings.*

10. Install bearings. Install the input shaft through the front of the case and insert snapring in the bearing groove.

11. Install the output shaft assembly in the case. Position the 2nd/3rd shift fork on the 2nd/3rd synchronizer.

12. Place a detent plug spring and a plug in the case. Place the 2nd/3rd synchronizer in the 2nd gear position (toward the rear of the case). Align the fork and install the 2nd/3rd shift rail. It will be necessary to depress the detent plug to install the shift rail in the bore. Move the rail forward until the detent plug enters the forward notch (2nd gear).

13. Secure the fork to the shift rail with a set screw and place the synchronizer in neutral.

14. Install the interlock plug in the case.

15. Place the 1st/reverse synchronizer in the 1st gear position (towards the front of the case). Place the shift fork in the groove of the synchronizer. Rotate the fork into position and install the shift rail. Move the shift rail inward until the center notch (neutral) is aligned with the detent bore. Secure shift fork with set screw.

16. Install a new shift rail expansion plug in the front of the case.

17. Hold the input shaft and blocking ring in position and move the output shaft forward to seat the pilot in the roller bearings on the input gear.

18. Tap the input gear bearing into place while holding the output shaft. Install the front bearing retainer and gasket. Torque attaching bolts to specifications.

19. Install the large snapring on the rear bearing. Place the bearing on the output shaft with the snapring end toward the rear of the shaft. Press the bearing into place using a special tool. Secure the bearing to the shaft with the snapring.

20. Hold the speedometer drive gear lock ball in the detent and slide the speedometer drive gear into position. Secure with snapring.

21. Place the transmission in the vertical position. Working with a screwdriver through the drain hole in the bottom of the case, align the bore of the countershaft gear and the thrust washer with the bore in the case.

22. Working from the rear of the case, push the dummy shaft out of the countershaft gear with the countershaft. Align the roll pin hole in the countershaft with the matching hole in the case. Drive the shaft into place and install the roll pin.

23. Position the new extension housing gasket on the case with sealer. Install the extension housing and torque to specification.

24. Place the transmission in gear and pour gear oil over entire gear train while rotating the input shaft.

25. Install the remaining detent plug and long spring in case.

26. Position cover gasket on case with sealer and install cover. Torque cover bolts to specifications.

27. Check operation of transmission in all gear positions.

Muncie 4-Speed (117mm, Top Cover)

TRANSMISSION UNIT

1. Remove transmission cover assembly. Move reverse shifter fork so that reverse idler gear is partially engaged before attempting to remove cover. Forks must be positioned so rear edge of the slot in the reverse fork is in line with the front edge of the slot in the forward forks as viewed through tower opening.

2. Lock transmission into two gears. Remove the universal joint flange nut, universal joint front flange and brake drum assembly.

NOTE: *On 4-wheel drive models, use a special tool to remove mainshaft rear lock nut.*

3. Remove parking brake and brake flange plate assembly on those vehicles having a driveshaft parking brake.

4. Remove rear bearing retainer and gasket.

5. Slide speedometer drive gear off mainshaft.

6. Remove clutch gear bearing retainers and gasket.

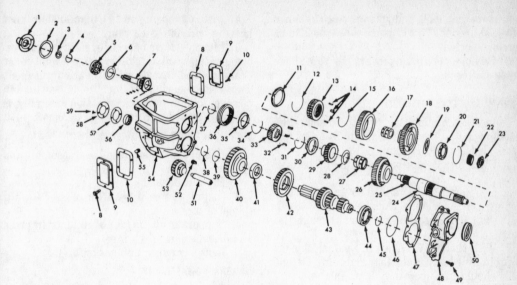

1. Drive gear bearing
2. Retainer gasket
3. Lip seal
4. Snap ring
5. Drive gear bearing
6. Oil slinger
7. Drive gear and pilot bearings
8. Power take-off cover gasket
9. Power take-off cover
10. Retaining screws
11. 1st-2nd speed blocker ring
12. Synchronizer spring
13. 1st-2nd speed synchronizer hub
14. Synchronizer keys
15. Synchronizer spring
16. Reverse driven gear
17. 1st gear bushing
18. 1st gear
19. Thrust washer
20. Rear main bearing

21. Bearing snap ring
22. Speedometer gear
23. Rear mainshaft lock nut
24. 2nd speed bushing (on shaft)
25. Mainshaft
26. 2nd speed gear
27. 3rd gear bushing
28. Thrust washer
29. 3rd speed gear
30. 3rd speed blocker ring
31. Synchronizer spring
32. Synchronizer keys
33. 3rd-4th synchronizer hub
34. Synchronizer spring
35. 3rd-4th speed blocker ring
36. 3rd-4th speed syncrhonizer sleeve
37. Snap ring
38. Snap ring
39. Thrust washer
40. Clutch countergear

41. Spacer
42. 3rd speed countergear
43. Countergear shaft
44. Countergear rear bearing
45. Snap ring
46. Bearing outer snap ring
47. Rear retainer gasket
48. Rear retainer
49. Retainer bolts
50. Retainer lip seal
51. Reverse idler shaft
52. Drain plug
53. Reverse idler gear
54. Case
55. Fill plug
56. Countergear front bearing
57. Gasket
58. Front cover
59. Cover screws

Exploded view-Muncie 4-speed (117mm-top cover)

7. Remove countergear front bearing cap and gasket.

8. Using a prybar, pry off countershaft front bearing.

9. Remove countergear rear bearing snaprings from shaft and bearing. Using special tool, remove countergear rear bearings.

10. Remove clutch gear bearing outer race to case retaining ring.

11. Remove clutch gear and bearing by tapping gently on bottom side of clutch gear shaft and prying directly opposite against the case and bearing snapring groove at the same time. Remove fourth gear synchronizer ring. Index cut out section of clutch gear in down position with countergear to obtain clearance for removing clutch gear.

12. Remove rear mainshaft bearing snapring and, using special tools, remove bearing from

case. Slide 1st speed gear thrust washer off mainshaft.

13. Lift mainshaft assembly from case. Remove synchronizer cone from shaft.

14. Slide reverse idler gear rearward and move countergear rearward, then lift to remove from case.

15. To remove reverse idler gear, drive reverse idler gear shaft out of case from front to rear using a drift. Remove reverse idler gear from case.

TRANSMISSION COVER DISASSEMBLY

1. Remove shifter fork retaining pins and drive out expansion plugs. The third and fourth shifter fork must be removed before the reverse shifter head pin can be removed.

2. With shifter shafts in neutral position, remove shafts. Care should be taken when remov-

ing the detent balls and springs since removal of the shifter shafts will cause these parts to be forcibly ejected.

3. Remove retaining pin and drive out reverse shifter shaft.

TRANSMISSION COVER ASSEMBLY

1. In reassembling the cover, care should be taken to install the shifter shafts in order, reverse, 3rd/4th and 1st/2nd.

2. Place fork detent ball springs and balls in cover.

3. Start shifter shafts into cover and, while depressing the detent balls, push the shafts over the balls. Push reverse shaft through the yoke.

4. With the 3rd/4th shaft in neutral, line up the retaining holes in the fork and shaft. Detent balls should line up with detents in shaft.

5. After 1st and 2nd fork is installed, place two interlock balls between the low speed shifter shaft and the high speed shifter shaft in the crossbore of the front support boss. Grease the interlock pin and insert it in the 3rd/4th shifter shaft hole. Continue pushing this shaft through cover bore and fork until retainer hole in fork lines up with hole in shaft.

6. Place two interlock balls in crossbore in front support boss between reverse and 3rd and 4th shifter shaft. Then push remaining shaft through fork and cover bore, keeping both balls in position between shafts until retaining holes line up in fork and shaft. Install retaining pin.

7. Install 1st/2nd fork and reverse fork retaining pins. Install new shifter shaft hole expansion plugs.

CLUTCH GEAR AND SHAFT ASSEMBLY

1. Remove mainshaft pilot bearing rollers from clutch gear if not already removed and remove roller retainer. Do not remove snapring on inside of clutch gear.

2. Remove snapring securing bearing on steam of clutch gear.

3. To remove bearing, position a special tool to the bearing and, with an arbor press, press gear and shaft out of bearing.

CLUTCH GEAR AND SHAFT ASSEMBLY

1. Press bearing and new oil slinger onto clutch gear shaft using a special tool. Slinger should be located flush with bearing shoulder on clutch gear. Be careful not to distort oil slinger.

2. Install bearing snapring on clutch gear shaft.

3. Install bearing retainer ring in groove on O.D. of bearing. The bearing must turn freely on the shaft.

4. Install snapring on I.D. of mainshaft pilot bearing bore in clutch gear.

5. Lightly grease bearing surface in shaft recess, install transmission mainshaft pilot roller bearings and install roller bearing retainer. This roller bearing retainer holds bearings in position and, in final transmission assembly, is pushed forward into recess by mainshaft pilot.

BEARING RETAINER OIL SEAL REPLACEMENT

1. Remove retainer and oil seal assembly and gasket.

2. Pry out oil seal.

3. Install new seal with lip of seal toward flange of tool.

4. Support front surface of retainer in press and drive seal into retainer.

5. Install retainer and gasket on case.

MAINSHAFT DISASSEMBLY

1. Remove first speed gear.

2. Remove reverse driven gear.

3. Press behind second speed gear to remove 3rd/4th synchronizer assembly, 3rd speed gear and 2nd speed gear along with 3rd speed gear bushing and thrust washer.

4. Remove 2nd speed synchronizer ring and keys.

5. Using a press, remove 1st speed gear bushing and 2nd speed synchronizer hub.

6. Without damaging the mainshaft, chisel out the 2nd speed gear bushing.

INSPECTION

Wash all parts in cleaning solvent and inspect them for excessive wear or scoring.

NOTE: *Third and fourth speed clutch sleeve should slide freely on clutch hub but clutch hub should fit snugly on shaft splines. Third speed gear must be running fit on mainshaft bushing and mainshaft bushing should be press fit on shaft. First and reverse sliding gear must be sliding fit on synchronizer hub and must not have excessive radial or circumferential play. If sliding gear is not free on hub, inspect for burrs which may have rolled up on front end of half tooth internal splines and remove by honing as necessary.*

MAINSHAFT ASSEMBLY

1. Lubricate with E.P. oil and press onto mainshaft. 1st, 2nd and 3rd speed gear bushings are sintered iron, exercise care when installing.

2. Press 1st and 2nd speed synchronizer hub onto mainshaft with annulus toward rear of shaft.

3. Install 1st and 2nd synchronizer keys and springs.

4. Press 1st speed gear bushing onto mainshaft until it bottoms against hub. Lubri-

cate all bushings with E.P. oil before installation of gears.

5. Install synchronizer blocker ring and 2nd speed gear onto mainshaft and against synchronize hub. Align synchronizer key slots with keys in synchronizer hub.

6. Install 3rd speed gear thrust washer onto mainshaft inserting washer tang in slotted shaft. Then press 3rd speed gear bushing onto mainshaft against thrust washer.

7. Install 3rd speed gear and synchronizer blocker ring against 3rd speed gear thrust washer.

8. Align synchronizer key ring slots with synchronizer assembly keys and drive 3rd and 4th synchronizer assembly onto mainshaft. Secure assembly with snapring.

9. Install reverse driven gear with fork groove toward rear.

10. Install 1st speed gear against 1st and 2nd synchronizer hub. Install 1st speed gear thrust washer.

COUNTERSHAFT DISASSEMBLY

1. Remove front countergear retaining ring and thrust washer. Do not re-use this snapring or any others.

2. Press countershaft out of clutch countergear assembly.

3. Remove clutch countergear and 3rd speed countergear retaining rings.

4. Press shift from 3rd speed countergear.

COUNTERSHAFT DISASSEMBLY

1. Press the 3rd speed countergear onto the shaft. Install gear with marked surface toward front of shaft.

2. Using snapring pliers, install new 3rd speed countergear retaining ring.

3. Install new clutch countergear rear retaining ring. Do not over stress snapring. Ring should fit tightly in groove with no side play.

4. Press countergear onto shaft against snapring.

5. Install clutch countergear thrust washer and front retaining ring.

TRANSMISSION UNIT ASSEMBLY

1. Lower the countergear into the case.

2. Place reverse idler gear in transmission case with gear teeth toward the front. Install idler gear shaft from rear to front, being careful to have slot in end of shaft facing down and flush with case.

3. Install mainshaft assembly into case with rear of shaft protruding out rear bearing hole in case. Rotate case onto front end. Install 1st speed gear thrust washer on shaft, if not previously installed.

4. Install snapring on bearing O.D. and place

rear mainshaft bearing on shaft. Drive bearing onto shaft and into case.

5. Install synchronizer cone on mainshaft and slide rearward to clutch hub. Make sure three cut out sections of 4th speed synchronizer cone align with three clutch keys in clutch assembly.

6. Install snapring on clutch gear bearing O.D. Index cut out portion of clutch gear teeth to obtain clearance over countershaft drive gear teeth and install into case.

7. Install clutch gear bearing retainer and gasket and torque 15-18 ft.lb.

8. Rotate case onto front end.

9. Install snapring on countergear rear bearing O.D. and drive bearing into place. Install snapring on countershaft at rear bearing.

10. Tap countergear front bearing assembly into case.

11. Install countergear front bearing cap and new gasket and torque 20-30 in.lb.

12. Slide speedometer drive gear over mainshaft to bearing.

13. Install rear bearing retainer with new gasket. Be sure snapring ends are in lube slot and cut out in bearing retainer. Install bolts and tighten 15-18 ft.lb. Install brake backing plate assembly on those models having driveshaft brake.

NOTE: *On models equipped with 4-wheel drive, install rear lock nut and washer and torque to 120 ft.lb. and bend washer tangs to fit slots in nut.*

14. Install parking brake drum and/or universal joint flange. Lightly oil seal surface.

15. Lock transmission in two gears at once. Install universal joint flange locknut and tighten 90-120 ft.lb.

16. Move all transmission gears to neutral except the reverse idler gear which should be engaged approximately ⅜" (leading edge of reverse idler gear taper lines up with the front edge of the 1st speed gear). Install cover assembly and gasket. Shifting forks must slide into their proper positions on clutch sleeves and reverse idler gear. Forks must be positioned as in removal.

17. Install cover attaching bolts and gearshift lever and check operation of transmission.

Muncie 4-Speed (Side Cover)
TRANSMISSION CASE DISASSEMBLY

1. Drain the lubricant. Remove the side cover and the shift forks.

2. Remove the clutch gear bearing retainer. Remove the bearing-to-gear stem snapring and pull out on the clutch gear until a small pry bar can be inserted between the bearing, the large snapring and case to pry the bearing off.

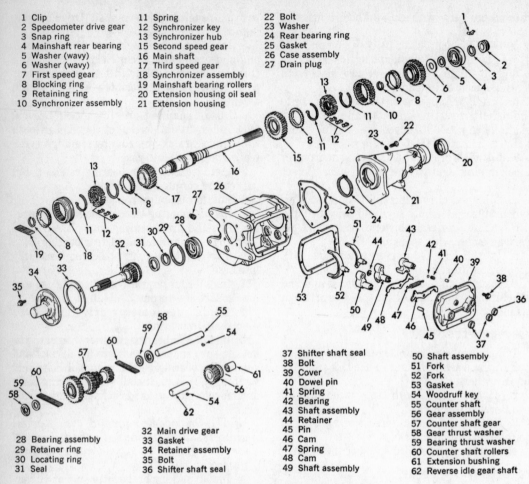

1 Clip
2 Speedometer drive gear
3 Snap ring
4 Mainshaft rear bearing
5 Washer (wavy)
6 Washer (wavy)
7 First speed gear
8 Blocking ring
9 Retaining ring
10 Synchronizer assembly
11 Spring
12 Synchronizer key
13 Synchronizer hub
15 Second speed gear
16 Main shaft
17 Third speed gear
18 Synchronizer assembly
19 Mainshaft bearing rollers
20 Extension housing oil seal
21 Extension housing
22 Bolt
23 Washer
24 Rear bearing ring
25 Gasket
26 Case assembly
27 Drain plug

28 Bearing assembly
29 Retainer ring
30 Locating ring
31 Seal
32 Main drive gear
33 Gasket
34 Retainer assembly
35 Bolt
36 Shifter shaft seal
37 Shifter shaft seal
38 Bolt
39 Cover
40 Dowel pin
41 Spring
42 Bearing
43 Shaft assembly
44 Retainer
45 Pin
46 Cam
47 Spring
48 Cam
49 Shaft assembly
50 Shaft assembly
51 Fork
52 Fork
53 Gasket
54 Woodruff key
55 Counter shaft
56 Gear assembly
57 Counter shaft gear
58 Gear thrust washer
59 Bearing thrust washer
60 Counter shaft rollers
61 Extension bushing
62 Reverse idle gear shaft

Exploded view-Muncie 4-speed (side cover)

NOTE: *The clutch gear bearing is a slip fit on the gear and in the case. Removal of the bearing will provide clearance for the clutch gear and the mainshaft removal.*

3. Remove the extension housing bolts, then remove the clutch gear, the mainshaft and the extension as an assembly.

4. Spread the snapring which holds the mainshaft rear bearing and remove the extension case.

5. Using a dummy shaft, drive the countershaft and its woodruff key out through the rear of the case. Remove the countergear assembly and the bearings.

6. Using a long drift, drive the Reverse idler shaft and the woodruff key through the rear of the case.

7. Expand and remove the 3rd/4th speed sliding clutch hub snapring from the mainshaft. Remove the clutch assembly, the 3rd gear blocking ring and the 3rd speed gear from the front of the mainshaft.

8. Press in the speedometer gear retaining

clip and slide the gear off the mainshaft. Remove the rear bearing snapring from the mainshaft.

9. Using an arbor press, support the 1st gear on press plates, then press the 1st gear, the thrust washer, the spring washer, the rear bearing and snapring from the rear of the mainshaft.

CAUTION: *Be sure to center the gear, the washers, the bearings and the snapring when pressing the rear bearing.*

10. Expand and remove the 1st/2nd sliding clutch hub snapring from the mainshaft, then remove the clutch assembly, the 2nd speed blocking ring and the 2nd speed gear from the rear of the mainshaft.

NOTE: *After thoroughly cleaning the parts and the transmission case, inspect and replace the damaged or worn parts. When checking the bearings, do not spin them at high speeds. Clean and rotate the bearings by hand to detect the roughness or unevenness. Spinning can damage the balls and the races.*

TRANSMISSION CASE ASSEMBLY

1. Grease both inside ends of the countergear. Install a dummy shaft into the countergear, then load a row of roller bearings (27) and thrust washers at each end of the countergear.

2. Position the countergear assembly into the case through the rear opening. Place a tanged thrust washer at each end of the countergear.

3. Install the countergear shaft and woodruff key from the rear of the case.

NOTE: *Make sure that the shaft engages both thrust washers and that the tangs align with their notches in the case.*

4. Install the Reverse idler gear, the shaft and the woodruff key. Install the extension-to-rear bearing snapring. Assemble the extension housing over the rear of the mainshaft and onto the rear bearing.

5. Install the 14 mainshaft pilot bearings into the clutch opening and the 4th speed blocking ring onto the clutching surface of the clutch gear (with the clutching teeth facing the gear).

6. Assemble the clutch gear, the pilot bearings and the 4th speed blocking ring unit over the front of the mainshaft. Do not assemble the bearing to the gear at this point.

CAUTION: *Be sure that the blocking ring notches align with the 3rd/4th synchronizer assembly keys.*

7. Install the extension-to-case gasket and secure it with grease. Install the clutch gear, the mainshaft and the extension housing as an assembly. Install the extension-to-case bolts (apply sealer to the bottom bolt) and torque to 45 ft.lb.

8. Install the outer snapring on the front bearing and place the bearing over the stem of the clutch gear and into the case bore.

9. Install the snapring to the clutch gear stem. Install the clutch gear bearing retainer and the gasket, with the retainer oil return hole at the bottom.

10. Place the synchronizer sleeves into the Neutral positions and install the cover, the gasket and the fork assemblies to the case; be sure the forks align with the synchronizer sleeve grooves. Torque the cover bolts to 22 ft.lb.

MAINSHAFT ASSEMBLY

Install the following parts with the front of the mainshaft facing up:

1. Install the 3rd speed gear with the clutching teeth up; the rear face of the gear will abut with the mainshaft flange.

2. Install a blocking ring (with the clutching teeth down) over the 3rd speed gear synchronizing surface.

NOTE: *The four blocking rings are the same.*

3. Press the 3rd/4th synchronizer assembly (with the fork slot down) onto the mainshaft splines until it bottoms.

CAUTION: *The blocking ring notches must align with the synchronizer assembly keys.*

4. Install the synchronizer hub-to-mainshaft snapring; both synchronizer snaprings are the same.

Install the following parts with the rear of the mainshaft facing up:

5. Install the 2nd speed gear with the clutching teeth up; the front face of the gear will abut with the flange on the mainshaft.

6. Install a blocking ring (with the clutching teeth down) over the 2nd speed gear synchronizing surface.

7. Press the 1st/2nd synchronizer assembly (with the fork slot down) onto the mainshaft.

WARNING: *The blocking ring notches must align with the synchronizer assembly keys.*

8. Install the synchronizer hub-to-mainshaft snapring.

9. Install a blocking ring with the notches down so they align with the 1st/2nd synchronizer assembly keys.

10. Install the 1st gear with the clutching teeth down. Install the 1st gear thrust washer and the spring washer.

11. Press the rear ball bearing (with the slot down) onto the mainshaft. Install the snapring. Install the speedometer gear and clip.

New Process (89mm)

TRANSMISSION DISASSEMBLY

1. Thoroughly clean the exterior of the transmission assembly.

2. Remove drain plug and drain lubricant from transmission.

3. Shift transmission into neutral position. Remove reverse shift lever, side cover bolts, side cover and shift forks. Remove reverse detent spring and ball from base in side of case.

4. Remove extension housing bolts and rotate the extension on the output shaft to expose the rear of the countershaft. Clearance has been provided on the extension in the inverted position to gain access for the countershaft removal.

5. With a centerpunch or drill, make a hole in the countershaft expansion plug at the front of the case.

6. Using this hole, push the countershaft rearward until the woodruff key is exposed. Remove key and push the countershaft forward against the expansion plug. Using a brass drift, tap the countershaft forward until the plug is driven out of the case.

7. Using tool J-29793 at the front of the countershaft, drive the shaft out of the rear of the case. Tool J-29793 will now hold the roller

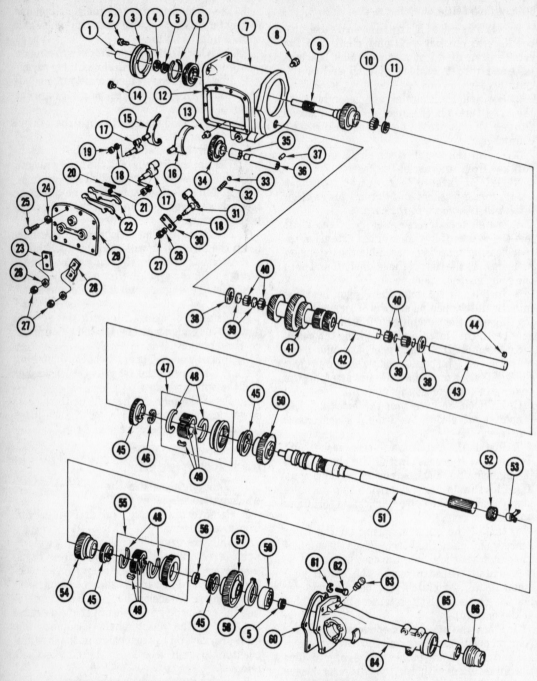

1. Retainer, clutch gear bearing
2. Bolt
3. Gasket, clutch gear bearing retainer
4. Seal, clutch gear bearing oil
5. Ring, main drive gear snap
6. Bearing, w/snap ring, main drive gear
7. Case, trans
8. Plug, sq hd, filler
9. Gear, clutch
10. Baring, mainshaft rollers
11. Ring, pilot bearing snap
12. Gasket, control lever housing

13. Plug, drain
14. Plug, expansion
15. Fork, shift 3rd & 4th
16. Fork, shift 1st & 2nd
17. Shaft, forward shift
18. Ring, "O" shift shaft seal
19. Retainer, shift shaft seal
20. Spring, detent
21. Ring, "E"
22. Cam, detent
23. Lever, control shift 3rd & 4th
24. Washer, lk

Exploded view-New Process 4-speed (89 mm)

bearings in position within the gear bore. Lower countershaft gear to bottom of case.

8. Rotate the extension housing back to its normal position.

9. Remove the drive gear bearing retainer bolts and slide retainer and gasket off the gear assembly.

10. Using a brass drift, tap the gear and bearing assembly forward and remove through front of case. Replacement of the drive gear or bearing require no further disassembly of the transmission. Replace the failed part and reassemble the transmission.

11. Slide third and overdrive (O/D) synchronizer sleeve slightly forward, slide reverse idler gear to center of its shaft, then using a soft faced hammer, tap on extension housing in a rearward direction. Slide housing and mainshaft assembly out and away from case.

12. Remove countershaft gear from bottom of case.

13. Remove the reverse idler gear shaft from transmission case. To remove the shaft, use a 3⁄8″ x 3½″ bolt with a free spinning nut and a 7⁄16″ deep socket 3⁄8″ drive. Place the bolt and socket in the case with the socket against the shaft and the head of the bolt against the case. Holding the head of the bolt, turn nut against the socket pushing shaft through its bore. Remove gear from shaft and remove shaft with woodruff key from transmission case.

14. Remove reverse gear shift lever from case by pushing shaft inward and remove it from the case. Remove O-ring and retainer from case bore.

15. Remove backup light switch from case.

MAINSHAFT DISASSEMBLY

1. Remove snapring that retains 3rd and O/D synchronizer clutch gear and sleeve assembly.

Then slide 3rd and O/D synchronizer assembly off end of mainshaft.

2. Slide O/D gear and stop ring off mainshaft. Mark and separate synchronizer parts for cleaning and inspection.

3. Using long nose pliers, spread snapring that retains mainshaft ball bearing in extension housing, then pull mainshaft assembly out of the extension housing.

4. Remove speedometer drive gear from mainshaft.

5. Remove snapring that retains mainshaft bearing on the shaft. Remove bearing from mainshaft by inserting steel plate on the front side 1st gear, then press mainshaft through bearing. (Be careful not to damage gear teeth).

6. Remove bearing, bearing retainer ring, 1st gear, and 1st speed stop ring from the shaft.

7. Remove snapring that retains 1st and 2nd clutch gear and sleeve assembly. Then slide 1st and 2nd gear and sleeve assembly from the mainshaft. Remove 2nd gear. Before cleaning, mark all parts for reassembly.

8. Inspect mainshaft gear bearing surfaces for signs of wear, scoring or any condition that would not allow shaft to be used.

9. Remove tool J-29793 from the countershaft gear, 76 needle type bearings, thrust washers and spacers.

10. Remove outer snapring on the drive gear. Using an arbor press, remove bearing from drive gear, if bearing is to be replaced.

11. Remove inner snapring and 16 bearing rollers from cavity of drive gear.

CLEANING AND INSPECTION

Transmission Case

1. Wash the transmission thoroughly inside and outside using a suitable solvent, then in-

25. Bolt
26. Washer, flat
27. Nut
28. Lever, control shift 1st & 2nd
29. Cover, trans.
30. Lever, reverse shift
31. Shaft, reverse shift
32. Spring, reverse shift shaft detent ball
33. Ball, steel
34. Gear, reverse idler
35. Bushing, reverse idler gear
36. Shaft, reverse idler
37. Key, reverse idler shaft
38. Washer, clutch counter gear thrust
39. Spacer, clutch counter gear bearing
40. Bearing, counter gear rollers
41. Gear, counter
42. Spacer, clutch counter gear bearing
43. Shaft, counter gear
44. Key, counter gear
45. Ring, syn blocking

46. Ring, syn 3rd & 4th snap
47. Synchronizer asm, trans 3rd & 4th
48. Spring, forward clutch key
49. Key, forward syn clutch
50. Gear, 4th speed
51. Shaft, main
52. Gear, speedo drive
53. Clip, speedo drive gear
54. Gear, 2nd speed
55. Synchronizer asm, trans 1st & 2nd
56. Ring, syn clutch gear snap
57. Gear, 1st speed
58. Ring, main shaft bearing outer snap
59. Bearing, clutch gear
60. Gasket, extension
61. Washer, lk
62. Screw
63. Ventilator, extension
64. Extension, trans
65. Bushing, trans extension
66. Seal, extension oil

Exploded view-New Process 4-speed (89 mm)

spect the case for cracks. The magnetic disc is glued in place, wipe with a clean cloth.

2. Check the front and rear faces for burrs and if present, dress them off with a fine mill file.

Roller Bearing Spacers

All main drive gear and countergear bearing rollers should be inspected closely and replaced if they show wear. Inspect countershaft and reverse idler shaft at the same time, replace if necessary. Replace all worn spacers.

Front and Rear Bearings

1. Wash the front and rear ball bearings thoroughly in a cleaning solvent.

2. Blow out bearings with compressed air. WARNING: *Do not allow the bearings to spin. Turn them slowly by hand. Spinning bearings may damage the race and balls.*

3. Lubricate bearings with a light oil and check them for roughness by slowly turning the race by hand.

Gears

1. Inspect all gears for excessive wear, chips or cracks and replace any that are worn or damaged.

2. Check oil seal contact area on the drive gear shaft, if its pitted, rusted or scratched, a new gear is recommended for best seal life.

3. Inspect interlock levers for cracks at detent and clearance notches at each end of levers.

4. Inspect shift forks for wear on pads and shafts. Inspect the fork shaft bores in the shift lever for galling.

SYNCHRONIZER KEYS AND SPRINGS REPLACEMENT

The synchronizer hubs and sliding sleeves are a selected assembly and should be kept together as originally assembled, but the keys and springs may be replaced if worn or broken.

1. If relation of hub an sleeve are not already marked, mark for assembly purposes.

2. Push the hub from the sliding sleeve, the keys will fall free and the spring may be easily removed.

3. Place the keys in position and while holding them in place, slide the sleeve onto the hub, aligning the marks made before disassembly.

4. Place the two springs in position (one on each side of hub), so all three keys are engaged by both springs.

EXTENSION OIL SEAL AND/OR BUSHING REPLACEMENT

1. Pry oil seal out of extension housing, using a screwdriver or small chisel.

2. Drive the brushing out of the housing, using tool J-8092 with J-21424-9.

3. Slide a new brushing tool J-23596 and drive bushing into place.

4. Position a new seal in opening of extension housing and drive it into the housing with tool J-21426.

DRIVE GEAR BEARING RETAINER OIL SEAL REPLACEMENT

1. Pry out old seal.

2. Using a new seal, install new seal into retainer using Tool J-23097 until it bottoms in bore. Lubricate I.D. of seal with transmission lubricant.

TRANSMISSION SIDE COVER

The following three steps need only be done if oil leakage is visible around gearshift lever shifts, or the interlock levers are cracked.

1. Remove the nuts that attach shift operating levers to the shafts. Disengage levers from flats on shafts and remove. Make sure shafts are free of burrs before removal, otherwise the bores may be scored resulting in leakage after assembly.

2. Pull gearshift lever shafts out of cover.

3. Remove O-ring retainers and O-rings from housing.

4. Remove E-ring from interlock lever pivot pin and remove interlock levers and spring from cover.

5. To assemble side cover, install interlock levers on pivot pin and fasten with E-ring. Use pliers to install spring on interlock lever hangers.

6. Grease housing bores and push each shaft into its proper bore followed by greased O-ring and retainer.

7. Install operating levers and tighten. Be sure 3rd-O/D operating levers point downward.

COUNTERGEAR ASSEMBLY

1. Coat inside bore of countergear at each end with a thin film of grease and install spacer with Tool J-29793 into gear. Center spacer and arbor.

2. Install 19 roller bearings, followed by a spacer ring and 19 more bearings and a spacer ring into each end of gear.

3. If countershaft thrush washers are worn or scored, install new thrust washers. Coat washers with grease and install one at the front of the countergear on the arbor with the tang side facing the case bore. Install the other washer after the countergear assemble is positioned in the bottom of the case.

DRIVE GEAR ASSEMBLY

1. Press drive gear bearing on drive gear seating bearing fully against shoulder on gear. Be sure outer snapring groove is toward the front.

2. Install a new snapring on shaft to retain

bearing. Be sure snapring is seated. This snapring is a select fit for minimum end play.

3. Place drive gear in a vise (with soft jaws), then install 16 bearing rollers in cavity of shaft. Coat bearing rollers with grease, then install retaining snapring in its groove.

MAINSHAFT ASSEMBLY

1. Slide second gear over mainshaft (synchronizer cone toward rear) and down against shoulder on shaft.

2. Slide 1st/2nd synchronizer assembly (including stop ring with lugs indexed in hub slots) over mainshaft, down against 2nd gear cone and secure with a new snapring. Slide next stop ring over shaft and index lugs into clutch hub slots.

3. Slide first gear (synchronizer cone toward clutch sleeve gear just installed) over mainshaft into position against clutch sleeve gear.

4. Install mainshaft bearing retainer ring, followed by mainshaft rear bearing.

Using an arbor and a suitable tool, drive or press bearing down into position. Install a new snapring on shaft to secure bearing. This snapring is a select fit for minimum end play.

5. Install partially assembled mainshaft into extension housing far enough to engage bearing retaining ring in slot in extension housing. Expand snapring with pliers so that mainshaft ball bearing can move in and bottom against its thrust shoulder in extension housing. Release ring and seat it all around its groove in extension housing.

6. Slide overdrive gear over mainshaft (with synchronizer cone toward front) followed by O/D gear stop ring.

7. Install 3rd-O/D snychronizer clutch gear assembly on mainshaft (shift fork slot toward rear) against O/D gear. Be sure to index rear stop ring with clutch gear struts. Install retaining snapring.

8. Using grease, position front stop ring over clutch gear, again indexing ring lugs with struts.

TRANSMISSION ASSEMBLY

1. Place the transmission case on its side with the shift cover opening toward the assembler.

2. Install countergear assembly into the case aligning the tangs on the front washer with the slots in the case. Next install the rear washer aligning the tans with the slot at the rear of the case and then let the countergear rest in the bottom of the case. (Be sure thrust washers stay in position).

3. Coat a new extension gasket with grease then place it in position on the extension.

4. Insert mainshaft assembly into the case tilting it as required to clear the countershaft gear.

5. Rotate the extension housing to expose the rear of the countershaft bore. Install one bolt to hole the extension in inverted position and prevent it from moving rearward.

6. Install drive gear assembly through the front of the case and position it in the front bore. Install outer snapring in bearing groove. Tap lightly into place using a soft faced hammer. If everything is in proper position, the outer snapring will bottom onto the case face without excessive effort. If not, check to see if a strut, roller bearing or a stop ring is out of position.

7. Raise the countgear assembly into position with the teeth meshed with the drive gear. Make sure thrust washer remain in position on ends of the arbor and tangs are aligned with slots in case.

8. Start the countershaft into the rear bore of the case and push forward until the shaft is approximately half way through the gear. Install woodruff key and push the shaft forward until end is flush with case. Remove arbor Tool J-29793.

9. Install reverse shift lever shaft in case bore followed by greased O-ring and retainer.

10. Remove extension housing bolt and rotate extension to provide clearance for installation of the reverse idler gear in end of case.

11. Push the shaft in far enough to position reverse idler gear on protruding end of shaft with fork slot toward rear. At the same time, engage slot with reverse shift fork.

12. Install woodruff key on shaft and install bolts. Torque housing bolts to 75 ft.lb.

13. Align extension housing to case and install bolts. Torque housing bolts to 50 ft.lb.

14. Install drive gear bearing retainer and gasket. Coat threads with sealing compound, then install bolts and torque to 30 ft.lb.

15. Install new expansion plug coated with sealing compound in countershaft bore at front of case.

16. Position both synchronizer sleeves in neutral. Place the 1st/2nd shift fork into the groove of the 1st/2nd synchronizer sleeve. Slide reverse idler gear to neutral.

17. Rotate each shift lever to neutral position (straight up) and install 3rd/overdrive shift fork into its bore and under both interlock levers.

18. Position side cover gasket on case using grease to retain it. Install reverse detent ball followed by the spring into its bore in the case.

19. Lower the side cover onto the case guiding the 3rd/overdrive shift fork into the synchronizer groove, then lead the shaft of the 1st/2nd shift fork into its bore in the side cover. Hold

the reverse interlock link against the 1st/2nd shift lever to provide clearance as the side cover is lowered into position. To finish the installation of the side cover, use a screwdriver and raise the interlock lever against its spring tension to allow the 1st/2nd shift fork to slip under the levers. Be sure the reverse detent spring is positioned in the cover bore.

20. Eight of the side cover bolts are shoulder bolts with one having a longer shoulder which acts as a dowel to accurately locate the side cover. The remaining two bolts are standard bolts. Install cover bolts finger tight and shift through all gears to insure proper operation.

21. Tighten side cover bolts evenly and torque to 15 ft.lb.

22. Install reverse shift lever, retaining nut and torque to 18 ft.lb.

23. Shift the transmission into each gear to insure correct shift travel and smooth operation. The reverse shift lever and 1st/2nd shift lever have cam surfaces which mate in reverse position to lock the 1st/2nd lever, fork and synchronzier in neutral position. Slight motion of the 1st/2nd shift lever toward low gear is normal during shifting into reverse gear.

24. Install backup light switch and torque to 15 ft.lb.

CLUTCH

Understanding the Clutch

The purpose of the clutch is to disconnect and connect engine power from the transmission. A car at rest requires a lot of engine torque to get all that weight moving. An internal combustion engine does not develop a high starting torque (unlike steam engines), so it must be allowed to operate without any load until it builds up enough torque to move the car. Torque increases with engine rpm. The clutch allows the engine to build up torque by physically disconnecting the engine from the transmission, relieving the engine of any load or resistance. The transfer of engine power to the transmission (the load) must be smooth and gradual; if it weren't, drive line components would wear out or break quickly. This gradual power transfer is made possible by gradually releasing the clutch pedal. The clutch disc and pressure plate are the connecting link between the engine and transmission. When the clutch pedal is released, the disc and plate contact each other (clutch engagement), physically joining the engine and transmission. When the pedal is pushed in, the disc and plate separate (the clutch is disengaged), disconnecting the engine from the transmission.

The clutch assembly consists of the flywheel, the clutch disc, the clutch pressure plate, the throwout bearing and fork, the actuating linkage and the pedal. The flywheel and clutch pressure plate (driving members) are connected to the engine crankshaft and rotate with it. The clutch disc is located between the flywheel and pressure plate, and splined to the transmission shaft. A driving member is one that is attached to the engine and transfers engine power to a driven member (clutch disc) on the transmission shaft. A driving member (pressure plate) rotates (drives) a driven member (clutch disc) on contact and, in so doing, turns the transmission shaft. There is a circular diaphragm spring within the pressure plate cover (transmission side). In a relaxed state (when the clutch pedal is fully released), this spring is convex; that it, it is dished outward toward the transmission. Pushing in the clutch pedal actuates an attached linkage rod. Connected to the other end of this rod is the throwout bearing fork. The throwout bearing is attached to the fork. When the clutch pedal is depressed, the clutch linkage pushes the fork and bearing forward to contact the diaphragm spring of the pressure plate. The outer edges of the spring are secured to the pressure plate and are pivoted on rings so that when the center of the spring is compressed by the throwout bearing, the outer edges bow outward and, by so doing, pull the pressure plate in the same direction — away from the clutch disc. This action separates the disc from the plate, disengaging the clutch and allowing the transmission to be shifted into another gear. A coil type clutch return spring attached to the clutch pedal arm permits full release of the pedal. Releasing the pedal pulls the throwout bearing away from the diaphragm spring resulting in a reversal of spring position. As bearing pressure is gradually released from the spring center, the outer edges of the spring bow outward, pushing the pressure plate into closer contact with the clutch disc. As the disc and plate move closer together, friction between the two increases and slippage is reduced until, when full spring pressure is applied (by fully releasing the pedal), The speed of the disc and plate are the same. This stops all slipping, creating a direct connection between the plate and disc which results in the transfer of power from the engine to the transmission. The clutch disc is now rotating with the pressure plate at engine speed and, because it is splined to the transmission shaft, the shaft now turns at the same engine speed. Understanding clutch operation can be rather difficult at first; if you're still confused after reading this, consider the following analogy. The action of the diaphragm spring can be compared to that of an oil can bottom. The bottom of an

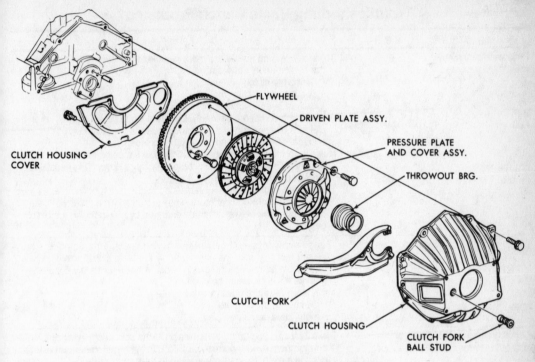

CLUTCH HOUSING COVER

FLYWHEEL

DRIVEN PLATE ASSY.

PRESSURE PLATE AND COVER ASSY.

THROWOUT BRG.

CLUTCH FORK

CLUTCH HOUSING

CLUTCH FORK BALL STUD

Exploded view of a typical diaphragm clutch

COAT THIS GROOVE

PACK THIS RECESS

Lubrication points of the throwout bearing

oil can is shaped very much like the clutch diaphragm spring and pushing in on the can bottom and then releasing it produces a similar effect. As mentioned earlier, the clutch pedal return spring permits full release of the pedal and reduces linkage slack due to wear. As the linkage wears, clutch free-pedal travel will increase and free-travel will decrease as the clutch wears. Free-travel is actually throwout bearing lash.

The diaphragm spring type clutches used are available in two different designs: flat diaphragm springs or bent spring. The bent fingers are bent back to create a centrifugal boost ensuring quick re-engagement at higher engine speeds. This design enables pressure plate load to increase as the clutch disc wears and makes low pedal effort possible even with a heavy duty clutch. The throwout bearing used with the bent finger design is 1¼" long and is shorter than the bearing used with the flat finger design. These bearings are not interchangeable. If the longer bearing is used with the bent finger clutch, free-pedal travel will not exist. This results in clutch slippage and rapid wear.

The transmission varies the gear ratio between the engine and rear wheels. It can be shifted to change engine speed as driving conditions and loads change. The transmission allows disengaging and reversing power from the engine to the wheels.

Two types of clutches are used. 6-cylinder engines use a single disc clutch with coil spring or diaphragm type pressure plates. V8 engines generally use a single disc with a coil spring pressure. Diaphragm type pressure plates operate with light pedal pressure, while coil spring

Troubleshooting Basic Clutch Problems

Problem	Cause
Excessive clutch noise	Throwout bearing noises are more audible at the lower end of pedal travel. The usual causes are: • Riding the clutch • Too little pedal free-play • Lack of bearing lubrication A bad clutch shaft pilot bearing will make a high pitched squeal, when the clutch is disengaged and the transmission is in gear or within the first 2″ of pedal travel. The bearing must be replaced. Noise from the clutch linkage is a clicking or snapping that can be heard or felt as the pedal is moved completely up or down. This usually requires lubrication. Transmitted engine noises are amplified by the clutch housing and heard in the passenger compartment. They are usually the result of insufficient pedal free-play and can be changed by manipulating the clutch pedal.
Clutch slips (the car does not move as it should when the clutch is engaged)	This is usually most noticeable when pulling away from a standing start. A severe test is to start the engine, apply the brakes, shift into high gear and SLOWLY release the clutch pedal. A healthy clutch will stall the engine. If it slips it may be due to: • A worn pressure plate or clutch plate • Oil soaked clutch plate • Insufficient pedal free-play
Clutch drags or fails to release	The clutch disc and some transmission gears spin briefly after clutch disengagement. Under normal conditions in average temperatures, 3 seconds is maximum spin-time. Failure to release properly can be caused by: • Too light transmission lubricant or low lubricant level • Improperly adjusted clutch linkage
Low clutch life	Low clutch life is usually a result of poor driving habits or heavy duty use. Riding the clutch, pulling heavy loads, holding the car on a grade with the clutch instead of the brakes and rapid clutch engagement all contribute to low clutch life.

pressure plates combine operating case with high torque capacity.

The operating controls are mechanical.

REMOVAL AND INSTALLATION

CAUTION: *The clutch driven disc contains asbestos, which has been determined to be a cancer causing agent. Never clean clutch surfaces with compressed air! Avoid inhaling any dust from any clutch surface! When cleaning clutch surfaces, use a commercially available brake cleaning fluid.*

Diaphragm Clutch

NOTE: *Before removing the bell housing (1973 and later) the engine must be supported. This can be done by placing a hydraulic jack, with a board on top, under the oil pan.*

1. Remove the transmission.

2. Disconnect the clutch fork pushrod and spring. Remove the clutch housing.

3. Remove the clutch fork by pressing it away from the ball mounting with a screwdriver until the fork snaps loose from the ball or remove the ball stud from the clutch housing. Remove the throwout bearing from the clutch fork.

4. Install a pilot tool (an old mainshaft makes a good pilot tool) to hold the clutch while you are removing it.

NOTE: *Before removing the clutch from the flywheel, mark the flywheel, clutch cover and one pressure plate lug, so that these parts may be assembled in their same relative positions. They were balanced as an assembly.*

5. Loosen the clutch attaching bolts one turn at a time to prevent distortion of the clutch cover until the tension is released.

6. Remove the clutch pilot tool and the clutch from the vehicle.

Check the pressure plate and flywheel for signs of wear, scoring, overheating, etc. If the clutch plate, flywheel, or pressure plate is oil-soaked, inspect the engine rear main seal and the transmission input shaft seal, and correct leakage as required. Replace any damaged parts.

To install:

7. Install the pressure plate in the cover assembly, aligning the notch in the pressure plate with the notch in the cover flange. Install pressure plate retracting springs, lockwashers and drive strap to pressure plate bolts. Tighten to 11 ft.lb. The clutch is now ready to be installed.

8. Turn the flywheel until the **X** mark is at the bottom.

9. Install the clutch disc, pressure plate and cover, using an old mainshaft as an aligning tool.

10. Turn the clutch until the **X** mark or painted white letter on the clutch cover aligns with the **X** mark on the flywheel.

11. Install the attaching bolts and tighten them a little at a time in a crossing pattern until the spring pressure is taken up.

12. Remove the aligning tool.

13. Pack the clutch ball fork seat with a small amount of high temperature grease and install a new retainer in the groove of the clutch fork.

WARNING: *Be careful not to use too much grease. Excessive amounts will get on the clutch fingers and cause clutch slippage.*

14. Install the retainer with the high side up with the open end on the horizontal.

15. If the clutch fork ball was removed, reinstall it in the clutch housing and snap the clutch fork onto the ball.

16. Lubricate the inside of the throwout bearing collar and the throwout fork groove with a small amount of graphite grease.

17. Install the throwout bearing. Install the clutch housing.

18. Install the transmission.

19. Further installation is the reverse of removal. Adjust the clutch.

Coil Spring Clutch

Basically, the same procedures apply to diaphragm clutch removal as to coil spring clutch removal.

1. Before removing the clutch, punch-mark the flywheel, clutch cover and one pressure plate lug so that the components can be reassembled in their original locations.

2. Loosen the attaching screws one turn at a time to prevent distortion.

3. When the clutch plate is removed, be sure to mark the flywheel side.

4. Place ⅜" wood or metal spacers between the clutch levers and the cover to hold the levers down as the holding screws are removed.

Free Pedal Travel Adjustment

1970-72

Only one adjustment is necessary to assure that the clutch operates efficiently. This adjustment is for the amount of free clutch pedal travel before the throwout bearing contacts the clutch fingers. The pedal should be adjusted at periodic intervals to provide ¾-1" of free pedal travel.

1. Disconnect the clutch fork return spring at the fork.

2. Loosen the nut (A) and back it off approximately ½" from the swivel.

3. Hold the clutch fork pushrod against the fork to move the throwout bearing against the clutch fingers. The pushrod will slide through the swivel at the cross-shaft.

4. Rotate the lever until the clutch pedal contacts the bumper mounted on the parking brake support.

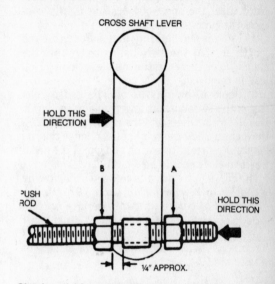

Clutch pedal free-play adjustment, 1970–72

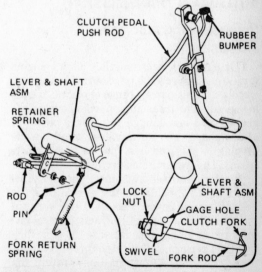

Clutch linkage adjustment, 1973 and later. Clutch pedal free play at the pedal should be about ¾ to 1 in.

5. Adjust nut (B) to obtain $^3/_{16}$-$^1/_4$" clearance between nut (B) and the swivel.

6. Release the pushrod, connect the return spring and tighten nut (A) to lock the swivel against nut (B).

7. Check the free pedal travel at the pedal and readjust as necessary.

1973 AND LATER

1. Disconnect the return spring at the clutch fork.

2. Rotate the clutch lever and shaft assembly until the clutch pedal is firmly against the rubber bumper on the brake pedal bracket.

3. Push the outer end of the clutch fork rearward until the throwout bearing lightly contacts the pressure plate levers.

4. Loosen the locknut and adjust the rod length so that the swivel slips freely into the gauge hole. Increase the rod length until all lash is removed.

5. Remove the swivel from the gauge hole. Insert the swivel in the lower hole in the lever. Install two washers and the cotter pin. Tighten the locknut, being careful not to change the rod length. Reinstall the spring and check the pedal free travel. It should be 1$^3/_8$-1$^5/_8$".

NOTE: *If you have a problem with driveline chatter in reverse on an early 1973 model, this can be corrected with a service kit (no. 340607) containing a new clutch cross shaft and relocated clutch fork springs. The kit components were installed at the factory in later models.*

AUTOMATIC TRANSMISSION

Understanding Automatic Transmissions

The automatic transmission allows engine torque and power to be transmitted to the rear wheels within a narrow range of engine operating speeds. The transmission will allow the engine to turn fast enough to produce plenty of power and torque at very low speeds, while keeping it at a sensible rpm at high vehicle speeds. The transmission performs this job entirely without driver assistance. The transmission uses a light fluid as the medium for the transmission of power. This fluid also works in the operation of various hydraulic control circuits and as a lubricant. Because the transmission fluid performs all of these three functions, trouble within the unit can easily travel from one part to another. For this reason, and because of the complexity and unusual operating principles of the transmission, a very sound un-derstanding of the basic principles of operation will simplify troubleshooting.

THE TORQUE CONVERTER

The torque converter replaces the conventional clutch. It has three functions:

1. It allows the engine to idle with the vehicle at a standstill, even with the transmission in gear.

2. It allows the transmission to shift from range to range smoothly, without requiring that the driver close the throttle during the shift.

3. It multiplies engine torque to an increasing extent as vehicle speed drops and throttle opening is increased. This has the effect of making the transmission more responsive and reduces the amount of shifting required.

The torque converter is a metal case which is shaped like a sphere that has been flattened on opposite sides. It is bolted to the rear end of the engine's crankshaft. Generally, the entire metal case rotates at engine speed and serves as the engine's flywheel.

The case contains three sets of blades. One set is attached directly to the case. This set forms the torus or pump. Another set is directly connected to the output shaft, and forms the turbine. The third set is mounted on a hub which, in turn, is mounted on a stationary shaft through a one-way clutch. This third set is known as the stator.

A pump, which is driven by the converter hub at engine speed, keeps the torque converter full of transmission fluid at all times. Fluid flows continuously through the unit to provide cooling.

Under low speed acceleration, the torque converter functions as follows:

The torus is turning faster than the turbine. It picks up fluid at the center of the converter and, through centrifugal force, slings it outward. Since the outer edge of the converter moves faster than the portions at the center, the fluid picks up speed.

The fluid then enters the outer edge of the turbine blades. It then travels back toward the center of the converter case along the turbine blades. In impinging upon the turbine blades, the fluid loses the energy picked up in the torus.

If the fluid were now to immediately be returned directly into the torus, both halves of the converter would have to turn at approximately the same speed at all times, and torque input and output would both be the same.

In flowing through the torus and turbine, the fluid picks up two types of flow, or flow in two separate directions. It flows through the turbine blades, and it spins with the engine. The stator, whose blades are stationary when the vehicle is being accelerated at low speeds, converts one type of flow into another. Instead of allowing the fluid to flow straight back into the torus, the stator's curved blades turn the fluid almost 90° toward the direction of rotation of the engine. Thus the fluid does not flow as fast toward the torus, but is already spinning when the torus picks it up. This has the effect of allowing the torus to turn much faster than the turbine. This difference in speed may be compared to the difference in speed between the smaller and larger gears in any gear train. The result is that engine power output is higher, and engine torque is multiplied.

As the speed of the turbine increases, the fluid spins faster and faster in the direction of engine rotation. As a result, the ability of the stator to redirect the fluid flow is reduced. Under cruising conditions, the stator is eventually forced to rotate on its one-way clutch in the direction of engine rotation. Under these conditions, the torque converter begins to behave almost like a solid shaft, with the torus and turbine speeds being almost equal.

THE PLANETARY GEARBOX

The ability of the torque converter to multiply engine torque is limited. Also, the unit tends to be more efficient when the turbine is rotating at relatively high speeds. Therefore, a planetary gearbox is used to carry the power output of the turbine to the driveshaft.

Planetary gears function very similarly to conventional transmission gears. However, their construction is different in that three elements make up one gear system, and, in that all three elements are different from one another. The three elements are: an outer gear that is shaped like a hoop, with teeth cut into the inner surface; a sun gear, mounted on a shaft and located at the very center of the outer gear; and a set of three planet gears, held by pins in a ring-like planet carrier, meshing with both the sun gear and the outer gear. Either the outer gear or the sun gear may be held stationary, providing more than one possible torque multiplication factor for each set of gears. Also, if all three gears are forced to rotate at the same speed, the gearset forms, in effect, a solid shaft.

Most modern automatics use the planetary gears to provide either a single reduction ratio of about 1.8:1, or two reduction gears: a low of about 2.5:1, and an intermediate of about 1.5:1. Bands and clutches are used to hold various portions of the gearsets to the transmission case or to the shaft on which they are mounted. Shifting is accomplished, then, by changing the portion of each planetary gearset which is held to the transmission case or to the shaft.

THE SERVOS AND ACCUMULATORS

The servos are hydraulic pistons and cylinders. They resemble the hydraulic actuators used on many familiar machines, such as bulldozers. Hydraulic fluid enters the cylinder, under pressure, and forces the piston to move to engage the band or clutches.

The accumulators are used to cushion the engagement of the servos. The transmission fluid must pass through the accumulator on the way to the servo. The accumulator housing contains a thin piston which is sprung away from the discharge passage of the accumulator. When fluid passes through the accumulator on the way to the servo, it must move the piston against spring pressure, and this action smooths out the action of the servo.

THE HYDRAULIC CONTROL SYSTEM

The hydraulic pressure used to operate the servos comes from the main transmission oil pump. This fluid is channeled to the various servos through the shift valves. There is generally a manual shift valve which is operated by the transmission selector lever and an automatic shift valve for each automatic upshift the transmission provides: i.e., 2-speed automatics have a low/high shift valve, while 3-speeds have a 1-2 valve, and a 2-3 valve.

There are two pressures which effect the operation of these valves. One is the governor pressure which is affected by vehicle speed. The other is the modulator pressure which is affected by intake manifold vacuum or throttle position. Governor pressure rises with an increase in vehicle speed, and modulator pressure rises as the throttle is opened wider. By responding to these two pressures, the shift valves cause the upshift points to be delayed with increased throttle opening to make the best use of the engine's power output.

Most transmissions also make use of an auxiliary circuit for downshifting. This circuit may be actuated by the throttle linkage or the vacuum line which actuates the modulator, or by a cable or solenoid. It applies pressure to a special downshift surface on the shift valve or valves.

The transmission modulator also governs the line pressure, used to actuate the servos. In this way, the clutches and bands will be actuated with a force matching the torque output of the engine.

Identification

Three automatic transmissions are used. The aluminum Powerglide was used from 1970 through 1971, when it was discontinued for use in trucks. The Turbo Hydra-Matic 350 and 400

Troubleshooting Basic Automatic Transmission Problems

Problem	Cause	Solution
Fluid leakage	• Defective pan gasket	• Replace gasket or tighten pan bolts
	• Loose filler tube	• Tighten tube nut
	• Loose extension housing to transmission case	• Tighten bolts
	• Converter housing area leakage	• Have transmission checked professionally
Fluid flows out the oil filler tube	• High fluid level	• Check and correct fluid level
	• Breather vent clogged	• Open breather vent
	• Clogged oil filter or screen	• Replace filter or clean screen (change fluid also)
	• Internal fluid leakage	• Have transmission checked professionally
Transmission overheats (this is usually accompanied by a strong burned odor to the fluid)	• Low fluid level	• Check and correct fluid level
	• Fluid cooler lines clogged	• Drain and refill transmission. If this doesn't cure the problem, have cooler lines cleared or replaced.
	• Heavy pulling or hauling with insufficient cooling	• Install a transmission oil cooler
	• Faulty oil pump, internal slippage	• Have transmission checked professionally
Buzzing or whining noise	• Low fluid level	• Check and correct fluid level
	• Defective torque converter, scored gears	• Have transmission checked professionally
No forward or reverse gears or slippage in one or more gears	• Low fluid level	• Check and correct fluid level
	• Defective vacuum or linkage controls, internal clutch or band failure	• Have unit checked professionally
Delayed or erratic shift	• Low fluid level	• Check and correct fluid level
	• Broken vacuum lines	• Repair or replace lines
	• Internal malfunction	• Have transmission checked professionally

Transmission Fluid Indications

The appearance and odor of the transmission fluid can give valuable clues to the overall condition of the transmission. Always note the appearance of the fluid when you check the fluid level or change the fluid. Rub a small amount of fluid between your fingers to feel for grit and smell the fluid on the dipstick.

If the fluid appears:	It indicates:
Clear and red colored	• Normal operation
Discolored (extremely dark red or brownish) or smells burned	• Band or clutch pack failure, usually caused by an overheated transmission. Hauling very heavy loads with insufficient power or failure to change the fluid, often result in overheating. Do not confuse this appearance with newer fluids that have a darker red color and a strong odor (though not a burned odor).
Foamy or aerated (light in color and full of bubbles)	• The level is too high (gear train is churning oil)
	• An internal air leak (air is mixing with the fluid). Have the transmission checked professionally.
Solid residue in the fluid	• Defective bands, clutch pack or bearings. Bits of band material or metal abrasives are clinging to the dipstick. Have the transmission checked professionally.
Varnish coating on the dipstick	• The transmission fluid is overheating

Lockup Torque Converter Service Diagnosis

Problem	Cause	Solution

No lockup	• Faulty oil pump
	• Sticking governor valve
	• Valve body malfunction
	  (a) Stuck switch valve
	  (b) Stuck lockup valve
	  (c) Stuck fail-safe valve
	• Failed locking clutch
	• Leaking turbine hub seal
	• Faulty input shaft or seal ring
		• Replace oil pump
		• Repair or replace as necessary
		• Repair or replace valve body or its internal components as necessary
		• Replace torque converter
		• Replace torque converter
		• Repair or replace as necessary

Will not unlock	• Sticking governor valve
	• Valve body malfunction
	  (a) Stuck switch valve
	  (b) Stuck lockup valve
	  (c) Stuck fail-safe valve
		• Repair or replace as necessary
		• Repair or replace valve body or its internal components as necessary

Stays locked up at too low a speed in direct	• Sticking governor valve
	• Valve body malfunction
	  (a) Stuck switch valve
	  (b) Stuck lockup valve
	  (c) Stuck fail-safe valve
		• Repair or replace as necessary
		• Repair or replace valve body or its internal components as necessary

Locks up or drags in low or second	• Faulty oil pump
	• Valve body malfunction
	  (a) Stuck switch valve
	  (b) Stuck fail-safe valve
		• Replace oil pump
		• Repair or replace valve body or its internal components as necessary

Sluggish or stalls in reverse	• Faulty oil pump
	• Plugged cooler, cooler lines or fittings
	• Valve body malfunction
	  (a) Stuck switch valve
	  (b) Faulty input shaft or seal ring
		• Replace oil pump as necessary
		• Flush or replace cooler and flush lines and fittings
		• Repair or replace valve body or its internal components as necessary

Loud chatter during lockup engagement (cold)	• Faulty torque converter • Failed locking clutch • Leaking turbine hub seal	• Replace torque converter • Replace torque converter • Replace torque converter
Vibration or shudder during lockup engagement	• Faulty oil pump • Valve body malfunction • Faulty torque converter • Engine needs tune-up	• Repair or replace oil pump as necessary • Repair or replace valve body or its internal components as necessary • Replace torque converter • Tune engine
Vibration after lockup engagement	• Faulty torque converter • Exhaust system strikes underbody • Engine needs tune-up • Throttle linkage misadjusted	• Replace torque converter • Align exhaust system • Tune engine • Adjust throttle linkage
Vibration when revved in neutral Overheating: oil blows out of dip stick tube or pump seal	• Torque converter out of balance • Plugged cooler, cooler lines or fittings • Stuck switch valve	• Replace torque converter • Flush or replace cooler and flush lines and fittings • Repair switch valve in valve body or replace valve body
Shudder after lockup engagement	• Faulty oil pump • Plugged cooler, cooler lines or fittings • Valve body malfunction • Faulty torque converter • Fail locking clutch • Exhaust system strikes underbody • Engine needs tune-up • Throttle linkage misadjusted	• Replace oil pump • Flush or replace cooler and flush lines and fittings • Repair or replace valve body or its internal components as necessary • Replace torque converter • Replace torque converter • Align exhaust system • Tune engine • Adjust throttle linkage

were installed in 1970-82 models. Some 1980 and later transmissions use the Torque Converter Clutch system. 1982 and later models are available with a 700-R4 4 speed automatic which incorporates the torque converter clutch. No band adjustments are necessary or possible on Turbo Hydra-Matic transmissions; they use clutches instead of bands. Pan removal, fluid and filter changes for all three transmissions are covered in Chapter 1.

Fluid Pan and Filter

REMOVAL AND INSTALLATION

1. Raise and support the vehicle with jackstands. This may not be necessary if there is enough clearance for you to work under the truck comfortably.

2. Place a large container under the transmission. Make sure the container is large enough to hold the amount of fluid contained in your particular transmission. Refer to the capacities chart to determine how much fluid your transmission holds.

3. Remove only enough bolts from the transmission pan to allow one corner to lower so that the fluid can flow into the container.

4. When the transmission pan has drained completely, remove the remaining bolts.

5. Drain the remainder of fluid from the pan, clean with a quality solvent and allow the pan to dry completely.

6. While the transmission pan is drying, remove the transmission filter by removing the two screws that secure it to the transmission.

7. Replace the old filter and the transmission pan gasket and reinstall. Permatex® can be used to hold the gasket in place, thus making installation easier.

8. Fill the transmission with new fluid, start the engine and check to see that the transmis-

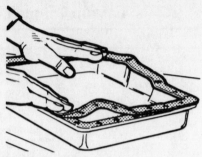

Install the new gasket to the pan

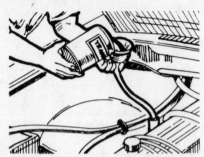

Transmission fluid is added through the dipstick tube

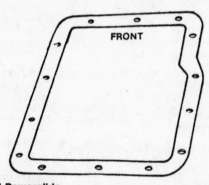

GM Powerglide

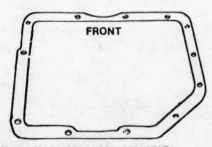

GM Turbo Hydra-Matic 250, 350, 375B

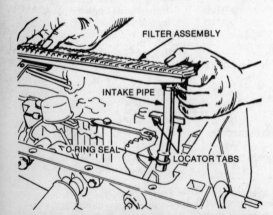

The Turbo Hydra-Matic 400 filter has an O-ring on the intake pipe; check the condition of this O-ring, and replace as necessary

sion fluid is at the proper level, and check for leaks.

NOTE: *Dexron® II is the recommended transmission fluid for all GM cars and trucks.*

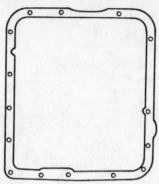

GM THM 700-R4

C 10, 20

Powerglide control rod adjustment

Low Band Adjustment

Powerglide

1. Raise and support the vehicle with jackstands.

2. Place the selector lever in Neutral.

3. Remove the protective cap from the low band adjusting screw.

4. Loosen the adjusting screw locknut ¼ turn and hold it in this position with a wrench.

5. Using an inch pound torque wrench, adjust the band adjusting screw to 70 in.lb., and back the screw off 4 complete turns for a band that has been in operation 6,000 miles or more; or 3 complete turns for a band that has been in operation less than 6,000 miles.

NOTE: *The back-off figure is not approximate; it must be exact.*

6. Tighten the adjusting screw locknut.

7. Lower the vehicle and road test.

Shift Linkage Adjustment

Powerglide

The shift tube and selector linkage must be free in the mast jacket.

1. Set the transmission lever in Drive (D).

Powerglide low band adjustment

NOTE: *Do not be guided by the position of the needle. Determine Drive by shifting the lever all the way to the right of the Low (L) detent. Rotate it back to the left, one detent, to Drive (D).*

2. Attach the control rod to the lever and inner lever of the shaft assembly with the retainers.

3. Assemble the swivel, clamp, grommet, bushing, washers and nut loosely on the selector lever.

4. Attach the control rod to the outer lever of the shaft assembly with the retainer.

5. Place the selector lever tang in the Neutral drive gate of the selector plate assembly and insert the control rod into the swivel.

6. Rotate the lever clockwise viewed looking down the steering column, until the tang contacts the drive side of the Neutral drive gate.

7. Tighten the nut.

Turbo Hydra-Matic 350, 400 and 700-R4

1970-72

1. The shift tube and levers located in the mast jacket of the steering column must move freely and must not bind.

2. Pull the shift lever toward the steering wheel and allow the lever to be positioned in Drive by the transmission detent. The pointer may be out of adjustment, so don't use the pointer on the column as a reference for positioning the lever. The pointer must be adjusted last.

3. Release the selector lever. The lever should not go into Low unless the lever is lifted.

4. Lift the lever toward the steering wheel and permit the lever to be placed in Neutral by the transmission detent.

5. Release the lever; it should not go into Reverse unless the lever is lifted.

6. If the linkage is adjusted correctly, the shift lever will not move past the Neutral detent and the Drive detent unless the lever is lifted so it can pass over the mechanical stop in the steering column.

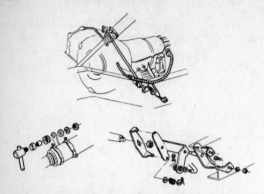

Turbo Hydra-Matic shift linkage, 1970–72

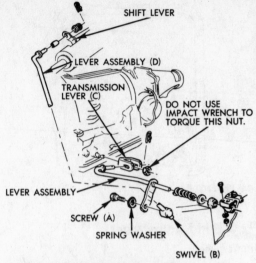

Turbo Hydra-Matic shift linkage, 1973–81

7. If adjustment is necessary, place the lever in the Drive or High detent position. If the indicator pointer is out of alignment, you must rely upon the detent position to determine what gear you are in (see Steps 2 and 3).

8. Loosen the adjustment swivel or clamp at the cross-shaft and move the shift lever so that it contacts the drive stop in the column.

9. Tighten the swivel and recheck the adjustment (see Steps 2 and 6).

10. If the indicator pointer fails to line up properly with the gear symbol (P, R, N, D, L) or aligns with a wrong symbol (being in Reverse when the pointer indicates Neutral, etc.), the cause may be a bent indicator wire. Inspect it and repair.

11. If necessary, readjust the neutral safety switch to agree with the detent positions. The ignition key should move into **lock** only when the shift lever is in Park.

WARNING: *The above adjustments must be made correctly to prevent early transmission failure caused by controls not being fully engaged with the detent. This results in a situation in which fluid pressure is reduced causing only partial engagement of the clutches. It may appear to run well but the pressure reduction may be just enough to cause clutch failure after only a few miles of operation.*

1973-81

1. The shift tube and lever assembly must be free in the mast jacket.

2. Lift the selector lever toward the steering wheel and allow the selector lever to be positioned in Drive by the detent. Do not use the selector lever pointer as a reference.

3. Release the selector lever. The lever should not be able to go into Low unless the lever is lifted.

4. Lift the selector lever toward the steering wheel and allow the lever to be positioned in Neutral by the transmission detent.

5. Release the selector lever. The lever should not be able to engage Reverse unless the

lever is lifted. A properly adjusted linkage will prevent the lever from moving beyond both the Neutral and Drive detents unless the lever is lifted.

6. If adjustment is required, remove the screw and spring washer from the swivel.

7. Set the transmission lever in Neutral by moving it counterclockwise to **L** and then three detents clockwise to Neutral.

8. Put the transmission selector lever in Neutral as determined by the mechanical stop in the steering column.

9. Do not use the pointer to determine these positions.

10. Assemble the swivel spring and washer to the lever and tighten to 20 ft.lb.

11. Readjust the Neutral safety switch if necessary.

12. Check the operation. With the key in RUN, and the transmission in Reverse, be sure that the key cannot be removed and the steering wheel is not locked.

With the key in LOCK and the shift lever in PARK, be sure that the key can be removed, the steering wheel is locked, and that the transmission remains in PARK when the steering column is locked.

NOTE: *Any inaccuracies in the above adjustments may result in premature transmission failure, due to operation of the transmission with the controls not in the full detent. Partial engagement of clutches and other internal parts will result in transmission failure after only a few miles.*

1982 AND LATER

1. Set the transmission lever **A** in the neutral position by moving it clockwise to the Park detent, then counterclockwise two detents to Neutral.

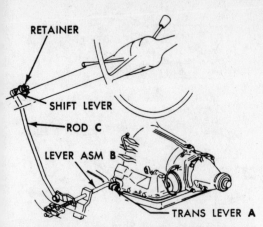

1982 and later Turbo Hydra-Matic automatic transmission linkage adjustment, column shift shown

2. Set the column shift lever to the Neutral gate notch, by rotating it until the shift lever drops in the Neutral gate. Do not use the indicator pointer as a reference to position the shift lever, as this will not be accurate.

3. Attach rod **C** to the transmission shaft assembly as shown.

4. Slide the swivel and clamp onto rod **C** and align it with the column shift lever. Complete the attachment.

5. Hold the column lever against the Neutral stop on the Park position side. Tighten the nut.

Throttle Valve Linkage Adjustment

Powerglide

6-CYLINDER ENGINES

1. With the accelerator depressed, the bellcrank on the engine must be in the wide open throttle position.

2. The dash lever must be $\frac{1}{64}$-$\frac{1}{16}$" off the lever stop and the transmission lever must be against the transmission internal stop.

V8 ENGINES

1. Remove the air cleaner.

2. Disconnect the accelerator linkage at the carburetor.

3. Disconnect the accelerator return spring and throttle valve rod return springs.

4. Pull the throttle valve rod forward until the transmission is through the detent. Open

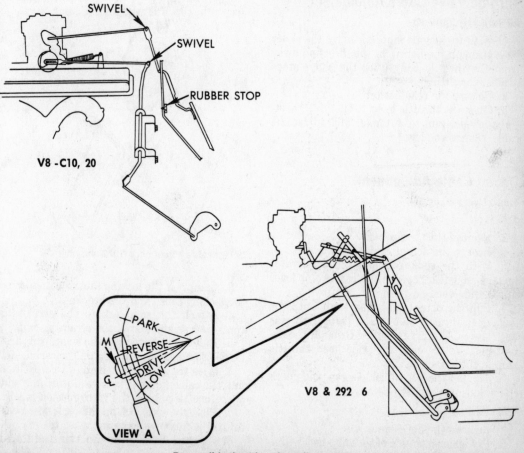

Powerglide throttle valve adjustment

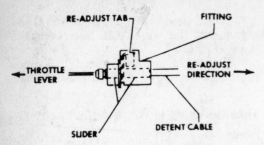

Turbo Hydra-Matic T.V cable (self adjusting)

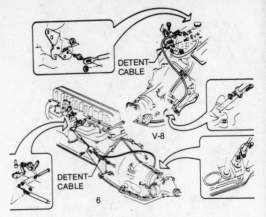

Detent cable adjustment, 1970–72

the carburetor to the wide-open throttle position. The carburetor must reach the wipe-open throttle position at the same time that the ball stud contacts the end of the slot in the upper throttle valve rod.

5. Adjust the swivel on the end of the upper throttle valve rod as per Step 4. The allowable tolerance is approximately $\frac{1}{32}$".

6. Connect and adjust the accelerator linkage.

7. Check for freedom of operation. Install the air cleaner.

Throttle Valve Cable Adjustment

All Turbo Hydra-Matic

1. With the engine stopped, move the slider back through the fitting in the direction away from the throttle body until the slider stops against the fitting.

2. Release the readjust tab.

3. Open the throttle lever to the "full throttle stop" position to automatically adjust the cable. release the lever.

Detent Cable Adjustment

Turbo Hydra-Matic 350

1970-71

1. Remove the air cleaner.

2. Loosen the detent cable screw.

3. With the choke off and the accelerator linkage adjusted, position the carburetor lever in the wide open position.

4. Pull the detent cable rearward until the wide open throttle stop in the transmission is felt. The cable must be pulled through the detent position to reach the wide open throttle stop in the transmission.

5. Tighten the detent cable screw and check the linkage for proper operation.

1972

1. Remove the air cleaner.

2. Pry up on each side of the snap-lock with a screwdriver to release the lock.

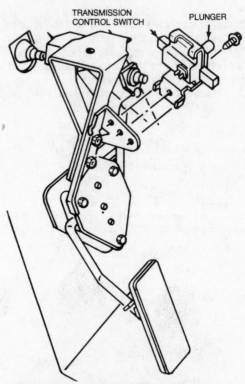

Detent cable adjustment, 1972 and later

3. Compress the locking tabs and disconnect the locking tabs from the bracket.

4. Attach the snap-lock to the accelerator control lever and install the retaining ring.

5. Pull the carburetor to the wide open throttle position against the stop on the carburetor.

6. With the carburetor held in this position, pull the cable housing rearward until the wide open throttle stop in the transmission is felt.

7. Push the snap lock on the cable downward until it is flush with the cable.

8. Do not lubricate the cable. Install the air cleaner.

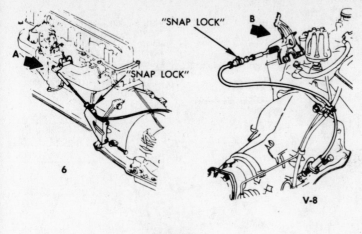

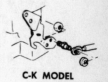

C-K MODEL

C-K MODEL
V-8 350 ENGINE
VIEW B

C-K MODEL
VIEW A

Detent cable adjustment, 1972 and later

1973 and Later

With the snap-lock disengaged from the bracket, position the carburetor at the wide open throttle position. Push the snap-lock downward until the top is flush with the rest of the cable.

Detent Switch Adjustment

Turbo Hydra-Matic 400

1970-71

Adjust the detent switch as shown in the accompanying illustrations.

1972 and Later

1. Install the detent switch as shown.
2. After installing the switch, press the

396 V8
ADJUST KICKDOWN SWITCH (A)
SO THAT ACTUATING LEVER (B)
RESTS AGAINST THREADED BARREL
OF SWITCH WHEN CARB LEVER IS
IN WIDE OPEN THROTTLE POSITION

CARB LEVER   ACTUATING
LEVER (B)

VIEW A   SWITCH (A)

Detent switch adjustment, 1970 396 V8

switch plunger as far forward as possible. This will preset the switch for adjustment. The switch will automatically adjust itself with the first wide open throttle application of the accelerator pedal.

Neutral Safety/Backup Light Switch Replacement And Adjustment

This switch is on top of the steering column, behind the instrument panel. It prevents the starting circuit from being completed unless the shift lever is in Neutral or Park. The same switch causes the backup light to go on in Reverse.

NOTE: *The 3-speed manual transmission backup light switch is on the column. On the 4-speed, it is on the transmission, near the top cover.*

Neutral Safety Switch Adjustment

1970-71 Powerglide

1. Align the slot in the contact support with the hole in the switch and insert a $^3/_{32}$" pin to hold it in this position.
2. The switch is now in the drive position.
3. Place the contact support drive slot over the shifter tube drive tang and tighten the screws.
4. Remove the clamp pin.
5. Check the operation of the switch. The engine should not be able to be started in any drive gear.

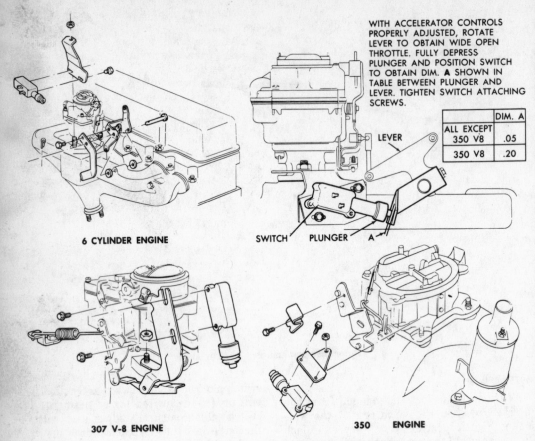

WITH ACCELERATOR CONTROLS
PROPERLY ADJUSTED, ROTATE
LEVER TO OBTAIN WIDE OPEN
THROTTLE. FULLY DEPRESS
PLUNGER AND POSITION SWITCH
TO OBTAIN DIM. **A** SHOWN IN
TABLE BETWEEN PLUNGER AND
LEVER. TIGHTEN SWITCH ATTACHING
SCREWS.

	DIM. A
ALL EXCEPT 350 V8	.05
350 V8	.20

6 CYLINDER ENGINE

SWITCH   PLUNGER   A

307 V-8 ENGINE   350   ENGINE

Detent switch adjustment, 1970–71 except 396 V8

1970-72 Turbo Hydra-Matic

1. Disconnect the wiring plug. Remove the screws and the switch.

2. Place the shift lever in Drive. Locate the lever tang against the transmission selector plate.

3. Align the slot in the contact support with the hole in the switch and insert a $\frac{3}{32}''$ drill bit to hold the support in place.

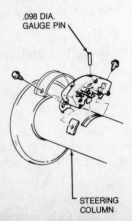

.098 DIA.
GAUGE PIN

STEERING
COLUMN

Neutral start switch adjustment, 1973 and later

4. Place the contact support drive slot over the shifter tube drive tang and tighten the screws. Remove the bit.

5. Connect the wiring plug and check that the engine will start only in Neutral and Park (foot on the brake!) and that the backup lights work only in reverse. Loosen the screws and move the switch to correct.

1973 and Later

1. Disconnect the switch wiring plug. Remove the screws and the switch.

2. Place the shift lever in Neutral.

3. Insert a $\frac{3}{32}''$ drill bit, ⅜" into the switch hole on a used switch. A new switch is held in the Neutral position by a plastic shear pin, so the bit isn't needed.

4. Insert the switch tang into the column slot and install the screws.

5. Remove the locating bit. With a new switch, shift out of neutral to shear the plastic pin.

6. Connect the wiring plug and check that the engine will start only in neutral and Park (foot on the brake!) and that the backup lights work only in Reverse. Loosen the screws and move the switch to correct.

Transmission

REMOVAL AND INSTALLATION

NOTE: *It would be best to drain the transmission before starting.*

It may be necessary to disconnect and remove the exhaust crossover pipe on V8s, and to disconnect the catalytic converter and remove its support bracket, on models so equipped.

2-Wheel Drive

1. Disconnect the battery ground cable. Disconnect the detent cable at the carburetor.
2. Raise and support the truck on jackstands.
3. Remove the driveshaft, after matchmarking its flanges.
4. Disconnect the speedometer cable, downshift cable, vacuum modulator line, shift linkage, throttle linkage and fluid cooler lines at the transmission. Remove the filler tube.
5. Support the transmission and unbolt the rear mount from the crossmember. Remove the crossmember.
6. Remove the torque converter underpan, matchmark the flywheel and converter, and remove the converter bolts.
7. Support the engine and lower the transmission slightly for access to the upper transmission to engine bolts.
8. Remove the transmission to engine bolts and pull the transmission back. Rig up a strap or keep the front of the transmission up so the converter doesn't fall out.
9. Reverse the procedure for installation. Bolt the transmission to the engine first (34 ft.lb.), then the converter to the flywheel (50 ft.lb.). Make sure that the converter attaching lugs are flush and that the converter can turn freely before installing the bolts. Tighten the bolts finger tight, then torque to specification, to insure proper converter alignment.

NOTE: *Lubricate the internal yoke splines at the transmission end of the driveshaft with lithium base grease. The grease should seep out through the vent hole.*

1970-72 4-Wheel Drive

1. Disconnect the battery ground cable. Disconnect the detent cable at the carburetor.
2. Raise and support the truck.
3. Remove the driveshafts, after matchmarking their flanges.
4. Remove the transfer case shift lever.
5. Disconnect the speedometer cable, downshift cable, vacuum modulator line, shift linkage, throttle linkage and fluid cooler lines at the transmission. Remove the filler tube.

6. Support the transmission and transfer case separately. Remove the transmission to adapter case bolts. Unbolt the transfer case from the frame bracket and remove it.
7. Procede with Steps 5 through 9 of the two wheel drive procedure. See transfer case Removal and Installation for adapter bolt torques.

1973 and Later 4-Wheel Drive

1. Disconnect the battery ground cable and remove the transmission dipstick. Detach the downshift cable at the carburetor. Remove the transfer case shift lever knob and boot.
2. Raise and support the truck on jackstands.
3. Remove the skid plate, if any. Remove the flywheel cover.
4. Matchmark the flywheel and torque converter, remove the bolts, and secure the converter so it doesn't fall out of the transmission.
5. Detach the shift linkage, speedometer cable, vacuum modulator line, downshift cable, throttle linkage and cooler times at the transmission. Remove the filler tube.
6. Remove the exhaust crossover pipe to manifold bolts.
7. Unbolt the transfer case adapter from the crossmember. Support the transmission and transfer case. Remove the crossmember.
8. Move the exhaust system aside. Detach the driveshafts after matchmarking their flanges. Disconnect the parking brake cable.
9. Unbolt the transfer case from the frame bracket. Support the engine. Unbolt the transmission from the engine, pull the assembly back, and remove.
10. Reverse the procedure for installation. Bolt the transmission to the engine first (34 ft.lb.), then the converter to the flywheel (50 ft.lb.). Make sure that the converter attaching lugs are flush and that the converter can turn freely before installing the bolts. See Transfer Case Removal and Installation for adapter bolt torques.

TRANSFER CASE

There are three cases used. The New Process 205 is used in part time systems with all transmissions through 1975, and in 1980, and with manual transmissions only 1976-79. It has a large New Process emblem on the back of the case. The full time new Process 203 is used with all transmissions in 1974 and early 1975, and only with automatics from mid-1975, to 1979. It can be identified by the H-LOC and L-LOC positions on the shifter. 1981 and later ½ and ¾ ton trucks use the model 208 transfer case. All 1 ton trucks use model 205.

CHILTON TIP: *Models with the new process 203 full time 4-wheel drive transfer case, especially with manual transmissions, may give a front wheel chatter or vibration on sharp turns. This is a normal characteristic of this drivetrain combination. If it occurs shortly after shifting out of a LOC position, the transfer case is probably still locked up. This should correct itself after about a mile of driving, or can be alleviated by backing up for a short distance.*

WARNING: *Owners of full time 4-wheel drive trucks (New Process 203 transfer case) often consider either removing the front driveshaft, or installing locking front hubs and operating in a LOC position, as a means of improving gas mileage. This practice will submit the transfer case to stresses beyond its design limits and will void all warranties. Use of any lubricant additive in the transfer case is also not recommended.*

REMOVAL AND INSTALLATION

All Models

NOTE: *See illustrations of 205 and 208 series transfer cases under Transmission Removal in this chapter.*

1. Raise and support the truck.
2. Drain the transfer case.

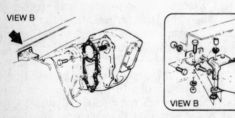

1970–72 manual transmission transfer case mounting

Automatic transmission transfer case mounting, 1970–72

3. Disconnect the speedometer cable, back-up light switch, and the TCS switch.
4. If necessary, remove the skid plate and crossmember support.
5. Disconnect the front and rear driveshafts and support them out of the way.
   a. On New Process 205 models, disconnect the shift lever rod from the shift rail link.
   b. On New Process 203 models, disconnect the shift levers at the transfer case.
6. Remove the transfer case-to-frame mounting bolts.
7. Support the transfer case and remove the bolts attaching the transfer case to transmission adaptor.
8. Move the transfer case to the rear until the input shaft clears the adaptor and lower the transfer case from the truck.
9. Installation is the reverse of removal.

SHIFT LINKAGE ADJUSTMENT

New Process Model 203

The 203 full time 4-wheel drive transfer case is the only one on which linkage adjustment is possible.

1. Place the selector lever in the cab in the Neutral position.
2. Detach the adjustable rod ends from the transfer case levers.
3. Insert an $^{11}/_{64}$" drill bit through the alignment holes in the shifter levers. This will lock the shifter in the neutral position with both levers vertical.
4. Place the range shift lever (the outer lever) on the transfer case in the Neutral position.
5. Place the lockout shift lever (the inner lever) on the transfer case in the unlocked position. Both levers should now be vertical.
6. Adjust the rods so that the linkage fits together. The indicator plate can be moved to align with the correct symbol.
7. Remove the drill bit.

New Process Model 203 Overhaul

The New Process Model 203 transfer case is a full-time 4WD unit that operates in 4WD at all times. The unit incorporates a differential similar to axle differentials; compensating for different speeds of the front and rear axles resulting from varying speeds while turning and operating over different surfaces.

There are five shift positions with this transfer case; Neutral, High and High Lock, and Low and Low Lock. The Lock positions are used under low traction conditions. In the Lock position, the differential action of the transfer case

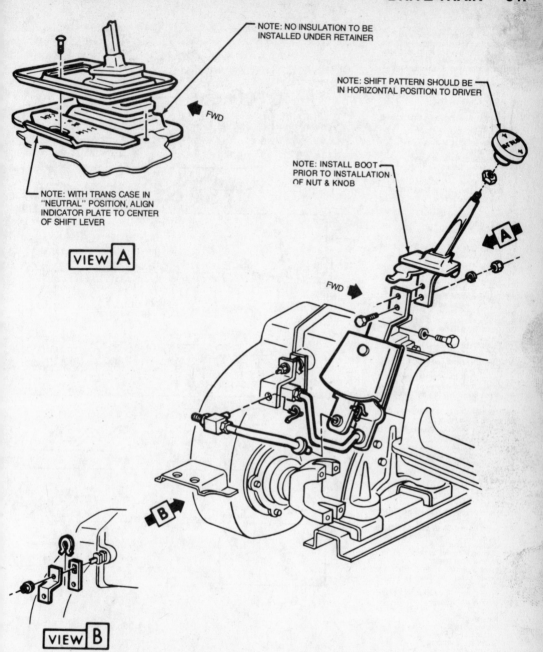

NOTE: NO INSULATION TO BE INSTALLED UNDER RETAINER

NOTE: SHIFT PATTERN SHOULD BE IN HORIZONTAL POSITION TO DRIVER

NOTE: INSTALL BOOT PRIOR TO INSTALLATION OF NUT & KNOB

NOTE: WITH TRANS CASE IN "NEUTRAL" POSITION, ALIGN INDICATOR PLATE TO CENTER OF SHIFT LEVER

FWD

VIEW A

FWD

A

VIEW B

B

New Process model 203 transfer case shift linkage adjustment

is eliminated, by locking the front and rear output shafts together. In this mode, neither the front or rear axle can rotate independently of the other.

CASE DISASSEMBLY

1. Loosen rear output shaft flange retaining nut and remove front output shaft flange and washer.

2. Tap the front output shaft dust seal away from case assembly. Remove front output shaft bearing retainer and gasket.

3. Position transfer case assembly on blocks with input shaft facing downward.

4. Remove rear output shaft assembly from transfer case. Slide the differential carrier off the shaft.

5. Place a 1½-2″ band type hose clamp on input shaft to retain bearings.

6. Lift shift rail and driveout pin retaining shift fork.

7. Remove shift rail poppet ball plug, gasket and ball from case. Use a magnet to remove poppet ball.

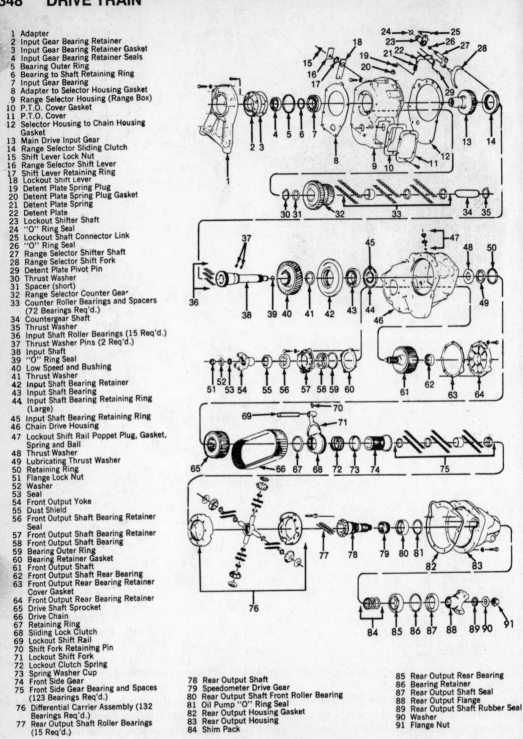

1 Adapter
2 Input Gear Bearing Retainer
3 Input Gear Bearing Retainer Gasket
4 Input Gear Bearing Retainer Seals
5 Bearing Outer Ring
6 Bearing to Shaft Retaining Ring
7 Input Gear Bearing
8 Adapter to Selector Housing Gasket
9 Range Selector Housing (Range Box)
10 P.T.O. Cover Gasket
11 P.T.O. Cover
12 Selector Housing to Chain Housing Gasket
13 Main Drive Input Gear
14 Range Selector Sliding Clutch
15 Shift Lever Lock Nut
16 Range Selector Shift Lever
17 Shift Lever Retaining Ring
18 Lockout Shift Lever
19 Detent Plate Spring Plug
20 Detent Plate Spring Plug Gasket
21 Detent Plate Spring
22 Detent Plate
23 Lockout Shifter Shaft
24 "O" Ring Seal
25 Lockout Shaft Connector Link
26 "O" Ring Seal
27 Range Selector Shifter Shaft
28 Range Selector Shift Fork
29 Detent Plate Pivot Pin
30 Thrust Washer
31 Spacer (short)
32 Range Selector Counter Gear
33 Counter Roller Bearings and Spacers (72 Bearings Req'd.)
34 Countergear Shaft
35 Thrust Washer
36 Input Shaft Roller Bearings (15 Req'd.)
37 Thrust Washer Pins (2 Req'd.)
38 Input Shaft
39 "O" Ring Seal
40 Low Speed and Bushing
41 Thrust Washer
42 Input Shaft Bearing Retainer
43 Input Shaft Bearing
44 Input Shaft Bearing Retaining Ring (Large)
45 Input Shaft Bearing Retaining Ring
46 Chain Drive Housing
47 Lockout Shift Rail Poppet Plug, Gasket, Spring and Ball
48 Thrust Washer
49 Lubricating Thrust Washer
50 Retaining Ring
51 Flange Lock Nut
52 Washer
53 Seal
54 Front Output Yoke
55 Dust Shield
56 Front Output Shaft Bearing Retainer Seal
57 Front Output Shaft Bearing Retainer
58 Front Output Shaft Bearing
59 Bearing Outer Ring
60 Bearing Retainer Gasket
61 Front Output Shaft
62 Front Output Shaft Rear Bearing
63 Front Output Rear Bearing Retainer Cover Gasket
64 Front Output Rear Bearing Retainer
65 Drive Shaft Sprocket
66 Drive Chain
67 Retaining Ring
68 Sliding Lock Clutch
69 Lockout Shift Rail
70 Shift Fork Retaining Pin
71 Lockout Shift Fork
72 Lockout Clutch Spring
73 Spring Washer Cup
74 Front Side Gear
75 Front Side Gear Bearing and Spaces (123 Bearings Req'd.)
76 Differential Carrier Assembly (132 Bearings Req'd.)
77 Rear Output Shaft Roller Bearings (15 Req'd.)

78 Rear Output Shaft
79 Speedometer Drive Gear
80 Rear Output Shaft Front Roller Bearing
81 Oil Pump "O" Ring Seal
82 Rear Output Housing Gasket
83 Rear Output Housing
84 Shim Pack

85 Rear Output Rear Bearing
86 Bearing Retainer
87 Rear Output Shaft Seal
88 Rear Output Flange
89 Rear Output Shaft Rubber Seal
90 Washer
91 Flange Nut

Disassembled view of the 203 transfer case

8. Push shift rail down, lift up on lockout clutch and remove shift fork from clutch assembly.

9. Remove front output shaft rear bearing retainer. It may be necessary to gently tap front of shaft or cautiously pry retainer from case.

Make certain that no roller bearings are lost from rear cover.

10. When necessary, remove rear bearing by pressing.

11. Pry front output shaft front bearing from lower side of case.

12. Remove front output shaft assembly from case.

13. Lift intermediate housing from range box, after removing bolts.

14. Remove chain from intermediate housing.

15. Remove lockout clutch, drive gear and input shaft from range box.

16. Install a 1½-2″ band type hose clamp on end of input shaft to retain roller bearings.

17. Pull up on shift rail and remove rail from link.

18. Lift input shaft assembly from range box.

CASE ASSEMBLY

1. Position range box with input gear side down, on wood blocks.

2. Place gasket on input housing.

3. Install lockout clutch and drive sprocket on input shaft assembly. Install a 2″ band type hose clamp on end of input shaft to prevent loss of bearings during installation.

4. Place input shaft, lockout clutch and drive sprocket in range box. Align tab on bearing retainer with notch in gasket.

5. Engage lockout clutch shift rail to the connector link. Position rail in housing bore and turn shifter shaft lowering rail into the housing. This will prevent the link and rail from becoming disconnected.

6. Place the drive chain in housing with the chain around the outer wall.

7. Secure the chain housing to the range box. Be sure that the shift rail engages the channel of the housing. Place the chain on the input drive sprocket.

8. Place the front output sprocket in transfer case. Turn the clutch drive gear to assist in positioning chain on sprocket.

9. Position the shift fork and rail on the clutch assembly. Install the clutch assembly completely into the drive sprocket. Insert retaining pin in shift fork and rail.

10. Install front output bearing, gasket, retainer, bolts, flange, gasket, seal, washer and retaining nut.

11. If rear bearing was removed from front output shaft, press a new bearing into the outside face of cover until bearing is flush with opening.

12. Install front output shaft, rear bearing, retainer, gasket and bolts.

13. Slip differential carrier assembly on the input shaft. Bolts on carrier must face rear of shaft.

14. Load bearings in pinion shaft, install rear output housing assembly, gasket and bolts.

15. Install a dial indicator on the rear housing. The indicator must contact the end of the output shaft. While holding the rear flange, rotate the front output shaft and find the highest

point of gear hop. Reset indicator and with rear output shaft at high point, pull up on the end of the shaft to determine end-play. Remove indicator and install shim pack to control end-play to between 0 and 0.005″. The shim pack is positioned on the shaft in front of the rear bearing. Check for binding of rear output shaft.

16. Insert lockout clutch shift rail poppet ball, spring and screw plug in transfer case.

17. Install poppet plate spring, gasket and plug, if they were not previously installed.

18. Install shift levers on the range box, if these were not left on vehicle.

19. Torque all bolts, locknuts and plugs to the following specifications:

- Adapter-to-case: 38 ft.lb.
- Adapter-to-transmission: 40 ft.lb.
- Upper case-to-frame: 50 ft.lb.
- Lower case-to-frame: 65 ft.lb.
- Shift lever nuts: 25 ft.lb.
- Shift lever rod-to-swivel: 50 ft.lb.
- Shift lever locking arm nut: 150 in.lb.
- Skid plate nuts: 45 ft.lb.
- Crossmember nuts: 45 ft.lb.
- Adapter mount bolts: 25 ft.lb.
- Intermediate case-to-range box: 30 ft.lb.
- Front output bearing retainer: 30 ft.lb.
- Output shaft yoke nut: 150 ft.lb.
- Differential assembly screws: 45 ft.lb.
- Rear output shaft housing: 30 ft.lb.
- Poppet ball retainer nut: 15 ft.lb.
- PTO cover bolts: 15 ft.lb.
- Front input bearing retainer: 20 ft.lb.
- Filler plug: 25 ft.lb.

20. Fill transfer case with specified lubricant until the proper level is reached. Secure filler plug.

SUBASSEMBLIES OVERHAUL

Lockout Clutch

DISASSEMBLY

1. Remove front side gear from input shaft assembly.

2. Remove thrust washer, roller bearings and spacers from front side gear bore. The position of the spacers must be noted.

3. Remove the snapring which holds the drive sprocket to clutch assembly. Slip the drive sprocket from the front side gear.

4. Remove the lower snapring.

5. Remove sliding gear, spring and spring cup washer from the front side gear.

6. Thoroughly clean and inspect all component parts. Replace any component that is worn or defective.

ASSEMBLY

1. Place spring cup washer, spring and sliding clutch gear on front side gear.

2. Secure sliding clutch to front side gear with a snapring.

3. Spread petroleum jelly on front side gear and install roller bearings and spacers.

4. Place thrust washer in gear end of front side gear.

5. Slide drive sprocket on clutch splines and secure with snapring.

Differential Carrier

DISASSEMBLY

1. Separate differential carrier sections and lift out pinion gear and spider assembly.

2. Note that undercut side of pinion gear spider faces toward front of side gear.

3. Remove pinion thrust washers, pinion roller washer gears and roller bearings from spider unit.

4. Thoroughly clean and inspect all component parts. Replace any component that is worn or damaged.

ASSEMBLY

1. Spread petroleum jelly on pinion gears and install roller bearings.

2. Position on the leg of each spider, pinion roller washer, pinion gear and thrust washer.

3. Position the spider assembly in front half of the carrier. The undercut surface of the spider thrust surface face downward or toward teeth.

4. Secure carrier halves together. Make certain the marks are aligned. Torque all bolts to specifications. See the above list.

Input Shaft

DISASSEMBLY

1. Remove thrust washer and spacer from shaft.

2. Remove bearing retainer assembly from input shaft.

3. Hold low speed gear and lightly tap shaft from gear. Note the position of the thrust washer pins in input shaft.

4. Remove snapring holding input bearing in retainer using a screw driver. Lightly tap rear bearing out of retainer.

5. Remove pilot roller bearing and O-ring from end of input shaft.

6. Thoroughly clean and inspect all component parts. Replace any component that is worn or damaged.

ASSEMBLY

1. Tap or press input bearing into retainer. Be sure that ball loading slots are toward concave side of retainer. Install securing snap ring.

Make certain that selective snapring of proper thickness is used to provide tightest fit.

2. Position low speed gear on shaft, clutch end facing gear end of input shaft.

3. Place thrust washers on input shaft, align slot in washer with pin in shaft. Slide or tap washers into position.

4. Place input bearing retainer on shaft and secure with snapring. Snaprings are selective. Use snapring that provides tightest fit.

5. Slip spacer and thrust washer on shaft and align with locating pin.

6. Spread heavy grease on end of shaft and install roller bearings.

7. Install rubber O-ring at end of shaft.

Range Box

DISASSEMBLY

1. Remove poppet plate spring, plug and gasket.

2. Remove clutch fork and sliding gear by disengaging sliding clutch gear from input gear.

3. Remove upper shift lever from shifter shaft.

4. Remove snapring and lower shift lever.

5. Push shifter shaft assembly down and remove lockout clutch connector link. The long end of connector link engages poppet plate.

6. Remove shifter shaft assembly and separate shafts. Remove O-rings.

7. When necessary to remove poppet plate, drive pivot shaft out and remove plate and spring from bottom of case.

8. Remove input gear bearing retainer and seal assembly. Release snapring from retainer and tap bearing out of assembly.

9. Release snapring holding input shaft bearing to shaft and remove bearing.

10. Remove countershaft from cluster gear and case assembly from intermediate case side. Remove cluster gear assembly from range box.

11. Remove cluster gear thrust washers from case.

12. Thoroughly clean and inspect all component parts. Replace any component that is worn or damaged.

ASSEMBLY

1. Spread heavy grease in cluster bore and using proper tool install roller bearings and spacers.

2. Spread heavy grease on case and install thrust washers. Engage tab on thrust washers with slot in case.

3. Place cluster gear assembly in case and install countershaft through front of range box and into gear assembly. Flat face of countershaft must be aligned with case gasket.

4. Place bearing on input gear shaft with snapring groove facing out, install a new retaining ring. Insert input gear and bearing in housing. The retaining ring used in this operation is a select fit. Use ring that provides the tightest fit.

5. Secure input gear and bearing with a snapring.

6. Match up oil slot in retainer with drain hole in case and insert input gear bearing retainer and gaskets. Install bolts and torque to 20 ft.lb.

7. Spread sealant on pin and install poppet pin and pivot pin in housing.

8. Lubricate and install new O-rings on inner and outer shifter shafts.

9. Insert shifter shafts in housing and engage long end of lockout clutch connector link with outer shifter shaft. Complete this operation before assembly bottoms out.

10. Install lower shift lever and retaining ring.

11. Install upper shift lever and shaft retaining nut.

12. Install shift fork and sliding clutch gear. Push fork up into shifter shaft and engage poppet plate. Move sliding clutch gear onto input shaft gear.

13. Insert poppet plate spring, gasket and plug in housing top. Make certain that spring engages poppet plate.

Input Gear Bearing

REPLACEMENT

1. Remove bearing retainer and gasket from housing.

2. Remove and discard snapring holding bearing in retainer.

3. Pry bearing from case and remove from shaft.

4. Inspect input gear and bearing retainer for damage or wear. Replace if necessary.

5. Place new bearing and snapring on input gear. Using a soft hammer, tap bearing into position. Secure snapring.

6. Insert bearing retainer into housing and secure with attaching bolts. Tighten bolts to 20 ft.lb.

Input Gear Seal

REPLACEMENT

1. Remove bearing retainer from housing.

2. Remove seal from retainer by prying.

3. Place new seal on retainer and install with proper seal driver.

4. Install bearing retainer in housing and secure with attaching bolts. Tighten bolts to 20 ft.lb.

Rear Output Shaft Housing

DISASSEMBLY

1. Remove speedometer driven gear from housing.

2. Remove rear output flange and washer, if they have not been removed previously.

3. Using a soft hammer tap on flange end of pinion and remove the pinion. If speedometer drive gear does not come off with pinion reach into case and remove.

4. Remove old seal from bore with suitable prying tool.

5. Remove snap ring retaining rear output rear bearing.

6. Tap bearing out of housing.

7. Install a long drift into rear opening of housing and drive out front output bearing. Remove seal and discard.

ASSEMBLY

1. Spread grease on front bearing seal and place in bore. Place bearing in bore and press until it bottoms in housing.

2. Using a soft hammer tap rear bearing into place. Secure with proper snapring. Snaprings are selective, use the one that provides the tightest fit.

3. Place rear seal in bore and drive into position with suitable tool. When seal is in position it should be approximately $1/8''$ to $3/16''$ below housing face.

4. Place speedometer drive gear on output shaft with shims of approximately 0.050" thickness. Insert output shaft into carrier through housing front opening.

5. Install flange and washer on output shaft. Leave retaining nut loose until shim requirements are known.

6. Install speedometer driven gear.

Front Output Shaft Bearing Seal

REPLACEMENT

1. Remove old seal from retainer bore.

2. Inspect and clean retainer.

3. Spread sealer on outer edge of new seal.

4. Place new seal in retainer bore and drive into position with proper tool.

Front Output Bearing

REPLACEMENT

1. Remove rear cover from case assembly and discard gasket.

2. Press old bearing from cover.

3. Place new bearing on outside face of cover. Cover bearing with a wood block and press into cover until bearing is flush with opening.

4. Place gasket on transfer case and tap cover into position using a soft hammer. Secure

cover with attaching bolts and tighten to 30 ft.lb.

New Process Model 205 Transfer Case Overhaul

The New Process Model 205 transfer case is a two-speed gearbox mounted between the main transmission and the rear axle. The gearbox transmits power from the transmission and engine to the front and rear driving axles.

CASE DISASSEMBLY

1. Clean the exterior of the case.
2. Remove the nuts from the universal joint flanges.
3. Remove the front output shaft rear bearing retainer, front bearing retainer and drive flange.
4. Tap the front output shaft assembly from the case with a soft hammer. Remove the sliding clutch, front output high gear, washer and bearing from the case.
5. Remove the rear output shaft housing attaching bolts and remove the housing, output shaft, bearing retainer and speedometer gear.
6. Slide the rear output shaft from the housing.

NOTE: *Be careful not to lose the 15 needle bearings that will be loose when the rear output shaft is removed.*

7. Drive the two ¼" shift rail pin access hole plugs into the transfer case with a punch and hammer.

8. Remove the two shift rail detent nuts and springs from the case. Use a magnet to remove the two detent balls.
9. Position both shift rails in neutral and remove the shift fork retaining roll pins with a long punch.
10. Remove the clevis pin from one shift rail and rail link.
11. Remove the range shift rail first, then the 4WD shift rail.
12. Remove the shift forks and and sliding clutch from the case. Remove the input shaft bearing retainer, bearing and shaft.
13. Remove the cup plugs and rail pins, if they were driven out, from the case.
14. Remove the locknut from the idler gear shaft.
15. Remove the idler gear shaft rear cover.
16. Remove the idler gear shaft, using a soft hammer and a drift.
17. Roll the idler gear assembly to the front output shaft hole and remove the assembly from the case.

REAR OUTPUT SHAFT AND YOKE

1. Loosen rear output shaft yoke nut.
2. Remove shaft housing bolts, then remove the housing and retainer assembly.
3. Remove retaining nut and yoke from the shaft, then remove the shaft assembly.
4. Remove and discard snapring.
5. Remove thrust washer and pin.
6. Remove tanged bronze washer. Remove

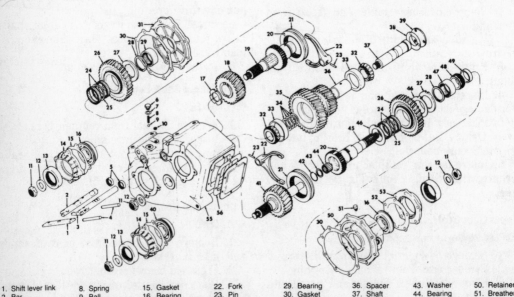

1. Shift lever link	8. Spring	15. Gasket	22. Fork	29. Bearing	36. Spacer	43. Washer	50. Retainer
2. Bar	9. Ball	16. Bearing	23. Pin	30. Gasket	37. Shaft	44. Bearing	51. Breather
3. Bar	10. Plug	17. Washer	24. Bearing	31. Retainer	38. Gasket	45. Gear	52. Gasket
4. Plunger	11. Nut	18. Gear	25. Spacer	32. Cone	39. Cover	46. Washer	53. Retainer
5. Seal	12. Washer	19. Shaft	26. Gear	33. Cup	40. Bearing	47. Bearing	54. Seal
6. Screw	13. Seal	20. Pin	27. Washer	34. Shim set	41. Shaft	48. Gear	55. Case
7. Gasket	14. Retainer	21. Clutch	28. Ring	35. Gear	42. Ring	49. Spacer	56. Gasket

Disassembled view of the 205 transfer case

gear needle bearings, spacer and second row of needle bearings.

7. Remove tanged bronze thrust washer.

8. Remove pilot rollers, retainer ring and washer.

9. Remove oil seal retainer, ball bearing, speedometer gear and spacer. Discard gaskets.

10. Press out bearing.

11. Remove oil seal from the retainer.

FRONT OUTPUT SHAFT

1. Remove lock nut, washer and yoke.

2. Remove attaching bolts and front bearing retainer.

3. Remove rear bearing retainer attaching bolts.

4. Tap output shaft with a soft-faced hammer and remove shaft, gear assembly and rear bearing retainer.

5. Remove sliding clutch, gear, washer and bearing from output high gear.

6. Remove sliding clutch from the high output gear; then remove gear, washer and bearing.

7. Remove gear retaining snap-ring from the shaft, using large snapring picks. Discard ring.

8. Remove thrust washer and pin.

9. Remove gear, needle bearings and spacer.

10. Replace rear bearing, if necessary.

WARNING: *Always replace the bearing and retainer as an assembly. Do not try to press a new bearing into an old retainer.*

SHIFT RAILS AND FORKS

1. Remove the two poppet nuts, springs, and using a magnet, the poppet balls.

2. Remove cup plugs on top of case, using a ¼" punch.

3. Position both shift rails in neutral, then remove fork pins with a long handled screw extractor.

4. Remove clevis pins and shift rail link.

5. Lower shift rails; upper rail first and then lower.

6. Remove shift forks and sliding clutch.

7. Remove the front output high gear, washer and bearing. Remove the shift rail cup plugs.

INPUT SHAFT

1. Remove snapring in front of bearing. Tap shaft out rear of case and bearing out front of case, using a soft-faced hammer or mallet.

2. Tilt case up on power take-off and remove the two interlock pins from inside.

IDLER GEAR

1. Remove idler gear shaft nut.

2. Remove rear cover.

3. Tap out idler gear shaft, using a soft-faced hammer and a drift approximately the same diameter as the shaft.

4. Remove idler gear through the front output shaft hole.

5. Remove two bearing cups from the idler gear.

CASE ASSEMBLY

1. Assemble the idler shaft gears, bearings, spacer and shims, and bearings on a dummy shaft tool and install the assembly into the case through the front output shaft bore, large end first.

2. Install the idler shaft from the large bore side, using a soft hammer to drive it through the bearings, spacer, gears, and shims.

3. Install a washer and new locknut on the end of the idler shaft. Check to make sure the idler gear rotates freely. Tighten the locknut to 150 ft.lb.

4. Install the idler shaft cover with a new gasket so the flat side faces the rear bearing retainer of the front output shaft. Install and tighten the two retaining screws to the proper torque.

5. Install the interlock pins into the interlock bore through the front of the output shaft opening.

6. Start the 4WD shift rail into the front of the case, solid end of the rail first, with the detent notches facing up.

7. Position the shift fork onto the shift rail with the long end facing inward. Push the rail through the fork and into the Neutral position.

8. Position the input shaft and bearing in the case.

9. Start the range shift rail into the case from the front, with the detent notches facing up.

10. Position the sliding clutch to the shift fork. Place the sliding clutch on the input shaft and align the fork with the shift rail. Push the rail through the fork into the Neutral position.

11. Install the roll pins that lock the shift forks to the shift rails with a long punch.

12. Position the front wheel drive high gear and its thrust washer in the case. Position the sliding clutch in the shift fork. Shift the rail and fork into the front wheel drive (4WD-Hi) position, while at the same time, meshing the clutch with the mating teeth on the front wheel drive high gear.

13. Align the thrust washer, high gear and sliding clutch with the bearing bore in the case and insert the front output shaft and low gear into the high gear assembly.

14. Install a new seal in the front bearing retainer of the front output shaft, and install the bearing and retainer and new gasket in the

case. Tighten the bearing retainer cap screws to the proper torque.

15. Lubricate the roller bearing in the front output shaft rear bearing retainer, which is the aluminum cover, and install it over the front output shaft and to the case. Install and tighten the retaining screws to the proper torque.

16. Move the range shift rail to the High position and install the rear output shaft and retainer assembly to the housing and input shaft. Use one or two new gaskets, as required, to adjust the clearance on the input shaft pilot. Install the rear output shaft housing retaining bolts and tighten them to 35 ft.lb.

17. Using a punch and sealing compound, install the shift rail pin access plugs.

18. Install the fill and drain plugs and the cross-link clevis pin.

IDLER GEAR

1. Press the two bearing cups in the idler gear.

2. Assemble the two bearing cones, spacer, shims and idler gear on a dummy shaft, with bore facing up. Check end-play.

3. Install idler gear assembly (with dummy shaft) into the case, large end first, through the front output shaft bore.

4. Install idler shaft from large bore side, driving it through with a soft-faced hammer or mallet.

5. Install washer and new locknut. Check for free rotation and measure end-play. Endplay should be 0-0.002" Torque locknut to 150 ft.lb.

6. Install idler shaft cover and new gasket. Torque cover bolts to 20 ft.lb.

NOTE: *Flat side of cover must be positioned towards front output shaft rear cover.*

SHIFT RAILS AND FORKS

1. Press the two rail seals into the case.

NOTE: *Install seals with metal lip outward.*

2. Install interlock pins from inside case.

3. Insert slotted end of front output drive shift rail (with poppet notches up) into back of case.

4. While pushing rail through to neutral position, install shift fork (long end inward).

5. Install input shaft and bearing into case.

6. Install end of range rail (with poppet notches up) into front of case.

7. Install sliding clutch on fork, then place over input shaft in case.

8. Push range rail, while engaging sliding clutch and fork, through to neutral position.

9. Drive new lockpins into forks through holes at top of case.

NOTE: *Tilt case on power take-off opening to install range rail lockpin.*

FRONT OUTPUT SHAFT AND GEAR

1. Install two rows of needle bearings in the front low output gear and retain with grease.

NOTE: *Each row consists of 32 needle bearings and the two rows are separated by a spacer.*

2. Position front output shaft in a soft-jaw vise, with spline end down. Place front low gear over shaft with clutch gear facing down; then install thrust washer pin, thrust washer and new snapring.

NOTE: *Position snapring gap opposite the thrust washer pin.*

3. Place front drive high gear and washer in case. Install sliding clutch in the shift fork, then put fork and rail into 4-High position, meshing front drive high gear and clutch teeth.

4. Align washer, high gear and sliding clutch and bearing bore. Insert front output shaft and low gear assembly through the high gear assembly.

5. Install front output bearing and retainer with a new seal in the case.

6. Clean and grease rollers in front output rear bearing retainer. Install on case with one gasket and bolts coated with sealant. Torque bolts to 35 ft.lb.

7. Install front output yoke, washer and locknut. Torque locknut to 150 ft.lb.

REAR OUTPUT SHAFT

1. Install two rows of needle bearings into the output low gear, retaining them with grease.

NOTE: *Each row consists of 32 needle bearings and the two rows are separated by a spacer.*

2. Install thrust washer (with tang down in clutch gear groove) onto the rear output shaft.

3. Install output low gear onto shaft with clutch teeth facing downward.

4. Install thrust washer over gear with tab pointing up and away. Install washer pin.

5. Install large thrust washer over shaft and pin. Turn washer until tab fits into slot located approximately 90° away from pin.

6. Install snapring and measure shaft endplay. Endplay should be 0.00-0.027".

7. Grease pilot bore and install needle bearings.

NOTE: *There are 15 pilot needle bearings.*

8. Install thrust washer and new snapring in pilot bore.

9. Press new bearing into retainer housing.

10. Install housing on output shaft assembly.

11. Install spacer and speedometer gear. Install rear bearing.

12. Install rear bearing retainer seal.

13. Install bearing retainer assembly on hous-

ing, using one or two gaskets to achieve specified clearance. Torque attaching bolts to 35 ft.lb.

14. Install yoke, washer and locknut on output shaft.

15. Position range rail in high, then install output shaft and retainer assembly on case. Torque the yoke nut to 150 ft.lb.

CASE ASSEMBLY

1. Install power take-off cover and gasket. Torque attaching bolts to 15 ft.lb.

2. Install cup plugs at rail pin holes.

NOTE: *After installing, seal the cup plugs.*

3. Install drain and filler plugs. Torque to 30 ft.lb.

4. Install shift rail cross link, clevis pins and lock pins.

New Process 208 Transfer Case Overhaul

The NP208 is a part-time unit with a two piece aluminum housing. On the front case half, the front output shaft, front input shaft, four wheel drive indicator switch and shift lever assembly are located. On the rear case half, the rear output shaft, bearing retainer and drain and fill plugs are located.

DISASSEMBLY

1. Drain the fluid from the case.

2. Remove the attaching nuts from the front and rear output yokes. Remove the yokes and sealing washers.

3. Remove the four bolts and separate the rear bearing retainer from the rear case half.

4. Remove the retaining ring, speedometer drive gear nylon oil pump housing, and oil pump gear from the rear output shaft.

5. Remove the eleven bolts and separate the case halves by inserting a screw driver in the pry slots on the case.

6. Remove the magnetic chip collector from the bottom of the rear case half.

7. Remove the thick thrust washer, thrust bearing and thin thrust washer from the front output shaft assembly.

8. Remove the drive chain by pushing the front input shaft inward and by angling the gear slightly to obtain adequate clearance to remove the chain.

9. Remove the output shaft from the front case half and slide the thick thrust washer, thrust bearing and thin thrust washer off the output side of the front output shaft.

10. Remove the screw, poppet spring and check ball from the front case half.

11. Remove the four wheel drive indicator switch and washer from the front case half.

12. Position the front case half on its face and lift out the rear output shaft, sliding clutch and clutch shift fork and spring.

13. Place a shop towel on the shift rail. Clamp the rail with a vise grip pliers so that they lay between the rail and the case edge. Position a pry bar under the pliers and pry out the shift rail.

14. Remove the snap ring and thrust washer from the planetary gear set assembly in the front case half.

15. Remove the annulus gear assembly and thrust washer from the front case half.

16. Lift the planetary gear assembly from the front case half.

17. Lift out the thrust bearing, sun gear, thrust bearing and thrust washer.

18. Remove the six bolts and lift the gear locking plate from the front case half.

19. Remove the nut retaining the external shift lever and washer. Press the shift control shaft inward and remove the shift selector plate and washer from the case.

20. From the rear output shaft, remove the snap-ring and thrust washer retaining the chain drive sprocket and slide the sprocket from the drive gear.

21. Remove the retaining ring from the sprocket carrier gear.

22. Carefully slide the sprocket carrier gear from the rear output shaft. Remove the two rows of 60 loose needle bearings. Remove the three separator rings from the output shaft.

ASSEMBLY

1. Slide the thrust washer against the gear on the rear output shaft.

2. Place the three space rings in position on the rear output shaft. Liberally coat the shaft with petroleum jelly and install the two rows (60 each) of needle bearings in position on the rear output shaft.

3. Carefully slide the sprocket gear carrier over the needle bearings. Be careful not to dislodge any of the needles.

4. Install the retaining ring on the sprocket gear.

5. Slide the chain drive sprocket onto the sprocket carrier gear.

6. Install the thrust washer and snap ring on the rear output shaft.

7. Install the shift selector plate and washer through the front of the case.

8. Place the shift lever assembly on the shift control shaft and torque the nut to 14-20 ft. lbs.

9. Place the locking plate in the front case half and torque the bolts to 25-35 ft. lbs.

10. Place the thrust bearing and washer over the input shaft of the sun gear. Insert the input

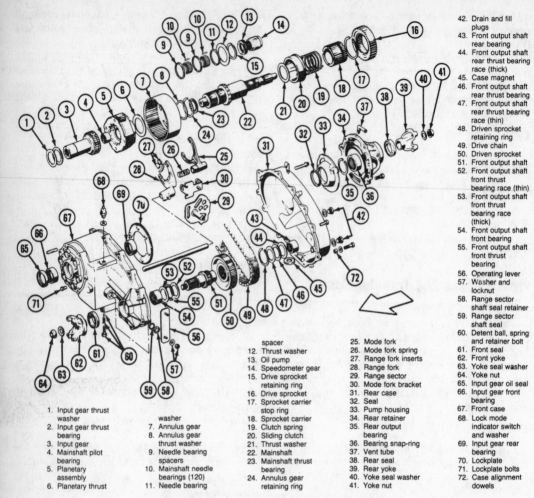

42. Drain and fill plugs
43. Front output shaft rear bearing
44. Front output shaft rear thrust bearing race (thick)
45. Case magnet
46. Front output shaft rear thrust bearing
47. Front output shaft rear thrust bearing race (thin)
48. Driven sprocket retaining ring
49. Drive chain
50. Driven sprocket
51. Front output shaft
52. Front output shaft front thrust bearing race (thin)
53. Front output shaft front thrust bearing race (thick)
54. Front output shaft front bearing
55. Front output shaft front thrust bearing
56. Operating lever
57. Washer and locknut
58. Range sector shaft seal retainer
59. Range sector shaft seal
60. Detent ball, spring and retainer bolt
61. Front seal
62. Front yoke
63. Yoke seal washer
64. Yoke nut
65. Input gear oil seal
66. Input gear front bearing
67. Front case
68. Lock mode indicator switch and washer
69. Input gear rear bearing
70. Lockplate
71. Lockplate bolts
72. Case alignment dowels

1. Input gear thrust washer
2. Input gear thrust bearing
3. Input gear
4. Mainshaft pilot bearing
5. Planetary assembly
6. Planetary thrust washer
7. Annulus gear
8. Annulus gear thrust washer
9. Needle bearing spacers
10. Mainshaft needle bearings (120)
11. Needle bearing
12. Thrust washer
13. Oil pump
14. Speedometer gear
15. Drive sprocket retaining ring
16. Drive sprocket
17. Sprocket carrier stop ring
18. Sprocket carrier
19. Clutch spring
20. Sliding clutch
21. Thrust washer
22. Mainshaft
23. Mainshaft thrust bearing
24. Annulus gear retaining ring
25. Mode fork
26. Mode fork spring
27. Range fork inserts
28. Range fork
29. Range sector
30. Mode fork bracket
31. Rear case
32. Seal
33. Pump housing
34. Rear retainer
35. Rear output bearing
36. Bearing snap-ring
37. Vent tube
38. Rear seal
39. Rear yoke
40. Yoke seal washer
41. Yoke nut

Disassembled view of the 208 transfer case

shaft through the front case half from the inside and insert the thrust bearing.

11. Install the planetary gear assembly so the fixed plate and planetary gears engage the sun gear.

12. Slide the annulus gear and clutch assembly with the shift fork assembly engaged, over the hub of the planetary gear assembly. The shift fork pin must engage the slot in the shift selector plate. Install the thrust washer and snap ring.

13. Position the shift rail through the shift fork hub in the front case. Tap lightly with a soft hammer to seat the rail in the hole.

14. Position the sliding clutch shift fork on the shift rail and place the sliding clutch and clutch shift spring into the front case half. Slide the rear output shaft into the case.

15. On the output side of the front output shaft, assemble the thin thrust washer, thrust bearing, and thick thrust washer and partially insert the front output shaft into the case.

16. Place the drive chain on the rear output shaft drive gear. Insert the rear output shaft into the front case half and engage the drive chain on the front output shaft drive gear. Push the front output shaft into position in the case.

17. Assemble the thin thrust washer, thrust bearing and thick thrust washer on the inside of the front output shaft drive gear.

18. Position the magnetic chip collector into position in the front case half.

19. Place a bead of RTV sealant completely around the face of the front case half and assemble the case halves being careful that the shift rail and forward output shafts are properly retained.

20. Alternately tighten the bolts to 20-25 ft. lbs.

21. Slide the oil pump gear over the input shaft and slide the spacer collar into position.

22. Engage the speedometer drive gear onto the rear output shaft and slide the retaining ring into position.

23. Use petroleum jelly to hold the nylon oil pump housing in position at the rear bearing retainer. Apply a bead of RTV sealant around the mounting surface of the retainer and carefully position the retainer assembly over the output shaft and onto the rear case half. The retainer must be installed so that the vent hole is vertical when the case is installed.

24. Torque the retainer bolts alternately to 20-25 ft. lbs.

25. Place a new thrust washer under each yoke and install the yokes on their respective shafts. Place the oil slinger under the front yoke. Torque the nuts to 90-130 ft. lbs.

26. Install the poppet ball, spring and screw in the front case half. Torque the screw to 20-25 ft. lbs.

27. Install the 4WD indicator switch and washer and tighten to 15-20 ft. lbs.

28. Fill the unit with 6 pints of DEXRON®II.

DRIVELINE

Tubular driveshafts are used on all models, incorporating needle bearing U-joints. An internally splined sleeve at the forward end compensates for variation in distance between the rear axle and the transmission.

The number of driveshafts used is determined by the length of the wheelbase. On trucks that use two driveshafts there is a center support incorporating a rubber cushioned ball bearing mounted in a bracket attached to the frame crossmember. The ball bearing is permanently sealed and lubricated. 4-WD models use a front driveshaft with a constant velocity joint.

Extended lift U-joints have been incorporated on most models and can be identified by the absence of a lubrication fitting.

Front Driveshaft
REMOVAL AND INSTALLATION
4-WD Only

Chevrolet and GMC use U-bolts or straps to secure the driveshaft to the pinion flange. Use the following procedure to remove the driveshaft.

1. Jack up your vehicle and support it with jackstands.

2. Scribe aligning marks on the driveshaft and the pinion flange to aid in reassembly.

3. Remove the U-bolts or straps at the axle end of the shaft. Compress the shaft slightly and tape the bearings into place to avoid losing them.

4. Remove the U-bolts or straps at the transfer case end of the shaft. Tape the bearings into place.

5. Remove the driveshaft.

6. Installation is the reverse of removal. Make certain that the marks made earlier line up correctly to prevent possible imbalances. Be sure that the constant velocity joint is at the transfer case end.

Rear Driveshaft
REMOVAL AND INSTALLATION
All Models

1. Jack up your truck and support it with jackstands.

Troubleshooting Basic Driveshaft and Rear Axle Problems

When abnormal vibrations or noises are detected in the driveshaft area, this chart can be used to help diagnose possible causes. Remember that other components such as wheels, tires, rear axle and suspension can also produce similar conditions.

BASIC DRIVESHAFT PROBLEMS

Problem	Cause	Solution
Shudder as car accelerates from stop or low speed	• Loose U-joint • Defective center bearing	• Replace U-joint • Replace center bearing
Loud clunk in driveshaft when shifting gears	• Worn U-joints	• Replace U-joints
Roughness or vibration at any speed	• Out-of-balance, bent or dented driveshaft • Worn U-joints • U-joint clamp bolts loose	• Balance or replace driveshaft • Replace U-joints • Tighten U-joint clamp bolts
Squeaking noise at low speeds	• Lack of U-joint lubrication	• Lubricate U-joint; if problem persists, replace U-joint
Knock or clicking noise	• U-joint or driveshaft hitting frame tunnel • Worn CV joint	• Correct overloaded condition • Replace CV joint

Troubleshooting Basic Driveshaft and Rear Axle Problems (cont.)

BASIC REAR AXLE PROBLEMS

First, determine when the noise is most noticeable.

Drive Noise: Produced under vehicle acceleration.

Coast Noise: Produced while the car coasts with a closed throttle.

Float Noise: Occurs while maintaining constant car speed (just enough to keep speed constant) on a level road.

Road Noise

Brick or rough surfaced concrete roads produce noises that seem to come from the rear axle. Road noise is usually identical in Drive or Coast and driving on a different type of road will tell whether the road is the problem.

Tire Noise

Tire noises are often mistaken for rear axle problems. Snow treads or unevenly worn tires produce vibrations seeming to originate elsewhere. **Temporarily** inflating the tires to 40 lbs will significantly alter tire noise, but will have no effect on rear axle noises (which normally cease below about 30 mph).

Engine/Transmission Noise

Determine at what speed the noise is most pronounced, then stop the car in a quiet place. With the transmission in Neutral, run the engine through speeds corresponding to road speeds where the noise was noticed. Noises produced with the car standing still are coming from the engine or transmission.

Front Wheel Bearings

While holding the car speed steady, lightly apply the footbrake; this will often decease bearing noise, as some of the load is taken from the bearing.

Rear Axle Noises

Eliminating other possible sources can narrow the cause to the rear axle, which normally produces noise from worn gears or bearings. Gear noises tend to peak in a narrow speed range, while bearing noises will usually vary in pitch with engine speeds.

NOISE DIAGNOSIS

The Noise Is	Most Probably Produced By
• Identical under Drive or Coast	• Road surface, tires or front wheel bearings
• Different depending on road surface	• Road surface or tires
• Lower as the car speed is lowered	• Tires
• Similar with car standing or moving	• Engine or transmission
• A vibration	• Unbalanced tires, rear wheel bearing, unbalanced driveshaft or worn U-joint
• A knock or click about every 2 tire revolutions	• Rear wheel bearing
• Most pronounced on turns	• Damaged differential gears
• A steady low-pitched whirring or scraping, starting at low speeds	• Damaged or worn pinion bearing
• A chattering vibration on turns	• Wrong differential lubricant or worn clutch plates (limited slip rear axle)
• Noticed only in Drive, Coast or Float conditions	• Worn ring gear and/or pinion gear

2. Scribe alignment marks on the driveshaft and flange of the rear axle, and transfer case or transmission. If the truck is equipped with a two piece driveshaft, be certain to also scribe marks at the center joint near the splined connection. When reinstalling driveshafts, it is necessary to place the shafts in the same position from which they were removed. Failure to reinstall the driveshaft properly will cause driveline vibrations and reduced component life.

3. Disconnect the rear universal joint by removing U-bolts or straps. Tape the bearings into place to avoid losing them.

4. If there are U-bolts or straps at the front end of the shaft, remove them. Tape the bearings into place. For trucks with two piece shafts, remove the bolts retaining the bearing support to the frame crossmember. Compress the shaft slightly and remove it.

5. If there are no fasteners at the front end of the transmission, there will only be a splined fitting. Slide the shaft forward slightly to disen-

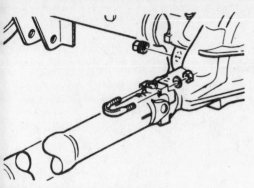

Rear drive shaft U-bolt attachment

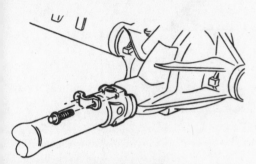

Rear driveshaft strap attachment

gage the axle flange, lower the rear end of the shaft, then pull it back out of the transmission. Most two wheel drive trucks are of this type. For trucks with two piece driveshafts, remove the bolts retaining the bearing support to the frame crossmember.

6. Reverse the procedure for installation. It may be tricky to get the scribed alignment marks to match up on trucks with two piece driveshafts. For those models only, the following instructions may be of some help. First, slide the grease cap and gasket onto the rear splines.

• 1977 and later K models with 16 splines, after installing the front shaft to the transmission and bolting the support to the crossmember, arrange the front trunnion vertically and the second trunnion horizontally.

• 1973 C and K models, 1974 C models, 1975 and later models with 32 splines have an alignment key. The driveshaft cannot be replaced incorrectly. Simply match up the key with the keyway.

• 1975-76 K models with 16 splines, align the trunnions vertically. The shafts should not be rotated before installing the rear shaft to the front shaft.

• 1975-76 C models with 16 splines, after installing the front shaft to the transmission or transfer case, must align the trunnions vertically, then the rear shaft must be rotated four

splines (90 degrees) to the left (driver's) side before installing the rear shaft to the front shaft.

• 1971-72 C and K models and 1974 K models, after installing the front shaft to the transmission or transfer case and bolting the support to the crossmember, rotate all the U-joints so the trunnions are vertical, then rotate the rear shaft four splines towards the left (driver's) side of the truck before installing the rear shaft to the front shaft.

7. On two wheel drive automatic transmission models, lubricate the internal yoke splines at the transmission end of the shaft with lithium base grease. The grease should seep out through the vent hole.

NOTE: *A thump in the rear driveshaft sometimes occurs when releasing the brakes after braking to a stop, especially on a downgrade. This is most common with automatic transmission. It is often caused by the driveshaft splines binding and can be cured by removing the driveshaft, inspecting the splines for rough edges, and carefully lubricating. A similar thump may be caused by the clutch plates in Positraction limited slip rear axles binding. If this isn't caused by wear, it can be cured by draining and refilling the rear axle with the special lubricant and adding Positraction additive, both of which are available from dealers.*

1973 C-10 and C-1500 long wheelbase pickups equipped with either the Turbo Hydra-Matic 350 or 400 transmission may suffer from a driveline shudder during acceleration. This can be corrected by installing a spacer between the driveshaft center bearing support and the hanger to which it is attached. The spacer should measure 7¾″ long and 1¼″ wide, and be ½″ thick. Two ½″ diameter holes should be drilled at either end, centered $\frac{9}{16}$″ from the end in the long dimension and ⅝″ on the short dimension. This places the centers of the holes ⅝″ apart. Install the spacer between the center bearing support and the hanger using bolts ½″ longer than the ones removed.

U-Joints
OVERHAUL

There are three types of U-joints used in these trucks. The first is held together by wire snaprings in the yokes. The second type, first used in 1975, is held together with injection molded plastic retainer rings. This type cannot be reassembled with the same parts, once disassembled. However, repair kits are available. The third type (4-wheel drive models only) is the large constant velocity joint which looks

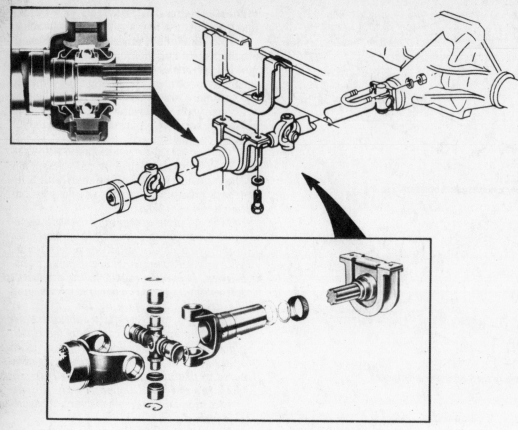

Driveshaft, U-joint and bearing support, 1971 and later

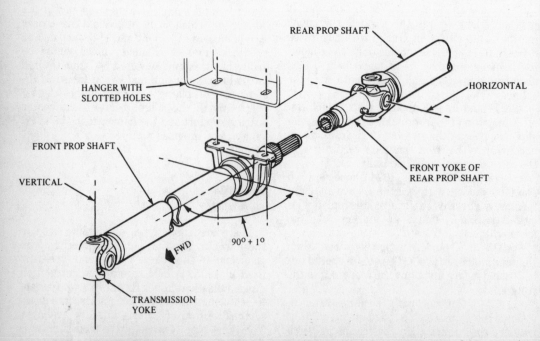

REAR PROP SHAFT

HANGER WITH
SLOTTED HOLES

HORIZONTAL

FRONT PROP SHAFT

FRONT YOKE OF
REAR PROP SHAFT

VERTICAL

FWD

90° + 1°

TRANSMISSION
YOKE

U-joint alignment, 1977 and later K models with two piece driveshafts only

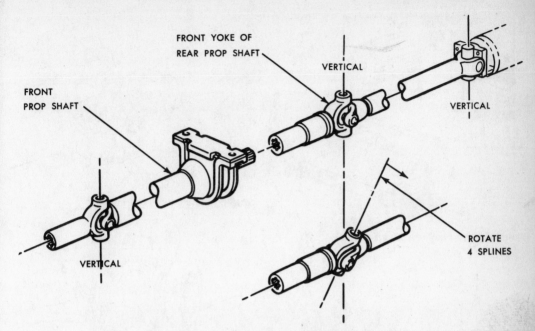

U-joint alignment, 1971–72 C and K, 1974 K models

like a double U-joint, located at the transfer case end of the front driveshaft.

Snapring Type

1. Remove the driveshaft(s) from the truck.
2. Remove the lockrings from the yoke and remove the lubrication fitting.
3. Support the yoke in a bench vise. Never clamp the driveshaft tube.

4. Use a soft drift pin and hammer to drive against one trunnion bearing to drive the opposite bearing from the yoke.

NOTE: *The bearing cap cannot be driven completely out.*

5. Grasp the cap and work it out.
6. Support the other side of the yoke and drive the other bearing cap from the yoke and remove as in Steps 4 and 5.

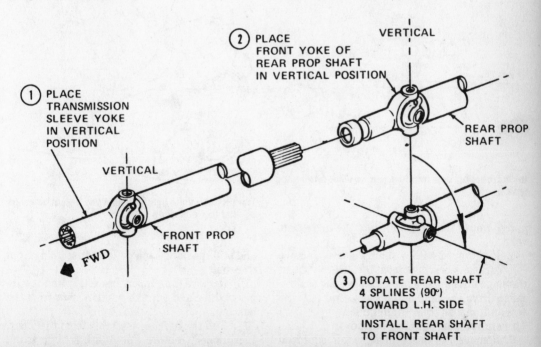

U-joint alignment, 1975–76 C models with 16 splines,; for 1975–76 K models follow steps 1 and 2 only

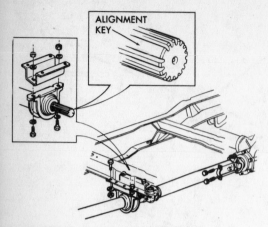

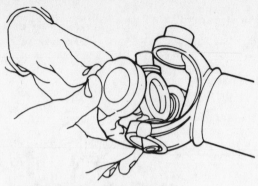

Installing trunnion into bearing yoke

U-joint alignment keyway, 32-spline shaft

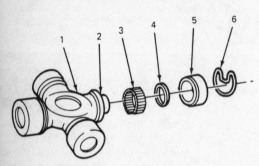

1. TRUNNION
2. SEAL
3. BEARINGS
4. WASHER
5. CAP
6. SNAP RING

U-joint repair kit, snap-ring types

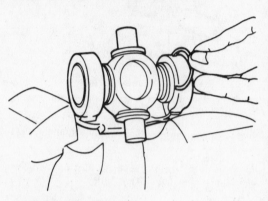

Installing U-joint snap-rings

STRIKE TUBE YOKE
EAR IN THIS AREA

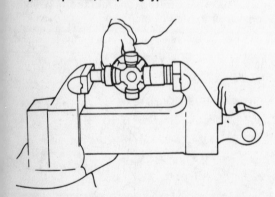

U-joint bearing cup removal with a vise, snap-ring type

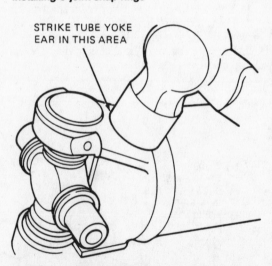

Tap the tube yoke lightly to seat the U-joint bearings against the lock rings

7. Remove the trunnion from the driveshaft yoke.

8. If equipped with a sliding sleeve, remove the trunnions bearings from the sleeve yoke in the same manner as above. Remove the seal retainer from the end of the sleeve and pull the seal and washer from the retainer.

To remove the bearing support:

9. Remove the dust shield, or, if equipped with a flange, remove the cotter pin and nut and pull the flange and deflector assembly from the shaft.

10. Remove the support bracket from the rubber cushion and pull the cushion away from the bearing.

11. Pull the bearing assembly from the shaft. If equipped, remove the grease retainers and slingers from the bearing.

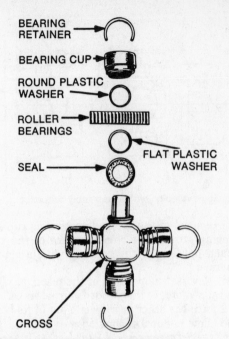

- BEARING RETAINER
- BEARING CUP
- ROUND PLASTIC WASHER
- ROLLER BEARINGS
- FLAT PLASTIC WASHER
- SEAL
- CROSS

Injected molded retainer U-joint repair kit

Assemble the bearing support as follows:

12. Install the inner deflector on the driveshaft and punch the deflector on 2 opposite sides to be sure that it is tight.

13. Pack the retainers with special high melting grease. Insert a slinger (if used) inside one retainer and press this retainer over the bearing outer race.

14. Start the bearing and slinger on the shaft journal. Support the driveshaft and press the bearing and inner slinger against the shoulder of the shaft with a suitable pipe.

15. Install the second slinger on the shaft and press the second retainer on the shaft.

16. Install the dust shield over the shaft (small diameter first) and depress it into position against the outer slinger or, if equipped with a flange, install the flange and deflector. Align the centerline of the flange yoke with the centerline of the driveshaft yoke and start the flange straight on the splines of the shaft with the end of the flange against the slinger.

17. Force the rubber cushion onto the bearing and coat the outside diameter of the cushion with clean brake fluid.

18. Force the bracket onto the cushion.

Assemble the trunnion bearings:

19. Repack the bearings with grease and replace the trunnion dust seals after any operation that requires disassembly of the U-joint. But be sure that the lubricant reservoir at the end of the trunnion is full of lubricant. Fill the reservoirs with lubricant from the bottom.

20. Install the trunnion into the driveshaft

yoke and press the bearings into the yoke over the trunnion hubs as far as it will go.

21. Install the lockrings.

22. Hold the trunnion in one hand and tap the yoke slightly to seat the bearings against the lockrings.

23. On the rear driveshafts, install the sleeve yoke over the trunnion hubs and install the bearings in the same manner as above.

Molded Retainer Type

An injection molded plastic retainer is used on some 1975 and later models. A service repair kit is available for overhaul.

1. Remove the driveshaft.

2. Support the driveshaft in a horizontal position. Place the U-joint so that the lower ear of the shaft yoke is supported by a 1⅛" socket. Press the lower bearing cup out of the yoke ear. This will shear the plastic retaining the lower bearing cup.

NOTE: *Never clamp the driveshaft tubing in a vise.*

3. If the bearing cup is not completely removed, lift the cross, insert a spacer and press the cup completely out.

4. Rotate the driveshaft, shear the opposite plastic retainer, and press the other bearing cup out in the same manner.

5. Remove the cross from the yoke. Production U-joints cannot be reassembled. There are no bearing retainer grooves in the cups. Discard all parts that we removed and substitute those in the overhaul kit.

6. Remove the sheared plastic bearing retainer. Drive a small pin or punch through the injection holes to aid in removal.

7. If the front U-joint is serviced, remove the bearing cups from the slip yoke in the manner previously described.

8. Be sure that the seals are installed on the service bearing cups to hold the needle bearings in place for handling. Grease the bearings if they aren't pregreased.

9. Install one bearing cup partway into one side of the yoke and turn this ear to the bottom.

10. Insert the opposite bearing cup partway. Be sure that both trunnions are started straight into the bearing cups.

11. Press against opposite bearing cups, working the cross constantly to be sure that it is free in the cups. If binding occurs, check the needle rollers to be sure that one needle has not become lodged under an end of the trunnion.

12. As soon as one bearing retainer groove is exposed, stop pressing and install the bearing retainer snaping.

13. Continue to press until the opposite bearing retainer can be installed. If difficulty installing the snaprings is encountered, rap the

yoke with a hammer to spring the yoke ears slightly.

14. Assemble the other half of the U-joint in the same manner.

Constant Velocity (CV) Joint

4-WHEEL DRIVE MODELS ONLY

1. Using a punch, mark the link yoke and the adjoining yokes before disassembly to ensure proper reassembly and driveshaft balance.

NOTE: *It is easier to remove the universal joint bearings from the flange yoke first. The first pair of flange yoke universal joint bearings to be removed is the pair in the link yoke.*

2. With the driveshaft in a horizontal position, solidly support the link yoke (a 1⅛″ pipe will do).

3. Apply force to the bearing cup on the opposite side with a 1⅛″ pipe or a socket the size of the bearing cup. Use a vise or press to apply force. Force the cup inward as far as possible.

NOTE: *In the absence of a press, a heavy vise may be used, but make sure that the universal to be removed is at a right angle to the jaws of the vise. Do not cock the bearing cups in their bores.*

4. Remove the pieces of pipe and complete

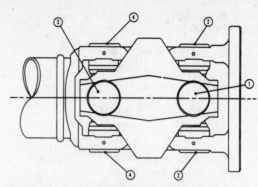

Constant velocity joint disassembly sequence

the removal of the protruding bearing cup by tapping around the circumference of the exposed portion of the bearing with a small hammer.

5. Reverse the position of the pieces of pipe and apply force to the exposed journal end. This will force the other bearing cup out of its bore and allow removal of the flange.

NOTE: *There is a ball joint located between the two universals. The ball portion of this joint is on the inner end of the flange yoke. Prior to 1973, the ball was not replaceable. Beginning 1973, the ball, as well as the ball seat parts, is replaceable. Care must be taken not to damage the ball. The ball portion of this joint is on the driveshaft. To remove the seat, pry the seal out with a screwdriver.*

6. To remove the journal from the flange, use steps two through five.

7. Remove the universal joint bearings from the driveshaft using the steps from two through five. The first pair of bearing caps that should be removed is the pair in the link yoke.

8. Examine the ball stud seat and ball stud for scores or wear. Worn seats can be replaced with a kit. A worn ball, however, requires the replacement of the entire shaft yoke and flange assembly. Clean the ball seat cavity and fill it with grease. Install the spring, washer, ball seats, and spacer, if removed.

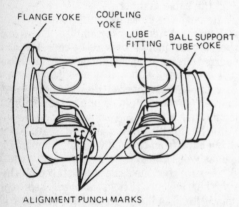

Constant-velocity joint showing alignment marks punched for reassembly

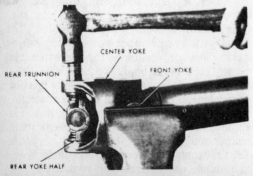

Driving out the bearing cup constant velocity joint

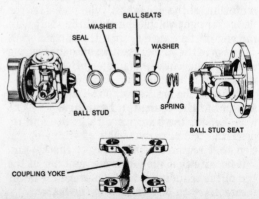

Exploded view of a constant velocity joint

9. Install the universal joints opposite the order in which they were disassembled.

10. Install a bearing ¼ of the way into one side of the yoke.

11. Insert the journal into the yoke so that an arm of the journal seats into the bearing.

12. Press the bearing in the remaining distance and install its snapring.

13. Install the opposite bearing. Do not allow the bearing rollers to jam. Continually check for free movement of the journal in the bearings as they are pressed into the yoke.

14. Install the rest of the bearings in the same manner.

NOTE: *The flange yoke should snap over center to the right or left and up or down by the pressure of the ball seat spring.*

REAR AXLE

Understanding Drive Axles

The drive axle is a special type of transmission that reduces the speed of the drive from the engine and transmission and divides the power to the wheels. Power enters the axle from the driveshaft via the companion flange. The flange is mounted on the drive pinion shaft. The drive pinion shaft and gear which carry the power into the differential turn at engine speed. The gear on the end of the pinion shaft drives a large ring gear the axis of rotation of which is 90 degrees away from the of the pinion. The pinion and gear reduce the gear ratio of the axle, and change the direction of rotation to turn the axle shafts which drive both wheels. The axle gear ratio is found by dividing the number of pinion gear teeth into the number of ring gear teeth.

The ring gear drives the differential case. The case provides the two mounting points for the ends of a pinion shaft on which are mounted two pinion gears. The pinion gears drive the two side gears, one of which is located on the inner end of each axle shaft.

By driving the axle shafts through the arrangement, the differential allows the outer drive wheel to turn faster than the inner drive wheel in a turn.

The main drive pinion and the side bearings, which bear the weight of the differential case, are shimmed to provide proper bearing preload, and to position the pinion and ring gears properly.

WARNING: *The proper adjustment of the relationship of the ring and pinion gears is critical. It should be attempted only by those with extensive equipment and/or experience.*

Limited-slip differentials include clutches which tend to link each axle shaft to the differential case. Clutches may be engaged either by spring action or by pressure produced by the torque on the axles during a turn. During turning on a dry pavement, the effects of the clutches are overcome, and each wheel turns at the required speed. When slippage occurs at either wheel, however, the clutches will transmit some of the power to the wheel which has the greater amount of traction. Because of the presence of clutches, limited-slip units require a special lubricant.

Identification

All models use conventional hypoid axles. Half ton models use semi-floating axles, while ¾ and 1 ton models use full floating axles. Semi-floating axles use one bearing at the end of the axle housing next to the wheel hub. These bearings do not require adjustment. Full floating axles use two bearings, and must be adjusted (in much the same manner as front wheel bearings) if removed or replaced. Full floating axle housings carry the entire weight of the chassis and cargo, permitting the axle shafts to be removed without disturbing the differential.

Determining Axle Ratio

Axle ratios available in these trucks range from 2.56:1 to 4.47:1 with nine stops in between. However, not all ratios are available with all axles. If you are contemplating a change of axle ratios, your dealer can advise you as to what gears are available for your particular axle.

Front axle ratios installed on 4-wheel drive models are the same as the rear.

An axle ratio is obtained by dividing the number of teeth on the drive pinion gear into the number of teeth on the ring gear. For instance, on a 4.11 ratio, the driveshaft will turn 4.11 times for every turn of the rear wheel.

The most accurate way to determine axle ratios is to drain the differential, remove the cover, and count the number of teeth on the ring and pinion.

An easier method is to jack and support the truck so that both rear wheels are off the ground. Make a chalk mark on the rear wheel and the driveshaft. Block the front wheels and put the transmission in Neutral. Turn the rear wheel one complete revolution and count the number of turns made by the driveshaft. The number of driveshaft rotations is the axle ratio. You can get more accuracy by going more than one tire rotation and dividing the result by the number of tire rotations.

The axle ratio is also identified by the axle serial number prefix on the axles. Dana axles usually have a tag under one of the cover bolts, giving either the ratio or the number of pinion/ring gear teeth.

Axle Shaft, Bearings, and Seal
REMOVAL AND INSTALLATION

All ½ Ton Trucks Except 1974 And Later w/ Locking Differential

This procedure applies to all standard rear axles and to those with the optional Positraction Limited slip differential.

1. Support the axle on jackstands.
2. Remove the wheels and brake drums.
3. Clean off the differential cover area, loosen the cover to drain the lubricant, and remove the cover.
4. Turn the differential until you can reach the differential pinion shaft lockscrew. Remove the lockscrew and the pinion shaft.
5. Push in on the axle end. Remove the C-lock from the inner (bottom) end of the shaft.
6. Remove the shaft, being careful of the oil seal.
7. You can pry the oil seal out of the housing by placing the inner end of the axle shaft behind the steel case of the seal, then prying it out carefully.
8. A puller or a slide hammer is required to remove the bearing from the housing.
9. Pack the new or reused bearing with wheel bearing grease and lubricate the cavity between the seal lips with the same grease.
10. The bearing has to be driven into the housing. Don't use a drift, you might cock the bearing in its bore, use a large socket instead. Drive only on the outer bearing race. In a similar manner, drive the seal in flush with the end of the tube.
11. Slide the shaft into place, turning it slowly until the splines are engaged with the differential. Be careful of the oil seal.
12. Install the C-lock on the inner axle end. Pull the shaft out so that the C-lock seats in the counterbore of the differential side gear.
13. Position the differential pinion shaft

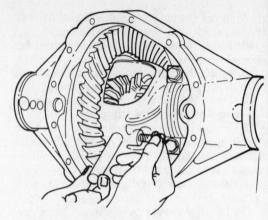

Removing the differential pinion shaft lock pin, all ½ ton trucks, except with locking differential

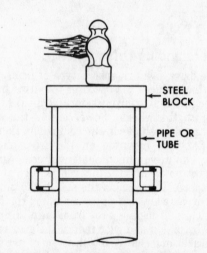

STEEL BLOCK

PIPE OR TUBE

The correct way to install a bearing. Note that the one illustrated is being driven down over a shaft. When installing the axle tube bearing, you would drive on the outer bearing race to prevent damaging the bearing rollers. The pipe exerts even pressure all around so that the bearing goes on straight

Removing the full floating axle shaft, 1970–72; 1973 and later similar

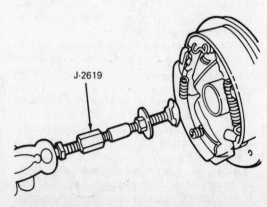

J-2619

Wheel bearing puller. This tool can usually be rented from tool rental shops

through the case and the pinion gears, aligning the lockscrew hole. Install the lockscrew.

14. Install the cover with a new gasket and tighten the bolts evenly in a crisscross pattern.

15. Fill the axle with lubricant.

16. Replace the brake drums and wheels.

1974-80 Series 10 and 1500 With Locking Differential

This axle uses a thrust block on the differential pinion shaft.

1. Follow Steps 1-3 of the proceeding procedure.

2. Rotate the differential case so that you can remove the lockscrew and support the pinion shaft so it can't fall into the housing. Remove the differential pinion shaft lockscrew.

3. Carefully pull the pinion shaft partway out and rotate the differential case until the shaft touches the housing at the top.

4. Use a drift pin to position the C-lock with its open end directly inward. You can't push in the axle shaft till you do this.

5. Push the axle shaft in and remove the C-lock.

6. Follow Steps 6-11 of the proceeding procedure.

7. Keep the pinion shaft partway out of the differential case while installing the C-lock on the axle shaft. Put the C-lock on the axle shaft and carefully pull out on the axle shaft until the C-lock is clear of the thrust block.

8. Follow steps 13-16 of the previous procedure.

1970-82 ¾ and 1 Ton

These models all use axles of full floating design. The procedures are the same for locking and non-locking axles. Some 1970-72 trucks use Dana axles, but the same procedures should be used.

The best way to remove the bearings from the wheel hub is with an arbor press. Use of a press reduces the chances of damaging the bearing races, cocking the bearing in its bore, or scoring the hub walls. A local machine shop is probably equipped with the tools to remove and install bearings and seals. However, if one is not available, the hammer and drift method outlined can be used.

1. Support the axle on jacking stands.

2. Remove the wheels.

3. Remove the bolts and lock washers that attach the axle shaft flange to the hub.

4. On 1970-72 trucks, install two ½" by 13" bolts in the threaded holes provided in the axle shaft flange. By turning these bolts alternately the axle shaft may be easily started and then removed from the housing.

5. On 1973 and later trucks, rap on the flange with a soft faced hammer to loosen the shaft. Grip the rib on the end of the flange with a pair of locking pliers and twist to start shaft removal. Remove the shaft from the axle tube.

6. The hub and drum assembly must be removed to remove the bearings and oil seals. You will need a large socket to remove and later adjust the bearing adjustment nut.

7. Remove the locknut retainer, then the locknut.

8. Remove the adjusting nut from the housing tube.

9. Remove the thrust washer from the housing tube.

10. Pull the hub and drum straight off the axle housing.

11. Remove the oil seal and discard.

12. Use a hammer and a long draft pin to knock the inner bearing, cup, and oil seal from the hub assembly.

13. Remove the outer bearing snapring with a pair of pliers. It may be necessary to tap the bearing outer race away from the retaining ring slightly by tapping on the ring to remove the ring.

14. Drive the outer bearing from the hub with a hammer and drift pin.

15. To reinstall the bearings, place the outer bearing into the hub. The larger outside diameter of the bearing should face the outer end of the hub. Drive the bearing into the hub using a washer that will cover both the inner and outer races of the bearing. Place a socket on the top of this washer, then drive the bearing into place with a series of light taps. If available, an arbor press should be used for this job.

16. Drive the bearing past the snapring groove, and install the snapring. Then, turning the hub assembly over, drive the bearing back against the snapring. Again, protect the bearing by placing a washer on top of it. You can use the thrust washer that fits between the bearing and the adjusting nut for this job.

17. Place the inner bearing into the hub. The thick edge should be toward the shoulder in the hub. Press the bearing into the hub until it seats against the shoulder, using a washer and socket as outlined earlier. Make certain that the bearing is not cocked and that it is fully seated on the shoulder.

18. Pack the wheel bearings with the grease, and lightly coat the inside diameter of the hub bearing contact surface and the outside diameter of the axle housing tube.

19. Make sure that the inner bearing, oil seal, axle housing oil deflector, and outer bearing are properly positioned. Install the hub and drum assembly on the axle housing, exercising care so as not to damage the oil seal or dislocate other internal components.

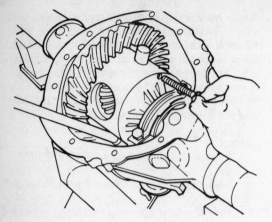

Removing the lock screw

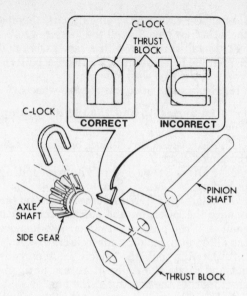

Correct C-lock positioning, 1974–80 locking differential

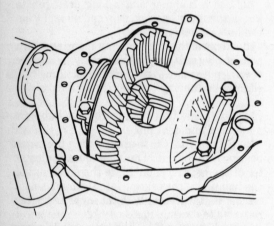

Positioning the differential case for best clearance for pinion shaft removal, 1974 and later locking differential.

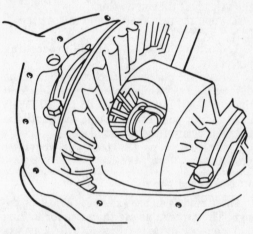

Push the axle shaft inward to remove the C-lock

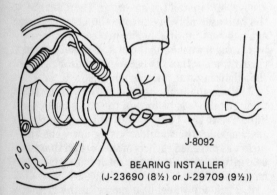

J-8092

BEARING INSTALLER
(J-23690 (8½) or J-29709 (9½))

Rear wheel bearing installation tool

20. Install the thrust washer so that the tang on the inside diameter of the washer is in the keyway on the axle housing.

21. Install the adjusting nut. Tighten to 50 ft.lb., at the same time rotating the hub to make sure that all the bearing surfaces are in

This tool is available for removing and adjusting the bearing locknut and adjusting nut

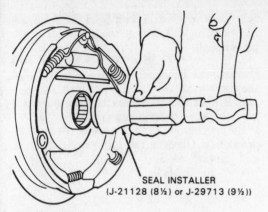

SEAL INSTALLER
(J-21128 (8½) or J-29713 (9½))

Seal installation

contact. Back off the nut and retighten to 35 ft.lb., then back off ¼ of a turn.

22. Install the tanged retainer against the inner adjusting nut. Align the adjusting nut so that the short tang of the retainer will engage the nearest slot on the adjusting nut.

23. Install the outer locknut and tighten to 65 ft.lb. Bend the long tang of the retainer into the slot of the outer nut. This method of adjustment should provide 0.001-0.010″ of endplay.

24. Place a new gasket over the axle shaft and position the axle shaft in the housing so that the shaft splines enter the differential side gear. Position the gasket so that the holes are in alignment, and install the flang-to-hub attaching bolts. Torque to 90 ft.lb. through 1975, 115 ft.lb. 1976 and later.

NOTE: *To prevent lubricant from leaking through the flange holes, apply a nonhardening sealer to the bolt threads. Use the sealer sparingly.*

25. Replace the wheels.

Pinion Seal

REMOVAL AND INSTALLATION

All Except 8½″, 8⅞″, 9½″ Chevrolet ring gears

1. Raise and support the vehicle safely. Matchmark the driveshaft and the pinion flange.

2. Disconnect the driveshaft from the rear differential. Position the driveshaft out of the way.

3. Mark the position of the pinion flange, pinion shaft and nut. Using the proper flange removal tools, remove the pinion flange nut and washer.

4. Remove the pinion flange. Position a drain pan under the assembly to catch any excess lubricant.

5. Using a centerpunch, remove the seal from its mounting.

6. Installation is the reverse of the removal procedure. Be sure to replace any lost lubricant. On all axles except those equipped with the Chevrolet 12¼″ and the Rockwell 12″ ring gears tighten the nut flush, then tighten to the original line scribed during disassemnly. On the Chevrolet 12¼″ torque the nut to 220 ft.lb. and on the Rockwell 12″ torque the nut to 350 ft.lb.

8½″, 8⅞″, 9½″ Chevrolet ring gears

1. Raise the vehicle and support it safely.

2. Disconnect the driveshaft from the axle.

3. Position the propeller shat to one side and tie it to the frame side rail.

4. Measure the torque required to rotate the pinion and record the torque for later reference.

5. Mark the position of the pinion flange, pinion shaft and nut. Count the number of exposed threads on the pinion stem, and record for later reference.

6. Install Tool No. J-8614-11 on the pinion flange and remove the pinion flange self-locking washer faced nut. Position the tool on the flange so that the four notches are toward the flange. Save the scribed nut for reinstallation.

7. Thread the pilot end of Tool J-8614-3 into the small O.D. end of Tool J-8614-2. Then with Tool J-8614-11 installed as in step 6, insert J-8614-2 into J-8614-11 and turn 45° to the locked position. Remove the flange by turning J-8614-3 while turning J-8614-11.

8. Using a suitable tool pry the old seal out of the bore.

9. To install, lubricate the cavity between the seal lips of the pinion flange oil seal with a lithium-base extreme pressure lubricant.

10. Position the seal in the bore and place gauge plate J-22804-1 over the seal and against the seal flange. This tool assures proper seating of the seal.

11. Using tool J-21057 or J-22388 for the 9½″ ring gear, to press the seal into the carrier bore until the gauge plate is flush with the carrier shoulder and seal flange. Turn the gauge plate 180° from the installed position; the seal must be square in the carrier bore to seal properly against the pinion flange.

12. Pack the cavity between the ends of the pinion splines and pinion flange with a nonhardening sealer such as Permatex® Type A or equivalent prior to installing the washer and nut on the pinion.

13. Using Tool J-8614-11, install the flange onto the pinion. Install the washer and nut and tighten the nut to the original position. Refer to the scribe nuts and number of threads recorded earlier.

14. Measure the rotating torque of the pinion and compare with the torque recorded before removal. Tighten the pinion nut in additional

small increments until the torque necessary to rotate the pinion exceeds the original figure by 1-5 in. lbs. Do not exceed the original torque by more than 5 in.lb.

15. Reattach the driveshaft, brake drums and wheels.

Axle Housing

REMOVAL AND INSTALLATION

1. Raise and support the vehicle safely. Remove the tire and wheel assemblies. Properly support the rear axle assembly.

2. Disconnect the shock absorbers from the anchor plate. Matchmark the driveshaft and the pinion flange. Remove the driveshaft and position it out of the way.

3. Remove the brake line junction block from the axle housing. Disconnect the axle vent hose from the vent connector and position it to the side.

4. Remove the brake drums. Disconnect the parking brake cables at the actuating levers and at the flange plate.

5. Remove the U-bolts and anchor plates. Remove the axle housing from the vehicle.

8. Installation is the reverse of the removal procedure.

Differential Carrier

REMOVAL AND INSTALLATION

Dana 9¾″ And 10½″

1. Raise and support the vehicle safely. Allow the rear axle assembly to hang freely. Remove the tire and wheel assemblies. Drain the lubricant.

2. Remove the axle shaft to hub retaining nuts. Rap the axle shaft to loosen it from the hub. Remove the shafts.

3. Remove the cap screws and lock washers retaining the cover to the carrier. Remove the carrier cover and gasket.

4. Mark one side of the carrier and matching cap for reassembly in the same position. Remove the bearing caps.

5. Using a spreader tool and a dial indicator gauge, spread the carrier assembly to a maximum of 0.015″.

6. Remove the dial indicator tool. Use a prybar and remove the differential case from the carrier.

7. Record the dimension and location of the side bearing shims. Remove the spreader tool.

8. Installation is the reverse of the removal procedure.

Rockwell 12″

1. As required, raise and support the vehicle safely. Drain the lubricant.

2. Remove the axle shaft from the drive unit and housing. Disconnect the universal at the pinion shaft.

3. Remove the carrier to housing stud nuts and washers. Loosen the two top nuts and leave the studs to prevent the carrier from falling.

4. Break the carrier loose from the axle housing using the proper hammer.

5. Installation is the reverse of the removal procedure. Observe the following carrier-to-housing torques:
- ½″-20: 102 ft.lb.
- ⅝″-18: 205 ft.lb.
- ¾″-16: 360 ft.lb.

FRONT DRIVE AXLE 4-WHEEL DRIVE ONLY

Front Hub

Locking front hubs are standard equipment on 1975 and later 4-wheel drive models and optional on earlier years, with the exception of 1973-79 full time 4-wheel drive trucks. The purpose of locking hubs is to reduce friction and wear by disengaging the front axle shaft, differential, and driveline from the front wheels when 4-wheel drive is not being used.

The engagement and disengagement of the hubs is a manual operation which must be performed to each hub assembly. Unlocking should only take place when the transfer case lever is in the two wheel drive position. The hubs should be placed in the full Lock or full Free position or damage will result.

WARNING: *Do not use 4-wheel drive unless the hubs are in the Lock position.*

Locking hubs should be run in the Lock position for at least 10 miles each month to assure proper differential lubrication.

REMOVAL AND INSTALLATION

Including Wheel Bearings

NOTE: *This procedure requires snapring pliers and a special hub nut wrench. It is not very easy without them.*

1. Raise and support the front end on jackstands.

2. Remove the wheels.

3. For 1970 and later ½ and ¾ ton trucks with locking front hubs: lock the hubs. Remove the outer retaining plate Allen head bolts and take off the plate, O-ring, and knob. Take out the large snapring inside the hub and remove the outer clutch retaining ring and actuating cam body. This is a lot easier with snapring pliers. Relieve pressure on the axle shaft snapring and remove it. Take out the axle shaft sleeve and clutch ring assembly and the inner clutch

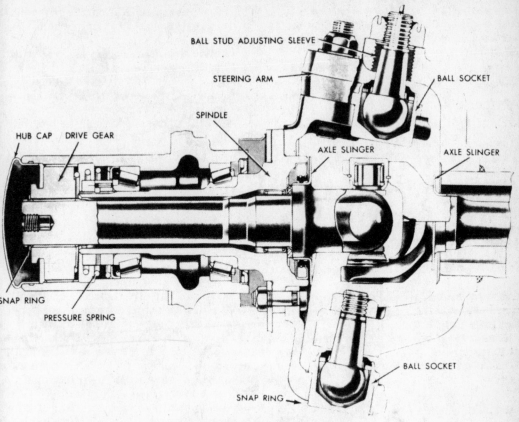

BALL STUD ADJUSTING SLEEVE

STEERING ARM

SPINDLE

BALL SOCKET

HUB CAP   DRIVE GEAR

AXLE SLINGER

AXLE SLINGER

SNAP RING

PRESSURE SPRING

BALL SOCKET

SNAP RING

Four wheel drive steering knuckle

ring and bushing assembly. Remove the spring and retainer plate.

4. For ¾ ton truck models 1970-76, with locking front hubs, turn the hub key to the **Free** position. Remove the Allen head bolts securing the retainer cap assembly to the wheel hub. Pull off the hub cap extension housing and its gasket.

NOTE: *You will have to modify this procedure for either of the models mentioned above if you have non-factory installed locking hubs.*

5. If you don't have locking front hubs, remove the hub cap and snapring. Next, remove the drive gear and pressure spring. To prevent the spring from popping out, place a hand over the drive gear and use a screwdriver to pry the gear out. Remove the spring.

6. Remove the wheel bearing outer lock nut, lock ring, and wheel bearing inner adjusting nut. A special wrench is required.

7. Remove the brake disc assembly and outer wheel bearing. Remove the spring retainer plate if you don't have locking hubs. See Chapter 9 for details on brake drum or disc and caliper removal.

8. Remove the oil seal and inner bearing cone

from the hub using a brass drift and hammer. Discard the oil seal. Use the drift to remove the inner and outer bearing cups.

9. Check the condition of the spindle bearing. If you have drum brakes, remove the grease retainer, gasket, and backing plate after removing the bolts. Unbolt the spindle and tap it with a soft hammer to break it loose. Remove the spindle and check the condition of the thrust washer, replacing it if worn. Now you can remove the oil seal and spindle roller bearing.

NOTE: *The spindle bearings must be greased each time the wheel bearings are serviced.*

10. Clean all parts in solvent, dry, and check for wear or damage.

11. Pack both wheel bearings (and the spindle bearing) using wheel bearing grease. Place a healthy glob of grease in the palm of one hand and force the edge of the bearing into it so that grease fills the bearing. Do this until the whole bearing is packed. Grease packing tools are available to make this job easier.

12. To reassemble the spindle: drive the repacked bearing into the spindle and install the grease seal onto the slinger with the lip toward

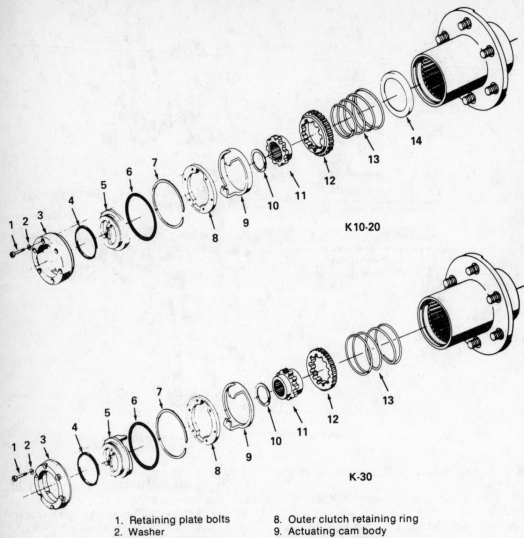

K10-20

K-30

1. Retaining plate bolts
2. Washer
3. Hub ring retaining knob
4. Actuator knob "O" ring
5. Actuator knob
6. "O" ring
7. Internal snap ring
8. Outer clutch retaining ring
9. Actuating cam body
10. Axle shaft snap ring
11. Axle shaft sleeve and ring
12. Inner clutch ring
13. Pressure spring
14. Spring retainer plate

Exploded view, manual-locking free wheeling hubs

the spindle. It would be best to replace the axle shaft slinger when the spindle seal is replaced. See Axle Shaft Removal and Overhaul for details.

CHILTON TIP: *An improved spindle seal (no. 376855) and axle seal (no. 376851) were introduced during the 1976 model year. These can be installed on earlier (late 1972 and up) models. See the note under Axle Shaft Removal and Installation in this chapter for details on identifying late 1972 models.*

If you are using the improved seals, fill the seal end of the spindle with grease. If not, apply grease only to the lip of the seal. Install the thrust washer over the axle shaft. On late 1972 through 1982 models, the chamfered side of the thrust washer should be toward the slinger. Replace the spindle and torque the nuts to 45 ft.lb. through 1976, 25 ft.lb., 1977-78, 33 ft.lb., 1979-80, 65 ft.lb. 1981 and later.

WHEEL BEARING ASSEMBLY AND ADJUSTMENT

1. To reassemble the wheel bearings: drive the outer bearing cup into the hub, replace the inner bearing cup, and insert the repacked bearing.

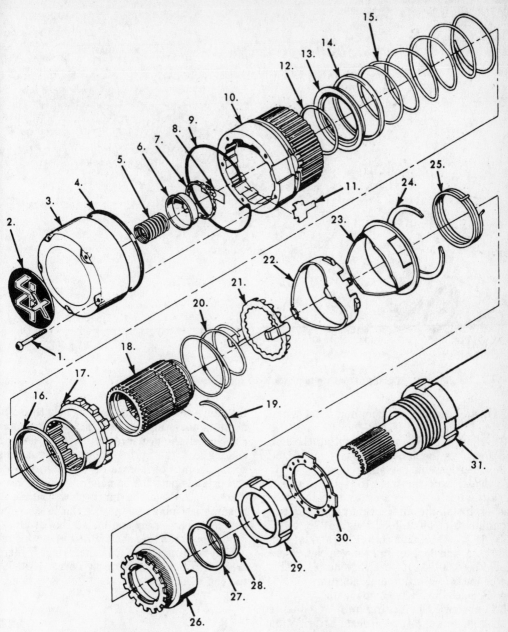

1. Machine screw
2. Cover plate
3. Cover
4. Sealing ring
5. Bearing race spring
6. Bearing inner race
7. Bearing
8. Bearing retainer clip
9. Wire retaining ring
10. Outer clutch housing
11. Seal bridge—retainer
12. Retaining ring
13. Spring support washer
14. Spring retainer
15. Return spring
16. Spring retainer

17. Clutch gear
18. Hub sleeve
19. "C" type retaining ring
20. Conical spring
21. Cam follower
22. Outer cage
23. Inner cage
24. Snap ring
25. Brake band
26. Drag sleeve and detent
27. Small spacer
28. Retaining ring
29. Lock nut
30. Drag sleeve retainer washer
31. Adjusting nut, wheel bearing

Exploded view—automatic free wheeling hubs

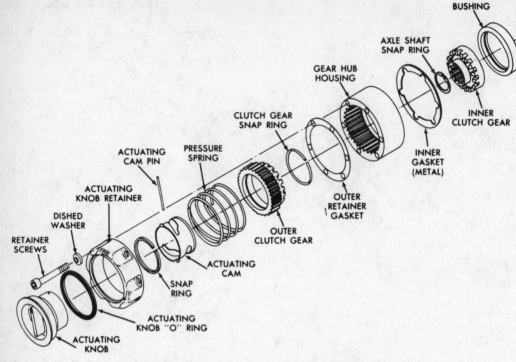

RETAINER SCREWS

DISHED WASHER

ACTUATING KNOB RETAINER

ACTUATING CAM PIN

PRESSURE SPRING

CLUTCH GEAR SNAP RING

GEAR HUB HOUSING

AXLE SHAFT SNAP RING

BUSHING

INNER CLUTCH GEAR

INNER GASKET (METAL)

OUTER RETAINER GASKET

OUTER CLUTCH GEAR

ACTUATING CAM

SNAP RING

ACTUATING KNOB "O" RING

ACTUATING KNOB

Details of locking hubs for K-20 and K-2500 models, 1970–77

2. Install the disc or drum and outer wheel bearing to the spindle.

3. Adjust the bearings by rotating the hub and torquing the inner adjusting nut to 50 ft.lb., then loosening it and retorquing to 35 ft.lb. Next, back the nut off ⅜ turn or less. Turn the nut to the nearest hole in the lockwasher. Install the outer locknut and torque to a minimum of 50 ft.lb. through 1978, or 80 ft.lb., 1979-80, 160-205 ft.lb. 1981 and later ½ and ¾ ton, and 65 ft.lb. on 1 ton vehicles. There should be 0.001-0.010″ bearing end play. This can be measured with a dial indicator.

4. Replace the brake components.

5. Lubricate the locking hub components with high temperature grease. Lubrication must be applied to prevent component failure. For ½ ton 1970-82 and 1977-84 ¾ and 1 ton models, install the spring retainer plate with the flange side facing the bearing over the spindle nuts and seat it against the bearing outer cup. Install the pressure spring with the large end against the spring retaining plate. The spring is an interference fit; when seated, its end extends past the spindle nuts by approximately ⅞″. Place the inner clutch ring and bushing assembly into the axle shaft sleeve and clutch ring assembly and install that as an assembly onto the axle shaft. Press in on this assembly and install the axle shaft ring. If there are two axle shaft snapring grooves (1976-79) use the inner one.

This special four wheel drive bearing adjusting wrench is available at four wheel drive suppliers and truck parts outlets

Driving out the bearing cups

NOTE: *You can install a $7/16$" bolt in the axle shaft end and pull outward on it to aid in seating the snapring.*

Install the actuating cam body in the cams facing outward, the outer clutch retaining ring, and the internal snapring. Install a new O-ring on the retaining plate, and then install the actuating knob in the Lock position. Install the retaining plate. The grooves in the knob must fit into the actuator cam body. Install the seals and six cover bolts and torque them to 30 ft.lb. Turn the knob to the Free position and check for proper operation.

6. For ¾ and 1 ton models, 1970-76, apply grease generously to the axle splines and teeth of the inner and outer clutch gears.

NOTE: *Remove the head from a 5" long ⅜" bolt and use this to align the hub assembly.*

Install the headless bolt into one of the hub housing bolt holes. Install a new exterior sleeve extension housing gasket, the housing, and a new hub retainer cap assembly gasket, and the cap assembly. Install the six Allen head bolts and their washers, and torque them to 30 ft.lb. Turn the knob to Lock and check engagement.

7. Without locking hubs, replace the snapring and hub cap. If there are two axle shaft snapring grooves (1976-79), use the inner one.

Axle Shaft

REMOVAL AND INSTALLATION

NOTE: *The front spindles and universal joints were changed during the 1972 model year. You must know which one you have to order the correct parts. The early design is stamped 603351 or 603352 on the front of the left axle tube; the later design is 603333 or 603334. The only interchangeable part is the inner hub seal.*

1. Follow the steps of the Front Hub section above.

2. Pull out the axle shaft and universal joint assembly.

3. When installing the axle shaft, turn the shaft slowly to align the splines with the differential.

4. Reassemble everything and adjust the wheel bearings following the steps in the Front Hub section in this chapter.

AXLE SHAFT U-JOINT OVERHAUL

1. Remove the axle shaft.

2. Squeeze the ends of the trunnion bearings in a vise to relieve the load on the snaprings. Remove the snaprings.

3. Support the yoke in a vise and drive on one end of the trunnion bearing with a brass drift enough to drive the opposite bearing from the yoke.

4. Support the other side of the yoke and drive the other bearing out.

5. Remove the trunnion.

6. Clean and check all parts. You can buy U-joint repair kits to replace all the worn parts.

7. Lubricate the bearings with wheel bearing grease.

8. Replace the trunnion and press the bearings into the yoke and over the trunnion hubs far enough to install the lock rings.

9. Hold the trunnion in one hand and tap the yoke lightly to seat the bearings against the lock rings.

10. The axle slingers can be pressed off the shaft.

NOTE: *Always replace the slingers if the spindle seals are replaced.*

11. Replace the shaft.

Pinion Seal

REMOVAL AND INSTALLATION

1. Using a Holding Bar Tool J-8614-1, attached to the pinion shaft flange, remove the self locking nut and washer from the pinion shaft.

2. Install Tool J-8614-2, and 3 into the holding bar and remove the flange from the drive pinion. Remove the drive pinion from the carrier.

3. With a long drift, tap on the inner race of the outer pinion bearing to remove the seal.

4. Install the oil seal, gasket and using Tool J-22804 install the oil seal.

5. Install the flange, washer and nut and torque the nut to 270 ft. lbs.

Axle Housing

REMOVAL AND INSTALLATION

1. Raise and support the vehicle safely. Remove the driveshaft.

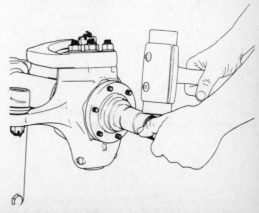

Removing the spindle

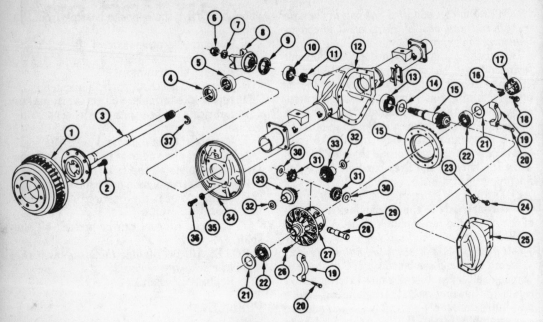

1. Drum
2. Bolt, rr whl
3. Shaft, rr axle
4. Seal, rr axle shaft
5. Bearing, rr axle whl
6. Nut, pinion flange
7. Washer, pinion flange
8. Flange, w/defl, pinion
9. Seal, pinion flange
10. Bearing, pinion frt
11. Spacer, pinion bearing
12. Carrier & tube, diff
13. Bearing, pinion gear rr

14. Shim kit, pinion brg
15. Gear, ring and pinion
16. Lock
17. Nut, diff brg adj
18. Bolt, adj nut lock
19. Cap, diff brg
20. Bolt, diff brg cap
21. Shim, diff brg
22. Bearing, differential
23. Clip, rr brk c/ovr pipe
24. Bolt, diff carrier cover
25. Cover, diff carrier

26. Bolt, hyp drive gear
27. Case, diff
28. Shaft, diff pinion
29. Screw, diff pinion shaft
30. Washer, diff png thrust
31. Pinion, diff
32. Washer, si gear thrust
33. Gear, diff side
34. Plate, rr brk flg
35. Washer, lk (½")
36. Bolt, hex (½"-20 x 1")
37. Lock, axle shaft

9½ in. ring gear axle, exploded view

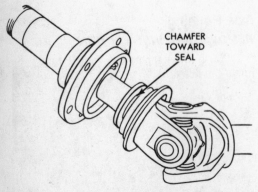

CHAMFER
TOWARD
SEAL

Replacing the spindle thrust washer and spindle; the components are removed from the truck for clarity

2. Disconnect the connecting rod from the steering arm. Disconnect the brake caliper and properly position it to the side.

3. Disconnect the shock absorbers from the axle brackets. As required, remove the front stabilizer bar.

4. Disconnect the axle vent tube clip at the differential housing. Properly support the axle assembly using a suitable jack.

5. Remove the U-bolts from the axle and separate the axle from the springs. Remove the axle assembly from the vehicle.

6. Installation is the reverse of the removal procedure.

Suspension and Steering

8

FRONT SUSPENSION

All models except four wheel drive use an independent front suspension with upper and lower control arms and coil springs. 4-wheel drive pick-ups are tapered leaf springs and the traditional solid front axle.

CAUTION: *Coil springs are under considerable tension. Be very careful when removing and installing them; they can exert enough force to cause serious injury.*

Coil Spring

REMOVAL AND INSTALLATION

1. Raise and support the truck under the frame rails. The control arms should hang free.

2. Disconnect the shock absorber at the lower end and move it aside. Disconnect the stabilizer bar from the lower control arm.

3. Support the cross-shaft and install a spring compressor or chain the spring to the control arm as a safety precaution.

4. Raise the jack to remove the tension from the lower control arm cross-shaft and remove the two U-bolts securing the crosshaft to the crossmember.

CAUTION: *The cross-shaft and lower control arm keeps the coil spring compressed. Use care when you lower the assembly.*

5. Slowly release the jack and lower the control arm until the spring can be removed. Be sure that all compression is relieved from the spring.

6. Remove the spring.

7. Installation is the reverse of removal, with the following recommendations: Position the control arm cross-shaft on the crossmember and install the U-bolts. Be sure that the front indexing hole in the cross-shaft is aligned with the crossmember attaching saddle stud.

Have the front suspension alignment

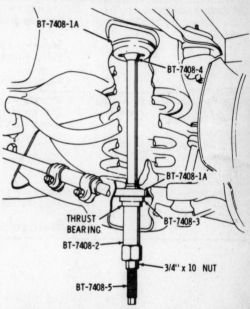

Front coil spring removal showing spring compressor. Make sure the fork in the top of the spring compressor is in position whenever the tool is used

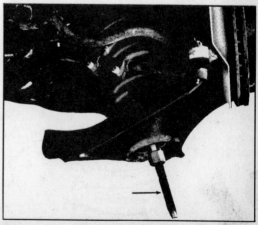

Coil spring compressed. The lower control arm pivot bolts have been removed.

Troubleshooting Basic Steering and Suspension Problems

Problem	Cause	Solution
Hard steering (steering wheel is hard to turn)	• Low or uneven tire pressure • Loose power steering pump drive belt • Low or incorrect power steering fluid • Incorrect front end alignment • Defective power steering pump • Bent or poorly lubricated front end parts	• Inflate tires to correct pressure • Adjust belt • Add fluid as necessary • Have front end alignment checked/adjusted • Check pump • Lubricate and/or replace defective parts
Loose steering (too much play in the steering wheel)	• Loose wheel bearings • Loose or worn steering linkage • Faulty shocks • Worn ball joints	• Adjust wheel bearings • Replace worn parts • Replace shocks • Replace ball joints
Car veers or wanders (car pulls to one side with hands off the steering wheel)	• Incorrect tire pressure • Improper front end alignment • Loose wheel bearings • Loose or bent front end components • Faulty shocks	• Inflate tires to correct pressure • Have front end alignment checked/adjusted • Adjust wheel bearings • Replace worn components • Replace shocks
Wheel oscillation or vibration transmitted through steering wheel	• Improper tire pressures • Tires out of balance • Loose wheel bearings • Improper front end alignment • Worn or bent front end components	• Inflate tires to correct pressure • Have tires balanced • Adjust wheel bearings • Have front end alignment checked/adjusted • Replace worn parts
Uneven tire wear	• Incorrect tire pressure • Front end out of alignment • Tires out of balance	• Inflate tires to correct pressure • Have front end alignment checked/adjusted • Have tires balanced

Spring compressed and ready to install

checked. Torque the U-bolts to 45 ft.lb., 1970-75 ½ ton trucks, 110 ft.lb. ¾ and 1 ton models; all other trucks 85 ft.lb.

Leaf Spring

REMOVAL AND INSTALLATION

1. Raise and support the vehicle so that all tension is taken off of the front suspension.
2. Remove the shackle upper retaining bolt and the front spring eye bolt.
3. Remove the spring-to-axle U-bolt nuts. Pull of the spring, the lower plate, and the spring pads.
4. Remove the shackle-to-spring bolt, bushings, and shackle.

To replace the bushing, place the spring in a press or vise and press out the bushing. Press in the new bushing. The new bushing should protrude evenly on both sides of the spring.

5. Installation is the reverse of removal. The following torques are necessary: 1970-72 U-Bolts 120 ft.lb. 1973 and later 150 ft.lb., Spring Shackle 50 ft.lb., Front eye bolt 90 ft.lb., Rear eye bolt 50 ft.lb.

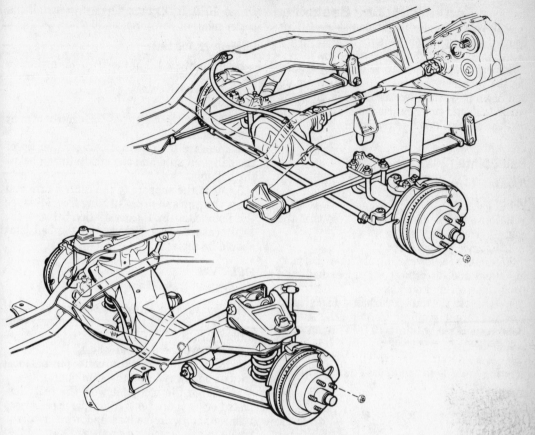

Typical front suspensions. 4X4 top, 2WD lower

Shock Absorbers

REMOVAL AND INSTALLATION

1. Raise and support the truck.
2. Remove the nuts and eye bolts securing the upper and lower shock absorber eyes.
3. Remove the shock absorber and inspect the rubber eye bushings. If these are defective, replace the shock absorber assembly.
4. Installation is the reverse of removal.

TESTING

Adjust the tire pressure before testing the shocks. If the truck is equipped with heavy duty

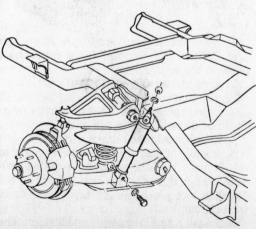

Two wheel drive front shock absorber

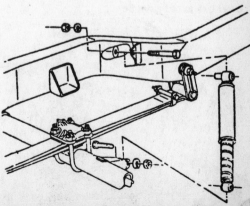

Four wheel drive front shock absorber

equipment, this can sometimes be misleading. A stiff ride normally accompanies a stiff or heavy duty suspension. Be sure that all weight in the truck is distributed evenly.

Each shock absorber can be tested by bouncing the corner of the truck until maximum up and down movement is obtained. Let go of the truck. It should stop bouncing in 1-2 bounces. If not, the shock should be replaced.

Ball Joints (2-Wheel Drive)
INSPECTION
Upper — 1970-71

1. Raise and support the truck so that the control arms hang free.
2. Remove the wheel.
3. Support the lower control arm with a jacking stand and disconnect the upper ball stud from the steering knuckle.
4. Reinstall the nut on the ball stud and measure the torque required to rotate the stud. If the torque is not within 1-10 ft.lb., replace the ball joint.
5. If no defects are evident, connect the steering knuckle to the upper stud and torque

Lower ball joint inspection

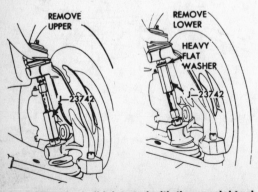

Loosening the ball joint stud with the special tool

the to 70 ft.lb. Tighten further to install the cotter pin, but don't exceed 90 ft.lb.

Upper 1972 And Later

Perform Steps 1-3 of the 1970-71 inspection procedure.

Lower

1. Support the weight of the control arm at the wheel hub.
2. Measure the distance between the tip of the ball joint stud and the grease fitting below the ball joint.
3. Move the support to the control arm and allow the hub and drum to hang free. Measure the distance again. If the variation between the two measurements exceeds $3/32''$ the ball joint should be replaced.

REMOVAL
Lower

1. Raise and support the truck with jackstands. Support the lower control arm with a floor jack.
2. Remove the tire and wheel.
3. Remove the lower stud cotter pin and loosen, but do not remove, the stud nut.
4. Loosen the ball joint with the tool illustrated or its equivalent. It may be necessary to remove the brake caliper and wire it to the frame to gain enough clearance.
5. When the stud is loose, remove the tool and ball stud nut.
6. Install a spring compressor on the coil spring for safety.
7. Pull the brake disc and knuckle assembly up and off the ball stud and support the upper arm with a block of wood.
8. Remove the ball joint from the control arm with a ball joint fork or another suitable tool.

INSTALLATION
Lower

1. Start the new ball joint into the control arm. Position the bleed vent in the rubber boot facing inward.
2. Turn the screw until the ball joint is seated in the control arm.
3. Lower the upper arm and match the steering knuckle to the lower ball stud.
4. Install the brake caliper, if removed.
5. Install the ball stud nut and torque it to 80-100 ft.lb. plus the additional torque necessary to align the cotter pin hole. Do not exceed 130 ft.lb. or back the nut off to align the holes with the pin.
6. Install a new lube fitting and lubricate the new joint.

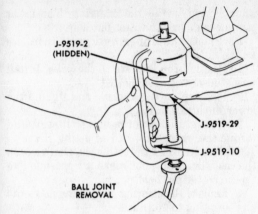

Pressing out the 2WD lower ball-joint using a ball-joint tool

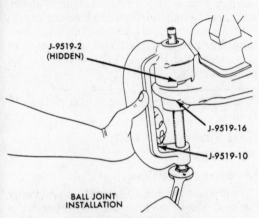

Installing the lower ball-joint, 2WD models

7. Install the tire and wheel.
8. Lower the truck.

REMOVAL AND INSTALLATION

Upper

1. Raise and support the truck with jackstands. Remove wheel.

2. Support the lower control arm with a floor jack.

3. Remove the cotter pin from the upper ball stud and loosen, but do not remove the stud nut.

4. Using the special tool or its equivalent, loosen the ball stud in the steering knuckle. When the stud is loose, remove the tool and the stud nut. It may be necessary to remove the brake caliper and wire it to the frame to gain clearance.

5. Drill out the rivets. Remove the ball joint assembly.

To Install:

6. Install the service ball joint, using the nuts supplied or special hardened fasteners.

7. Torque the ball stud nut as follows: ½ ton

trucks: 60 ft.lb. plus the additional torque to align the cotter pin. Do not exceed 90 ft.lb. and never back the nut off to align the pin. ¾ and 1 ton trucks: 80-100 ft.lb. plus additional torque necessary to align the cotter pin. Do not exceed 130 ft.lb. and never back off the nut to align the pin.

8. Install a new cotter pin.

9. Install a new lube fitting and lubricate the new joint.

10. If removed, install the brake caliper.

11. Install the wheel and lower the truck.

Ball Joints (4-Wheel Drive)
REMOVAL AND INSTALLATION
All Except K30 Series

The steering knuckle pivot ball joints may need replacement when there is excessive steering play, hard steering, irregular tire wear (especially on the inner edge), or persistent tie rod loosening.

This procedure requires the removal of the steering knuckle before the ball joints can be removed. K30 models with kingpins have their

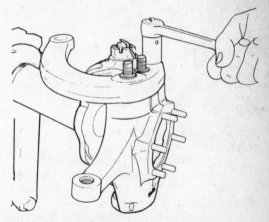

Removing the steering arm nuts, 4X4 models. Replace the nuts with new ones when installing

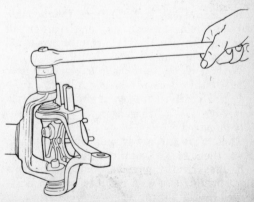

Removing the ball socket retaining nuts on 4X4s

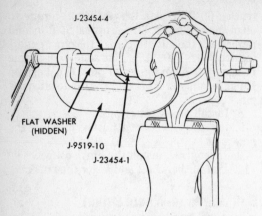

Pressing the lower ball-joint out of the knuckle

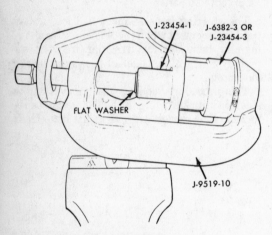

Lower ball-joint removal, 4X4s.

own knuckle removal procedure later in this chapter.

1. Support the front axle on jackstands.

2. Remove the axle shaft as detailed earlier.

3. Remove the steering linkage. The best method is to use a tire rod end puller.

4. If you remove the steering arm from the top of the knuckle, the nuts cannot be reused.

5. Remove the cotter pin and ball joint stud nuts.

6. Remove the knuckle from the housing yoke by forcing a wedge between the lower ball stud and the yoke, then between the upper ball stud and the yoke.

WARNING: *If you have to loosen the upper ball stud adjusting sleeve to remove the knuckle, don't loosen it more than two threads. The soft threads in the yoke are easily damaged.*

7. Remove the lower ball joint snapring. Press the lower ball joint out first.

8. Press out the upper ball joint and unscrew the adjusting sleeve. A spanner wrench is required for the sleeve.

9. Press the new lower ball joint into the

knuckle and install the snapring. The lower joint doesn't have a cotter pin hole.

10. Press the upper ball joint into the knuckle.

11. Position the knuckle to the yoke. Install new stud nuts finger tight.

12. Push up on the knuckle and tighten the lower nut to 70 ft.lb.

13. Using a spanner wrench, install and torque the upper ball stud adjusting sleeve to 100 ft.lb. and install the cotter pin. Don't loosen the castellated nut, but make it tighter to line up the cotter pin hole.

14. Replace the steering arm, using new nuts and torquing to 90 ft.lb.

15. Check the knuckle turning torque with a spring scale hooked to the tie rod hole in the steering arm. With the knuckle straight ahead, measure the right angle pull to keep the knuckle turning after initial breakaway, in both directions. The pull should be 25 lbs. or less for axles assembled after Feb. 10, 1976, and 33 lbs. for earlier models.

16. Replace the axle shaft and other components. Tighten the steering linkage nuts to 45 ft.lb.

King Pins

REPLACEMENT

K30 Series 4-Wheel Drive

1. Remove the hub and spindle as previously outlined. Check the bronze spacer between the axle shaft joint assembly and bearing, if worn it must be replaced.

2. Remove the upper king pin cap nuts alternately, as the spring pressure will be forcing the cap up.

3. Remove the cap, compression spring, and gasket. Discard the gasket.

4. Remove the four cap screws from the lower king pin bearing cap. Remove the gearing cap and king pin.

5. Remove the upper king pin tapered bush-

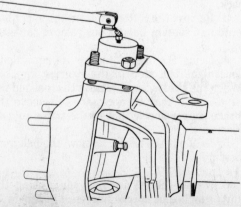

Remove the upper king pin cap nuts alternately

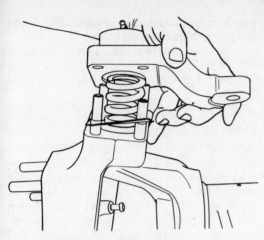

Removing the cap, spring and gasket

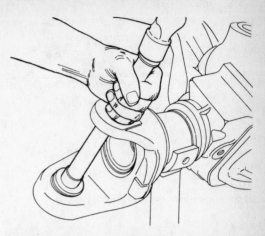

Remove the cap, cone and seal. Discard the seal and replace with a new one during assembly. If the grease retainer is damaged, replace it

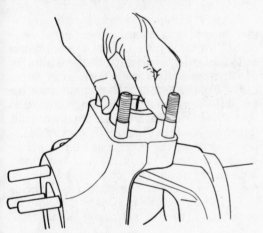

Removing the tapered bushing

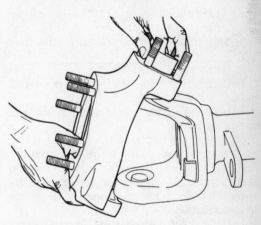

Installing the knuckle to the yoke

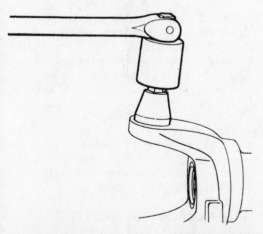

Use a large breaker bar to remove the upper king pin. When installing the king pin, torque to 500–600 ft. lbs.

ing and knuckle from the yoke. Remove the felt seal and remove the knuckle.

6. Remove the upper king pin from the yoke with a large breaker bar.

7. Remove the lower king pin bearing cup, cone, grease retainer, and seal. Discard the seal. If the grease retainer is damaged, replace it.

Install in the following manner:

1. Install the new grease retainer and lower king pin bearing cup using special tool J-7817 or its equivalent.

2. Fill the grease retainer, grease the bearing and install. Install the lower seal using tool J22281 or its equivalent.

WARNING: *Do not distort the oil seal. It will protrude slightly from the surface of the yoke when installed.*

3. Install the upper king pin using tool J18871 or its equal. Torque to 500-600 ft.lb.

4. Install the felt seal on the king pin.

5. Install the knuckle and tapered bushing over the king pin.

6. Install the lower bearing cap and king pin. Torque the cap screws to 90 ft.lb.

7. Place the compression spring on the upper king pin bushing. Install the bearing cap with a new gasket. Torque the nuts to 90 ft.lb.

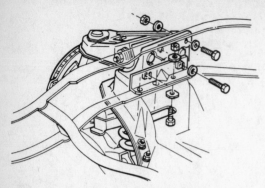

Upper control arm mounting, 2WD models

Upper Control Arm

REMOVAL AND INSTALLATION

1. Raise and support the truck on jackstands.

2. Support the lower control arm with a floor jack.

3. Remove the wheel and tire.

4. Remove the cotter pin from the upper ball joint and loosen the stud nut one turn.

5. Install a spring compressor on the coil spring for safety.

6. Loosen the upper ball joint using a ball joint removal tool. Remove the nut from the ball joint and raise the upper arm to clear the steering knuckle. It may be necessary to remove the brake caliper and wire it to the frame to gain clearance.

7. Remove the nuts securing the control arm shaft studs to the crossmember bracket and remove the control arm.

8. Tape the shims and spacers together and tap for proper reassembly.

9. Installation is the reverse of removal. Before tightening the nuts to 70 ft.lb. for ½ ton trucks, or 105 ft.lb. for ¾ and 1 ton models. Have the front alignment checked, and adjusted.

Lower Control Arm

REMOVAL AND INSTALLATION

1. Raise and support the truck on jackstands.

2. Remove the spring (see Spring Removal and Installation).

3. Support the inboard end of the control arm after spring removal.

4. Remove the cotter pin from the lower ball joint and loosen the nut one turn.

5. Loosen the lower ball joint using a ball joint removal tool. When the stud is loose, remove the nut from the stud. It may be neces-

sary to remove the brake caliper and wire it to the frame to gain clearance.

6. Remove the lower control arm.

7. Reverse the above to install. Refer to the Spring Removal and Installation for bolt torques.

Front End Alignment

Correct alignment of the front suspension is necessary to provide optimum tire life and for proper and safe handling of the vehicle. Caster and camber cannot be set or measured accurately without professional equipment. Toe-in can be adjusted with some degree of success without any special equipment.

CASTER

Caster is the tilt of the front steering axis either forward or backward away from the vertical. A tilt toward the rear is said to be positive and a forward tilt is negative. Caster is calculated with a special instrument but one can see the caster angle by looking straight down from the top of the upper control arm. You will see that the ball joints are not aligned if the caster angle is more or less than 0 degrees. If the vehicle has positive caster, the lower ball joint would be ahead of the upper ball joint center line. Caster is designed into the four wheel drive front suspension. Small caster adjustments can be made on four wheel drive front axles by the use of tapered shims between the springs and the axle.

CAMBER

Camber is the slope of the front wheels from the vertical when viewed from the front of the vehicle. When the wheels tilt outward at the top, the camber is positive. When the wheels tilt inward at the top, the camber is negative. The amount of positive and negative camber is measured in degrees from the vertical and the measurement is called camber angle. Camber is designed into the front axle of all four wheel drive vehicles. Small camber adjustments can be made on four wheel drive front axles by the use of an adjusting shim between the spindle and the steering knuckle. Any major corrections require axle straightening equipment.

CASTER AND CAMBER ADJUSTMENTS
2-Wheel Drive

Caster and camber adjustments are made by removing or adding shims between the upper control arm shaft and the mounting bracket which is attached to the suspension crossmember.

Front wheel alignment on Chevrolet and GMC trucks is a complex operation. Specifica-

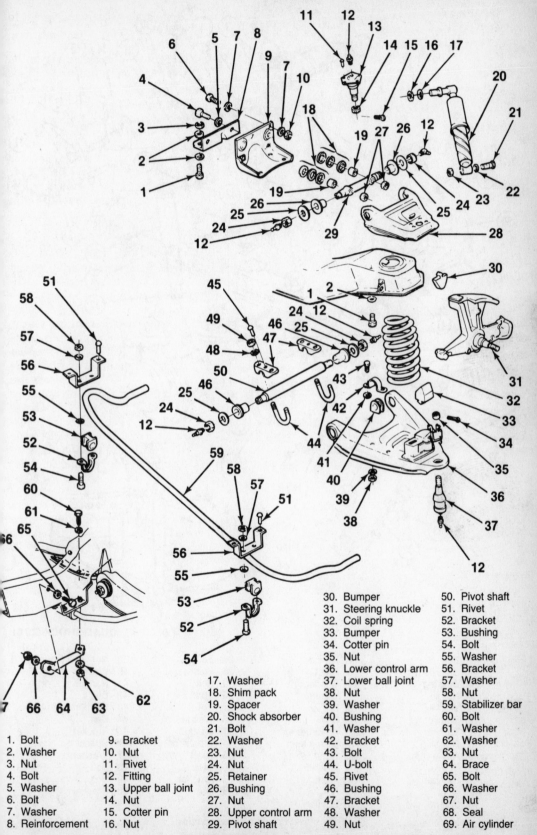

17. Washer	30. Bumper	50. Pivot shaft
18. Shim pack	31. Steering knuckle	51. Rivet
19. Spacer	32. Coil spring	52. Bracket
20. Shock absorber	33. Bumper	53. Bushing
21. Bolt	34. Cotter pin	54. Bolt
22. Washer	35. Nut	55. Washer
23. Nut	36. Lower control arm	56. Bracket
24. Nut	37. Lower ball joint	57. Washer
25. Retainer	38. Nut	58. Nut
26. Bushing	39. Washer	59. Stabilizer bar
27. Nut	40. Bushing	60. Bolt
28. Upper control arm	41. Washer	61. Washer
29. Pivot shaft	42. Bracket	62. Washer
1. Bolt	43. Bolt	63. Nut
2. Washer	44. U-bolt	64. Brace
3. Nut	45. Rivet	65. Bolt
4. Bolt	46. Bushing	66. Washer
5. Washer	47. Bracket	67. Nut
6. Bolt	48. Washer	68. Seal
7. Washer	49. Nut	69. Air cylinder
8. Reinforcement		
9. Bracket		
10. Nut		
11. Rivet		
12. Fitting		
13. Upper ball joint		
14. Nut		
15. Cotter pin		
16. Nut		

Two wheel drive front suspension

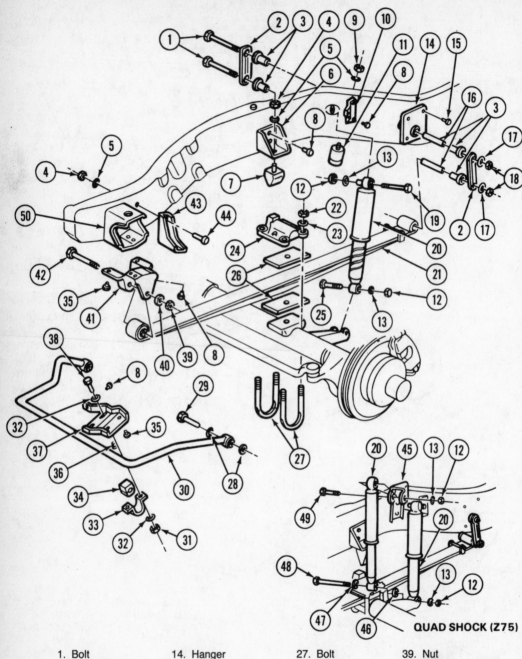

1. Bolt	14. Hanger	27. Bolt	39. Nut
2. Shackle asm	15. Rivet	28. Washer	40. Washer
3. Bushing	16. Spacer	29. Bolt	41. Hanger
4. Nut	17. Washer	30. Shaft	42. Bolt
5. Washer	18. Nut	31. Nut	43. Reinforcement
6. Bracket	19. Bolt	32. Washer	44. Bolt
7. Bumper	20. Absorber asm	33. Bracket	45. Bracket
8. Rivet	21. Spring asm	34. Brushing	46. Spacer
9. Nut	22. Nut	35. Rivet	47. Washer
10. Bracket	23. Washer	36. Rivet	48. Bolt
11. Bumper	24. Plate	37. Bracket	49. Bolt
12. Nut	25. Bolt	38. Bolt	50. Bracket
13. Washer	26. Spacer		

Four wheel drive front suspension

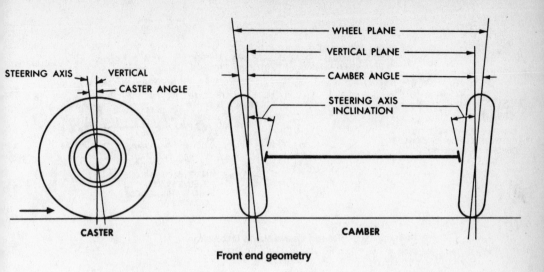

Front end geometry

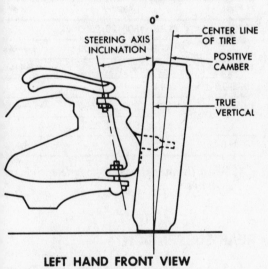

LEFT HAND FRONT VIEW

Front wheel camber

tions for camber and caster are given in relation to a measurement (the distance from the lower control arm to the bump stop bracket). This takes into account all sorts of individuality among trucks: heavy duty suspensions, tires, spring rates, and even wear on the front suspension. As a result specifications are not included in this book. Camber should not vary more than ½° from side to side.

TOE-IN

Toe-in is the amount, measured in a fraction of an inch, that the wheels are closer together in front than at the rear.

Virtually all trucks are set with toe-in. Some four wheel drive trucks require toe-out to prevent excessive toe-in under power.

NOTE: *Some alignment specialists set toe-in to the lower specified limit on vehicles with radial tires. The reason is that radial tires*

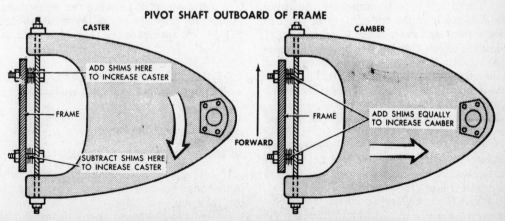

2WD front suspension showing caster adjustment shims

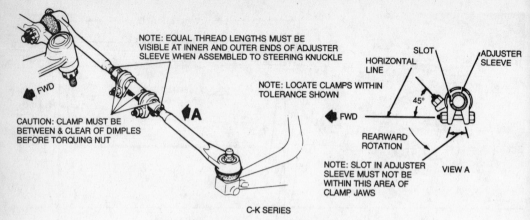

NOTE: EQUAL THREAD LENGTHS MUST BE VISIBLE AT INNER AND OUTER ENDS OF ADJUSTER SLEEVE WHEN ASSEMBLED TO STEERING KNUCKLE

CAUTION: CLAMP MUST BE BETWEEN & CLEAR OF DIMPLES BEFORE TORQUING NUT

FWD

NOTE: LOCATE CLAMPS WITHIN TOLERANCE SHOWN

SLOT

HORIZONTAL LINE

ADJUSTER SLEEVE

45°

REARWARD ROTATION

FWD

NOTE: SLOT IN ADJUSTER SLEEVE MUST NOT BE WITHIN THIS AREA OF CLAMP JAWS

VIEW A

C-K SERIES

Tie-rod sleeve clamp installation

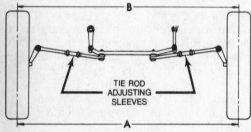

"B" IS LESS THAN "A" WHEN WHEELS TOE-IN

TIE ROD ADJUSTING SLEEVES

Toe-in adjustment

Toe-in (in.)

Year	Model	Toe-in
1970	C-10, 1500, 20, 2500	⅛–¼
	K-10, 1500, 20, 2500	³⁄₃₂–³⁄₁₆
1971	All	⅛–¼
1972–73	All	³⁄₁₆
1974–80	C-10, 1500, 20, 2500	³⁄₁₆
	K-10, 1500, 20, 2500	0
1981–87	All	³⁄₁₆

have less drag, and therefore a lesser tendency to toe-out at speed. By the same reasoning, off-road tires would require the upper limit of toe-in.

Toe-in must be checked after caster and camber have been adjusted, but it can be adjusted without disturbing the other two settings. You can make this adjustment without special equipment, if you make careful measurements. The adjustment is made at the tie rod sleeves. The wheels must be straight ahead.

1. Toe-in can be determined by measuring the distance between the centers of the tire treads, front and rear. If the tread pattern of your tires makes this impossible, you can measure between the edges of the wheel rims, but make sure to move the truck forward and measure in a couple of places to avoid errors caused by bent rims or wheel runout.

2. Loosen the clamp bolts on the tie rod sleeves.

3. Rotate the sleeves equally (in opposite directions) to obtain the correct measurement. If the sleeves are not adjusted equally, the steering wheel will be crooked.

NOTE: *If your steering wheel is already crooked, it can be straightened by turning the sleeves equally in the same direction.*

4. *When the adjustment is complete, tighten the clamps.*

REAR SUSPENSION

All two wheel drive trucks from 1970-72 use a coil spring with lateral control arm rear suspension. An auxiliary leaf spring is also used on ½ and ¾ ton trucks. In 1973 this was changed to a conventional leaf spring rear suspension. Four wheel drive trucks in all years use the traditional leaf springs in the rear. All models use one shock absorber at each rear wheel.

CAUTION: *Springs are under considerable tension. Be careful when removing and installing them; they can exert enough force to cause very serious injuries.*

Coil Spring

REMOVAL AND INSTALLATION

1. Jack up the vehicle and support it with jackstands. Position another jack under the control arm.

2. Remove the lower shock absorber bolt from its mounting on the lower control arm.

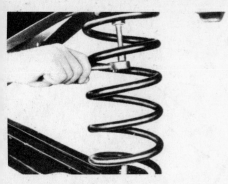

Removing the upper clamp bolt from the rear coil spring

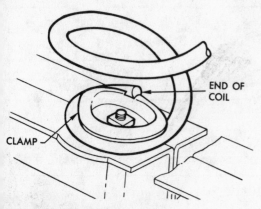

END OF COIL

CLAMP

Lower clamp bolt, rear coil spring

3. Remove the upper and lower clamps from the spring by releasing the lower bolt from the lower side of the control arm. The upper bolt is situated in the middle of the spring.

Insert a safety chain through the spring and lower control arm to prevent the spring from flying out.

4. Lower the jack under the control arm slowly until there is sufficient room to remove the spring.

5. Installation is the reverse of removal.

Auxiliary Spring (1970-72)
REMOVAL AND INSTALLATION

The auxiliary spring is attached to the frame and is removed as follows.

1. Remove all tension from the spring before attempting to remove it. Be certain that the spring leaf does not contact the bumper on the control arm.

2. Pull the cotter pin from the spring retaining bolt and then remove the nut. Remove the spring from the frame bracket.

3. If you are removing the contact bumper, support the axle with a jack, remove the U-bolts, and remove the bumper.

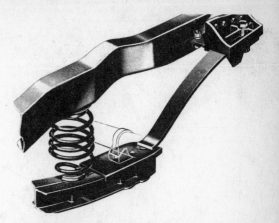

Auxiliary rear spring, 1970–72 C series

To install:

4. Place the spring bumper between the control arm and the axle housing. Make certain that the holes in the spring bracket are aligned with those in the control arm. Place the shock absorber bracket on the underside of the control arm. Place the U-bolt over the axle and through the auxiliary spring control arm and shock absorber bracket. Tighten the U-bolt retaining nuts alternately to 150 ft.lb.

5. Position the auxiliary spring assembly in the frame bracket so that the free end of the spring is above the bumper and aligned with the spring-to-bracket bolt holes. Place the bolt and washer through the top side of the bracket and then install the nut and washer on the bolt. The nut should be torqued to 370 ft.lb. Install the cotter pin.

Leaf Spring
REMOVAL AND INSTALLATION

1. Raise the vehicle and support it so that there is no tension on the leaf spring assembly.

2. Loosen the spring-to-shackle retaining bolts. (Do not remove these bolts).

3. Remove the securing bolts which attach the shackle to the spring hanger.

4. Remove the nut and bolt which attach the spring to the front hanger.

5. Remove the U-bolt nuts and remove the spring plate.

6. Pull the spring from the vehicle.

7. Inspect the spring and replace any damaged components.

NOTE: *If the spring bushings are defective, use the following procedures for removal and installation. 1975 and later ¾ ton and 1 ton trucks use bushings that are staked in place. The stakes must first be straightened. When a new bushing is installed stake it in 3 equally spaced locations.*

Using a press or vise, remove the bushing and install the new one.

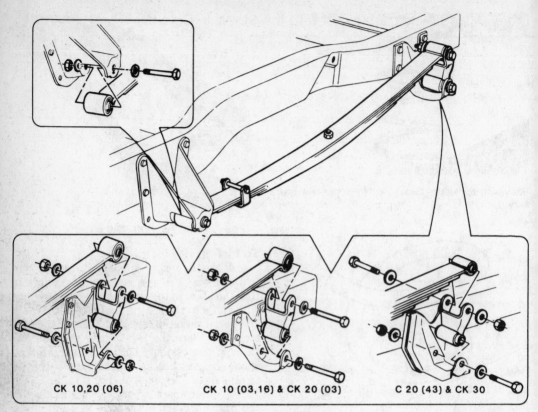

CK 10,20 (06)   CK 10 (03,16) & CK 20 (03)   C 20 (43) & CK 30

Leaf spring installation

8. Place the spring assembly onto the axle housing

NOTE: *The shackle assembly must be attached to the rear spring eye before the rear shackle is installed.*

9. Position the spring retaining plate and the U-bolts (loosely).

10. It will be necessary to jack the frame in some manner to align the spring and shackle with the spring hangers.

11. Install the shackle bolt and nut and reposition the spring if necessary in order to align the front eye. Position the front eyebolt and nut.

12. Torque the hanger and shackle fasteners to 110 ft.lb. 1977 and later, 90 ft.lb. 1973-76.

NOTE: *Make sure that the bolts are free turning in their bushings prior to torquing.*

13. Lower the truck so that the weight is on the suspension components. Torque the U-bolt nuts to 140 ft.lb.

14. Lower the truck completely and remove the jacks.

Shock Absorbers

REMOVAL AND INSTALLATION

1. Raise and support the truck.
2. Support the rear axle with a floor jack.

3. If the truck is equipped with air lift shocks, bleed the air from the lines and disconnect the line from the shock absorber.

4. Disconnect the shock absorber at the top by removing the nut and washers.

5. Remove the nut, washers and bolt from the bottom mount.

6. Remove the shock from the truck.

7. Installation is the reverse of removal. Torque the upper mount to 140 ft.lb. through 1977, or 150 ft.lb., 1978 and later; the lower to 115 ft.lb.

TESTING

See Shock Absorber Testing under Front Suspension.

STEERING

Steering Wheel

REMOVAL AND INSTALLATION

1. Disconnect the battery ground cable.
2. Remove the horn button and the receiving cap, belleville washer and bushing (if equipped).
3. Mark the steering wheel-to-steering shaft relationship.
4. On 1975 and later models, remove the snapring from the steering shaft.

Troubleshooting the Steering Column

Problem	Cause	Solution
Will not lock	• Lockbolt spring broken or defective	• Replace lock bolt spring
High effort (required to turn ignition key and lock cylinder)	• Lock cylinder defective	• Replace lock cylinder
	• Ignition switch defective	• Replace ignition switch
	• Rack preload spring broken or deformed	• Replace preload spring
	• Burr on lock sector, lock rack, housing, support or remote rod coupling	• Remove burr
	• Bent sector shaft	• Replace shaft
	• Defective lock rack	• Replace lock rack
	• Remote rod bent, deformed	• Replace rod
	• Ignition switch mounting bracket bent	• Straighten or replace
	• Distorted coupling slot in lock rack (tilt column)	• Replace lock rack
Will stick in "start"	• Remote rod deformed	• Straighten or replace
	• Ignition switch mounting bracket bent	• Straighten or replace
Key cannot be removed in "off-lock"	• Ignition switch is not adjusted correctly	• Adjust switch
	• Defective lock cylinder	• Replace lock cylinder
Lock cylinder can be removed without depressing retainer	• Lock cylinder with defective retainer	• Replace lock cylinder
	• Burr over retainer slot in housing cover or on cylinder retainer	• Remove burr
High effort on lock cylinder between "off" and "off-lock"	• Distorted lock rack	• Replace lock rack
	• Burr on tang of shift gate (automatic column)	• Remove burr
	• Gearshift linkage not adjusted	• Adjust linkage
Noise in column	• One click when in "off-lock" position and the steering wheel is moved (all except automatic column)	• Normal—lock bolt is seating
	• Coupling bolts not tightened	• Tighten pinch bolts
	• Lack of grease on bearings or bearing surfaces	• Lubricate with chassis grease
	• Upper shaft bearing worn or broken	• Replace bearing assembly
	• Lower shaft bearing worn or broken	• Replace bearing. Check shaft and replace if scored.
	• Column not correctly aligned	• Align column
	• Coupling pulled apart	• Replace coupling
	• Broken coupling lower joint	• Repair or replace joint and align column
	• Steering shaft snap ring not seated	• Replace ring. Check for proper seating in groove.
	• Shroud loose on shift bowl. Housing loose on jacket—will be noticed with ignition in "off-lock" and when torque is applied to steering wheel.	• Position shroud over lugs on shift bowl. Tighten mounting screws.
High steering shaft effort	• Column misaligned	• Align column
	• Defective upper or lower bearing	• Replace as required
	• Tight steering shaft universal joint	• Repair or replace
	• Flash on I.D. of shift tube at plastic joint (tilt column only)	• Replace shift tube
	• Upper or lower bearing seized	• Replace bearings
Lash in mounted column assembly	• Column mounting bracket bolts loose	• Tighten bolts
	• Broken weld nuts on column jacket	• Replace column jacket
	• Column capsule bracket sheared	• Replace bracket assembly

Troubleshooting the Steering Column (cont.)

Problem	Cause	Solution
Lash in mounted column assembly (cont.)	• Column bracket to column jacket mounting bolts loose	• Tighten to specified torque
	• Loose lock shoes in housing (tilt column only)	• Replace shoes
	• Loose pivot pins (tilt column only)	• Replace pivot pins and support
	• Loose lock shoe pin (tilt column only)	• Replace pin and housing
	• Loose support screws (tilt column only)	• Tighten screws
Housing loose (tilt column only)	• Excessive clearance between holes in support or housing and pivot pin diameters	• Replace pivot pins and support
	• Housing support-screws loose	• Tighten screws
Steering wheel loose—every other tilt position (tilt column only)	• Loose fit between lock shoe and lock shoe pivot pin	• Replace lock shoes and pivot pin
Steering column not locking in any tilt position (tilt column only)	• Lock shoe seized on pivot pin	• Replace lock shoes and pin
	• Lock shoe grooves have burrs or are filled with foreign material	• Clean or replace lock shoes
	• Lock shoe springs weak or broken	• Replace springs
Noise when tilting column (tilt column only)	• Upper tilt bumpers worn	• Replace tilt bumper
	• Tilt spring rubbing in housing	• Lubricate with chassis grease
One click when in "off-lock" position and the steering wheel is moved	• Seating of lock bolt	• None. Click is normal characteristic sound produced by lock bolt as it seats.
High shift effort (automatic and tilt column only)	• Column not correctly aligned	• Align column
	• Lower bearing not aligned correctly	• Assemble correctly
	• Lack of grease on seal or lower bearing areas	• Lubricate with chassis grease
Improper transmission shifting— automatic and tilt column only	• Sheared shift tube joint	• Replace shift tube
	• Improper transmission gearshift linkage adjustment	• Adjust linkage
	• Loose lower shift lever	• Replace shift tube

Troubleshooting the Ignition Switch

Problem	Cause	Solution
Ignition switch electrically inoperative	• Loose or defective switch connector	• Tighten or replace connector
	• Feed wire open (fusible link)	• Repair or replace
	• Defective ignition switch	• Replace ignition switch
Engine will not crank	• Ignition switch not adjusted properly	• Adjust switch
Ignition switch wil not actuate mechanically	• Defective ignition switch	• Replace switch
	• Defective lock sector	• Replace lock sector
	• Defective remote rod	• Replace remote rod
Ignition switch cannot be adjusted correctly	• Remote rod deformed	• Repair, straighten or replace

Troubleshooting the Turn Signal Switch

Problem	Cause	Solution
Turn signal will not cancel	• Loose switch mounting screws	• Tighten screws
	• Switch or anchor bosses broken	• Replace switch
	• Broken, missing or out of position detent, or cancelling spring	• Reposition springs or replace switch as required

Troubleshooting the Turn Signal Switch (cont.)

Problem	Cause	Solution
Turn signal difficult to operate	• Turn signal lever loose • Switch yoke broken or distorted • Loose or misplaced springs • Foreign parts and/or materials in switch • Switch mounted loosely	• Tighten mounting screws • Replace switch • Reposition springs or replace switch • Remove foreign parts and/or material • Tighten mounting screws
Turn signal will not indicate lane change	• Broken lane change pressure pad or spring hanger • Broken, missing or misplaced lane change spring • Jammed wires	• Replace switch • Replace or reposition as required • Loosen mounting screws, reposition wires and retighten screws
Turn signal will not stay in turn position	• Foreign material or loose parts impeding movement of switch yoke • Defective switch	• Remove material and/or parts • Replace switch
Hazard switch cannot be pulled out	• Foreign material between hazard support cancelling leg and yoke	• Remove foreign material. No foreign material impeding function of hazard switch—replace turn signal switch.
No turn signal lights	• Inoperative turn signal flasher • Defective or blown fuse • Loose chassis to column harness connector • Disconnect column to chassis connector. Connect new switch to chassis and operate switch by hand. If vehicle lights now operate normally, signal switch is inoperative • If vehicle lights do not operate, check chassis wiring for opens, grounds, etc.	• Replace turn signal flasher • Replace fuse • Connect securely • Replace signal switch • Repair chassis wiring as required
Instrument panel turn indicator lights on but not flashing	• Burned out or damaged front or rear turn signal bulb • If vehicle lights do not operate, check light sockets for high resistance connections, the chassis wiring for opens, grounds, etc. • Inoperative flasher • Loose chassis to column harness connection • Inoperative turn signal switch • To determine if turn signal switch is defective, substitute new switch into circuit and operate switch by hand. If the vehicle's lights operate normally, signal switch is inoperative.	• Replace bulb • Repair chassis wiring as required • Replace flasher • Connect securely • Replace turn signal switch • Replace turn signal switch
Stop light not on when turn indicated	• Loose column to chassis connection • Disconnect column to chassis connector. Connect new switch into system without removing old. Operate switch by hand. If brake lights work with switch in the turn position, signal switch is defective.	• Connect securely • Replace signal switch

Troubleshooting the Turn Signal Switch (cont.)

Problem	Cause	Solution
Stop light not on when turn indicated (cont.)	• If brake lights do not work, check connector to stop light sockets for grounds, opens, etc.	• Repair connector to stop light circuits using service manual as guide
Turn indicator panel lights not flashing	• Burned out bulbs • High resistance to ground at bulb socket • Opens, ground in wiring harness from front turn signal bulb socket to indicator lights	• Replace bulbs • Replace socket • Locate and repair as required
Turn signal lights flash very slowly	• High resistance ground at light sockets • Incorrect capacity turn signal flasher or bulb • If flashing rate is still extremely slow, check chassis wiring harness from the connector to light sockets for high resistance • Loose chassis to column harness connection • Disconnect column to chassis connector. Connect new switch into system without removing old. Operate switch by hand. If flashing occurs at normal rate, the signal switch is defective.	• Repair high resistance grounds at light sockets • Replace turn signal flasher or bulb • Locate and repair as required • Connect securely • Replace turn signal switch
Hazard signal lights will not flash—turn signal functions normally	• Blow fuse • Inoperative hazard warning flasher • Loose chassis-to-column harness connection • Disconnect column to chassis connector. Connect new switch into system without removing old. Depress the hazard warning lights. If they now work normally, turn signal switch is defective. • If lights do not flash, check wiring harness "K" lead for open between hazard flasher and connector. If open, fuse block is defective	• Replace fuse • Replace hazard warning flasher in fuse panel • Conect securely • Replace turn signal switch • Repair or replace brown wire or connector as required

Troubleshooting the Power Steering Gear

Problem	Cause	Solution
Hissing noise in steering gear	• There is some noise in all power steering systems. One of the most common is a hissing sound most evident at standstill parking. There is no relationship between this noise and performance of the steering. Hiss may be expected when steering wheel is at end of travel or when slowly turning at standstill.	• Slight hiss is normal and in no way affects steering. Do not replace valve unless hiss is extremely objectionable. A replacement valve will also exhibit slight noise and is not always a cure. Investigate clearance around flexible coupling rivets. Be sure steering shaft and gear are aligned so flexible coupling rotates in a flat plane and is not distorted as shaft rotates. Any metal-to-metal contacts through flexible coupling will transmit valve hiss into passenger compartment through the steering column.

Troubleshooting the Power Steering Gear (cont.)

Problem	Cause	Solution
Rattle or chuckle noise in steering gear	• Gear loose on frame	• Check gear-to-frame mounting screws. Tighten screws to 88 N·m (65 foot pounds) torque.
	• Steering linkage looseness	• Check linkage pivot points for wear. Replace if necessary.
	• Pressure hose touching other parts of car	• Adjust hose position. Do not bend tubing by hand.
	• Loose pitman shaft over center adjustment	• Adjust to specifications
	NOTE: A slight rattle may occur on turns because of increased clearance off the "high point." This is normal and clearance must not be reduced below specified limits to eliminate this slight rattle.	
	• Loose pitman arm	• Tighten pitman arm nut to specifications
Squawk noise in steering gear when turning or recovering from a turn	• Damper O-ring on valve spool cut	• Replace damper O-ring
Poor return of steering wheel to center	• Tires not properly inflated	• Inflate to specified pressure
	• Lack of lubrication in linkage and ball joints	• Lube linkage and ball joints
	• Lower coupling flange rubbing against steering gear adjuster plug	• Loosen pinch bolt and assemble properly
	• Steering gear to column misalignment	• Align steering column
	• Improper front wheel alignment	• Check and adjust as necessary
	• Steering linkage binding	• Replace pivots
	• Ball joints binding	• Replace ball joints
	• Steering wheel rubbing against housing	• Align housing
	• Tight or frozen steering shaft bearings	• Replace bearings
	• Sticking or plugged valve spool	• Remove and clean or replace valve
	• Steering gear adjustments over specifications	• Check adjustment with gear out of car. Adjust as required.
	• Kink in return hose	• Replace hose
Car leads to one side or the other (keep in mind road condition and wind. Test car in both directions on flat road)	• Front end misaligned	• Adjust to specifications
	• Unbalanced steering gear valve	• Replace valve
	NOTE: If this is cause, steering effort will be very light in direction of lead and normal or heavier in opposite direction	
Momentary increase in effort when turning wheel fast to right or left	• Low oil level	• Add power steering fluid as required
	• Pump belt slipping	• Tighten or replace belt
	• High internal leakage	• Check pump pressure. (See pressure test)
Steering wheel surges or jerks when turning with engine running especially during parking	• Low oil level	• Fill as required
	• Loose pump belt	• Adjust tension to specification
	• Steering linkage hitting engine oil pan at full turn	• Correct clearance
	• Insufficient pump pressure	• Check pump pressure. (See pressure test). Replace relief valve if defective.
	• Pump flow control valve sticking	• Inspect for varnish or damage, replace if necessary
Excessive wheel kickback or loose steering	• Air in system	• Add oil to pump reservoir and bleed by operating steering.

Troubleshooting the Power Steering Gear (cont.)

Problem	Cause	Solution
		Check hose connectors for proper torque and adjust as required.
	• Steering gear loose on frame	• Tighten attaching screws to specified torque
	• Steering linkage joints worn enough to be loose	• Replace loose pivots
	• Worn poppet valve	• Replace poppet valve
	• Loose thrust bearing preload adjustment	• Adjust to specification with gear out of vehicle
	• Excessive overcenter lash	• Adjust to specification with gear out of car
Hard steering or lack of assist	• Loose pump belt • Low oil level **NOTE:** Low oil level will also result in excessive pump noise	• Adjust belt tension to specification • Fill to proper level. If excessively low, check all lines and joints for evidence of external leakage. Tighten loose connectors.
	• Steering gear to column misalignment	• Align steering column
	• Lower coupling flange rubbing against steering gear adjuster plug	• Loosen pinch bolt and assemble properly
	• Tires not properly inflated	• Inflate to recommended pressure
Foamy milky power steering fluid, low fluid level and possible low pressure	• Air in the fluid, and loss of fluid due to internal pump leakage causing overflow	• Check for leak and correct. Bleed system. Extremely cold temperatures will cause system aeriation should the oil level be low. If oil level is correct and pump still foams, remove pump from vehicle and separate reservoir from housing. Check welsh plug and housing for cracks. If plug is loose or housing is cracked, replace housing.
Low pressure due to steering pump	• Flow control valve stuck or inoperative	• Remove burrs or dirt or replace. Flush system.
	• Pressure plate not flat against cam ring	• Correct
Low pressure due to steering gear	• Pressure loss in cylinder due to worn piston ring or badly worn housing bore	• Remove gear from car for disassembly and inspection of ring and housing bore
	• Leakage at valve rings, valve body-to-worm seal	• Remove gear from car for disassembly and replace seals

Troubleshooting the Power Steering Pump

Problem	Cause	Solution
Chirp noise in steering pump	• Loose belt	• Adjust belt tension to specification
Belt squeal (particularly noticeable at full wheel travel and stand still parking)	• Loose belt	• Adjust belt tension to specification
Growl noise in steering pump	• Excessive back pressure in hoses or steering gear caused by restriction	• Locate restriction and correct. Replace part if necessary.
Growl noise in steering pump (particularly noticeable at stand still parking)	• Scored pressure plates, thrust plate or rotor • Extreme wear of cam ring	• Replace parts and flush system • Replace parts

Troubleshooting the Power Steering Pump (cont.)

Problem	Cause	Solution
Groan noise in steering pump	• Low oil level • Air in the oil. Poor pressure hose connection.	• Fill reservoir to proper level • Tighten connector to specified torque. Bleed system by operating steering from right to left—full turn.
Rattle noise in steering pump	• Vanes not installed properly • Vanes sticking in rotor slots	• Install properly • Free up by removing burrs, varnish, or dirt
Swish noise in steering pump	• Defective flow control valve	• Replace part
Whine noise in steering pump	• Pump shaft bearing scored	• Replace housing and shaft. Flush system.
Hard steering or lack of assist	• Loose pump belt • Low oil level in reservoir **NOTE:** Low oil level will also result in excessive pump noise • Steering gear to column misalignment • Lower coupling flange rubbing against steering gear adjuster plug • Tires not properly inflated	• Adjust belt tension to specification • Fill to proper level. If excessively low, check all lines and joints for evidence of external leakage. Tighten loose connectors. • Align steering column • Loosen pinch bolt and assemble properly • Inflate to recommended pressure
Foaming milky power steering fluid, low fluid level and possible low pressure	• Air in the fluid, and loss of fluid due to internal pump leakage causing overflow	• Check for leaks and correct. Bleed system. Extremely cold temperatures will cause system aeriation should the oil level be low. If oil level is correct and pump still foams, remove pump from vehicle and separate reservoir from body. Check welsh plug and body for cracks. If plug is loose or body is cracked, replace body.
Low pump pressure	• Flow control valve stuck or inoperative • Pressure plate not flat against cam ring	• Remove burrs or dirt or replace. Flush system. • Correct
Momentary increase in effort when turning wheel fast to right or left	• Low oil level in pump • Pump belt slipping • High internal leakage	• Add power steering fluid as required • Tighten or replace belt • Check pump pressure. (See pressure test)
Steering wheel surges or jerks when turning with engine running especially during parking	• Low oil level • Loose pump belt • Steering linkage hitting engine oil pan at full turn • Insufficient pump pressure	• Fill as required • Adjust tension to specification • Correct clearance • Check pump pressure. (See pressure test). Replace flow control valve if defective.
Steering wheel surges or jerks when turning with engine running especially during parking (cont.)	• Sticking flow control valve	• Inspect for varnish or damage, replace if necessary
Excessive wheel kickback or loose steering	• Air in system	• Add oil to pump reservoir and bleed by operating steering. Check hose connectors for proper torque and adjust as required.

Troubleshooting the Power Steering Pump (cont.)

Problem	Cause	Solution
Low pump pressure	• Extreme wear of cam ring	• Replace parts. Flush system.
	• Scored pressure plate, thrust plate, or rotor	• Replace parts. Flush system.
	• Vanes not installed properly	• Install properly
	• Vanes sticking in rotor slots	• Freeup by removing burrs, varnish, or dirt
	• Cracked or broken thrust or pressure plate	• Replace part

5. Remove the nut and washer from the steering shaft.

6. Remove the steering wheel with a puller. WARNING: *Don't hammer on the steering shaft.*

7. Installation is the reverse of removal. The turn signal control assembly must be in the Neutral position to prevent damaging the cancelling cam and control assembly. Tighten the nut to 40 ft.lb. 1970-72, 30 ft.lb. 1973 and later.

NOTE: *A steering wheel puller can be made by drilling two holes in a piece of steel the same distance apart as the two threaded holes in the steering wheel. Sometimes an old spring shackle will have the right dimensions. Drill another hole in the center. Place a center bolt with the head against the steering shaft and a nut against the bottom of the homemade puller bar. Thread the two outer bolts into the holes into the wheel. Unscrew the nut on the center bolt to draw the wheel off the shaft.*

Turn Signal Switch
REPLACEMENT
1970-72

1. Disconnect the battery ground cable.

2. Remove the steering wheel, preload spring, and concelling cam.

3. Remove the shaft lever roll pin and shaft lever (if applicable).

4. Remove the turn signal lever screw and the lever.

5. Push the hazard warning knob in. This must be done to avoid damaging the switch.

6. Disconnect the switch wire from the chassis harness located under the dash.

7. Remove the mast jacket upper bracket.

8. Remove the switch wiring cover from the column.

9. Unscrew the mounting screws and remove the switch, bearing housing, switch cover, and shaft housing from the column.

10. Installation is the reverse of removal.

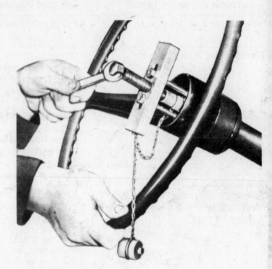

Steering wheel removal

1973 and Later

1. Remove the steering wheel as previously outlined.

2. Loosen the three cover screws and lift the cover off the shaft. On 1976-80 models, place a drift pin in the cover slot and pry out to free the cover.

3. The round lockplate must be pushed down to remove the wire snapring from the shaft. A special tool is available to do this. The tool is an inverted U-shape with a hole for the shaft. The shaft nut is used to force it down. Pry the wire snapring out of the shaft groove. Discard the snapring.

4. Remove the tool and lift the lockplate off the shaft.

5. Slip the cancelling cam, upper bearing preload spring, and thrust washer off the shaft.

6. Remove the turn signal lever. Push the flasher knob in and unscrew it.

7. Pull the switch connector out of the mast jacket and tape the upper part to facilitate switch removal. On tilt wheels, place the turn signal and shifter housing in Low position and remove the harness cover.

8. Remove the three switch mounting screws. Remove the switch by pulling it straight

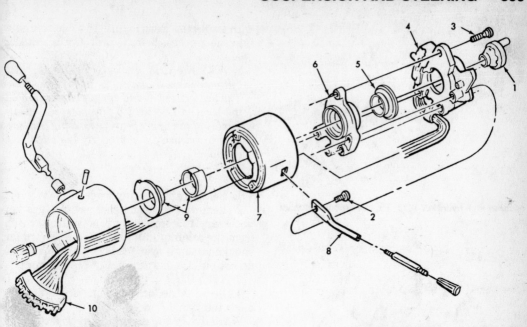

1. Cancelling cam
2. Directional lever retaining screw
3. Switch mounting screw
4. Switch
5. Upper bearing

6. Bearing support
7. Switch cover
8. Lever arm
9. Washer
10. Wiring connector

1970–72 turn signal switch

up while guiding the wiring harness cover through the column.

9. Install the replacement switch by working the connector and cover down through the housing and under the bracket. On tilt models, the connector is worked down through the housing, under the bracket, and then the cover is installed on the harness.

10. Install the switch mounting screws and the connector on the mast jacket bracket. Install the column-to-dash trim plate.

11. Install the flasher knob and the turn signal lever.

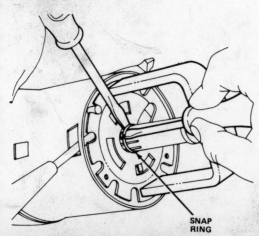

SNAP
RING

Removing the lockplate retaining ring

12. With the turn signal lever in neutral and the flasher knob out, slide the thrust washer, upper bearing preload spring, and cancelling cam into the shaft.

13. Position the lockplate on the shaft and press it down until a new snapring can be inserted in the shaft groove.

14. Install the cover and the steering wheel.

Lock Cylinder
REMOVAL AND INSTALLATION
1973-78

1. Remove steering wheel and turn signal switch.
   NOTE: It is not necessary to completely remove the turn signal switch. Pull the switch over the end of the shaft; no further.
2. Place lock cylinder in Run position.
   NOTE: *Do not remove the ignition key buzzer.*
3. Insert a small drift pin into the turn signal housing slot. Keeping the drift pin to the right side of the slot, break the housing flash loose and depress the spring latch at the lower end of the lock cylinder. Remove the lock cylinder.
   WARNING: *Considerable force may be necessary to break this casting flash, but be careful not to damage any other parts. When ordering a new lock cylinder, specify a cylinder*

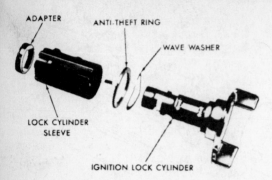

Ignition lock cylinder, 1973–78; later models similar

Ignition lock cylinder removal, 1973–78

assembly. This will save assembling the cylinder, washer, sleeve and adapter.

4. To install, hold the lock cylinder sleeve and rotate the knob clockwise against the stop. Insert the cylinder into the housing, aligning the key and keyway. Hold a 0.070″ drill between the lock bezel and housing. Rotate the cylinder counterclockwise, maintaining a light pressure until the drive section of the cylinder mates

with the sector. Push in until the snapring pops into the grooves. Remove drill. Check cylinder operation.

NOTE: *The drill prevents forcing the lock cylinder inward beyond its normal position. The buzzer switch and spring latch can hold the lock cylinder in too far. Complete disassembly of the upper bearing housing is necessary to release an improperly installed lock cylinder.*

1979 and Later

1. Remove the steering wheel.
2. Remove the turn signal switch. It is not necessary to completely remove the switch from the column. Pull the switch rearward far enough to slip it over the end of the shaft, but do not pull the harness out of the column.
3. Turn the lock to Run.
4. Remove the lock retaining screw and remove the lock cylinder.

WARNING: *If the retaining screw is dropped on removal, it may fall into the column, requiring complete disassembly of the column to retrieve the screw.*

5. To install, rotate the key to the stop while holding onto the cylinder.
6. Push the lock all the way in.
7. Install the screw. Tighten the screw to 3 ft.lb. for regular columns, 2 ft.lb. for adjustable columns.
8. Install the turn signal switch and the steering wheel.

Ignition Switch

REMOVAL AND INSTALLATION

1973 And Later

The switch is on the steering column, behind the instrument panel.

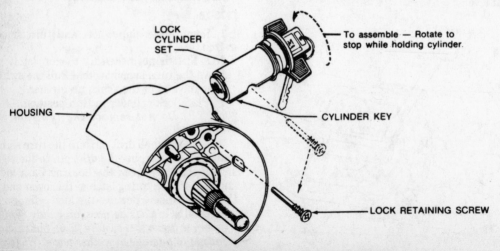

1979 and later ignition lock cylinder removal and installation

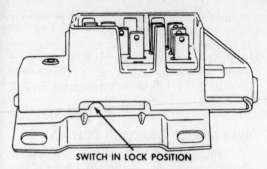

SWITCH IN LOCK POSITION

1973 and later ignition switch assembly showing switch in "Lock" position for removal

1. Lower the steering column, making sure that it is supported.

WARNING: *Extreme care is necessary to prevent damage to the collapsible column.*

2. Make sure that the switch is in the Lock position. If the lock cylinder is out, pull the switch rod up to the stop, then go down one detent.

3. Remove the two screws and the switch.

4. Before installation, make sure the switch is in the Lock position.

5. Install the switch using the original screws.

CAUTION: *Use of screws that are too long could prevent the column from collapsing on impact.*

6. Replace the column.

Steering Column

To perform service procedures on the steering column upper end components, it is not necessary to remove the column from the vehicle.

The steering wheel, horn components, directional signal switch, and ignition lock cylinder may be removed with the column remaining in the vehicle as described earlier in this section.

WARNING: *The outer most jacket shift tube, steering shaft and instrument panel mount-*

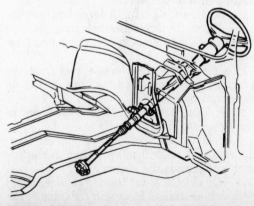

Steering Column

ing bracket are designed as energy absorbing units. Because of the design of these components, it is absolutely necessary to handle the column with care when performing any service operation. Avoid hammering, jarring, dropping or leaning on any portion of the column. When reassembling the column components, use only the specified screws, nuts and bolts and tighten to specified torque. Care should be exercised in using over-length screws or bolts as they may prevent a portion of the column from compressing under impact.

INSPECTION

To determine if the energy absorbing steering column components are functioning as designed, or if repairs are required, a close inspection should be made. Inspection is called for in all cases where damage is evident or whenever the vehicle is being repaired due to a front end collision. Whenever a force has been exerted on the steering wheel or steering column, or its components, inspection should also be made. If damage is evident, the affected parts must be replaced.

The inspection procedure for the various steering column components on all C-K Series Trucks is as follows:

Column Support Bracket

Damage in this area will be indicated by separation of the mounting capsules from the bracket. The bracket will have moved forward toward the engine compartment and will usually result in collapsing of the jacket section of the steering column.

Column Jacket

Inspect jacket section of column for looseness, and/or bends.

Shifter Shaft

Separation of the shifter shaft sections will be internal and cannot be visually identified. Hold lower end of the shifter shaft and move shift lever on column through its ranges and up and down. If there is little or no movement of the shifter shaft, the plastic joints are sheared.

Steering Shaft

If the steering shaft plastic pins have been sheared, the shaft will rattle when struck lightly from the side and some lash may be felt when rotating the steering wheel while holding the rag joint. It should be noted that if the steering shaft pins are sheared due to minor collision the vehicle can be safely steered; however, steering shaft replacement is recommended.

Because of the differences in the steering col-

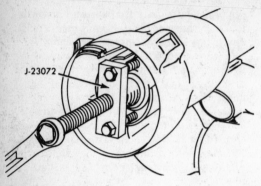

Removing Shift Tube

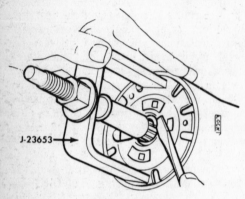

Removing Lock Plate Retaining Ring

umn types, be sure to refer to the set of instructions below which apply to the column being serviced.

REMOVAL

Front of dash mounting plates must be loosened whenever the steering column is to be lowered from the instrunet panel.

1. Disconnect the battery ground cable.

2. Remove the steering wheel as outlined under Steering Wheel Removal.

3. Remove the nuts and washers securing the flanged end of the steering shaft to the flexible coupling.

4. Disconnect the transmission control linkage from the column shift tube levers.

5. Disconnect the steering column harness at the connector. Disconnect the neutral start switch and back-up lamp switch connectors if so equipped.

6. Remove the floor pan trim cover screws and remove the cover.

7. Remove the transmission indicator cable, if so equipped.

8. Remove the screws securing the two halves of the floor pan cover, then remove the screws securing the halves and seal to the floor pan and remove the covers.

9. Move the front seat as far back as possible to provide maximum clearance.

10. Remove the two column bracket-to-instrument panel nuts and carefully remove from vehicle. Additional help should be obtained to guide the lower shift levers through the firewall opening.

DISASSEMBLY STANDARD COLUMN

1. Remove the four dash panel bracket-to-column screws and lay the bracket in a safe place to prevent damage to the mounting capsules.

2. Place the column in a vise using both weld nuts of either Set A or B or shown in Figure. The vise jaws must clamp onto the sides of the weld nuts indicated by arrows shown on Set B.
WARNING: *Do not place the column in a vise by clamping onto one weld nut of both sets A and B or by clamping onto the sides not indicated by arrows, since damage to the column could result.*

3. Remove the Directional Signal Switch, Lock Cylinder, and Ignition Switch as outlined previously in this section.

4. Column Shift Models — Drive out the upper shift lever pivot pin and remove the shift lever.

5. Remove the upper bearing thrust washer. Remove the four screws attaching the turn signal and ignition lock housing to the jacket and remove the housing assembly.

6. Remove the thrust cap from the lower side of the housing.

7. Lift the ignition switch actuating rod and rack assembly, the rack preload spring and the shaft lock bolt and spring assembly out of the housing.

8. Remove the shift lever detent plate (shift gate).

9. Remove the ignition switch actuator sector through the lock cylinder hole by pushing firmly on the block tooth of the sector with a blunt punch or screwdriver.

10. Remove the gearshift lever housing and shroud from the jacket assembly (transmission control lock tube housing and shroud on floor shift models).

11. Remove the shift lever spring from the gearshift lever housing (lock tube spring on floor shift models).

12. Pull the steering shaft from lower end of the jacket assembly.

13. Remove the two screws holding the back-up switch or neutral safety switch to the column and remove the switch.

14. Remove the lower bearing retainer clip.

15. Automatic and Floorshift Columns — Remove the lower bearing retainer, bearing adapt-

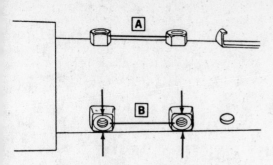

Installing Steering Column in Vise

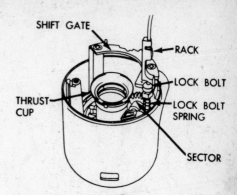

Turn Signal Housing Assembly

SHIFT GATE
RACK
THRUST CUP
LOCK BOLT
LOCK BOLT SPRING
SECTOR

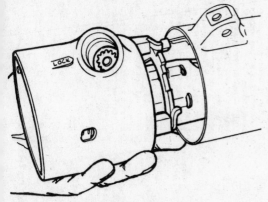

Removing Turn Signal Housing

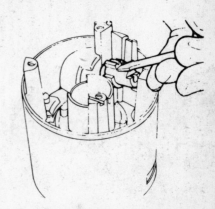

Removing Ignitiion Switch Actuator Sector

er assembly, shift tube thrust spring and washer. The lower bearing may be removed from the adapter by light pressure on the bearing outer race. Slide out the shift tube assembly.

Manual Transmission – Column Shift – Remove the lower bearing adapter, bearing and the first reverse shift lever. The lower bearing may be removed from the adapter by light pressure on the bearing outer race. Remove the three screws from bearing at the lower end and slide out the shift tube assembly. Remove the gearshift housing lower bearing from the upper end of the mast jacket.

ASSEMBLY STANDARD COLUMNS

Apply a thin coat of lithium soap grease to all friction surfaces.

1. Install the sector into the turn signal and lock cylinder housing. Install the sector in the lock cylinder hole over the sector shaft with the tang end to the outside of the hole. Press the sector over the shaft with a blunt tool.

2. Install the shift lever detent plate onto the housing.

3. Insert the rack preload spring into the housing from the bottom side. The long section should be toward the handwheel and hook onto the edge of the housing.

4. Assemble the locking bolt onto the crossover arm on the rack and insert the rack and lock bolt assembly into the housing from the bottom with the teeth up (toward handwheel) and toward the centerline of the column. Align the 1st tooth on the sector with the 1st tooth on the rack; if aligned properly, the block teeth will line up when the rack assembly is pushed all the way in.

5. Install the thrust cup on the bottom hub of the housing.

6. Install the gearshift housing lower bearing. Insert the bearing from the very end of the

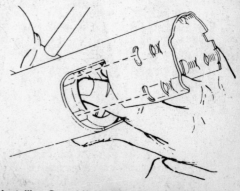

Installing Gearshift Housing Lower Bearing

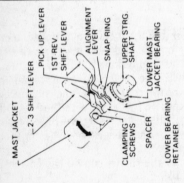

MAST JACKET
2-3 SHIFT LEVER
PICK UP LEVER
1ST-REV. SHIFT LEVER
ALIGNMENT LEVER
SNAP RING
UPPER STRG. SHAFT
LOWER MAST JACKET BEARING
CLAMPING SCREWS
.005 IN. SHIM
SPACER
LOWER BEARING RETAINER

A. TO REDUCE CLEARANCE
SLIDE THE CLAMPING SCREWS AROUND THE MAST JACKET IN THE DIRECTION OF ARROW A.

B. TO INCREASE CLEARANCE
SLIDE THE CLAMPING SCREWS AROUND THE MAST JACKET IN THE DIRECTION OF ARROW B

ADJUSTMENT PROCEDURE

1. WITH THE TRANSMISSION IN NEUTRAL DISCONNECT THE TRANSMISSION RODS.
2. TEST FOR ROTATIONAL DRAG BY TURNING THE SHIFT LEVER (INSIDE TRUCK) THROUGH THE 2-3 SHIFT ARC. DRAG MEASURED AT THE SHIFT KNOB MUST BE NO MORE THAN 2.0 LBS. IF DRAG IS MORE THAN 2.0 LBS. CORRECTIONS MUST BE MADE BEFORE PROCEEDING WITH THIS ADMUSTMENT.
3. LOOSEN THE THREE CLAMPING SCREWS.
4. INSTALL A .005 IN. THICK SHIM BETWEEN THE SPACE AND EITHER OF THE SHIFT LEVERS. THE ABOVE ILLUSTRATION SHOWS THE SHIM BETWEEN THE SPACER AND THE 2-3 SHIFT LEVER.
5. SLIDE THE CLAMPING SCREWS IN DIRECTION OF ARROW B UNTIL THE SYSTEM IS LOOSE. THEN SLIDE THE SCREWS IN OPPOSITE DIRECTION UNTIL A DEFINITE DRAG IS FELT AT THE 1ST-REV. SHIFT LEVER.
6. TIGHTEN THE CLAMPING SCREWS.
7. REMOVE THE SHIM.
8. REINSTALL THE TRANSMISSION RODS.

NOTE: IF THERE IS NO PROBLEM WITH STEERING COLUMN DRAG. THIS ADJUSTMENT CAN BE MADE BY DISCONNECTING ONLY THE 1ST. REV. TRANSMISSION ROD AND OMITTING STEP. 2.

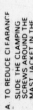

MAST JACKET
2-3 SHIFT LEVER
PICK UP LEVER
1ST-REV. SHIFT LEVER
ALIGNMENT LEVER
SNAP RING
UPPER STRG. SHAFT
LOWER MAST JACKET BEARING
CLAMPING SCREWS
SPACER
LOWER BEARING RETAINER

A. TO REDUCE CLEARANCE
SLIDE THE CLAMPING SCREWS AROUND THE MAST JACKET IN THE DIRECTION OF ARROW A.

B. TO INCREASE CLEARANCE
SLIDE THE CLAMPING SCREWS AROUND THE MAST JACKET IN THE DIRECTION OF ARROW B

ADJUSTMENT PROCEDURE

1. WITH THE TRANSMISSION IN NEUTRAL DISCONNECT THE TRANSMISSION RODS.
2. TEST FOR ROTATIONAL DRAG BY TURNING THE SHIFT LEVER (INSIDE TRUCK) THROUGH THE 2-3 SHIFT ARC. DRAG, MEASURED AT THE SHIFT KNOB, MUST BE NO MORE THAN 2.0 LBS. IF DRAG IS MORE THAN 2.0 LBS. CORRECTIONS MUST BE MADE BEFORE PROCEEDING WITH THE ADJUSTMENT.
3. LOOSEN THE THREE CLAMPING SCREWS.
4. INCREASE CLEARANCE BY SLIDING THE CLAMPING SCREWS IN DIRECTION OF ARROW "B" ABOVE UNTIL THE 1ST-REV. SHIFT LEVER COMPLETELY FREE OF DRAG.
5. DECREASE CLEARANCE BY SLIDING THE CLAMPING SCREWS IN DIRECTION OF ARROW "A" ABOVE UNTIL A SLIGHT DRAG IS FELT AT THE 1ST-REV. SHIFT LEVER.
6. TIGHTEN THE THREE CLAMPING SCREWS.
7. RECONNECT THE TRANSMISSION RODS.

NOTE: IF NO PROBLEM WITH STEERING COLUMN DRAG IS INVOLVED, THIS ADJUSTMENT CAN BE MADE BY DISCONNECTING ONLY THE 1ST. REV. TRANSMISSION ROD AND OMITTING STEP 2.

Adjusting Lower Bearing-Typical

jacket. Aligning the indentations in the bearing with the projections on the jacket. If the bearing is not installed correctly, it will not rest on all of the stops provided.

7. Install the shift lever spring into the gearshift lever (or lock tube) housing. Install the housing and shroud assemblies onto the upper end of the mast jacket. Rotate the housing to be sure it is seated in the bearing.

8. With the shift lever housing in place, install the turn signal and lock cylinder housing onto the jacket. The gearshift housing should be in **Park** position and the rack pulled downward. Be sure the turn signal housing is seated on the jacket and drive the four screws.

9. Press the lower bearing into the adapter assembly.

10. Insert the shift tube assembly into the lower end of the jacket and rotate until the upper shift tube key slides into the housing keyway.

11. Automatic and Floor Shift Columns — Assemble the spring and lower bearing and adapter assembly into the bottom of the jacket. Holding the adapter in place, install the lower bearing reinforcement and retainer clip. Be sure the clip snaps into the jacket and reinforcement slots.

12. Manual Transmission — Column Shift — Loosely attach the three screws in the jacket and shift tube bearing. Assemble the 1st/Reverse lever and lower bearing and adapter assembly into the bottom of the jacket. Holding the adapter in place, install the bearing reinforcement and retaining clip. Be sure the retaining clip snaps into the jacket and reinforcement slots.

13. Install the neutral safety or back-up switch as outlined in Section 8 of this manual.

14. Slide the steering shaft into the column and install the upper bearing thrust washer.

15. Install the turn signal switch, lock cylinder assembly and ignition switch as previously outlined in this section.

16. Install the shift lever and shift lever pivot pin.

17. Remove the column from the vise.

18. Install the dash bracket to the column; torque the screws to specifications.

DISASSEMBLY

Tilt Columns

Steps 3-14 may be performed with the steering column in the vehicle.

1. Remove the four screws retaining the dash mounting bracket to the column and set the bracket aside to protect the breakaway capsules.

2. Mount the column in a vise using both weld nuts of either Set A or B. The vise jaws must clamp onto the sides of the weld nuts indicated by arrows shown on Set B.

WARNING: *Do not place the column in a vise by clamping onto only one weld nut, by clamping onto one weld nut of both Sets A and B or by clamping onto the sides not indicated by arrows, since damage to the column could result.*

3. Remove the directional signal switch, lock cylinder and ignition switch as outlined previously in this section.

4. Remove the tilt release lever. Drive out the shift lever pivot pin and remove the shift lever from the housing.

5. Remove the three turn signal housing screws and remove the housing.

6. Install the tilt release lever and place the column in the full up position. Remove the tilt lever spring retainer using a #3 phillips screwdriver that just fits into the slot opening. Insert the phillips screwdriver in the slot, press in approximately $3/16''$, turn approximately ⅛ turn counterclockwise until the ears align the the grooves in the housing and remove the retainer, spring and guide.

7. Remove the pot joint to steering shaft clamp bolt and remove the intermediate shaft and pot joint assembly. Push the upper steering shaft in sufficiently to remove the steering shaft upper bearing inner race and seat. Pry off the lower bearing retainer clip and remove the bearing reinforcement, bearing and bearing adapter assembly from the lower end of the mast jacket.

8. Remove the upper bearing housing pivot pins using Tool J-21854-1.

9. Install the tilt release lever and disengage the lock shoes. Remove the bearing housing by pulling upward to extend the rack full down, and then moving the housing to the left to disengage the ignition switch rack from the actuator rod.

10. Remove the steering shaft assembly from the upper end of the column.

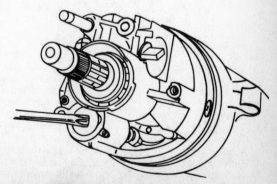

Removing Tilt Lever Spring Retainer

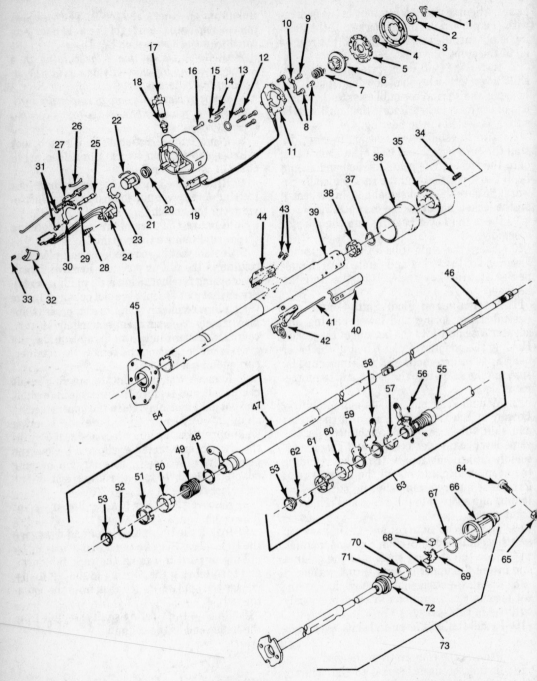

Standard steering column-column shift

1. Retainer	13. Washer	25. Shaft lock bolt
2. Nut	14. Tone alarm switch	26. Switch rack preload spring
3. Lock plate cover	15. Retainer clip	27. Actuator rack
4. Retainer	16. Retainer screw	28. Actuator pivot pin
5. Lock plate	17. Ignition lock	29. Washer
6. Cancelling cam	18. Actuator sector	30. Shift lever gate
7. Bearing preload spring	19. Housing assembly	31. Shift lever screw
8. Turn signal screws	20. Bearing	32. Housing cover
9. Tap screw	21. Bushing	33. Cover screw
10. Actuator arm	22. Horn contact	34. Shift lever spring
11. Turn signal switch	23. Upper bearing retainer	35. Gear shift housing
12. Turn signal housing screws	24. Dimmer pivot and wiper switch	36. Gear shift shroud

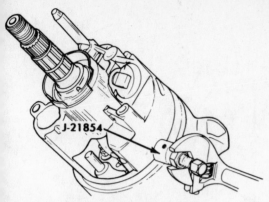

Removing Bearing Housing Pivots Pins

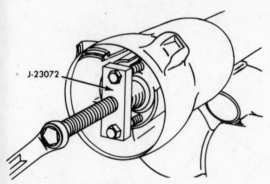

Removing Shift Tube

11. Disassemble the steering shaft by removing the centering spheres and the anti-lash spring.

12. Remove the transmission indicator wire, if so equipped.

13. Remove the four steering shaft bearing housing support to gearshift housing screws and remove the bearing housing support. Remove the ignition switch actuator rod.

14. Remove the shift tube retaining rings with a screwdriver and then remove the thrust washer.

15. Install Tool J-23072 into the lock plate, making sure that the tool screws have good thread engagement in the lock plate, then turning the center screw clockwise, force the shift tube from the housing. Remove the shift tube (transmission control lock tube on floor shift models) from the lower end of the mast jacket. Remove Tool J-23072.

WARNING: *When removing the shift tube, be sure to guide the lower end through the slotted opening in the mast jacket. If the tube is allowed to interfere with the jacket in any way, damage to the tube and jacket could result.*

16. Remove the bearing housing support lock plate by sliding it out of the jacket notches, tipping it down toward the housing hub at the 12 o'clock position and sliding it under the jacket opening. Remove the wave washer.

17. All columns — Remove the shift lever housing from the mast jacket (transmission control lock tube housing on floor shift models). Remove the shift lever spring by winding the spring up with pliers and pulling it out. On floor shift models, remove the spring plunger.

18. Disassemble the bearing housing as follows:

a. Remove the tilt lever opening shield.

b. Remove the lock bolt spring by removing the retaining screw and moving the spring clockwise to remove it from the bolt.

c. Remove the snaping from the sector driveshaft. With a small punch, lightly tap the driveshaft from the sector. Remove the driveshaft, sector and lock bolt. Remove the rack and rack spring.

d. Remove the tilt release lever pin with a punch and hammer. Remove the lever and release lever spring. To relieve the load on the release lever, hold the shoes inward and wedge a block between the top of the shoes (over slots) and bearing housing.

e. Remove the lock shoe retaining pin with a punch and hammer. Remove the lock shoes and lock shoe springs. With the tilt lever opening on the left side and shoes facing up, the four slot shoe is on the left.

37. Washer	50. Adapter	62. Adapter clip
38. Gear shift housing bearing	51. Reinforcement	63. Manual transmission
39. Jacket	52. Adapter clip	64. Bolt
40. Wiring protector	53. Lower bearing	65. Nut
41. Actuator rod	54. Automatic transmission	66. Coupling
42. Dimmer switch	55. Shift tube	67. Retainer
43. Ignition switch screw	56. Bolt	68. Bearing
44. Ignition switch	57. Spacer	69. Spring
45. Dash seal	58. Lower shift lever	70. Washer
46. Shaft	59. Adapter plate	71. Pin
47. Shift tube	60. Adapter	72. Seal
48. Washer	61. Retainer	73. Intermediate shaft
49. Spring		

Standard steering column-column shift

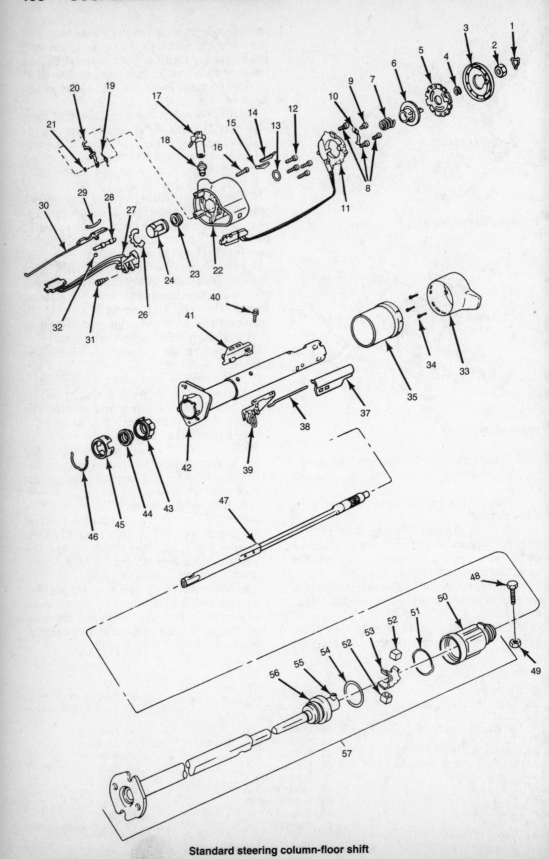

Standard steering column-floor shift

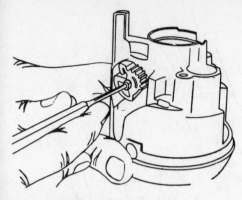

Removing Sector Drive Shaft

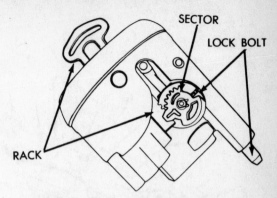

Installaing Lock Bolt and Rack Assemblies

f. Remove the bearings from the bearing housing only if they are to be replaced. Remove the separator and balls from the bearings. Place the housing on work bench and with a pointed punch against the back surface of the race, carefully hammer the race out of the housing until a bearing puller an be used. Repeat for the other race.

ASSEMBLY

Tilt Columns

Apply a thin coat of lithium grease to all friction surfaces.

1. If the bearing housing was disassembled, repeat the following steps:

a. Press the bearings into the housing, if removed, using a suitable size socket. Be careful not to damage the housing or bearing during installation.

b. Install the lock shoe springs, lock shoes and shoe pin in the housing. Use an approximate 0.180" rod to line up the shoes for pin installation.

c. Install the shoe release lever, spring and

pin. To relieve the load on the release lever, hold the shoes inward and wedge a block between the top of the shoes (over slots) and bearing housing.

d. Install the sector driveshaft into the housing. Lightly tap the sector onto the shaft far enough to install the snapring. Install the snapring.

e. Install the lock bolt and engage it with the sector cam surface. Then install the rack and spring. The block tooth on the rack should engage the block tooth on the sector. Install the external tilt release lever.

f. Install the lock bolt spring and retaining screw. Tighten the screw to 35 in.lb.

2. Install the shift lever spring into the housing by winding it up with pliers and pushing it into the housing. On floor shift models, install the plunger, slide the gearshift lever housing onto the mast jacket.

3. Install the bearing support lock plate wave washer.

4. Install the bearing support lock plate. Work it into the notches in the jacket by tipping it toward the housing hub at the 12 o'clock posi-

1. Retainer	20. Key release lever	39. Dimmer switch
2. Nut	21. Key release washer	40. Ignition switch screw
3. Lock plate cover	22. Housing assembly	41. Ignition switch
4. Retainer	23. Bearing	42. Dash seal
5. Lock plate	24. Bushing	43. Adapter
6. Cancelling cam	25. Horn contact	44. Bearing
7. Bearing preload spring	26. Upper bearing retainer	45. Reinforcement
8. Turn signal screws	27. Dimmer pivot and wiper switch	46. Adapter clip
9. Tap screw	28. Shaft lock bolt	47. Shaft
10. Actuator arm	29. Switch rack preload spring	48. Bolt
11. Turn signal switch	30. Actuator rack	49. Nut
12. Turns ignal housing screws	31. Actuator pivot pin	50. Coupling
13. Washer	32. Washer	51. Retainer
14. Tone alarm switch	33. Gear shift housing	52. Bearing
15. Retainer clip	34. Signal switch mounting screws	53. Spring
16. Retainer screw	35. Gear shift housing	54. Washer
17. Ignition lock	36. Jacket	55. Pin
18. Actuator sector	37. Wiring protector	56. Seal
19. Key release spring	38. Actuator rod	57. Intermediate shaft

Standard steering column-floor shift

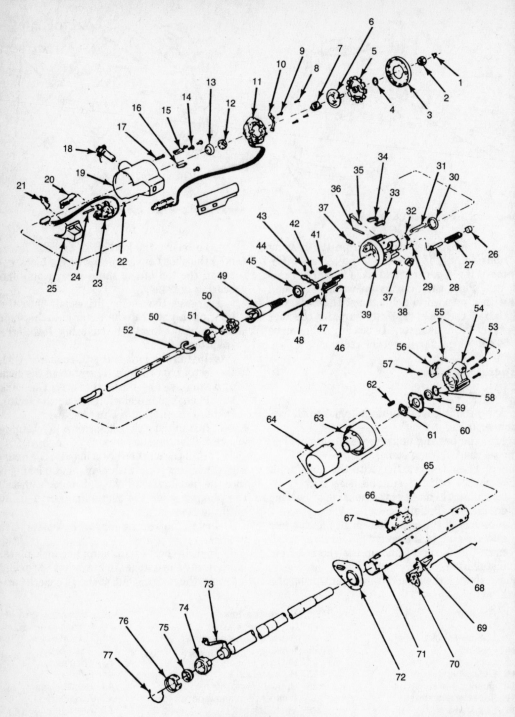

Tilt steering column-column shift

1. Retainer	11. Turn signal switch	21. Shield
2. Nut	12. Inner race seat	22. Pin preload spring
3. Lock plate cover	13. Bearing race	23. Pivot switch
4. Retainer	14. Screw	24. Actuator pivot pin
5. Lock plate	15. Tone arlarm switch	25. Cap
6. Cancelling cam	16. Retainer clip	26. Retainer
7. Bearing preload spring	17. Lock retainer screw	27. Tilt spring
8. Turn signal screws	18. Ignition lock	28. Spring guide
9. Tap screw	19. Housing cover	29. Screw
10. Actuator arm	20. Dimmer switch actuator	30. Bearing

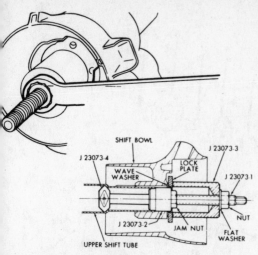

SHIFT BOWL

J 23073-4

J 23073-3

WAVE WASHER

LOCK PLATE

J 23073-1

J 23073-2

NUT

JAM NUT

FLAT WASHER

UPPER SHIFT TUBE

Installing Shift Tube

tion and sliding it under the jacket opening. Slide the lock plate into the notches in the jacket.

5. Carefully install the shift tube into the lower end of the mast jacket. Align keyway in the tube with the key in the shift lever housing. Install the wobble plate end of Tool J-23073 into the upper end of the shift tube far enough to reach the enlarged portion of the tube. Then install the adapter over the end of the tool, seating it against the lock plate. Place the nut on the threaded end of the tool and pull the shift tube into the housing. Remove Tool J-23073.

WARNING: *Do not push or tap on the end of the shift tube. Be sure that the shift tube lever is aligned with the slotted opening at the lower end of the mast jacket or damage to the shift tube and mast jacket could result.*

6. Install the bearing support thrust washer and retaining ring by pulling the shift lever housing up far enough to compress the wave washer.

7. Install the bearing support by aligning the

V in the support with the V in the jacket. Insert the screws through the support and into the lock plate and torque to 60 in.lb.

8. Align the lower bearing adapter with the notches in the jacket and push the adapter into the lower end of the mast jacket. Install lower bearing, bearing reinforcement and retaining clip, being sure that the clip is aligned with the slots in the reinforcement, jacket and adapter.

9. Install the centering spheres and anti-lash spring in the upper shaft. Install the lower shaft from the same side of the spheres that the spring ends protrude.

10. Install the steering shaft assembly into the shift tube from the upper end. Carefully guide the shaft through the shift tube and bearing.

11. Install the ignition switch actuator rod through the shift lever housing and insert in the slot in the bearing support. Extend the rack downward from the bearing housing.

12. Assemble the bearing housing over the steering shaft and engage the rack over the end of the actuator rod.

13. With the external release lever installed, hold the lock shoes in the disengaged position and assemble the bearing housing over the steering shaft until the pivot pin holes line up.

14. Install the pivot pins.

15. Place the bearing housing in the full up position and install the tilt lever spring guide, spring and spring retainer. With a suitable screwdriver, push the retainer in and turn clockwise to engage in the housing.

16. Install the upper bearing inner race and race seat.

17. Install the tilt lever opening shield.

18. Remove the tilt release lever, install the turn signal housing and torque the three retaining screws to 45 in.lb.

19. Install the tilt release lever and shift lever. Drive the shift lever pin in.

20. Install the lock cylinder, turn signal

1. Lock bolt
2. Lock bolt spring
3. Lock shoe
4. Lock shoe
5. Sector shaft
6. Lock shoe pin
7. Pivot pin
8. Actuator sector
9. Housing assembly
1. Shoe release springs
2. Spring
3. Shoe release lever pin
4. Shoe release lever
5. Lower bearing
6. Rack preload spring
7. Actuator rack

48. Ignition switch actuator
49. Sphere spring
50. Centering spheres
51. Spring
52. Lower steering shaft
53. Housing support screws
54. Housing support
55. Pin
56. Shift lever gate
57. Detent plate screw
58. Retaining ring
59. Washer
60. Lock plate
61. Wave washer
62. Gear shift lever spring

63. Gear shift lever bowl
64. Shroud
65. Screw
66. Stud
67. Switch
68. Dimmer switch rod
69. Nut
70. Dimmer switch
71. Jacket
72. Dash seal
73. Shift tube
74. Adapter
75. Lower bearing
76. Retainer
77. Adapter clip

Tilt steering column-column shift

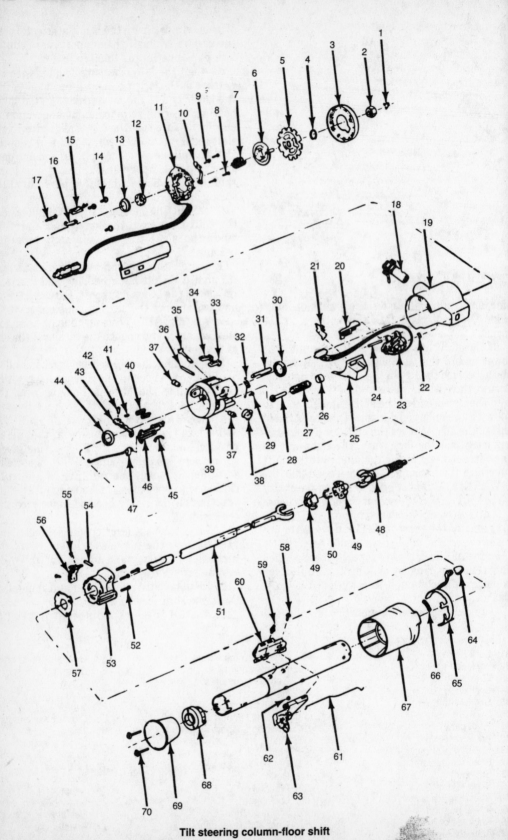

Tilt steering column-floor shift

switch and ignition switch as outlined previously in this section.

21. Align the groove across the upper end of the pot joint with the flat on the steering shaft. Assemble the intermediate shaft assembly to the upper shaft. Install the clamp and bolt and torque the nut to specifications.

WARNING: *The clamp bolt must pass through the shaft undercut, or damage may occur to the components.*

22. Install the neutral safety switch or back-up switch as outlined in this chapter.

23. Install the four dash panel bracket to column screws and torque to specifications.

NOTE: *Be sure that the slotted openings in the bracket (for the mounting capsules) face the upper end of the steering column.*

COLUMN INSTALLATION MANDATORY SEQUENCE

Mandatory Preliminary Instructions

1. Assemble the lower dash cover and upper dash cover to the seal with fasteners that are part of the seal.

2. Attach bracket to jacket and tighten four bolts to specified torque.

Mandatory Installation Sequence

1. Position column in body and position flange to rag joint and install lock washers and nuts (May be tightened to specified torque at this time). Coupling on manual steering must be installed prior to column installation.

2. Loosely assemble (2) capsules nuts at the instrument panel bracket.

3. Position lower clamp and tighten attaching nuts to specified torque.

4. Tighten two nuts at capsules to specified torque.

5. Install seal and covers to dash.

6. Install attaching screws and tighten to specified torque.

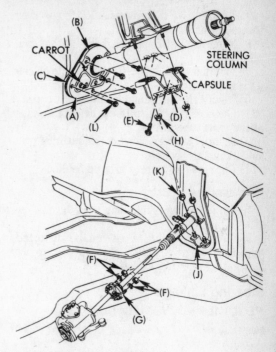

Steering Column Installation

1. Retainer	25. Cap	48. Sphere spring
2. Nut	26. Retainer	49. Centering spheres
3. Lock plate cover	27. Tilt spring	50. Spring
4. Retainer	28. Spring guide	51. Lower steering shaft
5. Lock plate	29. Screw	52. Housing support screws
6. Cancelling cam	30. Bearing	53. Housing support
7. Bearing preload spring	31. Lock bolt	54. Pin
8. Turn signal screws	32. Lock bolt spring	55. Shift lever gate
9. Tap screw	33. Lock shoe	56. Detent plate screw
10. Actuator arm	34. Lock shoe	57. Lock plate
11. Turn signal switch	35. Sector shaft	58. Screw
12. Inner race seat	36. Lock shoe pin	59. Stud
13. Bearing race	37. Pivot pin	60. Switch
14. Screw	38. Actuator sector	61. Dimmer switch rod
15. Tone alarm switch	39. Housing assembly	62. Nut
16. Retainer clip	40. Shoe release springs	63. Dimmer switch
17. Lock retainer screw	41. Spring	64. Pad
18. Ignition lock	42. Shoe release lever pin	65. Key release lever
19. Housing cover	43. Shoe Release lever	66. Key release spring
20. Dimmer switch actuator	44. Lower bearing	67. Shroud
21. Shield	45. Rack preload spring	68. Lower bearing
22. Pin preload spring	46. Actuator rack	69. Retainer
23. Pivot switch	47. Ignition switch actuator	70. Screws
24. Actuator pivot pin		

Tilt steering column-floor shift

7. Tighten two nuts at capsules to specified torque if not already done.

8. Remove plastic spacers from flexible coupling pins.

9. Install transmission indicator cable on column automatics.

10. Install the instrument panel trim cover.

11. Connect the transmission control linkage at the shift tube levers.

12. Install the steering wheel as outlined previously in this section.

13. Connect the battery ground cable.

Mandatory System Requirements

1. Pot joint operating angle must be $1\frac{1}{2}° \pm 4°$.

2. Flexible coupling must not be distorted greater than $\pm 0.06''$ due to pot joint bottoming, in either direction.

Steering Linkage

REMOVAL AND INSTALLATION

Pitman Arm

REMOVAL

1. Raise vehicle on hoist.

2. Remove nut from pitman arm ball stud.

3. Remove pitman arm or relay rod from ball stud by tapping on side of rod or arm (in which the stud mounts) with a hammer while using a heavy hammer or similar tool as a backing. Pull on linkage to remove from stud.

4. Remove pitman arm nut from pitman shaft or clamp bolt from pitman arm, and mark relation of arm position to shaft.

5. Remove pitman arm, using Tool J-6632 or J-5504.

INSTALLATION

1. Install pitman arm on pitman shaft, lining up the marks made upon removal.

NOTE: *If a clamp type pitman arm is used, spread the pitman arm just enough, with a wedge, to slip arm onto pitman shaft. Do not spread pitman arm more than required to slip over pitman shaft with hand pressure. Do not hammer or damage to steering gear may result. Be sure to install the hardened steel washer before installing the nut.*

2. Make sure that threads on ball studs and in ball stud nuts are clean and smooth. If threads are not clean and smooth, ball studs may turn in sockets when attempting to tighten nut. Check condition of ball stud seals; replace if necessary.

3. Install pitman shaft nut or pitman arm clamp bolt and torque to specifications.

4. Position ball stud onto pitman arm or relay rod. Use a ⅝"-18 free spinning nut to seat the tapers, as shown.

5. Lubricate ball studs.

6. Lower the vehicle to the floor.

Idler Arm

Use of the proper diagnosis and checking procedure is essential to prevent needless replacement of good idler arms.

1. Raise the vehicle in such a manner as to allow the front wheels to rotate freely and the steering mechanism freedom to turn. Position the wheels in a straight ahead position.

2. Using a spring scale located as near the relay rod end of the idler arm as possible, exert a 25 lb. force upward and then downward while noticing the total distance the end of the arm moves. This distance should not exceed $\pm \frac{1}{16}''$ for a total acceptable movement of ⅛". It is necessary to ensure that the correct load is applied to the arm since it will move more when higher loads are applied. It is also necessary that a scale or ruler be rested against the frame and used to determine the amount of movement since observers tend to over-estimate the acutal movement when a scale is not used. The idler arm should always be replaced if it fails this test.

Jerking the right front wheel and tire assembly back and forth, thus causing an up and down movement in the idler arm is not an acceptable method of checking since there is no control on the amount of force being applied.

Caution should be used in assuming shimmy complaints are caused by loose idler arms. Before suspecting suspension or steering components, technicians should eliminate shimmy excitation factors, such as dynamic imbalance, run-out or force variation of wheel and tire assemblies and road surface irregularities.

REMOVAL

1. Raise vehicle on a hoist.

2. Remove the nut from ball stud at the relay rod. Remove the ball stud from the relay rod by

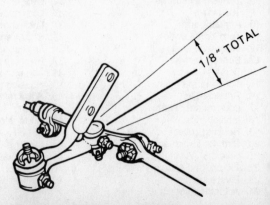

Checking Idler Movement, Typical

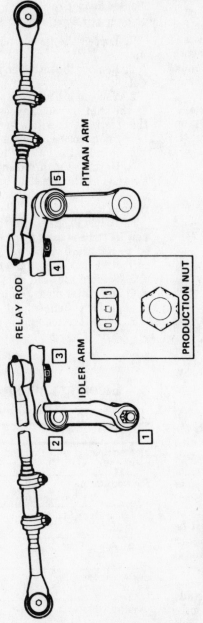

PITMAN ARM

RELAY ROD

IDLER ARM

5

4

3

2

1

PRODUCTION NUT

Typical Crimp Nut Locations

IMPORTANT

WHENEVER ANY OF THE CRIMP NUTS OR STUDS AT THE (5) LOCATIONS SHOWN ARE LOOSENED OR REMOVED, THE FOLLOWING STEPS MUST BE TAKEN:

A. WHEN RE-ATTACHING ANY TWO COMPONENTS BY MEANS OF A BALL STUD, CAREFULLY POSITION THE TWO PARTS. THEN INSTALL A FREE-SPINNING NUT, AND DRAW THE ITEMS TOGETHER TO SEAT THE TAPER, TORQUE NUT TO 54 N·m (40 FT-LBS), THEN REMOVE NUT.

B. THEN USE A TORQUE PREVAILING SERVICE REPLACEMENT NUT (#351249) AND TORQUE TO 90 N·m (66 FT-LBS).

tapping on the relay rod boss with a hammer, while using a heavy hammer as a backing.

3. Remove the idler arm to frame bolt and remove the idler arm assembly.

INSTALLATION

1. Position the idler arm on the frame and install the mounting bolts (special plain washers under bolt heads); torque.

2. Make sure that the threads on the ball stud and in the ball stud nut are clean and smooth. If threads are not clean and smooth, ball stud may turn in the socket when attempting to tighten nut. Check condition of ball stud seal; replace if necessary.

3. Install the idler arm ball stud in the relay rod, making certain the seal is positioned properly. Use a ⅝″-18 free-spinning nut to seat the tapers, as shown.

4. Lower the vehicle to the floor.

Center Link

REMOVAL

1. Raise and support the vehicle with jackstands.

2. Remove the inner ends of the tie rods from the center link.

3. Remove the nuts from the pitman and idler arm ball studs at the center link.

4. Remove the center link from the pitman and idler arms by tapping on the center link ball stud bosses with a hammer, while using a heavy hammer as backing.

5. Remove the center link from the vehicle.

INSTALLATION

WARNING: *These fasteners are important attaching parts in that they could affect the performance of vital components and systems, and/or could result in major repair expense. They must be replaced with one of the same part number or with an equivalent part if replacement becomes necessary. Do not use a replacement part of lesser quality or substitute design. Torque values must be used as specified during reassembly to assure proper retention of these parts. For the nut(s) and bolt(s) torque specifications please, refer to the chart which follows.*

1. Make sure that threads on the ball studs and in the ball stud nuts are clean and smooth. If the threads are not clean and smooth, ball studs may turn in sockets when attempting to tighten nut. Check condition of ball stud seals; replace if necessary.

2. Install the center link to the idler arm and pitman arm ball studs, making certain the seals are in place. Use a free-spinning nut to seat the tapers, as shown.

3. Install the tie rods to the center link as previously described under Tie Rod Installation. Lubricate the tie rod ends.

4. Lower the vehicle to the floor.

5. Adjust toe-in and align steering wheel as described previously.

Tie Rod Ends

REMOVAL AND INSTALLATION

1. Loosen the tie rod adjuster sleeve clamp nuts.

2. Remove the tie rod end stud cotter pin and nut.

3. You can use a tie rod removal tool to loosen the stud, or you can loosen it by tapping on the steering arm with a hammer while using a heavy hammer as a backup.

4. Remove the inner stud in the same way.

5. Unscrew the tie rod end from the threaded sleeve. The threads may be left or right hand threads. Count the number of turns required to remove it.

6. To install, grease the threads and turn the new tie rod end in as many turns as were needed to remove it. This will give approximately correct toe-in. Tighten the clamp bolts.

7. Tighten the stud nuts to 45 ft.lb. and install new cotter pins. You may tighten the nut to align the cotter pin, but don't loosen it.

8. Adjust the toe-in.

Steering Linkage Torque— Thru 1985

	C	K
Steering Knuckle to Tie Rod End	55 N·m (41 ft. lb.)	55 N·m (41 ft. lb.)
Toe Rod Clamp	16 N·m (12 ft. lb.)	16 N·m (12 ft. lb.)
Tie Rod to Relay Rod	55 N·m (41 ft. lb.)	55 N·m (41 ft. lb.)
Pitman Arm to Gear	220 N·m (148 ft. lb.)	110 N·m (74 ft. lb.)
Idler Arm to Relay Rod	55 N·m (41 ft. lb.)	— —
Idler Arm to Frame	34 N·m (25 ft. lb.)	— —
Steering Damper to Rod	— —	55 N·m (41 ft. lb.)
Steering Damper to Frame	— —	90 N·m (66 ft. lb.)
Rod, Pitman Arm to Knuckle	— —	110 N·m (74 ft. lb.)

Steering Linkage Torque—1986–87

	R, C Models		V, K Models	
	N·m	Ft. Lbs.	N·m	Ft. Lbs.
Tie Rod (3) End To Steering Knuckle (4)*	62	46	55	40
Tie Rod (3) Adjuster Tube Bolts	19	14	55	40
Tie Rod (3) To Relay Rod (2)	90	66	—	—
Idler Arm (1) to Relay Rod (2)	90	66	—	—
Idler Arm (1) To Frame	40	30	—	—
Pitman Arm (5) To Relay Rod (2)	90	66	—	—
Pitman Arm (5) To Steering Gear (6)	250	184	125	92
Bolt To Shock Absorber Bracket (9)	—	—	—	—
Shock Absorber (7) To Tie Rod (3)*	—	—	62	46
Shock Absorber (7) To Frame	—	—	110	81
Shock Absorber (7) To Idler Arm (1)*	—	—	—	—
Connecting Rod (8) To Adjuster Tube Bolts	—	—	54	40
Connecting Rod (8) To Pitman Arm (5)*	—	—	120	89
Connecting Rod (8) To Steering Knuckle (4)*	—	—	120	89
Connecting Rod (8) To Relay Arm (11)*	—	—	—	—
Support Assemblies (10) To Frame	—	—	—	—
Idler Arm (1) And Relay Arm (11) To Support Assemblies (10)	—	—	—	—
Relay Rod (2) To Relay Arm (11)	—	—	—	—
Tie Rod Jam Nut (K10, 20)	—	—	125	92

* Tightening Procedure (Castellated Nuts)
1. Tighten to the specified torque.
2. Advance the nut to align the nut slot with the cotter pin hole.
3. Insert a new cotter pin of the correct size.

Manual Steering Gear

LUBRICATION

The manual steering gear is factory filled with steering gear lubricant. Seasonal change of this lubricant should not be performed and the housing should not be drained. No lubrication is required for the life of the steering gear.

According to the intervals listed in Section 0B, the manual gear should be inspected for seal leakage (actual solid grease, not just oily film). If a seal is replaced or the gear is overhauled, the gear housing should be refilled with 1051052 (13 oz. container) Steering Gear Lubricant which meets GM Specification GM 4673M, or its equivalent.

WARNING: *Do not use EP Chassis Lube, which meets GM Specification GM 6031M, to lubricate the gear DO NOT OVER-FILL the gear housing, or damage may occur to the gear.*

ADJUSTMENTS

NOTE: *Before any adjustments are made to the steering gear to attempt to correct complaints of loose or hard steering, or other wheel disturbances, a careful check should be made of front end alignment, shock absorbers, wheel balance and tire pressure for possible steering system problems. See the Troubleshooting Charts at the end of this section.*

Correct adjustment of steering gear is very important. While there are but two adjustments to be made, the following procedure must be followed step-by-step in the order given.

1. Disconnect the battery ground cable.
2. Raise the vehicle.
3. Remove the pitman arm nut. Mark the relationship of the pitman arm to the pitman shaft. Remove the pitman arm with Tool J-6632 or J-5504 as shown.
4. Loosen the steering gear adjuster plug

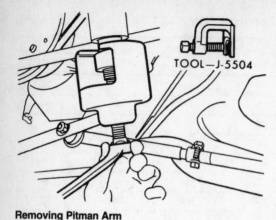

Removing Pitman Arm

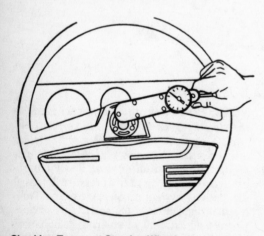

Steering Gear Adjustment Points-Typical

Checking Torque at Steering Wheel

locknut and back the adjuster plug off ¼ turn.

5. Remove the horn shroud or button cap.

6. Turn the steering wheel gently in one direction until stopped by the gear; then turn back ½ turn.

WARNING: *Do not turn the steering wheel hard against the stops when the steering linkage is disconnected from the gear as damage to the ball guides could result.*

7. Measure and record bearing drag by applying a torque wrench with a socket on the steering wheel nut and rotating through a 90 degree arc. Do not use a torque wrench having a maximum torque reading of more than 50 in.lb.

8. Adjust thrust bearing preload by tightening the adjuster plug until the proper thrust loading preload is obtained (See specifications section). When the proper preload has been obtained, tighten the adjuster plug locknut to specifications and recheck torque. If the gear feels lumpy after adjustment, there is probably damage in the bearings due to severe impact or improper adjustment; the gear must be disassembled and inspected for replacement of damaged parts.

9. Adjust over-center preload as follows:

a. Turn the steering wheel gently from one stop all the way to the other carefully counting the total number of turns. Turn the wheel back exactly half-way, to center position.

b. Turn the lash adjuster screw clockwise to take out all lash between the ball nut and pitman shaft sector teeth and then tighten the locknut.

c. Check the torque at the steering wheel, taking the highest reading as the wheel is turned through center position. See Specifications for proper over-center prelaod.

d. If necessary, loosen locknut and re-adjust lash adjuster screw to obtain proper torque. Tighten the locknut to specifications and again check torque reading through center of travel. If maximum specification is exceeded, turn lash adjuster screw counterclockwise, then come up on adjustment by turning the adjuster in a clockwise motion.

10. Reassemble the pitman arm to the pitman shaft, lining up the marks made during disassembly. Torque the pitman shaft nut to specifications.

If a clamp type pitman arm is used, spread the pitman arm just enough, with a wedge, to slip the arm onto the pitman shaft. Do not spread the clamp more than required to slip over pitman shaft with hand pressure. Do not hammer the pitman arm onto the pitman shaft. Be sure to install the hardened steel washer before installing the nut.

11. Install the horn button cap or shroud and connect the battery ground cable.

12. Lower the vehicle to the floor.

HIGH POINT CENTERING

1. Set front wheels in straight ahead position. This can be checked by driving vehicle a short distance on a flat surface to determine steering wheel position at which vehicle follows a straight path.

2. With front wheels set straight ahead, check position of mark on wormshaft designating steering gear high point. This mark should be at the top side of the shaft at 12 o'clock position and lined up with the mark in the coupling lower clamp.

3. If the gear has been moved off high point when setting wheel in straight ahead position, loosen adjusting sleeve clamps on both left and right hand tie rods. Then turn both sleeves an equal number of turns in the same direction to bring gear back on high point.

Turning the sleeves an unequal number of turns or in different directions will disturb the toe-in setting of the wheels.

4. If the gear has been moved off high point when setting wheels in straight ahead position, loosen adjusting sleeve clamps on the connecting rod. Then turn sleeve to bring gear back on high point.

5. Readjust toe-in as outlined previously.

6. Be sure to properly orient sleeves and clamps when fastening and torqueing clamps to proper specifications.

STEERING GEAR

REMOVAL

1. Set the front wheels in straight ahead position by driving vehicle a short distance on a flat surface.

2. Remove the flexible coupling to steering shaft flange bolts.

3. Mark the relationship of the pitman arm to the pitman shaft. Remove the pitman shaft nut or pitman arm pinch bolt and then remove the pitman arm from the pitman shaft using Puller J-6632.

4. Remove the steering gear to frame bolts and remove the gear assembly.

5. Remove the flexible coupling pinch bolt and remove the coupling from the steering gear wormshaft.

INSTALLATION

1. Install the flexible coupling onto the steering gear wormshaft, aligning the flat in the coupling with the flat on the shaft. Push the coupling onto the shaft until the wormshaft bottoms on the coupling reinforcement. Install the pinch bolt and torque to specifications. The coupling bolt must pass through the shaft undercut.

2. Place the steering gear in position, guiding the coupling bolt into the steering shaft flange.

3. Install the steering gear to frame bolts and torque to specifications.

4. If flexible coupling alignment pin plastic spacers were used, make sure they are bottomed on the pins, torque the flange bolt nuts

to specifications and then remove the plastic spacers.

5. If flexible coupling alignment pin plastic spacers were not used, center the pins in the slots in the steering shaft flange and then install and torque the flange bolt nuts to specifications.

PITMAN SHAFT SEAL REPLACEMENT

A faulty seal may be replaced without removal of steering gear by removing pitman arm as outlined earlier and proceed as follows:

1. Rotate the steering wheel from stop to stop, counting the total number of turns. Then turn back exactly half-way, placing the gear on center (the wormshaft flat should be at the 12 o'clock position).

2. Remove the three self-locking bolts attaching side cover to the housing and lift the pitman shaft and side cover assembly from the housing.

3. Pry the pitman shaft seal from the gear housing using a screwdriver and being careful not to damage the housing bore.

WARNING: *Inspect the lubricant in the gear for contamination if the lubricant is contaminated in any way, the gear must be removed from the vehicle and completely overhauled as outlined in the Unit Repair Manual, or damage to the gear could result.*

4. Coat the new pitman shaft with Steering Gear Lubricant meeting GM Specification GM4673M (or equivalent). Position the seal in the pitman shaft bore and tap into position using a suitable size socket.

5. Remove the lash adjuster lock nut. Remove the side cover from the pitman shaft assembly by turning the lash adjuster screw clockwise.

6. Place the pitman shaft in the steering gear such that the center tooth of the pitman shaft

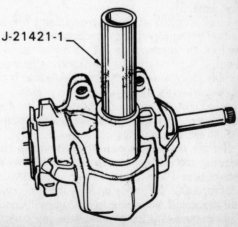

J-21421-1

Pitman Shaft Seal Replacement

sector enters the center tooth space of the ball nut.

7. Fill the steering gear housing with Steering Gear Lubricant meeting GM Specification GM4673M (or equivalent).

8. Install a new side cover gasket onto the gear housing.

9. Install the side cover onto the lash adjuster screw by reaching through the threaded hole in the side cover with a small screwdriver and turning the lash adjuster screw counterclockwise until it bottoms and turns back in ¼ turn.

10. Install the side cover bolts and torque to specifications.

11. Install the lash adjuster screw locknut, perform steering gear adjustment and install the pitman arm.

Power Steering Gear and Pump

GENERAL DESCRIPTION

The steering gear is of the recirculating ball type. This gear provides for ease of handling by transmitting forces from the wormshaft to the pitman shaft through the use of ball bearings.

LUBRICATION OF THE PUMP

Check the fluid level in the pump reservoir according to the intervals listed in Section OB. Use only an approved power steering lubricant in the pump.

WARNING: *Never use brake fluid in the power steering pump, or damage may occur.*

ADJUSTMENTS

Adjustment of the steering gear in the vehicle is not recommended because of the difficulty encountered in adjusting the worm thrust bearing preload and the confusing effects of the hydraulic fluid in the gear. Since a gear adjustment is made only as a correction and not as a periodic adjustment, it is better to take the extra time and make the adjustment correctly the first time.

Since a handling stability complaint can be caused by improperly adjusted worm bearings a well as an improper gear over-center adjustment, it is necessary that the steering gear assembly be removed from the vehicle and both thrust bearing and over-center preload be checked and corrected as necessary. An in-vehicle check of the steering gear will not pinpoint a thrust bearing looseness.

Before any adjustments are made to the steering gear attempt to correct complaints of loose or hard steering, or other wheel disturbances, a careful check should be made of front end alignment, shock absorbers, wheel balance and tire pressure for possible steering system problems.

Steering Gear High Point Centering

1. Set front wheels in straight ahead position. This can be checked by driving vehicle a short distance on a flat surface to determine steering wheel position at which vehicle follow a straight path.

2. With front wheels set straight ahead check position of mark on wormshaft designating steering gear high point. This mark should be at the top side of the shaft at 12 o'clock position and lined up with the mark in the coupling lower clamp.

3. On the C series if gear has been moved of high point when setting wheel in straight ahead position, loosen the adjusting sleeve clamps on both left and right hand tie rods. Then turn both sleeves an equal number of turns in the same direction to bring gear back on high point.

Turning the sleeves an unequal number of turns or in different directions will disburb the toe-in setting of the wheels.

4. On K series, if the gear has been moved of high point when setting wheels in straight ahead position, loosen the adjusting sleeve clamps on the connecting rod. Then turn sleeve to bring gear back on high point.

5. Readjust toe-in (if necessary).

6. Be sure to properly orient sleeves and clamps, when fastening and torquing clamps to proper specifications.

Pump Belt Tension Adjustment

1. Loosen pivot bolt and pump brace adjusting nuts.

WARNING: *Do not move pump by prying against reservoir or by pulling on filler neck, or damage to the pump could occur.*

2. Move pump, with belt in place until belt is tensioned to specifications as indicated by Tool J-23600.

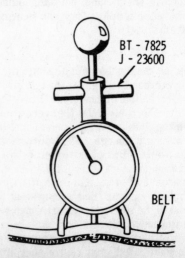

BT - 7825
J - 23600

BELT

Checking Belt Tension with J-23600

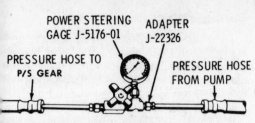

POWER STEERING GAGE J-5176-01   ADAPTER J-22326

PRESSURE HOSE TO P/S GEAR

PRESSURE HOSE FROM PUMP

Checking Power Steering Pressures

3. Tighten pump brace adjusting nut. Then tighten pivot bolt nut.

Fluid Level Adjustment

1. Check oil level in the reservoir by checking the dipstick when oil is at operating temperature. On models equipped with remote reservoir, the oil level should be maintained approximately ½-1" from top with wheels in full left turn position.

2. Fill, if necessary, to proper level with GM Power Steering Fluid or equivalent.

WARNING: *Never use brake fluid in the power steering pump, or damage may occur.*

BLEEDING HYDRAULIC SYSTEM

1. Fill oil reservoir to proper level and let oil remain undisturbed for at least two minutes.

2. Start engine and run only for about two seconds.

3. Add oil if necessary.

4. Repeat above procedure until oil level remains constant after running engine.

5. Raise front end of vehicle so that wheels are off the ground.

6. Increase engine speed to approximately 1500 rpm.

7. Turn the wheels (off ground) right and left, lightly contacting the wheel stops.

8. Add oil if necessary.

9. Lower the vehicle and turn wheels right and left on the ground.

10. Check oil level and refill as required.

11. If oil is extremely foamy, allow vehicle to stand a few minutes with engine off and repeat above procedure.

   a. Check belt tightness and check for a bent or loose pulley. (Pulley should not wobble with engine running).

   b. Check to make sure hoses are not touching any other parts of the truck, particularly sheet metal except where design calls for a clamp.

   c. Check oil level, filling to proper level if necessary, following operations 1 through 10. This step and Step d are extremely important as low oil level and/or air in the oil are the most frequent causes of objectional pump noise.

   d. Check the presence of air in the oil. If air is present, attempt to bleed system as described in operations 1 through 10. If it becomes obvious that the pump will not bleed after a few trials, proceed as outlined under Hydraulic System Checks.

HYDRAULIC SYSTEM CHECKS

The following procedure outlines methods to identify and isolate power steering hydraulic circuit difficulties. The test provides means of determining whether power steering system hydraulic parts are actually faulty. This test will result in readings indicating faulty hydraulic operation, and will help to identify the faulty component.

Before performing hydraulic circuit test, carefully check belt tension, fluid level and condition of driving pulley.

Engine must be at normal operating temperature. Inflate front tires to correct pressure. All tests are made with engine idling. Check idle adjustment and, if necessary, adjust engine idle speed to correct specifications and proceed as follows:

1. With engine NOT running disconnect pressure hose from pump and install Tool J-5176 using a spare pressure hose between gage and pump. Gage must be between shut-off valve and pump. Open shut-off valve.

2. Remove filler cap from pump reservoir and check fluid level. Fill pump reservoir to full mark on dipstick. Start engine and, momentarily holding steering wheel against stop, check connections at Tool J-5176 for leakage.

3. Bleed system as outlined under Maintenance and Adjustments.

4. Insert thermometer (Tool J-5421) in reservoir filler opening. Move steering wheel from stop to stop several times until thermometer indicates that hydraulic fluid in reservoir has reached temperature of 150 degrees to 170 F.

WARNING: *To prevent scrubbing flat spots on tires, do not turn steering wheel more than five times without rolling vehicle to change tire-to-floor contact area.*

5. Start engine and check fluid level adding any fluid if required. When engine is at normal operating temperature, the initial pressure read on the gage (valve open) should be in the 80-125 PSI range. Should this pressure be in excess of 200 PSI, check the hoses for restrictions and the poppet valve for proper assembly.

6. Close gate valve fully 3 times. Record the highest pressure attained each time.

   a. If the pressures recorded are within the listed specs and the range of readings are within 50 PSI, the pump is functioning within specs. (Ex. Spec. 1250-1350 PSI readings − 1270-1280).

b. If the pressures recorded are high, but do not repeat with 50 PSI, the flow controlling valve is sticking. Remove the valve, clean it and remove any burrs using crocus cloth or fine home. If the system contains some dirt, flush it. If it is exceptionally dirty, both the pump and the gear must be completely disassembled, cleaned, flushed and reassembled before further usage.

c. If the pressures recorded are constant, but more than 100 PSI, below the low listed spec., replace the flow control valve and recheck. If the pressures are still low, replace the rotating group in the pump.

7. If the pump checks within specifications, leave the valve open and turn (or have turned) the steering wheel into both corners. Record the highest pressures and compare with the maximum pump pressures recorded. If this pressure cannot be built in either (or one) side of the gear, the gear is leaking internally and must be disassembled and repaired.

8. Shut off engine, remove testing gage, spare hose, reconnect pressure hose, check fluid level and/or make needed repairs.

Power Steering Gear

REMOVAL

1. Disconnect hoses at gear. When hoses are disconnected, secure ends in raised position to prevent drainage of oil. Cap or tape the ends of the hoses to prevent entrance of dirt.

2. Install two plugs in gear fittings to prevent entrance of dirt.

3. Remove the flexible coupling to steering shaft flange bolts.

4. Mark the relationship of the pitman arm to the pitman shaft. Remove the pitman shaft nut or pitman arm pinch bolt and then remove the pitman arm from the pitman shaft using Puller J-6632.

5. Remove the steering gear to frame bolts and remove the gear assembly.

6. Remove the flexible coupling pinch bolt and remove the coupling from the steering gear stub shaft.

INSTALLATION

1. Install the flexible coupling onto the steering gear stub shaft, aligning the flat in the coupling with the flat on the shaft. Push the coupling onto the shaft until the stub shaft bottoms on the coupling reinforcement. Install the pinch bolt and torque to specifications.
WARNING: *The coupling bolt must pass through the shaft undercut, or damage to the components could occur.*

2. Place the steering gear in position, guiding the coupling bolt into the steering shaft flange.

3. Install the steering gear to frame bolts and torque to specifications.

4. If flexible coupling alignment pin plastic spacers were used, make sure they are buttomed on the pins, tighten the flange bolt nuts to specifications and then remove the plastic spacers.

5. If flexible coupling alignment pin plastic spacers were not used, center the pins in the slots in the steering shaft flange and then install and torque the flange bolt nuts to specifications.

6. Install the pitman arm onto the pitman shaft, lining up the marks made at removal. Install the pitman shaft nut or pitman arm pinch bolt and torque to specifications.

7. Remove the plugs and caps from the steering gear and hoses and connect the hoses to the gear. Tighten the hose fillings to specified torque.

Power Steering Pump

REMOVAL

1. Disconnect hoses at pump. When hoses are disconnected, secure ends in raised position to prevent drainage of oil. Cap or tape the ends of the hoses to prevent entrance of dirt.

On Models with remote reservoir, disconnect reservoir hose at pump and secure in raised position. Cap hose pump fittings.

2. Install two caps at pump fittings to prevent drainage of oil from pump.

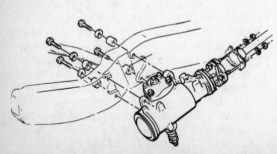

Power Steering Gear Mounting-Typical

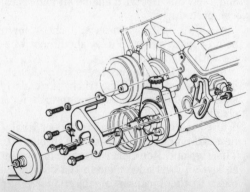

Typical Power Steering Pump Mounting

3. Loosen bracket-to-pump mounting nuts.

4. Remove pump belt.

5. Remove pump from attaching parts and remove pump from vehicle.

INSTALLATION

1. Position pump assembly on vehicle and install attaching parts loosely.

2. Connect and tighten hose fillings.

3. Fill reservoir. Bleed pump by turning pulley backward (counterclockwise as viewed from front) until air bubbles cease to appear.

4. Install pump belt over pulley.

5. Tension belt as outlined under Pump Belt Tension Adjustment in this section.

6. Bleed as outlined under Bleeding Power Steering System.

Brakes

BASIC OPERATING PRINCIPLES

Hydraulic systems are used to actuate the brakes of all automobiles. The system transports the power required to force the frictional surfaces of the braking system together from the pedal to the individual brake units at each wheel. A hydraulic system is used for two reasons.

First, fluid under pressure can be carried to all parts of an automobile by small pipes and flexible hoses without taking up a significant amount of room or posing routing problems.

Second, a great mechanical advantage can be given to the brake pedal end of the system, and the foot pressure required to actuate the brakes can be reduced by making the surface area of the master cylinder pistons smaller than that of any of the pistons in the wheel cylinders or calipers.

The master cylinder consists of a fluid reservoir and a double cylinder and piston assembly. Double type master cylinders are designed to separate the front and rear braking systems hydraulically in case of a leak.

Steel lines carry the brake fluid to a point on the vehicle's frame near each of the vehicle's wheels. The fluid is then carried to the calipers and wheel cylinders by flexible tubes in order to allow for suspension and steering movements.

In drum brake systems, each wheel cylinder contains two pistons, one at either end, which push outward in opposite directions.

In disc brake systems, the cylinders are part of the calipers. One cylinder in each caliper is used to force the brake pads against the disc.

All pistons employ some type of seal, usually made of rubber, to minimize fluid leakage. A rubber dust boot seals the outer end of the cylinder against dust and dirt. The boot fits around the outer end of the piston on disc brake calipers, and around the brake actuating rod on wheel cylinders.

The hydraulic system operates as follows: When at rest, the entire system, from the piston(s) in the master cylinder to those in the wheel cylinders or calipers, is full of brake fluid. Upon application of the brake pedal, fluid trapped in front of the master cylinder piston(s) is forced through the lines to the wheel cylinders. Here, it forces the pistons outward, in the case of drum brakes, and inward toward the disc, in the case of disc brakes. The motion of the pistons is opposed by return springs mounted outside the cylinders in drum brakes, and by spring seals, in disc brakes.

Upon release of the brake pedal, a spring located inside the master cylinder immediately returns the master cylinder pistons to the normal position. The pistons contain check valves and the master cylinder has compensating ports drilled in it. These are uncovered as the pistons reach their normal position. The piston check valves allow fluid to flow toward the wheel cylinders or calipers as the pistons withdraw. Then, as the return springs force the brake pads or shoes into the released position, the excess fluid reservoir through the compensating ports. It is during the time the pedal is in the released position that any fluid that has leaked out of the system will be replaced through the compensating ports.

Dual circuit master cylinders employ two pistons, located one behind the other, in the same cylinder. The primary piston is actuated directly by mechanical linkage from the brake pedal through the power booster. The secondary piston is actuated by fluid trapped between the two pistons. If a leak develops in front of the secondary piston, it moves forward until it bottoms against the front of the master cylinder, and the fluid trapped between the pistons will operate the rear brakes. If the rear brakes develop a leak, the primary piston will move forward until direct contact with the secondary piston takes place, and it will force the secondary piston to actuate the front brakes. In either case, the brake pedal moves farther when the brakes are applied, and less braking power is available.

All dual circuit systems use a switch to warn the driver when only half of the brake system is operational. This switch is located in a valve body which is mounted on the firewall or the frame below the master cylinder. A hydraulic piston receives pressure from both circuits, each circuit's pressure being applied to one end of the piston. When the pressures are in balance, the piston remains stationary. When one circuit has a leak, however, the greater pressure in that circuit during application of the brakes will push the piston to one side, closing the switch and activating the brake warning light.

In disc brake systems, this valve body also contains a metering valve and, in some cases, a proportioning valve. The metering valve keeps pressure from traveling to the disc brakes on the front wheels until the brake shoes on the rear wheels have contacted the drums, ensuring that the front brakes will never be used alone. The proportioning valve controls the pressure to the rear brakes to lessen the chance of rear wheel lock-up during very hard braking.

Warning lights may be tested by depressing the brake pedal and holding it while opening one of the wheel cylinder bleeder screws. If this does not cause the light to go on, substitute a new lamp, make continuity checks, and, finally, replace the switch as necessary.

The hydraulic system may be checked for leaks by applying pressure to the pedal gradually and steadily. If the pedal sinks very slowly to the floor, the system has a leak. This is not to be confused with a springy or spongy feel due to the compression of air within the lines. If the system leaks, there will be a gradual change in the position of the pedal with a constant pressure.

Check for leaks along all lines and at wheel cylinders. If no external leaks are apparent, the problem is inside the master cylinder.

Disc Brakes
BASIC OPERATING PRINCIPLES

Instead of the traditional expanding brakes that press outward against a circular drum, disc brake systems utilize a disc (rotor) with brake pads positioned on either side of it. Braking effect is achieved in a manner similar to the way you would squeeze a spinning phonograph record between your fingers. The disc (rotor) is a casting with cooling fins between the two braking surfaces. This enables air to circulate between the braking surfaces making them less sensitive to heat buildup and more resistant to fade. Dirt and water do not affect braking action since contaminants are thrown off by the centrifugal action of the rotor or scraped off the by the pads. Also, the equal clamping action of the two brake pads tends to ensure uniform, straight line stops. Disc brakes are inherently self-adjusting.

There are three general types of disc brake:
1. A fixed caliper.
2. A floating caliper.
3. A sliding caliper.

The fixed caliper design uses two pistons mounted on either side of the rotor (in each side of the caliper). The caliper is mounted rigidly and does not move.

The sliding and floating designs are quite similar. In fact, these two types are often lumped together. In both designs, the pad on the inside of the rotor is moved into contact with the rotor by hydraulic force. The caliper, which is not held in a fixed position, moves slightly, bringing the outside pad into contact with the rotor. There are various methods of attaching floating calipers. Some pivot at the bottom or top, and some slide on mounting bolts. In any event, the end result is the same.

All the cars covered in this book employ the sliding caliper design.

Drum Brakes
BASIC OPERATING PRINCIPLES

Drum brakes employ two brake shoes mounted on a stationary backing plate. These shoes are positioned inside a circular drum which rotates with the wheel assembly. The shoes are held in place by springs. This allows them to slide toward the drums (when they are applied) while keeping the linings and drums in alignment. The shoes are actuated by a wheel cylinder which is mounted at the top of the backing plate. When the brakes are applied, hydraulic pressure forces the wheel cylinder's actuating links outward. Since these links bear directly against the top of the brake shoes, the tops of the shoes are then forced against the inner side of the drum. This action forces the bottoms of the two shoes to contact the brake drum by rotating the entire assembly slightly (known as servo action). When pressure within the wheel cylinder is relaxed, return springs pull the shoes back away from the drum.

Most modern drum brakes are designed to self-adjust themselves during application when the vehicle is moving in reverse. This motion causes both shoes to rotate very slightly with the drum, rocking an adjusting lever, thereby causing rotation of the adjusting screw.

Power Boosters

Power brakes operate just as non-power brake systems except in the actuation of the master cylinder pistons. A vacuum diaphragm is located on the front of the master cylinder and assists the driver in applying the brakes, reducing both the effort and travel he must put into moving the brake pedal.

The vacuum diaphragm housing is connected to the intake manifold by a vacuum hose. A check valve is placed at the point where the hose enters the diaphragm housing, so that during periods of low manifold vacuum brake assist vacuum will not be lost.

Depressing the brake pedal closes off the vacuum source and allows atmospheric pressure to enter on one side of the diaphragm. This causes the master cylinder pistons to move and apply the brakes. When the brake pedal is released, vacuum is applied to both sides of the diaphragm, and return springs return the diaphragm and master cylinder pistons to the released position. If the vacuum fails, the brake pedal rod will butt against the end of the master cylinder actuating rod, and direct mechanical application will occur as the pedal is depressed.

The hydraulic and mechanical problems that apply to conventional brake systems also apply to power brakes, and should be checked for if the tests below do not reveal the problem.

Test for a system vacuum leak as described below:

1. Operate the engine at idle without touching the brake pedal for at least one minute.
2. Turn off the engine, and wait one minute.
3. Test for the presence of assist vacuum by depressing the brake pedal and releasing it several times. Light application will produce less and less pedal travel, if vacuum was present. If there is no vacuum, air is leaking into the system somewhere.

Test for system operation as follows:

1. Pump the brake pedal (with engine off) until the supply vacuum is entirely gone.
2. Put a light, steady pressure on the pedal.
3. Start the engine, and operate it at idle. If the system is operating, the brake pedal should fall toward the floor if constant pressure is maintained on the pedal.

Power brake systems may be tested for hydraulic leaks just as ordinary systems are tested.

BRAKE SYSTEM

All Chevrolet and GMC trucks from 1970 are equipped with a split hydraulic braking system. The system is designed with separate systems for the front and rear brakes using a dual master cylinder with separate reservoirs. If a wheel cylinder or brake line should fail in either the front or the rear system, the truck can still be stopped with reasonable control.

In 1970, trucks were equipped drum brakes front and rear. The front brakes are duo-servo anchor pin type which are self-adjusting. The rear brakes are of the same basic type.

Beginning in 1971, trucks were equipped with disc brakes at the front and drum brakes at the rear. The drum brakes are still of the duo-servo anchor pin self-adjusting type, while the front disc brakes are single piston sliding caliper types. The front disc brakes are self-adjusting.

The parking brake is either hand or foot operated, but in any event, acts upon the rear service brakes.

ADJUSTMENT

Front or Rear Drum Brakes

These brakes are equipped with self-adjusters and no manual adjustment is necessary, except when brake linings are replaced.

Front Disc Brakes

These brakes are self-adjusting and no adjustment is possible.

Brake Pedal

Brake pedal adjustment is made by removing the cotter pin, nut and bolt from the pedal rod end and screwing the rod end in or out to achieve the proper pedal travel.

PEDAL TRAVEL

At reasonably frequent intervals, the brakes should be inspected for pedal travel, which is the distance the pedal moves toward the floor from a fully released position. Inspection should be made with the brake pedal firmly depressed (approximately 90 lbs.) while the brakes are cold.

- Manual.......4.5″ (115mm)
- Power........3.5″ (90mm)

On power brake equipped vehicles, pump the pedal a minimum of 3 times with the engine off before making pedal travel checks. This exhausts all vacuum from the power booster or fluid from the hydro-boost accumulator.

Brake Light Switch

ADJUSTMENT

The design of the switch and valve mounting provides for automatic adjustment when the brake pedal is manually returned to its mechanical stop as follows:

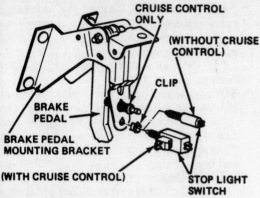

Stoplight Switch

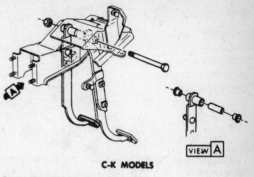

C-K MODELS

Brake Pedal Installation

1. With brake pedal depressed, insert switch and/or valve assembly into tubular clip until switch body and/or valve assembly seats on the tube clip. Note that audible clicks can be heard as threaded portion of switch and valve are pushed through the clip toward the brake pedal.

2. Pull brake pedal fully rearward against pedal stop, until audible click sounds can no longer be heard. Switch and/or valve assembly will be move in tubular clip providing proper adjustment.

3. Release brake pedal, then repeat Step 2 to assure that no audible click sounds remain.

Electrical contact should be made when the brake pedal is depressed 1.0-1.24″ (25-31 mm) from its fully released position.

REMOVAL AND INSTALLATION

1. Remove the clip and the electrical connector from the brake light switch and remove it from the brake pedal mounting bracket.

2. Reverse procedure to install.

Master Cylinder
REMOVAL AND INSTALLATION

1. Using a clean cloth, wipe the master cylinder and its lines to remove excess dirt and then

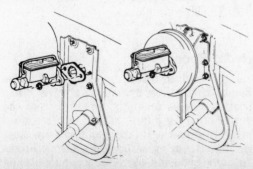

Typical master cylinder installations

place cloths under the unit to absorb spilled fluid.

WARNING: *Clean master cylinder parts in alcohol or brake fluid. Never use mineral based cleaning solvents such as gasoline, kerosene, carbon tetrachloride, acetone, or paint thinner as these will destroy rubber parts.*

2. Remove the hydraulic lines from the master cylinder and plug the outlets to prevent the entrance of foreign material.

3. Disconnect the brake pushrod from the brake pedal (non-power brakes).

4. Remove the attaching bolts and remove the master cylinder from the firewall or the brake booster. Remove the master cylinder from the booster.

5. Connect the pushrod to the brake pedal with the pin and retainer.

6. Connect the brake lines and fill the master cylinder reservoirs to the proper levels.

7. Bleed the brake system.

8. If necessary, adjust the brake pedal freeplay.

OVERHAUL

In most years, there are two sources for master cylinders: Delco-Moraine and Bendix. The Bendix unit can readily be identified by the secondary stop bolt on the bottom, which is not present on the Delco-Moraine unit. Master cylinders bearing identifying code letters should only be replaced with cylinders bearing the same code letters. Secondary pistons are also coded by rings or grooves on the shank or center section of the piston, and should only be replaced with pistons having the same code. The primary pistons also are of two types. One has a deep socket for the pushrod and the other has a very shallow socket. Be sure to replace pistons with identical parts. Failure to do this could result in a malfunction of the master cylinder.

NOTE: *This a tedious, time consuming job. You can save yourself trouble if you buy a rebuilt or new master cylinder.*

1. Remove the secondary piston stop screw

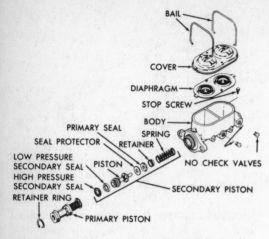

BAIL

COVER

DIAPHRAGM

STOP SCREW

BODY

PRIMARY SEAL

SPRING

SEAL PROTECTOR

RETAINER

LOW PRESSURE
SECONDARY SEAL   PISTON

HIGH PRESSURE
SECONDARY SEAL

RETAINER RING

NO CHECK VALVES

SECONDARY PISTON

PRIMARY PISTON

Exploded view of a typical master cylinder

(if equipped) which is located at the bottom of the master cylinder front reservoir.

2. Position the master cylinder is a vise covering the jaws with cloth to prevent damage. Do not tighten the vise too tightly!

3. Remove the lockring from the inside of the piston bore. Once this is done, the primary piston assembly may be removed.

4. The secondary piston, piston spring, and the retainer may be removed by blowing compressed air through the stop screw hole. If compressed air is not available, the piston may be removed with a small piece of wire. Bend the wire ¼" from the end into a right angle. Hook this end to the edge of the secondary piston and pull it from the bore. The brass insert should not be removed unless it is being replaced.

5. Inspect the piston bore for corrosion or other obstructions. Make certain that the outer ports are clean and the fluid reservoirs are free of foreign matter. Check the by-pass and the compensation ports to see if they are clogged.

6. Remove the primary seal, seal protector, and secondary seals from the secondary piston.

Clean all parts in denatured alcohol or brake fluid. Use a soft brush to clean metal parts and compressed air to dry all parts. If corrosion is found inside the housing, either a crocus cloth or fine emery paper can be used to remove these deposits. Remember to wash all parts after this cleaning. Be sure to keep the parts clean until assembly. All rubber parts should be clean and free of fluid. Check each rubber part for cuts, nicks or other damage. If there is any doubt as to the condition of any rubber part, it is best to replace it.

NOTE: *Since there are differences between master cylinders, it is important that the assemblies are identified correctly. There is a two-letter metal stamp located at the end of the master cylinder. The stamp indicates the*

displacement capabilities of the particular *master cylinder. If the master cylinder is replaced, it must be replaced with a cylinder with the same markings.*

7. Install the new secondary piston assembly.

NOTE: *The seal which is nearest the flat end has its lips facing toward the flat end. On Delco units, the seal in the second groove has its lips facing toward the compensating holes of the secondary piston. On Bendix units, the seal is an O-ring.*

8. Install the new primary seal and seal protector over the end of the secondary piston opposite the secondary seals. It should be positioned so that the flat side of the seal seats against the flange of the piston with the compensation holes.

NOTE: *The seal protector isn't used on 1977 and later models.*

9. Install the complete primary piston assembly included in every repair kit.

10. Coat the master cylinder bore and the primary and secondary seals with brake fluid. Position the secondary seal spring retainer into the secondary piston spring.

11. Place the retainer and spring over the end of the secondary piston so that the retainer is placed inside the lips of the primary seal.

12. Seat the secondary piston. It may be necessary to manipulate the piston to get it to seat.

13. Position the master cylinder with the open end up and coat the primary and secondary seal on the primary piston with brake fluid. Push the primary piston into the bore of the master cylinder. Hold the piston and position the lockring.

14. Still holding the piston down, install and tighten the stop screw to a torque of 25 to 40 in.lb.

15. Install the reservoir cover and also the cover on the master cylinder and its retaining clip.

16. Bleed the master cylinder of air. Do this by positioning the cylinder with the front slightly down, filling it with brake fluid, and working the primary piston until all the bubbles are gone.

Hydro-Boost

Diesel engined trucks are equipped with the Bendix Hydro-boost system. This power brake booster obtains hydraulic pressure from the power steering pump, rather than vacuum pressure from the intake manifold as in most gasoline engine brake booster systems. Procedures for removing, overhauling, and replacing the master cylinder are the same as previously outlined. The master cylinder uses the same DOT 3 brake fluid recommended for other systems.

HYDRO-BOOST SYSTEM CHECKS

1. A defective Hydro-Boost cannot cause any of the following conditions:
   a. Noisy brakes
   b. Fading pedal
   c. Pulling brakes

If any of these occur, check elsewhere in the brake system.

2. Check the fluid level in the master cylinder. It should be within ¼" of the top. If it isn't, add only DOT-3 or DOT-4 brake fluid until the correct level is reached.

3. Check the fluid level in the power steering pump. The engine should be at normal running temperature and stopped. The level should register on the pump dipstick. Add power steering fluid to bring the reservoir level up to the correct level. Low fluid level will result in both poor steering and stopping ability.

WARNING: *The brake hydraulic system uses brake fluid only, while the power steering and Hydro-Boost systems use power steering fluid only. Don't mix the two.*

4. Check the power steering pump belt tension, and inspect all of the power steering/Hydro-Boost hoses for kinks or leaks.

5. Check and adjust the engine idle speed, as necessary.

6. Check the power steering pump fluid for bubbles. If air bubbles are present in the fluid, bleed the system:
   a. Fill the power steering pump reservoir to specifications with the engine at normal operating temperature.
   b. With the engine running, rotate the steering wheel through its normal travel 3 or 4 times, without holding the wheel against the stops.
   c. Check the fluid level again.

7. If the problem still exists, go on to the Hydro-Boost test sections and troubleshooting chart.

HYDRO-BOOST TESTS

Functional Test

1. Check the brake system for leaks or low fluid level. Correct as necessary.

2. Place the transmission in Neutral and stop the engine. Apply the brakes 4 or 5 times to empty the accumulator.

3. Keep the pedal depressed with moderate (25-40 lbs.) pressure and start the engine.

4. The brake pedal should fall slightly and then push back up against your foot. If no movement is felt, the Hydro-Boost system is not working.

Accumulator Leak Test

1. Run the engine at normal idle. Turn the steering wheel against one of the stops; hold it there for no longer than 5 seconds. Center the steering wheel and stop the engine.

2. Keep applying the brakes until a hard pedal is obtained. There should be a minimum of 1 power assisted brake application when pedal pressure of 20-25 lbs. is applied.

3. Start the engine and allow it to idle. Rotate the steering wheel against the stop. Listen for a light hissing sound; this is the accumulator being charged. Center the steering wheel and stop the engine.

4. Wait one hour and apply the brakes without starting the engine. As in step 2, there should be at least 1 stop with power assist. If not, the accumulator is defective and must be replaced.

HYDRO-BOOST SYSTEM BLEEDING

The system should be bled whenever the booster is removed and installed.

1. Fill the power steering pump until the fluid level is at the base of the pump reservoir neck. Disconnect the battery lead from the distributor.

NOTE: *Remove the electrical lead to the fuel solenoid terminal on the injection pump before cranking the engine.*

2. Jack up the front of the car, turn the wheels all the way to the left, and crank the engine for a few seconds.

3. Check steering pump fluid level. If necessary, add fluid to the **Add** mark on the dipstick.

4. Lower the car, connect the battery lead, and start the engine. Check fluid level and add fluid to the **Add** mark if necessary.

With the engine running, turn the wheels from side to side to bleed air from the system. Make sure that the fluid level stays above the internal pump casting.

5. The Hydro-Boost system should now be fully bled. If the fluid is foaming after bleeding, stop the engine, let the system set for one hour, then repeat the second part of Step 4.

The preceding procedures should be effective in removing excess air from the system, however sometimes air may still remain trapped. When this happens the booster may make a gulping noise when the brake is applied. Lightly pumping the brake pedal with the engine running should cause this noise to disappear. After the noise stops, check the pump fluid level and add as necessary.

HYDRO-BOOST TROUBLESHOOTING

HIGH PEDAL AND STEERING EFFORT (IDLE)

1. Loose/broken power steering pump bilt.
2. Low power steering fluid level.
3. Leaking hoses or fittings.
4. Low idle speed.
5. Hose restriction.
6. Defective power steering pump

HIGH PEDAL EFFORT (IDLE)

1. Binding pedal/linkage.
2. Fluid contamination.
3. Defective Hydro-Boost unit

POOR PEDAL RETURN

1. Binding pedal linkage.
2. Restricted booster return line.
3. Internal return system restriction

PEDAL CHATTER/PULSATION

1. Power steering pump drive belt slipping.
2. Low power steering fluid level.
3. Defective power steering pump.
4. Defective Hydro-Boost unit

BRAKES OVERSENSITIVE

1. Binding linkage.
2. Defective Hydro-Boost unit

NOISE

1. Low power steering fluid level.
2. Air in the power steering fluid.
3. Loose power steering pump drive belt.
4. Hose restrictions

OVERHAUL

GM Hydro-Boost units may be rebuilt. Kits are available through auto parts jobbers and GMC/Chevrolet truck dealers.

NOTE: *Have a drain pan ready to catch and discard leaking fluid during disassembly.*

Use the accompanying illustrations to overhaul the Hydro-Boost system. If replacing the power piston/accumulator, dispose of the old one as shown.

HYDRO-BOOST UNIT REMOVAL AND INSTALLATION

WARNING: *Power steering fluid and brake fluid cannot be mixed. If brake seals contact the steering fluid or steering seals contact the brake fluid, damage will result.*

1. Turn the engine off and pump the brake pedal 4 or 5 times to deplete the accumulator inside the unit.
2. Remove the two nuts from the master cylinder, and remove the cylinder keeping the brake lines attached. Secure the master cylinder out of the way.
3. Remove the three hydraulic lines from the booster.
4. Remove the booster unit from the firewall.
5. To install, reverse the removal procedure, torque the booster retaing bolts to 25 ft. lbs. and bleed the Hydro-Boost system.

SPOOL VALVE PLUG AND SEAL REMOVAL AND INSTALLATION

1. Turn the engine off and pump the brake pedal 4 or 5 times to deplete the accumulator inside the boost unit.
2. Remove the master cylinder from the boost unit with the brake lines attached. Fasten the master cylinder out of the way with tape or wire.
3. Push the spool valve plug in and use a small screwdriver to carefully remove the retaining ring.
4. Remove the spool valve plug and O-ring.
5. Installation is the reverse of removal.

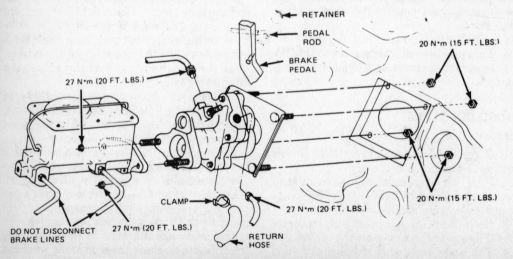

RETAINER

PEDAL ROD

BRAKE PEDAL

20 N•m (15 FT. LBS.)

27 N•m (20 FT. LBS.)

CLAMP

DO NOT DISCONNECT BRAKE LINES

27 N•m (20 FT. LBS.)

27 N•m (20 FT. LBS.)

RETURN HOSE

20 N•m (15 FT. LBS.)

Removal and installation of Hydro-Booster

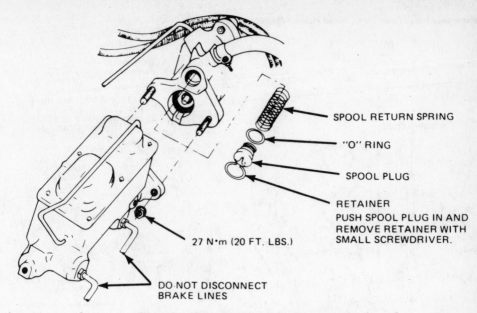

Removing Hydro-Boost spool valve and seal

Within the diagram: SPOOL RETURN SPRING, "O" RING, SPOOL PLUG, RETAINER PUSH SPOOL PLUG IN AND REMOVE RETAINER WITH SMALL SCREWDRIVER., 27 N·m (20 FT. LBS.), DO NOT DISCONNECT BRAKE LINES

Bleed the system upon installation, following the above bleeding instructions.

Combination Valve

This valve is used on all models with disc brakes. The valve itself is a combination of: 1) the metering valve, which will not allow the front disc brakes to engage until the rear brakes contact the drum; 2) the failure warning switch, which notifies the driver if one of the systems has a leak; 3) the proportioner which limits rear brake pressure and delays rear wheel skid.

CENTERING THE SWITCH

Whenever work on the brake system is done it is possible that the brake warning light will come on and refuse to go off when the work is finished. In this event, the switch must be centered.

1. Raise and support the truck.

2. Attach a bleeder hose to the rear brake bleed screw and immerse the other end of the hose in a jar of clean brake fluid.

3. Be sure that the master cylinder is full.

4. When bleeding the brakes, the pin in the end of the metering portion of the combination valve must be held in the open position (with the tool described in the brake bleeding section installed under the pin mounting bolt). Be sure to tighten the bolt after removing the tool.

5. Turn the ignition key ON. Open the bleed screw while an assistant applies heavy pressure on the brake pedal. The warning lamp should light. Close the bleed screw before the helper releases the pedal.

To reset the switch, apply heavy pressure to the pedal. This will apply hydraulic pressure to the switch which will recenter it.

6. Repeat Step 5 for the front bleed screw.

7. Turn the ignition OFF and lower the truck.

NOTE: *If the warning lamp does not light during Step 5, the switch is defective and must be replaced.*

VALVE REPLACEMENT

1. Disconnect the hydraulic lines and plug to prevent dirt from entering the system.

2. Disconnect the warning switch harness.

3. Remove the retaining bolts and remove the valve.

4. Install in reverse of removal and bleed the brake system.

Bleeding the Brakes

The brake system must be bled when any brake line is disconnected or there is air in the system.

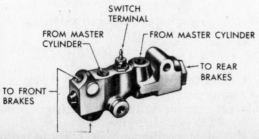

Within the diagram: SWITCH TERMINAL, FROM MASTER CYLINDER, FROM MASTER CYLINDER, TO REAR BRAKES, TO FRONT BRAKES

Combination valve

Remove And Install Spool Valve, Power Piston/Acuumulator And Seal.

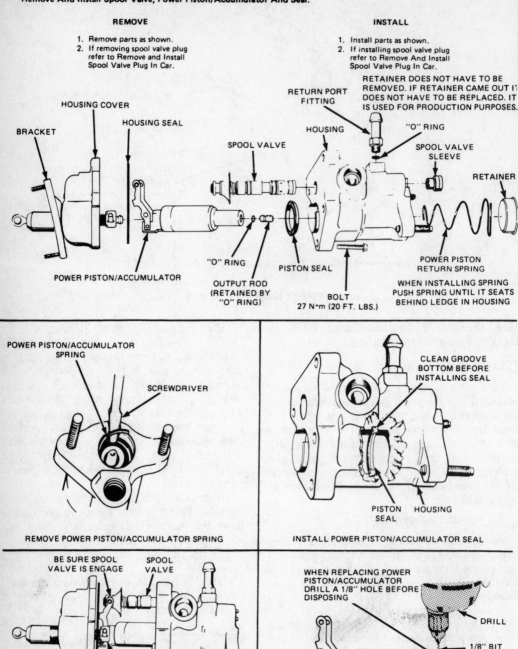

REMOVE

1. Remove parts as shown.
2. If removing spool valve plug refer to Remove and Install Spool Valve Plug In Car.

BRACKET

HOUSING COVER

HOUSING SEAL

SPOOL VALVE

POWER PISTON/ACCUMULATOR

"O" RING

OUTPUT ROD (RETAINED BY "O" RING)

PISTON SEAL

INSTALL

1. Install parts as shown.
2. If installing spool valve plug refer to Remove And Install Spool Valve Plug In Car.

RETAINER DOES NOT HAVE TO BE REMOVED. IF RETAINER CAME OUT IT DOES NOT HAVE TO BE REPLACED. IT IS USED FOR PRODUCTION PURPOSES.

RETURN PORT FITTING

HOUSING

"O" RING

SPOOL VALVE SLEEVE

RETAINER

POWER PISTON RETURN SPRING

BOLT 27 N·m (20 FT. LBS.)

WHEN INSTALLING SPRING PUSH SPRING UNTIL IT SEATS BEHIND LEDGE IN HOUSING

POWER PISTON/ACCUMULATOR SPRING

SCREWDRIVER

REMOVE POWER PISTON/ACCUMULATOR SPRING

CLEAN GROOVE BOTTOM BEFORE INSTALLING SEAL

PISTON SEAL   HOUSING

INSTALL POWER PISTON/ACCUMULATOR SEAL

BE SURE SPOOL VALVE IS ENGAGE

SPOOL VALVE

BE SURE "U" SHAPE BRACKET ON INPUT ROD IS ENGAGED WITH LOWER LEVER PINS.

INSTALL SPOOL VALVE

WHEN REPLACING POWER PISTON/ACCUMULATOR DRILL A 1/8" HOLE BEFORE DISPOSING

DRILL

1/8" BIT

DISPOSE POWER PISTON/ACCUMULATOR

Hydro Boost overhaul

NOTE: *Never bleed a wheel cylinder when a drum is removed.*

1. Clean the master cylinder of excess dirt and remove the cylinder cover and the diaphragm.

2. Fill the master cylinder to the proper lev-el. Check the fluid level periodically during the bleeding process, and replenish it as necessary. Do not allow the master cylinder to run dry, or you will have to start over.

3. Before opening any of the bleeder screws, you may want to give each one a shot of pene-

fill the master cylinder, install its cover and diaphragm, and discard the fluid bled from the brake system.

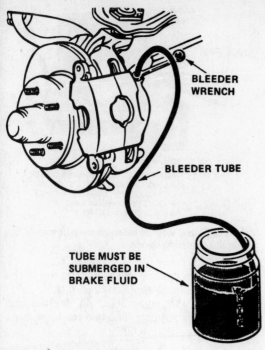

Brake bleeding equipment

trating solvent. This reduces the possibility of breakage when they are unscrewed.

4. Attach a length of vinyl hose to the bleeder screw of the brake to be bled. Insert the other end of the hose into a clear jar half full of brake fluid, so that the end of the hose is beneath the level of fluid. The correct sequence for bleeding is to work from the brake farthest from the master cylinder to the one closest; right rear, left rear, right front, left front.

5. The combination valve (all vehicles with disc brakes) must be held open during the bleeding process. A clip, tape, or other similar tool (or an assistant) will hold the metering pin in.

6. With power brakes, depress and release the brake pedal three or four times to exhaust any residual vacuum.

7. Have an assistant push down on the brake pedal. Open the bleeder valve slightly. As the pedal reaches the end of its travel, close the bleeder screw.

Repeat this process until no air bubbles are visible in the expelled fluid.

NOTE: *Make sure your assistant presses the brake pedal to the floor slowly. Pressing too fast will cause air bubbles to form in the fluid.*

8. Repeat this procedure at each of the brakes. Remember to check the master cylinder level occasionally. Use only fresh fluid to refill the master cylinder, not the stuff bled from the system.

9. When the bleeding process is complete, re-

DRUM BRAKES

Brake Drums
REMOVAL AND INSTALLATION

Drums on all models can be removed by raising the vehicle, removing the wheel lugs and the tire, and pulling the drum from the brake assembly. If the brake drums have been scored from worn linings, the brake adjuster must be backed off so that the brake shoes will retract from the drum. Some drums are retained by two screws to the hub, and can be removed after removing the screws.

The adjuster can be backed off by inserting a brake adjusting tool through the access hole provided. In some cases the access hole is provided in the brake drum. A metal cover plate is over the hole. This may be removed by using a hammer and chisel.

NOTE: *Make sure all metal particles are removed from the brake drum before reassembly.*

To install, reverse the removal procedure.

CAUTION: *Do not blow the brake dust out of the drums with compressed air or lung power. The brake linings contain asbestos, a known cancer causing agent. Wipe the drums and linings with a clean, grease-free rag, and dispose of the rag immediately.*

INSPECTION

Lining

Remove the drum and inspect the lining thickness on both brake shoes. A front brake lining should be replaced if it is less than $1/8''$ thick at the lowest point on the brake shoe. The limit for rear brake linings is $1/16''$. However, these lining thickness measurements may disagree with your state inspection laws.

NOTE: *Brake shoes should always be replaced in axle sets.*

NEW SHOE & LINING   **READY FOR REPLACEMENT**

New and worn brake pads

Drum

When a drum is removed, it should be inspected for cracks, scores, or other imperfections. These must be corrected before the drum is replaced.

If the drum is found to be cracked, replace it. Do not attempt to service a cracked drum.

Minor drum score marks can be removed with fine emery cloth. Heavy score marks must be removed by "turning" the drum. This procedure removes metal from the entire inner surface of the drum in order to level the surface. Automotive machine shops and some parts stores are equipped to perform this operation.

If the drum is not scored, it should be polished with fine emery cloth before replacement. If the drum is resurfaced, it should not be enlarged past 0.060″ of the original diameter.

NOTE: *All brake drums have a maximum diameter number cast into their outer surface. This number is a maximum wear diameter and not a refinish diameter. Do not refinish a brake drum that will not meet specifications after refinishing.*

It is advisable, while the drums are off, to check them for out-of-round. An inside micrometer is necessary for an exact measurement; therefore unless this tool is available, the drums should be taken to a machine shop to be checked. Any drum which is more than 0.006″ out-of-round will result in an inaccurate brake adjustment and should be refinished or replaced.

NOTE: *If the micrometer is available, make all measurements at right angles to each other and at the open and closed edges of the drum machined surface.*

Check the drum with a micrometer in the following manner:

1. Position the drum on a level surface.
2. Insert the micrometer with its adapter bars if necessary.

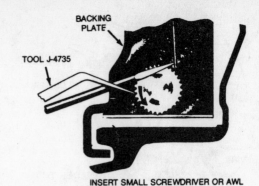

INSERT SMALL SCREWDRIVER OR AWL THROUGH BACKING PLATE SLOT AND HOLD ADJUSTER LEVER AWAY FROM SPROCKET BEFORE BACKING OFF BRAKE SHOE ADJUSTMENT

Cross-sectional view of drum brake adjustment using brake adjusting spoon

3. Obtain a reading on the micrometer at the point of maximum contact. Record this.
4. Rotate the micrometer 45 degrees and take a similar reading. The two readings must not vary more than 0.006″.

Brake Shoes

REMOVAL

NOTE: *Disassemble and assemble one wheel at a time so that you will have an example to refer to while you are reassembly the shoes.*

1. Jack up and support your vehicle with jackstands.
2. Remove the check nuts from the end of the parking brake equalizer bracket and remove all tension on the brake cable (rear brakes only).
3. Remove the brake drums.

NOTE: *The brake pedal must not be depressed while the drums are removed.*

4. Using a brake tool, remove the shoe springs from their holder.
5. Remove the self-adjuster actuator spring.
6. Remove the spring from the secondary shoe by pulling it from the anchor pin.
7. Remove the holddown pins. They can be removed with a pair of pliers. Reach around the rear of the backing plate and hold the back of the pin. Turn the top of the pin retainer with the pliers. This will align the elongated tang with the slot in the retainer. Be careful, as the pin is spring-loaded and may fly off when released. Use the same procedure for the other pin assembly.
8. Remove the adjuster actuating lever assembly by removing the holddown pin which is attached to the secondary brake shoe.

NOTE: *Since the actuator, pivot, and override spring are considered an assembly it is not recommended that they be disassembled.*

Measure the drum inside diameter with an inside micrometer

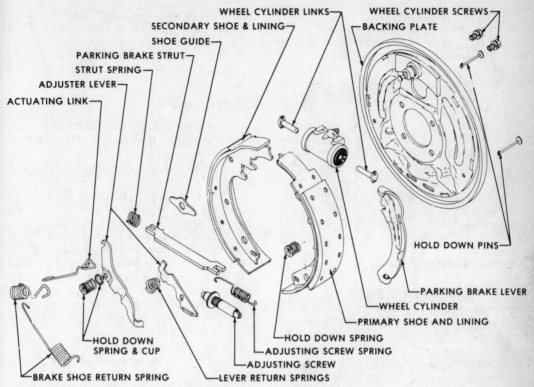

WHEEL CYLINDER LINKS
SECONDARY SHOE & LINING
SHOE GUIDE
PARKING BRAKE STRUT
STRUT SPRING
ADJUSTER LEVER
ACTUATING LINK

WHEEL CYLINDER SCREWS
BACKING PLATE

HOLD DOWN PINS
PARKING BRAKE LEVER
WHEEL CYLINDER
PRIMARY SHOE AND LINING

HOLD DOWN SPRING & CUP
BRAKE SHOE RETURN SPRING
HOLD DOWN SPRING
ADJUSTING SCREW SPRING
ADJUSTING SCREW
LEVER RETURN SPRINGS

Exploded view of a typical drum brake

9. Remove the shoes from the backing plate. Make sure that you have a secure grip on the assembly as the bottom spring will still exert pressure on the shoes. Slowly let the tops of the shoes come together and the tension will decrease and the adjuster and spring may be removed.

NOTE: *If the linings are to be reused, mark them for identification.*

10. Remove the parking brake lever from the secondary shoe (rear brakes). Using a pair of pliers, pull back on the spring which surrounds the cable. At the same time, remove the cable from the notch in the shoe bracket. Make sure that the spring does not snap back or injury may result.

11. Use a cloth to remove dirt from the brake drum. Check the drums for scoring and cracks. Have the drums checked for out-of-round and service the drums as necessary.

12. Check the wheel cylinders by carefully pulling the lower edges of the wheel cylinder

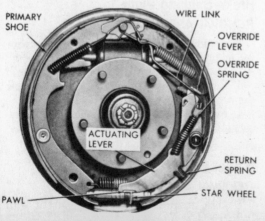

PRIMARY SHOE
WIRE LINK
OVERRIDE LEVER
OVERRIDE SPRING
ACTUATING LEVER
RETURN SPRING
PAWL
STAR WHEEL

Self-adjusting brake, assembled

Unhooking the pull-back springs

Removing the hold-down springs

Checking the actuator

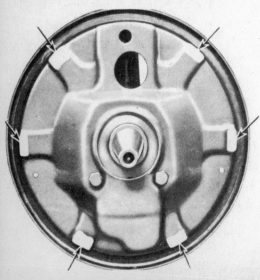

Lubricate the brake backing plate pads

boots away from the cylinders. Excessive leakage requires rebuilding or replacement of the wheel cylinder.

NOTE: *A small amount of fluid will be present to act as a lubricant for the wheel cylinder pistons.*

INSTALLATION

1. Install the parking brake lever to the secondary shoe with the washer and retaining ring.

2. Install the adjusting screw assembly and spring.

NOTE: *The coils of the spring must not be over the star wheel. Left and right hand springs are different do not interchange.*

3. Spread the shoe and lining assemblies to clear the axle flange, and connect the parking brake cable and install the parts on the truck.

4. Install the parking brake strut and spring by spreading the shoes apart. The strut end without the spring engages the parking brake lever. The end with the spring engages the opposite shoe.

5. Install the shoe guide.

6. Install the actuator lever and return spring.

7. Install the hold down pins, lever pivot and hold down springs.

8. Install the actuating link on the anchor pin.

9. Lift up on the actuatoor lever and hook the link into the lever.

10. Install the shoe return springs, using brake spring pliers.

11. Adjust the brakes if necessary.

CAUTION: *It is important to keep your hands free of dirt and grease when handling the brake shoes. Foreign matter will be absorbed into the linings and result in unpredictable braking.*

Brake Backing Plate
REMOVAL AND INSTALLATION

1. Remove the brake shoes and wheel cylinder as previously outlined.

2. Remove the axles as outlined in Chapter 7.

3. Remove the attaching bolts and pull off the backing plate.

4. Install all parts as outlined and torque the backing plate retaining bolts to 25-30 ft. lbs.

Wheel Cylinders
REMOVAL AND INSTALLATION

1. Jack up your truck and support it with jackstands.

2. Remove the wheel and tire.

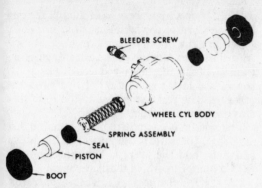

Wheel cylinder, exploded view

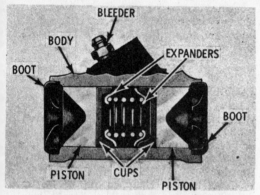

Sectional view of an assembled wheel cylinder

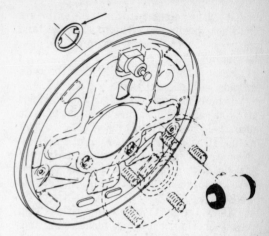

Later wheel cylinders are held in place by a retainer (arrow)

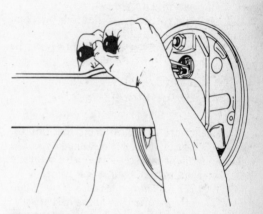

Bend back the tabs on the retainer using two awls simultaneously

3. Back off the brake adjustment and remove the drum.

4. Disconnect and plug the brake line.

5. Remove the brake shoe pull-back springs.

6. Remove the screws securing the wheel cylinder to the backing plate. Later models have their wheel cylinders retained by a round retainer. To release the locking tabs, insert two awls (see illustration) into the access slots to bend the tabs back. Install the new retainer over the wheel cylinder abutment using a 1⅛", 12-point socket and socket extension.

7. Disengage the wheel cylinder pushrods from the brake shoes and remove the wheel cylinder.

8. To install, place the wheel cylinder into position and torque the retaining bolts to 180 in. lbs., install the pushrods and install the inlet tube and torque to 120-280 in. lbs. Bleed the brake system.

OVERHAUL

As in the case with master cylinders, overhaul kits for wheel cylinders are readily available. When rebuilding and installing wheel cylinders, avoid getting any contaminants into the system. Always install clean, new high-quality brake fluid. If dirty or improper fluid has been

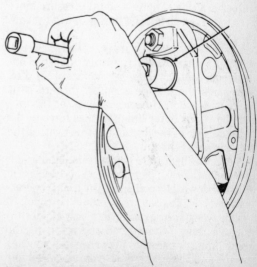

Install the new retainer over the wheel cylinder using a 1⅛ in., 12-point socket and extension

used, it will be necessary to drain the entire system, flush the system with proper brake fluid, replace all rubber components, refill, and bleed the system.

1. Remove the rubber boots from the cylinder ends with pliers. Discard the boots.

2. Remove and discard the pistons and cups.

3. Wash the cylinder and metal parts in denatured alcohol or clean brake fluid.

CAUTION: *Never use a mineral-based solvent such as gasoline, kerosene, or paint thinner for cleaning purposes. These solvents will swell rubber components and quickly deteriorate them.*

4. Allow the parts to air dry or use compressed air. Do not use rags for cleaning since lint will remain in the cylinder bore.

5. Inspect the piston and replace it if it shows scratches.

6. Lubricate the cylinder bore and counterbore with clean brake fluid.

7. Install the rubber cups (flat side out) and then the pistons (flat side in).

8. Insert new boots into the counterbores by hand. Do not lubricate the boots.

FRONT DISC BRAKES

All models from 1971 have front disc brakes. This single piston caliper is a sliding type. No brake adjustment is necessary once the brake pads have been seated against the rotor.

NOTE: *1977 and later vehicles (Over 9000 GVWR) use a Bendix disc brake assembly.*

The single piston system is a closed system with fluid pressure being exerted on two surfaces: on the piston itself and in the opposite direction against the bottom of the bore of the caliper housing. There is equal pressure since the area of the piston and the bottom of the caliper bore are equal.

When hydraulic pressure is applied to the piston, it is transmitted to the inner brake pad lining which contacts the inner surface of the disc. This pulls the caliper assembly inboard as it slides on the four rubber bushings. As the caliper slides, the outer lining applies force to the outer surface of the disc and in this manner the two surfaces brake the vehicle.

Since the hydraulic pressure is equally applied to both brake pads there will be no flexing or distortion of the pad and if the unit is operating correctly, the pad wear should be equal.

This type of disc brake uses a very small running clearance between pad and rotor. As the brake linings wear, the caliper assembly moves inward and the brake fluid from the reservoir fills the area behind the piston so that brake pedal travel is not increased. Therefore, you

will still have a high pedal even though the pad could be worn to the metal backing.

Because the brake pads are in close contact with the rotor, this gives the advantage of increased brake response, reduced brake pedal travel, and faster generation of hydraulic line pressure. The pad being close to the rotor disc also cleans it of foreign material.

The system is composed of the hub and disc assembly, the shield, the support, the caliper assembly, and the linings. The disc is vented with cooling fins which dissipate heat.

CAUTION: *Brake shoes contain asbestos, which has been determined to be a cancer causing agent. Never clean the brake surface with compressed air! Avoid inhaling any dust from any brake surface! When cleaning brake surfaces, use a commercially available brake cleaning fluid.*

Brake Pads

INSPECTION

NOTE: *The Bendix system does not use a wear warning sensor.*

Support the front suspension or axle on jackstands and remove the wheels. Look in at the ends of the caliper to check the lining thickness of the outer pad. Look through the inspection hole in the top of the caliper to check the thickness of the inner pad. Minimum acceptable pad thickness is $\frac{1}{32}''$ from the river heads on original equipment riveted linings and $\frac{1}{32}''$ lining thickness on bonded linings.

NOTE: *These manufacturer's specifications may not agree with your state inspection law.*

All original equipment pads are the riveted type; unless you want to remove the pads to measure the actual thickness from the rivet heads, you will have to make the limit for visual inspection $\frac{1}{16}''$ or more. The same applies if you don't know what kind of lining you have. 1974 and later original equipment pads and GM replacement pads have an integral wear sensor. This is a spring steel tab on the rear edge of the inner pad which produces a squeal by rubbing against the rotor to warn that the pads have reached their wear limit. They do not squeal when the brakes are applied.

WARNING: *The squeal will eventually stop if the worn pads aren't replaced. Should this happen, replace the pads immediately to prevent expensive rotor (disc) damage.*

REMOVAL AND INSTALLATION

NOTE: *Remove one set of pads at a time so you have a reference for reassembly.*

Delco Type

1. Remove the cover on the master cylinder and siphon enough fluid out of the reservoirs to

bring the level to ⅓ full. This step prevents spilling fluid when the piston is pushed back. Discard the fluid.

2. Raise and support the vehicle. Remove the front wheels and tires.

3. Push the brake piston back into its bore using a C-clamp.

4. Remove the two Allen head bolts which hold the caliper and then lift the caliper off the disc.

WARNING: *Do not let the caliper assembly hang by the brake hose. Tie it out of the way with wire.*

5. Remove the inboard and outboard pads. The shoe support spring will come off with the inner pad.

6. Install rubber bushings on all four caliper ears.

NOTE: *It is essential that new sleeves and rubber bushings be used to ensure the proper function of the sliding caliper design. There is a special Tool recommended No. J-22835 for installing the sleeves.*

7. Position the sleeves so that the end toward the shoe and lining assemblies is flush with the machined surface of the ear.

8. Install the shoe support spring by replacing the single tang end of the spring over the notch in the center of the edge of the shoe. Then press the two tangs at the spring end of the inboard shoe spring over the bottom edge of the shoe so that they engage in the shoe securely.

9. Position the inboard shoe and lining assembly (with the spring attached) in the caliper so that the ear end of the shoe and lining is down and the bottom end up at an angle with the spring resting on the pisto I.D.. Press down on both ends of the shoe until the shoe is in a a flat position, resting on the piston. The spring end of the inboard shoe support spring should be resting on the I.D. of the piston.

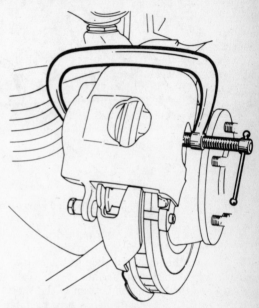

Use a C-clamp to retract the caliper piston

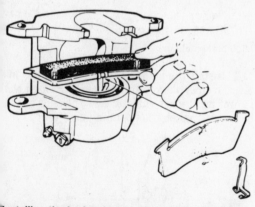

Installing the brake shoe; note proper shoe support spring installation

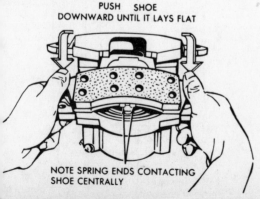

PUSH SHOE DOWNWARD UNTIL IT LAYS FLAT

NOTE SPRING ENDS CONTACTING SHOE CENTRALLY

Inner brake pad installation in caliper

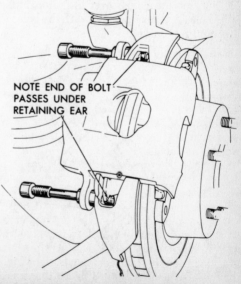

NOTE END OF BOLT PASSES UNDER RETAINING EAR

Disc brake caliper removal and installation

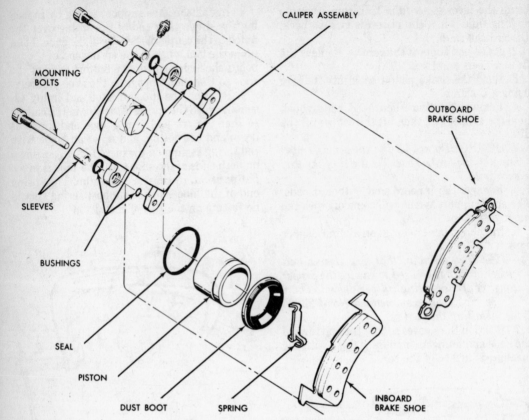

MOUNTING BOLTS

SLEEVES

BUSHINGS

SEAL

PISTON

DUST BOOT

SPRING

CALIPER ASSEMBLY

OUTBOARD BRAKE SHOE

INBOARD BRAKE SHOE

Exploded view of the Delco brake caliper

NOTE: *The wear sensor of the inborad shoe will be toward the rear of the caliper.*

10. Position the outboard shoe in the caliper with the ears at the top of the shoe over the caliper ears and the tab at the bottom of the shoe engaged in the caliper cutout. Be sure to note the right and left brake shoes.

11. Position the caliper over the rotor, lining up the holes in the caliper ears with the holes in the mounting bracket.

12. Install the bolts starting through the inboard caliper sleeves and ears and through the mounting bracket, making sure the ends of the bolts pass under the retaining ears on the in-

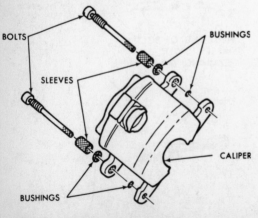

BOLTS

BUSHINGS

SLEEVES

BUSHINGS

CALIPER

▒ LUBRICATE AREAS INDICATED

Caliper lubrication points at installation

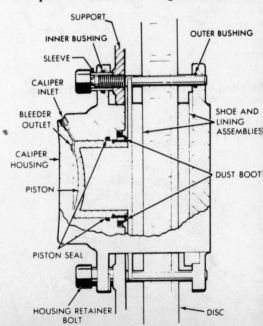

SUPPORT

INNER BUSHING

SLEEVE

CALIPER INLET

BLEEDER OUTLET

CALIPER HOUSING

PISTON

PISTON SEAL

HOUSING RETAINER BOLT

OUTER BUSHING

SHOE AND LINING ASSEMBLIES

DUST BOOT

DISC

Cross-section of a front disc brake caliper

board shoe. Push the bolts on through to engage the holes in the outboard shoes and the outboard caliper ears at the same time, threading the bolts into the mounting bracket. Torque the bolts to 35 ft. lbs.

13. Add fresh brake fluid as necessary to the master cylinder.

14. Pump the brake pedal to seat the linings against the rotor.

15. Clinch the upper ears of the outboard shoe by positiong channel lock pliers with one jaw on the top upper ear and one jaw on the notch on the bottom of the shoe opposite the upper ear. After clinching, the ears are to be flat against the caliper housing.

16. Install the wheel and tire assembly.

Bendix Type

1. Remove approximately ⅓ of the brake fluid from the master cylinder. Discard the used brake fluid.

2. Jack up your vehicle and support it with jackstands.

3. Push the piston back into its bore. This can be done by suing a C-clamp.

4. Remove the bolt at the caliper support key. Use a brass drift pin to remove the key and spring.

5. Tie the caliper out of the way with a piece of wire. Be careful not to damage the brake line.

6. Remove the inner shoe from the rear caliper support. Discard the inner shoe clip. Remove the outer shoe.

7. To install, lubricate the caliper support and support spring, with silicone.

8. Install a NEW inboard shoe clip in the steering knuckle or rear support. Install the lower end of the inboard shoe into the groove provided in the steering knuckle or support (against the spring clip). Slide the upper end of

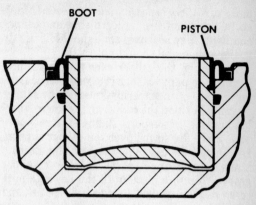

Piston boot seating

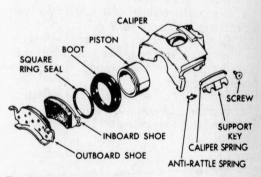

Removing the caliper support key

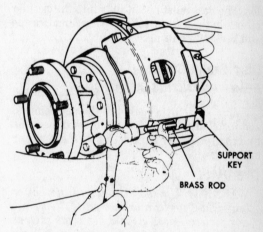

Bendix brake caliper assembly

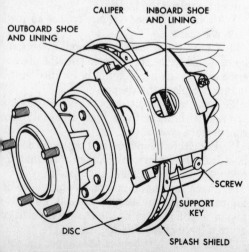

Bendix front disc brake assembly

the shoe into position. Be sure the clip remains in position.

9. Position the outboard shoe in the caliper with the ears at the top of the shoe over the caliper ears and the tab at the bottom of the shoe engaged in the caliper cutout. If assembly is difficult, a C-clamp may be used. Be careful not to mar the lining.

10. With both shoes installed, lift up the caliper and rest the bottom edge of the outboard lining on the outer edge of the brake disc to

make sure there is no clearance between the tab at the bottom of the outboard shoe and caliper abutment. The outboard shoe should fit tightly in the caliper and should not rattle.

11. Position the caliper over the brake disc, guiding the upper caliper groove onto the mating surface of the steering knuckle opr caliper support. Position the caliper to the lower steering knuckle (or support) sliding surface.

12. Place the spring over the caliper support key, install the assembly between the steering knuckle (or rear support) and lower caliper groove. Tap into place until the key retaining screw can be installed, using a brass punch and a light hammer.

13. Install the screw and torque to 12-18 ft. lbs. The boss must not fit fully into the circular cutout in the key. Install the wheel and tire and add brake fluid as necessary.

Disc Brake Caliper
REMOVAL AND INSTALLATION

Follow steps 1 through 4 of the pad removal and installation procedure then disconnect the hydraulic hose. Bleed the system after installing.

OVERHAUL

WARNING: *Use only denatured alcohol or brake fluid to clean caliper parts. Never use any mineral based cleaning solvents such as gasoline or kerosene as these solvents will deteriorate rubber parts.*

1. Remove the caliper, clean it and place it on a clean and level work surface.

2. Remove the brake hose from the caliper and discard the copper gasket. Check the brake hose for cracks or deterioration. Replace the hose as necessary.

3. Drain the brake fluid from the caliper.

4. Pad the interior of the caliper with cloth and then apply compressed air to the caliper inlet hose.

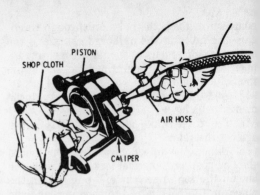

Piston removal using compressed air. Keep fingers out of the way of the piston when the air is applied.

CAUTION: *Do not place hands or fingers in front of the piston in an attempt to catch it. Use just enough air pressure to ease the piston out of the bore.*

5. Remove the piston dust boot by prying it out with a drift pin. Use caution when performing this procedure.

6. Remove the piston seal from the caliper piston bore using a small piece of wood or plastic. DO NOT use any type of metal tool for this procedure.

7. Remove the bleeder valve from the caliper. NOTE: *Dust boot, piston seal, rubber bushings and sleeves are included in every rebuilding kit. These should be replaced at every caliper rebuilt.*

8. Clean all parts in solvent and dry them completely.

WARNING: *The use of lubricated shop air may leave an oil film on metal parts. This may damage rubber parts.*

9. Examine the mounting bolts for rust or corrosion. Replace them as necessary.

10. Examine the piston for scoring, nicks, or worn plating. If any of these conditions are present, replace the piston.

WARNING: *Do not use any type of abrasive on the piston.*

11. Check the piston bore. Small defects can be removed with crocus cloth. (Do not use emery cloth.) If the bore cannot be cleaned in this manner, replace the caliper.

12. Lubricate the piston bore and the new piston seal with brake fluid. Place the seal in the caliper bore groove.

13. Lubricate the piston and position the new boot into the groove in the piston so that the fold faces the open end of the piston.

14. Place the piston into the caliper bore using caution not to damage the seal. Force the piston to the bottom of the bore. This will require a force of 50-100 lbs.

15. Place the dust boot in the caliper counter bore and seat the boot. Make sure that the boo

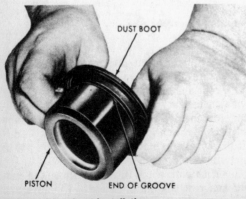

Caliper piston boot installation

...s positioned correctly and evenly. Proper seat-
...ng of the boot is very important for sealing out
...contaminants.

16. Lubricate the new sleeves and rubber
...bushings. Install the bushings in the caliper
...ears. Install the sleeves so that the end toward
...the disc pad is flush with the machined surface.

NOTE: *Lubrication of the sleeves and bushings is essential to ensure the proper operation of the sliding caliper design.*

17. Install the shoe support spring in the
...piston.

18. Install the disc pads in the caliper and re-
...mount the caliper in the hub. See pad removal
...and installation under Disc Brake Caliper.

19. Reconnect the brake hose to the steel
...brake line. Install the retainer clip. Bleed the
...brakes (see Brake Bleeding).

20. Replace the wheels, check the brake fluid
...level, check the brake pedal travel, and road
...est the vehicle.

Disc Brake Rotor

REMOVAL AND INSTALLATION

Two Wheel Drive

1. Remove the brake caliper as previously
...outlined.

2. Remove the outer wheel bearing. (Refer to
...Chapter 7 for the proper procedure).

3. Remove the rotor from the spindle.

4. Reverse procedure to install.

Four Wheel Drive

1. Remove the locking hubs as described in
...Chapter 7.

2. Remove the wheel bearing outer lock nut,
...retainer and and wheel bearing inner adjusting
...nut.

3. Remove the hub and disc assembly and
...outer wheel bearing.

4. Remove the oil seal and inner bearing cone
...from the hub using a brass drift and tapping
...with a hammer. Discard the oil seal.

5. Remove the inner and outer bearing cups
...using a brass drift and a hammer.

6. Clean, inspect and lubricate all parts as re-
...quire with a high speed grease.

WARNING: *Lubrication must be applied to
prevent deterioration before the unit is placed
in service.*

7. Assemble the outer wheel bearing cup into
...the wheel hub using Tool J-6368 and Driver
...Handle J-8092.

8. Assemble the inner wheel bearing cup into
...the wheel hub using Tool J-23448 and Driver
...Handle J-8092.

9. Pack the wheel bearing cone with a high
...melting point type wheel bearing grease and in-
...sert the cone into the cup.

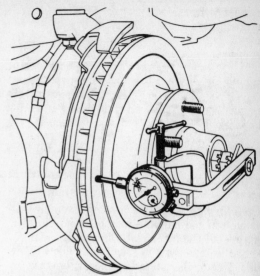

Measure the disc run-out with a dial indicator

10. Install thje hub and disc and wheel bearings to the spindle.

11. Adjust the wheel bearings.

INSPECTION

The minimum wear thickness, 1.215", is cast
into each disc hub. This is a minimum wear dimension and not a refinish dimension. If the
thickness of the disc after refinishing will be
1.230" or less, it must be replaced. Refinishing
is required whenever the disc surface shows
scoring or severe rust scale. Scoring not deeper
than 0.015" in depth can be corrected by
refinishing.

NOTE: *Some discs have an anti-squeal
groove. This should not be mistaken for
scoring.*

Wheel Bearings

Four wheel drive front wheel bearing service
is covered under 4-Wheel Drive Front Hub removal and installation in Chapter 7. The following wheel bearing service procedure is for
two wheel drive trucks only.

2-Wheel Drive

1. Remove the wheel, tire assembly, and the
brake drum or brake caliper.

2. Remove the hub and disc as an assembly.
Remove the caliper mounting bolts and insert a
block between the brake pads as the caliper is
removed. Remove the caliper and wire it out of
the way.

3. Pry off the grease cap, remove the cotter
pin, spindle nut, and washer, and then remove
the hub. Be careful that you do not drop the
wheel bearings.

4. Remove the outer roller bearing assembly

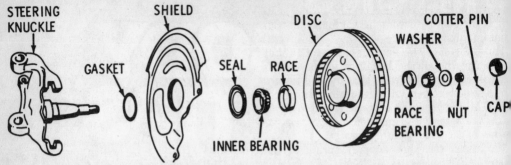

Exploded view of 2WD knuckle and hub assembly showing inner and outer wheel bearings

from the hub. The inner bearing assembly will remain in the hub and may be removed after prying out the inner seal. Discard this seal.

5. Clean all parts in solvent and allow to air dry. Check the parts for excessive wear or damage.

6. If the bearing cups are worn or scored, they must be replaced. Using a hammer and a drift, remove the bearing cups from the hub. When installing new cups, make sure that they are not cocked, and that they are fully seated against the hub shoulder.

7. Pack both wheel bearings using high melting point wheel bearing grease. Ordinary grease will melt, and ruin the pads. High temperature grease provides an extra margin of protection. Place a healthy glob of grease in the palm of one hand and force the edge of the bearing into it so that the grease fills the bearing. Do this until the whole bearing is packed. Grease packing tools are available to make this job a lot less messy. There are also tools which make it possible to grease the inner bearing without removing it or the disc from the spindle.

8. Place the inner bearing in the hub and install a new inner seal, making sure that the seal flange faces the bearing cup.

9. Carefully install the wheel hub over the spindle.

10. Using your hands, firmly press the outer bearing into the hub. Install the spindle washer and nut.

11. To adjust the bearings on 1970-71 models, tighten the adjusting nut to 15 ft.lb. while rotating the hub. Back the nut off one flat ($\frac{1}{6}$ turn) and insert a new cotter pin. If the nut and spindle hole do not align, back the nut off slightly. There should be 0.001-0.008″ end play in the bearing. This can be measured with a dial indicator, if you wish. Install the dust cap, wheel, and tire.

12. To adjust the bearings on 1972 through 1984 models, spin the wheel hub by hand and tighten the nut until it is just snug (12 ft.lb.). Back off the nut until it is loose, then tighten it finger right. Loosen the nut until either hole in

the spindle lines up with a slot in the nut, and insert a new cotter pin. There should be 0.001 0.008″ end play in the bearing through 1973 and 0.001-0.005″ 1974 and later. This can be measured with a dial indicator, if you wish. Replace the dust cap, wheel and tire.

PARKING BRAKE
ADJUSTMENT

The rear brakes serve a dual purpose. They are used as service brakes and as parking brakes. To obtain proper adjustment of the parking brake, the service brakes must first be properly adjusted as outlined earlier.

1. Apply the parking brake 1 notch from the fully released position, 4 notches for 1976 and later.

2. Raise and support the vehicle.

3. Loosen the jam nut at the equalizer.

4. Tighten or loosen the adjusting nut until light drag is felt when the rear wheels are rotated forward.

5. Tighten the check nut.

6. Release the parking brake and rotate the rear wheels. No drag should be felt. If even light drag is felt, readjust the parking brake.

7. Lower the vehicle.

NOTE: *If a new parking brake cable is being installed, pre-stretch it by applying the parking brake hard about three times before making adjustments.*

Parking Brake Cables
FRONT CABLE REPLACEMENT

1. Raise vehicle on hoist.

2. Remove adjusting nut from equalizer.

3. Remove retainer clip from rear portion of front cable at frame and from lever arm.

4. Disconnect front brake cable from parking brake pedal or lever assemblies. Remove front brake cable. On some models, it may assist in stallation of new cable if a heavy cord is tied to other end of cable in order to guide new cable through proper routing.

CHILTON'S
AUTO BODY
REPAIR TIPS

ools and Materials • Step-by-Step Illustrated Procedures

w To Repair Dents, Scratches and Rust Holes

pray Painting and Refinishing Tips

With a little practice, basic body repair procedures can be mastered by any do-it-yourself mechanic. The step-by-step repairs shown here can be applied to almost any type of auto body repair.

TOOLS & MATERIALS

You may already have basic tools, such as hammers and electric drills. Other tools unique to body repair — body hammers, grinding attachments, sanding blocks, dent puller, half-round plastic file and plastic spreaders — are relatively inexpensive and can be obtained wherever auto parts or auto body repair parts are sold. Portable air compressors and paint spray guns can be purchased or rented.

Auto Body Repair Kits

The best and most often used products are available to the do-it-yourselfer in kit form, from major manufacturers of auto body repair products. The same manufacturers also merchandise the individual products for use by pros.

Kits are available to make a wide variety of repairs, including holes, dents and scratches and fiberglass, and offer the advantage of buying the materials you'll need for the job. There is little waste or chance of materials going bad from not being used. Many kits may also contain basic body-working tools such as body files, sanding blocks and spreaders. Check the contents of the kit before buying your tools.

BODY REPAIR TIPS

Safety

Many of the products associated with auto body repair and refinishing contain toxic chemicals. Read all labels before opening containers and store them in a safe place and manner.

• Wear eye protection (safety goggles) when using power tools or when performing any operation that involves the removal of any type of material.

• Wear lung protection (disposab[le] mask or respirator) when grinding, sar[d] ing or painting.

Sanding

1 Sand off paint before using a de[nt] puller. When using a non-adhes[ive] sanding disc, cover the back of the di[sc] with an overlapping layer or two [of] masking tape and trim the edges. T[he] disc will last considerably longer.

2 Use the circular motion of the sar[d] ing disc to grind *into* the edge of t[he] repair. Grinding or sanding away fro[m] the jagged edge will only tear the sar[d] paper.

3 Use the palm of your ha[nd] flat on the panel to dete[ct] high and low spots. Do not use yo[ur] fingertips. Slide your hand slowly ba[ck] and forth.

WORKING WITH BODY FILLER

Mixing The Filler

...leanliness and proper mixing and ...application are extremely impor-...t. Use a clean piece of plastic or ...ss or a disposable artist's palette to ... body filler.

Allow plenty of time and follow di-...rections. No useful purpose will be ...ved by adding more hardener to ...ke it cure (set-up) faster. Less hard-...r means more curing time, but the ...xture dries harder; more hardener ...ans less curing time but a softer mix-...e.

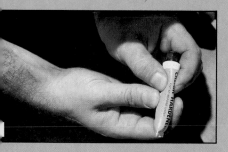

Both the hardener and the filler ...should be thoroughly kneaded or ...red before mixing. Hardener should ...a solid paste and dispense like thin ...thpaste. Body filler should be ...ooth, and free of lumps or thick ...ts.

...Getting the proper amount of hard-...r in the filler is the trickiest part of ...paring the filler. Use the same ...unt of hardener in cold or warm ...ather. For contour filler (thick coats), ...ead of hardener twice the diameter of ...filler is about right. There's about a ...% margin on either side, but, if in ...bt use less hardener.

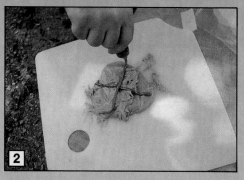

3 Mix the body filler and hardener by wiping across the mixing surface, picking the mixture up and wiping it again. Colder weather requires longer mixing times. Do not mix in a circular motion; this will trap air bubbles which will become holes in the cured filler.

Applying The Filler

1 For best results, filler should not be applied over 1/4″ thick.

Apply the filler in several coats. Build it up to above the level of the repair surface so that it can be sanded or grated down.

The first coat of filler must be pressed on with a firm wiping motion.

Apply the filler in one direction only. Working the filler back and forth will either pull it off the metal or trap air bubbles.

REPAIRING DENTS

Before you start, take a few minutes to study the damaged area. Try to visualize the shape of the panel before it was damaged. If the damage is on the left fender, look at the right fender and use it as a guide. If there is access to the panel from behind, you can reshape it with a body hammer. If not, you'll have to use a dent puller. Go slowly and work the metal a little at a time. Get the panel as straight as possible before applying filler.

1 This dent is typical of one that can be pulled out or hammered out from behind. Remove the headlight cover, headlight assembly and turn signal housing.

2 Drill a series of holes ½ the size of the end of the dent puller along the stress line. Make some trial pulls and assess the results. If necessary, drill more holes and try again. Do not hurry.

3 If possible, use a body hammer and block to shape the metal back to its original contours. Get the metal back as close to its original shape as possible. Don't depend on body filler to fill dents.

4 Using an 80-grit grinding disc on a electric drill, grind the paint from th surrounding area down to bare meta Use a new grinding pad to prevent hea buildup that will warp metal.

5 The area should look like this whe you're finished grinding. Knock th drill holes in and tape over small ope ings to keep plastic filler out.

6 Mix the body filler (see Body Repa Tips). Spread the body filler even over the entire area (see Body Repa Tips). Be sure to cover the area con pletely.

7 Let the body filler dry until the su face can just be scratched with yo fingernail. Knock the high spots fro the body filler with a body file ("Chees grater"). Check frequently with the pal of your hand for high and low spots.

8 Check to be sure that trim pieces that will be installed later will fit exactly. Sand the area with 40-grit paper.

9 If you wind up with low spots, you may have to apply another layer of filler.

10 Knock the high spots off with 40-grit paper. When you are satisfied with the contours of the repair, apply a thin coat of filler to cover pin holes and scratches.

11 Block sand the area with 40-grit paper to a smooth finish. Pay particular attention to body lines and ridges that must be well-defined.

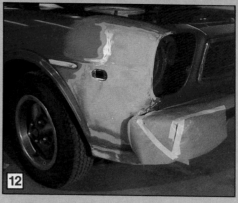

12 Sand the area with 400 paper and then finish with a scuff pad. The finished repair is ready for priming and painting (see Painting Tips).

Materials and photos courtesy of Ritt Jones Auto Body, Prospect Park, PA.

REPAIRING RUST HOLES

There are many ways to repair rust holes. The fiberglass cloth kit shown here is one of the most cost efficient for the owner because it provides a strong repair that resists cracking and moisture and is relatively easy to use. It can be used on large and small holes (with or without backing) and can be applied over contoured areas. Remember, however, that short of replacing an entire panel, no repair is a guarantee that the rust will not return.

1 Remove any trim that will be in the way. Clean away all loose debris. Cut away all the rusted metal. But be sure to leave enough metal to retain the contour or body shape.

2 Grind away all traces of rust with a 24-grit grinding disc. Be sure to grind back 3-4 inches from the edge of the hole down to bare metal and be sure all traces of paint, primer and rust are removed.

3 Block sand the area with 80 or 100 grit sandpaper to get a clear, shiny surface and feathered paint edge. Tap the edges of the hole inward with a ball peen hammer.

4 If you are going to use release film, cut a piece about 2-3″ larger than the area you have sanded. Place the film over the repair and mark the sanded area on the film. Avoid any unnecessary wrinkling of the film.

5 Cut 2 pieces of fiberglass matte to match the shape of the repair. One piece should be about 1″ smaller than the sanded area and the second piece should be 1″ smaller than the first. Mix enough filler and hardener to saturate the fiberglass material (see Body Repair Tips).

6 Lay the release sheet on a flat surface and spread an even layer of filler, large enough to cover the repair. Lay the smaller piece of fiberglass cloth in the center of the sheet and spread another layer of filler over the fiberglass cloth. Repeat the operation for the larger piece of cloth.

7 Place the repair material over the repair area, with the release film facing outward. Use a spreader and work from the center outward to smooth the material, following the body contours. Be sure to remove all air bubbles.

8 Wait until the repair has dried tack free and peel off the release sheet. The ideal working temperature is 60°-90° F. Cooler or warmer temperatures or high humidity may require additional curing time. Wait longer, if in doubt.

9 Sand and feather-edge the entire area. The initial sanding can be ~~o~~ne with a sanding disc on an electric ~~dr~~ill if care is used. Finish the sanding ~~wi~~th a block sander. Low spots can be ~~fil~~led with body filler; this may require ~~se~~veral applications.

10 When the filler can just be scratched with a fingernail, ~~kn~~ock the high spots down with a body ~~fil~~e and smooth the entire area with 80-~~gr~~it. Feather the filled areas into the sur-~~ro~~unding areas.

11 When the area is sanded smooth, mix some topcoat and hardener ~~an~~d apply it directly with a spreader. ~~Th~~is will give a smooth finish and pre-~~ve~~nt the glass matte from showing ~~th~~rough the paint.

12 Block sand the topcoat smooth with finishing sandpaper (200 grit), and 400 grit. The repair is ready for masking, priming and painting (see Painting Tips).

Materials and photos courtesy Marson Corporation, Chelsea, Massachusetts

PAINTING TIPS

Preparation

1 SANDING — Use a 400 or 600 grit wet or dry sandpaper. Wet-sand the area with a $1/4$ sheet of sandpaper soaked in clean water. Keep the paper wet while sanding. Sand the area until the repaired area tapers into the original finish.

2 CLEANING — Wash the area to be painted thoroughly with water and a clean rag. Rinse it thoroughly and wipe the surface dry until you're sure it's completely free of dirt, dust, fingerprints, wax, detergent or other foreign matter.

3 MASKING — Protect any areas you don't want to overspray by covering them with masking tape and newspaper. Be careful not get fingerprints on the area to be painted.

4 PRIMING — All exposed metal should be primed before painting. Primer protects the metal and provides an excellent surface for paint adhesion. When the primer is dry, wet-sand the area again with 600 grit wet-sandpaper. Clean the area again after sanding.

Painting Techniques

P aint applied from either a spray gun or a spray can (for small areas) will provide good results. Experiment on an old piece of metal to get the right combination before you begin painting.

SPRAYING VISCOSITY (SPRAY GUN ONLY) — Paint should be thinned to spraying viscosity according to the directions on the can. Use only the recommended thinner or reducer and the same amount of reduction regardless of temperature.

AIR PRESSURE (SPRAY GUN ONLY) — This is extremely important. Be sure you are using the proper recommended pressure.

TEMPERATURE — The surface to be painted should be approximately the same temperature as the surrounding air. Applying warm paint to a cold surface, or vice versa, will completely upset the paint characteristics.

THICKNESS — Spray with smooth strokes. In general, the thicker the coat of paint, the longer the drying time. Apply several thin coats about 30 seconds apart. The paint should remain wet long enough to flow out and no longer; heavier coats will only produce sags or wrinkles. Spray a light (fog) coat, followed by heavier color coats.

DISTANCE — The ideal spraying distance is 8"-12" from the gun or can to the surface. Shorter distances will produce ripples, while greater distances will result in orange peel, dry film and poor color match and loss of material due to overspray.

OVERLAPPING — The gun or can should be kept at right angles to the surface at all times. Work to a wet edge at an even speed, using a 50% overlap and direct the center of the spray at the lower or nearest edge of the previous stroke.

RUBBING OUT (BLENDING) FRESH PAINT — Let the paint dry thoroughly. Runs or imperfections can be sanded out, primed and repainted.

Don't be in too big a hurry to remove the masking. This only produces paint ridges. When the finish has dried for at least a week, apply a small amount of fine grade rubbing compound with a clean, wet cloth. Use lots of water and blend the new paint with the surrounding area.

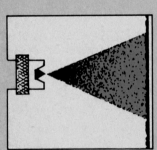

WRONG

Thin coat. Stroke too fast, not enough overlap, gun too far away.

CORRECT

Medium coat. Proper distance, good stroke, proper overlap.

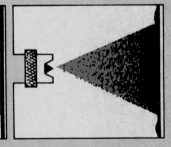

WRONG

Heavy coat. Stroke too slow, too much overlap, gun too close.

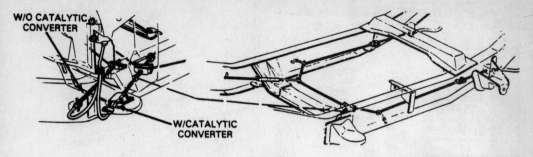

(C10-20)   **C MODELS (ALL)**

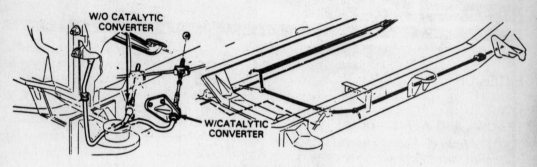

C100 (16) AND K MODELS

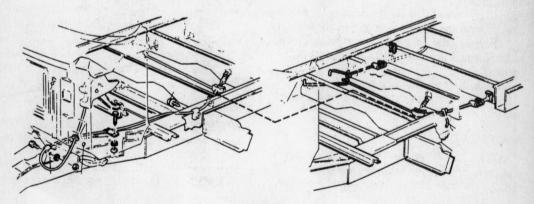

G MODELS

Parking Brake System, Typical

5. Install cable by reversing removal procedure.

6. Adjust parking brake.

CENTER CABLE REPLACEMENT

1. Raise vehicle on hoist.

2. Remove adjusting nut from equalizer.

3. Unhook connector at each end and disengage hooks and guides.

4. Install new cable by reversing removal procedure.

5. Adjust parking brake.

6. Apply parking brake 3 times with heavy pressure and repeat adjustment.

REAR PARKING BRAKE CABLE REPLACEMENT

1. Raise vehicle on hoist.

2. Remove rear wheel and brake drum.

3. Loosen adjusting nut at equalizer.

4. Disengage rear cable at connector.

5. Bend retainer fingers.

6. Disengage cable at brake shoe operating lever.

7. Install new cable by reversing removal procedure.

8. Adjust parking brake.

Body and Trim

10

EXTERIOR

Doors

REMOVAL AND INSTALLATION

NOTE: *If the door being removed is to be re-installed, matchmark the hinge position.*

1. If the door is to be replaced with a new one, remove the trim panels weathersheets and all molding.

2. If the door is to be replaced with a new one, remove the glass, locks and latches.

3. Support the door and remove the hinge-to-body attaching bolts. Lift the door from the truck.

4. Installation is the reverse of removal.

Perform the alignment procedures indicated below.

ALIGNMENT

NOTE: *The holes for the hinges are over-sized to provide for latitude in alignment.*

Align the door hinges first, then the striker.

Hinges

1. If a door is being installed, first mount the door and tighten the hinge bolts lightly.

If the door has not been removed, determine which hinge bolts must be loosed to effect alignment.

2. Loosen the necessary bolts just enough to allow the door to be moved with a padded prybar.

3. Move the door in small movements and check the fit after each movement.

Be sure that there is no binding or interference with adjacent panels.

Keep repeating this procedure until the door is properly aligned.

4. Tighten all the bolts.

NOTE: *Shims may be either fabricated or purchased to install behind the hinges as an aid in alignment.*

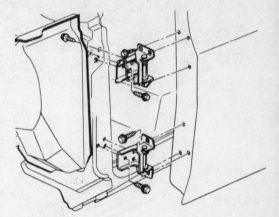

Door Hinge

Striker Plate

NOTE: *The striker is attached to the pillar using oversized holes, providing latitude in movement.*

Striker adjustment is made by loosening the bolts and moving the striker plate in the desired

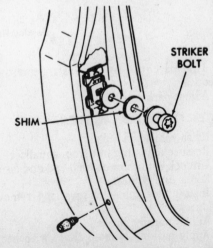

Typical Striker Bolt Adjustment

direction or adding or deleting the shims behind the plate, or both.

The striker is properly adjusted when the locking latch enters the striker without rubbing and the door closed fully and solidly, with no play when closed.

HOOD

REMOVAL AND INSTALLATION

NOTE: *You are going to need an assistant for this job.*

1. Open the hood and trace the outline of the hinges on the body.

2. While an assistant holds the hood, remove the hinge-to-body bolts and lift the hood off.

3. Installation is the reverse of removal.

● Align the outlines previously made.

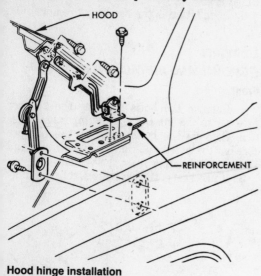

Hood hinge installation

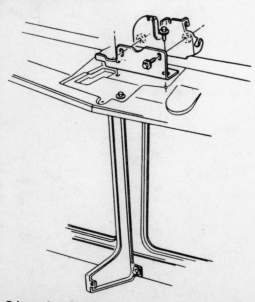

Primary hood latch

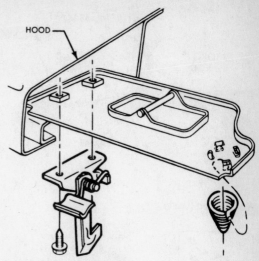

Secondary hood latch

● Check that the hood closes properly.
● Adjust hood alignment, if necessary.

ALIGNMENT

1. Hood alignment can be adjusted front-to-rear or side-to-side by loosening the hood-to-hinge or hinge-to-body bolts.

2. The front edge of the hood can be adjusted for closing height by adding or deleting shims under the hinges.

3. The rear edge of the hood can be adjusted for closing height by raising or lowering the hood bumpers.

Tailgate

REMOVAL AND INSTALLATION

1. Open and support the tailgate.

2. Remove the four bolts securing hinge to body on each side.

3. Disconnect the wiring harness if so equipped.

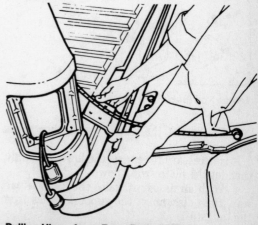

Pulling Hinge Away From Body (Utility)

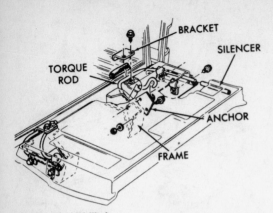

Torque Rod (Utility)

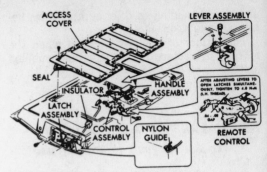

Latch and Remote Controls (Suburban)

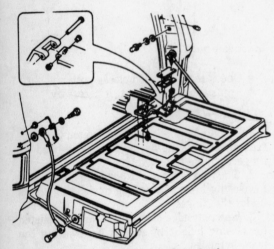

Endgate, Hinges and Supports-(Suburban)

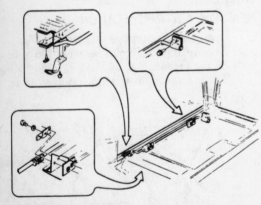

Torque Rod (Suburban)

4. Disconnect the torque rod anchor plates on each side.

It is necessary to remove the lower bolt only, then let the plate swing down.

4. With an assistant, raise the tailgate part way, then disconnect the support cables from the tailgate.

5. Remove the tailgate by pulling the discon-nected hinge from the body, then grasping the torque rod with one hand and pulling torque rod over the gravel deflector and lift off the tailgate.

6. Installation is the reverse of removal.

Bumpers

REMOVAL AND INSTALLATION

Front

1. Remove the bolts securing the bumper face bar to the left and right bumper brackets.

2. Remove the bolts securing the bumper face bar to the left and right bumper braces and remove the bumper from the vehicle.

3. If necessary, the brackets and braces may

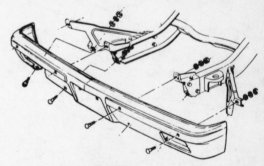

Front bumper installation

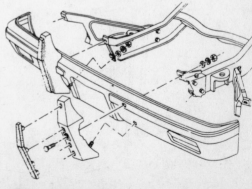

Front bumper guards

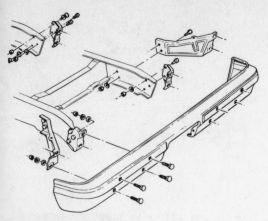

Rear bumper installation

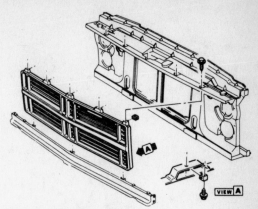

Typical grille installation

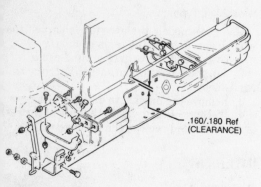

.160/.180 Ref
(CLEARANCE)

Rear step bumper

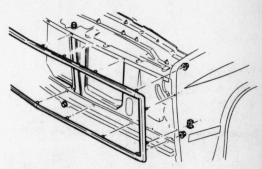

Typical grille moulding installation

be removed from the frame by removing the retaining bolts.

4. For ease of installation use something to support the bumper and tighten all bolts securely.

Rear

1. Remove the bolts securing the bumper face bar to the left and right bumper braces. Disconnect the license lamp wiring.

2. Remove the bolts securing the bumper face bar to the left and right bumper brackets and remove the bumper from the vehicle.

3. If necessary, the brackets, braces and rear stone shield may be removed from the frame by removing the retaining bolts.

4. For ease of installation use something to support the bumper and tighten all bolts securely. Connect the license lamp wiring.

Grille

REMOVAL AND INSTALLATION

1. Most grilles are attached to the radiator support. Some may have braces in between. Re-

move the grille retaining screws and remove the grille.

2. Grille mouldings are usually held in place by retaining nuts which may be removed from under the hood.

Outside Rear View Mirror

REMOVAL AND INSTALLATION

Standard Type

1. Remove the mirror to bracket screw and remove the mirror from the door.

2. Remove the bracket to door bolts and remove the bracket and gasket from the vehicle.

3. Install in reverse of above.

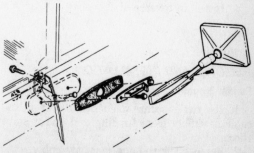

Standard rear view mirror

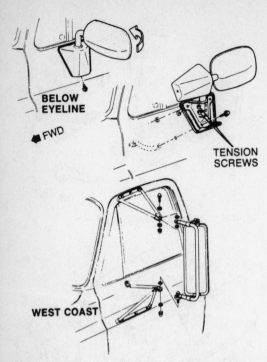

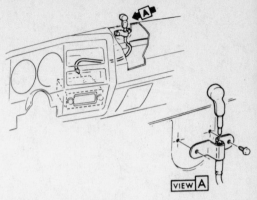

Antenna lead location for windshield type antennas

Below eye level and West Coast mirror installation

Below Eyeline Type

1. Remove the mirror cover screw and lift the cover and pivot the mirror towards the window.

2. Remove the mirror to door bolts and remove the mirror and seal from the door.

3. To install, position the mirror and seal to the door and install the retaining bolts.

4. Pivot the mirror away from the window, and lower the mirror cover.

5. Install the mirror cover screw

West Coast Type

1. Remove the mirror bracket to door bracket nuts, bolts and bushings.

2. Remove the mirror bracket from the vehicle.

3. Remove the door bracket nuts and bolts and remove the bracket from the door.

4. Install in reverse of above.

Antenna

REMOVAL AND INSTALLATION

Fender Mounted Type

1. Use two separate wrenches to prevent the cable assembly from turning and and remove the mast nut.

2. Remove the rod and mast assembly.

3. Reverse the above to install.

Windshield Type

On these models the antenna is part of the windshield. Replace the cable as follows:

1. Disconnect the battery ground cable.

2. Unsnap the antenna cable from the windshield.

3. Remove the bracket to dash panel screws.

4. Disconnect the cable at the rear of the radio receiver and remove the cable assembly.

INTERIOR

Door Panels

REMOVAL

1. Remove the window handle by removing the retaining clip.

2. Remove the door lock knob and arm rest.

3. Remove the four screws securing the lower edge of trim panel.

4. Remove the screw at the door handle cover plate and the screw located under the arm rest pad.

5. Remove the screws retaining the assist strap, if so equipped.

6. Remove the trim panel by carefully prying out at the trim retainers located around the perimeter of the panel.

INSTALLATION

NOTE: *Before installing the door trim assembly, check that all trim retainers are se-*

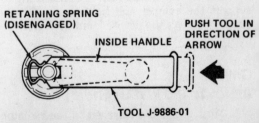

Clip Retained Inside Handle Removal

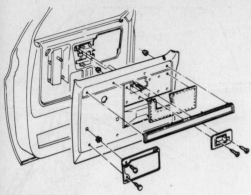

Door Trim Panel

curely installed to the assembly and are not damaged.

1. Pull the door inside handle inward, then position trim assembly to inner panel, inserting door handle through handle hole in panel.

2. Position rim assembly to door inner panel so trim retainers are aligned with attaching holes in panel and tap retainers into holes with a clean rubber mallet.

3. Install previously removed items.

Door Ventilator Assembly

REMOVAL

NOTE: *The channel between the door window glass and door vent is removed as part of the vent assembly.*

1. Regulate the door window glass to the full down position.

2. Remove the clip from the window regulator handle, and knob from the lock rod.

3. Remove arm rest screws and trim panel.

4. Remove the screws attaching the ventilator lower assembly to the door panel.

5. Remove the three screws at the upper front of the door frame.

6. Pull upper portion of the vent assembly rearward and raise upward while rotating counter clockwise.

7. Turn vent assembly 90° and carefully remove by guiding it up and out.

Ventilator Glass Replacement

1. Using an oil can, squirt Prepsol® or an equivalent on the glass filler all around the glass channel or frame to soften the old seal. When the seal is softened, remove the glass from the channel.

2. Thoroughly clean the inside of the glass channel with sandpaper, removing all rust etc.

3. Using new glass channel filler, cut the piece to be installed two inches longer than necessary for the channel.

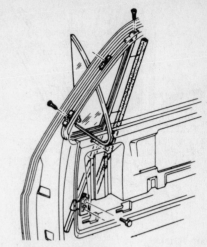

Door Ventilator Assembly

Removing Ventilator Assembly

Place this piece of filler (sandstoned side of filler away from glass) evenly over the edge of the glass which will fit in the channel.

The extra filler extending beyond the rear edge of the glass should be pinched together to hold it in place during glass installation.

4. Brush the inside of the channel with ordinary engine oil.

This will enable the glass and filler to slide freely into the channel.

Push the glass with the filler around it into the channel until it is firmly seated.

After the glass is firmly in place, the oil softens the filler, causing it to swell, thereby making a water tight seal.

Trim off all excess filler material around the channel.

NOTE: *Glass should be installed so that the rear edge is parallel to the division post.*

Allow full cure before water testing.

Adjusting Tension

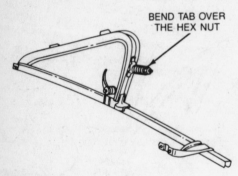

Bend Tabs Over Hex Nut

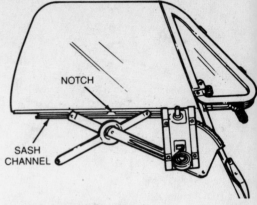

Door Window and Regulator

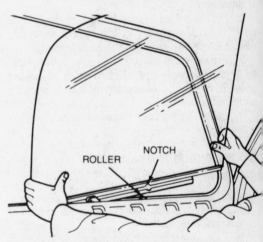

Removing Door Glass

VENTILATOR INSTALLATION

1. Lower the ventilator assembly into the door frame.
2. Make sure the rubber lip is positioned inside the inner and outer panel before tightening the screws.
3. Reinstall all screws and tighten.
4. Install and tighten the three screws at the upper front of the door.

ADJUSTMENT

1. Adjust the ventilator by placing a wrench on the adjusting nut through the access hole and turning vent window to the desired tension.
2. After making adjustment bend tabs over the hex nut on the base of the assembly.
3. Install arm rest screws and trim panel.
4. Install window regulator handle.

Door Glass and Regulator
REMOVAL AND INSTALLATION

1. Lower the door glass completely.
2. Remove the trim panel from the door.
3. Remove the ventilator assembly as previously outlined.

4. Slide the glass forward until the front roller is in line with the notch in the sash channel.
5. Push window forward and tilt the front portion of window up until rear roller is disengaged.
6. Put window assembly in normal position (level) and raise straight up and out.
7. Installation is the reverse of removal.

Power Window Regulator and Motor
REMOVAL AND INSTALLATION

1. Raise the glass to the full up position and tape it to the door frame with fabric tape.
2. Disconnect the negative battery cable.
3. Remove the door trim panel.
4. Remove the remote control bolts and lay the control aside for access.
5. Remove the regulator to door panel attaching bolts.
6. Disconnect the harness from the regulator.

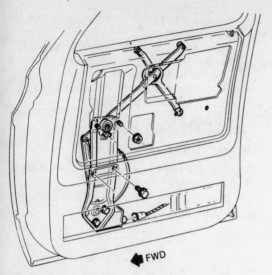

Power window regulator and motor

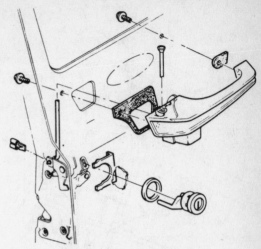

Door lock cylinder and outside handle

7. Slide the regulator assembly rearward, disengaging the rollers from the sash panel.
NOTE: *A notch is provided in the sash panel to allow disengagement of the forward roller on the window regulator.*
8. Remove the regulator assembly through the access hole in the door.
CAUTION: *Step 9 must be performed when the regulator is removed from the door. The regulator lift arms are under tension from the counterbalance spring and can cause serious injury if the motor is removed without locking the sector gear in position.*
9. Drill a hole through the regulator sector gear and back plate. DO NOT drill a hole closer than ½" to the edge of the sector gear or back plate. Install a pan head sheet metal tapping screw (No. 10-12 × ¾") in the drilled hole to lock the sector gear in position.
10. Remove the motor to regulator attaching screws and remove the motor from the regulator.
11. Prior to installation, lubricate the motor drive gear and regulator sector teeth.
12. Install the motor to the regulator. Make sure the motor and sector gear teeth mesh properly before installing the retaining screws.
13. Remove the screw locking the sector gear in the fixed position.
14. Reposition the motor in the door and install the wiring connector.
15. Attach the regulator to the door.

Door Lock Cylinder
REMOVAL AND INSTALLATION

NOTE: *A key code is stamped on the lock cylinder to aid in replacing lost keys.*

1. Remove the door trim panel.
2. Pull the weathersheet, gently, away from the door lock access holes.
3. Using a suitable tool, push the lock cylinder retaining clip upward, noting the position of the lock cylinder.
4. Remove the lock cylinder from the door.
5. Install the lock cylinder in reverse of removal.
It's a good idea to open the window before checking the lock operation, just in case it doesn't work properly.

Door Lock Assembly
REMOVAL

1. Raise the window completely.
2. Remove the door trim panel.
3. Using a suitable flat bladed tool, push on the top of the door lock rod clips and pivot the clip away from the rod.
4. Disconnect the door handle to lock rod from the lock.
5. Disconnect the outside door handle to lock rod clip, using the same procedure as in step 3.
6. Remove the inside door lock knob.
7. Remove the door to lock assembly screws, then tilt the lock assembly away from the outside lock cylinder. Pull the lock assembly downward to make clearance for the inside lock rod and remove the lock assembly from the door.

INSTALLATION

1. Align the lock rod to the hole in the door panel. Tilt the lock assembly onto the outside lock cylinder.
2. Install the door to lock assembly screws.
3. Install the inside door lock knob.

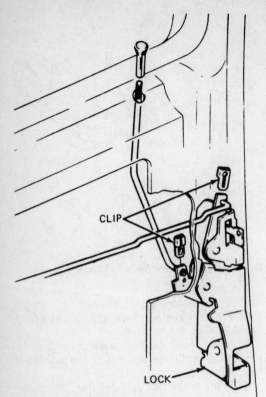

Door Lock Assembly and Rods

4. Install the outside door handle to lock rod onto the lock assembly.

5. Pivot the clip up and onto the lock rod.

6. Install the inside door handle to the lock rod onto the lock assembly.

7. Pivot the clip up and onto the lock rod.

8. Install the door trim panel.

Inside Rear View Mirror

REPLACEMENT

1. Remove the screw retaining the mirror to its glass mounted bracket.

2. Install the mirror to the bracket and tighten as necessary.

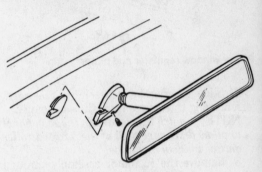

Inside rear view mirror installation

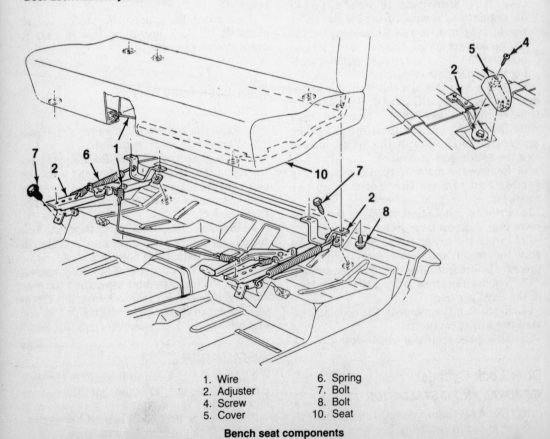

1. Wire
2. Adjuster
4. Screw
5. Cover
6. Spring
7. Bolt
8. Bolt
10. Seat

Bench seat components

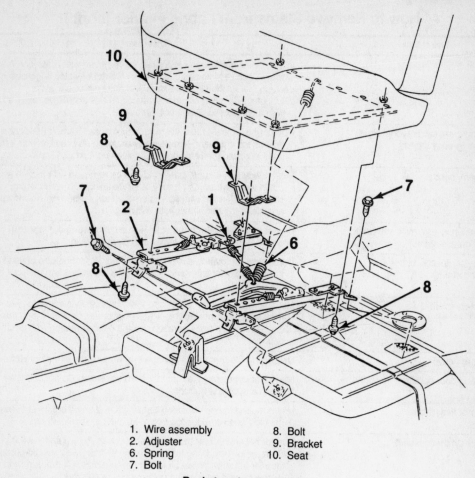

1. Wire assembly
2. Adjuster
6. Spring
7. Bolt

8. Bolt
9. Bracket
10. Seat

Bucket seat components

Seats

REMOVAL AND INSTALLATION

1. Remove the bolt covers, if so equipped.
2. Remove the seat adjuster to floor panel bolts.

3. Remove the seat with the adjuster from the vehicle.
4. The seat adjusters may be removed by removing the retaining bolts.
5. Reverse the above to install.

How to Remove Stains from Fabric Interior

For rest results, spots and stains should be removed as soon as possible. Never use gasoline, lacquer thinner, acetone, nail polish remover or bleach. Use a 3′ x 3″ piece of cheesecloth. Squeeze most of the liquid from the fabric and wipe the stained fabric from the outside of the stain toward the center with a lifting motion. Turn the cheesecloth as soon as one side becomes soiled. When using water to remove a stain, be sure to wash the entire section after the spot has been removed to avoid water stains. Encrusted spots can be broken up with a dull knife and vacuumed before removing the stain.

Type of Stain	How to Remove It
Surface spots	Brush the spots out with a small hand brush or use a commercial preparation such as K2R to lift the stain.
Mildew	Clean around the mildew with warm suds. Rinse in cold water and soak the mildew area in a solution of 1 part table salt and 2 parts water. Wash with upholstery cleaner.

How to Remove Stains from Fabric Interior (cont.)

Type of Stain	How to Remove It
Water stains	Water stains in fabric materials can be removed with a solution made from 1 cup of table salt dissolved in 1 quart of water. Vigorously scrub the solution into the stain and rinse with clear water. Water stains in nylon or other synthetic fabrics should be removed with a commercial type spot remover.
Chewing gum, tar, crayons, shoe polish (greasy stains)	Do not use a cleaner that will soften gum or tar. Harden the deposit with an ice cube and scrape away as much as possible with a dull knife. Moisten the remainder with cleaning fluid and scrub clean.
Ice cream, candy	Most candy has a sugar base and can be removed with a cloth wrung out in warm water. Oily candy, after cleaning with warm water, should be cleaned with upholstery cleaner. Rinse with warm water and clean the remainder with cleaning fluid.
Wine, alcohol, egg, milk, soft drink (non-greasy stains)	Do not use soap. Scrub the stain with a cloth wrung out in warm water. Remove the remainder with cleaning fluid.
Grease, oil, lipstick, butter and related stains	Use a spot remover to avoid leaving a ring. Work from the outisde of the stain to the center and dry with a clean cloth when the spot is gone.
Headliners (cloth)	Mix a solution of warm water and foam upholstery cleaner to give thick suds. Use only foam—liquid may streak or spot. Clean the entire headliner in one operation using a circular motion with a natural sponge.
Headliner (vinyl)	Use a vinyl cleaner with a sponge and wipe clean with a dry cloth.
Seats and door panels	Mix 1 pint upholstery cleaner in 1 gallon of water. Do not soak the fabric around the buttons.
Leather or vinyl fabric	Use a multi-purpose cleaner full strength and a stiff brush. Let stand 2 minutes and scrub thoroughly. Wipe with a clean, soft rag.
Nylon or synthetic fabrics	For normal stains, use the same procedures you would for washing cloth upholstery. If the fabric is extremely dirty, use a multi-purpose cleaner full strength with a stiff scrub brush. Scrub thoroughly in all directions and wipe with a cotton towel or soft rag.

Mechanic's Data

General Conversion Table

Multiply By	To Convert	To	
	LENGTH		
2.54	Inches	Centimeters	.3937
25.4	Inches	Millimeters	.03937
30.48	Feet	Centimeters	.0328
.304	Feet	Meters	3.28
.914	Yards	Meters	1.094
1.609	Miles	Kilometers	.621
	VOLUME		
.473	Pints	Liters	2.11
.946	Quarts	Liters	1.06
3.785	Gallons	Liters	.264
.016	Cubic inches	Liters	61.02
16.39	Cubic inches	Cubic cms.	.061
28.3	Cubic feet	Liters	.0353
	MASS (Weight)		
28.35	Ounces	Grams	.035
.4536	Pounds	Kilograms	2.20
—	To obtain	From	Multiply by

Multiply By	To Convert	To	
	AREA		
.645	Square inches	Square cms.	.155
.836	Square yds.	Square meters	1.196
	FORCE		
4.448	Pounds	Newtons	.225
.138	Ft./lbs.	Kilogram/meters	7.23
1.36	Ft./lbs.	Newton-meters	.737
.112	In./lbs.	Newton-meters	8.844
	PRESSURE		
.068	Psi	Atmospheres	14.7
6.89	Psi	Kilopascals	.145
	OTHER		
1.104	Horsepower (DIN)	Horsepower (SAE)	.9861
.746	Horsepower (SAE)	Kilowatts (KW)	1.34
1.60	Mph	Km/h	.625
.425	Mpg	Km/1	2.35
—	To obtain	From	Multiply by

Tap Drill Sizes

National Coarse or U.S.S.

Screw & Tap Size	Threads Per Inch	Use Drill Number
No. 5	40	.39
No. 6	32	.36
No. 8	32	.29
No. 10	24	.25
No. 12	24	.17
1/4	20	8
5/16	18	F
3/8	16	5/16
7/16	14	U
1/2	13	27/64
9/16	12	31/64
5/8	11	17/32
3/4	10	21/32
7/8	9	49/64

National Coarse or U.S.S.

Screw & Tap Size	Threads Per Inch	Use Drill Number
1	8	7/8
1 1/8	7	63/64
1 1/4	7	1 7/64
1 1/2	6	1 11/32

National Fine or S.A.E.

Screw & Tap Size	Threads Per Inch	Use Drill Number
No. 5	44	.37
No. 6	40	.33
No. 8	36	.29
No. 10	32	.21

National Fine or S.A.E.

Screw & Tap Size	Threads Per Inch	Use Drill Number
No. 12	28	.15
1/4	28	3
6/16	24	1
3/8	24	Q
7/16	20	W
1/2	20	29/64
9/16	18	33/64
5/8	18	37/64
3/4	16	11/16
7/8	14	13/16
1 1/8	12	1 3/64
1 1/4	12	1 11/64
1 1/2	12	1 27/64

Drill Sizes In Decimal Equivalents

Inch	Decimal	Wire	mm
1/64	.0156		.39
	.0157		.4
	.0160	78	
	.0165		.42
	.0173		.44
	.0177		.45
	.0180	77	
	.0181		.46
	.0189		.48
	.0197		.5
	.0200	76	
	.0210	75	
	.0217		.55
	.0225	74	
	.0236		.6
	.0240	73	
	.0250	72	
	.0256		.65
	.0260	71	
	.0276		.7
	.0280	70	
	.0292	69	
	.0295		.75
	.0310	68	
1/32	.0312		.79
	.0315		.8
	.0320	67	
	.0330	66	
	.0335		.85
	.0350	65	
	.0354		.9
	.0360	64	
	.0370	63	
	.0374		.95
	.0380	62	
	.0390	61	
	.0394		1.0
	.0400	60	
	.0410	59	
	.0413		1.05
	.0420	58	
	.0430	57	
	.0433		1.1
	.0453		1.15
	.0465	56	
3/64	.0469		1.19
	.0472		1.2
	.0492		1.25
	.0512		1.3
	.0520	55	
	.0531		1.35
	.0550	54	
	.0551		1.4
	.0571		1.45
	.0591		1.5
	.0595	53	
	.0610		1.55
1/16	.0625		1.59
	.0630		1.6
	.0635	52	
	.0650		1.65
	.0669		1.7
	.0670	51	
	.0689		1.75
	.0700	50	
	.0709		1.8
	.0728		1.85

Inch	Decimal	Wire	mm
	.0730	49	
	.0748		1.9
	.0760	48	
	.0768		1.95
5/64	.0781		1.98
	.0785	47	
	.0787		2.0
	.0807		2.05
	.0810	46	
	.0820	45	
	.0827		2.1
	.0846		2.15
	.0860	44	
	.0866		2.2
	.0886		2.25
	.0890	43	
	.0906		2.3
	.0925		2.35
	.0935	42	
3/32	.0938		2.38
	.0945		2.4
	.0960	41	
	.0965		2.45
	.0980	40	
	.0981		2.5
	.0995	39	
	.1015	38	
	.1024		2.6
	.1040	37	
	.1063		2.7
	.1065	36	
	.1083		2.75
7/64	.1094		2.77
	.1100	35	
	.1102		2.8
	.1110	34	
	.1130	33	
	.1142		2.9
	.1160	32	
	.1181		3.0
	.1200	31	
	.1220		3.1
1/8	.1250		3.17
	.1260		3.2
	.1280		3.25
	.1285	30	
	.1299		3.3
	.1339		3.4
	.1360	29	
	.1378		3.5
	.1405	28	
9/64	.1406		3.57
	.1417		3.6
	.1440	27	
	.1457		3.7
	.1470	26	
	.1476		3.75
	.1495	25	
	.1496		3.8
	.1520	24	
	.1535		3.9
	.1540	23	
5/32	.1562		3.96
	.1570	22	
	.1575		4.0
	.1590	21	
	.1610	20	

Inch	Decimal	Wire & Letter	mm
	.1614		4.1
	.1654		4.2
	.1660	19	
	.1673		4.25
	.1693		4.3
	.1695	18	
11/64	.1719		4.36
	.1730	17	
	.1732		4.4
	.1770	16	
	.1772		4.5
	.1800	15	
	.1811		4.6
	.1820	14	
	.1850	13	
	.1850		4.7
	.1870		4.75
3/16	.1875		4.76
	.1890		4.8
	.1890	12	
	.1910	11	
	.1929		4.9
	.1935	10	
	.1960	9	
	.1969		5.0
	.1990	8	
	.2008		5.1
	.2010	7	
13/64	.2031		5.16
	.2040	6	
	.2047		5.2
	.2055	5	
	.2067		5.25
	.2087		5.3
	.2090	4	
	.2126		5.4
	.2130	3	
7/32	.2188		5.5
	.2205		5.6
	.2210	2	
	.2244		5.7
	.2264		5.75
	.2280	1	
	.2283		5.8
	.2323		5.9
	.2340	A	
15/64	.2344		5.95
	.2362		6.0
	.2380	B	
	.2402		6.1
	.2420	C	
	.2441		6.2
	.2460	D	
	.2461		6.25
	.2480		6.3
1/4	.2500	E	
	.2520		6.
	.2559		6.5
	.2570	F	
	.2598		6.6
	.2610	G	
	.2638		6.7
17/64	.2656		6.74
	.2657		6.75
	.2660	H	
	.2677		6.8

Inch	Decimal	Letter	mm
	.2717		6.9
	.2720	I	
	.2756		7.0
	.2770	J	
	.2795		7.1
	.2810	K	
9/32	.2812		7.14
	.2835		7.2
	.2854		7.25
	.2874		7.3
	.2900	L	
	.2913		7.4
	.2950	M	
	.2953		7.5
19/64	.2969		7.54
	.2992		7.6
	.3020	N	
	.3031		7.7
	.3051		7.75
	.3071		7.8
	.3110		7.9
5/16	.3125		7.93
	.3150		8.0
	.3160	O	
	.3189		8.1
	.3228		8.2
	.3230	P	
	.3248		8.25
	.3268		8.3
21/64	.3281		8.33
	.3307		8.4
	.3320	Q	
	.3346		8.5
	.3386		8.6
	.3390	R	
	.3425		8.7
11/32	.3438		8.73
	.3445		8.75
	.3465		8.8
	.3480	S	
	.3504		8.9
	.3543		9.0
	.3580	T	
	.3583		9.1
23/64	.3594		9.12
	.3622		9.2
	.3642		9.25
	.3661		9.3
	.3680	U	
	.3701		9.4
	.3740		9.5
3/8	.3750		9.52
	.3770	V	
	.3780		9.6
	.3819		9.7
	.3839		9.75
	.3858		9.8
	.3860	W	
	.3898		9.9
25/64	.3906		9.92
	.3937		10.0
	.3970	X	
	.4040	Y	
13/32	.4062		10.31
	.4130	Z	
	.4134		10.5
27/64	.4219		10.71

Inch	Decimal	mm
	.4331	11.0
7/16	.4375	11.11
	.4528	11.5
29/64	.4531	11.51
15/32	.4688	11.90
	.4724	12.0
31/64	.4844	12.30
	.4921	12.5
1/2	.5000	12.70
	.5118	13.0
33/64	.5156	13.09
17/32	.5312	13.49
	.5315	13.5
35/64	.5469	13.89
	.5512	14.0
9/16	.5625	14.28
	.5709	14.5
37/64	.5781	14.68
	.5906	15.0
19/32	.5938	15.08
39/64	.6094	15.47
	.6102	15.5
5/8	.6250	15.87
	.6299	16.0
41/64	.6406	16.27
	.6496	16.5
21/32	.6562	16.66
	.6693	17.0
43/64	.6719	17.06
11/16	.6875	17.46
	.6890	17.5
45/64	.7031	17.85
	.7087	18.0
23/32	.7188	18.25
	.7283	18.5
47/64	.7344	18.65
	.7480	19.0
3/4	.7500	19.05
49/64	.7656	19.44
	.7677	19.5
25/32	.7812	19.84
	.7874	20.0
51/64	.7969	20.24
	.8071	20.5
13/16	.8125	20.63
	.8268	21.0
53/64	.8281	21.03
27/32	.8438	21.43
	.8465	21.5
55/64	.8594	21.82
	.8661	22.0
7/8	.8750	22.22
	.8858	22.5
57/64	.8906	22.62
	.9055	23.0
29/32	.9062	23.01
	.9219	23.41
59/64	.9252	23.5
15/16	.9375	23.81
	.9449	24.0
61/64	.9531	24.2
	.9646	24.5
31/32	.9688	24.6
	.9843	25.0
63/64	.9844	25.0
1	1.0000	25.4

GLOSSARY OF TERMS

AIR/FUEL RATIO: The ratio of air to gasoline by weight in the fuel mixture drawn into the engine.

AIR INJECTION: One method of reducing harmful exhaust emissions by injecting air into each of the exhaust ports of an engine. The fresh air entering the hot exhaust manifold causes any remaining fuel to be burned before it can exit the tailpipe.

ALTERNATOR: A device used for converting mechanical energy into electrical energy.

AMMETER: An instrument, calibrated in amperes, used to measure the flow of an electrical current in a circuit. Ammeters are always connected in series with the circuit being tested.

AMPERE: The rate of flow of electrical current present when one volt of electrical pressure is applied against one ohm of electrical resistance.

ANALOG COMPUTER: Any microprocessor that uses similar (analogous) electrical signals to make its calculations.

ARMATURE: A laminated, soft iron core wrapped by a wire that converts electrical energy to mechanical energy as in a motor or relay. When rotated in a magnetic field, it changes mechanical energy into electrical energy as in a generator.

ATMOSPHERIC PRESSURE: The pressure on the Earth's surface caused by the weight of the air in the atmosphere. At sea level, this pressure is 14.7 psi at 32°F (101 kPa at 0°C).

ATOMIZATION: The breaking down of a liquid into a fine mist that can be suspended in air.

AXIAL PLAY: Movement parallel to a shaft or bearing bore.

BACKFIRE: The sudden combustion of gases in the intake or exhaust system that results in a loud explosion.

BACKLASH: The clearance or play between two parts, such as meshed gears.

BACKPRESSURE: Restrictions in the exhaust system that slow the exit of exhaust gases from the combustion chamber.

BAKELITE: A heat resistant, plastic insulator material commonly used in printed circuit boards and transistorized components.

BALL BEARING: A bearing made up of hardened inner and outer races between which hardened steel ball roll.

BALLAST RESISTOR: A resistor in the primary ignition circuit that lowers voltage after the engine is started to reduce wear on ignition components.

BEARING: A friction reducing, supportive device usually located between a stationary part and a moving part.

BIMETAL TEMPERATURE SENSOR: Any sensor or switch made of two dissimilar types of metal that bend when heated or cooled due to the different expansion rates of the alloys. These types of sensors usually function as an on/off switch.

BLOWBY: Combustion gases, composed of water vapor and unburned fuel, that leak past the piston rings into the crankcase during normal engine operation. These gases are removed by the PCV system to prevent the build-up of harmful acids in the crankcase.

BRAKE PAD: A brake shoe and lining assembly used with disc brakes.

BRAKE SHOE: The backing for the brake lining. The term is, however, usually applied to the assembly of the brake backing and lining.

BUSHING: A liner, usually removable, for a bearing; an anti-friction liner used in place of a bearing.

BYPASS: System used to bypass ballast resistor during engine cranking to increase voltage supplied to the coil.

CALIPER: A hydraulically activated device in a disc brake system, which is mounted straddling the brake rotor (disc). The caliper contains at least one piston and two brake pads. Hydraulic pressure on the piston(s) forces the pads against the rotor.

CAMSHAFT: A shaft in the engine on which are the lobes (cams) which operate the valves. The camshaft is driven by the crankshaft, via a belt, chain or gears, at one half the crankshaft speed.

CAPACITOR: A device which stores an electrical charge.

CARBON MONOXIDE (CO): a colorless, odorless gas given off as a normal byproduct of combustion. It is poisonous and extremely dangerous in confined areas, building up slowly to toxic levels without warning if adequate ventilation is not available.

CARBURETOR: A device, usually mounted on the intake manifold of an engine, which mixes the air and fuel in the proper proportion to allow even combustion.

CATALYTIC CONVERTER: A device installed in the exhaust system, like a muffler, that converts harmful byproducts of combustion into carbon dioxide and water vapor by means of a heat-producing chemical reaction.

CENTRIFUGAL ADVANCE: A mechanical method of advancing the spark timing by using flyweights in the distributor that react to centrifugal force generated by the distributor shaft rotation.

CHECK VALVE: Any one-way valve installed to permit the flow of air, fuel or vacuum in one direction only.

CHOKE: A device, usually a moveable valve, placed in the intake path of a carburetor to restrict the flow of air.

CIRCUIT: Any unbroken path through which an electrical current can flow. Also used to describe fuel flow in some instances.

CIRCUIT BREAKER: A switch which protects an electrical circuit from overload by opening the circuit when the current flow exceeds a predetermined level. Some circuit breakers must be reset manually, while other reset automatically

COIL (IGNITION): A transformer in the ignition circuit which steps of the voltage provided to the spark plugs.

COMBINATION MANIFOLD: An assembly which includes both the intake and exhaust manifolds in one casting.

COMBINATION VALVE: A device used in some fuel systems that routes fuel vapors to a charcoal storage canister instead of venting them into the atmosphere. The valve relieves fuel tank pressure and allows fresh air into the tank as fuel level drops to prevent a vapor lock situation.

COMPRESSION RATIO: The comparison of the total volume of the cylinder and combustion chamber with the piston at BDC and the piston at TDC.

CONDENSER: 1. An electrical device which acts to store an electrical charge, preventing voltage surges.
2. A radiator-like device in the air conditioning system in which refrigerant gas condenses into a liquid, giving off heat.

CONDUCTOR: Any material through which an electrical current can be transmitted easily.

CONTINUITY: Continuous or complete circuit. Can be checked with an ohmmeter.

COUNTERSHAFT: An intermediate shaft which is rotated by a mainshaft and transmits, in turn, that rotation to a working part.

CRANKCASE: The lower part of an engine in which the crankshaft and related parts operate.

CRANKSHAFT: The main driving shaft of an engine which receives reciprocating motion from the pistons and converts it to rotary motion.

CYLINDER: In an engine, the round hole in the engine block in which the piston(s) ride.

CYLINDER BLOCK: The main structural member of an engine in which is found the cylinders, crankshaft and other principal parts.

CYLINDER HEAD: The detachable portion of the engine, fastened, usually, to the top of the cylinder block, containing all or most of the combustion chambers. On overhead valve engines, it contains the valves and their operating parts. On overhead cam engines, it contains the camshaft as well.

DEAD CENTER: The extreme top or bottom of the piston stroke.

DETONATION: An unwanted explosion of the air fuel mixture in the combustion chamber caused by excess heat and compression, advanced timing, or an overly lean mixture. Also referred to as "ping".

DIAPHRAGM: A thin, flexible wall separating two cavities, such as in a vacuum advance unit.

DIESELING: A condition in which hot spots in the combustion chamber cause the engine to run on after the key is turned off.

DIFFERENTIAL: A geared assembly which allows the transmission of motion between drive axles, giving one axle the ability to turn faster than the other.

DIODE: An electrical device that will allow current to flow in one direction only.

DISC BRAKE: A hydraulic braking assembly consisting of a brake disc, or rotor, mounted on an axle, and a caliper assembly containing, usually two brake pads which are activated by hydraulic pressure. The pads are forced against the sides of the disc, creating friction which slows the vehicle.

DISTRIBUTOR: A mechanically driven device on an engine which is responsible for electrically firing the spark plug at a predetermined point of the piston stroke.

DOWEL PIN: A pin, inserted in mating holes in two different parts allowing those parts to maintain a fixed relationship.

DRUM BRAKE: A braking system which consists of two brake shoes and one or two wheel cylinders, mounted on a fixed backing plate, and a brake drum, mounted on an axle, which revolves around the assembly. Hydraulic action applied to the wheel cylinders forces the shoes outward against the drum, creating friction and slowing the vehicle.

DWELL: The rate, measured in degrees of shaft rotation, at which an electrical circuit cycles on and off.

ELECTRONIC CONTROL UNIT (ECU): Ignition module, module, amplifier or igniter. See Module for definition.

ELECTRONIC IGNITION: A system in which the timing and firing of the spark plugs is controlled by an electronic control unit, usually called a module. These systems have not points or condenser.

ENDPLAY: The measured amount of axial movement in a shaft.

ENGINE: A device that converts heat into mechanical energy.

EXHAUST MANIFOLD: A set of cast passages or pipes which conduct exhaust gases from the engine.

FEELER GAUGE: A blade, usually metal, of precisely predetermined thickness, used to measure the clearance between two parts. These blades usually are available in sets of assorted thicknesses.

F-Head: An engine configuration in which the intake valves are in the cylinder head, while the camshaft and exhaust valves are located in the cylinder block. The camshaft operates the intake valves via lifters and pushrods, while it operates the exhaust valves directly.

FIRING ORDER: The order in which combustion occurs in the cylinders of an engine. Also the order in which spark is distributed to the plugs by the distributor.

FLATHEAD: An engine configuration in which the camshaft and all the valves are located in the cylinder block.

FLOODING: The presence of too much fuel in the intake manifold and combustion chamber which prevents the air/fuel mixture from firing, thereby causing a no-start situation.

FLYWHEEL: A disc shaped part bolted to the rear end of the crankshaft. Around the outer perimeter is affixed the ring gear. The starter drive engages the ring gear, turning the flywheel, which rotates the crankshaft, imparting the initial starting motion to the engine.

FOOT POUND (ft.lb. or sometimes, ft. lbs.): The amount of energy or work needed to raise an item weighing one pound, a distance of one foot.

FUSE: A protective device in a circuit which prevents circuit overload by breaking the circuit when a specific amperage is present. The device is constructed around a strip or wire of a lower amperage rating than the circuit it is designed to protect. When an amperage higher than that stamped on the fuse is present in the circuit, the strip or wire melts, opening the circuit.

GEAR RATIO: The ratio between the number of teeth on meshing gears.

GENERATOR: A device which converts mechanical energy into electrical energy.

HEAT RANGE: The measure of a spark plug's ability to dissipate heat from its firing end. The higher the heat range, the hotter the plug fires.

HUB: The center part of a wheel or gear.

HYDROCARBON (HC): Any chemical compound made up of hydrogen and carbon. A major pollutant formed by the engine as a byproduct of combustion.

HYDROMETER: An instrument used to measure the specific gravity of a solution.

INCH POUND (in.lb. or sometimes, in. lbs.): One twelfth of a foot pound.

INDUCTION: A means of transferring electrical energy in the form of a magnetic field. Principle used in the ignition coil to increase voltage.

INJECTION PUMP: A device, usually mechanically operated, which meters and delivers fuel under pressure to the fuel injector.

INJECTOR: A device which receives metered fuel under relatively low pressure and is activated to inject the fuel into the engine under relatively high pressure at a predetermined time.

INPUT SHAFT: The shaft to which torque is applied, usually carrying the driving gear or gears.

INTAKE MANIFOLD: A casting of passages or pipes used to conduct air or a fuel/air mixture to the cylinders.

JOURNAL: The bearing surface within which a shaft operates.

KEY: A small block usually fitted in a notch between a shaft and a hub to prevent slippage of the two parts.

MANIFOLD: A casting of passages or set of pipes which connect the cylinders to an inlet or outlet source.

MANIFOLD VACUUM: Low pressure in an engine intake manifold formed just below the throttle plates. Manifold vacuum is highest at idle and drops under acceleration.

MASTER CYLINDER: The primary fluid pressurizing device in a hydraulic system. In automotive use, it is found in brake and hydraulic clutch systems and is pedal activated, either directly or, in a power brake system, through the power booster.

MODULE: Electronic control unit, amplifier or igniter of solid state or integrated design which controls the current flow in the ignition primary circuit based on input from the pick-up coil. When the module opens the primary circuit, the high secondary voltage is induced in the coil.

NEEDLE BEARING: A bearing which consists of a number (usually a large number) of long, thin rollers.

OHM: (Ω) The unit used to measure the resistance of conductor to electrical flow. One ohm is the amount of resistance that limits current flow to one ampere in a circuit with one volt of pressure.

OHMMETER: An instrument used for measuring the resistance, in ohms, in an electrical circuit.

OUTPUT SHAFT: The shaft which transmits torque from a device, such as a transmission.

OVERDRIVE: A gear assembly which produces more shaft revolutions than that transmitted to it.

OVERHEAD CAMSHAFT (OHC): An engine configuration in which the camshaft is mounted on top of the cylinder head and operates the valve either directly or by means of rocker arms.

OVERHEAD VALVE (OHV): An engine configuration in which all of the valves are located in the cylinder head and the camshaft is located in the cylinder block. The camshaft operates the valves via lifters and pushrods.

OXIDES OF NITROGEN (NOx): Chemical compounds of nitrogen produced as a byproduct of combustion. They combine with hydrocarbons to produce smog.

OXYGEN SENSOR: Used with the feedback system to sense the presence of oxygen in the exhaust gas and signal the computer which can reference the voltage signal to an air/fuel ratio.

PINION: The smaller of two meshing gears.

PISTON RING: An open ended ring which fits into a groove on the outer diameter of the piston. Its chief function is to form a seal between the piston and cylinder wall. Most automotive pistons have three rings: two for compression sealing; one for oil sealing.

PRELOAD: A predetermined load placed on a bearing during assembly or by adjustment.

PRIMARY CIRCUIT: Is the low voltage side of the ignition system which consists of the ignition switch, ballast resistor or resistance wire, bypass, coil, electronic control unit and pick-up coil as well as the connecting wires and harnesses.

PRESS FIT: The mating of two parts under pressure, due to the inner diameter of one being smaller than the outer diameter of the other, or vice versa; an interference fit.

RACE: The surface on the inner or outer ring of a bearing on which the balls, needles or rollers move.

REGULATOR: A device which maintains the amperage and/or voltage levels of a circuit at predetermined values.

RELAY: A switch which automatically opens and/or closes a circuit.

RESISTANCE: The opposition to the flow of current through a circuit or electrical device, and is measured in ohms. Resistance is equal to the voltage divided by the amperage.

RESISTOR: A device, usually made of wire, which offers a preset amount of resistance in an electrical circuit.

RING GEAR: The name given to a ring-shaped gear attached to a differential case, or affixed to a flywheel or as part a planetary gear set.

ROLLER BEARING: A bearing made up of hardened inner and outer races between which hardened steel rollers move.

ROTOR: 1. The disc-shaped part of a disc brake assembly, upon which the brake pads bear; also called, brake disc.
2. The device mounted atop the distributor shaft, which passes current to the distributor cap tower contacts.

SECONDARY CIRCUIT: The high voltage side of the ignition system, usually above 20,000 volts. The secondary includes the ignition coil, coil wire, distributor cap and rotor, spark plug wires and spark plugs.

SENDING UNIT: A mechanical, electrical, hydraulic or electromagnetic device which transmits information to a gauge.

SENSOR: Any device designed to measure engine operating conditions or ambient pressures and temperatures. Usually electronic in nature and designed to send a voltage signal to an on-board computer, some sensors may operate as a simple on/off switch or they may provide a variable voltage signal (like a potentiometer) as conditions or measured parameters change.

SHIM: Spacers of precise, predetermined thickness used between parts to establish a proper working relationship.

SLAVE CYLINDER: In automotive use, a device in the hydraulic clutch system which is activated by hydraulic force, disengaging the clutch.

SOLENOID: A coil used to produce a magnetic field, the effect of which is produce work.

SPARK PLUG: A device screwed into the combustion chamber of a spark ignition engine. The basic construction is a conductive core inside of a ceramic insulator, mounted in an outer conductive base. An electrical charge from the spark plug wire travels along the conductive core and jumps a preset air gap to a grounding point or points at the end of the conductive base. The resultant spark ignites the fuel/air mixture in the combustion chamber.

SPLINES: Ridges machined or cast onto the outer diameter of a shaft or inner diameter of a bore to enable parts to mate without rotation.

TACHOMETER: A device used to measure the rotary speed of an engine, shaft, gear, etc., usually in rotations per minute.

THERMOSTAT: A valve, located in the cooling system of an engine, which is closed when cold and opens gradually in response to engine heating, controlling the temperature of the coolant and rate of coolant flow.

TOP DEAD CENTER (TDC): The point at which the piston reaches the top of its travel on the compression stroke.

TORQUE: The twisting force applied to an object.

TORQUE CONVERTER: A turbine used to transmit power from a driving member to a driven member via hydraulic action, providing changes in drive ratio and torque. In automotive use, it links the driveplate at the rear of the engine to the automatic transmission.

TRANSDUCER: A device used to change a force into an electrical signal.

TRANSISTOR: A semi-conductor component which can be actuated by a small voltage to perform an electrical switching function.

TUNE-UP: A regular maintenance function, usually associated with the replacement and adjustment of parts and components in the electrical and fuel systems of a vehicle for the purpose of attaining optimum performance.

TURBOCHARGER: An exhaust driven pump which compresses intake air and forces it into the combustion chambers at higher than atmospheric pressures. The increased air pressure allows more fuel to be burned and results in increased horsepower being produced.

VACUUM ADVANCE: A device which advances the ignition timing in response to increased engine vacuum.

VACUUM GAUGE: An instrument used to measure the presence of vacuum in a chamber.

VALVE: A device which control the pressure, direction of flow or rate of flow of a liquid or gas.

VALVE CLEARANCE: The measured gap between the end of the valve stem and the rocker arm, cam lobe or follower that activates the valve.

VISCOSITY: The rating of a liquid's internal resistance to flow.

VOLTMETER: An instrument used for measuring electrical force in units called volts. Voltmeters are always connected parallel with the circuit being tested.

WHEEL CYLINDER: Found in the automotive drum brake assembly, it is a device, actuated by hydraulic pressure, which, through internal pistons, pushes the brake shoes outward against the drums.

ABBREVIATIONS AND SYMBOLS

A: Ampere

AC: Alternating current

A/C: Air conditioning

A-h: Ampere hour

AT: Automatic transmission

ATDC: After top dead center

μA: Microampere

bbl: Barrel

BDC: Bottom dead center

bhp: Brake horsepower

BTDC: Before top dead center

BTU: British thermal unit

C: Celsius (Centigrade)

CCA: Cold cranking amps

cd: Candela

cm^2: Square centimeter

cm^3, cc: Cubic centimeter

CO: Carbon monoxide

CO_2: Carbon dioxide

cu.in., in^3: Cubic inch

CV: Constant velocity

Cyl.: Cylinder

DC: Direct current

ECM: Electronic control module

EFE: Early fuel evaporation

EFI: Electronic fuel injection

EGR: Exhaust gas recirculation

Exh.: Exhaust

F: Fahrenheit

F: Farad

pF: Picofarad

μF: Microfarad

FI: Fuel injection

ft.lb., ft. lb., ft. lbs.: foot pound(s)

gal: Gallon

g: Gram

HC: Hydrocarbon

HEI: High energy ignition

HO: High output

hp: Horsepower

Hyd.: Hydraulic

Hz: Hertz

ID: Inside diameter

in.lb.; in. lb.; in. lbs: inch pound(s)

Int.: Intake

K: Kelvin

kg: Kilogram

kHz: Kilohertz

km: Kilometer

km/h: Kilometers per hour

kΩ: Kilohm

kPa: Kilopascal

kV: Kilovolt

kW: Kilowatt

l: Liter

l/s: Liters per second

m: Meter

mA: Milliampere

mg: Milligram

mHz: Megahertz

mm: Millimeter

mm^2: Square millimeter

m^3: Cubic meter

MΩ: Megohm

m/s: Meters per second

MT: Manual transmission

mV: Millivolt

μm: Micrometer

N: Newton

N-m: Newton meter

NOx: Nitrous oxide

OD: Outside diameter

OHC: Over head camshaft

OHV: Over head valve

Ω: Ohm

PCV: Positive crankcase ventilation

psi: Pounds per square inch

pts: Pints

qts: Quarts

rpm: Rotations per minute

rps: Rotations per second

R-12: A refrigerant gas (Freon)

SAE: Society of Automotive Engineers

SO$_2$: Sulfur dioxide

T: Ton

t: Megagram

TBI: Throttle Body Injection

TPS: Throttle Position Sensor

V: 1. Volt; 2. Venturi

μV: Microvolt

W: Watt

$\propto$: Infinity

<: Less than

>: Greater than

Index